Key Science 4
– in 2 volumes –
with Resource Bank
and Teacher's Guide

Titles of Related Interest

Basic Chemistry Questions for GCSE
(National Curriculum Edition)
Bernard Abrams

Basic Physics Questions for GCSE
(National Curriculum Edition)
Bernard Abrams

Basic Biology Questions for GCSE
(National Curriculum Edition)
Chris Rouan

KEY SCIENCE 4

BOOK 2

Eileen Ramsden BSc PhD DPhil
Formerly of Wolfreton School, Hull

Jim Breithaupt BSc MSc
Head of Science and Mathematics, Wigan Campus, Wigan and Leigh College

David Applin BSc MSc PhD FRES
Head of Science, Chigwell School

Gareth Williams BSc FIBiol
Head of Biology, Poynton County High School

Stanley Thornes (Publishers) Limited

First published in 1992 by:
Stanley Thornes (Publishers) Ltd
Ellenborough House
Wellington Street
CHELTENHAM GL50 1YD
England

Reprinted 1993 (twice)
Reprinted 1994

A catalogue record of this book is available from the British Library.
ISBN 0-7487-0494-9 Book 2
    (0-7487-0492-2 Book 1)
    (0-7487-1719-6 Resource Bank)
    (0-7487-1723-4 Teacher's Guide)

Design and artwork by Cauldron Design Studio, Auchencrow,
Berwickshire.
Typeset by Word Power, Auchencrow, Berwickshire.
Printed and bound in Hong Kong

Contents

Contents of Book 1

Acknowledgements

We would like to express our thanks to Dr Jerry Wellington and Mr Jon Scaife who have provided some excellent material on information technology.

We thank the following organisations and people who have supplied photographs.

Allsport: Figures 36.4A (Vandystadt), 49.1B (Gray Mortimore)

Ardea London: 41.2D (Valerie Taylor), 55.1D(b) (Jack Swedburg), 55.2A, 55.5M (J-P Ferrero), 55.5A, 55.5N(e) (Francois Gohier), 55.5I, p. 433 (Peter Green), 55.5J (Adrian Warren), 55.5N(b) (Peter Steyn)

BBC Photographic Library: Figures A, 31.4F

Biofotos: Figure 52.1B(d) (S Summerhays)

Biophoto Associates: Figures 30.5G(b), 38.1B, 38.1E, 38.2B, 38.2G, 38.3C, 39.2B(a), 51.5A, 53.7A(e), (f), (g), 53.7B, 53.7D, 54.3A(a), (b), 54.3C(b)

British Rail: 50.6A

B Sky B: 33.3E

Cheltenham General Hospital Medical Photography: Figure 39.5M

Dr David Applin: Figures 39.2A, 39.2D, 39.2E, p.159, 39.3D(a), (b), 39.3E, 39.3F, 39.6C, 52.1A(a), (b), (c), (d), (e), (f), 52.2B, 52.5B, 53.5C, 55.1H(a), (b)

Dr Eileen Ramsden: Figures 48.2B, 51.3C, 51.3D, 51.4B

Heather Angel: Figures 30.4E, 32.5A, 35.1A, 39.2C, 39.3B(a), (b), 39.3C, 50.10A, 52.1B(b), 52.1D(c)

Hulton-Deutsch Collection: Figures 35.5D, 44.2H(a), 44.5A(b), 55.1F

InterCity: p.234

International Centre for Conservation Education: Figures 48.1B (Mark Tasker), 49.1A, 52.1C(b), (b) (Mark Boulton), 50.12B (Rob Cousins), 53.2A (WWF/Rautkari), 53.7A(a) (Manfred Kage), 53.7A(b) (Cath Wadforth), 53.7A(c) (Eric Grove), 53.7A(d) (EM Unit, CVL Webridge)

Jim Breithaupt: Figure 30.5I

John Innes Institute: Figure 54.5A

Mark Boulton: Figures A, 30.2E(b), 30.3A, 32.1G, 32.3A, 32.4A, p.47, 33.2B, 34.1A, 34.5A, 35.2A, 35.6A, 35.6C, 35.6D, p.115, 37.3B(b), 39.1A(b), 39.5D, 39.5Q, 39.5R, 40.1A(b), 42.4A, 43.2A, 43.2F(b), 43.4C(a), (b), 44.1F, 44.3F, 45.1A, 45.5E(c), 45.8A, 45.8C(a), (b), 50.11A(b), (c), 51.1A, 51.1E, 51.1G, 51.3A, 51.3L, 52.1B(a), (e), 52.2A, 53.5B(b), 54.1A, 54.2A, 55.5N(a), (c), (d)

Mary Evans Picture Library: Figures 34.2A(a), 37.2A, 37.3B(a), 40.2G, p.407, 55.1A, 55.1C, 55.1G, 55.2D, 55.3A

MIRA: Figures 36.2A, 36.7A, p.61

NASA: Figures 34.1E, 36.8A, 36.8F

National Medical Slide Bank: Figures A, 39.5B(c), 39.5T, 40.3B

Natural History Photographic Agency: 30.1E, p.122 (Stephen Dalton), 39.1A(a) (Karl Switak), 55.1E(b) (Philippa Scott), 55.5K(a), (Dave Watts/ANT), 55.5K(b) (ANT)

Oxford Scientific Films Ltd: Figures 39.1B(d), 39.1I, 39.1J, 39.6B, 40.2J, 41.2C(a), (c) (London Scientific Films), 39.1 H (Barrie Watts), 39.1K, 53.6E (Michael Fogden), 39.1L, 40.1A(a), 51.1C(d), 52.5A, 53.5B(a), (c) (G I Bernard), 39.2B(b) (Gordon Maclean), 39.6E(a) (David Thompson, London Scientific Films), 39.6B(b) (Val Cooke, Marcia W Griffen/Animal Animals), 39.6F(a) (Rudie H Kuiter, Scott Camazine), 39.6F(b) (Breck P Kent/ Animals Animals, London Scientific Films), 40.1B (Breck P Kent/Earth Scenes), 41.2C(b) (C G Gardener), 52.1B(c) (Ronald Templeton), 52.1B(f), 53.1A(c), (Waina Cheng), 51.1C(e) (Ronald Toms), 53.1A(a), 55.1D(a) (Len Rue Jr./Animals Animals), 53.1A(c), 53.6H (Doug Allan), 52.1C(a) (Stephen Mills), 53.5A (Stan Osolinski), 53.6C (Len Zell), 53.6F (P and W Ward), 54.4B(b) (David Fox), 54.5C(d) (Edward Parker), 55.1E(a) (Peter Ryley), 55.4C (Peter Parks), 38.2A, 38.2C, 38.2F, 38.2H

Panos Pictures: 51.4D (David Hall)

Philips Research Laboratories: Figures 44.4B, 44.4D, p.12

Pilkington Glass plc: Figure51.1I

Rolls-Royce Motor Cars Ltd: p.216

Science Photo Library: Figures A (Salim Patel), (Jerry Mason), 31.2D, p.211, 45.8G(a), p.287, 51.1D (Martin Bond), 31.2E (CNRI), 31.4C (Jonathan Watts), 32.2A (Dr Beer-Gabel/CNRI), 33.1A, 35.6B (David Parker), 33.2C (Dr Ray Clark and Mervyn Goff), 33.2E (Alexander Tsiaras), 33.2F, 34.5B (Garvey Pincis), 35.2D (Labat/Lanceau, Jerrican), 37.2B, 44.2D, 50.11B (Alex Bartel), p.125 (G F Gennard), 38.3I (Sheila Terry), 39.1B(a), (b), 39.1C (M I Walker), 39.1B(c) (Phillipe Plailly), 39.1B(e), 39.2H (Dr Jeremy Burgess), 39.5A(e) (Andrew Syred), 39.5H (Petit Format/CSI), 39.5N (SIU), p.192 (Will and Deni McIntyre), p.200 (Science Source), 41.1A (Sinclair Stammers), 44.2G(a) (J-L Charmet), p.250, 54.3(a) (Peter Menzel), 45.7C (Astrid and Hanns-Frieder Michler), 48.4B (Harry Nor-Hansen), 50.1A (John Ross), p.265 (Michael Marten), p.405, 54.3C(a) (Richard Hutchings), 54.3E(b) (Biophoto Associates), 55.3B

Sonia Boulton: 34.5E

Sporting Pictures (UK) Ltd: Figures p.1, 34.2A(b), 36.5A, 36.6A, 40.1A(c), 40.3D, 54.4B(b)

Still Pictures: Figure 53.4C (Mark Edwards)

Sue Boulton: Figures 37.1F, 43.2F(a), 45.8C(c), 51.3B, 51.4A, 54.4B

The BBC Domesday Project 1986: p.280

The Environmental Picture Library: Figures 52.6A, 52.6E, 52.6F, 52.6G, 53.8A, 53.8B, 53.8C, 53.8D

The Forensic Science Service: Figure 54.6B

Woodmansterne: Figure 31.2C

Main cover photograph, mineral opal fire silica, supplied by **Geo Science Features Picture Library**.

Every effort has been made to contact copyright holders and the publishers apologise if any have been overlooked.

We thank the following examining groups for permission to reproduce questions from examination papers:
London East Anglian Examining Group, Midland Examining Group, Northern Examining Association, Northern Ireland Schools Examination Council, Southern Examining Group, Welsh Joint Education Committee.

The production of a science text book from manuscripts involves considerable effort, energy and expertise from many people, and we wish to acknowledge the work of all members of the publishing team. We are particularly grateful to Penelope Barber (Senior Publisher), Adrian Wheaton (Science Publisher) and Lorna Godson (Editor), for their advice and support.

Finally we thank our families for the tolerance which they have shown and the encouragement which they have given during the preparation of this book.

Eileen Ramsden
Jim Breithaupt
David Applin
Gareth Williams

Careers in Science

Now that you are midway through your GCSE science course, you need to find out about the opportunities available to you after the course is completed. Whatever career you choose to follow, you will almost certainly need to use your GCSE science skills and knowledge. Science is a feature of everyday life, at work or at home. Industry, hospitals, transport and agriculture are examples of major sectors of the economy that depend heavily on science. At home, almost all the things you do make use of science in some way.

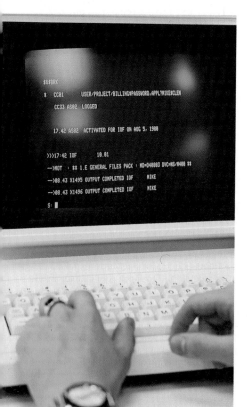

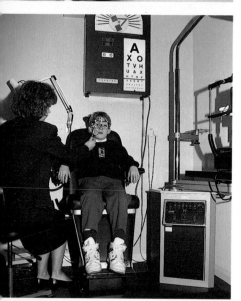

Figure A ● Science at work

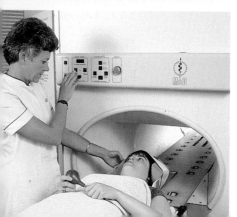

Your GCSE science course is designed to give you a good scientific background so that you can, if you wish, carry on with science studies after GCSE.

To work in science requires specific personal qualities in addition to academic qualifications. Scientists are very creative and imaginative people and the work of an individual scientist can bring huge benefits to everyone. For example, Alexander Fleming's discovery of penicillin has saved countless lives. But do not be misled into thinking that the life of a scientist is one of continual discoveries. Scientists have to be very patient and methodical to discover anything; they have to be good at working together and at communicating their ideas to each other and to other people. The qualifications needed to become a scientist are outlined on p. xii; the qualities needed to become a scientist are just the same as you need in your GCSE course – enthusiasm, hard work, imagination, awareness and concern.

What jobs are done by scientists? In industry, scientists design, develop and test new products. For example, scientists in the glass industry are developing amazingly clear glass for use as **optical fibres** in communication links. In medicine, scientists are continually finding applications for scientific discoveries; for example, medical scientists have developed a high-power ultrasonic transmitter for destroying kidney stones, thus avoiding a surgical operation. These are just two examples of the work of scientists. You will find scientists at work in research laboratories, industrial laboratories, forensic laboratories, hospitals, schools, on field trips, expeditions, radio, TV and lots of other places. Scientists have to be very versatile as science is a very wide and varied field.

The skills and knowledge you gain through studying science will enable you to gain the benefits of new technologies. Ask your parents what aspects of life have **not** changed since they were children – they may be stuck for an answer! New technologies force the pace of change and if you do not learn to use them, you will not share their benefits. Studying science encourages you to develop an open mind and to seek new approaches. That is why a wide range of careers involve further studies in science.

For many careers further studies in science are essential, for example, medicine, dentistry, pharmacy, engineering and computing. For other careers such as law, business studies, administration, the armed forces and retail management, studying science after GCSE will be helpful. Thus by continuing your science studies after GCSE, you keep many career options open, which is important when you are considering your choice of career.

LOOK AT LINKS
for **optical fibres**
See Theme H, Topic 32.2.

The next steps after GCSE

Read this section carefully, bearing in mind that your working life will probably be about forty years. If you want your life ahead to be interesting; if you want to make your own decisions about what you do; if you want to make the most of your talents; then you should continue your studies. After GCSE, you can continue in full-time education at school or at college, or you can train in a job through part-time study. If you take a job without training, you will soon find that your friends who stayed on have much better prospects.

Most students aiming for a career in science continue full-time study for two years, taking either GCE A and AS-levels or a BTEC National Diploma in Science. Successful completion of a suitable combination of these courses can then lead to a degree course at a polytechnic or a university or a college of higher education or, alternatively, straight into employment.

The Business and Technical Education Council (BTEC) National Diploma in Science is a two-year full time course covering biology, chemistry, mathematics, physics, computers, electronics and general studies. The course includes assignments, work experience in science laboratories and coursework assessments. Students completing the course successfully can progress to full-time degree courses in science, or work as a science technician in a science laboratory. The minimum entry qualifications for the BTEC National Diploma in Science are four GCSEs at grade C (including maths and science) or equivalent.

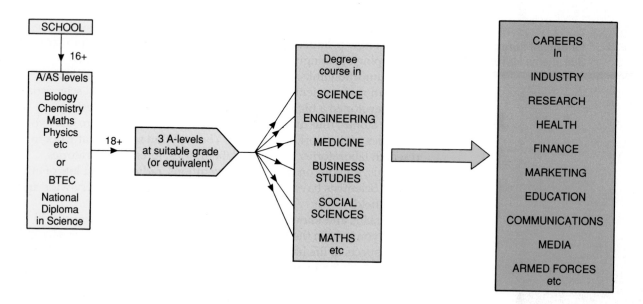

Figure B ● Career routes from GCSE

Using Waves

Wherever you are, you are probably using waves in one form or another. In the photograph, the surfrider is using waves for enjoyment. Sunbathers use ultra-violet waves from the Sun to become tanned, lifeguards use light waves to watch out for sharks and sirens can emit sound waves as a warning to swimmers.

TOPIC 30 WAVES

30.1 Making and using waves

This section introduces you to some different types of wave. What uses do you make of each type of wave you read about? Which devices that you use depend on waves?

Every day we use waves in one form or another. Waves carry energy. Figure 30.1A shows some 'snapshots' from a typical morning routine. An alarm clock wakes you up because it emits sound waves when it 'goes off'. The television set picks up signals in the form of radio waves and transforms them into a picture, which is carried to your eye by light waves. In these examples waves are being used to send information.

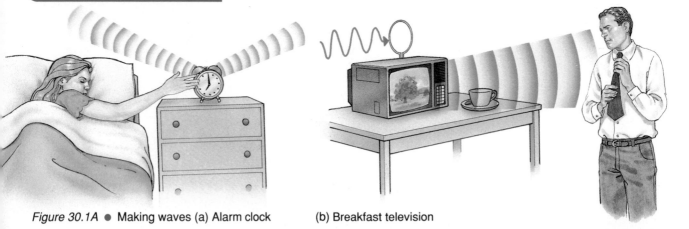

Figure 30.1A ● Making waves (a) Alarm clock   (b) Breakfast television

It is easy to make water waves. Drop a stone into a pond and you will see waves spread out in expanding circles. Anything floating on the water, like a duck or a toy boat, will bob up and down as the waves pass. At any point on the water surface, the water rises as each wave crest passes and then falls as each crest is followed by a trough.

To make waves in a rope, stretch the rope out with one end fixed, and move the free end from side to side repeatedly to send waves along it (Figure 30.1B). The strings of musical instruments, such as the piano, guitar and violin, vibrate to produce sound waves when they are plucked, struck or bowed. The human voice box, the larynx, works in the same way. It contains strings, the vocal cords, which vibrate to produce sound waves.

Direction of travel

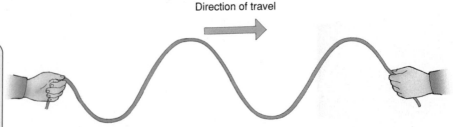

IT *Waves* (program)

Computers can be useful for showing how waves are made and what waves do. The program *Waves* lets you look at single pulses. Find out how pulses travel. *What happens when they come to the 'end of the line'?*

Figure 30.1B ● Making waves in a rope

Radio waves are produced by a radio transmitter which forces electrons to move up and down the transmitter aerial. The motion of electrons causes radio waves to be sent out from the aerial. The radio receiver aerial can pick up the radio waves.

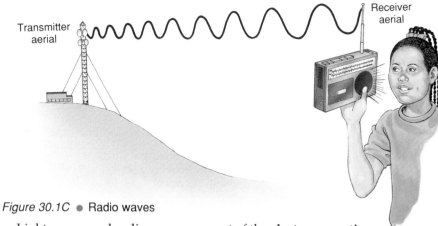

Figure 30.1C ● Radio waves

LOOK AT LINKS
for **electromagnetic spectrum**
See Theme H, Topic 33.2.

Light waves and radio waves are part of the **electromagnetic spectrum** of waves. All electromagnetic waves travel through space at a speed of 300 000 km/s. Light bulbs convert electrical energy into light energy.

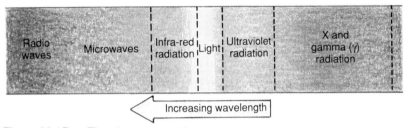

Figure 30.1D ● The electromagnetic spectrum

We make **sound waves** every time we speak. Our vocal cords vibrate, causing the air around them to vibrate and producing sound waves in the air. Anything that vibrates creates sound waves. A buzzing bee makes sound waves by moving its wings to and fro repeatedly very fast. A loudspeaker makes sound waves because it has a diaphragm that vibrates, pushing the air back and forth and making **compression waves** pass through the air. These waves can be detected by the human ear.

LOOK AT LINKS
for **compression waves**
See Theme H, Topic 30.4.

SUMMARY

Waves carry energy and they can be used to transmit information. Water waves, waves in a string, electromagnetic waves and sound waves are all examples of different forms of waves.

Figure 30.1E ● A natural buzzer

3

╱╱╱╱╱╱╱╱╱╱╱╱╱╱╱╱╱╱╱╱╱╱ CHECKPOINT ╱╱╱╱╱╱╱╱╱╱╱╱╱╱╱╱╱╱╱╱

❶ In each of the following situations, write down whether the waves are being used to transfer energy or information.
  (a) Microwaves used to cook a meal.
  (b) Light from the headlamps of a car.
  (c) Light from a flashing indicator of a car.
  (d) Sound from a loudspeaker.
  (e) Light from a laser used to destroy unwanted tissue in the human body.

❷ When a wave travels across the surface of water, the water does not travel with the wave. How would you prove this to a friend who thinks the water moves along with the wave?

❸ A 'tsunami' is a tidal wave created by an earthquake under the ocean. Such a wave can travel for thousands of kilometres and is capable of devastating coastal areas. Yet ships at sea 'ride out' these waves. Imagine you are on a ship at sea that rides out a tidal wave. Write a brief account of the events for the ship's log book.

❹ For each of the following sound producers, describe the sound and explain how it is produced.
  (a) Bluebottle.   (d) Drum.
  (b) Grasshopper.   (e) Whistle.
  (c) Cuckoo.

30.2 Investigating waves

All waves can be reflected, refracted and diffracted. This section explains their behaviour.

All types of wave have certain properties. For example, they can all be reflected. Sea waves reflect off sea walls; sound waves reflect to cause echoes; light waves reflect off mirrors. We can study the properties of water waves in carefully controlled conditions by using a **ripple tank**, as shown in Figure 30.2A.

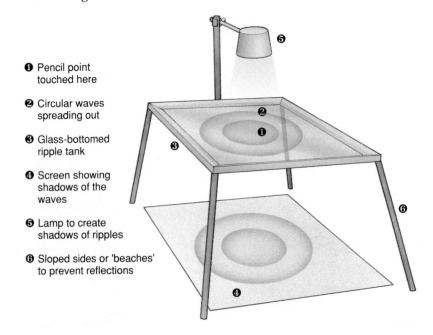

❶ Pencil point touched here

❷ Circular waves spreading out

❸ Glass-bottomed ripple tank

❹ Screen showing shadows of the waves

❺ Lamp to create shadows of ripples

❻ Sloped sides or 'beaches' to prevent reflections

Figure 30.2A ● The ripple rank

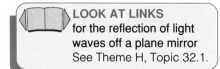

LOOK AT LINKS
for the reflection of light
waves off a plane mirror
See Theme H, Topic 32.1.

Reflection

The reflection of waves can be studied by putting differently shaped reflecting walls in the ripple tank and seeing how waves are reflected off them. Figure 30.2B shows the shape of some reflectors.

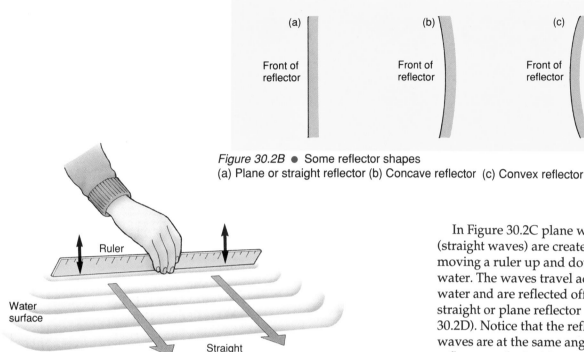

Figure 30.2B ● Some reflector shapes
(a) Plane or straight reflector (b) Concave reflector (c) Convex reflector

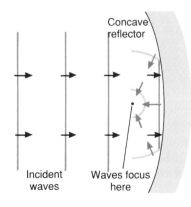

Figure 30.2C ● Making straight waves

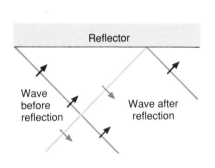

Figure 30.2D ● Reflection off a straight reflector

In Figure 30.2C plane waves (straight waves) are created by moving a ruler up and down in the water. The waves travel across the water and are reflected off a straight or plane reflector (Figure 30.2D). Notice that the reflected waves are at the same angle to the reflector as the incident waves. This can be demonstrated easily with light waves too.

In Figure 30.2E plane waves are being reflected by a concave reflector. Again, the reflected waves are at the same angle to the reflector as the incident waves. The reflected waves all meet at a point, called the **focus** of the reflector. Radio waves are reflected from concave reflectors in just the same way, which is why concave dishes are used to 'pick up' television programmes broadcast via satellites. The detector is actually at the focus of the dish, so the dish concentrates the signal by reflecting all the incoming radio waves to the detector.

Figure 30.2E ● (a) Reflection off a concave reflector (b) Television satellite dish with detector at the focus of the concave reflector

5

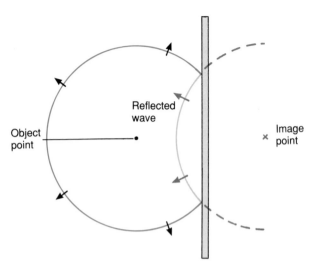

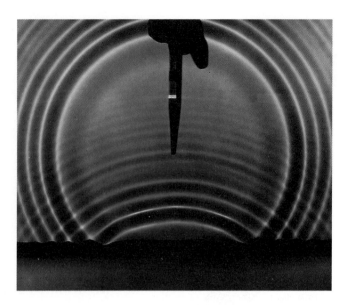

Figure 30.2F ● Formation of an image

Circular waves can be made by dipping a pencil in the tank. Figure 30.2F shows circular waves being reflected off a straight reflector. The reflected waves appear to come from an image point behind the reflector. Notice that the image point and the object point (where the waves come from) are both at the same distance from the reflector. The same happens with light waves. This is why your image in a plane mirror is the same distance behind the mirror as you are in front of it.

Refraction

All types of wave can be refracted. Refraction is a change of direction due to a change of speed. For example, water waves travel more slowly in shallow water than in deep water. Figure 30.2G shows how water waves change direction when they pass from deep to shallow water.

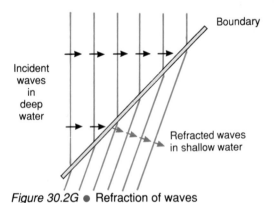

Figure 30.2G ● Refraction of waves

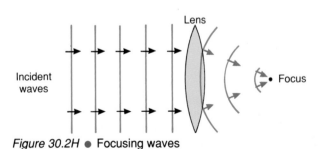

Figure 30.2H ● Focusing waves

Light waves are refracted when they pass between air and glass. Figure 30.2H shows how light waves are refracted (change direction) as they enter and leave a convex glass lens. They meet at a point. If a screen is put at this point, the light will be focused on the screen.

Diffraction

Diffraction is the name given to the way waves spread out when they pass through a gap or round an obstacle. The narrower the gap, the more the waves spread out (see Figure 30.2I). Sea waves passing into a harbour entrance spread out behind the harbour walls. You can demonstrate this for water waves using a ripple tank.

SUMMARY

All types of wave can be reflected, refracted and diffracted. Reflection is when waves bounce off a suitable reflector. Refraction of waves is when waves change direction due to change of speed. Diffraction happens when waves pass through a gap or round an obstacle and spread out.

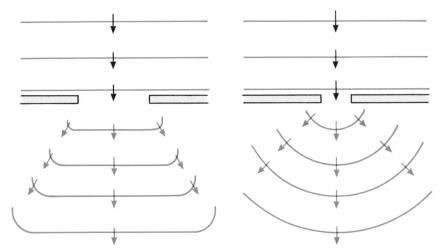

Figure 30.2I ● Diffraction at a gap (a) A wide gap (b) A narrow gap

CHECKPOINT

❶ Sea waves rolling up a sandy beach are not reflected. Why are 'beaches' used to line the sides of a ripple tank? What would happen if the 'beaches' were left out?

❷ Copy the sketches below showing circular waves produced near a concave reflector. In each case sketch in some reflected waves, indicating their direction. (Figure 30.2E will help you.)

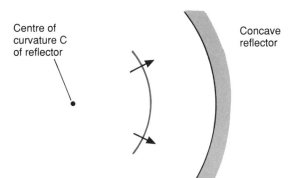

❸ (a) Sketch what you see when you look through a pinhole in metal foil at a distant light source.
(b) Try two more pinholes, one smaller and one larger than in (a). Is there any difference in what you see?

❹ Copy the sketch opposite, which shows plane waves passing from shallow to deep water. Draw in some refracted waves, indicating their direction. Remember that waves travel faster in deep water than in shallow water.

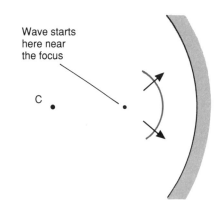

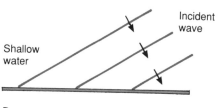

7

30.3 ● Measuring waves

This section explains how waves are measured and the uses we make of these measurements.

When the *Voyager 1* space probe flew past the planet Jupiter, it sent back amazing pictures of the planet and its moons. These pictures took about 40 minutes to reach Earth, even though they were carried by radio waves travelling at a speed of 300 000 km/s through space. All electromagnetic waves travel at this speed through space. Thus light from the Sun takes about eight minutes to reach Earth, a distance of about 150 million kilometres.

The **wavespeed**, *c*, of a wave is the distance travelled by the wavepeak per second. Sound waves in air travel at a speed of about 340 m/s. An aeroplane like Concorde can break the 'sound barrier' because it can travel faster than sound. However, nothing can travel faster than the speed of light, the 'cosmic speed limit'.

Water waves travel much more slowly than sound or light waves and they give a useful picture of measurements that can be made on any type of wave. Imagine you are fishing from a boat on a lake when a speedboat passes near. The speedboat creates waves that spread across the lake, and your boat goes up with each wavecrest (or wavepeak) and down with each wavetrough (Figure 30.3A). Each successive wave takes you through a cycle of motion.

Figure 30.3A ● Waves from a speedboat

The following terms that we use to describe waves are illustrated in Figure 30.3B.
- One **complete wave** is from one wavepeak to the next wavepeak.
- The **frequency**, *f*, is the number of complete waves passing a point in one second. The unit of frequency is the hertz, Hz, named after Heinrich Hertz who discovered how to produce and detect radio waves. A frequency of 1 hertz means one complete wave per second passes a given point.
- The **wavelength**, λ (Greek: pronounced 'lambda'), of a set of waves is the distance from one wavepeak to the next wavepeak.
- The **amplitude** of a wave is the height of its wavepeak or the depth of its wavetrough from the middle. The bigger the amplitude, the more energy the waves carry. Water waves decrease in height as they spread out. This is because the same amount of energy is being carried across a wider area.

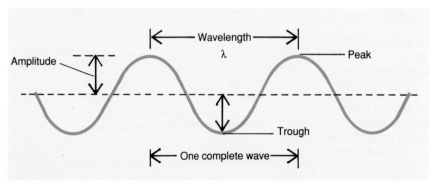

Figure 30.3B ● Parts of a wave

IT'S A FACT

It is possible to tune in to radio broadcasts from distant countries at night in summer. The Sun's radiation causes a layer of ions to form in the ionosphere (upper atmosphere). At night this layer cools and becomes dense enough to reflect radio waves. By being bounced off this layer, radio waves can reach distant continents.

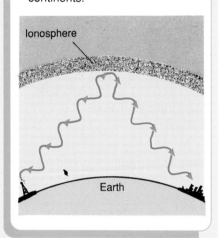

Tuning in

Now we will look at how these ideas apply to waves that cannot be seen. For example, radio waves from a transmitter aerial spread out as they travel away from the aerial. The amplitude of the waves becomes smaller as they spread out. This is why it is difficult to receive programmes from your local radio station when you travel away from your own area.

Each radio station has its own broadcasting frequency. *What is your favourite radio station? What frequency does it broadcast on?* To listen to it, you need to tune your radio in to that particular frequency. Radio programmes are broadcast using waves with frequencies ranging from about 1000 Hz (=1 kHz) up to about 1 000 000 Hz (= 1 MHz). Television programmes are carried by radio waves with much higher frequencies, usually around 100 MHz. This is sometimes called the ultra high frequency (or UHF) range.

Suppose a new radio station has started in your neighbourhood. You have read that it broadcasts at a frequency of 983 kHz, but your radio dial is marked in wavelengths in metres. You can work out the station wavelength using this formula.

$$\text{Frequency} \ f \quad \times \quad \text{Wavelength} \ \lambda \quad = \quad \text{Wavespeed} \ c$$

Radio waves travel at a speed of 3.00×10^8 m/s through air. Hence the wavelength for a frequency of 983 kHz is given by

$$983 \times 10^3 \quad \times \quad \text{Wavelength} \quad = \quad 3 \times 10^8$$

$$\text{thus} \quad \text{Wavelength} \quad = \quad \frac{3.00 \times 10^8}{983 \times 10^3} \quad = \quad 305 \text{ metres}$$

To prove the formula consider Figure 30.3C, which shows two stages of a ripple tank experiment in which straight waves are produced at a constant frequency, f.

Wave W moves forward from X to Y in time t.
Hence distance XY = Wavespeed x Time = $c \times t$. [1]

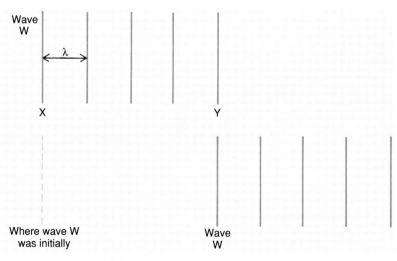

Figure 30.3C ● $c = f\lambda$ (a) Initially (b) After time t

Since the frequency, f, is the number of waves passing a point in one second, then $f \times t$ waves pass Y in time t. Therefore there are ft waves between X and Y.

SUMMARY

A complete wave is from one wavepeak to the next. One wavelength is the distance from one wavepeak to the next. The frequency is the number of complete waves passing a point per second. The amplitude of a wave is the height of the wavepeak above the middle.

So another way of finding the distance XY is

XY = Number of waves from X to Y x Wavelength
= $f \times t \times \lambda$ [2]

Combining [1] and [2] we have

$f \times t \times \lambda = c \times t$

and cancelling t on both sides gives

$f \times \lambda = c$

CHECKPOINT

❶ (a) Explain why you hear the sound of distant thunder some time after seeing the lightning flash that produced the thunder.
(b) In a thunderstorm, Katie observes that the interval between a lightning flash and its thunder is 6 seconds. She knows that sound travels at 340 m/s. How far away was the lightning strike?

❷ Radio waves travel through air at a speed of 300 000 km/s. Work out the frequency of the radio waves from each of the following radio stations.
(a) BBC Radio 4; $\lambda = 1500$ m (c) BBC Radio 3; $\lambda = 247$ m
(b) BBC Radio 1; $\lambda = 285$ m   (d) World Service; $\lambda = 463$ m

❸ Two fishermen in different boats are 30 m apart when a speedboat passes.
(a) The waves from the speedboat travel along the line between the two boats as in the illustration, causing the fishermen to bob up and down once every two seconds for a few minutes. What is the frequency of the waves?
(b) When one fisherman is on a wavepeak, the other is in a wavetrough as shown. Work out the wavelength and the wavespeed of the waves.

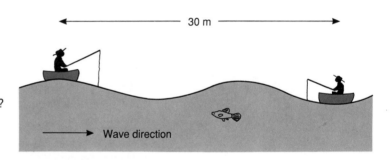

❹ Work out the wavelength of the sound waves produced in each of the following situations, given the speed of sound in air is 340 m/s.
(a) A tuning fork vibrating at a frequency of 512 Hz in air.
(b) A siren operating at 3000 Hz.
(c) A dog whistle emitting sound at 25 kHz.

30.4 🎯 Transverse and longitudinal waves

FIRST THOUGHTS

When you think about waves you probably picture water waves. This picture is reasonable for light waves and electromagnetic waves, but not for sound waves. Read on to find out why not.

In the previous sections, water waves have been used to explain some of the basic properties of all types of wave. When waves travel across water, objects floating on the water surface bob up and down along a vertical line. The objects are said to oscillate because they repeatedly move up and down along a line.

You can use a long rope to demonstrate wave properties, as shown in Figure 30.4A. By moving one end of the rope from side to side repeatedly, you can make waves travel along the rope towards the other end. Each point along the rope oscillates from side to side as the waves pass.

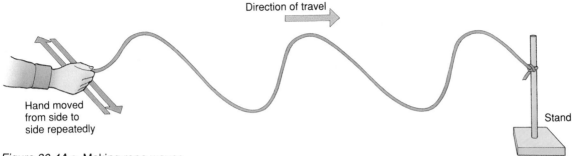

Figure 30.4A ● Making rope waves

Transverse waves

Water waves and waves in a rope are examples of **transverse waves**. Transverse means 'across' and transverse waves are waves where the oscillations are at right angles to (i.e. across) the direction in which the waves travel.

In water waves the motion is up and down, but in waves travelling along a rope, the oscillations can be along any line at right angles to the rope, not just up and down or side to side. To see this, try the demonstration shown in Figure 30.4B.

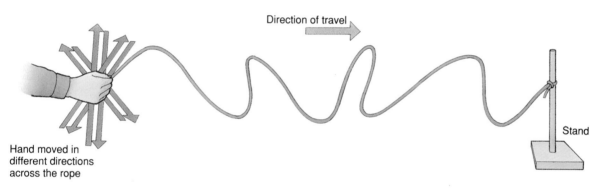

Figure 30.4B ● Unpolarised rope waves

Transverse waves are said to be **polarised** if they oscillate in one fixed direction only. Figure 30.4C shows polarised waves oscillating in a vertical direction. The waves in Figure 30.4B are unpolarised waves – the oscillations are in several different directions.

Light waves from a lamp bulb are unpolarised transverse waves. They can be polarised by being passed through special material called Polaroid®. This material only allows light waves through that are oscillating in a certain plane.

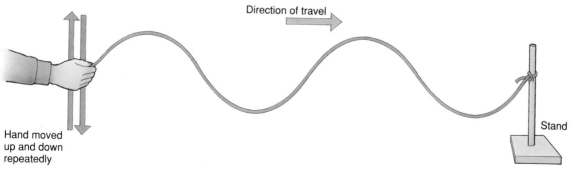

Figure 30.4C ● Polarised rope waves

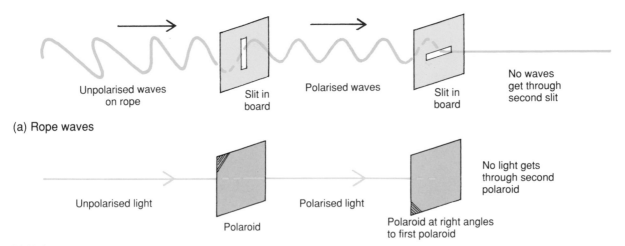

(a) Rope waves

(b) Light waves

Figure 30.4D ● Polarisers

The particular plane depends on the Polaroid molecules. Figure 30.4D shows how waves on a rope are polarised by being passed through a vertical slit that allows only vertical oscillations through. If the vertically polarised waves are then passed through a horizontal slit, no waves will come through at all. In the same way, light waves polarised in one direction by a piece of Polaroid cannot pass through a piece of the same Polaroid held at right angles to the first.

Polaroid filters are used in liquid crystal displays (LCDs) in calculators, and in Polaroid sunglasses. Look at an LCD through Polaroid sunglasses and rotate the display as you look. You should find that the display disappears then reappears as it is turned. This is because light from the LCD is polarised. Therefore it can only pass through the Polaroid sunglasses if the light is polarised in the 'correct' plane for the Polaroid molecules.

(a) Without Polaroid (b) With Polaroid

Figure 30.4E ● Polaroid sunglasses eliminate glare

Longitudinal waves

Sound waves are created by surfaces vibrating in air. The motion of a vibrating surface in air sends pressure waves through the air as the surface pushes and pulls repeatedly on the air surrounding it.

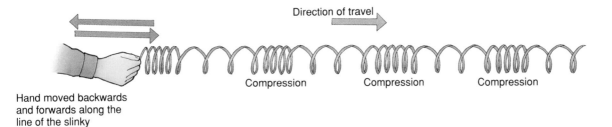

Figure 30.4F ● Making longitudinal waves in a slinky spring

IT
Waves
(program)

The *Waves* software shows how molecules move in the two types of wave: longitudinal and transverse. Slow the motion down so that you can see how the parts of the model move.

A slinky spring is useful for demonstrating how sound waves travel. If you move one end of the spring backwards and forwards repeatedly along the direction of the spring, you will see waves of compression travelling along it (Figure 30.4F). Each part of the slinky oscillates along the line of the spring. In the same way, when sound travels through air, each layer of air oscillates along the direction in which the sound travels (Figure 30.4G).

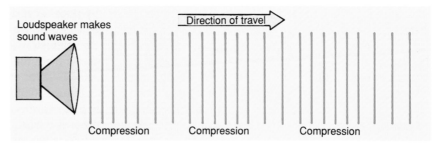

Figure 30.4G ● Making sound waves

SUMMARY

Transverse waves oscillate at right angles to the direction of travel of the waves. Longitudinal waves oscillate along the direction of travel of the waves. Transverse waves can be polarised.

Sound waves and compression waves along a slinky are examples of longitudinal waves, where the direction of oscillation is along the same line as the direction of travel of the wave itself. Like transverse waves, longitudinal waves can be reflected, refracted and diffracted. However, longitudinal waves cannot be polarised. Polarisation is a property of transverse waves only.

CHECKPOINT

❶ Describe how you would use a slinky to demonstrate to a friend the difference between longitudinal and transverse waves.

❷ If a beam of light is passed through two polaroid filters, as in the diagram, the beam can be stopped by turning one of the filters. Explain why this happens.

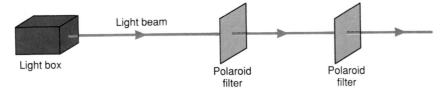

❸ (a) Susan's mother finds driving to work difficult because of the 'glare' of the Sun on the road. She thinks Polaroid sunglasses might be useful. Test a piece of Polaroid to find out if it cuts out glare.
   (b) It is not advisable to wear Polaroid sunglasses for driving because the toughened zones on the windscreen may be polarised. Why does this make Polaroid sunglasses unsuitable?

30.5 Interference of waves

FIRST THOUGHTS

How do we know that light is a waveform? In this section you will learn about one of the most important experiments in the history of physics. It was first carried out in 1803 and proved that light is a waveform.

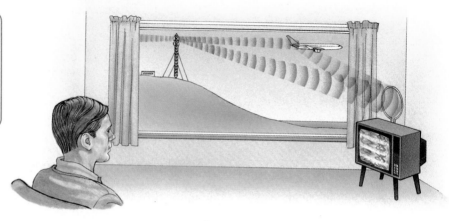

Figure 30.5A ● Television interference

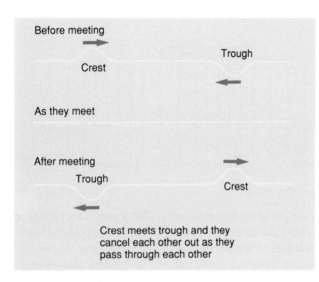

(a) Crest meets trough

Television programmes can sometimes be disturbed by poor reception when a low-flying aircraft passes near. Radio waves reflected from the aircraft arrive at the television aerial at the same time as radio waves direct from the transmitter (Figure 30.5A). The two sets of waves are said to **interfere** where they meet.

Figure 30.5B(a) shows two waves travelling along a rope towards each other. One wave is a **crest** and the other is a **trough**. They meet and pass through each other. When they meet, they **cancel** each other out at that instant. Figures 30.5B(b) and (c) show what happens when a crest meets a crest or a trough meets a trough. In these cases the waves are 'added together' to make a larger crest or trough. These are examples of **interference**.

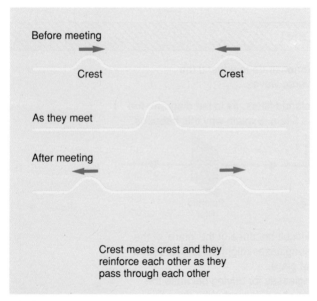

(b) Crest meets crest
Figure 30.5B ● Waves meeting

(c) Trough meets trough

❶ Lamp casts shadows of ripples on to screen ❹
❷ Beam and dippers suspended by elastic bands. The electric motor on the beam makes it vibrate, hence creating waves where the dippers ❸ touch the water

(a) Using the ripple tank

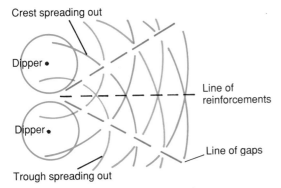

Crest spreading out

Dipper ●

Line of reinforcements

Dipper ●

Line of gaps

Trough spreading out

(b) Pattern on the screen

Figure 30.5C ● Interference of water waves

All types of wave can be made to interfere. Figure 30.5C shows what happens in a ripple tank when two sets of water waves overlap. Gaps are seen where crests from one dipper cancel troughs from the other dipper. The gaps are **points of cancellation**.

Between these gaps, there are **points of reinforcement** where crests (or troughs) from one dipper arrive at the same time as crests (or troughs) from the other dipper. The pattern of cancellations and reinforcements is called an **interference pattern**.

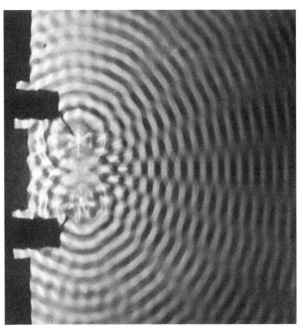

(c) What you see

Investigating interference

● ***Using microwaves***
Microwaves are short wavelength radio waves. Figure 30.5D shows how to produce an interference pattern using microwaves. You cannot see the pattern, but by moving a microwave detector you can locate the points of cancellation and reinforcement.

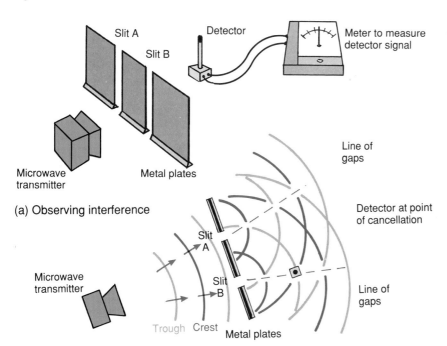

Slit A
Slit B
Detector
Meter to measure detector signal
Microwave transmitter
Metal plates

(a) Observing interference

Line of gaps
Slit A
Detector at point of cancellation
Microwave transmitter
Slit B
Line of gaps
Trough Crest   Metal plates

(b) The interference pattern

Figure 30.5D ● Using microwaves to investigate interference

Waves
(program)

Use *Waves* to find out what happens when waves bounce back and meet more waves coming in. In this program you can change the way the wave is reflected. *Does this change the interference pattern? Could you do this with a real wave in the laboratory?*

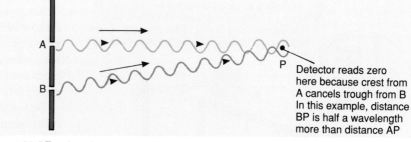

Detector reads zero here because crest from A cancels trough from B In this example, distance BP is half a wavelength more than distance AP

Figure 30.5E ● Interference conditions

Suppose the detector is moved to a point P where the meter reads zero (Figure 30.5E). This is a point of cancellation. At this point, waves from slit A cancel out waves from slit B. This is because a crest from one slit arrives at P at the same time as a trough from the other slit.

In fact, cancellation happens wherever the distances AP and BP differ by one half-wavelength or three half-wavelengths or five half-wavelengths, etc. Then crests from one slit arrive at P half a cycle later than crests from the other slit. Hence the two sets of waves cancel.

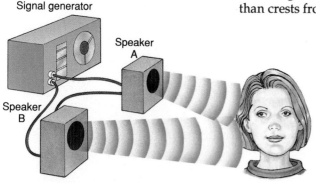

Figure 30.5F ● Interference of sound waves

● Using sound waves

Use two loudspeakers working from the same signal generator and walk about in front of the speakers (Figure 30.5F). You will hear the sound intensity vary from place to place. At each position of minimum intensity, crests from one speaker are arriving at the same time as troughs from the other speaker, and cancellation is taking place.

How does the interference pattern change if the wavelength of the sound waves is increased? The points of cancellation and reinforcement are now further apart.

● Using light

Observe the light from a narrow slit through a pair of slits, as shown in Figure 30.5G. A pattern of alternate bright and dark fringes will be seen stretching outwards from the double slits.

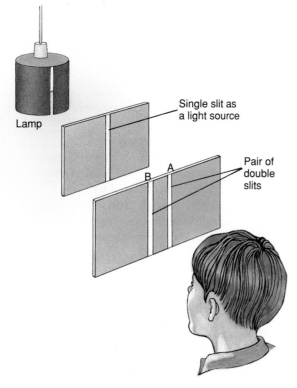

Single slit as a light source

Pair of double slits

Lamp

Figure 30.5G ● Interference of light
(a) Observing interference

(b) Interference pattern

SUMMARY

When two waves meet, they pass
through each other. Where a
crest meets a trough, they cancel
as they pass through each other.
Where a crest meets a crest or a
trough meets a trough, they
reinforce as they pass through
each other.

Young's Fringes
(program)

Young's Fringes is a program
which shows how light from two
slits can form an interference
pattern. The pattern changes
depending on how far apart the
slits are, what colour the light is
and also on where the screen is.
You can control these factors in the
program.

Light waves from the single slit source pass through each of the double slits. Where these two sets of waves overlap, interference takes place. Dark fringes occur where crests from one of the double slits arrive at the same time as troughs from the other double slit.

What happens if a different colour of light is used? Alternate bright and dark fringes are seen whatever colour is used. However, the spacing between adjacent fringes is greatest for red light and least for blue light (Figure 30.5H). This is because the wavelength of light waves differs for each colour; longest for red light and shortest for blue light.

Alternate bright and dark red fringes

(a) Red light

Alternate bright and dark blue fringes

(b) Blue light

Blue	Green	Yellow	Orange	Red
400 nm	500 nm	600 nm	700 nm	

(c) Wavelength and the colour of light

Figure 30.5H ● Interference patterns for different wavelengths of light

In the shadows

If you hold a coin in a beam of light from a torch in a darkened room, a sharp shadow of the coin is formed on the wall. In 1704 Sir Isaac Newton, the famous British scientist, put forward a theory of light to explain how shadows are formed.

Newton supposed that a ray of light consisted of tiny particles streaming out from the source of light. He called the particles corpuscles. Newton's theory was that a coin in the path of a beam of light casts a shadow because it stops the light particles. Newton also used his theory to explain other properties of light, such as reflection by mirrors. He imagined the corpuscles bouncing off the mirror like balls bouncing off a wall.

A different theory of light had been proposed by Christian Huygens in 1678 in the Netherlands. He imagined light as a waveform, spreading out from a point source like water waves spreading out from a stone dropped into water. He used his theory to explain reflection but was unable to explain how shadows are formed. According to wave theory, light passing the edge of a sharp object should be diffracted and spread out behind the object, making the edge of the shadow fuzzy rather than sharp. The sharpness of shadows was the main reason why Newton's theory was accepted, rather than Huygen's theory.

The corpuscular theory of light was unchallenged for a century until another British scientist, Thomas Young, discovered interference of light. He observed that light passing through two closely spaced slits produced a pattern of bright and dark fringes. This can be explained by wave theory but not by corpuscular theory.

The short-sighted policies of the ruling class in Britain restricted the development of science and technology in Britain for almost two decades. Pressure for change built up and the Reform Act of 1832 introduced democracy to Britain. The balance of power shifted from the landowning classes to the industrialists, and the importance of scientific and technical education to promote industrial and economic growth was recognised. As a result, institutes and colleges were established in many cities and towns.

Young presented his discovery to other scientists at a lecture to the Royal Society in 1803. However, although his discovery of interference of light was accepted, his fellow scientists would not accept that light was a waveform. They could not use Young's wave theory to explain why light passing through a calcite crystal formed a double image, as shown in Figure 30.5I. This was because they thought in terms of longitudinal waves, not transverse waves. Double refraction happens when light passes through calcite because the speed of light in calcite depends on the directions of vibration of the light waves.

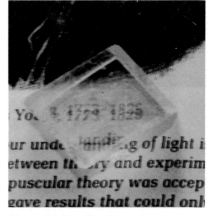
Figure 30.5I ● Double refraction

The solution did not occur to Young until 1818, when he realised that light waves are transverse not longitudinal. Augustin Fresnel, a French scientist, used this idea to give a complete explanation of double refraction. He then developed Young's theory to explain how fringe patterns are formed when light passes through any gap or round any obstacle. He also used wave theory to show that there should be a bright spot at the centre of the shadow of a coin in a beam of light. Scientists looked again at the sharpness of shadows. They used microscopes that had not been available to Huygens and observed the fringe patterns predicted by Fresnel. They found that there is indeed a bright spot at the centre of the shadow of a coin. Huygens had had the right idea after all!

Why did it take fifteen years for Thomas Young to realise that light waves are transverse, not longitudinal? At this time the ruling classes in Britain were worried that there could be a revolution as there had been in France. Britain was almost a police state and people were transported or imprisoned for opposition to the repressive government policies. Shortly before his 1803 lecture to the Royal Society, Young resigned from his post as assistant lecturer at the Royal Institution. Benjamin Thompson (who had appointed Young) had proposed radical plans to provide technical education for working people. The Royal Institution turned this down, since education could make the 'masses' more powerful. Thompson took his plans to Bavaria and Young, discouraged by the Institution's attitude, returned to his full-time medical practice.

LOOK AT LINKS
for Benjamin Thompson's contribution to science
See Theme B, Topic 7.3.

CHECKPOINT

❶ Simon notices that when he moves a metal tea tray near the aerial of a portable television, the television reception is affected. Why do you think this happens?

❷ In the microwave experiment to demonstrate interference (Figure 30.5D), the detector is placed at a point where its signal strength is zero. What would you expect to observe if each slit were blocked in turn?

❸ (a) In Figure 30.5D, the detector is moved to a point equidistant from the slits. The detector signal strength is then a maximum. Why?
(b) The detector is then moved to one side until the signal becomes zero. When it is moved further in the same direction the signal rises again. Explain these observations.

❹ In a microwave oven, microwaves are reflected from the inside surface of the oven. A metal 'paddle wheel' inside the oven spreads the reflected microwaves around. How would food being cooked in the microwave be affected if the wheel stopped turning during the cooking process?

❺ In Figure 30.5G, how would the pattern of light fringes change if:
(a) one of the double slits was covered completely,
(b) blue light was used instead of red light?

TOPIC 31 SOUND

 31.1 ● **Sound patterns**

FIRST THOUGHTS

In this section you will find out how characteristic sounds are produced.

Can you recognise people by the sound of their voices? How would you describe different voices? Loud, soft, deep, high-pitched; these are all terms we use to describe the human voice. Voice recognition locks are designed to open when commanded by the correct voice. Provided you don't have a cold, electronic voice recognition devices can use your voice to check your identity.

Investigating different sounds

Sound waves can be displayed using a microphone connected to an oscilloscope, which is an instrument designed to display waveforms on its screen (Figure 31.1A). The microphone converts sound waves into electrical waves, which are then supplied to the oscilloscope. The pattern on the oscilloscope screen shows how the amplitude of the sound waves changes with time.

Figure 31.1A ● Displaying sound waves

Figure 31.1B ● Tuning fork pattern

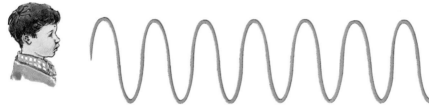

(a) Loud and high-pitched

The pattern for a tuning fork sounded near the microphone shows waves of constant frequency, as in Figure 31.1B. Whistling at a constant pitch at the microphone gives a pattern like that in Figure 31.1C. The way in which changing the pitch or the loudness alters the pattern is also shown in Figure 31.1C.

Playing a flute produces a pattern like that in Figure 31.1D. Unlike the previous examples, this pattern is a mixture of frequencies rather than a single frequency.

(b) Loud and low-pitched

(c) Quiet and high-pitched

Figure 31.1C ● Whistling wave patterns

Figure 31.1D ● Flute wave pattern

IT ***Sound/Ripples***
(program)

Use the *Sound/Ripples* disc to remind yourself of the way sound is produced and how it travels and then go on to the experiment part of the program. You can make a sound by choosing the amplitude and frequency of the wave. You are using the computer as a sound synthesiser. Try adding two sounds together – listen and look at the wave pattern on the screen.

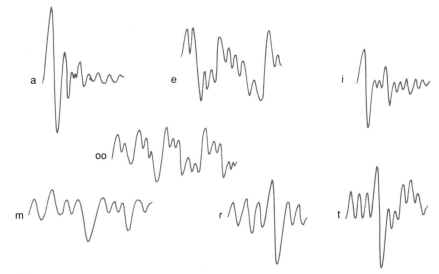

Figure 31.1E ● Making sounds

Speaking into the microphone produces changing patterns. Each voice sound produces a distinctive pattern. Some examples of patterns for different speech sounds are shown in Figure 31.1E.

The loudness of a sound depends on the amplitude of the sound waves. Increasing the 'volume' of a radio increases the amplitude of the sound waves produced by the radio's speaker, so the sound from the radio is louder. Changing the loudness does not alter the frequency of the sound.

The pitch depends on the frequency of the sound waves. Increasing the frequency makes the pitch higher. A signal generator is an electrical instrument that can be connected to a loudspeaker to produce sounds at different pitches.

The sound quality depends on how close the sound wave is to a wave with constant frequency. A high quality note is said to be more 'pure' than a low quality note. For example, in Figure 31.1E, the 'r' sound is a higher quality note than the 'i' sound.

SUMMARY

Sounds can be described in terms of loudness, pitch and quality. Increasing the amplitude of sound waves makes them louder. Increasing the frequency makes the pitch higher.

CHECKPOINT

❶ Use the patterns in Figure 31.1E to sketch the oscilloscope pattern produced when Marie says her name at the microphone.

❷ The patterns shown below are words made up of the sounds shown in Figure 31.1E. Work out what the words are.

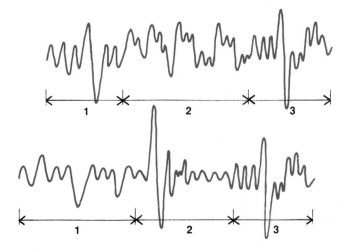

❸ The pattern produced by a tuning fork is shown in Figure 31.1B. Copy this pattern and sketch further patterns produced by:
(a) the same tuning fork making a louder sound,
(b) the same tuning fork making a softer sound,
(c) a higher pitched tuning fork making a louder sound,
(d) a lower pitched tuning fork making a sound of the same loudness as the one in Figure 31.1B.

❹ If you strike a tuning fork and hold it near your ear, you can hear it faintly for a long time. If you strike the same tuning fork and hold its base on a worktop, making the worktop vibrate as well, the sound is much louder but doesn't last as long. Try this for yourself and then explain the differences.

❺ Devise a voice recognition test, using a cassette recorder, and use your friends as 'guinea pigs'. Explain how you would test to find out if their voices can be recognised easily. If possible, conduct the test and present your findings to the group.

FIRST THOUGHTS

If you live near an airport the properties of sound affect you considerably. Read on to find out about the effects of different materials on sound.

31.2 ● The properties of sound

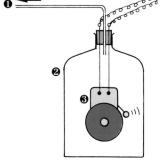

❶ Air removed using a vacuum pump
❷ Bell jar
❸ Bell works but cannot be heard
❹ Wires to bell battery

RESOURCE ACTIVITY PACK

Figure 31.2A ● Sound does not pass through a vacuum

Sound waves travel through solids and liquids as well as through gases. The apparatus shown in Figure 31.2A is used to demonstrate that sound cannot travel through a vacuum. As the air is pumped out of the flask, the sound of the ringing bell disappears. If the jar is filled with air again, the sound returns.

The speed of sound depends on the medium (i.e. type of material) the sound is travelling through. The speed of sound in a gas also depends on the temperature of the gas: the higher the temperature, the faster the sound travels.

TRY THIS

— Gun
Stopwatch

Figure 31.2B ● Measuring the speed of sound

● **Measuring the speed of sound in air**
You need two people for this. You and a friend should stand on opposite sides of a field as far apart as possible, but within sight of each other. If your friend fires a starting pistol in the air you will see the smoke from the pistol almost straight away. However, the 'bang' will be delayed because sound travels much more slowly than light. Use a stopwatch to time the interval between the smoke and the bang. This is the time taken for the sound to travel from your friend to you. Then measure the distance from your friend to where you did the timing. You can then work out the speed of sound using the formula

$$\text{Speed} = \frac{\text{Distance}}{\text{Time}}$$

SCIENCE AT WORK

Echo sounders are used at sea to measure the depth of the sea bed. Ultrasonics are used – high frequency sound waves that cannot be detected by the human ear. Ultrasonic pulses, beamed at the sea bed from the surface, reflect back to the surface. The pulses are timed and the timing is used to work out the depth.

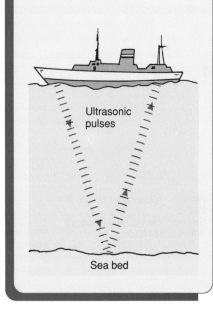

Ultrasonic pulses

Sea bed

Echoes

Echoes are sounds reflected off hard surfaces, such as bare walls and cliff faces. Shouting in a sports hall produces lots of echoes. Stand at the centre of a quiet hall facing a bare wall and clap your hands. You should be able to hear the echo of the clap. You may even be able to clap in time with the echoes.

To produce echoes the reflecting surface must be hard and smooth. If the surface is soft, the sound waves are absorbed by the surface instead of being reflected. If the surface is bumpy the waves are all reflected in different directions and the reflection is 'broken up', so no echo is heard. The sound is said to reverberate if it can still be heard after each clap. For example, in a curtain-lined hall no echoes are produced, so sound does not reverberate.

You can estimate the speed of sound by clapping near a bare wall. Suppose you stand 30 m from the bare wall and you clap in time with the echoes at a rate of six claps per second, timed by a friend.

Each clap travels a distance of 2 x 30 = 60 m from you to the wall and back again. Since each clap returns at the instant the next clap is being produced, it takes $\frac{1}{6}$th second to travel to the wall and back.

Figure 31.2C ● The Whispering Gallery, St Paul's Cathedral

Hence   Distance travelled   = 60 m
          Time taken   = $\frac{1}{6}$ s

Thus   Speed of sound   = $\frac{\text{Distance}}{\text{Time}}$ = $\frac{60}{\frac{1}{6}}$ = 360 m/s

Figure 31.2D ● A jumbo jet landing over houses

Noise

A school canteen at lunchtime is no place for anyone who wants a quiet rest. All the chatting and clattering can be very noisy. Noise is unwanted sound.

How could the din in a busy canteen be cut down? Eating in silence is not a practical proposition in a school. Wearing ear muffs is unrealistic too in this situation. A much more effective approach is to redesign the building to keep noise levels down.

Noise can be a problem in many situations. For example, people living near airports or busy motorways need protection in their homes from excessive noise. Noise can be cut down by:

• Reducing it at source; for example, cutting down on the number of flights allowed in and out of an airport or fitting quieter engines to jets.
• Absorbing it after it has been produced; for example, using fences or walls to shield homes in urban areas from traffic noise.

Ultrasonics

The human ear can detect sound waves in the frequency range from about 20 Hz to about 18 000 Hz. Sound waves above the upper frequency limit of the human ear are called ultrasonic waves. In hospitals, ultrasonic scanners are used to produce images of organs in the body or babies in the womb. Ships use ultrasonic depth gauges to locate the sea bed. Street lights are cleaned by immersing the lighting unit in a tank of water and passing ultrasonic waves through the water. The ultrasonic waves dislodge particles from the surfaces of the unit.

SUMMARY

Sound cannot travel through a vacuum. The speed of sound depends on the medium through which it passes. Echoes are caused by sound waves being reflected off hard surfaces.

Figure 31.2E ● An ultrasonic image of a baby in the uterus

CHECKPOINT

❶ (a) In an experiment to measure the speed of sound, a student fires a starting pistol. Another student 600 m away times the interval between the flash and the bang at 1.8 s. Work out the speed of sound.
(b) Does sound travel faster downwind than upwind? Design an outdoor experiment to find out if it does.

❷ Why would your voice echo more in an empty house than in a house that is carpeted and contains furniture?

❸ Concert halls are designed very carefully to eliminate unwanted echoes. However, the hall walls must not absorb the sound completely. How do you think a concert in a bare hall would sound compared with one in a hall with totally absorbing walls?

❹ Ultrasonics are used in hospitals to scan babies in the uterus. Figure 31.2E shows an image produced by an ultrasonic scan. A special device sends ultrasonic pulses into the mother's body. Tissue and bone boundaries reflect the pulses, which are detected and used to build up a picture of the baby on a monitor.
(a) Why is this method preferable to an internal examination of the mother?
(b) Why is it important to be able to see the placenta on the scan?
(c) What other things can a scan warn the doctor about?

❺ In a test to measure the depth of the sea bed, ultrasonic pulses took 0.4 s to travel from the surface to the sea bed and back. Given that the speed of sound in sea water is 1350 m/s, work out the depth of the sea bed.

31.3 The ear

FIRST THOUGHTS

Your ears are vital organs that enable you to receive information from other people. In this section you will find out how the ear works and how to test your own hearing response.

IT'S A FACT

The fleshy lobe of the outer ear is called the **pinna**. It funnels sound waves down the ear tube to the ear drum. Cats, dogs and other mammals can adjust the pinna and cock it towards sources of sound. In most humans it is fixed. The walls of the ear tube produce wax which keeps the ear drum soft and supple.

RESOURCE ACTIVITY PACK

Have you ever listened to the sound of your own voice played back on a tape recorder? Try it and you will hear yourself as others hear you. To you, your voice will sound different on the recording. When you hear yourself speak, sound waves from your voice travel through your head as well as through the air to reach your ears. Other people only receive the sound of you speaking through the air.

The human ear is a remarkable organ that can detect an enormous range of sound waves. The loudest sounds it can withstand carry over one million million times more energy than the quietest sounds it can hear. It can detect frequencies from about 20 Hz (a bee buzzing) to about 18 000 Hz (a very high-pitched whistle).

The ear sends signals to the brain in response to sound waves arriving at the **eardrum**. Sound waves arriving at the ear make the eardrum vibrate. These vibrations are passed through the middle ear by three tiny bones, the **hammer**, **anvil** and **stirrup**, to reach the **oval window** of the inner ear. The vibrations of the oval window are transmitted through the fluid of the **cochlea**, making the **basilar membrane** vibrate. Tiny hair cells, which are sound-sensitive receptors, are lined up on the basilar membrane. The vibrating membrane activates the hair cells, which fire off nerve impulses to the brain along the **auditory nerve**.

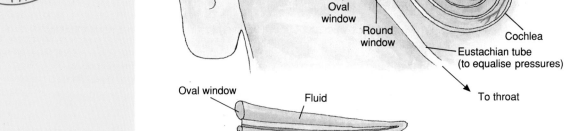

Figure 31.3A ● The human ear

What happens to the ear if very loud sound falls on it? If this happens too often, the ear becomes less and less sensitive and deafness can occur. One reason for this is that the bones of the middle ear vibrate too much and get worn down. They then become less effective at passing the vibrations from the ear drum to the oval window. Operators of noisy machines must wear ear pads or they suffer permanent loss of hearing. Protect your ears at noisy discos by putting cotton wool in your ears.

LOOK AT LINKS
find out more about the response of the human nervous system in Theme J, Topic 40.2.

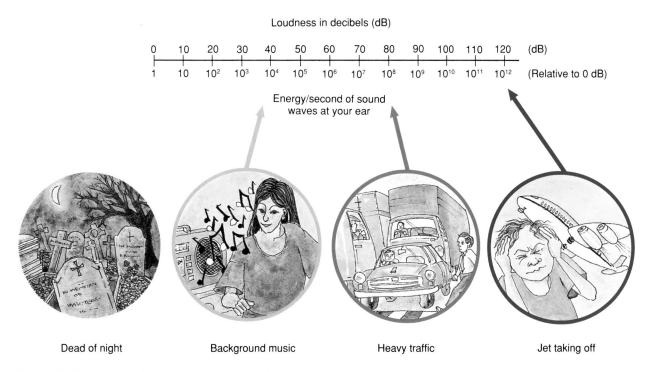

Figure 31.3B ● Decibel levels of everyday sounds

Your body is quite noisy. Lots of gurgling and pounding noises are produced by organs like your stomach and heart. Your doctor can hear all sorts of wheezing and whistling noises by listening with a stethoscope to your chest as you breathe. Yet these noises aren't usually detected by your own ears. This is because the bones of the middle ear help to filter out unwanted 'body' noise.

SUMMARY

The ear converts signals carried by sound waves into nerve impulses that it sends to the brain. The ear cannot detect frequencies above 18 000 Hz. Loudness levels above 120 decibels can cause deafness if the ear is not protected.

Loudness is measured in **decibels** (dB). The faintest sound that the ear can hear is defined as zero decibels (0 dB). Imagine steadily increasing the loudness of a radio from zero until it becomes too loud to bear. For every ten decibel (10 dB) increase in loudness, the energy of the sound waves is increased by a factor of 10. The sound would become too loud to bear at about 120 dB. Since this is 12 steps at 10 dB for each step, sound waves at this loudness carry $10 \times 10 \times 10 \times 10 \times 10 \times 10 \times 10 \times 10 \times 10 \times 10 \times 10 \times 10 = 10^{12}$ times as much energy as the faintest sound waves. Figure 31.3B shows the decibel levels of some everyday sounds.

The response of the ear to different levels of loudness varies with frequency, as shown in Figure 31.3C. The ear is most sensitive and can detect the softest sounds at about 3000 Hz. It is completely insensitive and cannot detect any sound over 18 000 Hz.

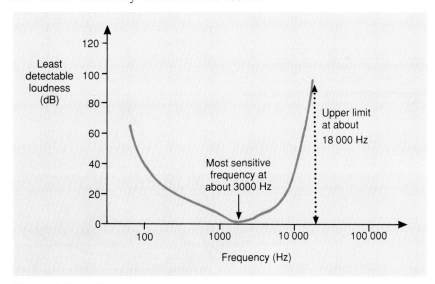

Figure 31.3C ● Frequency response of the ear

CHECKPOINT

❶ (a) One of the first hearing aids was the 'ear trumpet', which was a large hollow horn held to the ear. Why do you think this device improves hearing ability?

(b) Modern hearing aids are so small that they can be worn behind the ear. Such a device contains an electronic amplifier, a tiny microphone and an earpiece speaker. The amplifier makes electrical signals bigger without changing the frequency of the signal. What is the purpose of the microphone and what is the earpiece speaker for?

❷ What is the purpose of each of the following parts of the ear:
(a) the eardrum,
(b) the pinna,
(c) the bones of the middle ear,
(d) the oval window,
(e) the hair cells?

❸ Play back your own voice using a tape recorder. How does it differ from what you hear when you speak? Compare the voices of your friends on a tape recorder. Do their voices seem different from when they speak directly to you?

❹ Here is a passage from Claire's diary describing part of an evening out with her friends.
'It was very noisy and hot in the disco. We could only hear each other when the music stopped. I got a lift home with Michelle and her dad. There was a thunderstorm on the way home. When I got home, the TV was on very loud so I went to my bedroom for some peace and quiet.'
(a) When was the loudness level greatest and when was it least?
(b) Estimate the loudness when it was greatest.
(c) Which do you think was most damaging to the ears: the thunderclap or the disco noise?

---

o
o
o

31.4 Making music

How does music differ from other sounds? How is it produced? As you work through this section, think about your own experiences of making music, and perhaps try out some instruments.

Notes of music are sounds that are easy to listen to because they are rhythmic. The waves that carry these notes change smoothly and the wave pattern repeats itself regularly. Figure 31.1D shows the wave pattern for a note played on a flute, displayed on an oscilloscope connected to a microphone. Compare this note pattern with the pattern shown in Figure 31.1B produced by a tuning fork, which gives a note of constant frequency, sometimes called a **pure note**.

Wind instruments such as the trombone or the flute produce notes because the air inside the instrument is made to **resonate**. Anything that moves to and fro repeatedly can be made to resonate. For example, pushing a child on a swing every time the swing descends makes the swing resonate and the child go higher and higher (Figure 31.4A).

Figure 31.4A ● Making a swing resonate

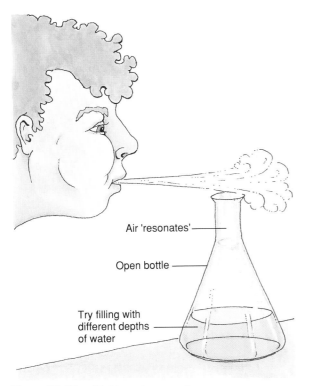

Figure 31.4B ● Making air resonate

Figure 31.4C ● Vibrating guitar strings

Air 'resonates'

Open bottle

Try filling with
different depths
of water

The most famous make of violin is the Stradivarius. This was made by Antonio Stradivari in the seventeenth century in Italy. He perfected the design to such an extent that no one since has ever surpassed it. Even attempts to reproduce the design have failed.

Blowing into a wind instrument makes the layers of air in the instrument oscillate so much that the instrument resonates with sound. You can make an empty bottle resonate by blowing gently across the top (Figure 31.4B). At the right speed, a booming sound is produced as the air inside resonates.

Percussion instruments such as the drum or the handbell are struck to produce sound. A drum has a tightly stretched membrane, the drum skin, which vibrates when it is struck. The vibrating drum skin pushes the surrounding air to and fro, making sound waves that travel outwards from the drum.

String instruments such as the guitar and the violin produce sound when the strings vibrate. A guitar string is plucked and vibrates, whereas a violin string vibrates when a bow is drawn across it. In both cases, the vibrating strings make the body of the instrument vibrate at the same frequency, which makes the surrounding air vibrate, so sound waves are produced.

A guitar has six strings, each of a different thickness. The pitch of the note produced by a plucked string is changed by making the string tighter or shorter. Pressing the string on the frets along the neck of the guitar makes the vibrating length shorter. Tuning the appropriate key changes the tension (i.e. tightness) of the string. *How would you make the pitch of a string higher? How does the pitch differ between a thin string and a thick string?*

Investigating the vibrations of a stretched string

Fix one end of a string to a vibrator driven by a signal generator and pass the other end over a pulley. Fix a weight on this end, as shown in Figure 31.4D overleaf. The string is then under constant tension and its length is

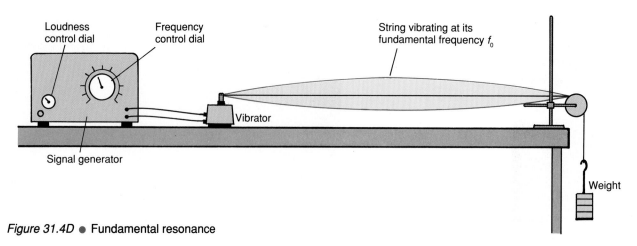

Figure 31.4D ● Fundamental resonance

fixed. The output frequency of the signal generator can be changed using the control dial. When the frequency is increased from zero, different patterns of vibration are produced in the string when it is made to resonate by the vibrator.

* The simplest pattern is called the **fundamental** pattern (Figure 31.4D). The vibrations are strongest at the middle of the string. The vibrating string produces sound waves at the same frequency as it is vibrating.
* Increasing the frequency produces more complicated patterns. These are called **overtones**. They occur at frequencies equal to two, three, four, etc. times the fundamental frequency. Figure 31.4E shows the patterns of the 1st and 2nd overtones.

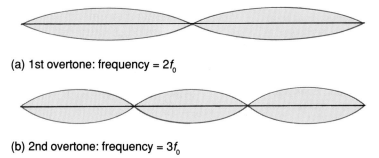

(a) 1st overtone: frequency = $2f_0$

(b) 2nd overtone: frequency = $3f_0$

Figure 31.4E ● Overtones

When a wire or a string is plucked it produces sound waves composed of a mixture of the fundamental note and the overtones. In comparison, a tuning fork produces a pure note (just the fundamental). The note from a wire sounds slightly different because of the presence of the overtones.

Synthesisers are electronic instruments that can make any type of sound (Figure 31.4F). Recording studios use them to make the sounds of other musical instruments and interesting sound effects for television, radio and films. A synthesiser has many channels, each of which can produce a pure note at a different frequency. The loudness of the note can be altered. To make a particular sound, different channels are selected, each feeding a note into a mixer circuit. The mixer adds the notes together and its output is then supplied to a loudspeaker. The loudness level of each channel can be adjusted to allow the user to produce the desired sound. The synthesiser can be linked up with a computer and programmed to produce different sounds in sequence.

SUMMARY

Musical notes are wave patterns that repeat themselves. Musical instruments are designed to vibrate, thus creating sound waves in the surrounding air. A synthesiser can produce the same note as any musical instrument.

Figure 31.4F ● Synthesiser in use

CHECKPOINT

❶ (a) List ten musical instruments, stating whether each one is a percussion instrument, a wind instrument or a string instrument.
(b) Why do you think big instruments usually produce deeper notes than small instruments?

❷ A guitar has six strings, each of a different thickness. The vibrating length of each string can be changed by pressing it against the frets. The string tension can be changed by using the tension keys.
(a) How does making the string (i) tighter (ii) shorter affect the pitch of the note produced by the string?
(b) How does the pitch of a note produced by a thin string compare with that of a note produced by a thick string at the same length and tension?

❸ (a) Design an experiment to test how the fundamental frequency of a vibrating string under constant tension varies with the length of the string.
(b) Here are some results from such an experiment. Can you see the connection between the frequency and the length? Plot a graph to show the relationship between these quantities.

Length (mm)	1000	800	600	400	200
Frequency (Hz)	96	120	160	240	480

❹ (a) Some wind instruments have a mouthpiece that contains a reed. Why?
(b) You can make some interesting sounds using a comb and paper. Try it and then explain how it works.
(c) Explain why a cracked handbell will not ring.
(d) Why do pianos need to be tuned regularly?

❺ Some types of microcomputer can be used as synthesisers. Here is a program that turns a BBC micro into a keyboard using the QWERTYUIOP keys. Do not worry about how it works. Key the program in and see if you can recognise the tune 'TTY5TY UUIUYT YT5T'.

```
10 *FX12, 4
20 *FX11, 4
30 S$ = "Q2W3ER5T6Y7UI9O0P"
40 REPEAT
50 SOUND &11, –15, INSTR (S$, GET$) *4, 1
60 UNTIL FALSE
```

TOPIC
32

LIGHT

32.1 **Mirror images**

Compare a photograph of yourself with your image in a mirror. Why do they differ? Images can be very deceptive.

Look in a mirror and you will see an image of yourself created by the **reflection** of light by the mirror. Your mirror image is reversed – use your left hand to wave at it and you will see that your image's right hand waves at you. However, provided your mirror is a plane (i.e. flat) mirror, your image has the same shape as you. In the 'Hall of Mirrors' at the funfair, using curved mirrors instead of plane mirrors gives very amusing images.

To understand how mirrors form images, we can reflect light rays off mirrors and then make scale drawings called ray diagrams to explain what we see. The light rays are drawn to show the direction in which the light waves travel (Figure 32.1A).

Figure 32.1A ● Rays and waves

Investigating reflection by plane mirrors

You can see how an image is formed by a plane mirror using the arrangement in Figure 32.1B. Look along the reflected rays and you will see an image of the ray box in the mirror. The image is called a **virtual image** because the reflected rays *appear* to come from it.

How far is the image behind the mirror? Remove the mirror and trace the ray paths on the paper to find out where they meet behind the mirror. This is where the image is formed. Compare the distance from the ray box to the mirror with the distance from the image to the mirror. Try the experiment again with the ray box in a different position. You should find that the image is always the same distance from the mirror as the object.

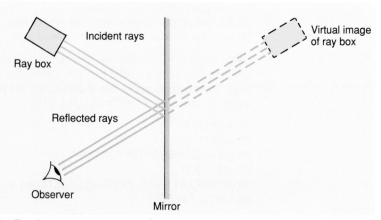

Figure 32.1B ● Investigating reflection

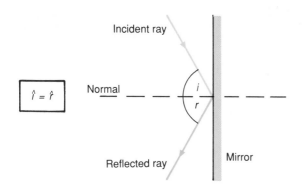

Figure 32.1C ● The law of reflection

To understand why this always happens, look carefully at Figure 32.1C. *Can you see that each ray reflects off the mirror at the same angle as it strikes the mirror?* To check this, use a protractor to measure the angles shown. Each angle is always measured from the light ray to the **normal**, which is the line at right angles to the mirror.

The **Law of Reflection** states that the angle between the incident ray and the normal is always equal to the angle between the reflected ray and the normal.

Investigating the concave mirror

You can use a concave mirror to form an image of a distant object on a screen. The ray diagram in Figure 32.1D shows how the light from the lamp shines through the slide on to the mirror and is reflected off the mirror on to the screen. An inverted image of the slide is formed on the screen. This image is called a **real image**, because it can be formed on a screen.

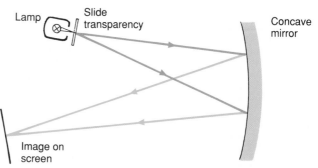

Figure 32.1D ● Investigating image formation

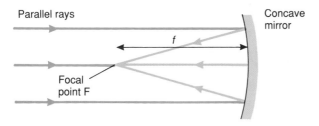

Figure 32.1E ● Focal length

Parallel rays of light always meet at the **focal point**, F, of the concave mirror after reflection (Figure 32.1E). Rays of light from a distant object reach the mirror as a parallel beam, so the image of a distant object is always formed at the focal point.

If you know the focal length, f, (the distance from the focal point to the mirror) you can draw a ray diagram to scale on graph paper to work out where an image is formed. How to do this is explained in Figure 32.1F, which is a ray diagram for a real image formed by reflection off a concave mirror. A real image is always formed if the object is outside the focal length of the mirror. It is always inverted, and its size depends on the distance of the object from the mirror.

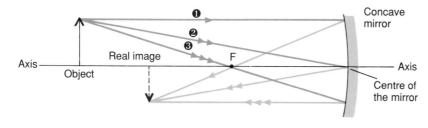

❶ Light ray parallel to the axis is reflected through F
❷ Light ray to centre of the mirror is reflected at an equal angle (Law of reflection)
❸ Light ray through F reflects parallel to the axis

Figure 32.1F ● Formation of a real image

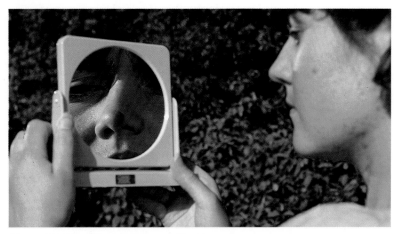

Figure 32.1G ● Forming a magnified image

A concave mirror can also be used as a face mirror (see Figure 32.1G). If you hold the mirror close up you will see a magnified image of your face. This is a virtual image, as it is formed where the reflected light appears to come from. This image cannot be formed on a screen. *Is it upright or inverted?*

A concave mirror forms a virtual image if the object is inside the focal length of the mirror. The image is always upright and enlarged. The ray diagram in Figure 32.1H shows how the image is formed.

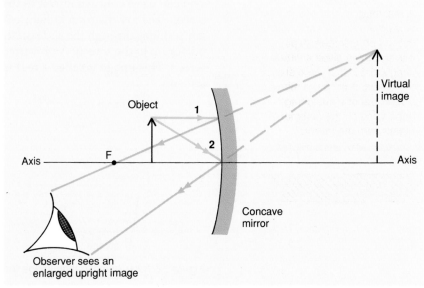

Figure 32.1H ● Formation of a virtual image

Uses of mirrors

Plane mirrors are used to see round awkward corners as well as to check personal appearance. They are also used in meters where a pointer has to be read against a scale (Figure 32.1I). For an accurate reading the image of the pointer must be under the pointer.

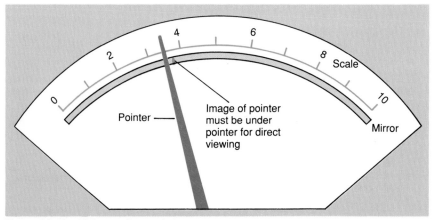

Figure 32.1I ● Using a plane mirror

Concave mirrors can be used as face mirrors, or to collect light or to project it. Sunlight can be focused to a tiny 'hot spot' by a concave mirror, as in a solar energy collector. To project light, a light bulb is placed at the focus of the mirror, which gives a parallel beam of reflected light, as shown in Figure 32.1J.

Convex mirrors are used as driving mirrors, as security mirrors in shops and to see around corners. Convex mirrors have a wide field of view. Figure 32.1K shows how a convex mirror reflects light falling on it.

SUMMARY

A real image can be formed on a screen. A virtual image cannot be formed on a screen. A plane mirror always gives a virtual image that is the same size as the object. A concave mirror can give a real or virtual image depending on the distance of the object from the mirror.

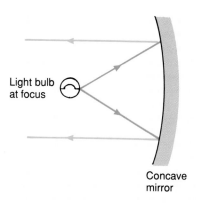

Light bulb at focus

Concave mirror

Figure 32.1J ● Projecting a parallel beam

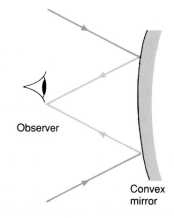

Observer

Convex mirror

Figure 32.1K ● A wide field of view

CHECKPOINT

❶ Test your drawing skills. A point object O is placed 50 mm from a plane mirror, as shown. Copy the figure and on your copy show the path of two rays from O that reflect off the mirror. Use the reflected rays to mark the image position I and show that the image is 50 mm behind the mirror.

Plane mirror

● Object
O

❷ Kim notices that letter 'p' held near a mirror appears as letter 'b' in the mirror. Are there any other pairs of letters that form mirror images of each other? Which letters appear the same in a plane mirror?

❸ Make your own 'Hall of Mirrors'. Suppose you are given a flexible plastic sheet with a mirror finish on one side. How would you bend it to make the image:
(a) thinner than normal, (c) longer and thinner than normal,
(b) shorter than normal, (d) wide at the bottom and thin at the top.

④ (a) A concave mirror can be used to form a real image of an object. Design an experiment, using a pair of crosswires as an object, to find out how the height (H) of the image varies with the distance (D) from the image to the mirror.

(b) The following measurements were made in such an experiment.

D (mm)	1000	850	700	550	400
H (mm)	46	37	26	17	6

Plot a graph of H on the vertical axis against D on the horizontal axis. Describe the connection between H and D that your graph shows. Can you write an equation to show this connection?

⑤ A concave mirror has a focal length of 250 mm. Make a scale drawing to locate the image formed by an object placed:
(a) 600 mm from the mirror,
(b) 400 mm from the mirror,
(c) 200 mm from the mirror.
In each case, write down whether the image is real or virtual.

FIRST THOUGHTS

32.2 Fibre optics

Surgeons and security firms use fibre optics for very different purposes. Read on to find out how fibre optics work.

Mr Green is in terrible pain. The surgeon thinks the cause may be a stomach ulcer. Fortunately for Mr Green the surgeon can find out without cutting into him, by using an **endoscope**. An endoscope is a thin, flexible tube, which the surgeon can pass down Mr Green's throat into his stomach. Light is sent down part of the tube and is reflected back along another part of the tube. It shows there is an angry-looking ulcer on the lining of Mr Green's stomach (Figure 32.2A).

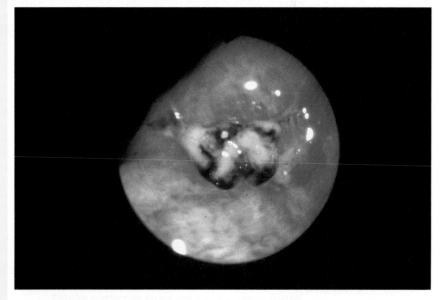

Figure 32.2A ● Stomach ulcer viewed through an endoscope

An endoscope contains a bundle of optical fibres, which are very thin strands of glass. Light enters the fibre at one end, passes along it, and comes out at the other end, even if the fibre is bent or twisted. Light passes along an optical fibre by **total internal reflection**.

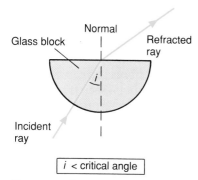

Figure 32.2B ● Refraction of light

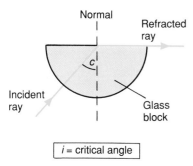

Figure 32.2C ● At the critical angle

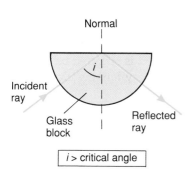

Figure 32.2D ● Total internal reflection

Investigating total internal reflection

You can use a semicircular glass block to investigate this. In Figure 32.2B the light ray is **refracted** by the glass and comes out through the straight edge of the block. Here the angle of incidence, i, is less than the **critical angle**, c. The critical angle for glass is about 42°, but varies for different types. If a light ray enters the block at the critical angle (Figure 32.2C) the refracted ray emerges along the straight edge of the block. If the angle of incidence of the light ray is greater than the critical angle, the light ray is totally internally reflected, as shown in Figure 32.2D. *What measurements would you make to show that the angle of reflection is equal to the angle of incidence?*

Light rays enter an optical fibre and are totally internally reflected from the sides of the fibre each time they hit the glass boundary at the edge of the fibre (Figure 32.2E). The fibres must be very thin. If the fibres were too thick, the angles of incidence of the light rays inside hitting the boundary would be smaller on average (see Figure 32.2F). If they were smaller than the critical angle, the light would not all be totally internally reflected, and some would be lost through the sides of the fibre. The thinner the fibre, the more it can be bent without light being lost.

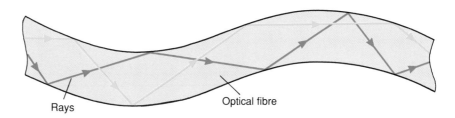

Figure 32.2E ● Fibre optics

In a thick fibre, angles of incidence are smaller than in a thin fibre.

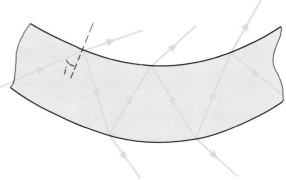

Figure 32.2F ● Thin and thick optical fibres

SUMMARY

Optical fibres are used to guide light rays. The fibres must be thin to ensure light does not escape through the sides of the fibre. They are used in medicine and in telecommunications.

Uses of optical fibres

Optical fibres are used in medicine, in endoscopes, and also in telecommunications. If a light source is switched on and off repeatedly, these signals can be carried by an optical fibre. Since light waves have a much higher frequency than radio waves, optical fibres can carry many more pulses than radio beams. Also, the light cannot be seen from outside the fibre, only by the receiver at the other end, so no-one can spy on the signals.

CHECKPOINT

❶ In medicine, separate 'bundles' of optical fibres are used to light up cavities in the body to enable doctors to see what is there.

(a) Why is it necessary to light up the cavity?
(b) Give two reasons why lots of thin fibres are used to make a bundle, rather than a few thick fibres.

❷ In telecommunications, messages carried by pulses of light can be sent along individual fibres.
(a) Why is it important that light does not leak between the fibres?
(b) Each fibre is coated with a special 'cladding' to prevent light leakage where fibres touch. What would happen if this cladding got rubbed away?

❸ The diagram shows a section of an optical fibre made of a material with a critical angle of 40°. Copy the diagram and complete the paths of the two rays marked X and Y.

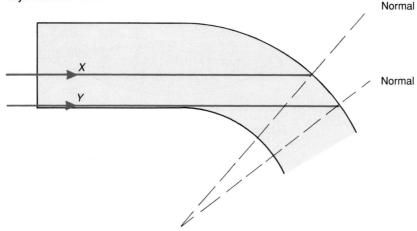

❹ A pulse of light is sent down an optical fibre as shown.
(a) The light rays that are reflected from side to side take longer to travel the length of the fibre than those that pass straight along. Why?
(b) Why does this time lag cause the light pulse reaching the far end to be 'smeared out'?

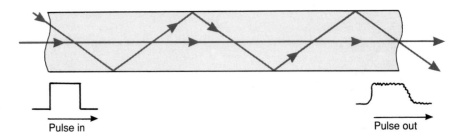

Pulse in

Pulse out

32.3 Refraction

Refraction is a property of every type of wave. In this section you will study refraction of light to give you the understanding necessary for work on lenses and optical instruments.

When you visit the swimming pool, take care near the deep end. It might seem shallow, but if you fall in you may be surprised. The water is deeper than it looks, because light from the bottom of the pool is bent (refracted) when it leaves the water, so the image of the bottom of the pool appears to be closer than it really is (Figure 32.3A).

Light is also refracted when it passes between air and glass. Light waves travel more slowly in glass than in air, because glass is more dense than air.

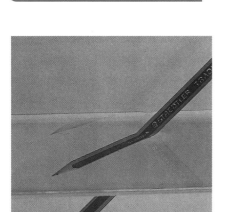

Figure 32.3A ● Refraction makes the water look shallower

LOOK AT LINKS
for **refraction**
See Theme H, Topic 30.2.

LOOK AT LINKS
for **total internal reflection**
See Theme H, Topic 32.2.

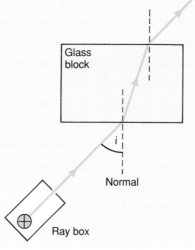

Figure 32.3B ● Refraction by a glass block

Refraction in a glass block

Direct a light ray from a ray box into a glass block, as shown in Figure 32.3B. *What can you say about the change of direction when the ray passes from the air into the glass? Is it towards or away from the normal? What about the change when it comes out of the glass? What happens if you change the angle of incidence, i?*

You will find that **the ray bends towards the normal when it goes into the glass and bends away from the normal when it leaves the glass**.

Refraction in a prism

Direct a light ray on to a prism as shown in Figure 32.3C. The ray is refracted as it enters and leaves the prism. Try altering the angle of incidence, *i*, to make the ray **reflect internally** off the second side of the prism.

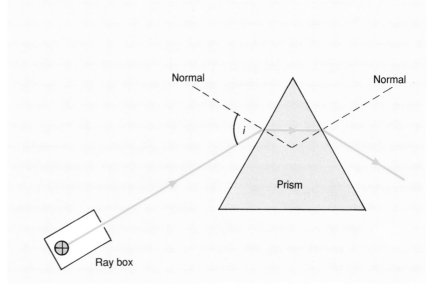

Figure 32.3C ● Refraction by a prism

Put a coin in an empty cup and position yourself so the coin is just out of sight below the rim of the cup. Then get a friend to pour water into the cup. Now you can see the coin. Why?

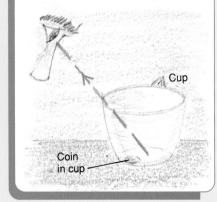

Cup

Coin in cup

IT

Optics
(program)

Using the *Optics* program you can enter your own distances and lengths to draw various objects and lenses. The computer traces light rays and shows how images are formed. You can select any of these options: concave lens, convex lens, concave mirror, convex mirror.

SUMMARY

When a light ray passes from air into glass, it bends towards the normal. A convex lens can make light rays converge.

Refraction in lenses

If you use a ray box plate with several slits you can produce several light rays at once. Aim the light rays at different shaped lenses and sketch the ray patterns for each one.

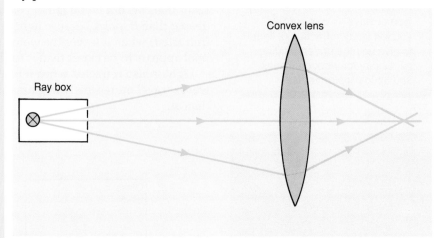

Convex lens

Ray box

Figure 32.3D ● The convex lens

Figure 32.3D shows a ray diagram for a convex lens, which makes the light rays converge (i.e. meet). However, if the lens is too close to the ray box, the lens just reduces the spreading of the rays, without making them actually meet. Imagine that the lens is divided into small sections (Figure 32.3E). Each section behaves like a small prism, refracting the rays at each glass–air boundary.

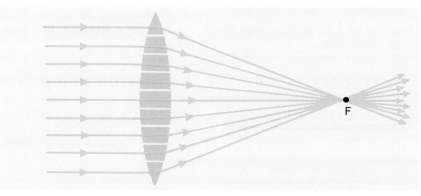

F

Figure 32.3E ●

A concave lens makes the light rays diverge (i.e. spread out), as in Figure 32.3F.

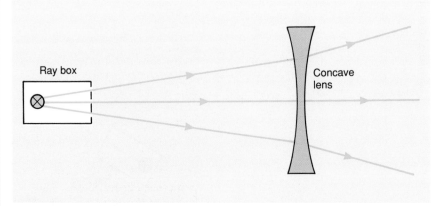

Ray box

Concave lens

Figure 32.3F ● The concave lens

❶ In an investigation of the refraction of light, a light ray was aimed at an air–glass boundary at different angles of incidence. For each angle, the ray path was drawn and the angles of incidence and refraction were measured, as shown below.

Angle of incidence i (°)	0	20	40	60	80
Angle of refraction r (°)	0	13	25	35	41

(a) Does the light ray always bend towards the normal when it passes into the glass?

(b) The ratio $\sin i / \sin r$ is a constant. This constant is known as the refractive index, n, of glass. Use the measurements above to work out n.

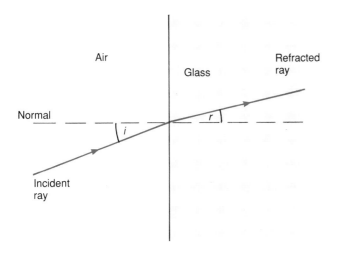

❷ Light bends when it passes from air into water. Copy the sketch and complete the ray path into air.

(a) Explain why the pond appears shallower than it really is.

(b) Would the fish be able to see the fly above the water?

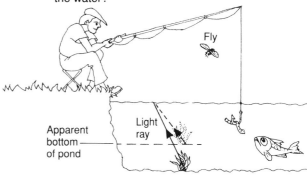

❸ Hold a pencil in water as shown in the diagram and it will appear bent. Copy and complete the diagram and use it to explain what you see.

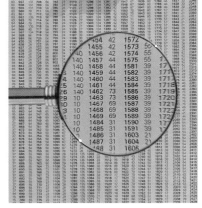

32.4 Lenses

FIRST THOUGHTS

The eye, the camera and the microscope are examples of optical instruments that use convex lenses. In this section you will find out about the action of convex lenses before studying optical instruments.

Our eyes contain lenses to enable us to see clearly. Cameras contain lenses to capture images on film. Microscopes contain lenses to magnify tiny objects. Film projectors use lenses to throw images onto screens. Telescopes and binoculars use lenses to enable us to see distant objects.

A **convex lens** can be used to project or to magnify images. Hold a convex lens over this page and you will see that it magnifies the print (see Figure 32.4A). The image of the print is a virtual

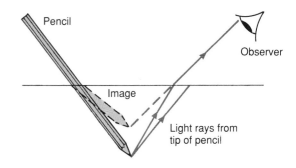

Figure 32.4A ● A convex magnifying lens

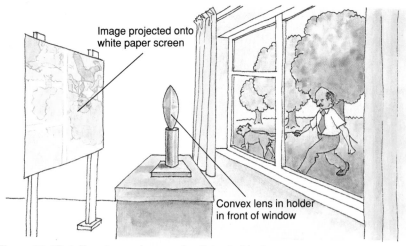

Figure 32.4B ● Forming an image of a distant object

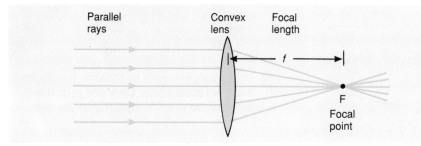

Figure 32.4C ● Focal length of a convex lens

image because it cannot be formed on a screen. It is formed at the point where the rays appear to come from.

Now hold the same lens up near a window and use it to form an image of a distant object on a sheet of white paper (Figure 32.4B). If you shine a torch bulb through the lens you should be able to project an image of the bulb onto a nearby screen or wall. This is a real image because it is formed on a screen.

The type of image formed by the lens depends on the distance of the object from the lens. The lens has a **focal point**, F, which is where parallel rays shining on the lens are brought to a focus. The distance from the focal point to the lens is called the **focal length**, f (Figure 32.4C).

Investigating the convex lens

Put the lens in a holder and place it facing an open window with a white screen behind it, as shown in Figure 32.4B. Move the screen until you can see a clear image of a distant object on the screen. The light rays from the distant object are almost exactly parallel by the time they reach the lens, and so are focused at the focal point. Thus the screen is at the focal point and you can measure the focal length, f, of the lens.

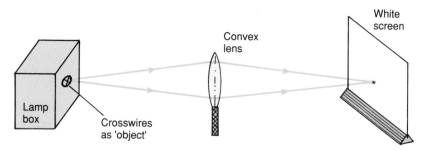

Figure 32.4D ● Investigating the convex lens

Now use a lamp box with a pair of crosswires as an object (Figure 32.4D). Set the object at distance $3f$ from the lens, and move the screen until you can see a clear image of the crosswires on it. Measure the image distance (the distance from the lens to the screen). Repeat this for different object distances. In each case, observe the image formed and measure the object and image distances. You should find that the screen needs to be placed nearer the lens as the object is moved further away.

Ray diagrams are useful to understand how a convex lens forms an image of an object. Three key rays from the object are used to locate the image. Figures 32.4E–G use these three key rays to show how a convex lens forms the different images you will have seen in your investigations.

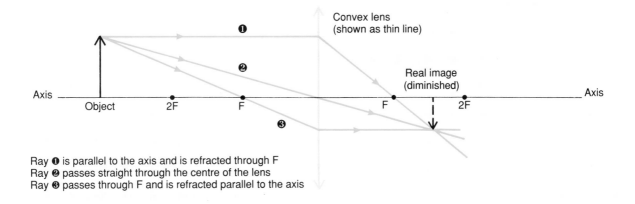

Convex lens
(shown as thin line)

Real image
(diminished)

Axis
Object   2F   F   F   2F   Axis

Ray ❶ is parallel to the axis and is refracted through F
Ray ❷ passes straight through the centre of the lens
Ray ❸ passes through F and is refracted parallel to the axis

Figure 32.4E ● Object outside 2F

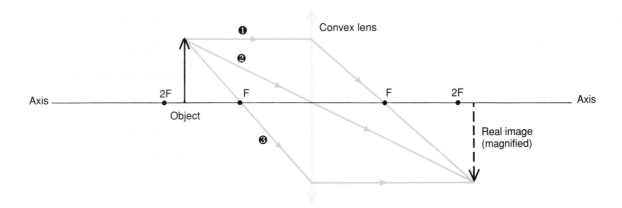

Convex lens

Axis
2F   F   F   2F   Axis
Object

Real image
(magnified)

Figure 32.4F ● Object between F and 2F

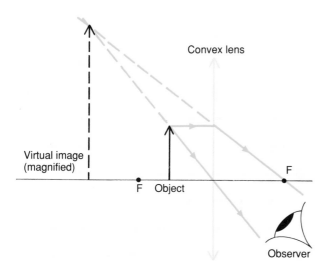

Convex lens

Virtual image
(magnified)

F   Object   F

Observer

Figure 32.4G ● Object inside F

If the image is larger than the object, it is said to be **magnified**. If the image is smaller than the object, it is said to be **diminished**.

The **camera** uses a convex lens to form a real image on a photographic film. 'Focusing' the camera adjusts the distance from the lens to the film, so that objects at different distances can be focused on to the film. Figure 32.4H explains how the camera works.

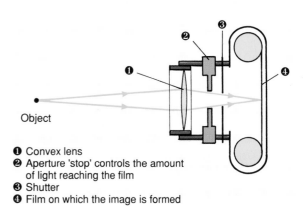

Object

❶ Convex lens
❷ Aperture 'stop' controls the amount of light reaching the film
❸ Shutter
❹ Film on which the image is formed

Figure 32.4H ● The camera

The **microscope** uses two convex lenses, the objective and the eyepiece, as shown in Figure 32.4I. The magnification can be changed by using different eyepieces. In this diagram the image is ten times bigger than the object, so the magnification is x10.

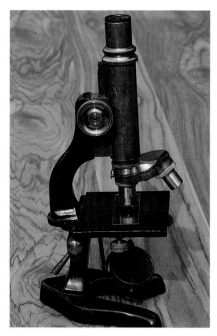

Figure 32.4I ● (a) The microscope
(b) Ray diagram of the microscope

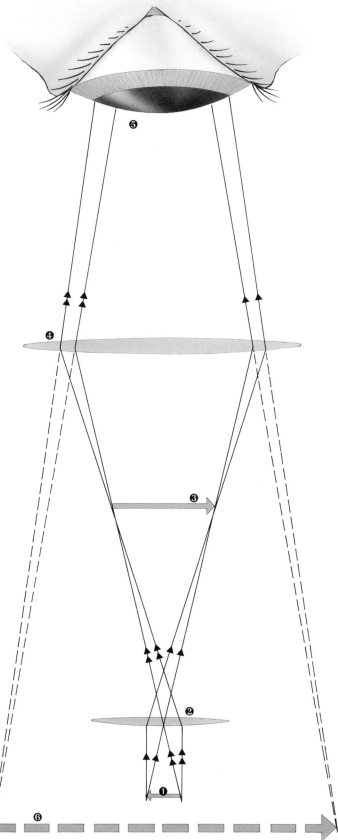

Objective magnification = $\dfrac{\text{Height of }❸}{\text{Height of }❶}$ = 3

Eyepiece magnification = $\dfrac{\text{Height of }❻}{\text{Height of }❸}$ = $\dfrac{10}{3}$

Overall magnification = 3 x $\dfrac{10}{3}$ = 10

❶ Object to be magnified on a slide
❷ Objective forms a real image ❸ of the object
❸ Real image formed by objective
❹ Eyepiece gives a magnified view of real image by forming a virtual image at ❻
❺ Viewer sees virtual image at ❻
❻ The virtual image is magnified and inverted

SUMMARY

The focal length, *f*, of a convex lens is the distance from the focal point, F, to the lens. A real image is always formed if the object is outside the focal length. A virtual image is formed if the object is inside the focal length.

CHECKPOINT

❶ Copy and complete the ray paths in each of the sketches below.

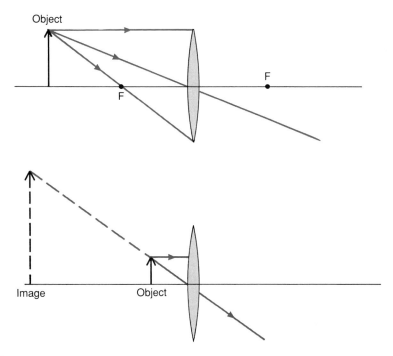

❷ With the aid of a ray diagram, explain how a single convex lens may be used as a magnifying glass.

❸ Draw ray diagrams to find the position of the image formed by a convex lens of focal length 15 cm when an object is placed:
(a) 30 cm from the lens,
(b) 20 cm from the lens,
(c) 10 cm from the lens.
In each case, describe the image formed.

❹ Ahmed has made a simple camera using a convex lens, a cardboard box and some greaseproof paper, as shown. He points the camera at a distant tree.
(a) Make a sketch of what he ought to see on the screen.
(b) Keith walks in front of the camera but his image is out of focus on the screen. What adjustment should be made to the camera to bring Keith's image into focus?
(c) Why should the inside of the camera be painted black?

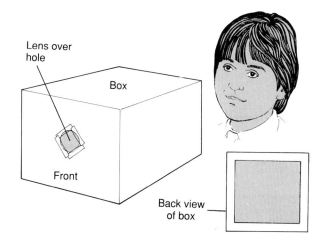

32.5 The eye

FIRST THOUGHTS

This section concentrates on the eye as an optical instrument rather than on its biological details. Read on to find out about sight defects and how they are corrected.

Have you ever been told to 'use your eyes' when you complain that you cannot find something or other? Think about what we use our eyes for. They tell us about colour, shape, position and movement. When you look at an object, each eye forms an image of it and sends signals to your brain. Your brain 'reads' these signals and you 'see' the object. Figure 32.5A shows four unusual views of everyday objects. *Can you recognise them?*

Figure 32.5A ● Recognising things

The front of the eye is covered by a thin transparent membrane called the conjunctiva. Dust particles that collect on the conjunctiva are washed away by a watery fluid from the tear glands, which are under the eyelids. This fluid contains lyosyme – a chemical that destroys germs. Blinking helps to spread the fluid across the conjunctiva. When the fluid reaches the lower part of the eye, it drains into a tube and goes down into the nose.

Figure 32.5B explains how the parts of the eye work. Light enters the eye through a tough transparent layer called the **cornea**. This protects the eye and it helps to focus the light onto the **retina**, the layer of light-sensitive cells at the back of the inside of the eye. The amount of light entering the eye is controlled by the iris, which adjusts the size of the pupil – the circular opening in its centre. The eye lens focuses the light to give a sharp image on the retina. Although the image on the retina is inverted, the brain interprets it so you see it the right way up.

1. Conjuctiva membrane
2. Cornea – helps to focus light on to retina
3. Aqueous humour – transparent watery liquid that supports the front of the eye
4. Iris – coloured ring of muscle that controls the amount of light entering the eye
5. Pupil – the central hole formed by the iris. Light enters the eye through the pupil
6. Eye lens – focuses light on to the retina
7. Ciliary muscles – attached to the lens by suspensory ligaments. The muscles change the thickness of the eye lens
8. Vitreous humour – transparent jelly-like substance that supports the back of the eye
9. Retina – the light-sensitive layer around the inside of the eye
10. Fovea – region of the retina where the retinal cells are densest
11. Blind spot – region where the retina is not sensitive to light (no light-sensitive cells present)
12. Choroid – black layer of blood vessels that carry food and oxygen to the eye and remove waste products
13. Eye muscles – move the eye in its socket
14. Optic nerve – carries nerve impulses from the retina to the brain

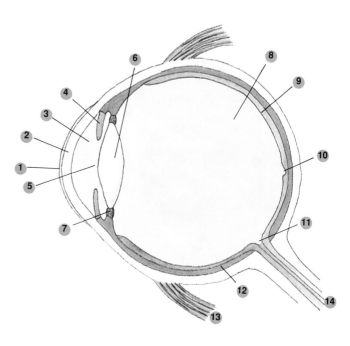

Figure 32.5B ● The human eye

Focusing

How does the eye focus on objects at different distances? If you look up from this book and gaze out of the window, your eye lens becomes thinner to keep your vision in focus. This is called **accommodation**. Your eye muscles alter the thickness of your eye lens. The muscles fibres run round the eye lens, so when they contract they shorten and squeeze the eye lens, making it thicker.

Human eyes are damaged by ultraviolet light, but insects' eyes can see in ultraviolet light. The honey guides on the petals of flowers stand out when photographed on film sensitive to ultraviolet light. Bees searching for nectar can see the honey guides very clearly.

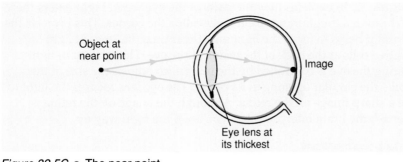

Figure 32.5C ● The near point

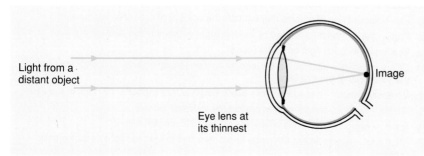

Figure 32.5D ● The far point

What is your range of vision? A normal eye can see clearly any object from far away to 25 cm from the eye.

- The **near point** of the eye is the closest point to the eye at which an object can be seen clearly. The eye lens is then at its thickest (Figure 32.5C).
- The **far point** of the eye is the furthest point from the eye at which an object can be seen clearly. The eye lens is then at its thinnest (Figure 32.5D).

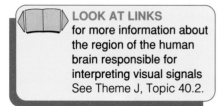

LOOK AT LINKS
for more information about the region of the human brain responsible for interpreting visual signals
See Theme J, Topic 40.2.

IT'S A FACT

There are more rods than cones. Reliable estimates are about 130 million rods and 7 million cones in a pair of human eyes.

LOOK AT LINKS
for **colour addition**
See Theme H, Topic 33.1.

Seeing shape and colour

How do we recognise the shape of an object? An image of the object is formed on the retina, which consists of lots of light-sensitive cells. When light falls on a cell, the cell sends an electrical impulse as a signal to the brain. The brain recognises the pattern of the signals from the cells covered by the image, and so recognises the object's shape.

How do we tell the colour of an object? There are two types of cells on the retina – **rods** and **cones** (Figure 32.5E). Rods occur mostly near the edges of the retina. They are not sensitive to colour and only respond to the brightness of light. Ask a friend to test you to see if you can tell the colour of something at the edge of your field of vision.

Cones are packed densely together at the middle of the retina. This area is called the **fovea**. Each cone is sensitive to red or blue or green light. For example, when red light falls on the retina, it 'activates' the red-sensitive cones, so you see red. Other colours activate more than one type of cone. For example, yellow light activates the red and the green cones, so they send messages to the brain. When the brain receives signals from adjacent red and green cones, it knows yellow light is on that part of the retina.

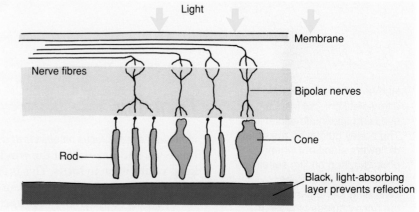

Figure 32.5E ● Rods and cones

Sight defects

Sight defects occur when the eye lens cannot form a sharp image on the retina. Spectacles contain lenses that compensate for sight defects.

Short sight is caused by over-strong eye muscles. A short-sighted eye cannot see far away objects clearly because the eye muscle cannot relax enough to make the eye lens thin enough. A suitable concave lens in front of the eye counteracts the effect of the over-strong eye lens (Figure 32.5F).

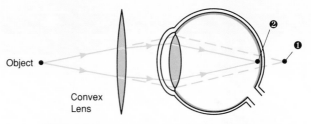

❶ Without the concave lens, the image is formed here
❷ With the concave lens, the image is formed on the retina

Figure 32.5F ● Short sight

Long sight is caused by weak eye muscles, and often develops as the muscles weaken with age. The muscles are unable to contract enough around the lens to make it thick enough to focus near objects. A suitable convex lens in front of the eye helps the eye lens to form a clear image on the retina (Figure 32.5G).

❶ Without the convex lens, the image is formed here
❷ With the convex lens, the image is formed on the retina

Figure 32.5G ● Long sight

IT

Blindspot
(program)

The *Blindspot* program shows screen models of the basic structure of a human eye. Using this program you can investigate where the blind spot in your right eye is and why it is called the blind spot.

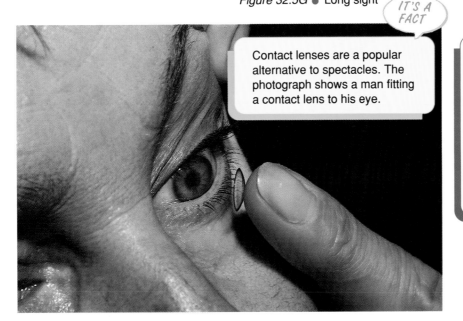

IT'S A
FACT

Contact lenses are a popular alternative to spectacles. The photograph shows a man fitting a contact lens to his eye.

SUMMARY

The eye lens forms a clear image on the retina. The iris controls the amount of light entering the eye. The thickness of the eye lens changes to accommodate (focus) objects at different distances. Spectacle lenses compensate for defects in the eye muscles controlling the eye lens, to give the wearer normal vision.

║///////////////////////////////// CHECKPOINT ///////////////////////////////////║

❶ (a) Why do your eye muscles relax when you look at a distant object and contract when you look at something close to you?

(b) Why is it easier to study an object in detail if you look straight at it?

(c) Why does the eye pupil dilate (i.e. widen) in dim light?

❷ Explain how (a) short sight and (b) long sight are caused and how they are corrected.

❸ Try these 'eye tests', which are explained below.

(a) The blind spot test.

(b) The sausage test.

(c) The birdcage test.

(d) The dark room test. Sit in a dark room for twenty minutes or more and you will discover your eyes can see in the dark. The rods become much more sensitive than normal in dark conditions and they make the most of whatever light there is.

(a)

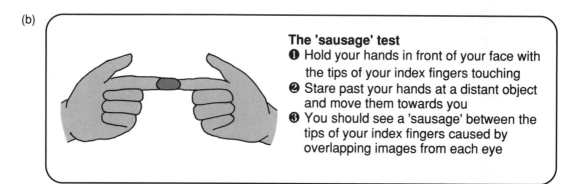

The blind spot test
❶ Position the black spot in front of your left eye. Cover your right eye
❷ Move the book closer and keep staring at the spot
❸ The X disappears when its image falls on the blind spot of your left eye

(b)

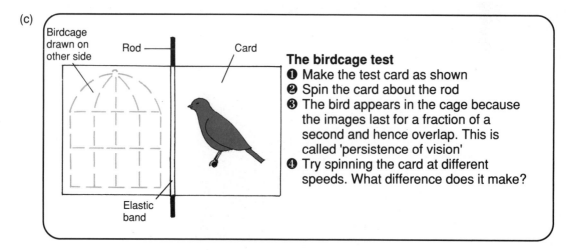

The 'sausage' test
❶ Hold your hands in front of your face with the tips of your index fingers touching
❷ Stare past your hands at a distant object and move them towards you
❸ You should see a 'sausage' between the tips of your index fingers caused by overlapping images from each eye

(c)

Birdcage drawn on other side   Rod   Card

Elastic band

The birdcage test
❶ Make the test card as shown
❷ Spin the card about the rod
❸ The bird appears in the cage because the images last for a fraction of a second and hence overlap. This is called 'persistence of vision'
❹ Try spinning the card at different speeds. What difference does it make?

║///║

ELECTROMAGNETIC WAVES

33.1 The spectrum

FIRST THOUGHTS

In this section you will find out what determines the colour of a surface. Objects on a stage change their appearance when the stage lights change colour. Read on to find out why.

Can you recall the colours of the rainbow? You can mak colours by shining a ray of white light through a pr White light is made up of a mixture of colours. The splits white light into these colours because it refrac colour by a different amount. Splitting white light in colours in this way is called **dispersion**. Seen on a w screen, the colours form a pattern called the **white l spectrum**, as shown in Figure 33.1A.

Figure 33.1A ● Splitting white light

Investigating colour

You can use colour filters to obtain colours of light. For example, if you beam of white light at a red filter, th that emerges is red (Figure 33.1B). T because the filter absorbs all the oth colours that make up white light.

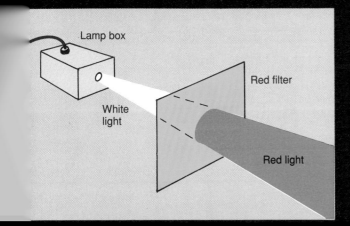

Lamp box

Red filter

White light

Red light

IT

Colour
(program)

A computer station with a colour screen is very good for showing the properties of coloured light. Use the *Colour* program to find answers to these questions:
• which are the primary colours,
• how are secondary colours produced,
• what is white light,
• why do coloured objects look black in certain kinds of light?

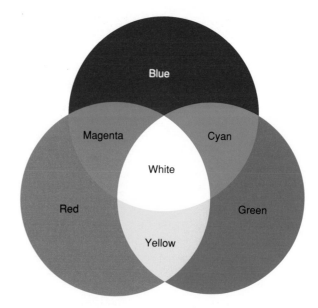

Figure 33.1C ● Overlapping colours

Red, blue and green are called the **primary** colours of light because they can be mixed to produce any other colour of the spectrum. Figure 33.1C shows the colours produced when light of the three primary colours is shone on a white screen. White light is seen where all three primary colours overlap. Two primary colours overlapping give a **secondary** colour. For example, red and green light give yellow, so yellow is one of the three secondary colours. Blue light added to yellow light gives white light, because yellow is made up of red and green.

The colour of a surface depends on the colour of the light falling on it, as well as the surface pigments. A book that is red in normal white light has a surface that absorbs all the colours of white light except red. When white light falls on its surface, only the red component of the incident white light is reflected (Figure 33.1D(a)).

What colour does the book appear if it is viewed in blue light? Since the incident light does not contain any red component, the surface absorbs all the light falling on it and reflects none (Figure 33.1D(b)), so the book appears black.

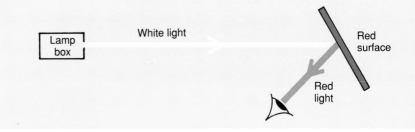

(a) Observing in white light (a red surface is seen)

SUMMARY

White light consists of all the colours of the spectrum. Any colour of the spectrum can be formed by mixing different proportions of red, blue and green light. These three colours are called the primary colours of light.

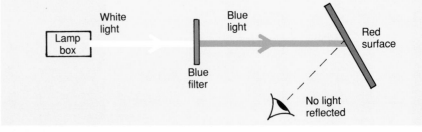

(b) Observing in blue light (a black surface is seen)
Figure 33.1D ● Observing in different coloured lights

❶ In the school's drama production, the first scene is a sunny day outdoors. The stage lights are red, green, blue and white. Each colour is controlled separately.

  (a) Which lights would you use for the first scene?
  (b) The scene then changes to a red sunset. How should the light be altered?
  (c) The leading actress wears a green dress in the first scene. What colour will it appear in the second scene?

❷ Explain why a blue book appears black in red light. What colour would it appear in green light?

❸ Top Gear Clothes Ltd want to advertise their name in discos so they have asked your school for some ideas. One suggestion is that the poster should have a red background with the words TOP GEAR in blue. How will this look in a disco where the lights flash red and blue alternately? Have you a better suggestion? If so, try it out.

❹ Suppose that in the experiment shown in Figure 33.1A the white light beam was shone through a beaker of chlorophyll before passing into the prism. Describe and explain what you would expect to see on the screen.

FIRST
THOUGHTS

33.2 The electromagnetic spectrum

Our eyes are sensitive to only a small part of the electro-magnetic spectrum. This section explains the properties and uses of other electromagnetic waves.

Light is just a small part of the spectrum of electromagnetic waves. Our eyes cannot detect the other parts. The world would appear very different to us if they could. The wavelengths of electromagnetic waves range from more than 1000 m (radio) to less than 10^{-12} m (X and γ (gamma) radiation).

Table 33.1 ● The electromagnetic spectrum

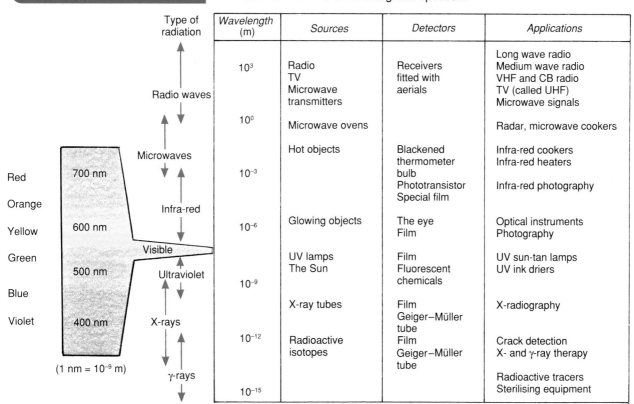

Wavelength (m)	Sources	Detectors	Applications
10^3	Radio TV Microwave transmitters	Receivers fitted with aerials	Long wave radio Medium wave radio VHF and CB radio TV (called UHF) Microwave signals
10^0	Microwave ovens		Radar, microwave cookers
10^{-3}	Hot objects	Blackened thermometer bulb Phototransistor Special film	Infra-red cookers Infra-red heaters Infra-red photography
10^{-6}	Glowing objects	The eye Film	Optical instruments Photography
10^{-9}	UV lamps The Sun	Film Fluorescent chemicals	UV sun-tan lamps UV ink driers
10^{-12}	X-ray tubes	Film Geiger–Müller tube	X-radiography
	Radioactive isotopes	Film Geiger–Müller tube	Crack detection X- and γ-ray therapy
10^{-15}			Radioactive tracers Sterilising equipment

Type of radiation: Radio waves, Microwaves, Infra-red, Visible, Ultraviolet, X-rays, γ-rays

Red 700 nm
Orange
Yellow 600 nm
Green
500 nm
Blue
Violet 400 nm

(1 nm = 10^{-9} m)

All electromagnetic waves travel at the same speed through a vacuum. However, the behaviour of electromagnetic waves in different materials depends on the wavelength and the type of material.

Radio waves

Radio waves are emitted when electrons are forced to move up and down an aerial by a specially designed electronic circuit called a radio transmitter connected to it. Lightning also produces radio waves, which is why radio programmes 'crackle' when there is a thunderstorm.

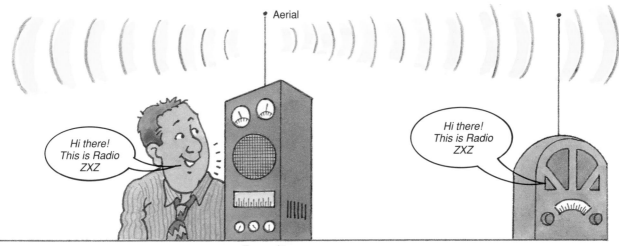

Figure 33.2A ● Local radio transmission

When radio waves pass across a wire aerial, the electrons in the wire are pushed to and fro along the wire by the radio waves. The motion of the electrons produces a tiny electrical voltage, which can be used to detect the radio waves (Figure 33.2A).

Portable radios have plastic cases with the aerial inside, but a car radio needs an aerial fitted to the car body. This is because radio waves can pass through non-conducting materials (e.g. plastic) but not through electrical conductors (e.g. metal).

Figure 33.2B ● Concave microwave receiving dish

Microwaves

Microwaves are used for cooking and in telecommunications. Food in a microwave oven cooks much faster than in a normal oven. The microwaves penetrate the food so it cooks from the inside as well as from the outside. Another advantage of a microwave oven is that the oven itself does not heat up. Microwaves cannot pass through metal, so food wrapped in aluminium foil will not cook in a microwave oven. Also the microwaves make the foil produce sparks.

In telecommunications, microwave beams can carry much more information than telephone wires can. Huge concave dishes are used to send and receive microwave signals (Figure 33.2B).

Figure 33.2C ● Infra-red imaging

Infra-red radiation

All objects emit infra-red radiation. The hotter an object is, the more energy it emits. Your body emits infra-red radiation. In medicine, infra-red scanners are used to detect 'hot spots' under the body's surface. Figure 33.2C shows an infra-red image of a man's head. Hot spots can often mean that the underlying tissue is unhealthy.

Infra-red radiation is just beyond the red part of the visible spectrum. A thermometer with a blackened bulb absorbs infra-red radiation. If the bulb is placed just beyond the red part of a visible spectrum in an experiment, the thermometer reading rises, because the bulb is absorbing infra-red energy.

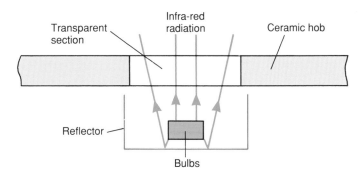

Figure 33.2D ● A ceramic hob

Cookers with ceramic hobs use special halogen lamp bulbs that emit mainly infra-red radiation. The radiation passes through the transparent part of the hob to heat up a saucepan placed on it (Figure 33.2D). A ceramic cooker ring has four 500 W bulbs above a silvered reflector. Most of the radiation from the bulbs is then directed upwards through the transparent hob.

A ceramic hob cooker cools quickly when the ring is switched off because the bulbs cool down fast when they are switched off. Ordinary cooker rings stay hot for much longer because they contain much more material than halogen lamps.

Figure 33.2E ● Goggles protect a woman's eyes from UV radiation while she uses a sunbed

Ultraviolet radiation

Ultraviolet (or UV) radiation is harmful to human eyes. Solar radiation contains UV radiation as well as light. UV radiation tans the skin, but does not heat it like infra-red radiation does. Too much UV radiation causes sunburn. It damages skin tissue, which then becomes painful and may blister. It can also cause skin cancer. To prevent sunburn, sunbathers should use skin creams that block UV radiation, preventing it from reaching the skin. Sunbed users should never exceed the exposure times recommended by the manufacturer.

Ozone in the atmosphere absorbs much of the ultraviolet radiation from the Sun, but there is much concern about damage to the ozone layer caused by aerosol propellants and other chemicals. Some scientists think that this is why skin cancer has become more common in recent years.

Ultraviolet radiation makes certain chemicals glow. Such chemicals in washing powder make clothes 'whiter than white'. The disco lighting that makes white clothes glow uses ultraviolet radiation.

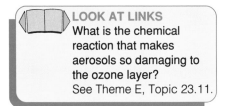

LOOK AT LINKS
What is the chemical reaction that makes aerosols so damaging to the ozone layer?
See Theme E, Topic 23.11.

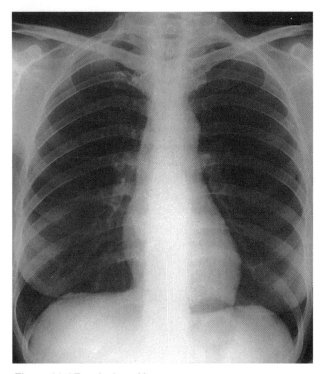

Figure 33.2F ● A chest X-ray

X-rays

X-radiation is used in hospitals to take X-ray pictures of limbs and organs (Figure 32.3F). X-rays pass through tissue but they are stopped by bones. To make a **radiograph** or X-ray picture, the radiographer places the patient between the X-ray tube and a photographic film in a cassette (Figure 33.2G). When the X-ray tube is switched on, X-rays pass through the patient's body and affect the film (Figure 33.2H). Too much X-radiation can induce cancer, so the radiographer and parts of the patient's body that do not need to be X-rayed are protected by thick lead screens, which stop the X-rays. X-rays and gamma rays can be used to destroy tumours inside the body.

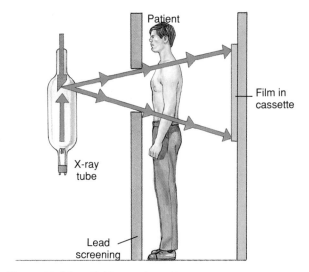

Figure 33.2G ● Taking a chest X-ray

SUMMARY

Light is part of the spectrum of electromagnetic waves. All electromagnetic waves travel at the same speed through a vacuum but their properties in materials depend on their wavelength and the type of material.

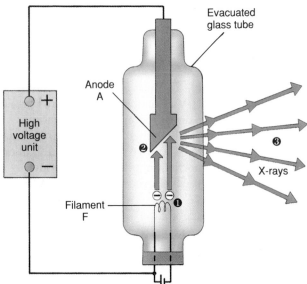

❶ Filament is heated by an electric current. Electrons escape from the filament
❷ Electrons from the filament are attracted on to the anode A and lose kinetic energy
❸ Kinetic energy of electrons is converted into X-ray energy

Figure 33.2H ● How an X-ray tube works

❶ (a) Microwave ovens should not be used to cook food wrapped in aluminium foil. Why?
(b) Why is it important that microwave ovens do not 'leak' microwaves when in use?
(c) A microwave oven operates at a frequency of 2500 MHz. Work out the wavelength of the microwaves. (The wavespeed in air is 3 x 10⁸ m/s.)

❷ The manager of a local cotton mill intends to use a 25 kW microwave oven to replace a 5 kW oven to dry large cotton reels at the end of the manufacturing process. This will cut the drying time from 10 hours to half an hour and so reduce the cost.
(a) How many kilowatt-hours of electricity does the 5 kW oven use to dry each batch?
(b) How many kilowatt-hours of electricity does the microwave oven use to dry each batch?
(c) How many kilowatt-hours per batch will be saved by using this process?

❸ High power ultraviolet lamps can be used to dry printing ink very quickly. Special UV sensitive ink is used so the ink dries without heating the paper.
(a) Test ordinary ink to see how long it takes to dry at room temperature.
(b) A continuous printing press delivers pages at a rate of 10 per second. Why is a UV drier better than drying the print using radiant heaters?

❹ Ceramic hobs for cooking use special bulbs.
(a) Why is a reflector fitted under each bulb?
(b) Why is the hob safer than an ordinary electric ring or a gas ring?
(c) Why is the hob easier to clean than an ordinary electric ring or a gas ring?

❺ Certain pens contain ink that is invisible in ordinary light but shows up in ultraviolet radiation. Suggest some uses for such a pen.

FIRST
THOUGHTS

33.3 ● Radio and television communications

Are you familiar with technical terms such as UHF waves and DBS systems? Read on to find out what they mean.

Where would you be without your favourite radio and television programmes? By using **satellites**, *we can watch events on the opposite side of the Earth as they happen. Yet radio broadcasting only began in the 1920s and television was not widely available until the 1960s.*

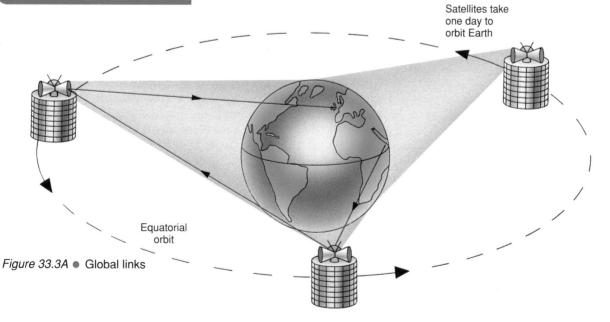

Satellites take one day to orbit Earth

Equatorial orbit

Figure 33.3A ● Global links

Sending information using radio waves

Morse code is the simplest way to send a message by radio. The operator uses a tapping key to switch the radio transmitter on and off repeatedly. Each burst of radio energy is made either short or long, corresponding to the dots and dashes of Morse code (Figure 33.3B).

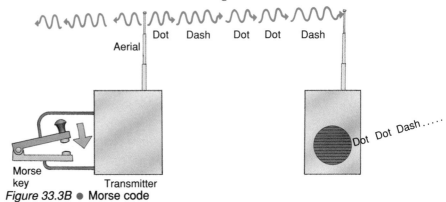

Figure 33.3B ● Morse code

Amplitude modulation (AM) is one way to send speech and music over the radio. A microphone and amplifier are used to convert the sound waves into electrical signals called **audio waves**. These signals are used to **modulate** or vary the amplitude of radio waves, as shown in Figure 33.3C. In this way, the radio waves 'carry' the audio waves, and are sometimes called **carrier waves**.

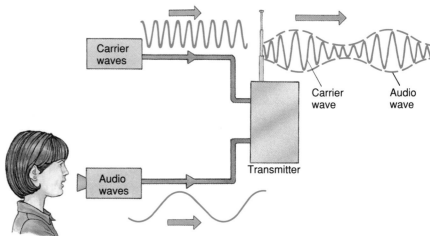

Figure 33.3C ● Amplitude modulation

The radio waves are picked up by a receiver and the carrier waves are filtered out. The audio waves are then amplified and converted back to sound, using speakers.

Television programmes are carried by ultra high frequency (UHF) waves. High frequency waves have a smaller wavelength than low frequency waves, so they can carry more information. UHF waves are used for television because much more information is needed for television pictures than for radio waves.

Why do we not use microwaves for television? Microwaves are electromagnetic waves with a much higher frequency than UHF radio waves. However, as microwaves spread out from a transmitter they get much weaker than UHF waves, so a special amplifier would be needed for microwave signals. Satellite television programmes are carried by microwaves, however. A direct broadcasting satellite (DBS) can supply several television channels to receivers on the ground, over a wide area.

LOOK AT LINKS
for **satellites**
See Theme I, Topic 36.8.

Each receiver must be connected to a dish aerial, which is necessary to collect sufficient power from the microwaves. (See Figures 33.3D and E.)

Microwave beams are also used to carry television signals and telephone calls between cities and, using satellite links, between continents.

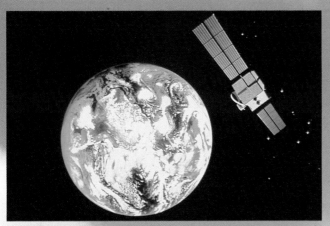

Figure 33.3D ● Television signals

SUMMARY

Radio waves carry radio and television programmes. The carrier frequency for television broadcasting needs to be much higher than for radio broadcasts. Microwaves are used to carry satellite television channels.

Figure 33.3E ● (a) A DB satellite

(b) A DB control room

(c) A DB dish aerial

❶ Electromagnetic waves travel through the atmosphere at 300 000 km/s, the same speed as through space. How long would a radio signal take to travel:

(a) across the Atlantic Ocean, a distance of 5000 km,
(b) to the Moon and back (Earth to Moon = 380000 km),
(c) to the nearest star, Proxima Centauri, which is 4.2 light years away?

❷ Radio waves at frequencies up to about 30 MHz are reflected from a layer in the upper atmosphere called the ionosphere, whereas higher frequencies pass out into space. Use this information to explain why people in Britain can listen to foreign radio programmes but cannot watch foreign television stations.

❸ Why is it important that each radio or television station is allocated a frequency (or 'channel') to broadcast on, which no other station can use?

❹ Direct broadcasting satellites must travel round the Earth over the equator, taking 24 hours for each orbit.
(a) A DB satellite in such an orbit always remains over the same point on the Earth. Why?
(b) Why is a dish needed to receive DBS signals?
(c) Why must the dish always be pointed in a certain direction to receive the signals?

❺ Most radios have at least three 'wavebands' labelled LW (long wave), MW (medium wave) and VHF (very high frequency).
(a) What is the wavelength range of each waveband?
(b) Which waveband would you use to listen to foreign radio programmes?
(c) Which waveband carries local radio programmes?

? THEME QUESTIONS

● Topic 30

1 The figure below shows some water waves made by a wave machine in a swimming pool, seen from the side.

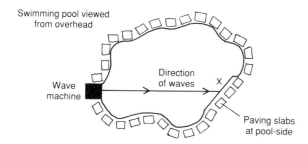

Waves from wave machine

Beach ball

(a) Which letter represents (i) the wavelength (ii) the amplitude?
(b) How many **complete** waves are shown in the diagram?
(c) How will the beach ball move as the waves reach it?
(d) If the wave moves from A to B in two seconds, what is its frequency?
(e) How many waves does the wave machine make in one minute?
(f) The figure below shows the position of the wave machine at the side of the pool.

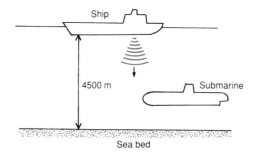

Swimming pool viewed from overhead

Wave machine

Direction of waves

X

Paving slabs at pool-side

Draw a line on a copy of the diagram to show the direction in which the waves will move after they hit the side of the pool at X.

(SEG)

2 Instruments on a ship send out an ultrasonic sound wave and detect an echo from the sea bed exactly six

Ship

4500 m

Submarine

Sea bed

seconds later. The water is 4500 metres deep.
(a) What is meant by 'ultrasonic'?
(b) How far, in metres, has the sound travelled in 6 seconds?
(c) Calculate the speed of sound in water.
(d) An echo is detected after 4 seconds as the ship passes over a submarine. How deep is the submarine?

(e) Suggest why ultrasonic echoes are sometimes preferred to X-rays for showing structures inside the human body.

(MEG)

● Topic 31

3 The bar chart below shows the loudness of various sounds.

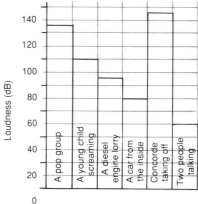

Loudness (dB)

A pop group
A young child screaming
A diesel engine lorry
A car from the inside
Concorde taking off
Two people talking

Sound can damage hearing and there are government regulations regarding the length of time that workers can be exposed to certain sounds.
Two examples are given below.
  1 A loudness of 90 decibels for up to 8 hours per day.
  2 A loudness of 100 decibels for up to 15 minutes per day.
(a) Use the bar chart to help you answer the following questions:
  (i) What is the maximum loudness of the pop group?
  (ii) Which **two** sounds would a worker not be allowed to work in for a quarter of an hour?
  (iii) Explain why it is likely that people who regularly attend pop concerts will become deaf.
(b) What can be done to protect workers from ear damage?
(c) A man was driving a car with a broken exhaust. He was breaking the law because he was guilty of noise pollution. Explain this statement.

(WJEC)

● Topic 32

4 (a) (i) The figure below shows a lamp bulb placed at the principal focus of a concave mirror. Draw on a copy of the diagram two rays of light which leave the lamp and reflect from the mirror.

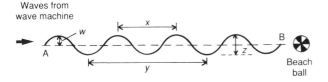

Concave mirror

Lamp bulb

(ii) Give **two** examples of devices which use concave reflectors for electromagnetic waves other than light. In each case, state which part of the electromagnetic spectrum is involved.

(b) The figure below shows a section of a rear reflector of a bicycle.

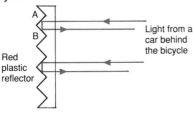

Red plastic reflector

Light from a car behind the bicycle

(i) What is the name of the effect at points A and B?
(ii) What are the **two** essential conditions for this effect to take place?
(iii) The figure below shows a section of an optical fibre which uses the above effect. State one use of optical fibres.

(NEA)

5 The diagram shows a screen with a lens in front of it. In front of the lens is a flower.

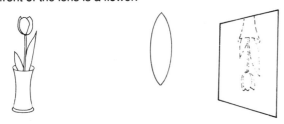

(a) The image of the flower on the screen is fuzzy. Suggest **two** ways in which you could make the image sharp.
(b) Once the image is sharp, the flower is moved a little way towards the lens. What must you now do with the screen to make the image sharp again?
(c) What difference would you see in the image if the lens was replaced by another of the same power, but with only half its diameter?

(MEG)

6 A camera forms on the film a well-focused image of an object. The diagram shows how the camera's lens produces this image.

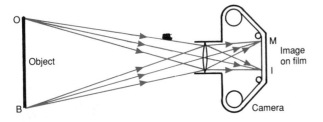

Object

O

B

M

I

Image on film

Camera

(a) Explain the following, referring to the diagram.
(i) The image which the camera produces is upside-down.
(ii) The size of the image remains unchanged if the size of the hole in front of the lens is decreased.
(b) The object moves further away from the camera. What adjustment will be needed to the lens to keep the image in sharp focus on the film?

(MEG)

● *Topic 33*

7 Infra-red radiation forms part of the electromagnetic spectrum.
(a) Name **two** other types of electromagnetic radiation.
(b) The figure below is a diagram of an infra-red wave.

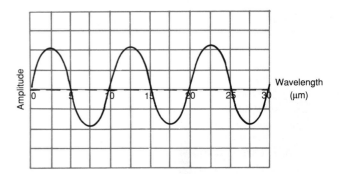

Amplitude

Wavelength (μm)

0   5   10   15   20   25   30

(i) What is the wavelength of this wave?
(ii) Copy the diagram and draw on it a wave with the **same** amplitude as the wave shown, but **twice** the wavelength.

The Acme Car Company checks the paintwork on new cars before they are sold. Some areas may have to be resprayed. The new paint on these areas must be heated to harden it.

(c) In the past the whole car was heated up in an oven for 35 minutes at 80 °C. Suggest **two** disadvantages of this process.

Nowadays the paint is hardened by a moving arch of infra-red lamps with a total power of 72 kilowatts. The arch moves over the car at 1 metre per minute.

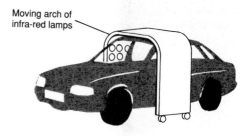

Moving arch of infra-red lamps

(d) A car is 6 metres long.
(i) How long would it take for the arch to pass over the car?
(ii) Write your answers to (i) as part of an hour.
(iii) How many kilowatt hours of electrical energy would be used by the infra-red lamps as they passed over the car?
(iv) The Acme Company pays 5p for a kilowatt hour of electrical energy. How much will it cost them to harden the paint on this car?

(LEAG)

THEME I
Forces

Car seat belts are designed to prevent car passengers being thrown forward in the event of a crash. The seat belts and fittings in a car are tested to ensure they can withstand the huge forces caused by an impact.

There are many situations where scientists need to measure forces and use their measurements. The test car in the photograph is fitted with sensors that measure the dummy's movement and the forces on it. Read on to find out how to measure motion and force.

TOPIC 34 ● FORCES IN BALANCE

34.1 What forces do

How many different types of force can you think of? For each type of force, think about a situation where the force acts.

Figure 34.1A ● Using force

Have you ever tried to push a piece of furniture across a room? Your push is opposed by the friction between the furniture and the floor. Not much push is needed if the floor is slippery, but if the floor is rough you may need help to move the furniture.

Work must be done to move a piece of furniture. Anything that can do work is called a **force**. Pushing on something is an example of applying a force.

Some more forces are illustrated in Figure 34.1B. *What is each force doing to the object it acts on?* A force acting on an object can change the shape or change the motion of the object. To bring about these changes, work is done by the force. Two or more forces acting on an object can keep it stationary. Since there is no movement, the forces do no work.

Two magnets do not need to be in contact to attract or repel each other. For this reason, magnetic forces are sometimes called action-at-a-distance forces. *Which other forces in Figure 34.1B act between objects that are not in direct contact?*

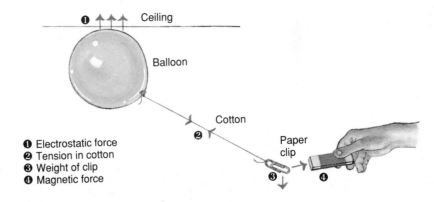

❶ Electrostatic force
❷ Tension in cotton
❸ Weight of clip
❹ Magnetic force

Figure 34.1B ● Some different forces

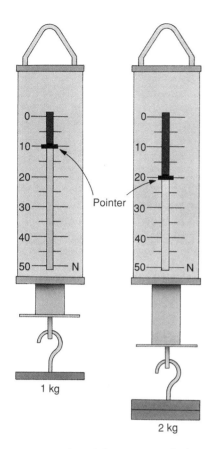

Figure 34.1C ● Using a newton balance

LOOK AT LINKS
for **newtons**
See Theme I, Topic 36.5.

The **newton,** N, is the unit of force. It is used to measure every type of force. It is defined as the force necessary to give a mass of 1 kg an acceleration of 1 m/s².

Weight

If you release any object above the ground it falls, because it is attracted towards the Earth. This force of attraction is called **gravity**. The Earth's gravity acts on every object near the Earth. The force of gravity on an object is its **weight**.

Weight is measured using a newton balance, which is a spring balance with a scale marked in newtons. Figure 34.1C shows different masses being weighed. A 1 kg mass has a weight of 10 N. A 2 kg mass has a weight of 20 N. *What is the weight of a 3 kg mass?* These results show that the strength of gravity on the Earth's surface is 10 N/kg. More accurate measurements give a result of 9.8 N/kg. This is usually denoted by the symbol *g*.

To work out the weight of an object from its mass, you can use the equation

Weight (in newtons)	=	Mass (in kg)	x	*g*

where *g* ≈ 10 N/kg.

You can reduce your weight by going to the equator. The strength of gravity varies slightly over the Earth's surface, and is least at the equator. However, your mass is constant, so you would not lose mass by going to the equator.

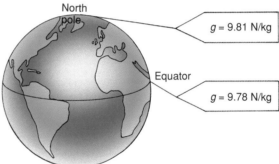

Figure 34.1D ● Variation of *g* with latitude

Figure 34.1E ● Astronauts weigh less on the Moon

The weight of astronauts is reduced when they go into space. Imagine you are an astronaut on a journey to the Moon. As your rocket moves away from the Earth, your weight becomes less because you are moving away from the Earth's gravity. Approaching the Moon, you begin to feel the effect of the Moon's gravity. On the Moon's surface your weight would be about one sixth of your weight on Earth, because lunar gravity is about one sixth of Earth's gravity at the surface.

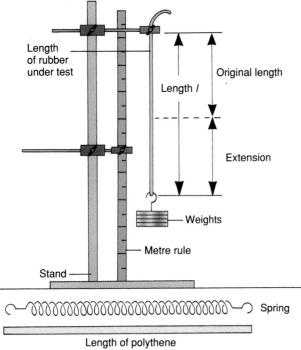

Length of rubber under test

Original length

Length *l*

Extension

Weights

Metre rule

Stand

Spring

Length of polythene

Figure 34.1F ● Investigating stretching

Force and shape

Squash players know that hitting a squash ball hard changes its motion and can even change its shape. Forces can change the motion or shape of an object. An object that regains its original shape when the force is removed is said to be elastic. For example, a rubber band that is stretched and then released usually returns to its original length. Rubber is an example of a material that possesses elasticity.

To investigate how easily a material stretches, you can hang weights from it as in Figure 34.1F. First, measure the initial length of the material. A small weight attached to the material will keep it straight. Then increase the amount of weight in steps, measuring and recording the length at each step. To check your measurements you can measure the material again as the weights are removed. For each step calculate the extension of the material – the increase in length from the initial length.

Plot your measurements on a graph, as extension (on the vertical axis) against weight. Some results for different materials are shown in Figure 34.1G.

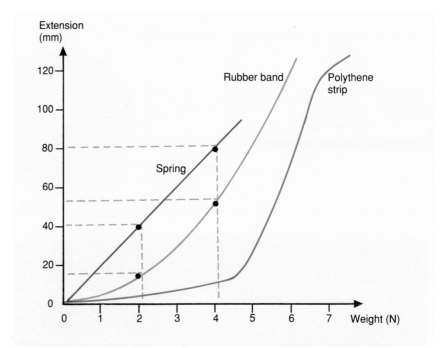

Figure 34.1G ● Graph of extension against weight for some different materials

The experiments show that the steel spring and the rubber band behave elastically. That is to say they regain their initial length after the weights are unloaded. The extension of the steel spring is proportional to the weight suspended on it. For example, doubling the weight from 2.0 N to 4.0 N doubles the extension of the spring. This is not true for the rubber band. When the weight on the band doubles from 2.0 N to 4.0 N, the extension of the rubber band more than doubles.

Robert Hooke carried out a series of investigations with springs in the seventeenth century. Hooke's Law for springs states that **the extension of**

a spring is proportional to the weight it supports. By applying this law you can weigh an object, or measure force, as shown in Figure 34.1H.

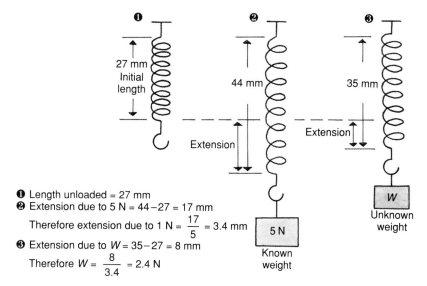

❶ Length unloaded = 27 mm
❷ Extension due to 5 N = 44 − 27 = 17 mm

Therefore extension due to 1 N = $\dfrac{17}{5}$ = 3.4 mm

❸ Extension due to W = 35 − 27 = 8 mm

Therefore $W = \dfrac{8}{3.4}$ = 2.4 N

Figure 34.1H ● Using Hooke's Law to find an unknown weight

SUMMARY

Forces can change the shape or change the motion of objects. The newton is the unit of force. Weight is the force of gravity on an object. A newton balance is used to weigh objects.

Although Hooke's Law refers only to springs, other materials are said to obey Hooke's Law if the extension is proportional to the stretching force. This may be written as an equation

Force = Constant x Extension

CHECKPOINT

❶ (a) Figure 34.1B shows different forces acting. Write down what each force is doing to the object it acts on.
(b) Name the forces acting in the diagram opposite. What is each force doing?

❷ Copy and complete the following table.

Mass (kg)	1.0	0.1	?	60	?
Weight (N)	10	?	25	?	0.2

❸ Suppose you were given several 1 kg masses, some string and a 'suspect' newton balance. Explain how you would check the accuracy of the balance.

❹ The strength of the Earth's gravity varies slightly over the Earth from 9.81 N/kg at the poles to 9.78 N/kg at the equator (Figure 34.1D). What would be the change in weight of a person of mass 60 kg who went from the equator to the North Pole?

❺ In a Hooke's Law test on a spring, the following results were obtained.

Weight (N)	0.0	1.0	2.0	3.0	4.0	5.0	6.0
Length (mm)	245	285	324	366	405	446	484

(a) Use these results to plot a graph of extension (on the vertical axis) against weight.
(b) How much weight is needed to extend the spring by (i) 100 mm, (ii) 1 mm?
(c) If an object produces an extension of 230 mm, what is its weight?
(d) Work out the mass of the object from its weight.

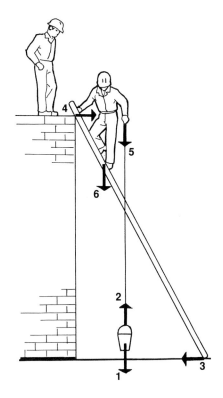

FIRST THOUGHTS

34.2 🍎 Centre of gravity

The design of racing cars has changed considerably since the first models. More powerful engines, better streamlining and less dense materials have all contributed to the improved performance of the modern racing car.

Figure 34.2A ●
(a) 1920s racing car design
(b) Modern racing car design

However, one feature that has not changed is the need to keep the car low. The weight of the car must be as near to the ground as possible, otherwise the car would overturn when cornering at high speeds.

The weight of a tractor also needs to be as low as possible, or it would tip over on rough ground. The top of the tractor cab may well be two or three metres above the ground. However, mounting the heavy parts like the engine as low as possible keeps the weight low and makes the tractor stable.

We can think of the weight of an object as if it acts at a single point. This point is called the **centre of gravity** of the object.

If you balance a ruler on the tip of your finger (Figure 34.2B) the point of balance is the centre of gravity of the ruler. The easiest way to carry a ladder is to lift it at its centre of gravity.

The centre of gravity of an object is the point where its entire weight seems to act.

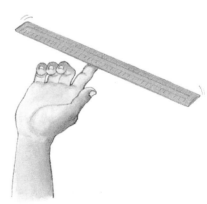

Figure 34.2B ● A balancing act

To find the centre of gravity of a flat card, hang the card from a pin so it is free to rotate, as in the diagram and let it come to rest. Use a plumbline to draw a vertical line from the pin downwards. The centre of gravity is somewhere along this line. Now repeat this step with the card hung at a different point. The centre of gravity is where the two lines drawn on the card meet. Test your results by seeing if you can balance the card at this point.

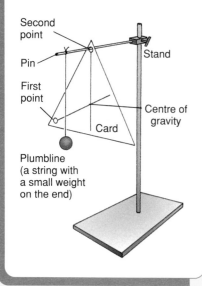

Stability

A card that hangs from a pin without moving is said to be in **equilibrium**. This means the forces acting on the object are balanced.

If the card is pushed to one side and then released, it swings back to its equilibrium position. This is an example of **stable equilibrium** as in the *Try this* diagram. The same card balanced on the tip of a pencil (Figure 34.2C) is in **unstable equilibrium**. A small push to one side will make the card fall off.

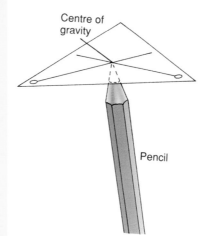

Figure 34.2C ● Unstable equilibrium

Tilting and toppling

How far can a tractor tilt before it topples over? How far can a pram with a bouncing baby tilt safely? Stand a brick on its end and then tilt it until it just balances on one edge. Figure 34.2D shows the idea. The brick will balance when its centre of gravity is directly above the edge on which it balances. The brick topples over if it is released when its centre of gravity is 'outside' this edge. The same applies to a vehicle when it tilts to one side. If the centre of gravity goes outside the wheel base, the vehicle topples over.

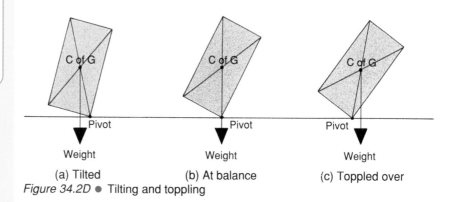

(a) Tilted (b) At balance (c) Toppled over
Figure 34.2D ● Tilting and toppling

The centre of gravity of an object is the point where its weight seems to act. An object in stable equilibrium returns to equilibrium when it is pushed and released.

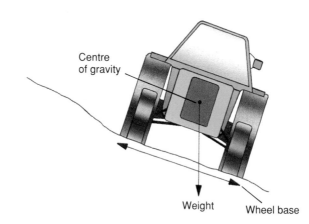

Figure 34.2E ● Forces on a tilting tractor

① (a) A tightrope walker often carries a long thin pole. How does this help the walker to balance on the rope?
(b) Balancing a spinning dinner plate on the end of a vertical pole is another circus trick. Why must the pole support the plate at its centre?

② Balance a parrot on your finger. Cut the parrot shape shown from a piece of card. Fix some paper clips to the parrot's tail. Why does this help to improve its stability?

③ Babies and young infants are often top-heavy. This is because a baby's head is usually large compared to its body. Why should a well-designed baby chair have a wide base? If the base was too narrow, what might happen if the baby leaned over the side of the chair?

④ (a) Filing cabinets are designed so that only one drawer at a time can be pulled out. What might happen if all the drawers, loaded with documents, were pulled out at the same time?
(b) High-sided lorries are at risk in strong winds. Why?

⑤ A Bunsen burner has a wide heavy base so it cannot be knocked over easily. How many other objects can you think of that are designed to be difficult to knock over? Make a list. Can you think of any object that needs to be redesigned because it is knocked over too easily?

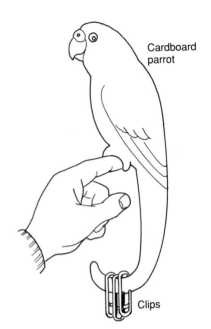

Cardboard parrot

Clips

o
o
o

34.3 Push and pull forces

In this section you will find out how to work out the effect of two forces acting on an object in opposite directions.

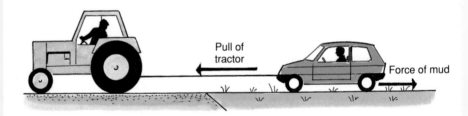

Pull of tractor

Force of mud

Figure 34.3A ● A muddy problem

John has just passed his driving test but he still has much to learn. He has reversed his car into a very muddy cart track and is stuck. He has had to ask a farmer with a tractor to pull his car out of the mud (Figure 34.3A).

One end of a rope is tied to the back of the tractor and the other end to the front of the car. At first, the car stays stuck in the mud. The pull of the tractor is not enough to overcome the force of the mud. As the tractor uses more power, the force it exerts becomes greater than the force of the mud and the car is pulled out.

The situation is like a tug-of-war; the winning team is the one that pulls with most force. If the two teams pull with equal force, there is stalemate. The rope is in equilibrium because the force at one end is equal and opposite to the force at the other end.

The size and direction of a force can be represented by a vector. A vector is an arrow whose length represents the magnitude (size) of the force and whose direction gives the direction of the force. Any force has magnitude and direction and so can be drawn as a vector.

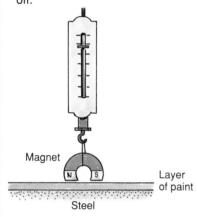
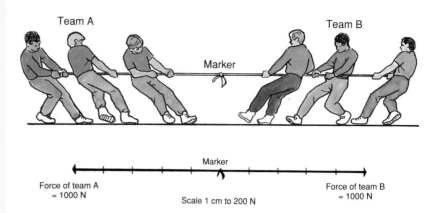

Team A

Team B

Marker

Marker

Force of team A = 1000 N

Force of team B = 1000 N

Scale 1 cm to 200 N

Figure 34.3B ● A tug-of-war

Figure 34.3B shows the pull of two tug-of-war teams as vectors. A scale of 1 cm to 200 N is used here, so the force of 1000 N is represented by a vector 5 cm long. The two vectors are the same length because the magnitudes of the forces are the same. Because the forces are in opposite directions, the two vectors point in opposite directions.

If one force were larger than the other, what would the overall effect be? In a tug-of-war, the team that exerts the larger force wins. Suppose one team pulls with a force of 1000 N and the other team with a force of 950 N (see Figure 34.3C). The smaller force nearly cancels out the other force, but not quite. The combined effect of these two forces is called the resultant. *What is the resultant here?* The stronger team can exert a force 50 N greater than the other team. So the resultant is 50 N.

Resultant force = 50 N

Force of team A = 1000 N

Force of team B = 950 N

Figure 34.3C ● Unequal forces

Another example of two forces in equilibrium is when an object is supported by a newton balance. The forces acting on the object are the force of gravity (i.e. its weight) and the pull of the spring balance. The weight of the object is equal and opposite to the pull of the balance.

What is the weight of the iron bar in Figure 34.3D(a)? Now suppose a magnet is brought near the iron bar as in Figure 34.3D(b). *If the newton balance reading increases to 5.5 N, what is the force on the bar due to the magnet?* The bar's weight is less than 5.5 N. The force due to the magnet must make up the difference.

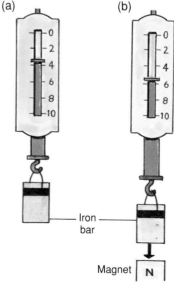

(a)

(b)

Iron bar

Magnet N

Figure 34.3D ● Measuring forces

▼ SUMMARY ▼

The magnitude and direction of any force can be represented on a diagram by a vector. An object is in equilibrium if the forces acting on it balance each other. If the forces do not balance, they do not cancel each other out. Their combined effect is called the resultant.

CHECKPOINT

① A trailer is attached to a car by a tow bar. The tow bar must be strong enough to withstand being pulled or pushed. Is the tow bar under tension or in compression when:
(a) the car and trailer drive off from rest,
(b) the car and trailer halt?
Make a sketch showing the trailer and the forces on it when the car drives off from rest.

② The diagrams opposite show several situations where two forces act on an object. In each case, work out the magnitude and direction of the resultant.

③ In the village of Much Watering, the highlight of the annual fair is when the tug-of-war team challenges the team from Little Steeping, the next village. The challenge takes place with the teams on opposite banks of the River Steeping. Each team is determined to pull the other team into the river. The team captains toss a coin to decide which side of the river to take. This is important because one bank is slightly higher than the other. Which bank would you take? Explain why.

④ A magnet of weight 2.4 N was hung from a newton balance. An identical magnet was hung from the first magnet. The second magnet was pulled down until it broke free from the first magnet. The spring balance reading just before the break was 9.6 N.
(a) What was the reading on the balance when it supported the first magnet only?
(b) What was the reading when the second magnet was hung on?
(c) What was the force of attraction between the two magnets just before they broke apart?

⑤ An empty car has a weight of 5500 N. Its driver has a weight of 600 N. The weight on each wheel should not be greater than 2500 N. In addition to the driver, how much extra weight can the car support safely?

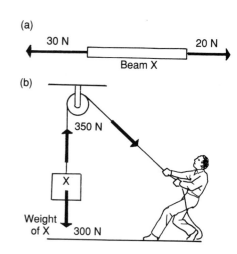

(a)

(b)

(c)

FIRST THOUGHTS

34.4 🍎 Turning forces

Your skeleton is a walking example of turning forces in action. Read on to find out about more turning forces.

To undo a very tight wheel nut on a bicycle you need a spanner. The force you apply to the spanner is called a **turning force**. Its effect is to turn the nut to undo it. *If you had the choice between a long-handled spanner and a short-handled one, which would you choose?*

Figure 34.4A ● A turning force

You cannot turn a tight nut with your fingers, but the spanner can turn it. Therefore the spanner must be exerting a bigger force on the nut than your fingers could. The spanner is an example of a **force multiplier**.

Figure 34.4B shows a crowbar being used to shift a heavy weight. The weight is called the **load**, and the force the person applies to the crowbar is called the **effort**. Using the crowbar, the effort needed to lift the safe is only a small fraction of its weight. A turning force is at work. The point about which the crowbar turns is called the **pivot** or the **fulcrum**. The crowbar is another example of a force multiplier.

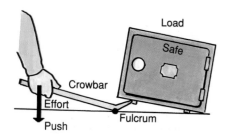

Figure 34.4B ● Using a crowbar

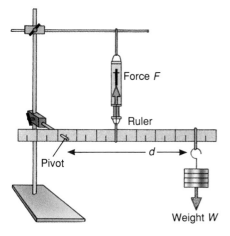

Figure 34.4C ● Investigating turning forces

Investigating the effect of a turning force

Figure 34.4C shows one way of investigating turning forces. The weight *W* is moved along the metre rule. *How do you think the reading on the balance compares with the weight? How does this reading change as the weight is moved away from the pivot?* Record the balance reading for different distances *d* from the pivot to the weight. The balance readings show that the force *F* needed to support the weight becomes larger as the weight is moved away from the pivot. The turning effect of the weight is called its **moment**.

The moment of a turning force is defined as

Moment = Force x Distance to the pivot (from the point where the force is applied)

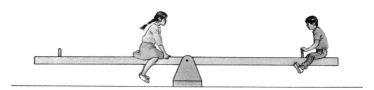

In Figure 34.4C, the moment of the weight is *W* x *d*. The greater the distance *d*, the bigger the moment. The weight tries to turn the bar clockwise. Force *F* tries to turn the bar anticlockwise. The moment of the weight is cancelled out by the moment of force *F*.

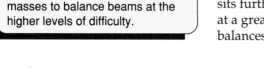

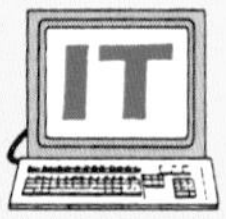

Figure 34.4D ● The seesaw

Moments
(program)

Use this program to study moments. You can use different masses to balance beams at the higher levels of difficulty.

A seesaw is another example where clockwise and anticlockwise moments balance an object. Figure 34.4D shows Vida sitting near the fulcrum to balance her younger brother, Tariq, at the far end of the seesaw. Vida's larger weight acting at a short distance from the fulcrum gives an anticlockwise moment. Tariq is not as heavy as his big sister and sits further away from the fulcrum on the other side. His smaller weight at a greater distance from the fulcrum gives a clockwise moment that balances Vida's anticlockwise moment.

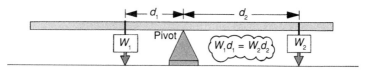

Figure 34.4E ● The principle of moments

This is an example of the **principle of moments**, which states that for an object in equilibrium,

Total clockwise moment = Total anticlockwise moment

Figure 34.4E shows how to test the principle. You will find that the beam is balanced when

$$\underset{\text{(clockwise moment)}}{W_1 \times d_1} = \underset{\text{(anticlockwise moment)}}{W_2 \times d_2}$$

This principle can be used to measure an unknown weight using a known weight.

LOOK AT LINKS
for more information about the human skeleton and how muscles make it move See Theme J, Topic 41.

In Figures 34.4D and E the beam is balanced at its centre of gravity. Its own weight acts at the pivot so has no turning effect. However, if the beam is balanced at another point then its weight does have a turning effect. Figure 34.4F shows how this can be used to find the weight of the beam using a known weight.

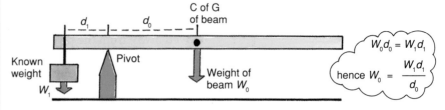

Figure 34.4F ● Finding the weight of a beam

The principle of moments explains why levers are so useful. Figure 34.4G shows some more examples that you may be familiar with. In each case, the effort provides a moment ($F_1 \times d_1$) that equals the moment of the load ($W_0 \times d_0$).

SCIENCE AT WORK

Artificial hip joints are used to replace diseased joints, releasing many people from pain and distress. The artificial joints are made from a plastic socket and a metallic alloy 'ball'. They have been developed by scientists and doctors working together. Hip joints must withstand huge forces, work smoothly at all times and never corrode. The joint is made from an alloy of chromium, cobalt and molybdenum. Titanium is used for the shaft. Titanium and chromium alloys do not corrode.

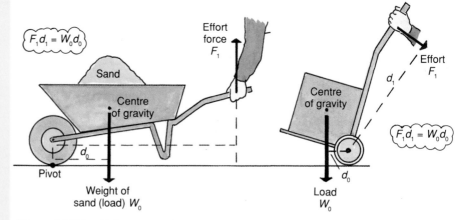

Figure 34.4G ● Using moments

Consider the wheelbarrow where $d_1 = 0.80$ m, $d_0 = 0.20$ m, $W_0 = 300$ N

$$\text{Since} \quad F_1 \times d_1 = W_0 \times d_0$$
$$\text{then} \quad F_1 \times 0.80 = 300 \times 0.20$$
$$\text{so} \quad F_1 = \frac{300 \times 0.20}{0.80} = 75 \text{ N}$$

Thus the wheelbarrow allows a load of 300 N weight to be shifted by applying an effort of 75 N.

The joints in the human body act as pivots. Each joint allows two bones to swivel about each other. The elbow allows the lower arm to swivel about the upper arm. The biceps muscle controls the movement of the lower arm. Compare Figures 34.4H and 34.4C. The muscle supports the lower arm in the same way as the balance supports the rule. In both cases, the force needed to support the weight is much larger than the weight itself.

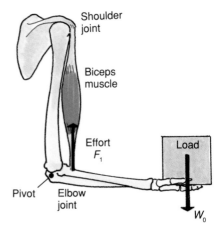

SUMMARY

The moment of a turning force is the product of the force and the distance to the pivot from the point where the force is applied. For any object in balance, the total clockwise moment is equal to the total anticlockwise moment.

Figure 34.4H ● Using your muscles

① Explain each of the following statements.
   (a) Trapping your finger in a door near the hinge can be very painful.
   (b) A claw hammer is easier to use if it has a long handle.
   (c) Using a wheelbarrow saves effort.

② For each of the balanced beams in the diagram opposite work out the unknown weight *W*.

③ Jill weighs 425 N and thinks she is the lightest girl in her class. Dawn claims she is lighter than Jill. They go to the local park to find out who weighs least. Dawn sits on the seesaw 2.50 m from the fulcrum. Jill balances the seesaw by sitting 2.00 m from the fulcrum on the other side of the pivot.
   (a) Who is the lighter?
   (b) What is Dawn's weight?
   (c) Dawn gets off the seesaw so John can sit on to balance Jill. His weight is 450 N. How far from the fulcrum should he sit?

④ The diagram opposite shows a bottle opener being used to remove a bottle top. Copy the diagram and add to it to show:
   (a) where the effort is applied,
   (b) where the bottle opener acts on the bottle top,
   (c) where the fulcrum is.
Explain how the bottle opener acts as a force multiplier.

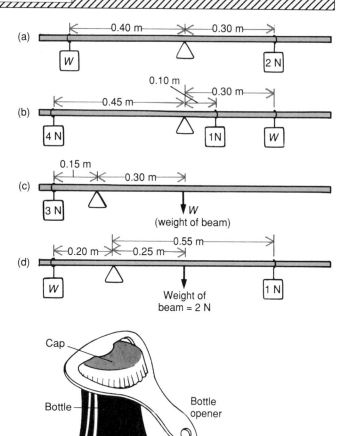

(a) 0.40 m | 0.30 m   *W*   2 N

(b) 0.10 m | 0.30 m   0.45 m   4 N   1 N   *W*

(c) 0.15 m | 0.30 m   3 N   *W* (weight of beam)

(d) 0.20 m | 0.25 m   0.55 m   *W*   Weight of beam = 2 N   1 N

Cap — Bottle — Bottle opener

34.5 Forces and frames

Architects, civil engineers and builders need to work out at the design stage what forces to expect in buildings.
Miscalculating the forces could be disastrous.

RESOURCE ACTIVITY PACK

Towers and bridges

The Eiffel Tower in Paris is one of the most famous buildings in the world. The iron tower, 300 m high, was the tallest building in the world when it was completed in 1889. If the upper section had been solid iron rather than a lattice of girders, perhaps it could have been made taller. *Why do you think a lattice of girders was used?* Modern skyscraper towers like the World Trade Centre in New York, which is 412 m high, are made from steel and concrete.

Figure 34.5A ●
The Eiffel Tower

Figure 34.5B ● (a) Coalbrookedale Iron Bridge

(b) Modern motorway bridge

The first iron bridge was constructed at Coalbrookedale, England in 1777 to span the River Severn. It was used for road traffic until the 1950s. Figure 34.5B shows this bridge in comparison with a modern motorway bridge made from steel and concrete.

Investigating bridges

Use a metre rule to make a simple beam bridge, as shown in Figure 34.5C. Load the rule at its centre with different weights and measure how much it sags.

Devise some means of reducing the 'sag' when the rule is loaded. Repeat your measurements and see how effective your design is. Some ideas are shown in Figure 34.5D.

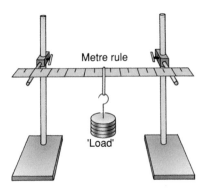

Figure 34.5C ● Testing a bridge

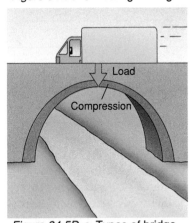

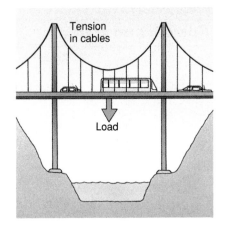

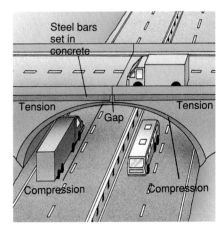

Figure 34.5D ● Types of bridge
(a) An arch bridge

(b) A suspension bridge

(c) A cantilever bridge

Bridge Building
(program)

Use this program to test different types of structure and the loads they can carry. Change the load on the bridge and its span. *What factors would you say are important in bridge building?*

- The arch bridge is strengthened by the arch under the span. The weight of the span and its load compresses (i.e. squeezes) the arch. The material of the arch must withstand huge compression forces.
- The suspension bridge roadway is supported by steel cables slung between towers. The weight of the roadway and traffic pulls on the cables. The cables must withstand very large tension forces.
- The cantilever bridge roadway consists of two beams that press against each other end-to-end. The upper part of each beam is in tension and the lower part is in compression. The beams are made from concrete reinforced with steel cables.

On the scaffold

Motorway flyovers are made from reinforced concrete. Unfortunately, the combined action of rain and salt (used in winter to prevent ice on roads) has weakened the concrete on some flyovers. Construction programmes are underway to strengthen them. Traffic delays are inevitable where flyovers are being repaired.

To build a high wall, builders stand on a scaffold platform erected alongside it. This is much safer than using a ladder. The scaffold needs to be strong to support the weight of the bricklayers and the bricks.

The scaffold is made of metal tubes clamped together. *Why are metal tubes used rather than metal bars?*

Some of the tubes are vertical, some horizontal and some are 'diagonal'. The horizontal tubes support the weight of the people and bricks on the platform. The vertical tubes support the horizontal tubes. *What are the diagonal tubes for?* If they were not included, the scaffold could collapse sideways. Their effect is to spread the weight of the people and bricks on the scaffold evenly across the structure.

SUMMARY

The design of any structure must take account of:
- the forces likely to act on the structure,
- how to strengthen the structure to withstand the forces on it,
- the best materials to use to make the structure, considering factors such as strength, weight and cost.

Figure 34.5E ● Scaffolding

CHECKPOINT

❶ Make a sketch of a well-known bridge and describe how the 'span' of the bridge is supported.

❷ (a) Explain why an arch bridge is much stronger than a simple beam bridge of the same length.
(b) Cardboard storage drums are much stronger than cardboard boxes. Why?

❸ (a) The diagram shows how reinforced concrete is used in the construction of a building. What is the purpose of the steel bars in the concrete?
(b) In the diagram, why is the steel bar in the top part of the concrete in the balcony section and in the lower part of the floor section?

❹ Elderly people often have difficulty in getting in and out of the bath. A 'bath seat' could be useful to an elderly person.
(a) Why can taking a bath be difficult for an elderly person?
(b) Design a bath seat to make it easier. Explain your choice of materials.

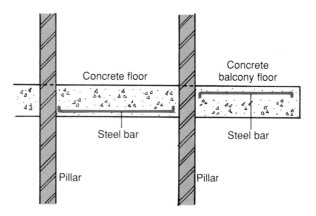

TOPIC 35  PRESSURE

35.1 What is pressure?

FIRST THOUGHTS

o
o
o

To estimate the pressure on your feet first draw around your shoes on centimetre squared paper. Count the number of squares in each footprint (ignoring any square less than half filled) to find the area of contact in square centimetres (cm²). Convert this to square metres (m²) using the conversion 10 000 cm² = 1 m².

Use bathroom scales to find your weight. If the scales read mass in kg, work out your weight in newtons using *g* = 10 N/kg.

Work out the pressure on your feet using

$$\text{Pressure} = \frac{\text{Weight}}{\text{Area}}$$

LOOK AT LINKS
for how to calculate weight
See Theme I, Topic 34.1.

SUMMARY

Pressure is force per unit area. The unit of pressure is the pascal, which is equal to 1 N/m².

If you have stood barefoot on a sharp object, you will have found out about **pressure** in a very painful way. All your weight acts on the tip of the object, so there is a huge pressure on your foot at the area of contact.

Pressure is caused when objects exert forces on each other. The pressure caused by any force depends on the area of contact where the force acts, as well as on the size of the force.

Ellen weighs 500 N. She stands barefoot on the kitchen floor. Then she puts on her stiletto heels and walks across the kitchen. Heelmarks appear on the vinyl floor wherever she treads in her high-heeled shoes. *Why has this happened?* Her weight has not changed, so the force she exerts on the floor has not changed. However, the area over which her weight acts has changed, changing the pressure that she exerts on the floor.

Snowshoes like those shown in Figure 35.1A are useful for walking across soft snow without sinking into it. Each showshoe has a much bigger area than the average human foot. The weight of the wearer is spread over a much bigger area of contact than in ordinary shoes. Therefore the pressure exerted on the snow by someone wearing snowshoes is much less than that exerted by the same person wearing ordinary shoes.

Figure 35.1A ●
Spreading the weight

Pressure is defined as force per unit area. The unit of pressure is the pascal (Pa), which is equal to one newton per square metre (N/m²).

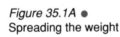

$$P = \frac{F}{A}$$ where *P* = pressure in pascals
A = area of contact in square metres
F = force in newtons acting at right angles to the surface

How much has the pressure Ellen exerts on the floor increased as a result of her wearing stiletto heels? Her weight is 500 N. The area of her bare foot in contact with the floor is 50 cm², which equals 0.0050 m². If she stands barefoot in the kitchen, the pressure she exerts on the floor with both feet is given by

$$P_1 = \frac{\text{Weight}}{\text{Contact area}} = \frac{500}{2 \times 0.0050} = 50\ 000 \text{ Pa}$$

The area of each stiletto heel is 1.0 cm² = 0.0001 m². Work out the pressure she exerts on the floor now. You should obtain a value equal to $50P_1$. In other words, the pressure is 50 times greater as a result of wearing the stiletto heels. No wonder the stiletto heels mark the floor.

CHECKPOINT

❶ Explain each of the following.
  (a) When you do a handstand, the pressure on your hands is greater than the pressure on your feet when you stand upright.
  (b) Caterpillar tracks are essential for vehicles used in the Arctic.
  (c) A sharp knife cuts meat more easily than a blunt one.

❷ Hospital patients confined to bed need to be moved to stop bed sores forming. These occur where the body presses on the bed for long periods. Estimate your area of contact when you lie on a bed and work out the pressure of your body on the bed.

❸ A concrete paving slab of weight 140 N has dimensions 1.00 m x 0.80 m x 0.050 m. What pressure does it exert when (a) it is laid flat on a bed of sand, (b) it stands upright on its shorter side?

❹ Skis are designed to allow the wearer to travel fast across snow. Why are skis made so much longer than even the largest human foot?

FIRST THOUGHTS

35.2 🍎 Pressure at work

Huge forces can be produced and huge loads shifted using hydraulic pressure systems. Read on to find out how hydraulic machines work.

Figure 35.2A ● Mechanical digger

IT

Working Under Pressure
(program)

Use this program in small groups to study the flow of gas in a pipeline. *How is pressure maintained along a pipeline? What factors affect the flow of gas in a pipe?*

Roadworks are an everyday feature of life in any town or city. Mains services such as water and gas reach our homes through underground pipes, usually beneath the road. Mechanical diggers are usually used to reach broken pipes. The 'grab' of the digger, designed to remove earth, operates by a hydraulic pressure system. Most machines that shift or lift things operate hydraulically. The hydraulic system of a machine is its 'muscle power'.

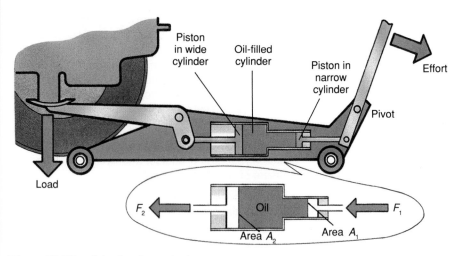

Figure 35.2B ● A hydraulic car jack

A car can be lifted 'by hand' using a hydraulic car jack (Figure 35.2B). When you press the handle down, a narrow piston is forced along an oil-filled cylinder. The oil is forced out of this cylinder along a pipe and into a wider cylinder. The pressure of the oil forces the piston in this cylinder outwards. The second piston acts on a lever to raise the car. The force applied to the narrow piston (the master piston) causes a large pressure on the oil. This pressure then acts on the wide piston (the slave). In Figure 35.2B the pressure on the narrow piston = F_1/A_1 so

Force F_2 on the large piston = Pressure x Area of large piston

$$F_2 = \frac{F_1}{A_1} \times A_2$$

Since area A_2 is much greater than area A_1, then F_2 is much greater than F_1. A force on the first piston supplies a bigger force to lift the car. The jack therefore acts as a 'force multiplier'.

Hydraulic brakes use pressure. When the driver presses the brake pedal of a car, pressure is exerted on the oil (or brake fluid) in the master cylinder (Figure 35.2C). This pressure is transmitted along oil-filled brake pipes to a slave cylinder at each wheel. The oil pressure forces the piston in each slave cylinder to push the brake disc pads on to the wheel disc.

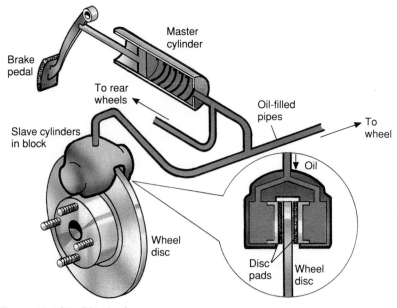

Figure 35.2C ● Disc brakes

Power-assisted brakes fitted to heavy goods vehicles and coaches use compressed air (air brakes). When the driver applies the brakes, compressed air at very high pressure is released to push on the piston in the master cylinder. The compressed air is used instead of the force of the brake pedal. That is why such vehicles hiss when the brakes are released.

Robots use hydraulics for 'muscle power'. Robots are used more and more in factories. Do not let your imagination run away with you though. The robot of science fiction is a long way off. Factory robots are fixed machines that operate such things as welding gear or paint sprays on assembly lines. They work non-stop without the need for a human operator. Robot muscles use compressed air.

Figure 35.2D ● Remote controlled robot used by bomb disposal teams for handling suspect packages

SUMMARY

Hydraulics are used to shift or lift heavy objects. The pressure in a hydraulic system is transmitted through the oil or air in the system. The force on the slave piston due to the oil pressure is much greater than the force applied to the master piston.

CHECKPOINT

❶ Write down as many things as you can think of that are operated hydraulically.

❷ Figure 35.2A shows the arm of a mechanical digger. Explain why the arm is raised when compressed air is released into cylinder X.

❸ The digger in Figure 35.2A has three levers in the control cab. One operates cylinder X, one cylinder Y and one cylinder Z. How would you use these controls to raise the earth-filled grab and dump the earth into a lorry?

❹ The hydraulic lift shown has four pistons, each of area 0.01 m², to lift the platform. The pressure in the system must not be greater than 500 kPa. The platform weight is 2 kN. What is the maximum load that can be lifted on the platform?

❺ Why is it important to ensure that air does not leak into the brake fluid of a car?

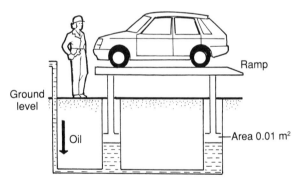

35.3 ● Pressure in liquids

FIRST THOUGHTS

In a two-storey house, why is the water pressure upstairs less than the pressure downstairs? Find out in this section.

Imagine you are swimming underwater with a snorkel tube. Provided the top of the tube is above water, you ought to be able to breathe air safely. *Why not give deep-sea divers very long snorkel tubes?* They would not work because of the huge pressure on the diver. The diver's chest muscles would not be strong enough to expand his or her chest muscles against the water pressure on his or her body. So the diver would be unable to draw air down the tube.

TRY THIS

The water table is the name given to the level of water beneath the ground. Dig a hole in the ground below the water table and water will fill the bottom of the hole. The bottom of a well should be below the water table. In dry weather, the water table may drop beneath the bottom of the well, so the well runs dry.

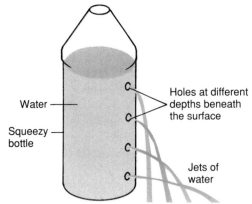

Figure 35.3A ● Pressure increases with depth

Holes at different depths beneath the surface

Water

Squeezy bottle

Jets of water

The pressure in a liquid increases with depth. A simple way to show this is to make small holes down the side of an empty plastic bottle. Then fill the bottle with water and place it in a bowl. A jet of water will emerge from each hole, as shown in Figure 35.3A. The deeper the hole is beneath the water level in the bottle, the greater the pressure of the jet.

The pressure along a fixed level is constant. Use the same bottle and make several holes around the bottle at the same level. The jets from these holes should be at the same pressure.

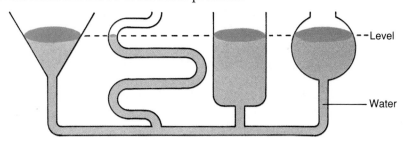

Level

Water

Figure 35.3B ● Pascal's vases

Pascal's vases, shown in Figure 35.3B, consist of several containers linked so that water can flow between them. When water is poured into one of them, the water level in each one rises until it is the same in all the containers. This is because the water will not come to rest until all the pressures on it are equalised. The pressure of the water in the container depends only on its depth, so if the depths are equal, the pressures are equal.

Pressure of a liquid column

How much pressure is exerted by a liquid column? Consider the column in Figure 35.3C.

Volume of liquid in the column = Area of cross-section A x Height H

Mass of liquid = Volume x Density of liquid ρ = A x H x ρ

Weight of liquid = Mass x g = A x H x ρ x g (where g = 10 N/kg)

Pressure at base of column $= \dfrac{\text{Weight of liquid}}{\text{Area of cross-section } A} = \dfrac{AH\rho g}{A} = H\rho g$

Therefore pressure of a liquid column of Height $H = H\rho g$

Where ρ = density of liquid.

The pressure of a liquid column depends on its height and the density of the liquid.

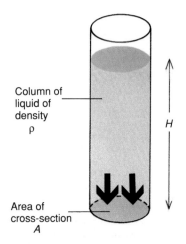

Column of liquid of density ρ

H

Area of cross-section A

Figure 35.3C ● Calculating liquid pressure

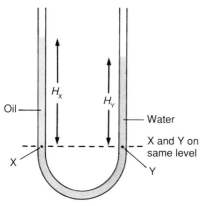

Figure 35.3D ● Comparing densities of liquids

The pressure depends on density. Suppose water is poured into a U-shaped tube, as in Figure 35.3D, until the level is about one third of the way up each side. Then oil is poured carefully down one side to form a column on top of the water. The oil level is higher than the water level because oil is less dense than water.

Worked example   Calculate the pressure due to sea water on the floor of the sea bed at a depth of 200 m. The density of sea water is 1050 kg/m^3. Assume $g = 10$ N/kg.

Solution   Consider a column of sea water of height 200 m above the sea bed.

Using $p = H\rho g$,

where $H = 200$ m, $\rho = 1050$ kg/m^3,

$p = 200 \times 1050 \times 10 = 2.10 \times 10^6$ Pa

SUMMARY

The pressure in a liquid increases with depth. Along a fixed level, the pressure does not change.

CHECKPOINT

❶ In most homes, the water pressure upstairs is less than the pressure downstairs. The diagram shows a house with a water tank in the loft to supply the hot water boiler.

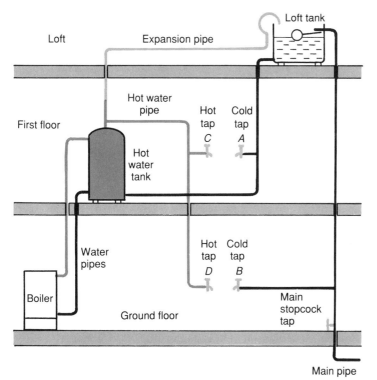

(a) Why is the cold water pressure upstairs (at tap A) less than downstairs (at tap B)?
(b) Is the hot water pressure at C less than the cold water pressure at A?
(c) How does hot water get from the boiler to the hot water tank?
(d) What is the function of the expansion pipe?

❷ Why is the wall of a dam thicker at the base than at the top?

❸ In a hydro-electric scheme, water is piped from an upland reservoir down to a generator station, 700 m below the reservoir. Work out the pressure in the water pipe from the reservoir when at the station. The density of water is 1000 kg/m^3. Assume $g = 10$ N/kg.

❹ A sink plug has an area of 0.0006 m^2. It is used to block the outlet of a sink filled with water to a depth of 0.09 m.
(a) What is the pressure on the plug due to the water?
(b) How much force is needed to remove the plug from the outlet? Use the values for ρ and g given in question 3.

35.4 Measuring pressure

In this section you will learn how pressure is measured and why such measurements are important.

Keeping the recommended pressure in a system means measuring the pressure regularly, so that action can be taken if the pressure is not at the correct level.

What do nurses, car mechanics, gas board officials and submariners have in common? They all need to measure pressure. Nurses measure blood pressure, car mechanics measure tyre pressure, gas board officials measure pressure to detect gas leaks and submariners use a pressure indicator as a depth gauge.

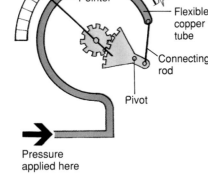

Figure 35.4A ● Bourdon gauge

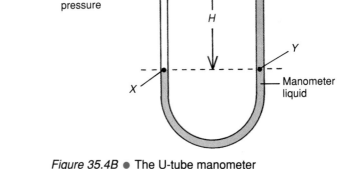

Figure 35.4B ● The U-tube manometer

LOOK AT LINKS
for **blood pressure**
See Theme J, Topic 38.3.

The **Bourdon gauge** contains a flexible copper tube (Figure 35.4A). When pressure is applied at the inlet, the tube uncurls a little. This movement is magnified by a lever to make a pointer move across a scale. Tyre pressure is measured using a Bourdon gauge. The reading is the excess pressure in the tyre above atmospheric pressure.

The **U-tube manometer** (Figure 35.4B) is a much simpler instrument than the Bourdon gauge. The gas pressure forces the manometer liquid up the open side of the U-tube until it remains steady when the difference in levels balances the gas pressure. The height difference between the levels, H, is measured. The equation $p = H\rho g$ gives the excess pressure of the gas (i.e. its pressure above atmospheric pressure) where ρ is the density of the manometer liquid.

SUMMARY

There are three main types of pressure-measuring instruments. They are the Bourdon gauge, the U-tube manometer and the electronic pressure gauge.

Electronic pressure gauges use special crystals that generate a voltage when squeezed. This is called the **piezoelectric effect**. You may have used a piezoelectric gas lighter: press the trigger of the lighter and the high voltage generated produces sparks. In this type of pressure gauge, the pressure to be measured squeezes the crystal. A voltmeter connected across the crystal measures the voltage generated and thus the pressure.

CHECKPOINT

1 In Figure 35.4B, atmospheric pressure acts at point Z. The gas pressure to be measured acts at X. How does the pressure at X compare with:
(a) the pressure at Z,
(b) the pressure at Y?
(c) The manometer liquid is water. Its density is 1000 kg/m³. If the difference in levels is 0.25 m, what is the difference between the pressure at X and at Z? Assume g = 10 N/kg.

② Typical values of car tyre pressures are in the range 150 to 200 kPa. What would be the height of a column of water that produced a pressure of 200 kPa at its base? Use the values of ρ and g in question 1. Why is a Bourdon gauge more suitable for measuring tyre pressure than a U-tube manometer?

③ Blood pressure is usually expressed in millimetres of mercury rather than in pascals. This unit is used because the most common type of blood pressure gauge contains a tube of mercury. The blood pressure of a healthy human is 120 mm of mercury, on average. Work out what this pressure is in pascals, given the density of mercury is 13 600 kg/m³ and $g = 10$ N/kg. (See Theme J, Topic 38.3 for more about blood pressure.)

④ State one advantage and one disadvantage of an electronic pressure gauge compared with (a) a Bourdon pressure gauge, (b) a U-tube manometer.

35.5 ● Atmospheric pressure

FIRST THOUGHTS

> The fact that the atmosphere exerts pressure was not proved until the seventeenth century. Changes in the weather can be predicted by measuring atmospheric pressure.

The Earth's atmosphere extends 100 km or more into space. It becomes less dense the higher it is above sea level, so atmospheric pressure falls with height. At sea level, atmospheric pressure varies from day to day, changing with weather conditions. Fine, clear weather usually occurs when atmospheric pressure is higher than average.

Investigating atmospheric pressure

*   You can use atmospheric pressure to siphon water from a tank (Figure 35.5A). Use a clean tube and suck water into it from the tank. Keep the end of the tube in the water. Take the other end from your mouth and hold it below the tank. *Why does water flow down the tube from the upper tank?*
*   Drinking through a straw makes use of atmospheric pressure (Figure 35.5B). Sucking on the straw reduces the pressure in the straw. The pressure of the atmosphere on the liquid in the glass then forces the liquid up the straw from outside.
*   Estimate atmospheric pressure using a suction cap (Figure 35.5C). Measure the area of the cap and then estimate the force needed to pull it off a wall. You can then work out the atmospheric pressure by Pressure = Force/Area. Its value is about 100 kPa.

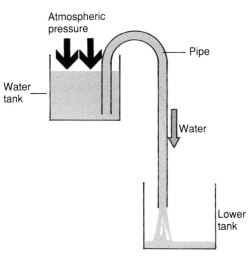

Figure 35.5A ● A siphon

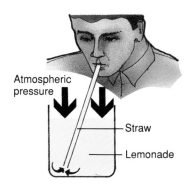

Figure 35.5B ● Sucking through a straw

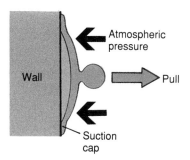

Figure 35.5C ● A suction cap

Pascal and pressure

Fill a milk bottle in a bowl of water and then hold the bottle upside down with its open end under the water. *Why doesn't the water fall out? What would remain in the bottle if the water did fall out?* The answer is nothing – a vacuum. Some people would say the water does not fall out because 'nature dislikes a vacuum'. *Do you think this is a satisfactory explanation?*

Blaise Pascal was a seventeenth century French scientist who did not think much of such vague statements. He carried out experiments to explain them scientifically. Here are some simplified versions of his experiments.

❶ The inverted bottle experiment uses a tube instead of a milk bottle. The tube is sealed at one end with a cork (Figure 35.5E). When the tube filled with water is inverted in a bowl of water, the water remains in the tube. *What happens if the tube is raised so its lower end is lifted out of the water?*

❷ Suppose the cork is removed from the inverted tube in Figure 35.5E. *What happens now?*

Figure 35.5D ● Blaise Pascal (1623-62)

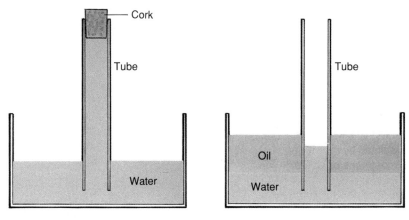

Figure 35.5E ●   *Figure 35.5F* ●

❸ Now suppose oil is poured onto the water outside the tube. Oil is less dense than water so it floats on the water surface. Water goes up the inside of the tube (Figure 35.5F). *Why?*

Pascal realised that the weight of the oil pushing on the water outside the tube forced water up the tube. *What do you think would happen if oil was poured on to the water inside the tube as well?*

Can you use these observations to explain why the water remains in the tube in Figure 35.5E until the cork is removed? In Figure 35.5F the weight of the oil on the water forces the water up the tube. *So why does the water drop out when the cork is removed?* Letting air into the tube at the top is like pouring oil on to water inside the tube. The water is pushed down the tube until it is at the same level as the water outside the tube.

Pascal realised that air has weight and the weight of the atmosphere creates pressure. Atmospheric pressure acting on the water outside the tube in Figure 35.5E pushes the water up inside the tube. When the cork is removed, atmospheric pressure now acts on the water in the tube as well as on the water outside. So the water in the tube is pushed down the to the same level as the water outside the tube.

In recognition of Pascal's work on pressure, the unit of pressure is named after him.

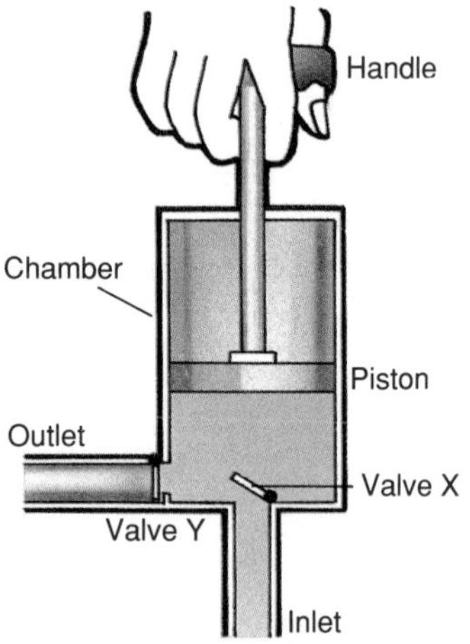

Instruments that use atmospheric pressure ▪

Pumps make use of atmospheric pressure. In Figure 35.5G, when the handle is pulled up, the piston is withdrawn from the pump chamber. Atmospheric pressure then forces water into the chamber through the inlet valve X. When the piston is pushed back in again, this valve closes and the outlet valve opens, so water leaves the chamber.

❶ Handle raised
❷ Piston pulled up
❸ Valve X opens, valve Y closes and chamber fills from inlet with water
❹ Handle pushed down, piston moves down
❺ Y opens, X closes and water forced through outlet

Figure 35.5G ● The force pump

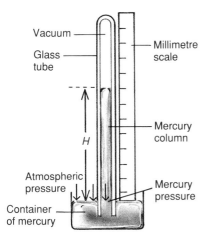

Figure 35.5H ● The mercury barometer

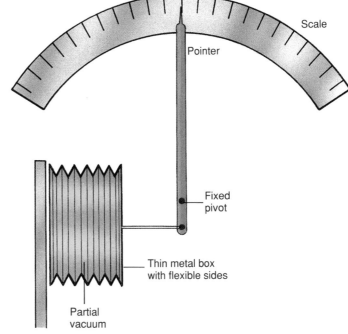

Figure 35.5I ● The aneroid barometer

The **barometer** is designed to measure atmospheric pressure. There are two common types:
• The **mercury barometer**, shown in Figure 35.5H, consists of an inverted tube of mercury with its lower end under the surface of mercury in a container. The top end of the tube is sealed and there is a vacuum above the mercury in the tube. *Why doesn't the mercury drop out of the tube?* The atmospheric pressure acting on the mercury in the container holds it up by balancing the pressure due to the column of mercury in the tube.

Atmospheric pressure = $H\rho g$

where H = height of the mercury column
       ρ = density of mercury,
       g = 10 N/kg

The average value of barometric height is 760 mm of mercury, often referred to as standard pressure. You can show that this is equal to 101 kPa, given that the density of mercury, ρ is 13 600 kg/m^3.
• The **aneroid barometer**, shown in Figure 35.5I, contains a sealed metal chamber with flexible sides. When atmospheric pressure increases, the box is squeezed in. The movement of its flexible sides makes a pointer move across a scale. The altimeter of an aircraft, used to measure its height, is an aneroid barometer with its dial marked in metres above sea level. It makes use of the fact that atmospheric pressure falls with increasing height above the ground.

SUMMARY

Atmospheric pressure at sea level changes slightly from day to day. Its average value is 760 mm of mercury. It can be measured using an aneroid barometer or a mercury barometer.

CHECKPOINT

❶ Explain how atmospheric pressure acts:
   (a) to keep a rubber sucker on a wall,
   (b) when you drink through a straw,
   (c) when water is siphoned from a tank.

❷ Atmospheric pressure is about 100 kPa. What depth of water will give the same pressure? The density of water is 1000 kg/m^3. Assume g = 10 N/kg.

③ How will the reading of a mercury barometer be affected if:
(a) some air leaks into the top of the tube,
(b) the tube and the scale tilt slightly?

④ The tyres of a car are at a pressure of 180 kPa above atmospheric pressure. Each of the four tyres has an area of contact with the ground of 0.015 m². Work out the weight of the car in newtons.

⑤ How would you find out if atmospheric pressure can be used to predict weather changes? Assume you have a barometer. What records would you keep each day?

FIRST THOUGHTS

35.6 Floating and sinking

Any object in a fluid is acted on by the pressure of the fluid. Find out why an object weighs less in water than in air.

Figure 35.6A ● Disabled people find it easier to move in water

When you go swimming, have you noticed that you feel lighter in the water? Disabled people often find it much easier to move in water than in air. Water exerts an upward force on a body in it. This force is called the **upthrust** of the water.

Floating and Sinking
(program)

This is a program which allows you to study different materials in different liquids. After using the program, make a list of how different factors determine whether an object floats or sinks.

Eureka!

Archimedes was one of the most famous scientists in Ancient Greece. His king asked him to find out if his new crown was made of pure gold, presumably to check that the royal crownmaker was not cheating. However, the king would not allow the crown to be damaged in any way.

After much thought Archimedes was no nearer solving the problem, so he decided to take a bath. In the bath he had a flash of inspiration. He realised that by weighing the crown in water and in air and making similar measurements on a piece of pure gold, he could tell whether the crown was pure gold. History records that he celebrated this discovery by running through the streets shouting 'Eureka!' (Greek for 'I've found it').

Archimedes realised that the upthrust on an object in water depended on how much water is **displaced** (i.e. pushed aside) by the object. He measured the amount of water displaced as illustrated in the *Try this* exercise on the next page, and discovered the following principle

> The upthrust is always equal to the weight of fluid displaced.
> This is called Archimedes' Principle.

TRY THIS

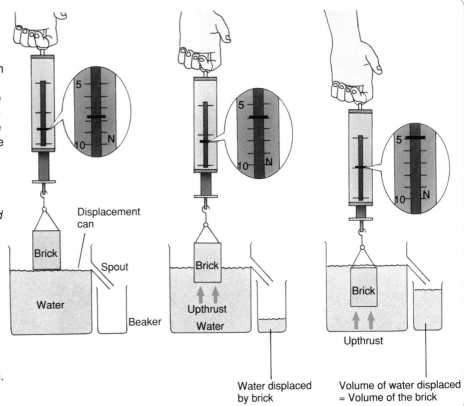

The diagram shows a brick being weighed in air and then in water. The reading on the spring balance is less when the brick is in water. The difference is caused by the upthrust of the water on the brick. Work out the upthrust on the brick in the diagram.

Why do you think the reading of the spring balance changes as the brick is lowered into the water? Try it and you will find that the upthrust increases as more of the brick enters the water.

The upthrust is due to the upward pressure of the water on the underside of the brick. As the brick is lowered into the water, the upthrust increases, because the pressure on the underside increases with depth.

Displacement can

Brick

Spout

Water

Beaker

Brick

Upthrust

Water

Brick

Upthrust

Water displaced by brick

Volume of water displaced = Volume of the brick

LOOK AT LINKS
Amphibians can live on land or in water. When an amphibian is in water, the upthrust from the water helps to support the creature.
See Theme A, Topic 3.5.

Will it float?

A busy waterway is fascinating to watch. Boats and ships laden with cargo float low in the water. A boat carrying cargo stays afloat provided the upthrust due to the water is equal to the total weight of the boat and its cargo.

A ship being loaded will float lower and lower in the water as the load increases. At any stage in the loading operation, the weight of water displaced by the ship is equal to the upthrust, which is greater than or equal to the total weight of the ship. If the ship is loaded too much, it sinks because the upthrust is unable to support the total weight of the ship.

Every ship has a horizontal line painted on its hull to show how low it can float safely in the water when loaded (see Figure 35.6C) — and also

Figure 35.6B ● Busy waterway

Figure 35.6C ● Loading lines and draft marks

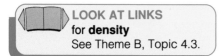

LOOK AT LINKS
for **density**
See Theme B, Topic 4.3.

IT

Upthrust and Flotation
(program)

Use this program to study the forces on balloons and other objects immersed in a fluid. *What does Archimedes principle tell you about the forces on objects in a fluid?*

SUMMARY

A body in water experiences an upthrust equal to the weight of the water it displaces. If the upthrust equals the weight of the body, the object does not sink.

---

the **Plimsoll line** after Samuel Plimsoll who guided the legislation through Parliament in 1875 to make this line compulsory. Before this time, many ships and crews were lost at sea due to overloading.

The hydrometer

In a brewery, the final product is tested by using a hydrometer to measure its density. If the beer's density is too low, it contains too much water; if the density is too high, the beer is too strong.

Figure 35.6D shows a hydrometer in use. The density of the liquid is given by the level of the liquid on the float. The density can be read off the scale.

Figure 35.6D ● Using a hydrometer

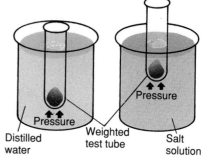

Figure 35.6E ● Using a weighted test tube as a hydrometer

A weighted test tube can be used as a hydrometer as shown in Figure 35.6E. The test tube floats higher in a salt solution than in pure water. Therefore the volume of salt solution displaced is less than the volume of pure water displaced. The weight of liquid displaced is the same in both cases, equal to the weight of the tube. Therefore the density of salt solution is greater than that of pure water.

CHECKPOINT

❶ (a) Why is it difficult to hold an inflated plastic ball under water?
(b) Why is cork a suitable material for filling life belts?
(c) When a submarine surfaces, it uses compressed air to push water out of its 'ballast' tanks. Why does this allow it to rise?

❷ In the diagram for *Try this* on the previous page work out:
(a) the mass of the brick, assuming a mass of 1 kg has a weight of 10 N,
(b) the upthrust on the brick when it is totally submerged,
(c) the density of the brick, assuming the density of water = 1000 kg/m³.

❸ (a) A block of wood of weight 5.0 N floats in water, as shown. What is the upthrust on the block?
(b) What weight of water is displaced by the block?
(c) Work out the mass of the water displaced, assuming a mass of 1 kg has a weight of 10 N.
(d) What can you say about the density of the block compared with the density of water?
(e) A solid object is released in water and it sinks. What does this tell you about (i) the upthrust on the object in relation to its weight, (ii) the density of the object in relation to the density of water?

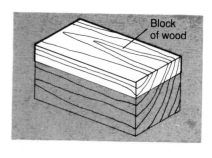

Block of wood

❹ (a) Ice floats on water. What does this tell you about the density of ice compared with that of water?
(b) In winter, why is it possible for fish to remain alive in ponds that are covered with ice?

TOPIC 36 *FORCE AND MOTION*

 FIRST THOUGHTS

36.1 **Maps and routes**

> After you have worked through this section you will be able to plan journeys with confidence.

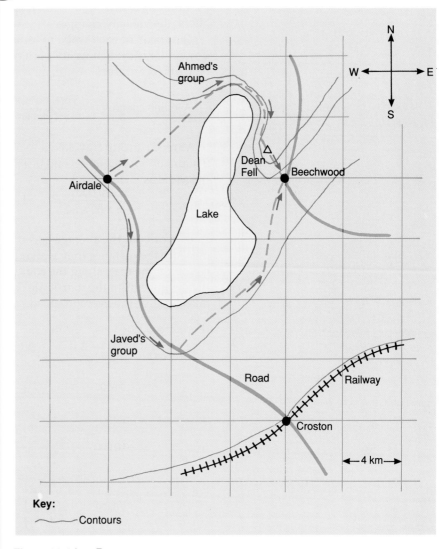

Figure 36.1A ● Routes

A group of friends are planning a walking holiday, stopping overnight at youth hostels. Figure 36.1A shows part of the route. They decide to stop for two nights at Airdale and then walk to Beechwood. The shortest distance from Airdale to Beechwood is 12 km but this route is not very sensible. *Can you see why?*

There are two possible routes, one following the map contours and a shorter route over Dean Fell. Ahmed wants to take the shorter route and measures the distance at 20 km. Javed wants to take the other route, even though it is considerably longer than 20 km. So the group decide to split into two for this part of the walk.

The two groups set off at 10 a.m. from Airdale. Javed and his group arrive at Beechwood at 4 p.m. only to find that the other group have arrived one hour earlier. Ahmed's group travelled 4 km per hour. Javed reckons his group walked faster, even though they arrived one hour after Ahmed's group. *Which group do you think walked at the greatest speed?*

Speed is defined as distance travelled per unit time. Its scientific unit is metres per second (m/s). Other units such as cm/s or km/h (kilometres per hour) are used, but they may need to be converted into m/s for calculations. For example, a speed of 20 cm/s is 0.20 m/s, since 20 cm = 0.20 m. Car speeds are often given in km/h. A speed of 110 km/h is approximately 31 m/s.

Velocity is speed in a given direction. The map shows that Ahmed's route changes direction. Even if speed is constant, where the direction alters, the velocity changes.

The speed of each walker would have varied during the journey, going downhill faster than uphill perhaps. The average speed of each group can be worked out from

$$\text{Average speed} \quad = \quad \frac{\text{Total distance travelled}}{\text{Total time taken}}$$

Ahmed's group travelled a total distance of 20 km (= 20 000 m) in 5 hours (= 5 x 60 x 60 seconds). The average speed was 4 km/h, which is the same as

$$\frac{20\,000}{5 \times 60 \times 60} \quad = \quad 1.11 \text{ m/s.}$$

To work out the average speed of Javed's group, use the map to measure the distance they walked. One way to do this is to lay a length of cotton on the map along the route and then straighten it out to measure the distance from the map scale. Then divide this distance by the time taken to give the average speed.

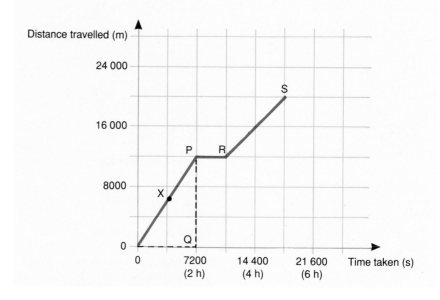

Figure 36.1B ● Ahmed's progress

Distance–time graphs are useful to illustrate a journey. From Figure 36.1B you can see that Ahmed's group travelled 12 km in the first two hours and then rested for an hour. Then they completed the remaining 8 km in two hours.

Uniform or constant speed is where the speed does not change. In Figure 36.1B the speed is uniform from O to P and from R to S. Uniform speed is shown on the graph by a constant gradient.

The speed at any point can be calculated from the **gradient** of the graph at that point. To find the gradient at any point, draw a 'gradient triangle'.

Consider point X in Figure 36.1B. The gradient triangle at X is labelled OPQ. Its height, PQ, represents distance travelled; its base, OQ, represents time taken.

$$\text{Speed at X} = \frac{\text{Distance}}{\text{Time taken}} = \frac{PQ}{OQ} = \frac{12\,000}{(7200)} = 1.67 \text{ m/s}$$

Where the speed changes, the gradient of the distance–time graph changes. Figure 36.1C is a distance–time graph for a cyclist going downhill. The increase in the cyclist's speed is shown by the increasing gradient. To find the speed at any point, a gradient triangle must be drawn at that point.

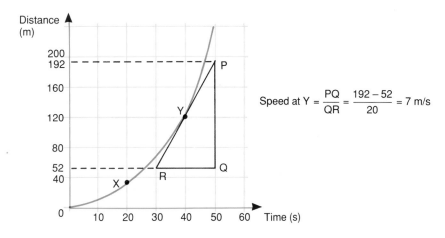

$$\text{Speed at Y} = \frac{PQ}{QR} = \frac{192 - 52}{20} = 7 \text{ m/s}$$

Figure 36.1C ● Using a distance-time graph

Consider point Y on Figure 36.1C. The graph is curved. The straight line touching Y is called the **tangent**. This is used to form the gradient triangle at Y. The height PQ of the triangle represents the distance moved; the base QR represents the time taken. Hence the speed can be calculated as shown.

SUMMARY

Speed is distance travelled per unit time. Velocity is speed in a given direction. The gradient of a distance–time graph gives the speed.

CHECKPOINT

❶ (a) The distance travelled by Javed's group was 28 km. Work out the average speed of Javed's group in km/h. Did they travel faster than Ahmed's group?
　(b) What is the average speed of Javed's group in m/s?

❷ (a) Use Figure 36.1B to work out the average speed of Ahmed's group in the two hours of their journey from R to S.
　(b) Why is their average speed for the whole journey, 1.1 m/s (see previous page), less than their speed for the first part of the journey?

❸ Javed's group walked 16 km from 10 a.m. until 12.30 p.m., when they took a break for an hour. Then they completed their journey without stopping. Sketch a distance–time graph for Javed and his friends.

❹ (a) Imagine you are a cyclist. How could you measure your average speed between two points on your route?
　(b) Work out the speed at point X of Figure 36.1C.

❺ The next part of our friends' journey is from Beechwood to the railway station at Croston which is 16.0 km due south of Beechwood.
　(a) What is the direct distance from Airdale to Croston?
　(b) Ahmed reckons the best route to Croston from Beechwood is 24 km. How long would it take the group to make this journey at an average speed of 1.00 m/s?

36.2 🍎 Acceleration

In this section you will need to remember how to rearrange equations and how to use equations to solve numerical problems.

The makers of a new type of car claim it can reach a certain speed faster than any other car. Their sales brochure states 'Under test conditions, this car accelerated more quickly than any of the other cars being tested'. Rival car makers are none too pleased by this claim and issue a challenge. Each car in turn is tested on the same racing circuit with a speed recorder fitted. The results for the two cars with the highest performances are shown below.

Figure 36.2A   New car on a test circuit

Table 36.1 ● Car test results

Time from a standing start (s)		0	20	40	60	80	100
Speed (m/s)	Car X	0	5	10	15	20	20
	Car Y	0	6	12	18	18	18

Which car accelerates more? The speed of X increases 5 m/s every 20 s, compared with 6 m/s every 20 s for Y. So Y **accelerates** more because its increase of speed in the same time is greater.

Investigating acceleration using a ticker timer

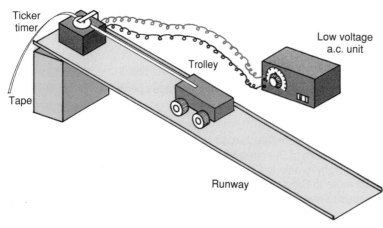

Figure 36.2B ● Investigating acceleration

The ticker timer is designed to print dots on to tape at a steady rate of 50 per second. Figure 36.2B shows how to use the ticker timer to record the motion of a trolley down a runway. As the trolley accelerates down the runway, it pulls the tape through the timer at a faster and faster rate. Figure 36.2C shows the result.

The dots become more widely spaced because the tape travels faster and faster. The time interval between successive dots is 0.02 s (= 1/50 s).

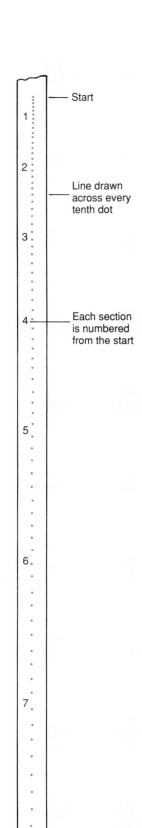

— Start

1

2

Line drawn
across every
tenth dot

3

4 — Each section
is numbered
from the start

5

6

7

8

Figure 36.2C ● A ticker tape

The tape can be marked into 10-dot sections, each section taking 0.20 s
(= 10/50 s) to pass through the machine. The sections get longer as the
tape goes through faster and faster.

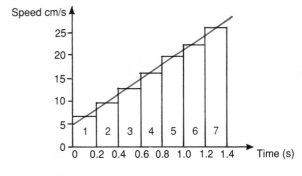

Figure 36.2D ● A tapechart

These sections can be made into a **tapechart** as shown in Figure 36.2D.
This example shows that the speed increases at a constant rate, because
the sections get longer at a steady rate. In effect, the tapechart is a graph
of speed against time for the trolley.

The time axis is marked in intervals of 0.2 s because each section took
0.2 s to travel through the timer. The speed axis is marked in intervals of
5 cm/s for each centimetre of the scale. This is because a section of length
1 cm would pass through the timer in 0.2 s. Hence its speed would be
1/0.2 = 5 cm/s.

The line through the tops of the sections has a constant gradient. The
speed rises steadily. This shows the acceleration is **uniform**.

Acceleration is defined as the change of velocity per unit time. The
unit of acceleration is the metre per second per second (m/s^2).

Since the direction in the car test example opposite is constant, the
acceleration can be worked out from the change of speed per second.

$$\text{Acceleration} = \frac{\text{Change of speed}}{\text{Time taken}}$$

For example, for car X,

$$\text{Acceleration} = \frac{\text{Change of speed}}{\text{Time taken}} = \frac{20}{80} = 0.25 \text{ m/s}^2$$

When a moving object slows down, it is said to **decelerate**. This is
represented by a negative-valued acceleration.

Speed–time graphs are used to show changes in motion. Figure 36.2E
shows the results for cars X and Y plotted on the same graph. Line OY is
steeper than line OX because Y accelerates more than X does.

**The acceleration of each car can be worked out from the gradient of
its line on the speed–time graph.** Figure 36.2E shows how to do this
for X.

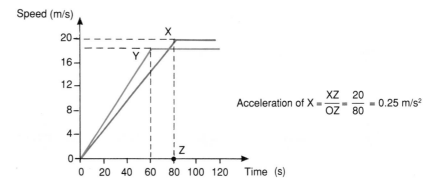

$$\text{Acceleration of X} = \frac{XZ}{OZ} = \frac{20}{80} = 0.25 \text{ m/s}^2$$

Figure 36.2E ● Speed–time comparison

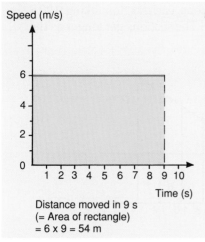

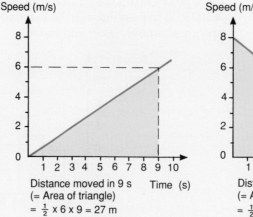

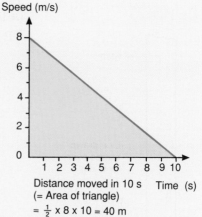

(a) Constant speed
Figure 36.2F ● Speed-time graphs

(b) Uniform acceleration

(c) Uniform deceleration

Graph (a) in Figure 36.2F is for an object moving at steady speed (acceleration = 0). The distance travelled in a certain time is given by Speed x Time. This is represented on the graph by Height x Base of the shaded rectangle, i.e. the area under the line.

For any speed–time graph the distance travelled by an object in a given time can be worked out from the area under the line. Graph (b) represents uniform acceleration and graph (c) represents uniform deceleration. In each case the area under the line is the area of the shaded triangle, which represents Average speed x Time taken = Distance moved.

Consider Figure 36.2E once again. *How far does car X move in 80 s from rest?* The area under the line OX is 1/2 x Height x Base of the triangle OXZ = 1/2 x 20 x 80 = 800 m.

SUMMARY

Acceleration is the change of velocity per unit time, which is equal to the change of speed per second for any object moving along a straight line. The gradient of a speed–time graph gives the acceleration; the area under the line gives distance travelled.

CHECKPOINT

❶ The diagram shows a tapechart made by Anna walking away from the timer while holding the end of the tape. Each section is a 10-dot length. The timer operated at 50 dots per second.
(a) Describe how Anna's speed changed as she walked away.
(b) How long did she take to reach her top speed?
(c) What was her top speed in (i) cm/s, (ii) m/s?

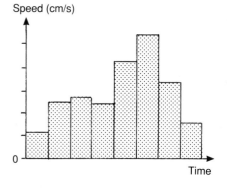

❷ (a) From Figure 36.2E work out the acceleration of car Y.
(b) How far did car Y travel in the first 60 s from rest?

❸ A ticker timer is designed to print dots on a tape at a rate of 50 per second. How would you test that it is printing at the correct rate?

❹ In a motor cycle test, the speed from rest was recorded at intervals.

Time (s)	0	5	10	15	20	25	30
Speed (m/s)	0	10	20	30	40	40	40

(a) Plot a speed–time graph of these results.
(b) What was the initial acceleration?
(c) How far did it move in (i) the first 20 s, (ii) the next 10 s?

❺ A rocket under test reaches a speed of 210 m/s from rest in 30 s before its fuel is used up. Assuming it accelerates uniformly, sketch a speed–time graph of its motion. Use the graph to work out how far it travelled in that time and what its acceleration was.

36.3 Equations for uniform acceleration

The study of motion is called dynamics. In this section you will study motion in a straight line.

Consider an object accelerating uniformly in a straight line from initial speed u to final speed v in time t. Its motion is shown by the graph in Figure 36.3A.

Its change of speed is $(v - u)$ and since its acceleration is given by Change of speed / Time taken, then

$$\text{Acceleration, } a = \frac{(v - u)}{t} \qquad [1]$$

Because the acceleration is uniform the speed increases steadily from u to v. The average speed is therefore $\frac{1}{2}(u + v)$.

Since	$\text{Average speed} = \dfrac{\text{Distance}}{\text{Time}}$
Rearranging gives	$\text{Distance} = \text{Average speed} \times \text{Time}$
So	$\text{Distance travelled, } s = \frac{1}{2}(u + v)t \qquad [2]$

We can combine equations [1] and [2] to eliminate v.

Rearranging $\quad a = \dfrac{(v - u)}{t}$ gives $at = (v - u)$

Hence $\quad v = u + at$

Substituting this value for v into equation [2] gives

$$\text{Distance, } s = \frac{1}{2}(u + u + at)t$$

Hence $\quad s = ut + \frac{1}{2}at^2 \qquad [3]$

Worked example 1 The speed of a train travelling between two stations changes with time as shown in the table.

Time (s)	0	50	100	150	200	250	300	350	400
Speed (m/s)	0	3.0	6.0	9.0	9.0	9.0	9.0	4.5	0

(a) Plot a speed–time graph of the journey.
(b) Work out the acceleration and distance travelled in each part of the journey.
(c) Work out the average speed for the whole journey.

Solution (a) The speed–time graph is shown in Figure 36.3B.
(b) The journey is in three parts, as shown in Figure 36.3B.

OA: $\text{Acceleration} = \dfrac{(v - u)}{t} = \dfrac{9.0 - 0.0}{150} = 0.06 \text{ m/s}^2$
$\text{Distance} = \frac{1}{2}(u + v)t = \frac{1}{2}(9.0 + 0.0) \times 150 = 675 \text{ m}$

AB: $\text{Acceleration} = 0$ (since the speed does not change here)
$\text{Distance} = \text{Speed} \times \text{Time} = 9.0 \times 150 = 1350 \text{ m}$

BC: $\text{Acceleration} = \dfrac{(v - u)}{t} = \dfrac{0.0 - 9.0}{100} = -0.09 \text{ m/s}^2$ (a deceleration)
$\text{Distance} = \frac{1}{2}(u + v)t = \frac{1}{2}(0.0 + 9.0) \times 100 = 450 \text{ m}$

(c) Total distance travelled = 675 + 1350 + 450 = 2475 m
Total time taken = 400 s
Hence Average speed for the whole journey $= \dfrac{\text{Distance}}{\text{Time}} = \dfrac{2475}{400} = 6.19 \text{ m/s}$

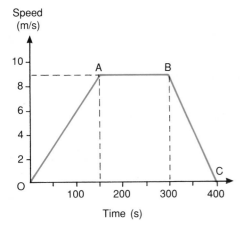

Figure 36.3A ● Uniform acceleration

IT

Uniformly Accelerated Motion (program)

Use this program and the voice-track to study:
• uniform velocity,
• uniform acceleration,
• free fall.
What is 'terminal velocity'?

Figure 36.3B ● Speed-time graph for the train

Worked example 2   A bullet travelling at a speed of 120 m/s hits a large piece of wood and penetrates it to a depth of 60 mm. Work out the time taken to bring the bullet to rest and the deceleration.

Solution   Initial speed u = 120 m/s, Final speed v = 0 m/s, Distance travelled s = 60 mm = 0.060 m

(a) To find the time taken, t, use

$$s = \tfrac{1}{2}(u + v)\,t$$
$$0.060 = \tfrac{1}{2}(120 + 0)\,t = 60t$$

Hence

$$t = \frac{0.060}{60} = 0.0010\text{s}$$

(b) To find the deceleration, use

$$a = \frac{(v - u)}{t}$$

$$a = \frac{(0 - 120)}{0.0010} = -120\,000 \text{ m/s}^2$$

SUMMARY

The three equations
$$a = \frac{v - u}{t}$$
$$s = \tfrac{1}{2}(u + v)t$$
$$s = ut + \tfrac{1}{2}at^2$$
can be used to solve problems where the acceleration is uniform.

CHECKPOINT

❶ A sprinter is capable of accelerating from rest to a speed of 10 m/s in 1.5 s. Work out her acceleration and the distance she travels in this time.

❷ The diagram shows a tapechart for a toy car released at the top of a ramp.
(a) How far did the car travel in 1 s from rest?
(b) Work out its average speed in the first second.
(c) Work out the increase of speed in 1 second by measuring the length of two 10-dot sections 1 s apart. Hence work out the acceleration.

❸ The speed of a car between two sets of traffic lights changes as shown in the table.

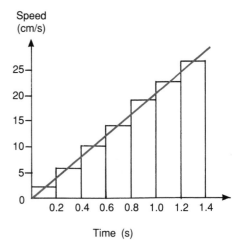

Speed (cm/s) vs Time (s)

Time (s)	0	20	40	60	80	100	120
Speed (m/s)	0	2.5	5.0	7.5	10.0	5.0	0

(a) Plot a speed–time graph of the motion.
(b) Work out the acceleration and distance travelled in (i) the first 80 seconds, (ii) the last 40 seconds.
(c) Work out the average speed of the car between the two sets of lights.

❹ In a test drive of a car on a dry road, the driver was instructed to travel at 30 m/s and to apply the brakes to stop the car when he passed a roadside marker X. The car stopped 75 m beyond X. This point was marked Y.
(a) What was (i) the initial speed, and (ii) the final speed of the car between X and Y.
(b) What was the average speed between X and Y?
(c) How long did the car take to stop and what was its deceleration?

❺ Simon is going on holiday with his parents. He knows that the runway at the airport is 3500 m in length. While waiting in the departure lounge, he times a jet taking off. The timing was 32.0 s from when the plane started accelerating along the runway to when its wheels lifted off the ground.
(a) What was the average speed of the plane during take-off?
(b) Assuming its initial speed was zero, what was its final speed?
(c) What was its acceleration?

36.4 Free fall

Now that you know how to use the dynamics equations for motion in a straight line, let's see how they apply to falling objects.

LOOK AT LINKS
for *g*
See Theme I, Topic 34.1.

IT'S A FACT

Seeds and spores released into the atmosphere fall to earth very slowly. Their terminal speeds are small. This allows the wind to blow them considerable distances. Cigarette smoke particles in the air fall to ground slowly, so the smoke takes a long time to clear. This is why people who do not smoke can be at risk from people who do smoke.

Figure 36.4A ● Free fall

Galileo Galilei was a famous scientist who lived in Italy in the seventeenth century. One of his best known experiments involved dropping objects from the top of the Leaning Tower of Pisa. He showed that different weights released at the same time reach the ground at the same time.

The **acceleration due to gravity,** *g*, is the same for all falling objects, provided there is no air resistance. The value of *g* near the Earth's surface is approximately 10 m/s².

Where there is air resistance the speed of a falling object builds up to a constant value. This value is called the **terminal speed** of the object. For example, a weight released under water falls at steady speed; so does a feather released in air. Because there is resistance acting against the motion these are not examples of free fall.

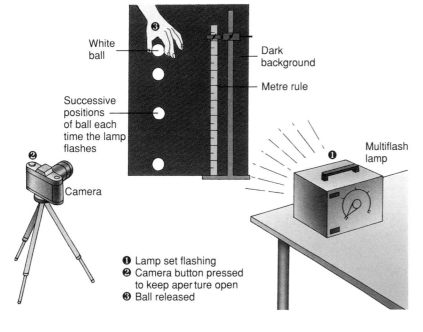

White ball

Dark background

Metre rule

Successive positions of ball each time the lamp flashes

Camera

Multiflash lamp

❶ Lamp set flashing
❷ Camera button pressed to keep aperture open
❸ Ball released

Multiflash photography

This is a method for investigating motion (Figure 36.4B). The aperture of a camera is kept open in a darkened room. A light flashes at a constant rate as the object under test moves. Each time the light flashes, an image of the object is recorded on the camera film. Figure 36.4C overleaf shows the result for two objects falling freely.

Figure 36.4B ●
Multiflash photography

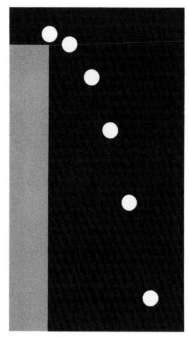

Figure 36.4C ● (a) Object A   (b) Object B

Gravity Pack
(program)

Use this program to study the way that moving objects are affected by gravity. *What path does a canonball follow if it is fired into the air?*

Object A falls vertically after being released from rest. Object B, released at the same time, is given a push sideways. Any object acted on by gravity alone after being given a push is called a **projectile**.

What do you notice about the motion of B compared with A? Both fall at the same rate; this is because gravity acts downwards on every object. However, B moves across as well. *What can you say about the horizontal motion of B?* The photograph shows that B moves equal distances horizontally in equal times.

Famine relief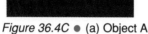

In 1986 in Ethiopia, RAF transport planes were used to drop food sacks to remote villages hit by famine. Since there were no runways to land on, each plane dropped its sacks as it approached a 'target' area.

What factors should the pilot take into account to make sure the sacks reach the target? Assume there is no wind. The height and speed of the aircraft must be considered. Suppose the plane approaches the target area in level flight at a speed of 80 m/s at 500 m height. Each sack released from the plane follows a path like that shown in Figure 36.4D.

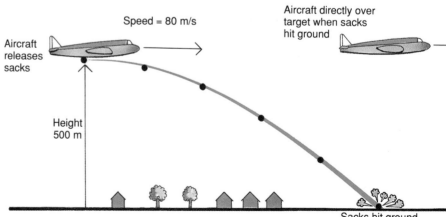

Figure 36.4D ● On target

How long does a sack take to reach the ground? A stationary sack released at the same height would take the same time. This time can be worked out as follows

Distance fallen, $s = 500$ m
Acceleration, $g = 10$ m/s^2
Initial **vertical** speed $u = 0$ (since the plane is moving horizontally).
To work out the time taken, t, use the equation $s = ut + \frac{1}{2}at^2$ to give
$500 = (0 \times t) + (\frac{1}{2} \times 10 \times t^2)$
$500 = 5t^2$
$t^2 = 100$
Therefore $t = 10$ s

How far does the sack travel horizontally in this time? As Figure 36.4C shows, the horizontal motion of a projectile is not affected by its vertical motion. The sack continues to move horizontally at the same speed as the plane (i.e. 80 m/s). Therefore in 10 seconds, the sack travels $80 \times 10 = 800$ m horizontally. The pilot must therefore release the sacks from the aircraft 800 m before the target area.

SUMMARY

All falling objects accelerate at the same rate, *g*, provided air resistance is negligible. The horizontal motion of a projectile is unaffected by its vertical motion.

CHECKPOINT

❶ A feather and a penny are released from the same height at the same time. Which one reaches the ground first? Explain why they do not reach the ground at the same time.

❷ (a) Test your reaction time. Ask a friend to help, as shown in the diagram.
(b) Rubinda and Karen try the test. The rule drops 0.20 m for Rubinda and 0.22 m for Karen. In both cases, the initial speed is zero. The girls use the equation $s = ut + \frac{1}{2}at^2$ to work out their reaction times.
(i) Rubinda reckons her reaction time works out at 0.20 s. Do you agree?
(ii) Work out Karen's reaction time.

❸ A stone released at the top of a well took 1.5 s to hit the water in the well. Use the equations of uniform acceleration to work out (a) the speed at which the stone hit the water, (b) the distance from the top of the well to the water. Assume $g = 10$ m/s^2.

❹ How fast can you throw a ball? One way to find out is to throw a ball directly up into the air and time its flight from launch to return. Suppose your timing is 4.2 s.
(a) How long did the ball take to reach maximum height from launch?
(b) At the instant it reaches maximum height, what was its speed?
(c) Use your values from (a) and (b) to work out its initial speed. Assume $g = 10$ m/s^2.

❺ Alan and Simon are on a cliff top overlooking an empty beach. Alan throws a stone horizontally from the cliff top while Simon times it. It takes 3.0 s to hit the beach. Then Simon throws another stone horizontally. It hits the beach further away than the first one.
(a) How do the flight times of the two stones compare?
(b) Which stone was given the greatest initial speed?
(c) Work out the height of the cliff top above the beach.
(d) If Simon's stone landed 60 m away from the foot of the cliff, work out the initial speed of the stone.

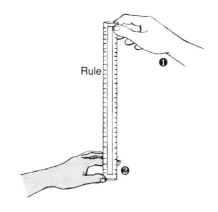

Rule

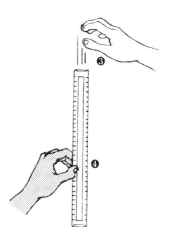

❶ Karen holds a metre rule
❷ Rubinda positions her hand at the zero mark, ready to catch the rule
❸ Karen lets go of the rule
❹ Rubinda catches the rule at the 0.20 m mark

36.5 Force and acceleration

The link between force and motion is not easy to discover, because of the effects of friction as a hidden force. Read on to find out what happens when friction is absent.

In winter, slides on icy playgrounds can be great fun if you manage to stay upright. Throw a stone across an icy pond and the stone will skid across the ice. Ice hockey players are experts at making pucks slide very fast across ice. In all these examples, friction is too small to affect the motion.

If you have ever tried to push a heavy crate across a rough concrete floor (Figure 36.5B) you will know about friction. The push force is opposed by friction and as soon as you stop pushing, friction stops the crate moving. If you do not know about friction, you might well think that a force is needed to keep an object moving.

Figure 36.5A ● Low friction motion

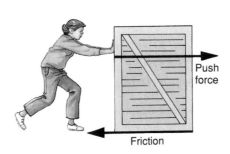

Push force

Friction

Figure 36.5B ● Overcoming friction

What if the floor is smooth? Friction is almost absent and so you do not have to push as hard to move the crate. If the floor is very smooth, the crate will continue to slide when you stop pushing. As friction is almost absent the crate keeps moving.

Figure 36.5C shows a linear air track where a glider floats on a cushion of air. Provided the track is level, the glider moves at constant speed along the track, because friction is absent.

Sir Isaac Newton was the first person to realise that objects either stay at rest or move with constant velocity unless acted on by a force. This is known as **Newton's First Law of Motion**. His discoveries made him the most famous scientist of his generation. He was able to show exactly how force affects motion and he showed that his theories apply everywhere.

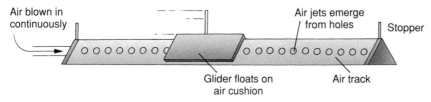

Air blown in continuously

Air jets emerge from holes

Stopper

Glider floats on air cushion

Air track

Figure 36.5C ● The linear air track

IT

Lift
(program)

Have you ever noticed the different feelings you experience in a lift? Using the program Lift, investigate the movement of Mabel inside a moving lift. Vary her mass and her acceleration. What effects do different changes have?

Investigating the link between force and motion

The way in which force affects motion can be seen by using the apparatus shown in Figure 36.5D. The runway is sloped to compensate for friction. This means that if the trolley is given a push, it will move at constant speed down the runway.

A constant force is applied to the trolley to pull it down the runway. The ticker timer records the motion of the trolley. The tape is cut into 10-dot lengths to make a tapechart.

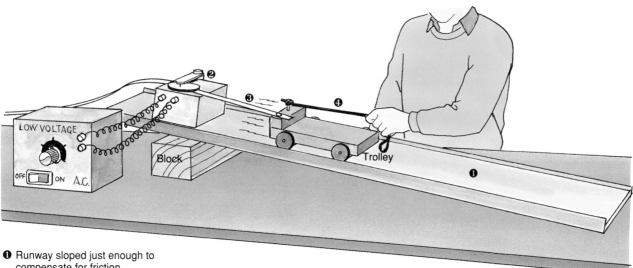

❶ Runway sloped just enough to compensate for friction
❷ Ticker timer prints 50 dots per second on the tape
❸ Tape records the trolley's motion
❹ Elastic bands stretched to the same length as the trolley pull it down the runway with constant force

Figure 36.5D ● Investigating the link between force and motion

Using one or more elastic bands, as in Figure 36.5D, different forces are applied to the trolley and a tapechart is made for each test. The tests can be repeated using a 'double decker' trolley. Figure 36.5E shows some of the tapecharts produced by these tests.

The tapecharts are speed–time graphs. Each has a constant gradient, which shows that the acceleration of the trolley is uniform. Thus the experiment shows that a constant force produces a uniform acceleration.

The acceleration in each test can be worked out. Each gradient triangle OPQ in Figure 36.5E has the same base length. So the triangle heights can be used to compare the accelerations. The results are as follows.

Table 36.2 ● Investigating force and motion

Force (no. of elastic bands)	1	2	3	1	2	3
Mass (no. of trolleys)	1	1	1	2	2	2
Acceleration	12	23	37	6	12	18
Mass x Acceleration	12	23	37	12	24	36

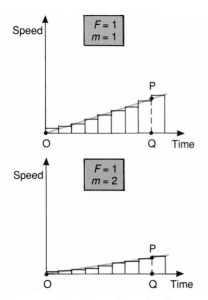
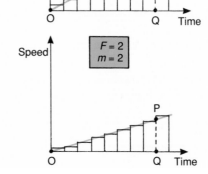
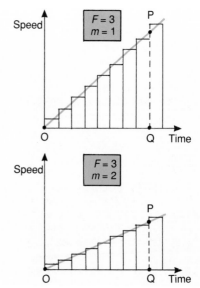

Figure 36.5E ● Tapecharts for *F = ma*

What do these results show? What would be the acceleration of a triple deck trolley pulled by two elastic bands? For this amount of force, Mass x Acceleration should be about 24. So the acceleration should be 8 for three trolleys.

The results show that

Force is proportional to Mass x Acceleration.

This link was another of Newton's discoveries, known as **Newton's Second Law**. It is used to define the unit of force, the newton.

The **newton, N,** is defined as **the force that will give a 1 kg mass an acceleration of 1 m/s².**

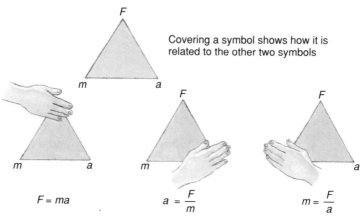

| Force | = | Mass | x | Acceleration |
| (N) | | (kg) | | (m/s²) |

Covering a symbol shows how it is related to the other two symbols

$F = ma$ $a = \dfrac{F}{m}$ $m = \dfrac{F}{a}$

Figure 36.5F ● Using Newton's Second Law

The force–mass–acceleration triangle in Figure 36.5F shows how these quantities are related. Cover one symbol to see how it is related to the other two.

Worked example 1   A car of mass 800 kg accelerates from rest to a speed of 8.0 m/s in 20 s. Work out (a) the acceleration of the car, (b) the force needed to produce this acceleration.

Solution
(a)

$$\text{Acceleration} = \frac{\text{Change of speed}}{\text{Time taken}} = \frac{8.0 - 0.0}{20} = 0.40 \text{ m/s}^2$$

(b)   Force = Mass x Acceleration = 800 kg x 0.40 m/s² = 320 N.

Worked example 2   A certain type of car has a braking force of 6000 N. Its total mass with four occupants is 1200 kg. How long does it take to stop from a speed of 30 m/s when the brakes are applied?

Solution   To work out the deceleration, use $F = ma$ with $F = 6000$ N and $m = 1200$ kg.
Thus $6000 = 1200 \times a$ which gives $a = \dfrac{6000}{1200} = 5.0$ m/s².

To work out the time taken, t, use $a = (v–u)/t$ with $v = 0$, $u = 30$ m/s and $a = –5.0$ m/s². (–ve sign denotes deceleration.)

Then $-5.0 = \dfrac{(0 - 30)}{t}$

which gives $-5.0\, t = -30$

and hence $t = \dfrac{-30}{-5.0} = 6.0$ s.

SUMMARY

Newton's First Law:
An object continues at rest or at uniform velocity unless acted on by a force.

Newton's Second Law:
Force = Mass x Acceleration

The unit of force is the newton. The weight of an object is equal to its mass x *g*.

Weight is the force of gravity on an object. Objects in free fall accelerate due to gravity. Newton's Second Law tells us that Force = Mass x Acceleration. Hence the force of gravity on an object in free fall is its Mass x *g*, where *g* is the acceleration due to gravity. Thus an object's weight can be worked out from its mass using the formula:

$$\text{Weight} = \text{Mass} \times g$$

An object that falls without any support is sometimes said to be weightless during its fall. For example, a person in free-fall from a plane has no support and could be described as weightless. However, this is misleading since gravity continues to pull the person downwards. It would be more accurate to describe the person as *unsupported*.

CHECKPOINT

1
(a) Why is it difficult to walk on an icy pavement?
(b) Why does oiling the wheel bearings of a bicycle make it easier to use?
(c) Why does streamlining the shape of a car reduce its fuel consumption?

2 Work out each of the following using Newton's Second Law.
(a) The force needed to give a 5.00 kg mass an acceleration of 0.30 m/s^2.
(b) The acceleration of a 0.20 kg mass when a force of 5.00 N is applied.
(c) The mass of an object that accelerates at 3.50 m/s^2 when a 14.0 N force is applied to it.
(d) The mass that must be added to a 0.80 kg trolley to give it an acceleration of 0.40 m/s^2 when a 0.50 N force is applied to it.

3
(a) A car of mass 800 kg is capable of reaching a speed of 20 m/s from rest in 36 s. Work out the force needed to produce this acceleration.
(b) What is the weight of the car?
(c) Work out the ratio of the car's accelerating force to its weight.

4 The engines of a ship have broken down. The ship is being towed into port by a tugboat at a steady speed of 4.0 m/s. The towing cable pulls the ship with a force of 22 500 N.
(a) The ship experiences a 'drag' force due to the water. This force opposes the motion of the ship. What is the size of the drag force?
(b) The total mass of the ship is 8.0 x 10^6 kg. When the cable is released, estimate how long the ship takes to stop, assuming the drag force does not change.

5 In an experiment to test the suitability of a playground surface, a heavy steel ball of mass 3.0 kg was dropped onto the surface from a height of 1.0 m. The ball made a dent in the surface of depth 4 mm. Assume *g* = 10 m/s^2.
(a) Work out the speed of the ball just before it hit the surface.
(b) Work out the time taken for the ball to come to rest after impact. The speed from (a) is the initial speed during the deceleration process. The final speed is zero. The distance moved during the impact is 4 mm.
(c) Work out the deceleration and the force of the impact.

FIRST THOUGHTS

36.6 Kinetic energy

In this section you will find out how to calculate the kinetic energy of an object from its mass and speed. The formula is valid provided speeds do not approach the speed of light.

Imagine you are cycling along a level road and there is a steep hill ahead. The hill will be easier to climb if you speed up as much as possible before you come to it. Speeding up increases your kinetic energy. As you climb the hill, you lose speed. Your kinetic energy (KE) is converted to potential energy (PE). If you start the hill climb at a slow speed, you need to use your muscles much more to increase your potential energy.

Figure 36.6A ● Cycling uphill

Investigating kinetic energy

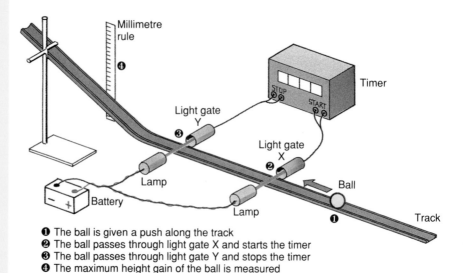

❶ The ball is given a push along the track
❷ The ball passes through light gate X and starts the timer
❸ The ball passes through light gate Y and stops the timer
❹ The maximum height gain of the ball is measured

Figure 36.6B ● Investigating kinetic energy

When you cycle up a hill, how does your height gain depend on your initial speed? Figure 36.6B shows one way to investigate this. The ball is timed, using the light gates, over a measured distance XY before it reaches the 'hill'. The height gained is measured. Some measurements with XY = 1.0 m for different speeds are shown below.

Table 36.3 ● Investigating kinetic energy

Height gained (m)	0.05	0.10	0.16	0.20
Time over XY (s)	0.98	0.72	0.58	0.50
Speed (m/s)	1.02	?	?	?

LOOK AT LINKS
for **kinetic energy** and **potential energy**
See Theme B, Topic 6.1.

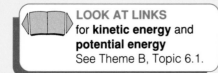

Work out the speed in each case. The first value has been worked out for you. *Can you see a link between speed and height gain?* Double the speed and the height gain increases by four times. The height gain is proportional to the (speed)². Check the other measurements to see if they fit this rule.

Now let us see if we can explain this link. The potential energy change is given by the equation Weight x Height change. Thus, for a mass m, the change of PE is given by the equation

Change in PE = mgh
where mg = weight and h = change in height

All the initial KE is converted into PE, so the height gain must be proportional to the initial KE. Since the experiment shows that the height gain is proportional to the (speed)², then the KE must be proportional to the (speed)².

To see the exact link between KE and speed, consider an object of mass m, initially at rest, acted on by a constant force F. Figure 36.6C shows the idea.

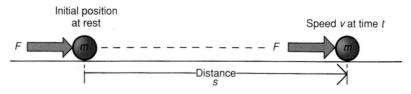

Figure 36.6C ● Gaining kinetic energy

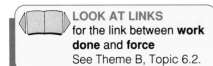

LOOK AT LINKS
for the link between **work done** and **force**
See Theme B, Topic 6.2.

In time t, the speed of the object increases from zero to v. The distance travelled, $s = \frac{1}{2}(u + v)t$

$$s = \frac{1}{2}(0 + v)t = \frac{1}{2}vt$$

Acceleration, $a = \dfrac{(v - u)}{t} = \dfrac{(v - 0)}{t} = \dfrac{v}{t}$

Using Newton's Second Law, Force = Mass × Acceleration,

$$F = ma = \frac{mv}{t}$$

Now   Work done = Force × Distance

$$= \frac{mv}{t} \times \tfrac{1}{2}vt$$

$$= \tfrac{1}{2}mv^2$$

Since the gain of kinetic energy is due to the work done, then

| Kinetic energy = $\frac{1}{2}$ × Mass × (Speed)^2 |
| KE = $\frac{1}{2}mv^2$ |

Worked example   A cyclist moving at a speed of 8.0 m/s along a level road reaches a steep hill. The mass of the cyclist and cycle is 55 kg.
  (a) Work out the initial KE of the cyclist.
  (b) What is the maximum height the cyclist can gain without pedalling? Assume $g = 10$ m/s^2.

SUMMARY

Kinetic energy = $\frac{1}{2}$ × Mass × (Speed)^2

Change of potential energy = Mass × g × Height change

Solution
(a)   KE = $\frac{1}{2}mv^2$ = $\frac{1}{2}$ × 55 × 8^2 = 1760 J
(b)   Assume   Gain of PE = Loss of KE
       Hence $mgh = \frac{1}{2}mv^2$

where h = height gain, $v = 8$ m/s and $g = 10$ m/s^2

Therefore $h = \dfrac{v^2}{2g} = \dfrac{8^2}{2 \times 10} = 3.2$ m

CHECKPOINT

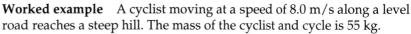

❶ (a) Consider the experiment shown in Figure 36.6B. Use the results given to plot a graph to check the link between height and speed.
   (b) Why is the cyclist going uphill unlikely to convert all the KE into PE?

❷ A car uses more fuel per kilometre when it keeps having to stop and start than when it travels at steady speed on a motorway. Why?

❸ Work out the kinetic energy of each of the following:
   (a) a 0.5 kg ball moving at a speed of 5.0 m/s,
   (b) a 1000 kg car moving at a speed of 20 m/s,
   (c) a 50 000 kg aeroplane moving at a speed of 200 m/s.

❹ A hot air balloon of mass 250 kg at a height of 150 m descends slowly into a field.
   (a) Work out the PE of the balloon before the descent.
   (b) What happens to this PE as a result of the descent?
   (c) If the balloon burst at 150 m height, what would be its speed of impact at the ground?

❺ A trolley of mass 45 kg is released at a height of 4.2 m at the top of a ramp.
   (a) Work out its PE at the top of the ramp.
   (b) What happens to its initial PE when it rolls down the ramp?
   (c) Work out its speed at the bottom of the ramp.

36.7 Collisions and explosions

A collision is when objects meet; an explosion is when they move apart. The same principle explains both collisions and explosions.

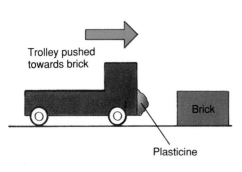

Trolley pushed towards brick

Brick

Plasticine

Figure 36.7B ● Investigating impacts

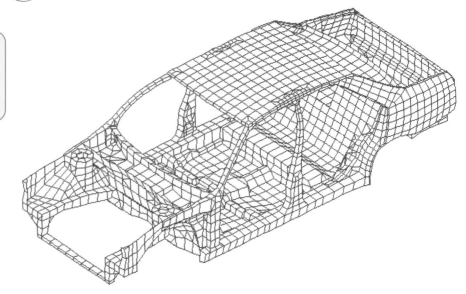

Figure 36.7A ● Car safety cage design

Safety is an important feature of car design. The structure of a well-designed car should protect the occupants in the event of a crash. The 'safety cage', where the occupants sit, is strengthened to protect those inside. The 'crumple zones' of a car are meant to lessen the force of an impact. Car manufacturers test the safety of their cars by driving them by remote control into brick walls.

Why are impacts lessened by using crumple zones? Consider the collision between a trolley and a brick as shown in Figure 36.7B. The Plasticine® flattens on impact, making the impact time longer. *Why does this lessen the impact?* Newton's Second Law has the answer.

Let the initial speed of the trolley be u. Assume its final speed v is zero. Suppose the time for the impact is t.

$$\text{Deceleration due to the impact} = \frac{(v-u)}{t} = \frac{-u}{t}$$

Using Newton's Second Law, Force = Mass x Acceleration

$$F = -\frac{mu}{t}$$

The minus sign tells us that the impact force is in the opposite direction to the initial velocity. The equation shows that making the impact time longer (increasing the value of t), makes the impact force smaller. Crumple zones in cars are designed to make impact times longer so impact forces are reduced.

The **momentum of a moving object** is defined as its Mass x Velocity. The unit of momentum is kg m/s.

The initial momentum of the above trolley is m x u. Its final momentum is zero. The impact force is given by

$$\text{Impact force} = \frac{\text{Change of momentum}}{\text{Time taken}}$$

Worked example   A car bumper is designed not to bend in impacts at less than 4 m/s. It was fitted to a car of mass 900 kg and tested by driving the car into a wall. The time of impact was measured and found to be 1.8 s. Work out the impact force.

IT   *Motion*
(visual database)

Use this program to study colliding cars. Describe what happens to the dummy passengers in a collision. *Why is it best for a car to 'crumple' when it collides with a wall?*

Solution

Initial momentum of car = Mass x Initial speed = 900 x 4 kg m/s,

Final momentum = 0 (assuming it is stopped by the impact).

Change of momentum = 900 x 4 = 3600 kg m/s.

$$\text{Force of impact} = \frac{\text{Change of momentum}}{\text{Time taken}} = \frac{3600}{1.8} = 2000 \text{ N}$$

Investigating collisions between moving objects

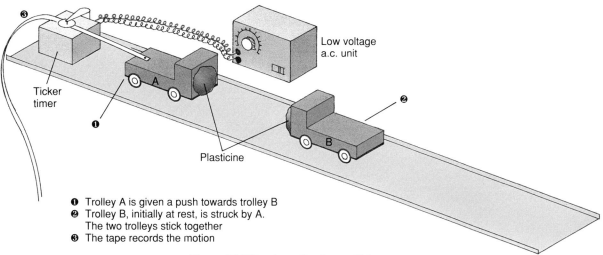

Ticker timer

Low voltage a.c. unit

A

Plasticine

B

❶ Trolley A is given a push towards trolley B
❷ Trolley B, initially at rest, is struck by A.
   The two trolleys stick together
❸ The tape records the motion

Figure 36.7C ● Investigating collisions

In Figure 36.7C one trolley is given a push so it collides with another. The two trolleys stick together after they collide. The tape records their motion, as shown on Tape 1 in Figure 36.7D.

Can you see on the tape where the trolleys collided? The spacing between the dots is less after the impact. The dots are twice as far apart before the impact as afterwards, which means the speed has been halved.

Let the trolleys A and B each have the same mass, m. The velocity of A at impact is v. Therefore the momentum of A before the impact is mv.

After the impact the mass is doubled and the speed is halved. The momentum of A and B after this impact is

$$(m + m)\,(\tfrac{1}{2}v)$$
$$= 2\,m \times \tfrac{1}{2}v$$
$$= mv$$

Thus the momentum before the impact is the same as the momentum afterwards.

What would the final speed be if a single trolley were pushed into a double trolley so they stuck together? In this case the combined mass would be three times the initial mass. Tape 2 in Figure 36.7D shows the result. The final speed is one third of the initial speed. Once again, the momentum is unchanged. Momentum is said to be **conserved**.

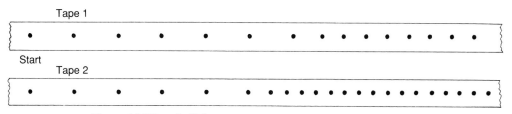

Tape 1

Start

Tape 2

Figure 36.7D ● Collision tapes

Momentum is conserved when objects interact, provided no external forces act on them. This principle applies to any type of collision. It also applies to explosions where objects fly apart.

Worked example   A rail wagon A of mass 3000 kg moving at a speed of 2.0 m/s collides with a stationary wagon B. The two wagons couple together and move at a speed of 1.2 m/s after the collision. What is the mass of the second wagon?

Solution   Let the mass of the second wagon = M
Initial momentum of A = 3000 x 2.0 = 6000 kg m/s
Initial momentum of B = 0
Therefore   Total initial momentum = 6000 kg m/s
Total final momentum of A and B = (3000 + M) x 1.2 kg m/s
Since momentum is conserved
Total final momentum = Total initial momentum
$$(3000 + M) \times 1.2 = 6000$$
$$(3000 + M) = \frac{6000}{1.2} = 5000$$
Hence $M = 2000$ kg

Explosions

When a bomb explodes, fragments of metal fly off in all directions. Their kinetic energy is produced from chemical energy. Figure 36.7E shows a rather more controlled explosion using trolleys.

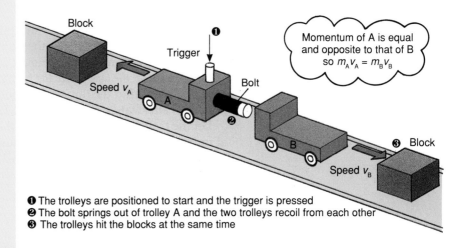

Block

Trigger

❶

Momentum of A is equal and opposite to that of B
so $m_A v_A = m_B v_B$

Speed v_A

Bolt

A

❷

B

❸ Block

Speed v_B

❶ The trolleys are positioned to start and the trigger is pressed
❷ The bolt springs out of trolley A and the two trolleys recoil from each other
❸ The trolleys hit the blocks at the same time

Figure 36.7E ● Investigating explosions

When the trigger rod is tapped, the bolt springs out and the trolleys recoil from each other. In order to compare the recoil speeds of A and B, blocks are positioned by trial and error on the runway so the trolleys reach them at the same time. Some results are shown in Figure 36.7F.

Two single trolleys travel the same distance in the same time. This shows that they recoil at equal speeds.

A double trolley only travels half the distance that a single trolley travels in the same time interval. Its speed is half that of the single trolley.

These results show that the trolleys recoil with equal and opposite momentum. The mass x speed of each trolley is the same and they recoil in opposite directions.

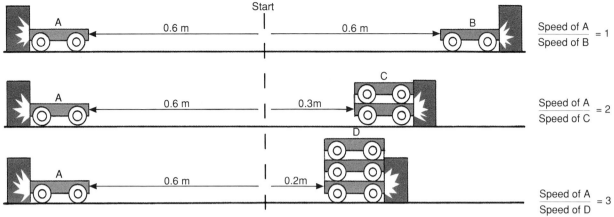

Figure 36.7F ● Using different masses

Momentum is conserved in an explosion. In the trolley examples, the initial momentum is zero. The total final momentum is also zero because the recoiling trolleys carry away equal amounts of momentum in opposite directions, which cancel each other out.

Worked example A bullet of mass 0.005 kg is fired from a rifle of mass 2.5 kg. The rifle recoils at a speed of 0.40 m/s. Work out the speed of the bullet when it leaves the rifle.

Solution Momentum of bullet = 0.005 x V where V is the bullet speed. Momentum of rifle = Mass x Recoil velocity = 1.5 x 0.40 = 0.60 kg m/s. Since the momentum of the bullet is equal and opposite to the momentum of the rifle, then

$$0.005 \times V = 0.60$$
$$V = \frac{0.60}{0.005} = 120 \text{ m/s}$$

SUMMARY

Momentum is defined as Mass x Velocity. In situations where no external force acts, momentum is conserved.

CHECKPOINT

❶ Explain each of the following:
   (a) An asphalt surface for a playground is safer than a concrete surface.
   (b) Catching a cricket ball is easier if you move your hand back as you catch the ball.
   (c) The soles of sports shoes are softer than normal shoe soles.

❷ (a) Work out the initial momentum of an 800 kg car travelling at 7.5 m/s.
   (b) What force is required to stop the car in (i) 12 s, (ii) 1.2 s?

❸ Simon is about to leap from a rowing boat on to the shore. His friends shout 'We are too far out at the moment!' Simon replies that he can easily jump the gap. He didn't. Why did he misjudge the jump?

❹ A railway wagon of mass 800 kg moving at a steady speed of 2.5 m/s collides with another wagon of mass 1000 kg. The two wagons couple together after the collision. Work out the final speed and the loss of kinetic energy if the second wagon was:
   (a) stationary,
   (b) moving at a steady speed of 2.0 m/s in (i) the same direction as the first wagon, (ii) the opposite direction to the first wagon.

❺ (a) Kim's skateboard recoils when she jumps off it. Explain why this happens.
   (b) The mass of the skateboard is 1.5 kg and Kim's mass is 40 kg. Work out the recoil speed of the skateboard if she jumps off at a speed of 1.2 m/s.

36.8 🍎 Rockets and satellites

The laws of motion are universal; they apply everywhere. They can be used to work out the flight paths of rockets and satellites.

Figure 36.8A ●
Rocket power

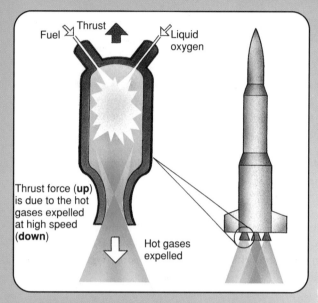

Fuel ☒ Thrust   ☒ Liquid oxygen

Thrust force (**up**) is due to the hot gases expelled at high speed (**down**)

Hot gases expelled

Figure 36.8B ● The rocket principle

Rockets

'Ten, nine, eight, seven, ..., two, one, ignition ... we have lift off!' A rocket launch is a spectacular event, the result of work by many scientists and engineers.

At lift-off, a mixture of fuel and liquid oxygen fed to the rocket engines is ignited. The gases produced by combustion are expelled downwards from the rocket engine at high speed. They thrust the rocket upwards. While the fuel continues to burn, the rocket gains speed as it lifts off the launch pad. This principle is illustrated in Figure 36.8B.

Motion in Space
(program)

Use this program to try out your own space mission. Try the mission which involves rebuilding a damaged satellite. Write down the differences between motion in space and motion on Earth, as we know it.

Rockets were used as weapons in China many centuries before they were first used in Europe. The gunpowder used as fuel burned very quickly after ignition so these rockets could not attain great heights. In 1895, the principles of modern space flight were set out by Konstantin Tsiolovsky in Russia. He predicted multistage rockets using liquid fuel (see Figure 36.8C)

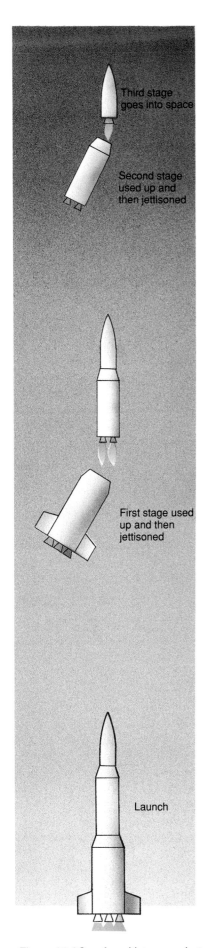

Figure 36.8C ● A multistage rocket

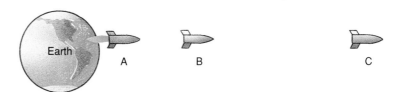

A → B Rocket uses fuel to attain high speed and to move away from Earth.

Chemical energy → KE + PE of rocket

B → C Rocket slows down as it moves away from Earth

KE → PE of rocket

Figure 36.8D ● Energy changes in a rocket leaving Earth

Tsiolovsky's ideas were first put into practice by Robert Goddard in 1926 in the US. His first rocket travelled just 55 m. In comparison, *Saturn V*, the most powerful rocket to date, is capable of carrying a 50 tonne cargo to the Moon.

Why do rockets for space travel need to be so powerful? Energy has to be used to move any object against the force of gravity. The force of the Earth's gravity stretches far into space, becoming weaker further from Earth. A rocket travelling into space has to use energy to move against the force of gravity. Chemical energy from the rocket fuel is converted into potential energy as the rocket rises above the Earth. Figure 36.8D explains this.

Satellites

Imagine launching a satellite into orbit round the Earth from the top of a very tall mountain, as in Figure 36.8E. If the satellite's initial speed is too low, it will fall to the ground. If its initial speed is too great, it will fly off into space. At the 'correct' speed, it orbits the Earth.

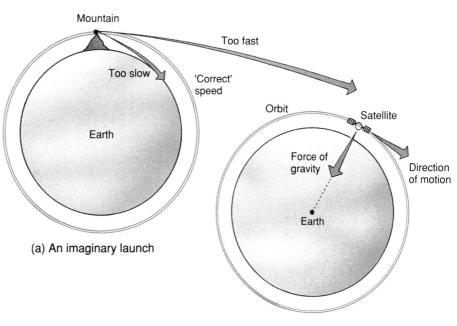

(a) An imaginary launch

(b) Gravity

Figure 36.8E ● Satellites

LOOK AT LINKS
for Newton's First Law of
Motion
See Theme I, Topic 36.5.

IT

***Newton and
the Shuttle***
(program)

Use this computer simulation to
launch a space shuttle and recover
a satellite from its orbit.

The first artificial satellite, *Sputnik 1*, was launched in 1957. It went round the Earth once every 96 minutes at a height of between 230 and 950 km. The Moon is the Earth's only natural satellite. Jupiter is known to have at least 15 natural satellites. The planets are satellites of the Sun.

What keeps a satellite going round and round? **Newton's First Law of Motion** tells us that an object travels at constant velocity unless acted on by a force. Velocity is speed in a given direction. An object going round in a circle at a steady rate does not have a constant velocity as its direction keeps changing. Therefore there must be a force acting on the object to keep it in circular motion.

Consider the motion of an object being whirled round at the end of a string. The tension in the string pulls the object round on a circular path. *What happens to the object if the string suddenly snaps?*

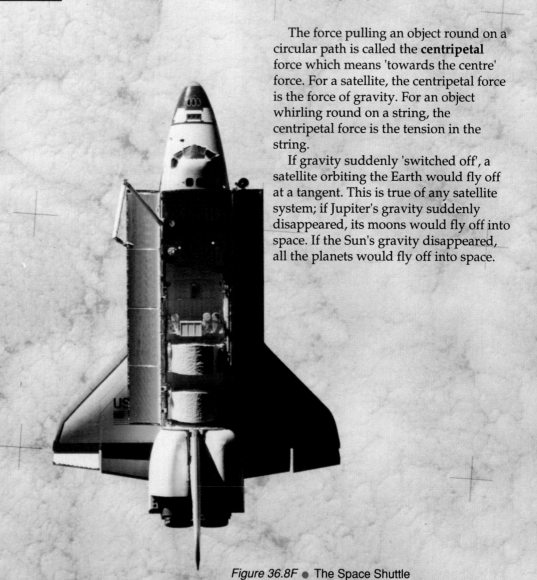

The force pulling an object round on a circular path is called the **centripetal** force which means 'towards the centre' force. For a satellite, the centripetal force is the force of gravity. For an object whirling round on a string, the centripetal force is the tension in the string.

If gravity suddenly 'switched off', a satellite orbiting the Earth would fly off at a tangent. This is true of any satellite system; if Jupiter's gravity suddenly disappeared, its moons would fly off into space. If the Sun's gravity disappeared, all the planets would fly off into space.

Figure 36.8F ● The Space Shuttle

The Space Shuttle is a reusable space vehicle, launched at high altitude from the top of a much larger aircraft. After launch, the shuttle flies under its own power into orbit round the Earth. In orbit, no fuel is used, since it stays at constant height. To return to the ground, the shuttle descends from orbit gradually and lands on a specially lengthened airstrip. The Shuttle is used to carry satellites into space.

Communications satellites

These are satellites that take exactly 24 hours to orbit the Earth directly above the Equator. The radius of orbit is approximately 42 000 km. At this distance from the centre of the Earth, they go round exactly once every 24 hours. Since they orbit Earth far above the atmosphere, they are unaffected by air resistance, so they stay in orbit indefinitely. Satellites that orbit closer to Earth are affected by air resistance and so eventually come back to Earth.

Because these satellites orbit at the same rate as the Earth spins, they are always over the same point on the Equator. Hence, a microwave beam from a transmitter on the ground can be aimed permanently at the satellite. The satellite detects the beam and transmits a second beam to a receiver station on the ground (see Figure 36.8G).

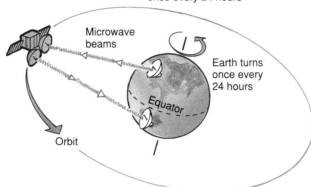

Satellite orbits Earth once every 24 hours

Microwave beams

Earth turns once every 24 hours

Equator

Orbit

Figure 36.8G ●
A communications satellite

CHECKPOINT

❶ (a) A rocket is used to launch an astronaut in a space capsule into orbit round the Earth. Describe the forces on the astronaut after lift-off.
(b) What are the advantages and disadvantages of using a rocket in comparison with a space shuttle?

❷ A rocket uses liquid hydrogen as its fuel. This is mixed and burned in the rocket engine with liquid oxygen.
(a) What are the likely products of combustion?
(b) Why doesn't a satellite carry fuel tanks?

❸ *Apollo 11* was the first successful mission to land astronauts on the Moon. The lunar module carried the astronauts back to the command module to return to Earth. Why did the lunar module not need huge fuel tanks to lift off the Moon?

❹ In 1618 Johannes Kepler established the laws of satellite motion by observing the motion of the planets round the Sun. He measured how long each planet took to go round the Sun and its distance from the Sun. His results are shown below.

	Mercury	Venus	Earth	Mars	Jupiter	Saturn
Time per orbit (years)	0.25	0.61	1.00	1.84	11.7	29.1
Distance (relative to Earth–Sun distance)	0.40	0.73	1.00	1.53	5.20	9.53

(a) Kepler worked out that $(Time)^2/(Distance)^3$ is the same for all the planets. Check this is so using the above values.
(b) The planet Uranus goes round the Sun once every 84 years. Use the link in (a) to work out its distance from the Sun.

❺ Imagine you are planning a mission to Mars. The journey is likely to take six months from Earth to Mars. Use the information in question 4 to make a scale drawing of the orbits of the two planets and sketch a possible flight path.

TOPIC 37 MACHINES AND ENGINES

37.1 Making jobs easier

Read on to find out how machines make jobs easier although they use more energy.

Kevin works for a builders' merchants and he has been told to load a truck with bags of cement. There are ten bags, each weighing 300 N. He struggles to lift the first one on to the truck. 'There must be an easier way than this' he thinks. He sees some planks of wood in the yard and decides to use them as a ramp (Figure 37.1A). He drags the next bag across the ground and up the ramp, which is slightly easier. Then he sees a wheelbarrow in a corner of the yard. Using this and the ramp, he completes the job much more easily than lifting each one directly.

Figure 37.1A ● Using a ramp

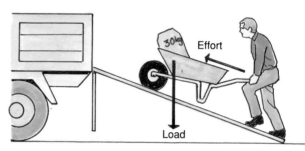

Figure 37.1B ● Making an effort

In the above example, the force that Kevin applies to the wheelbarrow is the **effort** (Figure 37.1B). The weight of the wheelbarrow and its contents is the **load**. The effort is much less than the load. That is why the job is easier using the ramp and wheelbarrow.

Pulleys can also be used to lift heavy objects. On the building site, Kevin's cement is mixed with sand and water to make mortar for bricks. The mortar has to be lifted to the top of some scaffolding. It could be carried by hand up the ladders. However, a winch consisting of two pulleys has been installed (Figure 37.1C). The bucket of mortar is the load and the pull on the rope is the effort. For a well-oiled pulley-system, the effort is much less than the load.

Some different pulley systems are shown in Figure 37.1D. The easiest one to use is the one with most sections of rope between the upper and lower pulleys. In effect, an equal fraction of the load is raised by each section.

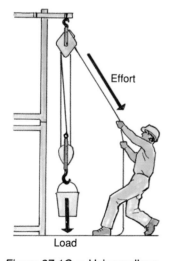

Figure 37.1C ● Using pulleys

RESOURCE ACTIVITY PACK

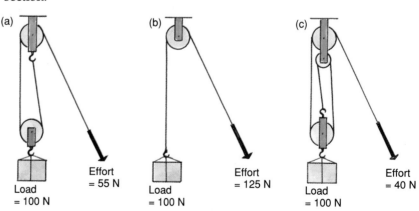

Figure 37.1D ● Different pulley systems

Investigating pulleys

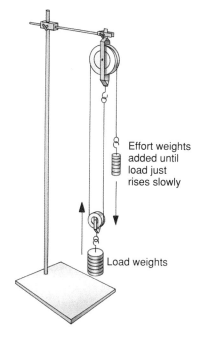

Figure 37.1E ● Investigating pulleys

Is a pulley system an energy saver? Pulleys make lifting easier because the effort is less than the load. *But is less energy used with the pulley system than without?* Figure 37.1E shows how this can be investigated.

The effort is measured by adding weights to the effort weight until the load just rises slowly. The height gain H of the load is measured. The corresponding distance moved down by the effort weights is also measured. Results for the pulley system shown in Figure 37.1E are as follows

Load = 9.0 N   Height gain, H, of load = 0.10 m
Effort = 6.0 N   Distance moved by effort, D = 0.20 m

These measurements show the effort has to move twice as far as the load, but the load is just 1.5 times the effort.

Work done by the effort = Effort x Distance = 6.0 x 0.20 = 1.2 J
PE gain of the load = Load x Height gain = 9.0 x 0.10 = 0.9 J

The calculations show that 1.2 J of work is done using the pulleys to lift the load. This is more than the PE gain of the load. So 0.3 J of energy is wasted using the pulleys. The waste energy is lost to the surroundings as heat.

The **efficiency** of a machine is defined as the percentage of the work done by the effort that is used to move the load.

$$\text{Efficiency} = \frac{\text{Useful energy supplied to load}}{\text{Work done by effort}} \times 100\%$$

No machine can ever be more than 100% efficient because the work done on the load can never be more than the work done by the effort. The useful energy from the machine is its **energy output**. The work done by the effort is the **energy input**. The energy output can never be more than the energy input.

In the example above, 0.9 J of useful energy is supplied by the pulley system to raise the load. The work done by the effort is 1.2 J, so the efficiency is 0.9/1.2 x 100 = 75%. The remaining 25% is wasted energy, lost to the surroundings as heat.

Worked example   To test the efficiency of a ramp, the force needed to pull a loaded trolley up the ramp was measured. The height gain and length of the ramp were measured. The measurements were as follows.
    Weight of loaded trolley = 350 N   Height gain = 1.2 m
    Effort (i.e. pull force) = 140 N   Length of ramp = 4.5 m
(a) Work out the efficiency of the ramp.
(b) How much energy was wasted in the test?

Solution
(a) Useful energy supplied to load = PE gain = Load x Height gain
                                  = 350 x 1.2 = 420 J

         Work done by effort = Effort x Length of ramp
                                   = 140 x 4.5 = 630 J

$$\text{Efficiency} = \frac{\text{PE gain}}{\text{Work done by effort}} \times 100$$

$$= \frac{420}{630} \times 100 = 67\%$$

(b) Wasted energy = 630 − 420 = 210 J

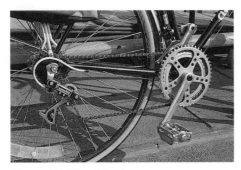

Figure 37.1F ● Bicycle gears

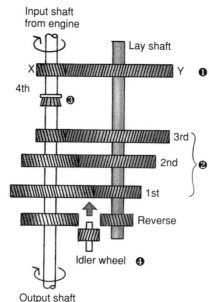

❶ The lay shaft is driven from the input shaft via gearwheels X and Y
❷ When 1st, 2nd or 3rd gear is selected, the appropriate gearwheel on the lay shaft is 'locked' on to the shaft. The other gearwheels turn freely
❸ When 4th gear is chosen, the output shaft is directly coupled to the input shaft
❹ When reverse gear is chosen, the idler wheel is pushed forwards as shown to make the lay shaft turn the output shaft

SUMMARY

Machines make jobs easier by reducing the effort needed to move a given load. The efficiency of a machine is the percentage of the work done by the effort that is used to move the load. No machine can ever be more than 100% efficient.

Figure 37.1G ● How car gears work

Gears are another mechanism for making jobs easier. A cyclist on a hill climb should use the lowest possible gear. This allows the cyclist to keep moving with the least possible effort. However, the work done by the effort is always more than the PE gain of the cyclist. Cycling is easier using gears but some energy is wasted. The cyclist's muscles do not need to pull as hard in low gear, although they have to work longer.

How the gears in a car work is explained in Figure 37.1G.

CHECKPOINT

❶ 'Cliff railways' are a tourist attraction in several seaside towns. Most were designed with twin tracks so that as one car climbs the track the other descends. An electric winch hauls the ascending car and its passengers up the track (see the diagram).
  (a) Why were they designed in this way?
  (b) The first cliff railway did not use an electric winch. Instead, each car included a 4500 litre water tank. The tank was filled with water when the car was at the top and then emptied when it reached the bottom. A steam-driven pump was used to pump water up to the top of the track. Explain why the system worked.

❷ Figure 37.1G shows the construction of part of a car gear box. There are four forward gears and reverse gear. The driver engages each gear using the gear lever. The gear system allows the input shaft to turn the output shaft easily.
  (a) In 4th gear, the output shaft is driven at the same speed as the input shaft. Does the output shaft turn faster or slower in 1st gear than in 4th gear?
  (b) Why is the idler gear essential to make the output shaft turn in reverse?

❸ A conveyor belt is used to transport boxes from the ground floor to the first floor of a factory. Each box weighs 150 N and is lifted through a height of 5.0 m. The belt is driven by a 2000 W electric motor and carries 15 boxes per minute up to the first floor.
  (a) How much energy is supplied by the 2000 W motor in one minute?
  (b) What is the gain of PE of each box?
  (c) Work out the efficiency of the system.

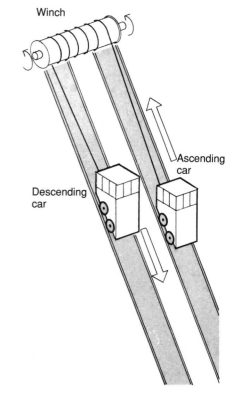

④ (a) The mechanical advantage of a machine is the ratio load/effort. Work this out for each of the pulley systems in Figure 37.1D. Which of the pulleys is easiest to use (has the greatest mechanical advantage)?

(b) The distance moved by the effort equals the height gain by the load x the number of sections of rope between the two pulleys. Why?

(c) Which of these pulleys systems is the most efficient? Work out its efficiency.

⑤ John Black Ltd have just bought an 'easilift' pulley system, guaranteed to be 90% efficient if it is maintained correctly. It is fitted to a steel jib at the top of a building, as shown. The manager decides to test it by lifting a crate of weight 1000 N through a height of 1.0 m. The effort he put in was 220 N.

(a) The distance moved by the effort was 5.0 m. How much work was done by the effort? What was the PE gain of the load?

(b) Work out the efficiency and compare it with the guaranteed value.

(c) What was the total force on the jib, ignoring the weight of the pulley, when it was used to lift the crate?

37.2 Engines

An engine uses fuel to do work. The steam engine and the petrol engine revolutionised transport. This section tells you how they work.

Figure 37.2A ● Mill steam engine

Steam engines revolutionised the world in the nineteenth century. No longer did people have to rely on muscle power, windmills or waterwheels to make things. In 1769 James Watt invented the steam engine which was later to power factories and mills throughout the world (Figure 37.2A). The fuel used was coal, which became a vital resource and has been ever since. Transport was also revolutionised by the invention of the steam locomotive and the steamship.

LOOK AT LINKS
for how a nuclear reactor works
See Theme C, Topic 12.6.

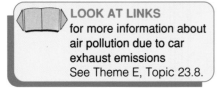

LOOK AT LINKS
for more information about air pollution due to car exhaust emissions
See Theme E, Topic 23.8.

LOOK AT LINKS
for **energy resources**
See Theme B, Topic 8.3.

Figure 37.2B ● Turbines in a power station

SCIENCE AT WORK

World oil reserves will probably be used up by the middle of the twenty-first century. How shall we manage without the petrol engine? Scientists in several countries are developing electric vehicles that are battery-powered. Another option is the production of oil from coal. Yet another development is to run cars using ethanol that has been made from sugar.

What has become of the steam engine? You may find steam locomotives still used as museum exhibits but most trains are now pulled by electric locomotives. Factories use electric motors supplied from the National Grid instead of steam engines. Electricity is produced in power stations by means of huge electricity generators.

What keeps these generators turning? **Steam turbines** are used in most power stations (Figure 37.2B). The means of producing steam depends on the type of power station. Coal-fired and oil-fired power stations burn their fuel to heat water to make steam. **Nuclear power stations** are designed to raise steam too, although the heat necessary is released as a result of nuclear fission. How a turbine works is illustrated in Figure 37.2C.

The **petrol engine** is used in most cars. Its fuel is a mixture of petrol and air. It is called an **internal combustion engine** because the fuel is burned inside the engine. It works on a four-stroke cycle, as shown in Figure 37.2D. Its efficiency is about 25%, which means it wastes about 75% of the energy from the fuel. Petrol engines also produce many pollutants in the exhaust gases, including carbon monoxide, sulphur dioxide and lead compounds. New cars are fitted with engines designed to use 'unleaded' petrol because of public concern about the harmful effects of lead compounds in the air we breathe.

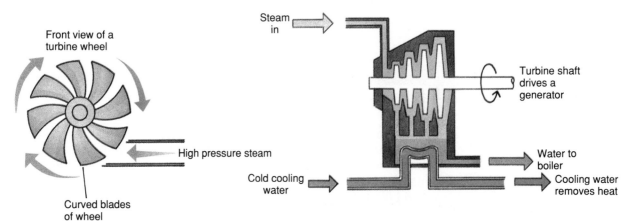

Figure 37.2C ● How a turbine works

SUMMARY

Engines produce useful energy from fuels. The petrol engine is used in most cars. The steam turbine is used in generators in power stations to produce electricity.

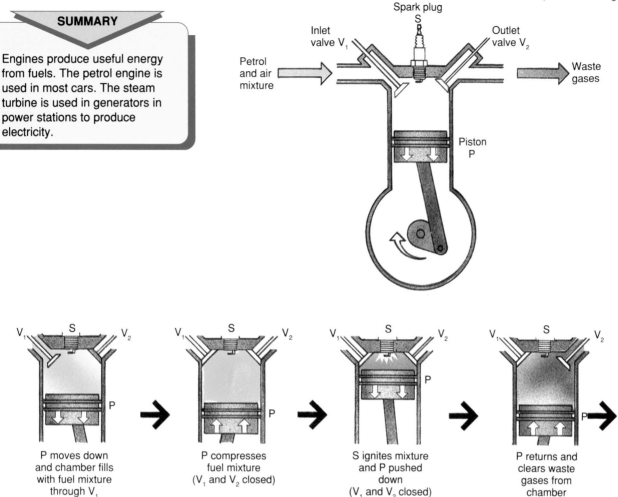

Figure 37.2D ● The four-stroke engine

CHECKPOINT

① Steam engines use coal and produce a lot of smoke and dust. Electric trains are more economical and produce no waste products. Explain why.

② Steam turbines in power stations must be supplied with cooling water to take away waste heat.
  (a) If the flow of cooling water became blocked, what would happen to the pressure in the turbine?
  (b) Why are power stations often sited on the coast or by a river or lake?

③ How would your life be changed if petrol supplies suddenly ceased everywhere?

④ The use of low density materials in cars saves fuel.
  (a) A car travels 12 000 km in one year and it uses 1 litre of petrol every 12 km travelled on average. How much fuel does it use in one year?
  (b) How much fuel would have been saved in one year if the car had travelled 14 km per litre on average?

⑤ Air pollution due to cars is a major problem in many countries. Controls on the emission of waste gases from car exhausts have been introduced in some of the worst-affected areas. Suppose you live in an area where air pollution is a problem, despite these controls. What other measures could be taken to deal with the problem effectively?

37.3 ● Flight

If you have ever flown in an aeroplane, you may know about rolling and diving. In this section you will find out how the motion of an aeroplane is controlled.

Figure 37.3A ● Taking off from London Heathrow Airport

In summer, millions of holidaymakers travel from northern Europe to countries bordering the Mediterranean Sea. At the busiest airports planes take off and land every few minutes. The skies above busy airports are crowded with planes. Air traffic controllers use powerful computers to keep track of them. The Wright brothers made the first powered flight in 1903. Now millions of people every year make routine journeys by aeroplane.

Airships were developed long before 1903. The balloon of an airship contains a gas such as helium, which is less dense than air, so the balloon is pushed upwards by the atmosphere. The force of gravity on the balloon is opposed by the upward force of the atmosphere on it. This force is called the **lift**. To make an airship float upwards, the lift must be greater than the total weight of the balloon and its load.

Hot air balloons get lift by trapping hot air. Hot air is less dense than cold air, so it rises. To make the balloon ascend, a burner is used to heat the air beneath the balloon.

Figure 37.3B ● (a) Airship

(b) Hot air balloons

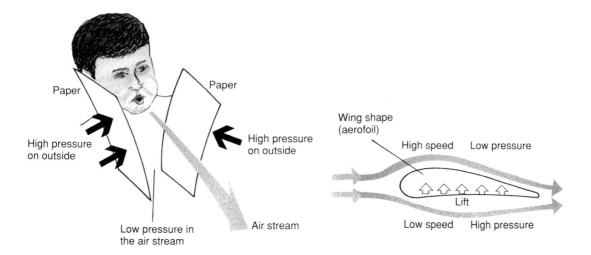

Figure 37.3C ● Making low pressure

Figure 37.3D ● How an aerofoil creates lift

Aeronautics (flight) is possible because the pressure of a stream of air depends on the air speed. This can be demonstrated by blowing between two pieces of paper, as in Figure 37.3C. The pressure in the fast-moving airstream is less than the atmospheric pressure outside, so the two pieces of paper are forced together.

The shape of an aeroplane wing is called an **aerofoil**. As the wing moves forwards through the air, the airstream is faster above than beneath it (Figure 37.3D). The air pressure above the wing is less than the pressure beneath it and the wing lifts. The lift on both wings opposes the weight of the aeroplane.

The amount of lift increases with speed, as the air moves faster over the wing, increasing the pressure difference. This is why an aeroplane needs to achieve a high speed to take off. The aeroplane's engines supply the thrust to enable it to reach the take-off speed. Figure 37.3E shows how a **jet engine** works.

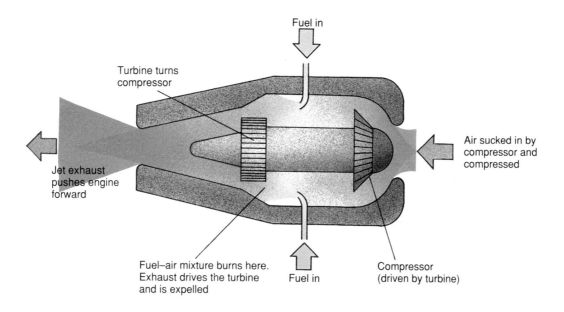

Figure 37.3E ● The jet engine

IT'S A FACT

Bird flight differs from powered flight because the thrust is supplied by the wings beating. A bird's wings are shaped to produce lift and the tail is for steering. Birds like the golden eagle, which can fly slowly, have slots in their wings. These slots make stalling less likely.

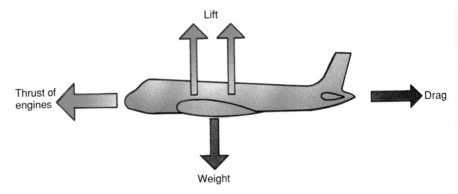

Figure 37.3F ● The forces on an aeroplane

The thrust of the engines is opposed by **drag** on the aeroplane due to air resistance. In level flight at steady speed, the drag is equal and opposite to the thrust and the lift is equal to the weight (see Figure 37.3F). The overall force on the aeroplane is zero so it continues to move at constant velocity.

How does an aeroplane gain height? The pilot pulls back on the control column to tilt the tailplane elevators as shown in Figure 37.3G. This increases the lift, so the aeroplane climbs. However, if the elevators are tilted too much, the aeroplane stalls. Altering the position of the rudder and ailerons makes the aeroplane turn and roll.

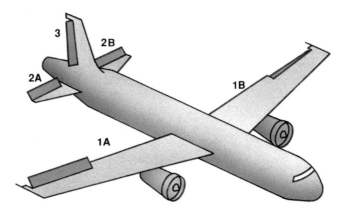

❶ Ailerons make the plane roll
❷ Elevators force the nose of the plane up or down
❸ Rudder turns the plane

Figure 37.3G ● Aeroplane controls

SUMMARY

Lift is essential for flight. Wings are shaped to produce lift. If the wings are at too great an angle to the airstream, the aeroplane or bird will stall.

CHECKPOINT

❶ (a) Explain why an airship can gain height by jettisoning unnecessary weight.
(b) How can an airship lose height?

❷ Imagine you are at the controls of an aeroplane. How would you use the controls to (a) gain height, (b) turn in a horizontal circle?

❸ Make a paper aeroplane. Bend the wings so it flies up.
(a) Why does it stall when it goes too high?
(b) How can you make it turn in a circle? Make a sketch showing how you did this.

❹ How does a bird in flight manage to land safely? Observe a bird landing and describe how it uses its wings to do this.

? THEME QUESTIONS

● *Topic 34*

1 The figure below shows a special type of spanner called a mole wrench. It is being used to unfasten a nut from a rusted bolt. The average force applied to the mole wrench is 20 newtons (N) and this force moves 30 centimetres (cm) when one quarter turn is made.

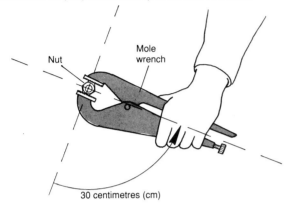

(a) (i) What is the pattern which links the energy transferred, distance moved and force applied?
(ii) What is the distance moved in metres (m) by the force when **one full turn** is made?
(iii) Calculate the energy transferred by the mole wrench when it makes **one full turn**. You should state the unit of energy in your answer.
(b) Suggest the name of the force which is **opposing** the rotation of the mole wrench.

(SEG)

● *Topic 35*

2 The diagram shows part of the disc brake system on a car.

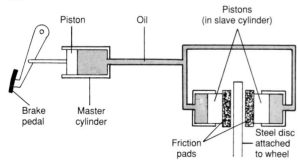

A force is applied to the brake pedal. This causes a force to act on the piston in the master cylinder.
(a) Explain how the friction pads are pushed against the rotating disc.
(b) Why do the brakes not work well if there is air in the oil?

(MEG)

● *Topic 36*

3 A ticker timer is a device that makes dots on a strip of paper at a steady rate of 50 dots every second.
In an experiment one end of a long strip of paper was pinned to a baby's clothes. As the baby walked forward,

she pulled the paper strip through a ticker timer. At the end of the experiment the marked paper was cut into 10-space pieces.
(a) There were twelve 10-space pieces of paper. They were stuck on to a chart in order. The figure below shows the chart.

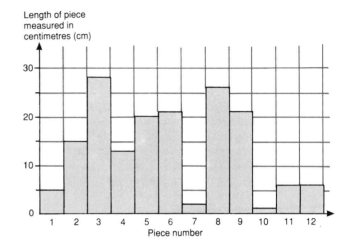

(i) Write down the number of the piece which shows the greatest speed.
(ii) Which **group of three** pieces shows when the baby was slowing down?
(b) The figure below shows the arrangement of dots on piece number 8.

(i) What length of **time** is shown by piece number 8?
(ii) Use the pattern

$$\text{Average speed} = \frac{\text{Distance}}{\text{Time}}$$

to calculate the average speed at which the baby moved to produce piece number 8.
(iii) Does the value you calculated in (c) (ii) represent the speed at which the baby was actually moving during that time? Explain how the evidence in piece number 8 supports your conclusion.

(SEG)

4 A man jumps from a balloon at a height of 400 m and his parachute opens immediately. Air resistance causes an upward force of 300 N to be exerted on him. The man has a mass of 80 kg. His parachute is very light and you can ignore its mass in this question.

(a) The gravitational field strength is 10 N/kg. What is the man's weight?

(b) Make a copy of the diagram and draw labelled arrows to show the forces acting on the man.

(c) What is the size of the resultant force acting on the man?

(d) Calculate his acceleration.

(e) Suppose that the air resistance force remains constant at 300 N until the man reaches the ground.
(i) Calculate the work done against air resistance as he falls 400 m.
(ii) Calculate also his loss of potential energy.
(iii) Hence find his kinetic energy as he reaches the ground.

(f) In practice the man will reach the ground with a far lower kinetic energy than you have just calculated. Explain this.

(MEG)

5 Mustafa usually cycles the short distance from his home to his school. The combined weight of Mustafa and his bicycle is 600 N. It is divided equally over each wheel. Each of Mustafa's tyres is in contact with the ground through a strip 12 cm by 2 cm.

(a) Calculate the area of each tyre in contact with the ground.

(b) Use the equation

$$\text{Pressure} = \frac{\text{Force}}{\text{Area}}$$

to calculate the pressure which Mustafa and his bicycle exert on the ground.

The graph below shows how Mustafa's velocity changes through the journey.

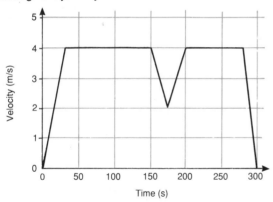

(c) Use the graph to find:
(i) the greatest velocity at which Mustafa travels,
(ii) the time taken for the whole journey.

(d) There is a pedestrian crossing in between Mustafa's home and the school. Sometimes he has to slow down or stop at it.
(i) How long after the start of his journey did Mustafa start to slow down for the pedestrian crossing?
(ii) Did Mustafa stop at the crossing? Explain how you worked out your answer.

(e) Use the equation

$$\text{Acceleration} = \frac{\text{Change of velocity}}{\text{Time}}$$

to calculate Mustafa's acceleration during the first thirty seconds of his journey.

(f) Calculate the distance between Mustafa's house and his school.

(LEAG)

6 Jean has a motor bike which she uses to get from her home to her work.

(a) Make a rough copy of the diagram above and draw three arrows on it to show the direction in which the following forces are acting.
(i) Gravity: label this arrow G.
(ii) Friction between tyres and the road: label this arrow F.
(iii) Air resistance: label this arrow A.

(b) Explain why the tyres do not grip the road as well in wet weather as they do in dry weather.

On the way to work Jean has to drive up a steep hill and sometimes she has to stop at a roundabout. The graph below shows how the distance travelled changes with time during Jean's journey.

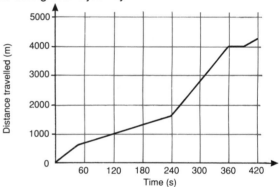

(c) Make a copy of the graph on graph paper. On your copy mark the letter:
(i) S where Jean is at the start of the hill,
(ii) F where Jean is at the finish of the hill,
(iii) R where Jean is stopped at the roundabout.

(d) Use the graph to find:
(i) the distance from Jean's home to her work.
(ii) Use the equation

$$\text{Speed} = \frac{\text{Distance}}{\text{Time}}$$

to find Jean's average speed for the whole journey.

(e) Here are some facts about Jean and her journey.
The height of the hill is 35 m.
The total weight of Jean and her motorbike is 2000 N.
The gain in potential energy when Jean drives to the top of the hill can be found using the equation
Gain in potential energy = Force x Height
When 1 g of petrol is burnt in the motorbike it produces 45 000 J of energy.
The motorbike uses 4 g of petrol climbing the hill.

$$\text{Efficiency} = \frac{\text{Gain in potential energy}}{\text{Energy obtained from petrol}}$$

Calculate the efficiency of the motorbike.

(LEAG)

THEME J
Life Processes 2

There are seven characteristics of life: nutrition, respiration, excretion, reproduction, growth, movement and sensitivity. The first three of these characteristics were examined in Theme F, the remaining four are discussed in this theme.

Life Processes 2 also examines the transport systems that plants and animals have developed to move food, oxygen, water and waste products around their bodies.

TOPIC 38 TRANSPORT IN LIVING THINGS

38.1 Transport in plants

FIRST THOUGHTS

How do adequate supplies of water and food reach all parts of a plant? A transport system is the answer! In this section we shall discuss the systems which transport water, minerals and food in a plant.

Water and food move into and out of plant cells by **osmosis**, **diffusion** and **active transport**. Flowering plants require special tissues for the transport of these materials to where they are needed. The tissues are xylem and phloem (see Figure 38.1A). Xylem transports water and phloem transports food. Xylem and phloem tissue form vascular bundles which is why flowering plants, along with conifers and ferns, are sometimes referred to as vascular plants.

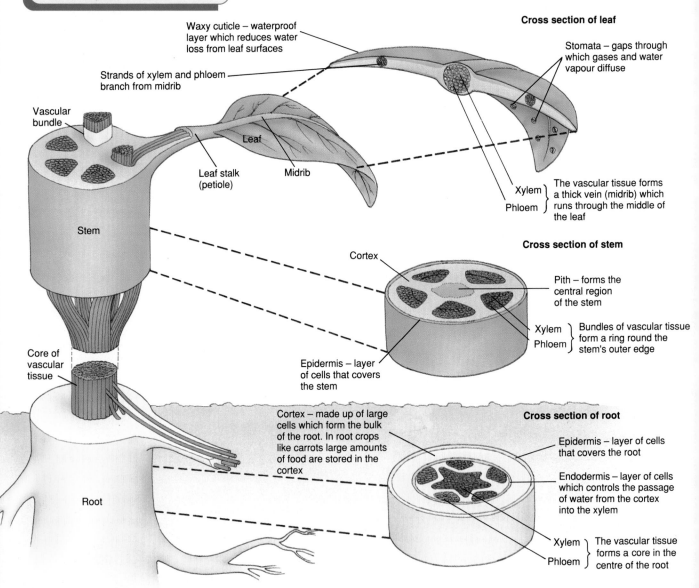

Cross section of leaf

Waxy cuticle – waterproof layer which reduces water loss from leaf surfaces

Stomata – gaps through which gases and water vapour diffuse

Strands of xylem and phloem branch from midrib

Vascular bundle

Leaf

Leaf stalk (petiole)

Midrib

Xylem
Phloem
The vascular tissue forms a thick vein (midrib) which runs through the middle of the leaf

Stem

Cross section of stem

Cortex

Pith – forms the central region of the stem

Xylem
Phloem
Bundles of vascular tissue form a ring round the stem's outer edge

Core of vascular tissue

Epidermis – layer of cells that covers the stem

Cortex – made up of large cells which form the bulk of the root. In root crops like carrots large amounts of food are stored in the cortex

Cross section of root

Epidermis – layer of cells that covers the root

Endodermis – layer of cells which controls the passage of water from the cortex into the xylem

Root

Xylem
Phloem
The vascular tissue forms a core in the centre of the root

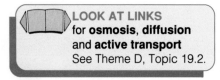

LOOK AT LINKS
for **osmosis, diffusion** and **active transport**
See Theme D, Topic 19.2.

Figure 38.1A ● The arrangement of xylem and phloem (vascular tissue) in a flowering non-woody plant. (Notice that the central core of vascular tissue in the root changes to a ring of bundles in the stem at ground level.)

Xylem transports water

Mature xylem cells are dead. They are cylindrical and join end-to-end to form strands of xylem tissue. The cross-walls separating adjoining cells break down so that each xylem strand becomes a long, hollow vessel through which water can pass freely (see Figure 38.1B). Xylem vessels run from the tips of roots, through the stem and out into every leaf as Figure 38.1A shows.

Water enters the plant through the root hairs by osmosis. It moves across the root cortex by osmosis and diffusion into the xylem vessels. Once in the xylem vessels, water forms unbroken columns from the roots, through the stem and into the leaves. Water evaporates from the leaves – mainly through the tiny pores in the underside of the leaf called stomata (see Figure 38.1C). The process is called **transpiration**.

Figure 38.1B ● Xylem in a stem – notice the rings of lignin, a substance which strengthens and waterproofs the cell walls of each vessel

IT'S A FACT

In 1872 an Australian eucalyptus tree was measured at 133 m – the tallest tree ever recorded. Today the tallest tree is a mountain ash growing in Tasmania. It measures 95 m.

TRY THIS

You need a white flower with a fairly long stem. Slit the stem lengthways from the bottom to half-way up. Place each half of the cut stem in a different pot of water. Add some red dye to one pot and blue dye to the other (or other available contrasting colours). After a day or so look at the flower and try to explain what has happened.

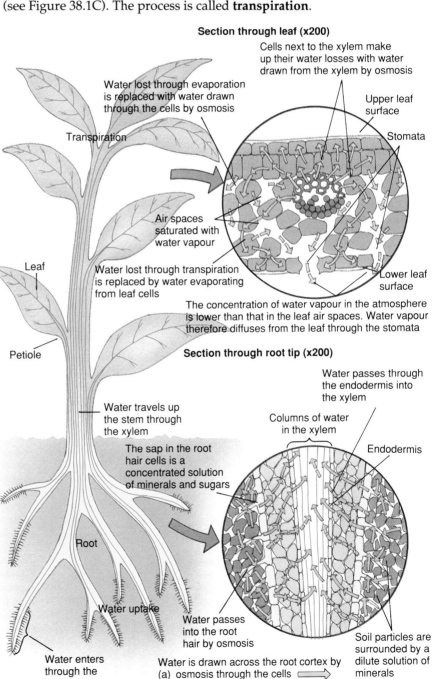

Section through leaf (x200)

Cells next to the xylem make up their water losses with water drawn from the xylem by osmosis

Water lost through evaporation is replaced with water drawn through the cells by osmosis

Upper leaf surface

Stomata

Transpiration

Air spaces saturated with water vapour

Water lost through transpiration is replaced by water evaporating from leaf cells

Lower leaf surface

The concentration of water vapour in the atmosphere is lower than that in the leaf air spaces. Water vapour therefore diffuses from the leaf through the stomata

Leaf

Petiole

Section through root tip (x200)

Water passes through the endodermis into the xylem

Columns of water in the xylem

Endodermis

Water travels up the stem through the xylem

The sap in the root hair cells is a concentrated solution of minerals and sugars

Root

Water uptake

Water enters through the root hairs

Water passes into the root hair by osmosis

Soil particles are surrounded by a dilute solution of minerals

Water is drawn across the root cortex by
(a) osmosis through the cells
(b) diffusion between the cells

Figure 38.1C ● The transpiration stream

127

Water Balance in Plants
(program)

Investigate the effect of varying water balance in plants using the program. You can look at the whole plant, individual tissues, single cells and also at the molecular level.

LOOK AT LINKS
for **turgor**
See Theme D, Topic 19.2.

As water transpires, more is drawn from the xylem. This movement of water exerts 'suction' on the water filling the xylem vessels of the stem. As the water is 'sucked' upwards through the xylem of the stem, more water is supplied to the bottom of the xylem by the roots. There is therefore a continuous moving column of water from the roots to the leaves. This is called the transpiration stream (see Figure 38.1C).

The force that drives the transpiration stream is equivalent to as much as thirty atmospheres pressure – sufficient to move water to the top of the tallest tree.

● *Factors affecting transpiration*

If the loss of water through transpiration is not made up by intake of water from the soil, then the stomata close. The closing of the stomata reduces transpiration. However, if the plant still does not get enough water, then its cells begin to lose **turgor** and the plant wilts.

Other factors in the environment also affect the rates of transpiration and water intake. For example, plants transpire more quickly (and therefore absorb more water from the soil) when it is light than when it is dark. Light stimulates the stomata to open wide. This means that water vapour can transpire more easily. Figure 38.1D shows the effects of other environmental factors on the rate of transpiration.

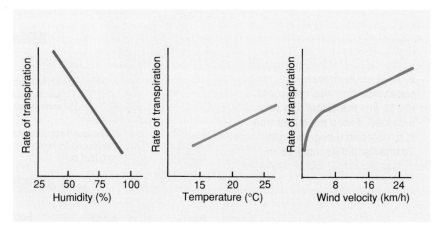

Figure 38.1D ● Environmental factors affecting the rate of transpiration

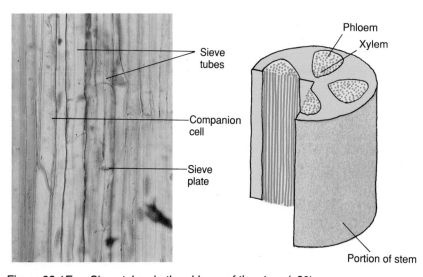

Figure 38.1E ● Sieve tubes in the phloem of the stem (x20)

Phloem transports food

Phloem tissue consists of different types of cell. **Sieve cells** and **companion cells** are the most important. Figure 38.1E shows that sieve cells are cylindrical and joined at their end walls to form strands of tissue called sieve tubes.

Mature sieve cells do not have nuclei. However, they are alive: each cell contains cytoplasm. The end walls, called sieve plates, are pierced with holes (hence their name). A companion cell lies next to each sieve cell. Companion cells and sieve cells work together to transport sugars to where they are needed in the plant. The movement of sugars and other substances from one region to another through the sieve cells is called **translocation**.

Which surface of a leaf transpires the most water? Cobalt chloride paper is blue when dry and pink when wet. Take a suitable plant and sandwich blue cobalt chloride papers against the upper and lower surfaces of some of its leaves. Record the time taken for each cobalt chloride paper to change colour. Explain your results.

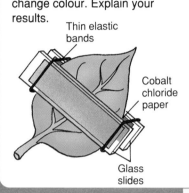

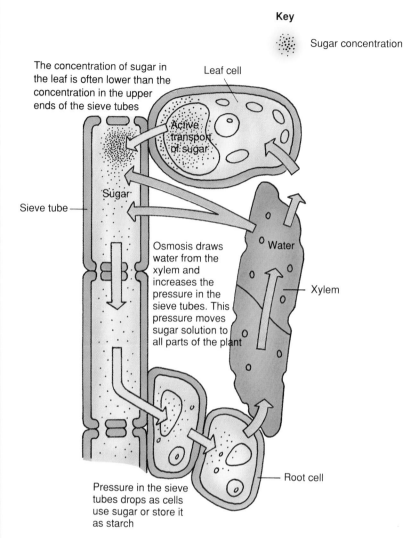

Figure 38.1F ● Translocation depends on the differences in concentration of sugar in different parts of the plant. Diffusion transports sugar from where it is in high concentration to where it is in low concentration.

Figure 38.1F shows how translocation takes place. Sugar passes from the leaf cells to the sieve cells by active transport. Once in the sieve tubes, the sugar, along with other substances, is carried to where it is needed. Sugar that passes to the roots can move out of the sieve tubes and into the cells of the cortex. The sugar is converted into starch and stored.

Scientists understood 300 years ago that xylem transports water in plants. *How do we know that phloem transports food?* The evidence is more recent. Two of the experiments that provided the answer are summarised below:

● **Tree ringing experiments** A ring of bark is cut from the stem of a woody plant. The strip of bark removed is just thick enough to contain phloem tissue from the vascular bundles. The xylem remains intact. After a few days there is a bulge of growth above the ring and no further growth below the ring. *Why do you think there is extra growth above the ring? Why does this result suggest that food is transported in the phloem? What will happen to the plant eventually?* (See Figure 38.1G overleaf.)

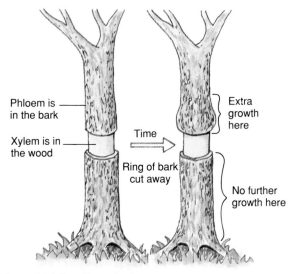

Figure 38.1G ● Tree ringing

Phloem is in the bark

Xylem is in the wood

Time

Ring of bark cut away

Extra growth here

No further growth here

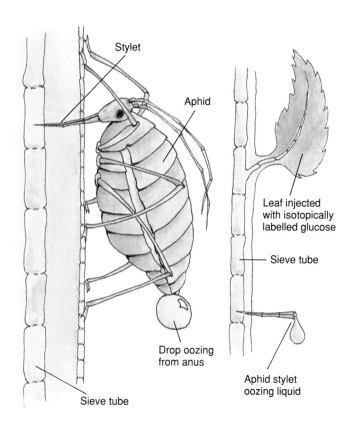

Stylet

Aphid

Leaf injected with isotopically labelled glucose

Sieve tube

Aphid stylet oozing liquid

Drop oozing from anus

Sieve tube

Figure 38.1H ● Aphids and isotopic tracers

IT'S A FACT

Do you know why a car parked under a lime tree is soon covered with a sticky substance? Aphids feeding on the tree sprinkle the juice which passes through them onto the car beneath.

- **Aphids and isotopic tracers** The aphid can be used to study the transport of sugar in the phloem sieve tubes. To feed, the aphid inserts its tube-like mouthparts (called a stylet) through the surface of a stem into a sieve tube. The pressure of the liquid in the sieve tube force-feeds the aphid to the point where drops ooze from its anus. When an aphid is cut from its stylet, liquid will continue to ooze from the stylet for several days. Isotopically labelled glucose is injected into a leaf and samples of liquid are collected regularly from a newly placed stylet. *What test would you do to find out if the liquid on which the aphid was feeding contains sugar? If sugar is transported in the phloem what change would you expect in the samples of liquid obtained from the stylet? How would you detect the change?* (See Figure 38.1H.)

CHECKPOINT

① With the help of diagrams describe the differences in structure between xylem and phloem.

② Distinguish between transpiration and translocation.

③ Describe the passage of a water molecule from the soil through a plant and out into the atmosphere.

④ Why does a plant lose more water on a dry, warm, windy day than when it is cool, still and wet?

⑤ By what route does sugar made in the leaves move to the roots?

⑥ Atmospheric pressure can support a column of water 11 metres high. How tall could a tree grow and water still reach its topmost branches?

38.2 Blood and its functions

Blood transports gases, food and other vital materials to the tissues of the body. It protects the body from disease by producing antibodies and forming clots. This topic explains how the blood in the human body performs these functions and many others beside.

IT'S A FACT

Anybody who is healthy, weighs over 50 kg and is between the ages of 18 and 65 can give blood. There are about five litres of blood in the body of an adult human. A donor may give up to half a litre of blood at one time. That is one tenth of the body's total blood content.

When a person is seriously injured or undergoes a major operation they often lose a lot of blood. The blood they lose is replaced by **blood transfusion** with blood from blood donors. A needle is inserted into a vein in the arm of the donor and blood flows through the needle and into a sterilised bottle via a tube. The blood is mixed with sodium citrate to stop it from clotting and stored at 5 °C in regional blood banks. When a hospital needs blood it should be available from its regional blood bank.

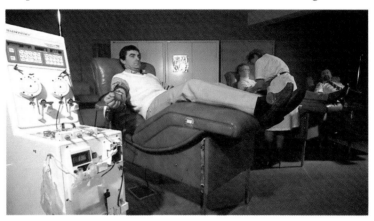

Figure 38.2A ● Giving blood

What is blood made of?

Figure 38.2B shows what happens when a sample of blood is spun for a time in a centrifuge. The blood separates into a straw coloured liquid called **plasma** and a dark red–brown mass of blood cells.

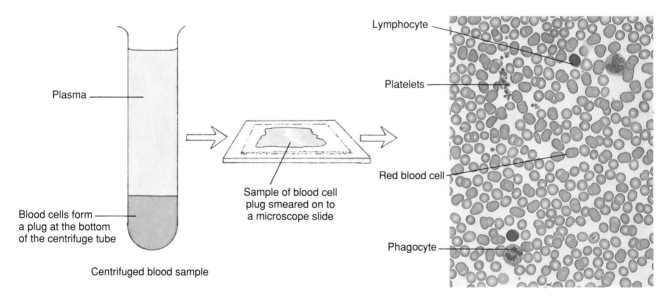

Plasma

Blood cells form a plug at the bottom of the centrifuge tube

Centrifuged blood sample

Sample of blood cell plug smeared on to a microscope slide

Lymphocyte

Platelets

Red blood cell

Phagocyte

LOOK AT LINKS
for **centrifuging**
See Theme D, Topic 15.5.

Figure 38.2B ● Human blood sample spun in a centrifuge and examined under a microscope. (Notice the characteristic shapes of the nuclei of phagocytes and lymphocytes.)

The plasma transports heat released by metabolism in the liver, muscles and fat to other parts of the body. The plasma consists of:

- Water – 90% by volume.
- Blood proteins – these include antibodies that help to protect the body from disease and fibrinogen, one of the proteins that helps blood to clot.
- Foods, vitamins and minerals (see Theme F, Topic 25).
- Urea (see Theme F, Topic 27).
- Hormones – substances which help to co-ordinate different body functions (see Theme J, Topic 40).

The red plug of blood cells at the bottom of the test-tube consists of:

- Red blood cells – the cells contain the red pigment haemoglobin that gives blood its colour. Red blood cells do not have nuclei.
- White blood cells – two types, lymphocytes and phagocytes. The nucleus of each type of white blood cell has a characteristic shape (see Figure 38.2B).
- Platelets – these look like fragments of red cells.

Red cells transport oxygen and carbon dioxide

Red cells are made in the marrow of the limb bones, ribs and vertebrae. Old red cells are destroyed in the liver. Red cells contain the protein **haemoglobin**. Haemoglobin readily combines with oxygen in tissues where the concentration of oxygen is high to form **oxyhaemoglobin**. Oxyhaemoglobin breaks down to release oxygen in tissues where the concentration of oxygen is low.

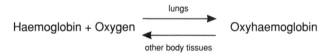

$$\text{Haemoglobin + Oxygen} \xrightleftharpoons[\text{other body tissues}]{\text{lungs}} \text{Oxyhaemoglobin}$$

LOOK AT LINKS
for **cellular respiration**
See Theme F, Topic 26.1.

Blood which contains a lot of oxyhaemoglobin is called **oxygenated blood** and is bright red in colour (see Figure 38.2C). Blood with little oxyhaemoglobin is called **deoxygenated blood** and looks a deep red–purple.

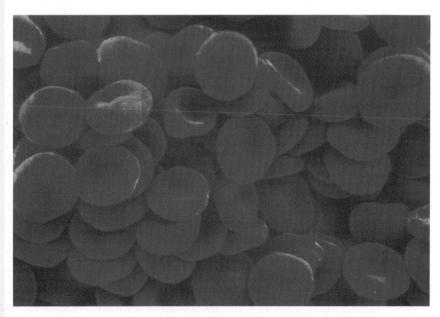

Figure 38.2C ● Oxygen makes the difference

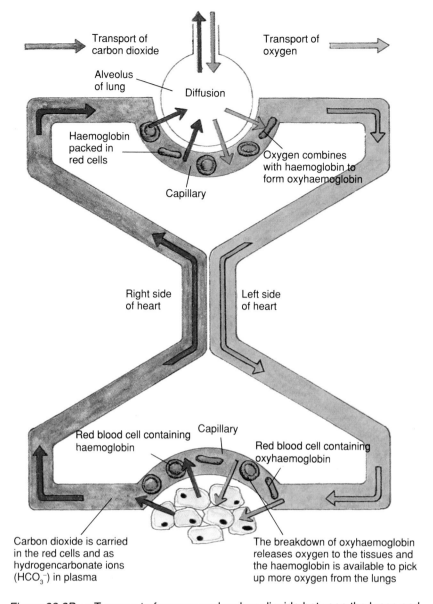

Figure 38.2D ● Transport of oxygen and carbon dioxide between the lungs and tissues of mammals

Cellular respiration releases carbon dioxide which diffuses into the blood. Some of it forms hydrogencarbonate ions (HCO_3^-) in the plasma. Haemoglobin carries the rest of the carbon dioxide in the red cells. When blood reaches the lungs, carbon dioxide diffuses from the plasma and red cells into the alveoli and is exhaled (see Figure 38.2D).

White cells protect the body

Some types of virus and bacteria enter (infect) the blood and tissues and cause disease. The two types of white blood cell, lymphocytes and phagocytes, protect the body by working quickly to destroy viruses and bacteria. Lymphocytes and phagocytes also destroy any other cells or substances which the body does not recognise as its own. Materials 'foreign' to the body are called **antigens**. When antigens come into contact with lymphocytes they stimulate the lymphocytes to produce proteins called **antibodies** which begin the process of destruction. The phagocytes finish the job. Figure 38.2E shows what happens.

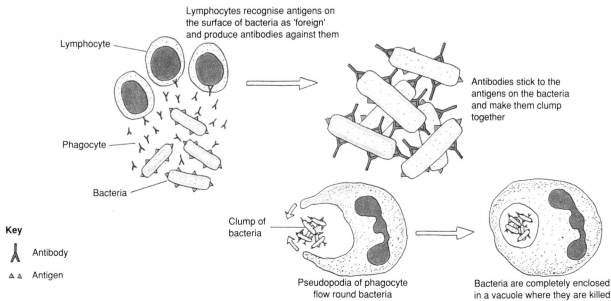

Figure 38.2E ● Lymphocytes and phagocytes at work

LOOK AT LINKS
Where white blood cells
are made in the body is
discussed in Theme J,
Topic 38.3.

● *Antibodies are specific*

Antibodies produced against a particular antigen will attack only that antigen. The antibody is said to be **specific** to that antigen. This means that antibodies produced against typhoid bacteria will not attack pneumonia bacteria. It seems that each of us can produce tens of millions of different antibodies to deal with all the antigens we are ever likely to meet in a life time.

● *Active immunity*

The action of lymphocytes and phagocytes against invading micro-organisms is called an **immune reaction**. The antibodies produced may stay in the body for some time ready to attack the same micro-organisms when next they invade the body. Even if the antibodies do not stay in the body for long, they are soon made again because the first-time battle between micro-organisms and lymphocytes primes the lymphocytes to recognise the same micro-organisms next time. This means that re-infection is dealt with by immune reactions which are even faster and more effective than the first reaction. In other words you become resistant. This is why you rarely catch diseases like chicken pox and measles more than once.

Immunisation

Immunisation promotes active immunity to disease-causing micro-organisms. It involves the doctor or nurse giving you an injection or asking you to swallow some substance. The substance injected or swallowed is called a vaccine and the process of being immunised is called immunisation or vaccination.

Vaccines are made from one of the following:
- Dead micro-organisms, e.g. whooping-cough vaccine is made from dead bacteria.
- A weakened form of micro-organism which is harmless. Vaccines made like this are called attenuated vaccines, e.g. the vaccine against tuberculosis and Sabin oral vaccine (the vaccine against poliomyelitis) are both attenuated vaccines.
- A substance from the micro-organism which does not cause the disease, e.g. diphtheria vaccine.

What effect does a vaccine have? Antigens from the dead or attenuated micro-organisms in the vaccine stimulate the lymphocytes to produce antibodies. So, when the same active, harmful micro-organisms invade the body, the antibodies made in response to the vaccine destroy them.

The active immunity produced by vaccines can protect a person from disease for a long time, although several more vaccinations called boosters may be needed after the first one. Boosters keep up the level of antibodies and so maintain a person's immunity.

Children in the UK are immunised against six diseases which used to cause many deaths. They are diphtheria, tetanus, whooping cough, poliomyelitis, tuberculosis and German measles. These diseases are now rare but those that spread through person-to-person contact would soon increase if the number of people vaccinated against them fell to levels where infections easily spread among unprotected individuals.

● *Whooping cough and German measles*

Whooping cough is a highly infectious disease caused by the bacterium *Bordetella pertussis*. The patient suffers from a wracking cough with characteristic 'whoops' which may last for 2–3 months. Whooping cough may make the patient vulnerable to bronchopneumonia and also increases the risk of brain damage. These complications and deaths from the disease are most common in babies under six months old.

Whooping cough vaccine is a suspension of killed *Bordetella pertussis*. It is usually given with diphtheria and tetanus vaccines in a triple vaccine.

Vaccination against whooping cough started in 1957. Before then about 100 000 cases of the disease were reported in the UK each year. By 1973 more than 80% of the population had been vaccinated and the number of annual cases had fallen to approximately 2400. However, there was a scare over the safety of the vaccine and vaccinations fell to around 30% in 1975. Epidemics of whooping cough followed in 1977–79 and 1981–83. Methods of producing the vaccine were improved. A publicity campaign pointed out the advantages of vaccination and helped to restore public confidence so that vaccination rose to 67% in 1986. This was enough to halt further epidemics.

Side-effects after injection of whooping cough vaccine occur in about one in 100 000 injections. Symptoms include fever and headache. In a very few cases there can be permanent brain damage. The fever soon goes away but the slight possibility of brain damage causes anxiety amongst parents. For this reason a double vaccine is available that contains diphtheria and tetanus vaccines but not the vaccine for whooping cough. Parents who choose the double vaccine have to decide whether the chances of their child catching whooping cough are less than the chances of their child suffering brain damage through having the vaccine.

If large numbers of children are not vaccinated against whooping cough then the level of protection for the population as a whole falls and outbreaks of the disease increase. The 'fors' and 'againsts' for whooping cough vaccination show how difficult it is to balance individual well-being and freedom of choice against what is good for everybody. *Where do you think the balance lies?* The information in Table 38.1 will help you to make a choice.

Table 38.1 ● Comparison of complications and side-effects with whooping cough and triple vaccine

Result of vaccination or illness	Vaccination with triple vaccine (incidence per 100 000 vaccinations)	Whooping cough (incidence per 100 000 cases)
Death	0.2	4000
Permanent brain damage	0.6	2000
Inflammation of the brain	3.0	4000
Convulsions	90	8000

The case for vaccination against the virus which causes German measles (rubella) is more straightforward, especially for girls. The vaccine does not have the same level of risk compared with whooping cough vaccine.

German measles in children is not serious. The body, arms, legs and face may be covered with pink spots and at worst there may be a fever and the lymph glands may swell up. These symptoms clear up after two or three days. However, it is much more serious if a woman catches German measles during the first four months of pregnancy. The virus can cross the placenta and affect the developing baby. The baby may be born dead or blind or deaf or with a damaged nervous system. Up to 90% of babies whose mothers catch the disease when pregnant are affected. This is why it is important for girls to be vaccinated against German measles before they have babies.

IT ABO Blood Grouping (program)

Find out how blood tests are carried out, using the program. The program takes you through the taking of blood samples, testing, transfusions, how blood forms clots, and the genetics of the ABO system.

● Passive Immunity

Not all vaccines contain antigens which stimulate the body to produce antibodies. Instead, antibodies can come ready-made from other animals. For example, anti-tetanus vaccine contains anti-tetanus antibodies produced by horses. The bacterium which causes tetanus lives in the soil and multiplies very rapidly in places where there is little air, such as in a deep wound. The bacterium produces a lethal poison which acts so quickly that the body's lymphocytes do not have time to make antibodies against it. This is why if you have a deep dirty cut you should be injected with vaccine containing anti-tetanus antibodies. These can act immediately to stop the disease from developing. Immunity which comes from antibodies made in another animal is called **passive immunity**.

Although it is short-lived, passive immunity is important for babies. While they are breast-feeding, babies receive antibodies from their mother's milk which protect them from disease-causing micro-organisms. By the time this protection wears off, the baby is able to make its own antibodies.

Blood groups

Although red blood cells all look alike under the microscope, they may carry different antigens called antigen A and antigen B on the cell surface. Plasma contains antibodies which attack foreign red cell antigens but does not contain antibodies which would attack a person's own red cell antigens. The possible combinations of antibody and antigen are shown in Table 38.2. These determine which blood group a person belongs to.

Table 38.2 ● Blood groups

Antigen on red cells	Antibody in plasma	Blood group	Percentage of UK population with blood group
A	Anti-B	A	40
B	Anti-A	B	10
A and B	Neither	AB	5
Neither	Anti-A and anti-B	O	45

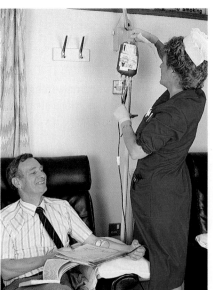

Figure 38.2F shows a patient having a transfusion. Blood at the right temperature is fed at the correct rate from the bag through the tube into a vein in the arm.

Before a person receives a blood transfusion it is important to know that the donor's blood group is compatible with that of the patient. If it is not then the donor's red blood cells clump in the patient's blood vessels and cause serious harm. Table 38.3 shows which blood groups are compatible. If a

Figure 38.2F ● A patient receiving a blood transfusion

donor's blood causes the patients red blood cells to clump, their blood groups are said to be incompatible.

Table 38.3 ● Blood transfusion: compatibility between donor and patient

Group	Donate to	Receive from
A	A and AB	A and O
B	B and AB	B and O
AB	AB	All groups
O	All groups	O

Group O people are called universal donors. *Why can they give blood to anybody?* Group AB people are universal recipients. *Why can they receive blood from anybody?*

Usually whole blood (plasma and cells) is given but sometimes plasma only is used to restore blood volume, especially in cases of serious burns or blood loss. It takes several weeks for the patient to make new blood cells to replace the ones lost.

Platelets help to stop bleeding

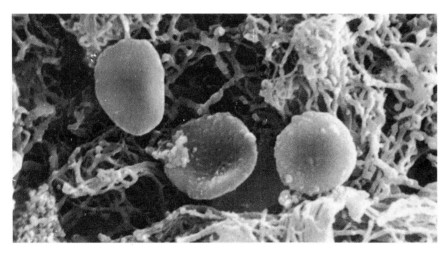

When you are cut a series of complex events begins which eventually stops the bleeding. A clot begins to form when platelets are damaged by the rough surface caused by a cut or torn tissue. They release a substance which results in the formation of an insoluble protein called fibrin . Fibrin forms a mesh of fibres across the wound that traps red cells, forming a clot (see Figure 38.2G).

Figure 38.2G ● A blood clot: red cells trapped by a mesh of fibrin fibres

Disorders of the blood

● Leukaemia

Leukaemia is a condition in which large numbers of immature white blood cells are produced and released into the blood stream. Overproduction of abnormal white cells results in the formation of too few red cells and other blood cells.

The microscopic examination of blood smears and bone marrow smears is an important tool in the diagnosis of leukaemia. The number of white cells and their appearance are helpful indicators to the presence of the disease.

Leukaemia can be treated with drugs and by radiotherapy. For some types of leukaemia the prospects of improvement and recovery in a patient are poor, but other types respond very well to treatment. For example, in about 90% of cases involving children with certain kinds of leukaemia, treatment stops the disease developing further and improves their chance of a healthy life. More than 50% of patients are cured.

IT'S A FACT

The drug vincristine has helped to improve the treatment of leukaemia. The drug is extracted from the rosy periwinkle plant which grows in the rain forests of Madagascar.

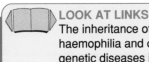

LOOK AT LINKS
The inheritance of haemophilia and other genetic diseases is described in Theme N, Topic 54.3.

● *Haemophilia*

Some people lose a lot of blood if they injure themselves because their blood does not clot properly. This disease is called haemophilia. In the most common form of the disease the blood lacks a substance called **factor VIII** which is one of the substances involved in the production of fibrin. Haemophiliacs are treated with injections of factor VIII. Haemophilia is a **genetic disease** that runs in families. Some of the royal families of Europe carry the genes for haemophilia.

● *AIDS*

AIDS (**A**cquired **I**mmune **D**eficiency **S**yndrome) is caused by a virus called the **Human Immunodeficiency Virus (HIV)** (see Figure 38.2H). The virus attacks the lymphocytes which play an important part in the body's defence against disease. This means that the body of a person with HIV is far less well protected than normal. It is not usually HIV itself which causes the suffering of AIDS patients: they may die from another infection, often a type of pneumonia, which develops after HIV has destroyed part of the body's defences. We call AIDS a **syndrome** as there are a variety of symptoms which an HIV-infected person may have. Many of these symptoms are the result of other infections.

Unlike many other viral infections, controlling AIDS presents a particular difficulty. There is a long time interval (from a few months to several years) between the virus getting into a person's body and symptoms developing. During this period the person is infectious and able to pass on the virus to other people without knowing it.

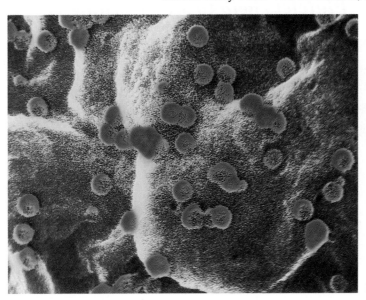

Figure 38.2H ● Human immunodeficiency virus (HIV)

CHECKPOINT

1. List the different types of blood cell.

2. What is meant by 'oxygenated blood' and 'deoxygenated blood'?

3. What is an antigen?

4. 'Antibodies are specific'. Briefly explain this statement.

5. Why are diseases like chicken pox and measles rarely caught more than once?

6. What is the difference between a vaccine and a vaccination?

7. What is an attenuated vaccine?

8. How do booster vaccinations help to maintain a person's immunity to disease?

9. What is the triple vaccination?

10 Briefly explain why it is important for women to be vaccinated against German measles before they have babies.

11 What is the difference between active immunity and passive immunity?

12 Briefly explain how the presence or absence of antigen A and antigen B determines a person's blood group.

13 Before a blood transfusion is given, why is it important to know that the donor's and patient's blood are compatible?

38.3 The blood system

How does the heart work? What is the role of arteries, veins and capillaries? Find out the answer to these questions in this section.

Why do we need a blood system? Small animals like flatworms do not have one. Osmosis, diffusion and active transport carry gases, minerals and other materials to where they are needed in the flatworm's body. However, large animals like humans require a system specialised to carry materials from one part of the body to another. This is the role of the blood system.

Blood vessels

The blood system consists of a network of tubes called blood vessels through which the heart pumps blood. The major blood vessels are the **arteries** and the **veins**. Table 38.4 compares arteries and veins.

Table 38.4 ● Arteries and veins compared. The smooth lining to the vessels helps bloodflow and prevents clots from forming.

Arteries	Veins
Thick outer wall, Narrow diameter, Thick layer of muscles and elastic fibres	Fairly thin outer wall, Large diameter, Thin layer of muscles and elastic fibres
Carry blood away from the heart to organs and tissues	Return blood to the heart from organs and tissues (except hepatic portal vein)
Blood at high pressure	Blood at low pressure. Body muscles squeeze the veins to help push the blood to the heart
Have a pulse because the vessel walls expand and relax as blood spurts from heart	Do not have a pulse since blood flows smoothly
Have thick walls to withstand pressure of blood	Have thin wall and large diameter reducing resistance to the flow of blood returning to the heart

Blood in the veins is at a much lower pressure than in the arteries. One-way valves inside the veins prevent blood from flowing backwards (see Figure 38.3A). The force of the heart beat keeps blood flowing away from the heart through the arteries, so there is no need for valves inside them.

The arteries and veins in the human body form two circuits: the lung circuit and the head and body circuit (see Figure 38.3B). The veins of the head and body bring deoxygenated blood to the heart. The heart pumps deoxygenated blood through the pulmonary arteries to the lungs, where it is oxygenated. The oxygenated blood returns to the heart through the pulmonary veins completing the lung circuit. The heart then pumps the oxygenated blood through the arteries of the head and body circuit.

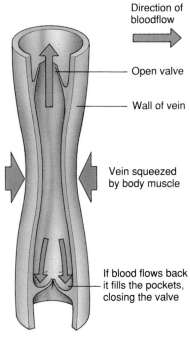

Direction of bloodflow

Open valve

Wall of vein

Vein squeezed by body muscle

If blood flows back it fills the pockets, closing the valve

Figure 38.3A ● Valves opening and closing inside a vein

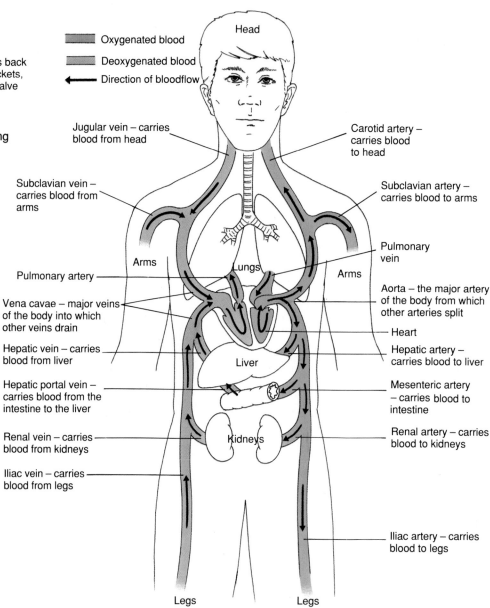

Oxygenated blood
Deoxygenated blood
Direction of bloodflow

Head

Jugular vein – carries blood from head

Carotid artery – carries blood to head

Subclavian vein – carries blood from arms

Subclavian artery – carries blood to arms

Arms

Lungs

Arms

Pulmonary vein

Pulmonary artery

Aorta – the major artery of the body from which other arteries split

Vena cavae – major veins of the body into which other veins drain

Heart

Hepatic vein – carries blood from liver

Liver

Hepatic artery – carries blood to liver

Hepatic portal vein – carries blood from the intestine to the liver

Mesenteric artery – carries blood to intestine

Renal vein – carries blood from kidneys

Kidneys

Renal artery – carries blood to kidneys

Iliac vein – carries blood from legs

Legs

Legs

Iliac artery – carries blood to legs

Figure 38.3B ● The lung circuit and the head and body circuit. Oxygen passes from tissue to blood and carbon dioxide passes from blood to tissue in the lungs. Oxygen passes from blood to tissue and carbon dioxide passes from tissue to blood in all other organs and tissues.

● *Capillaries*

Small blood vessels branch from the main arteries and veins. The vessels branching from arteries are called **arterioles**, those branching from veins are called **venules**. Arterioles and venules branch further to form capillaries. Capillaries join arterioles to venules and so link arteries and veins. Capillaries form dense networks, called beds, in the tissues of the body. This means that no cell is very far away from a capillary. (See Figure 38.3C.)

Capillaries are tiny vessels only 0.001 mm in diameter with walls one cell thick. The blood in capillaries supplies the nearby cells with the food, oxygen and other materials they need. The blood also carries away urea, carbon dioxide and other wastes produced by the cells' metabolism.

The pumping of the heart brings blood at high pressure to the arteriole end of the capillary network. The pressure forces plasma through the thin capillary walls. The liquid is now called tissue fluid and carries the food and oxygen to the cells which are not in direct contact with a capillary. (See Figure 38.3D.)

There is just enough room in the smallest capillaries for red cells to pass in single file. A lot of plasma is forced through the one-cell-thick walls as the red cells squeeze through the capillaries. The pressure drops as blood passes through the capillaries to the venule end of the bed. Tissue fluid can then seep back into the capillaries along with dissolved urea and carbon dioxide. Most tissue fluid returns to the blood by this route. The remaining small amount of fluid drains into the lymph vessels.

Figure 38.3C ● A capillary network

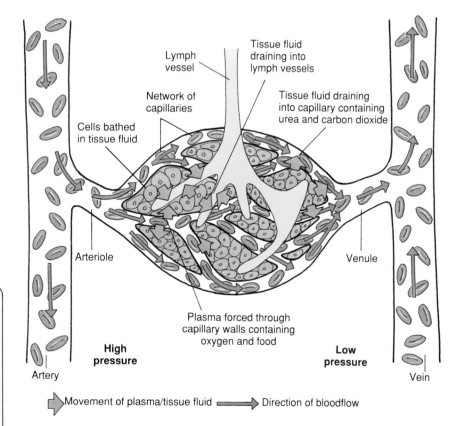

Figure 38.3D ● Capillaries at work

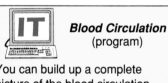

Blood Circulation
(program)

You can build up a complete picture of the blood circulation system using this program. Look at the models of heart structure. The program shows the way that blood flows through the heart.

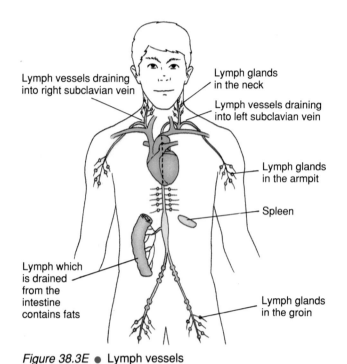

Figure 38.3E ● Lymph vessels

The lymph vessels

The lymph vessels return fluids to the blood system that would otherwise collect in the tissues. The smallest lymph vessels are the size of capillary blood vessels; the largest are the size of veins. Capillary lymph vessels are blind-ended tubes which form a network in the body's tissues. Tissue fluid diffuses through their walls and slowly passes into the larger lymph vessels. Figure 38.3E shows how the lymph vessels are arranged in the human body. The fluid, now called lymph, is moved by the contraction of the body's muscles during normal daily activity. Valves in the lymph vessels, similar to those found in veins, prevent the backflow of fluid.

The spleen is also part of the lymph vessel system. Lymphocytes are made in the spleen and in the lymph glands. The spleen also collects damaged and old red blood cells, breaking them down and releasing the haemoglobin in them. Iron in the haemoglobin is removed and re-used by bone marrow to make new haemoglobin.

If the circulation of lymph is upset by disease or poor diet, then fluid may gather in the tissues and cause swelling. This is called **oedema**.

The human heart

The heart is a pump which propels blood through the arteries and veins. It is made of a type of muscle called **cardiac muscle** which contracts and relaxes rhythmically for a lifetime. The more efficient the heart is, the more efficient are the exchanges of food, oxygen, carbon dioxide and other dissolved materials between the blood and the tissues of the body.

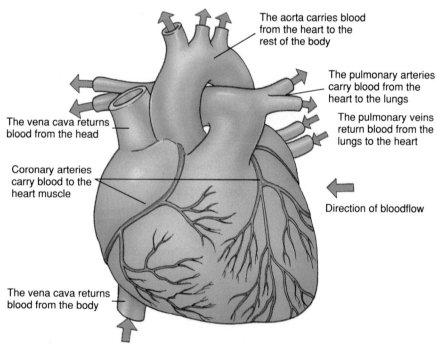

Figure 38.3F ● View of the heart from the front

● Heart structure

The heart lies in the chest cavity surrounded by a membrane called the **pericardium**. It is protected by the rib cage. Figures 38.3F and G show the heart and the blood vessels leading to and from it.

The heart is full of blood and it seems odd that heart muscle needs an additional blood supply. However, like other tissues, heart muscle needs a steady supply of the food and oxygen dissolved in blood. The walls of heart muscle are so thick that these materials cannot diffuse quickly enough from inside the heart to all of the heart muscle. So, some of the heart muscle is supplied with blood by the coronary arteries.

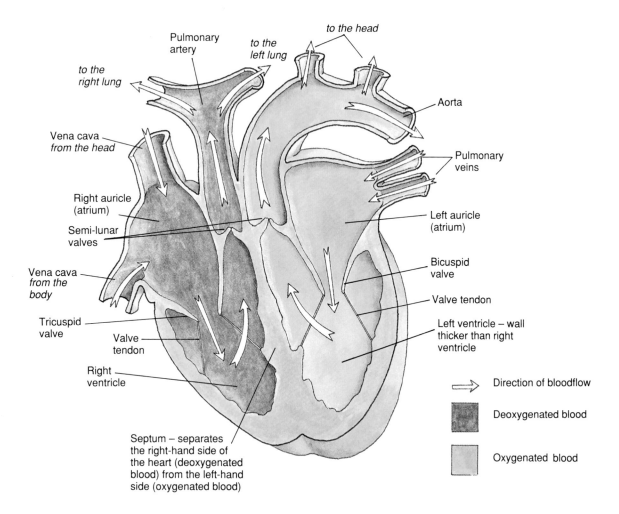

Figure 38.3G ● A cross-section of the heart viewed from the front

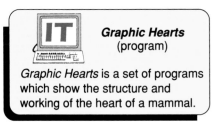

Graphic Hearts
(program)

Graphic Hearts is a set of programs which show the structure and working of the heart of a mammal.

═══ **SCIENCE AT WORK** ═══

Cancer cells that have broken loose from a cancer growth are often caught in the lymph glands. Lymph glands near to cancer growths under treatment are therefore usually removed by surgery.

● Flow of blood through the heart

When all the heart muscles relax (called diastole):
- deoxygenated blood from the head and body enters the right atrium through each vena cava,
- oxygenated blood from the lungs enters the left atrium through the pulmonary veins.

The atria fill with blood and then contract (called auricular systole). The increase in pressure opens the tricuspid and bicuspid valves and forces blood into the ventricles. When full, the ventricles contract (called ventricular systole). The increase in pressure closes the tricuspid and bicuspid valves and forces blood past the semi-lunar valves which guard the openings of the pulmonary artery and aorta. The right ventricle pumps blood into the pulmonary artery on its way to the lungs; the left ventricle pumps blood into the aorta which takes it round the rest of the body. The semi-lunar valves close when the ventricles relax.

In effect the heart is a double pump, each ventricle pumping blood along a different route through the body. Look back at Figure 38.3B. The distance travelled by blood through the head and body circuit is greater than the distance it travels through the lung circuit. This difference explains why the wall of the left ventricle is thicker than the wall of the right ventricle. Its contractions must be more powerful to pump blood the greater distance.

● The heartbeat

Diastole and systole produce an unmistakable two-tone sound which is easily heard through an instrument such as a stethoscope. This sound is the heartbeat. In a healthy adult the heart beats on average 72 times a minute but this can vary between 60 beats per minute and 80. Exercise makes the heart beat faster, bringing more blood to the muscles.

The beating of the heart is controlled by the pacemaker, which is a group of special cells in the right atrium. Occasionally the natural pacemaker goes wrong. The heart rate slows down causing drowsiness and shortage of breath. When the heart's natural pacemaker does not function properly an electronic pacemaker can be fitted which helps to keep the heart beating at the proper rate.

● The pulse

Each heart beat sets up a ripple of pressure which passes along the arteries. The ripple can be felt as a 'pulse' as the artery's muscular wall expands and relaxes.

Feeling a patient's pulse can help doctors and nurses to tell if the heart is beating properly. The neck pulse and wrist pulse are the most useful pulses (see Figure 38.3H). The pulse is felt with the finger tips pressed lightly over the artery (the thumb is not used since this has its own pulse). The number of beats in a minute are counted using the second hand of a watch.

Use a pulse sensor to measure your pulse rate. Compare the readings when you are relaxed and breathing easily with when you have exercised hard. You may be able to make the sensor beep in time to your heart beat.

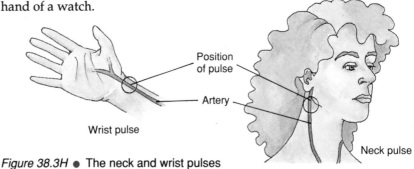

Figure 38.3H ● The neck and wrist pulses

Blood pressure

Figure 38.3I ● Measuring blood pressure with a sphygmomanometer

Blood flows along the blood vessels because it is under pressure. We call this **blood pressure**. It is measured with an instrument called a **sphygmomanometer** (see Figure 38.3I). An inflatable armband is wrapped around the patient's upper arm. The armband is inflated until it stops the blood from flowing along the main artery of the arm. The air is then let out of the armband very slowly while the doctor listens for the return of the pulse with a stethoscope placed below the armband. At the point when the blood moves back into the artery below the armband and the pulse returns, the pressure in the armband just equals the pressure of the blood.

LOOK AT LINKS
Blood pressure is measured in millimetres of mercury (mm Hg) rather than the SI unit of pressure, the pascal (Pa). A column of mercury 100 mm high exerts a pressure of 13 300 Pa at its base, so 1 mm Hg = 133 Pa. For more details, see Theme I, Topics 35.3 and 35.4.

Two readings are taken: the pressure of blood when the heart contracts (called systolic blood pressure) and the pressure of the blood when the heart relaxes (called diastolic blood pressure). The normal systolic pressure of a young adult is about 120 mm Hg; normal diastolic pressure is about 75 mm Hg.

Constant high blood pressure is harmful. It makes the heart work harder. Eventually the overworked heart may fail altogether. High blood pressure can also damage the kidneys and eyes, and increase the risk of an artery tearing open. A cerebral haemorrhage, or stroke, occurs when one of the arteries that supplies blood to the brain ruptures.

CHECKPOINT

1 Briefly explain the significance of the difference between arteries and veins.

2 How does blood, rich in digested food absorbed from the intestine, reach the liver?

3 Explain the function of the valves in the veins and in the lymph vessels.

4 What is oedema?

5 Briefly describe the function of lymph glands.

6

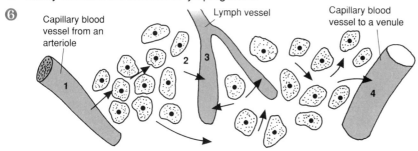

Capillary blood vessel from an arteriole
Lymph vessel
Capillary blood vessel to a venule

The diagram shows the movement of tissue fluid, plasma and lymph between capillary blood vessels, tissue cells and lymph vessels.
(a) Choose the word which correctly names the fluid in each of the locations numbered 1–4.
    water   lymph   salt solution   plasma   tissue fluid
(b) Explain why fluid leaves the capillary blood vessel at 1 but enters the capillary blood vessel at 4.

7 Describe the route that blood takes from the time it enters the heart to the time it reaches the lungs.

8 What are diastole and systole?

9 What does 'heart rate' mean?

10 What is meant by 'blood pressure'?

11 The diagram shows a section through the human heart viewed from the front.
(a) Name the parts of the heart labelled A–H.
(b) Which of the following sequences of letters describes the path taken by blood through the heart?
        G B A E H C D F   F D C H E A B G
        E A B G H C D F   H C D F G B A E
(c) Which two parts of the diagram show that chambers A and C are relaxed?
(d) Why is the wall of chamber D thicker than the wall of chamber B?

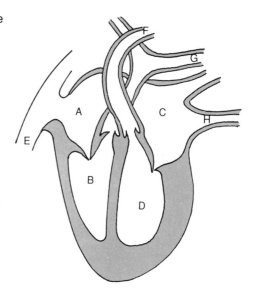

⑫

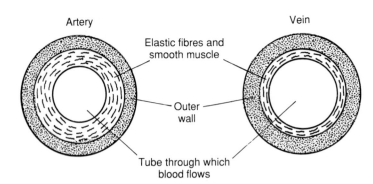

Artery

Vein

Elastic fibres and
smooth muscle

Outer
wall

Tube through which
blood flows

The diagram shows sections through an artery and a vein.
(a) Give two differences in structure between an artery and a vein.
(b) Briefly explain how the differences you have given in (a) are linked to the
way in which arteries and veins work.
(c) Complete the following:
An artery carries blood from the _____ at _____ pressure.
A vein carries blood to the _____ at _____ pressure.
Arteries and veins are linked by tiny blood vessels called capillaries
which are about _____ mm in diameter and have walls _____ _____
thick. Capillaries form at the end of small blood vessels branching from
the arteries and veins. The vessels branching from the arteries are called
_____; those branching from the veins are called _____ .

FIRST
THOUGHTS

38.4 ● Understanding heart disease

Heart disease is responsible for
more than a quarter of all
deaths in the UK. More people
in the world's developed
countries die from heart
disease than from any other
single cause. Why?

The smooth lining of healthy blood vessels allows blood to flow easily
through them. However, the lining can be damaged and roughened by a
fatty deposit called **atheroma**. The build-up of atheroma makes blood
vessels narrower and cuts down the flow of blood (see Figure 38.4A).
This increases the risk of blood clots forming. A blood clot can block a
blood vessel. The clot is called a **thrombus** and a blockage is called a
thrombosis.

Atheroma in the coronary arteries is one cause of heart disease. The
first signs of trouble may be cramp-like chest pain brought on by quick
walking, anger, excitement or any other activity or emotion that makes
the heart work harder than usual. The pain is called **angina**.

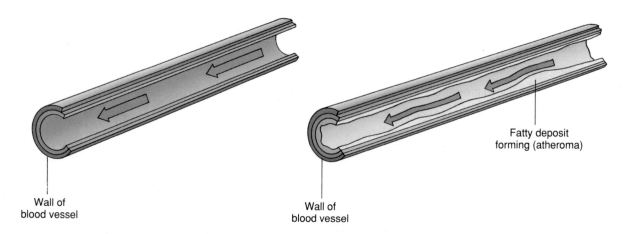

Wall of
blood vessel

Wall of
blood vessel

Fatty deposit
forming (atheroma)

Figure 38.4A ● Atheroma building up inside a blood vessel

People live with some types of angina for years but other types get worse and may later result in a heart attack (called a coronary thrombosis).

A heart attack happens when the blood supply to the heart is interrupted. This usually causes a gripping pain in the person's chest. The pain often spreads to the neck, jaw and arms, and the victim may also sweat and feel faint and sick.

The affected part of the heart is damaged and sometimes a heat attack is so severe that the heart stops beating altogether. This is called **cardiac arrest**. A victim of cardiac arrest will die unless the heart starts beating again within a few minutes.

Deaths from heart disease

Diseases of the heart and blood vessels kill more people in the UK than any other single cause (see Figures 38.4B and 38.4C). More than a quarter of all deaths are due to heart disease alone. This problem is not confined to the UK. Heart disease is the biggest single killer of middle-aged men in many of the world's developed countries.

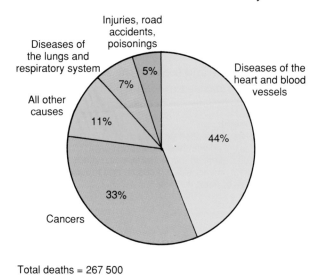

Total deaths = 267 500

Figure 38.4B ● Causes of death in people aged under 75 in the UK (Source: Office of Population Censuses and Surveys)

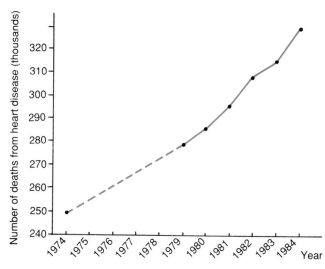

Figure 38.4C ● Deaths in the UK from heart disease between 1974 and 1984 (Source: Health and Personal Social Services statistics HMSO, 1986)

Risk factors

Research has identified some of the causes of heart disease by comparing groups of people who have high rates of heart disease with groups that have low rates. When a difference between the groups is found that might help to explain why some people are more likely to develop heart disease than others, it is called a **risk factor**.

Three risk factors are unavoidable:

- **Sex** – men are more likely to die of heart disease than women.
- **Age** – the risk of heart disease increases with a person's age.
- **Inherited genes** – the tendency to die from heart disease can run in families.

Being male, old or having a family history of heart disease does not mean that people in these categories will necessarily die from it. If the risk factors are known, people can live sensibly to increase their chances of reaching old age. Living sensibly means avoiding the other, controllable risk factors such as smoking and stress (see Figure 38.4D).

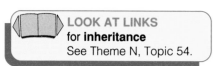

LOOK AT LINKS
for **inheritance**
See Theme N, Topic 54.

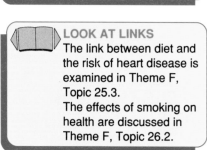

LOOK AT LINKS
The link between diet and the risk of heart disease is examined in Theme F, Topic 25.3.
The effects of smoking on health are discussed in Theme F, Topic 26.2.

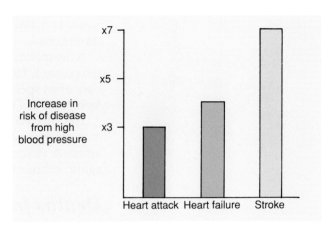

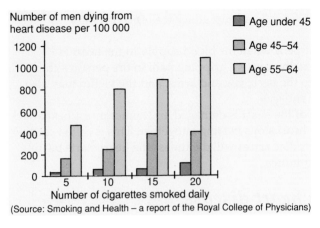

Figure 38.4D ● The evidence linking the risk of heart disease with avoidable risk factors
(a) Smoking and the risk of heart disease (b) High blood pressure and the risk of heart disease

Exercise and ...

Blood pressure
• Blood pressure is lower in physically fit people
• Regular exercise can help control high blood pressure and reduce the risk of heart disease

Regular exercise increases heart fitness but is there evidence that exercise directly reduces the risk of heart disease? Many different studies strongly support the idea that regular exercise protects against heart disease and some of the evidence is summarised in Figure 38.4E. *What conclusions can you make from the data?*

Overweight
• Overweight is often due to lack of exercise and is linked with high blood pressure
• Regular exercise increases fitness, reduces body fat, lowers blood pressure and reduces the risk of heart disease

Stress
• Stress increases blood pressure and the risk of heart disease as well as making people irritable and depressed
• Regular exercise reduces the risk of heart disease and gives an increased feeling of well being

London Transport Study
• The study found that bus drivers had twice as many fatal heart attacks as the conductors, who climbed the stairs and walked the aisles of the bus all day long

Coronary arteries
• Regular exercise reduces the build up of atheroma and makes coronary arteries wider reducing the risk of heart disease
• Exercise can promote the growth of new blood vessels after a heart attack

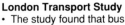

Figure 38.4E ● Exercise and heart disease

CHECKPOINT

❶ The bar chart compares deaths from diseases of the heart and blood vessels in 1900 and 1984.

1900 Total deaths from all causes = 587 830
1984 Total deaths from all causes = 566 881

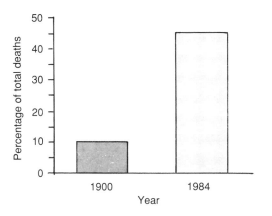

(a) How many people died from diseases of the heart and blood vessels in 1900 and 1984?
(b) How many times more likely is death from diseases of the heart and blood vessels in 1984 compared with 1900?
(c) Death from diseases of the heart and blood vessels is made more likely by risk factors.
  (i) What are 'risk factors'?
  (ii) Some risk factors cannot be avoided but others can. Give two examples of each type of risk factor.
  (iii) Briefly explain the evidence for one named risk factor.
  (iv) Do you think there are more risk factors in 1984 compared with 1900? Give reasons for your answer.

❷ The diagram shows three places A, B and C where blood vessels supplying blood to the heart could become blocked causing a heart attack.
(a) Name the blood vessels supplying blood to the heart.
(b) What is the blockage of the blood vessel called?
(c) Which of A, B or C would cause the most serious heart attack? Give reasons for your answer.

❸ The diagram shows lengthways sections of a healthy blood vessel and a diseased blood vessel.

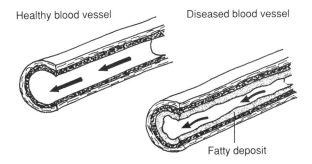

Healthy blood vessel   Diseased blood vessel

Fatty deposit

(a) What is the fatty deposit called?
(b) The artery narrows where the fatty deposit is forming. Briefly explain how the blood vessel could become completely blocked.
(c) What is a heart attack?
(d) Imagine you are walking along a busy street with someone who suddenly has a heart attack. The person remains conscious but needs your help. Explain what you should do.

❹ Briefly explain how a man with a family history of heart disease can cut down the risk of having a heart attack.

❺ 'Exercise is good for you' – so we are told. Using the data available, describe the effect of exercise on heart fitness.

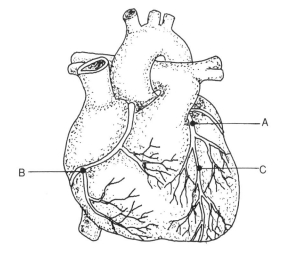

A

B

C

149

REPRODUCTION

39.1 Outlines of reproduction

> Reproduction more than anything else characterises living things. It continues the thread of life, unbroken from generation to generation. This section gives you an overview of the processes of reproduction.

All living things eventually die. They may be killed by other organisms or die of old age. Before dying, some individuals produce new individuals of their own kind. This is **reproduction** (see Figure 39.1A).

There are two basic types of reproduction:

- **Asexual reproduction** – one parent gives rise to new individuals which are genetically identical to it. The genetically identical individuals produced are called **clones**.
- **Sexual reproduction** – two parents give rise to new individuals. Offspring acquire genes from each parent and are therefore genetically different from one another and from their parents.

Figure 39.1A ● Reproduction (a) A female scorpion carrying her young

(b) A tree surrounded by its seedlings

Asexual reproduction

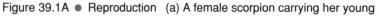

LOOK AT LINKS
for **mitosis** and **mutations**
See Theme D, Topic 19.4.

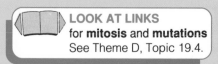

Figure 39.1B illustrates different ways in which asexual reproduction takes place. The offspring are identical to the parent because the cells divide by **mitosis** to give new daughter cells. During mitosis DNA replicates itself. Mistakes in DNA replication are called **mutations**, but they are rare.

Figure 39.1B ● Ways of reproducing asexually
(a) *Paramecium* dividing by fission – the parent divides into equal parts
(b) *Hydra* budding – outgrowths of the parent's body (buds) separate from the parent. Each one becomes a separate individual.
(c) Parts of the parent body grow into new individuals. For example parts of stems can sprout roots and grow into new plants.
(d) Regeneration – the parent body breaks into pieces, each piece can grow into a new individual
(e) A female aphid produces eggs which develop into new individuals without fertilisation

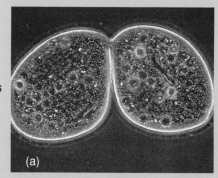
(a)

Sexual reproduction

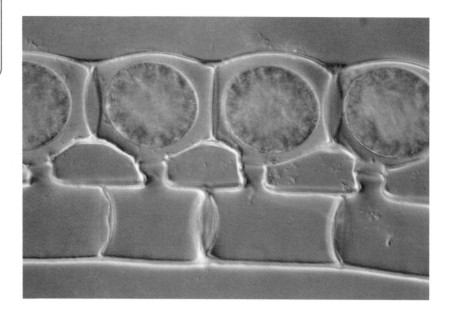

Figure 39.1C ● Maleness and femaleness in *Spirogyra* – a new strand of *Spirogyra* develops from the fused nuclei.

LOOK AT LINKS
for *Spirogyra*
See Theme A, Topic 3.5.

LOOK AT LINKS
The importance of genetic variation in evolution is discussed in Theme N, Topic 55.

Figure 39.1C shows strands of the green alga *Spirogyra* lying side-by-side. A cell of one of the strands is joined by a tube to a cell of the other strand. The content of one of the joined cells passes through the tube and the nucleus fuses with the nucleus of the other cell. The genetic material in each nucleus combines with the genetic material of its opposite number. The combination of genetic material is different from the combination in each of the parent cells. This is an important feature of sexual reproduction; the production of much more **genetic variation** is possible than by mutation alone. Figure 39.1C illustrates another important feature of sexual reproduction – maleness and femaleness. The male cell of *Spirogyra* is the empty one. Its contents have moved toward the female cell.

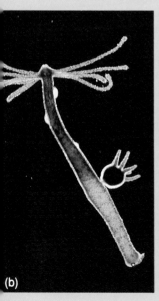

(b)

(c)

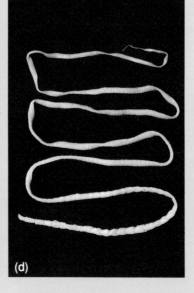

(d)

(e)

Seaweed

Mosses and liverworts

Sea-urchin

Rat

Chicken

● Sex cells

There are two types of sex cell: male sex cells called sperms and female sex cells called eggs. Sperms and eggs are called **gametes**.

Table 39.1 ● Comparing sperms and eggs

Sperms	Eggs
Small	Large
Move towards the egg	Do not move much
Have no food store	Have food store

The sperms of many types of organism are very similar (see Figure 39.1D). Human sperm is fairly typical (see Figure 39.1E). In fact, the sperm is little more than a mobile nucleus designed to bring genetic material from the male parent to the egg of the female parent.

Animal eggs are bigger than sperms because they contain yolk which is a food store. Some eggs have more yolk than others. This is why the eggs of different animals are different in size.

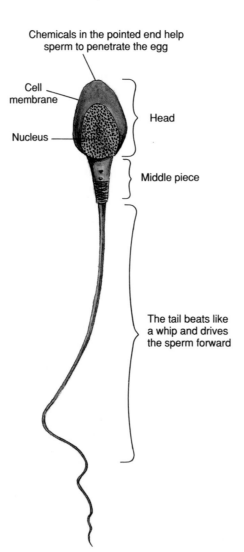

Chemicals in the pointed end help sperm to penetrate the egg

Cell membrane

Nucleus

Head

Middle piece

The tail beats like a whip and drives the sperm forward

● How many chromosomes?

Cells have a fixed number of chromosomes. For example, a human skin cell has 46 chromosomes and divides by mitosis to give daughter cells each with 46 chromosomes. Cells which, through mitosis, receive the full number of chromosomes from their parent cells and in turn hand them on to their daughter cells are described as **diploid** (or **2n**).

However, not all parent cells divide by mitosis to produce diploid daughter cells. When the cells that give rise to sex cells (sperms and eggs) divide, the diploid number of chromosomes in each nucleus is halved. For example, human sex cells each have 23 chromosomes compared with the normal diploid number of 46 chromosomes found in each body cell. The process which halves the diploid number of chromosomes is called **meiosis**. The half number – 23 chromosomes in the case of each human sperm and egg – is described as **haploid** (or **n**). Figure 39.1F shows the different stages of meiosis.

Figure 39.1D ● Plant and animal sperm   Figure 39.1E ● Human sperm

Parent cell

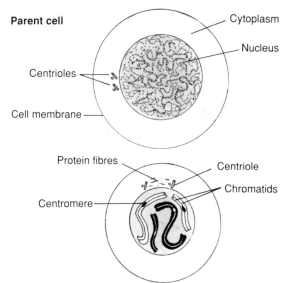

Cytoplasm

Nucleus

Centrioles

Cell membrane

Protein fibres

Centriole

Centromere

Chromatids

Stage 1 Chromosomes divide into pairs of identical chromatids joined to one another by the centromere. Centrioles move to opposite ends of the cell. Protein fibres form around each of them, just as in mitosis.

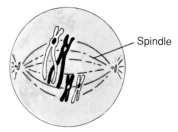

Stage 2 Chromosomes pair up. The two chromosomes of a pair are called **homologous chromosomes**. Notice the exchange of a segment of one chromosome with the corresponding segment of its homologous chromosome.

Spindle

Stage 3 The nuclear membrane disappears. A spindle forms between the centrioles just as in mitosis. Homologous pairs of chromosomes arrange themselves on the equator.

Stage 4 Homlogous pairs of chromosomes separate. Each chromosome (consisting of two chromatids) of the pair moves to opposite ends of the cell.

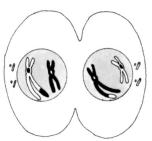

Stage 5 The chromosomes gather into two bunches. The cell begins to divide and a new nuclear membrane forms around each bunch.

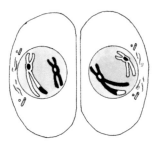

Stage 6 The cell divides.

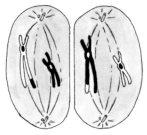

Stage 7 The nuclear membranes disappear and new spindles form at right angles to the first. The chromosomes (still as pairs of chromatids) arrange themselves on the equator.

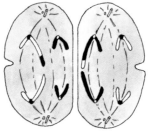

Stage 8 The centromeres divide. The chromatids separate and bunch at opposite ends of each cell. The chromatids are now the new chromosomes. Each cell begins to divide.

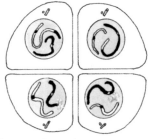

Stage 9 A nuclear membrane forms around each bunch of chromosomes and the cells divide.

Figure 39.1F ● The stages of meiosis. (Only four chromosomes are shown in detail.)

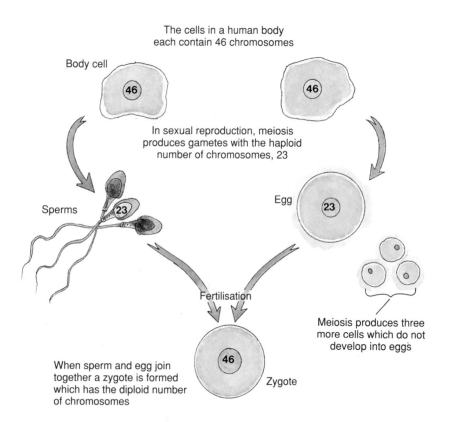

The cells in a human body each contain 46 chromosomes

Body cell

46

46

In sexual reproduction, meiosis produces gametes with the haploid number of chromosomes, 23

Sperms

23

Egg

23

Fertilisation

Meiosis produces three more cells which do not develop into eggs

When sperm and egg join together a zygote is formed which has the diploid number of chromosomes

46

Zygote

Why are sex cells haploid? During fertilisation (when sperm and egg join together) the sperm nucleus and the egg nucleus fuse. The chromosomes from each nucleus combine to produce new combinations of genes. Half come from the haploid sperm and half come from the haploid egg. The fertilised egg (called the zygote) is therefore diploid and develops into a new individual which inherits characteristics from both parents, not from just one as in asexual reproduction (see Figure 39.1G). *Can you think what would happen genetically in each generation of new individuals if sperms and eggs were diploid and not haploid?*

Figure 39.1G ● Fertilisation – restoring the diploid state

● Patterns of fertilisation

Sperms swim. Swimming brings sperms to eggs. Sperms and eggs must therefore be in a liquid for fertilisation to take place. Most aquatic organisms release sperms and eggs into the surrounding water where fertilisation takes place. This is called **external fertilisation** because it takes place outside the parent's body (see Figure 39.1H).

Although moss plants grow on land, even they need water to complete their life cycle. Without it moss sperms cannot swim to moss eggs to fertilise them (see Figure 39.1I). This is why mosses and other such plants grow in damp places.

Figure 39.1H ● Frogs mating. The male sheds sperms over the eggs which the female lays in the water.

Figure 39.1I ● Moss sperms are released in the film of water covering the plant. They swim towards the eggs.

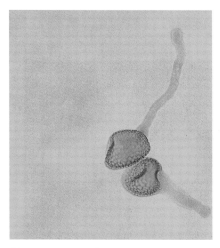

Figure 39.1J ● Sprouting pollen tubes

Without water sperms and eggs perish. *How do organisms that spend their lives on dry land overcome the problem?* Seed-producing plants can live in much drier places than moss plants. Their sperm is protected inside drought-resistant pollen grains. These are usually carried by animals or blown by the wind to the female part of the plant.

Each pollen grain sprouts a pollen tube which grows through the female tissues towards the eggs inside (see Figure 39.1J). Sperms pass down the pollen tube and one of them fertilises the egg. This is an example of **internal fertilisation**.

Internal fertilisation is one of the adaptations that insects, reptiles, birds and mammals have adopted for life on dry land. The male places sperm directly into the body of the female – a process that usually needs some kind of coupling, called **copulation**. Special organs help to transfer the sperm from male to female. In many insects, for example, sperm is transferred from male to female protected in a tiny package called the spermatophore (see Figure 39.1K).

In mammals the male has an organ called the penis which penetrates the opening to the reproductive system of the female (see Figure 39.1L). Sperms pass through the penis into her reproductive system where fertilisation takes place. The sperms swim towards the eggs in a liquid which is produced by the male reproductive system specially for the purpose and which is transferred to the female with the sperms.

Figure 39.1K ● Bush crickets transferring a spermatophore

Figure 39.1L ● Copulating zebras

CHECKPOINT

① What is asexual reproduction? Briefly describe the different ways it takes place.

② What are 'gametes'?

③ Explain, in simple terms, how sperms swim.

④ Why are eggs larger than sperms?

⑤ What is meant by the term 'fertilisation' and what is formed as a result of it?

⑥ What is 'meiosis'?

⑦ Briefly explain the meaning of 'diploid' and 'haploid'.

⑧ The nuclei of muscle cells in a species of lobster each contain 250 chromosomes. How many chromosomes would be found in the nucleus of each of the lobster's sperm?

⑨ 'The number of chromosomes in the nuclei of cells is kept constant from one generation to the next through meiosis and sexual reproduction.' Comment on this statement with reference to a named species.

39.2 Plant reproduction: flowers

How are flowers designed for sexual reproduction? What is the difference between pollination and fertilisation? This section gives you the answers.

Flowers are shoots which are specialised for sexual reproduction. Although flowers come in all shapes and sizes, they are all made up of similar parts. The sepals, petals, stamens and carpels of the buttercup are shown in Figure 39.2A.

Figure 39.2A ● The meadow buttercup

RESOURCE
ACTIVITY
PACK

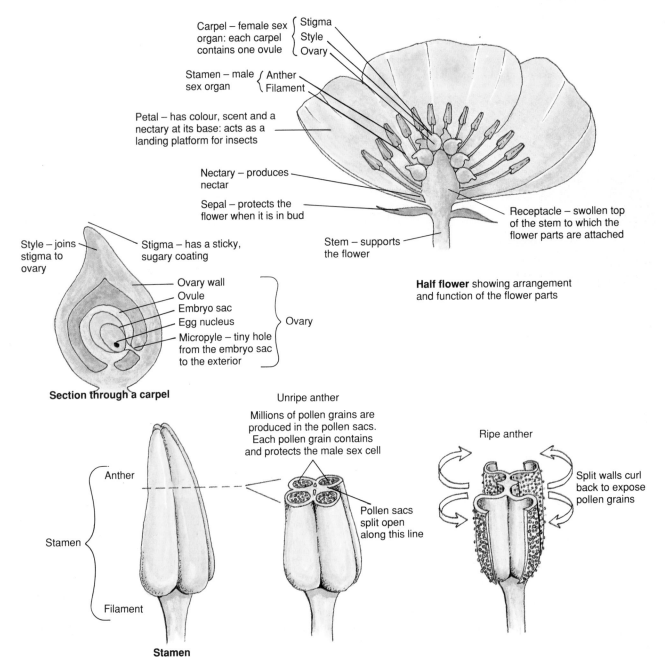

Carpel – female sex organ: each carpel contains one ovule { Stigma / Style / Ovary

Stamen – male sex organ { Anther / Filament

Petal – has colour, scent and a nectary at its base: acts as a landing platform for insects

Nectary – produces nectar

Sepal – protects the flower when it is in bud

Stem – supports the flower

Receptacle – swollen top of the stem to which the flower parts are attached

Half flower showing arrangement and function of the flower parts

Style – joins stigma to ovary

Stigma – has a sticky, sugary coating

Ovary wall
Ovule
Embryo sac
Egg nucleus
Micropyle – tiny hole from the embryo sac to the exterior
} Ovary

Section through a carpel

Unripe anther

Millions of pollen grains are produced in the pollen sacs. Each pollen grain contains and protects the male sex cell

Pollen sacs split open along this line

Ripe anther

Split walls curl back to expose pollen grains

Anther
Stamen
Filament

Stamen

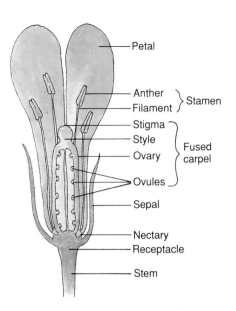

Petal

Anther ⎱
Filament ⎰ Stamen

Stigma ⎫
Style ⎬ Fused
Ovary ⎭ carpel
Ovules

Sepal

Nectary
Receptacle

Stem

Types of flower

Flowers like the buttercup are simple flowers. Their parts are free and separate from each other and they have many stamens and carpels. The parts of other types of flower may be arranged differently with some parts joined together or have fewer parts than the buttercup has. Figure 39.2B illustrates examples of different arrangements.

Figure 39.2B ● Arrangements of flower parts
(a) Half-flower of the wallflower. The one large carpel is formed from a number of carpels fused together. You can tell that the carpel is fused because it contains a number of ovules.

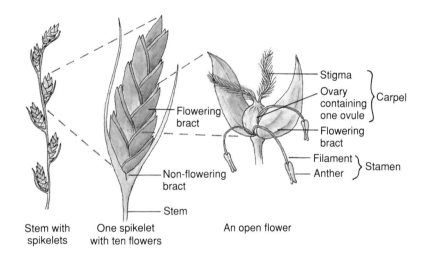

Flowering
bract

Non-flowering
bract

Stem

Stigma
Ovary ⎫
containing ⎬ Carpel
one ovule ⎭

Flowering
bract

Filament ⎱
Anther ⎰ Stamen

Stem with
spikelets

One spikelet
with ten flowers

An open flower

(b) Rye grass flowers have no sepals or petals

Pollination

The pollen grain must pass from the anther to the stigma before the male sex cell inside it can fertilise the female sex cell in the ovule. This transfer of pollen is called pollination.

● Wind pollination
Wind-pollinated flowers are adapted in ways that make sure that pollen is widely scattered. Some have long, slender anthers which hang clear of the sepals and petals, which otherwise might get in the way of the pollen being blown away. The flowers of different grasses (for example rye grass in Figure 39.2B) do not have sepals or petals at all. The dangling male catkins of the hazel tree produce a cloud of pollen which is blown away well before the leaves, which could get in the way, are fully open (see Figure 39.2C).

Figure 39.2C ● The anthers of hazel flowers produce large amounts of pollen. Notice that the leaves are in tight buds.

● Insect pollination

Insects carry pollen from the anthers of one flower on to the stigmas of another flower. Insect-pollinated flowers, therefore, are adapted to attract insects to them. They are often large, brightly coloured and sweetly scented. They also produce a sweet liquid called nectar. Insects visit flowers to feed on pollen and nectar, attracted by the colour and scent. Marks on the petals called honey guides lead the insect to the nectar (see Figure 39.2D). As insects feed at the flower, their bodies become covered in pollen which is carried to the next flower the insect visits (see Figure 39.2E).

Figure 39.2D ● Hibiscus flowers showing strongly marked honey guides

Pollination need not always lead to fertilisation. Chemicals in the stigma stop pollen from a different species growing pollen tubes. In the case of self-pollination the pollen tube may not grow as fast, if at all, as that of pollen from another flower.

Figure 39.2E ● Pollen sticking to the body and legs of a honey bee on a dandelion. Pollen is carried by the bee in pollen sacs, one on each of the back legs: one pollen sac can be seen. The curled stigmas of the dandelion florets can also be seen.

The differences between wind-pollinated and insect-pollinated flowers are summarised in Table 39.2.

Table 39.2 ● Comparing insect-pollinated and wind-pollinated flowers

Part of flower	Insect-pollinated		Wind-pollinated	
Petals	Brightly coloured Usually scented Most have nectaries	} Large flowers which attract insects	If present, green or dull colour No scent No nectaries	} Small flowers
Anthers	Positioned where insects are likely to brush against them		Hang loosely on long thin filaments so that they shake easily in the wind	
Stigma	Positioned where insects can brush against them Sticky and flat or lobe-shaped		Long, branching and feathery to make a large area for catching wind-blown pollen grains	
Pollen	Small amounts produced Large grains Rough or sticky surface which catches on the insects' bodies		Large amounts produced Small, light grains with smooth surfaces – easily carried on the wind	

● *Self-pollination and cross-pollination*

The wild arum is a trap for small insects. Insects that feed on dung and rotting flesh are attracted by its horrible smell. They fall down the slippery tube-like bract to the nectar at the bottom, brushing pollen on to the stigmas of the carpels as they fall. The insects cannot escape because of the downward pointing hairs. The anthers ripen within hours of pollination taking place, the hairs wither and the insect crawls out. As they brush past the anthers they are covered with fresh pollen which is transferred to another arum when the insect is trapped again.

LOOK AT LINKS
What are the advantages of cross-pollination compared with self-pollination? It increases genetic variation
See Theme N, Topic 55.

Figure 39.2F ●
(a) Self-pollination. Pollen is transferred from the anthers to the stigma(s) of the same flower or the anthers of one flower to the stigma(s) of another flower on the same plant

(b) Cross-pollination. Pollen is transferred from the anthers of a flower on one plant to the stigma(s) of a flower on a different plant

Figure 39.2F shows the difference between self-pollination and cross-pollination and how self-pollination can take place. Different adaptations make cross-pollination more likely than self-pollination. For example, self-pollination is less likely to occur if anthers and stigmas on the same flower or different flowers on the same plant are ripe at different times. The two possibilities are that:

● The anthers ripen and pollen falls before the stigma is ripe.
● The stigma is ready to receive pollen before the anthers are ripe.

However, pollination would not occur at all if all of the anthers (or stigmas) in flowers of a particular species were ripe at a time when all of the stigmas (or anthers) were not. Success depends on some anthers and some stigmas in different flowers being ripe at the same time.

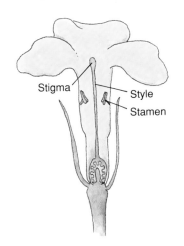

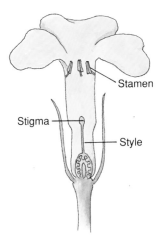

Figure 39.2G ●
(a) Half-flower of the pin-eye primrose with long style and stigma above stamens

(b) Half-flower of the thrum-eye primrose with short style and stigma below stamens

The primrose shown in Figure 39.2G illustrates another method for making cross-pollination more likely. When a bee pushes into a thrum-eyed flower in search of nectar, its head is dusted with pollen. If the next flower it visits is pin-eyed some pollen will brush onto the stigma. When a bee visits a pin-eyed flower, pollen sticks to its mouthparts at the place where it will touch the stigma of a thrum-eyed flower. Also, thrum-eyed flowers have large pollen grains and stigmas with small pits, pin-eyed flowers have small pollen grains and stigmas with large pits. Since large pollen grains fit best into large pits and small grains into small pits, cross-pollination is more likely.

The only way to make sure of cross-pollination is for a plant to have either all male or all female flowers. Few plants are like this but examples are the poplar, ash and willow trees.

Figure 39.2H ● Pollen grains on the surface of a stigma

Fertilisation

Pollination brings pollen grains to the stigma (see Figure 39.2H). A male sex cell is inside each pollen grain. *How does it reach the egg cell in the ovule inside the ovary?* The sugar coating the stigma's surface helps pollen grains to stick to it. If conditions are right pollen grains begin to grow pollen tubes (see Figure 39.2I). The pollen tube grows down through the style to the micropyle. The tube nucleus dies and the two male nuclei pass down the pollen tube and into the embryo sac. There, one nucleus fuses with the egg nucleus. This fusion of male and female nuclei is **fertilisation**. (See Figure 39.2J.)

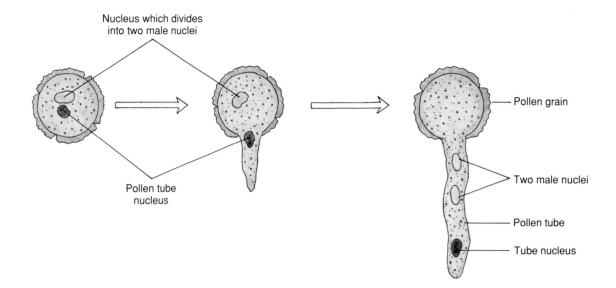

Figure 39.2I ● Growth of the pollen tube – notice the different nuclei

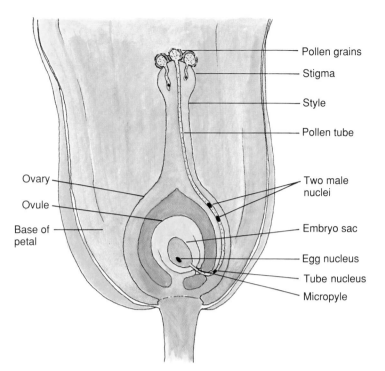

Figure 39.2J ● The male nucleus fertilises the egg nucleus

Although more than one pollen grain may grow a pollen tube, it is a male nucleus of the first pollen tube to reach the egg nucleus which fertilises it. In an ovary which has more than one ovule each egg nucleus fuses with only one male nucleus.

The fertilised egg divides and develops into the embryo which will become the new plant. The other male nucleus from the pollen tube fuses with two more nuclei in the embryo sac, developing into a special tissue which forms a food store for the embryo to use when it grows.

CHECKPOINT

❶ Look at Figure 39.2A

(a) Which parts are the male and female sex organs?
(b) The male sex organs produce millions of tiny pollen grains. What is inside each pollen grain?
(c) Which part of the female sex organ contains the ovule?
(d) What does the ovule contain?

❷ What is pollination?

❸ Pollination usually happens by wind or by insects. Choose one wind-pollinated flower and one insect-pollinated flower from Figures 39.2A–39.2D and study the pictures carefully. How is each flower you have chosen adapted for the way it is pollinated?

❹ Briefly describe different ways flowers are adapted to make cross-pollination more likely than self-pollination.

❺ Does pollination take place before or after fertilisation?

❻ What is the name of the tiny hole through which the pollen tube goes to the ovule?

❼ What happens when the pollen tube reaches the ovule?

39.3 ⛰ Plant reproduction: seeds and fruits

This section discusses seeds and fruits and the ways in which seeds are dispersed. As you read it think about:
- how seeds are formed,
- what fruits are,
- types of fruit,
- why dispersal of seeds is important,
- how fruits help the dispersal of seeds.

A seed is a fertilised ovule. The embryo plant and its store of food inside are covered by a tough seedcoat called the **testa**.

When the embryo is almost fully developed the tissues round it lose water, leaving the seed hard and dry. The seed can stay like this for a long time until conditions are right for it to grow.

Food may be stored in a thick, fleshy, wing-like structure called the **cotyledon**. Figure 39.3A shows that the seed of the broad bean has two cotyledons. Seeds like this are called **dicotyledonous** seeds. Figure 39.3A also shows which parts of the embryo will grow into which parts of a new plant.

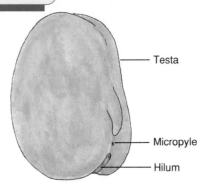

(a) The outside of the whole seed

Testa
Micropyle
Hilum

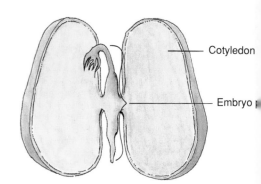

(b) The two cotyledons slightly separated showing the embryo plant between them

Cotyledon
Embryo

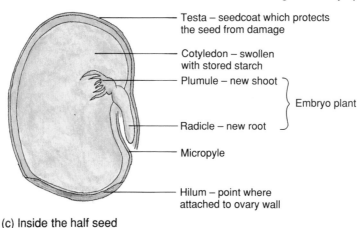

Testa – seedcoat which protects the seed from damage
Cotyledon – swollen with stored starch
Plumule – new shoot ⎫
Radicle – new root ⎬ Embryo plant
⎭
Micropyle
Hilum – point where attached to ovary wall

(c) Inside the half seed

Figure 39.3A ● The broad bean seed

Grasses produce seeds which store food in only one cotyledon. They are called **monocotyledonous** seeds.

After fertilisation it is usually the ovary which develops into the fruit. The wall of the ovary is then called the **pericarp**. As the fruit develops the pericarp becomes either dry and hard (examples are acorn, dandelion, wallflower, sycamore and poppy) or juicy and fleshy (examples are plum, tomato, blackberry, rosehip, honeysuckle and holly). Juicy fruits are more correctly called **succulent fruits** (see Figure 39.3B).

The fruit contains the seed or seeds. The number of seeds in a fruit depends on how many ovules there were in the ovary to begin with and how many were fertilised.

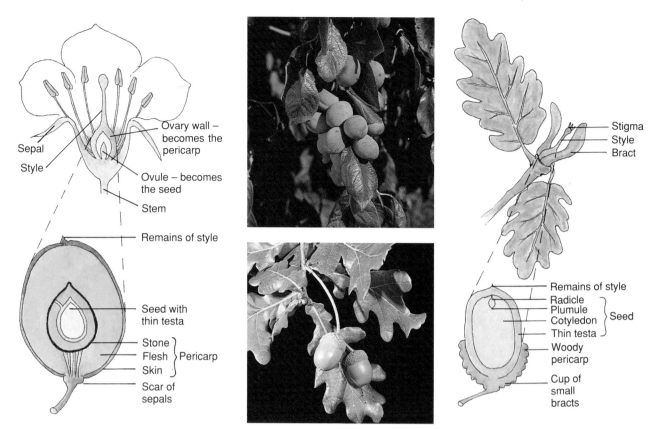

Figure 39.3B ● The parts of the flower that develop into parts of the fruit
(a) Plum – a succulent fruit with one seed inside the stone

(b) Acorn – a dry fruit

In some plants, parts of the flower other than the ovary develop into the fruit. These are called **false fruits**. In many false fruits the receptacle grows to form the fruit (see Figure 39.3C).

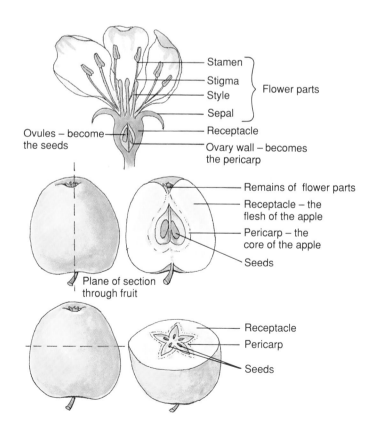

Figure 39.3C ● The apple is an example of a false fruit. The receptacle forms the fleshy fruit around the pericarp which contains the seeds.

Parachutes carry the
fruits on the wind

Dandelion

Wings enable the fruits
to float in the wind

Sycamore

Ash

Elm

Thistle

Poppy

The fruit sways in the wind and
its seeds are shaken out through
holes in the sides like pepper
from a pepper pot

Dispersal of fruits and seeds

When a fruit is ripe it breaks away from the parent plant and its seeds are scattered. The scattering is called **dispersal**. It is important that seeds are dispersed far and wide so that the plants which grow from them will not be overcrowded.

The two main ways of dispersal are by wind and by animals. The pericarps of different fruits develop in different ways for different methods of dispersal (see Figure 39.3D).

Figure 39.3D ● Methods of fruit and seed dispersal
(a) Wind-dispersed fruits and seeds. 'Parachute', 'wing' and 'pepper-pot' mechanisms all help dispersal. The photograph shows the fruits of Old Man's Beard – the hairs make a large surface area which catches the wind

Hooks on the fruit wall
cling to the bodies of
passing animals

Burdock

Cleavers
(goosegrass)

Hazelnut

Horse chestnut

Gooseberry

Bright colours attract birds and other animals to eat these fruits. The tough testa protects the seed from the digestive juices in the animals' intestine. Eventually the seeds pass out of the animal in the faeces

Rosehip

(b) Animal-dispersed fruits and seeds. Hooks and bright colours aid dispersal. Hazelnuts and horse chestnuts are often stored by squirrels and then forgotten. The photographs show the brightly coloured fruits of the honeysuckle and the wild rose.

The fruit wall of some plants dries and splits open. As it does so the seeds are thrown out. Examples of fruits that disperse seeds in this way are shown in Figure 39.3E. A few fruits are dispersed by water currents. Examples are the waterlily and the coconut (see Figure 39.3F).

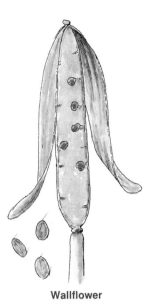

Wallflower

Honesty

Figure 39.3E ● Self-dispersal. The fruit dries and splits and the seeds fall out. The photograph shows the fruit of broom, split open with some of the seeds still in place.

Figure 39.3F ● Coconuts float and are dispersed by water currents. The outer fibres of the coconuts pictured have been removed. The coconut is thought to have come originally from South America and the water currents in the Pacific Ocean could have dispersed the coconut from South America to the South Sea Islands.

CHECKPOINT

❶ Which part of the flower usually develops into the fruit?

❷ What is the fruit wall called?

❸ Describe which parts of the flower have developed into the fruits illustrated in Figures 39.3B and 39.3C.

❹ Why is dispersal of seeds important?

39.4 ● Asexual reproduction in plants

This section deals with asexual reproduction in flowering plants. As you read it think about:
- vegetative parts of flowering plants,
- organs of asexual reproduction and organs which store food,
- cuttings and grafting.

RESOURCE
–ACTIVITY–
PACK

Many different plants can reproduce asexually. The root, leaf or more often the stem may grow into new plants. These parts are called **vegetative parts** and asexual reproduction in flowering plants is sometimes called **vegetative reproduction**. Since new plants come from one parent plant, they are genetically the same.

The strawberry plant shown in Figure 39.4A reproduces asexually by stems called runners which grow horizontally on the surface of the soil.

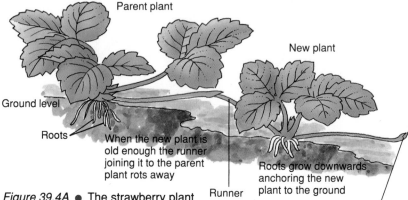

Parent plant

New plant

Ground level

Roots

When the new plant is old enough the runner joining it to the parent plant rots away

Runner

Roots grow downwards anchoring the new plant to the ground

Terminal bud – produces shoots which grow upwards

Figure 39.4A ● The strawberry plant

Many plants reproduce vegetatively underground. Figure 39.4B shows the thick, fleshy iris rhizome which is an example of a stem that grows horizontally underground. It branches at intervals from buds growing next to small leaves called scale leaves (leaves without chlorophyll). Because of the branching growth and the eventual dying of the old part of the rhizome, iris plants seem to move their position from year to year in the soil.

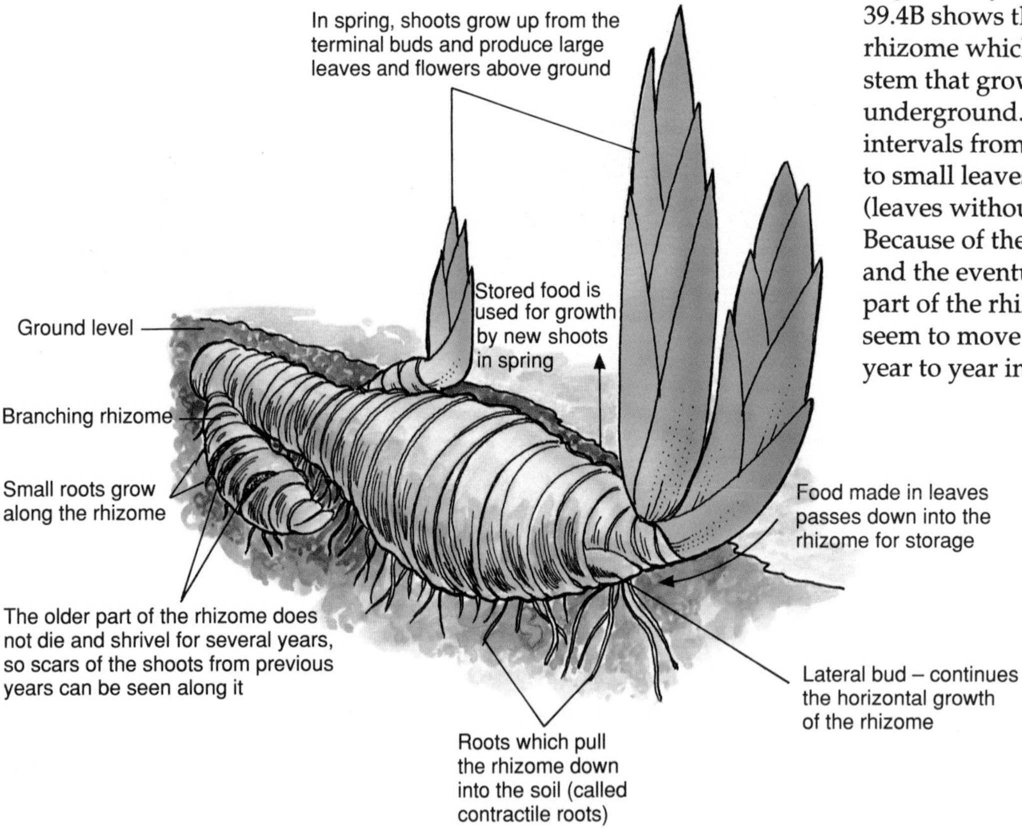

In spring, shoots grow up from the terminal buds and produce large leaves and flowers above ground

Stored food is used for growth by new shoots in spring

Ground level

Branching rhizome

Small roots grow along the rhizome

The older part of the rhizome does not die and shrivel for several years, so scars of the shoots from previous years can be seen along it

Food made in leaves passes down into the rhizome for storage

Lateral bud – continues the horizontal growth of the rhizome

Roots which pull the rhizome down into the soil (called contractile roots)

Figure 39.4B ● The thick, fleshy iris rhizome grows and branches horizontally underground. The arrows show the movement of stored food. *In which directions is the rhizome growing underground?*

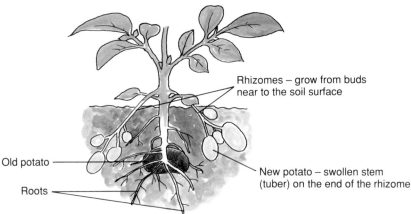

Rhizomes – grow from buds near to the soil surface

Old potato

Roots

New potato – swollen stem (tuber) on the end of the rhizome

Figure 39.4C shows the potato plant. The potato is a swelling of stored food at the end of a rhizome. It is called a stem tuber. Leaves on shoots which grow above ground make starch which passes down the stem into the rhizomes. The old tuber rots away at the end of the growing season.

(a) Rhizomes grow from the buds nearest to the soil's surface. 'New' potatoes form at their tips

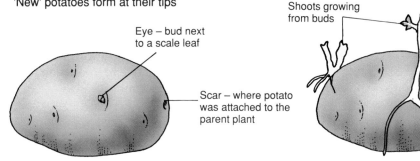

Eye – bud next to a scale leaf

Scar – where potato was attached to the parent plant

Shoots growing from buds

Roots

(b) A resting potato in winter showing 'eyes' which are buds next to scale leaves

Figure 39.4C ● The potato

(c) A sprouting potato in spring showing the growth of new shoots and roots from the 'eyes'

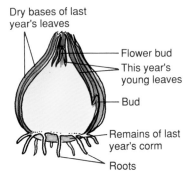

Dry bases of last year's leaves

Flower bud

This year's young leaves

Bud

Remains of last year's corm

Roots

(a) Resting corm, showing the parts which will grow next season

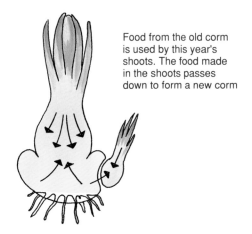

Food from the old corm is used by this year's shoots. The food made in the shoots passes down to form a new corm

(b) Growing leaves and flowers use up food stored in the old corm and a new corm begins to form on top of it (arrows show movement of stored food)

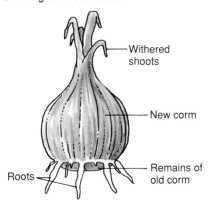

Withered shoots

New corm

Roots

Remains of old corm

(c) New corm which stores food for the next year – the new corn separates from the remains of the old corn at the end of the growing season

Figure 39.4D ● The crocus corm

A corm is a short, swollen, underground stem and a bulb is a large underground bud. At the end of a growing season the leaves make food which is stored in the corm or bulb underground until it is used the next year for the growth of new leaves and flowers. Daughter corms or bulbs develop from buds on the side of the parent organ and when they are large enough they break off and become independent plants. (See Figure 39.4D.)

167

Bulbs, corms, tubers and most rhizomes are not only organs of asexual reproduction but also organs which store food. They fill up with starch during the summer when the plants which have grown from them are in leaf and making food by photosynthesis. In the autumn the plants die down but the organs underground, full of stored food, survive the winter and produce new plants the following year. Because these organs asexually reproduce new plants year after year they are called **perennials**.

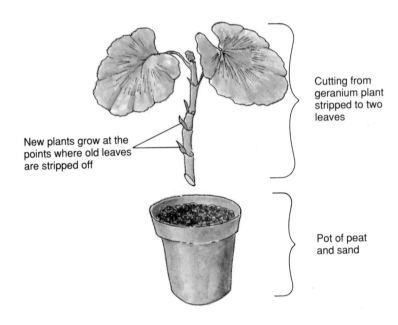

Cutting from geranium plant stripped to two leaves

New plants grow at the points where old leaves are stripped off

Pot of peat and sand

Figure 39.4E ● A cutting from a geranium plant

Artificial vegetative reproduction

Gardeners and farmers need to produce fresh stocks of plants with desirable characteristics like disease-resistance, colour of fruit or shape of flower. They exploit vegetative reproduction to achieve these aims.

● Cuttings

Figure 39.4E shows a geranium cutting. Short pieces of stem are cut just below the point where a leaf joins the stem. Most of the leaves are stripped from the stem. New shoots grow at the points where the old leaves are stripped off.

● Grafting

Grafting is often used for reproducing roses and fruit trees. A twig is cut from the tree to be reproduced and replaced in a slit in the stem of an already well-rooted tree so that the cut surfaces are brought together. The tissues of the twig and the tree join together and the graft grows on the rooted tree.

Budding is another type of grafting. A bud is used instead of a twig. Several buds can be grown on one root stock, each growing into an individual plant.

The plants produced by these methods are the same genetically as the parents from which they are taken. This means that the desirable qualities of the parent are preserved in the offspring, guaranteeing plant quality from one generation to the next.

CHECKPOINT

❶ What are the vegetative parts of flowering plants?

❷ Briefly compare the similarities and differences between a runner and a rhizome.

❸ What is a tuber?

❹ Look at Figure 39.4D. Describe the movement of food in a corm from the beginning of the growing season to the end.

39.5 Human reproduction

FIRST THOUGHTS

This section begins by asking you to explore the development of a sexual relationship. This puts in context the facts on human reproduction.

Getting to know you

Getting to know you charts the relationships between two imaginary people. Look at the different stages of their developing relationship.

Who is this person?
• Handsome • Pretty
What makes you notice someone of the opposite sex?

Attraction
• Caring • Easy to talk to
• Similar interests and opinions
Why do you want to see more of the other person?

Getting to know you
• You want to touch and kiss
• Are you nervous?
Why do you want to get closer to the other person?

Loving you
• Sharing your life with someone else
• Having children is a possibility
Why do you want to commit yourself to the other person?

• What points do you think are important at each stage of the developing relationship?
• Do you agree with the order of the different stages of *Getting to know you*?
How would you describe each stage?
• What do you think the role of love is in a relationship?
• How do you think the responsibility of children should be shared between partners?

Sexual feelings for someone of the opposite sex are called heterosexuality. Homosexuality is having sexual feeling for someone of your own sex. Homosexual feelings are not uncommon in adolescents who, as a result, often feel guilty and different from other people. Talking about homosexual feelings to parents, friends or a counsellor can help to keep problems in proportion. What is important about relationships is that they should be based on trust, love and understanding of one another.

The human reproductive system

The visible parts of the reproductive system are called the **genitalia**. A man's genitalia consist of the **penis** and the **testes** which are contained in a bag-like scrotum which hangs down between the legs. This position protects the testes from injury. It also keeps them about 3 °C lower than body temperature. This is important because sperms only develop properly inside the testes in these slightly cooler conditions. The reproductive system of a man is illustrated in Figure 39.5A.

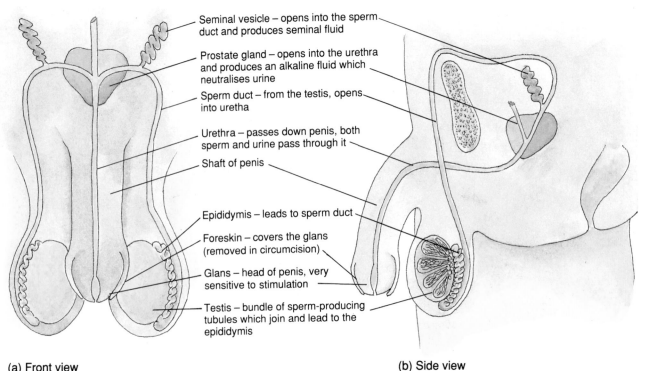

Seminal vesicle – opens into the sperm duct and produces seminal fluid

Prostate gland – opens into the urethra and produces an alkaline fluid which neutralises urine

Sperm duct – from the testis, opens into uretha

Urethra – passes down penis, both sperm and urine pass through it

Shaft of penis

Epididymis – leads to sperm duct

Foreskin – covers the glans (removed in circumcision)

Glans – head of penis, very sensitive to stimulation

Testis – bundle of sperm-producing tubules which join and lead to the epididymis

(a) Front view

(b) Side view

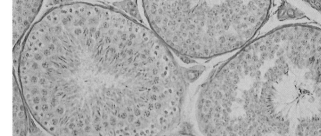

(c) Cross section through a sperm-producing tubule showing sperms clustered inside. Stretched out end-to-end the tubules inside each testis are more than 500 m long. (x200)

Figure 39.5A ● The male reproductive system

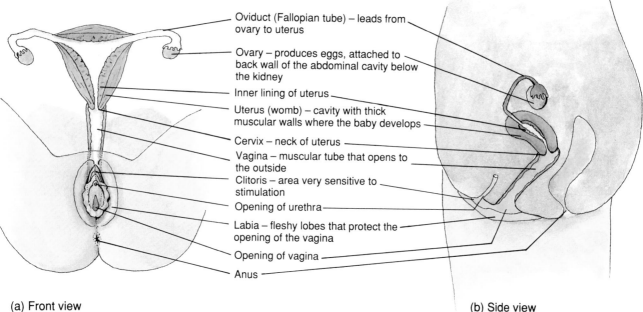

Oviduct (Fallopian tube) – leads from ovary to uterus

Ovary – produces eggs, attached to back wall of the abdominal cavity below the kidney

Inner lining of uterus

Uterus (womb) – cavity with thick muscular walls where the baby develops

Cervix – neck of uterus

Vagina – muscular tube that opens to the outside

Clitoris – area very sensitive to stimulation

Opening of urethra

Labia – fleshy lobes that protect the opening of the vagina

Opening of vagina

Anus

(a) Front view

(b) Side view

(c) Section through an ovary showing an egg surrounded by the cells which form the follicle (x200). Each follicle contains one egg. At birth each ovary contains approximately 300 000 follicles. Of these, approximately 300 complete their development in a woman's lifetime.

Figure 39.5B ● The female reproductive system

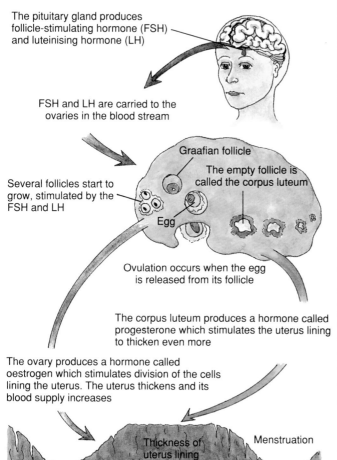

The pituitary gland produces follicle-stimulating hormone (FSH) and luteinising hormone (LH)

FSH and LH are carried to the ovaries in the blood stream

Several follicles start to grow, stimulated by the FSH and LH

Graafian follicle

The empty follicle is called the corpus luteum

Egg

Ovulation occurs when the egg is released from its follicle

The corpus luteum produces a hormone called progesterone which stimulates the uterus lining to thicken even more

The ovary produces a hormone called oestrogen which stimulates division of the cells lining the uterus. The uterus thickens and its blood supply increases

Thickness of uterus lining   Menstruation

0   14   28

Days

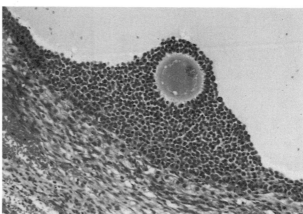

The reproductive system of a woman is illustrated in Figure 39.5B. The genitalia cover and protect the opening to the rest of the reproductive system inside her body.

Menstrual cycle

The human female usually produces one mature egg each month from the onset of puberty (age 11–14 years) to the beginning of the menopause (age about 45 years). This monthly cycle is called the **menstrual cycle** (from the Latin *mensis* meaning month). Egg production becomes more and more irregular during the menopause and stops altogether usually by about the age of 50. Figure 39.5C shows how the different events of the menstrual cycle fit together.

Figure 39.5C ● The menstrual cycle. A sharp increase in the level of luteinising hormone causes ovulation. The intervals of time for each stage may vary depending on the individual. For example, ovulation may occur earlier or later in the cycle than shown.

LOOK AT LINKS
for **hormones**
See Theme J, Topic 40.3.

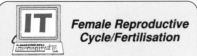

**Female Reproductive
Cycle/Fertilisation**

The disk shows the stages in the
menstrual cycle. You can also
investigate the process of
fertilisation and implantation.

The changes occuring during the menstrual cycle prepare the uterus to receive an egg if it is fertilised. If the egg is not fertilised, the production of the **hormones** oestrogen and progesterone tails off and the thick lining of the uterus begins to break down as Figure 39.5C shows. The release of blood and tissue through the vagina is called menstruation and is what is meant by 'having a period'. It lasts for several days. A new menstrual cycle then begins.

Blood released during a period can be absorbed by a sanitary towel, which a woman wears as a lining to her underwear, or as an alternative she can put a tampon made of cotton wool in her vagina (see Figure 39.5D).

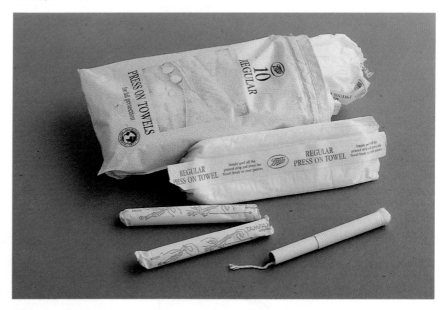

Figure 39.5D ● Hygiene during a period. Sanitary towels come in different thicknesses. The woman can choose which type suits her best depending on how much blood and tissue is released during her period. The tampon is removed from the vagina by its thread.

The menstrual cycle can affect a woman's emotions. How a woman feels depends on the individual. Some have few problems but others feel irritable and below their best just before and during menstruation.

How do sperms meet eggs?

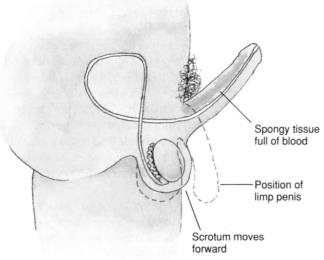

Spongy tissue
full of blood

Position of
limp penis

Scrotum moves
forward

Figure 39.5E ● An erection

An erect penis is a sign that a man is sexually excited. The penis stiffens and lengthens as blood fills the spongy tissue of the shaft (see Figure 39.5E). Signs of sexual excitement in women are less obvious. The labia fill with blood and swell a little. All of these changes in a man and woman help to prepare them for sexual intercourse.

The swollen labia help to guide the erect penis into the vagina. The muscles of the vagina wall relax, helping entry. Fluid produced by the vaginal wall lubricates the

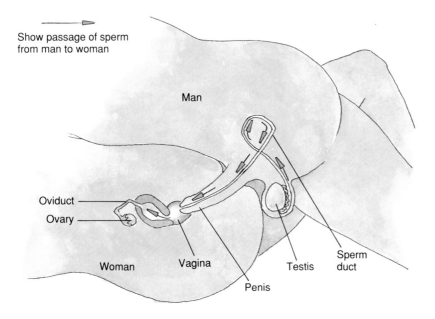

Show passage of sperm from man to woman

Figure 39.5F ● Sexual intercourse

movements of the penis during sexual intercourse. These movements stimulate the muscles in the scrotum and around the epididymis and sperm ducts to contract, pushing sperm from the testes along the sperm ducts to the urethra. During this journey the sperm mix with fluids from the seminal vesicles and prostate gland. These fluids and the sperm form semen. Continuing stimulation results in ejaculation which is a series of contractions that propel semen through the urethra into the vagina (see Figure 39.5F).

Semen is white and sticky. It contains sugars which are an energy source for the sperms as they swim up through the vagina and uterus to the oviducts.

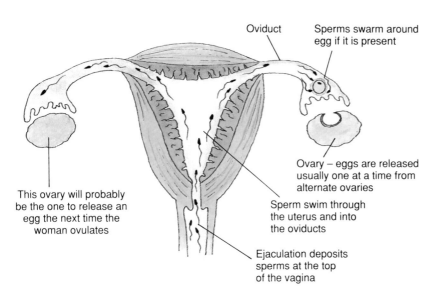

Figure 39.5G ● How sperms meet an egg. Sperms reach the top of the oviduct approximately 40 minutes after ejaculation

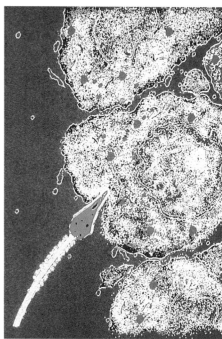

Figure 39.5H ● One sperm penetrates the membrane surrounding an egg

During ejaculation the man experiences a pleasant feeling called an orgasm. The woman may experience an orgasm as well. The muscles of the vagina gently relax and contract around the penis. The woman's orgasm is usually caused by gentle pressure stimulating the clitoris.

We have seen that ovulation releases an egg from the ovary into the opening of the oviduct (see Figure 39.5C). If a sperm is to meet an egg it must make its way from the vagina, through the uterus to the oviduct. Figure 39.5G shows the distance a sperm must travel. The journey is not an easy one. Of the hundreds of millions of sperm deposited in the vagina only a million or so make it through the cervix into the uterus. Of these, only a few thousand arrive at the end of the opening of the oviduct. Here they swarm around the egg if one is present (see Figure 39.5H).

Fertilisation and development of the embryo

Although thousands of sperms may reach an egg only one enters it. The tail of the successful sperm is left outside as the head travels through the cytoplasm of the egg to the nucleus. Fertilisation occurs when the sperm nucleus fuses with the egg nucleus to form a zygote (see Figure 39.5I). This is the moment of conception and the woman is now pregnant.

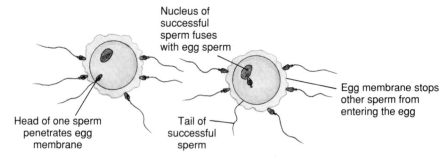

Figure 39.5I ● Fertilisation of the egg

Figure 39.5J shows what happens next. The zygote travels down the oviduct, dividing by mitosis as it goes, forming a ball of cells. The journey may take up to seven days. By the time the ball of cells reaches the uterus it has formed an **embryo**. Remember that at this stage of the menstrual cycle (see Figure 39.5C) the wall of the uterus has a thick lining. The embryo sinks into it – a process called implantation.

Finger-like extensions called villi project from the embryo into the lining of the uterus. The surfaces firmly bind together forming a region called the placenta. In the next few weeks the embryo develops into a foetus which is attached to the placenta by the umbilical cord. An artery and a vein run through the umbilical cord and connect the foetus' blood system to the placenta. Figure 39.5K shows that the foetus' blood system is not directly connected to the blood system of the mother. The exchange of oxygen, food and wastes between mother and foetus depends on diffusion across the thin wall of the placenta.

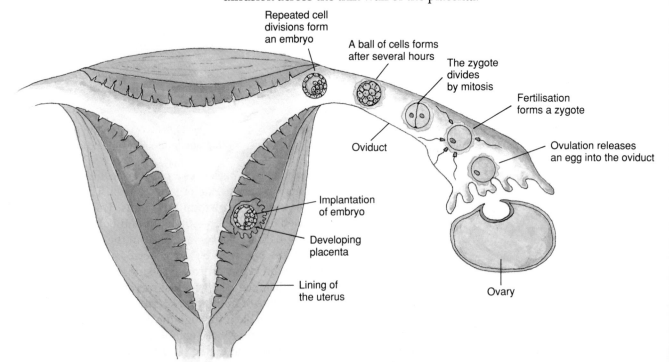

Figure 39.5J ● The stages from ovulation to implantation

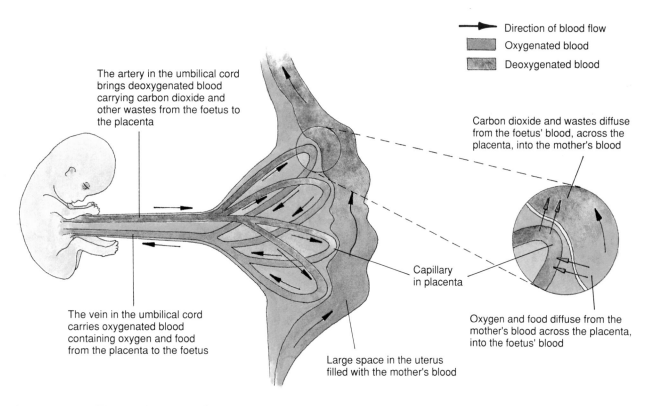

Figure 39.5K ● The blood systems of mother and foetus exchange material by diffusion across the placenta

The time taken for the foetus to develop from conception into a baby is called the **gestation period**. It usually lasts nine months in humans. Figure 39.5L shows the growth and development of the foetus from the early stages of pregnancy to just before the time the baby is due to be born.

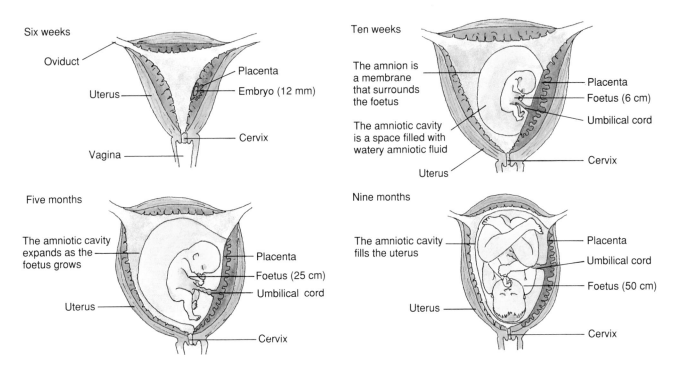

Figure 39.5L ● Growth and development of the foetus in the uterus. The amniotic fluid in the amniotic cavity cushions the baby from bumps as the mother moves

Figure 39.5M ● Chartered physiotherapist teaching a group of antenatal mothers

Birth

The mothers pictured in Figure 39.5M are heavily pregnant. It will not be long before they give birth to their babies. They are visiting an antenatal clinic where a doctor will check that all is well with each mother and her baby. The mothers also receive advice on how best to prepare for the baby's birth.

Figure 39.5N shows childbirth in progress. Safely delivered, the baby starts to breathe, sometimes helped by a tap on the back which causes a surprised intake of breath. Now that the baby can breathe for itself, the placenta and umbilical cord are no longer needed. The placenta comes away from the uterus wall and passes out through the vagina as the afterbirth. The umbilical cord is clamped near to where it joins the baby and is cut. This does not hurt the baby because there are no nerves in the cord. The stump that remains becomes the baby's navel.

Babies born before the ninth month of pregnancy are described as premature. They have a good chance of survival providing they are not too small and weak. Premature babies are often kept in incubators. An incubator is a cabinet with a controlled environment that keeps the baby warm and provides extra oxygen to help with breathing. The baby stays in the incubator until he or she is strong enough to survive independently.

In humans, pregnancy usually results in the birth of only one baby. However, sometimes two babies are born one after the other. They are called twins and Figure 39.5O shows how this arises. The twins develop together in the uterus, each with its own placenta and umbilical cord.

Occasionally ovulation releases three or more eggs into the uterus at the same time, especially if the woman has been given a fertility drug to help her to become pregnant. These multiple pregnancies can be difficult because of the space taken up in the uterus by the growing foetuses. Very often the mother gives birth early at around the seventh month and some of the babies may die.

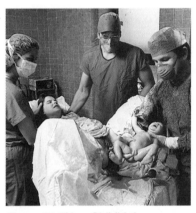

Figure 39.5N ● Childbirth

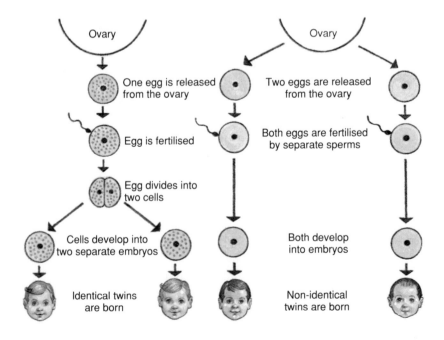

Figure 39.5O ●
(a) Identical twins are alike because they each have the same genes

(b) Non-identical or fraternal twins are different from one another because they do not have the same genes

Gestation periods are:
- Mouse – 18 days
- Cat – 2 months
- Horse – 11 months
- Elephant – 20 months

Usually the larger the animal, the longer the gestation period.

Animal mothers very often eat the afterbirth because the smell of blood might attract hungry predators. The afterbirth contains a lot of iron compounds and other nutritious substances.

Looking after baby

A newborn baby will naturally suck at the nipple of the mother's breast. Figure 39.5P shows that glands (called mammary glands) inside the breast secrete milk. This happens soon after birth and is called lactation. Mother's milk is perfect food for the baby. It contains all the necessary nutrients as well as the mother's antibodies which help to protect the baby from diseases during the first few months of life. Sometimes a mother does not produce enough milk, so the baby has to be bottle-fed (see Figure 39.5Q).

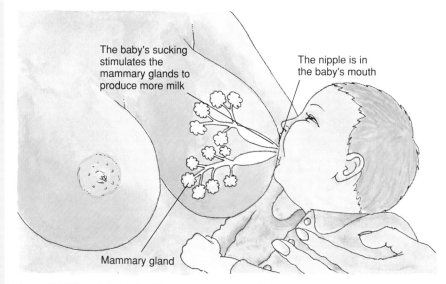

The baby's sucking stimulates the mammary glands to produce more milk

The nipple is in the baby's mouth

Mammary gland

Figure 39.5P ● A baby feeding from the mother's breast

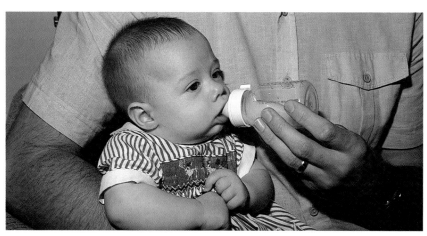

Figure 39.5Q ● Bottle feeding

A newborn baby cannot take in solid food because he or she has no teeth to chew it with. Also the digestive system is unable to deal with solid food. After about six months the first teeth appear and solid food can now be added to the baby's diet. At this stage the baby's milk intake decreases. **Weaning** is the word used to describe the change from a diet of milk to one of solid food.

Looking after a baby is time-consuming and exhausting. Apart from feeding, the baby must be kept clean and warm. It is also very important that the emotional needs of the baby are cared for. Keeping the baby interested, stimulated and happy is just as important as looking after the baby's physical needs.

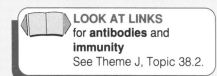
LOOK AT LINKS
for **antibodies** and **immunity**
See Theme J, Topic 38.2.

LOOK AT LINKS
for **teeth**
See Theme F, Topic 25.4.

Preventing pregnancy

Whether to have children or not is a choice open to everyone involved in sexual relationships. If a couple want to have sexual intercourse but do not want to have children they must use some form of contraception to prevent pregnancy. Using methods of contraception enables people to choose when they want children and how many children they want. This choice is called **family planning** or **birth control**.

To prevent pregnancy, the method of contraception must either:
* stop sperm from reaching the egg,
* stop eggs from being produced,
* or stop the fertilised egg from developing in the uterus.

Six methods of contraception are described below and illustrated in Figure 39.5R.

* **Intrauterine devices (IUDs)**. IUDs are fitted inside the uterus by a doctor. The IUD touches the inner wall of the uterus and prevents implantation of the embryo. The IUD can be removed by a doctor by pulling on the strings attached to it which pass through the cervix. IUDs are usually only used by women who have already had a child. (See Figure 39.5R(a)).

* **Diaphragms**. The diaphragm or cap is a dome-shaped device which fits over the cervix. They come in different sizes and a woman must be taught to insert the diaphragm by her doctor or at a family planning clinic. A diaphragm can be inserted immediately before intercourse but must remain in place for sometime after intercourse. Diaphragms offer more protection when used with a spermicide. (See Figure 39.5R(b)).

* **Spermicides**. Spermicidal creams kill sperms. A woman uses an applicator to put spermicide inside her vagina just before intercourse. Spermicides are not very effective on their own and are more often used as 'back-up' for other methods. (See Figure 39.5R(c)).

* **Sheaths (condoms)**. The condom is a thin sheath which the man rolls on to his erect penis before intercourse. The penis must be removed from the woman's vagina immediately after ejaculation to avoid any spillage of sperm. (See Figure 39.5R(d)).

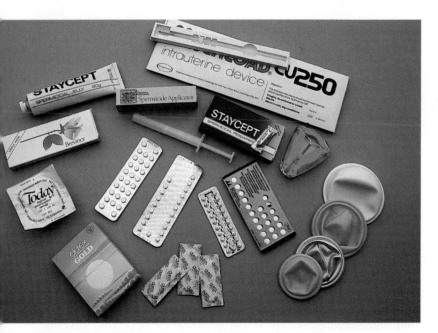

Figure 39.5R ● Methods of contraception

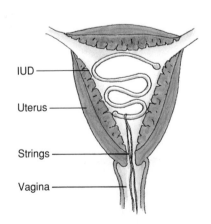

(a) Intrauterine device

LOOK AT LINKS
for **hormones**
See Theme J, Topic 40.3.

Contraception Update

The female condom is a thin sheath which lines the vagina. It is closed at one end and open at the other. A ring at the closed end helps the woman to insert the condom before sexual intercourse. A ring at the open end remains outside the body, pushed flat against the labia. The penis is guided into the sheath and moves inside the lining during intercourse. When the penis is removed after ejaculation; the ring at the open end is twisted to make sure no sperm is spilt, and the sheath gently pulled from the vagina.

Injected contraceptives contain the hormone progesterone. Once injected into the arm, the hormone is slowly released into the body over the next two or three months. Like the mini-pill (a make of pill that contains only progesterone), it stops the ovaries from producing eggs. Injected contraceptives are useful for women who find it difficult to take the pill or experience problems with other methods of contraception.

- **The pill**. The contraceptive pill contains one or both of the hormones oestrogen and progesterone. The concentration of the hormones stops the ovaries from producing eggs. The woman takes a pill every day for 21 days of her menstrual cycle. When she stops taking the pill menstruation occurs. The woman begins taking the pill again on day one of her next menstrual cycle. If the woman forgets to take a pill on one day then the protection is not complete and another form of contraception must be used until the woman's next menstrual cycle begins.

   Another type of pill is the morning-after pill. It delivers a large dose of hormones which prevents implantation of the embryo. The morning-after pill must be taken within three days of intercourse to be effective.

- **Sterilisation**. Both men and women can be sterilised. Sterilisation involves a minor operation. In a man, the sperm ducts are tied off and cut by the surgeon. The man can still ejaculate as the ducts are cut below the seminal vesicles which produce seminal fluid, but his semen will not contain any sperms. In a woman, the oviducts are tied off and cut. This prevents the sperm from reaching the egg. Although some sterilisation operations can be reversed, this is not usually the case so a man or woman who is sterilised has to be very sure that he or she does not want any more children. (See Figure 39.5R(e)).

All the methods of contraception described above, and shown in Figure 39.5R depend on surgery, chemicals or a mechanical device to be effective. The rhythm method does not use any of these aids but depends on the woman (and possibly her partner) understanding how her menstrual cycle works. Look at Figure 39.5C once more and calculate at what time in the menstrual cycle intercourse is most likely to lead to pregnancy. *Why is pregnancy not possible at other times – the so-called safe period?*

Figure 39.5S (overleaf) shows the changes in a woman's body temperature during her menstrual cycle. Notice the slight increase in body temperature when she ovulates. *How do you think the woman can use the information to help her prevent pregnancy?*

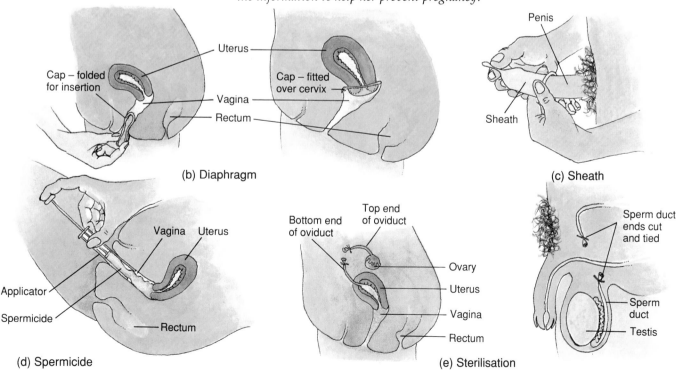

(b) Diaphragm

(c) Sheath

(d) Spermicide

(e) Sterilisation

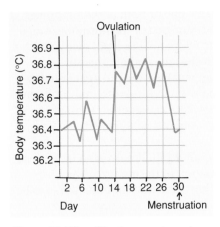

Figure 39.5S ● The temperature rise at ovulation is about 0.5 °C

Unfortunately the menstrual cycle is not always predictable. The cycle can vary a good deal, especially in teenagers, which makes it difficult to predict whether or not it is safe to have intercourse. However, the rhythm method is a natural form of contraception and it is used mostly by people whose religion does not allow other methods.

Table 39.3 compares the reliability of different methods of contraception. However you should not think that it is a matter of just looking down the list, choosing one that suits best and having intercourse when you please and with whom you please. A close physical relationship is only part of the relationship you have with a member of the opposite sex. It means that you must be old enough to take responsibility not only for your own actions and feelings but also for your partner's actions and feelings as well. Look back at *Getting to know you* on page 169 and think again about your answers to the questions now that you have read most of this section. *Have your opinions changed?*

Table 39.3 ● The reliability of contraceptive methods

Method	Percentage of pregnancies	How reliable is the method?
No method	54	Very unreliable
Rhythm method	17	Unreliable without expert help
Diaphragm with spermicide	12	Quite reliable when fitted well
Sheath	8	Quite reliable if used properly
IUDs	2	Reliable
The pill	0	Very reliable

Sexually transmitted diseases

Sexually transmitted diseases (sometimes called venereal diseases or VD) are a group of diseases which can pass from person to person during sexual activity. Syphilis and gonorrhea are both sexually transmitted.

Syphilis is caused by the bacterium *Treponema pallidum*. The bacterium can live for only a short time outside the body and is very quickly killed by heat, lack of water and antiseptics. The bacterium that causes gonorrhea is quickly killed in similar fashion. This is why it is very

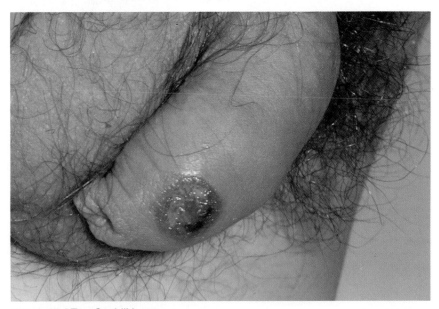

Figure 39.5T ● Syphilitic sore

Table 39.4 ● Syphilis and gonorrhea in men and women

Syphilis		Gonorrhea	
Men	Women	Men	Women
Sores appear on the genitals weeks or sometimes months after sexual intercourse		Becomes painful to pass urine; yellow discharge from penis	Many women show no symptoms but it may become painful to pass urine and there may be a yellow discharge from the vagina
Symptoms disappear		Symptoms disappear	
If syphilis is not treated, years later it can cause blindness, heart trouble, insanity and eventually leads to death	Same effects as in men In addition, babies can be badly affected in the uterus	In the long term, sperm ducts become blocked leading to sterility. May also lead to bladder problems	Oviducts become blocked resulting in sterility. Babies affected in the uterus may be born blind

difficult to pick up syphilis and gonorrhea other than by the intimate contact between two people having sex. Figure 39.5T shows a syphilitic sore and Table 39.4 summarises the symptoms of the two diseases in men and women.

Other diseases that may be passed from person to person by sexual activity include:

- Herpes – which is caused by a virus similar to the kinds that cause cold sores and chicken pox. Blisters appear, usually on the glans of the penis and inside the vagina. Unfortunately, once infected a person remains infected for life and the blisters often recur.
- AIDS – which is caused by the human immunodeficiency virus (HIV).

LOOK AT LINKS
for **AIDS**
See Theme J, Topic 38.2.

These diseases are not always caught through having sex with an infected person. AIDS, for example, is spread when a person's blood infected with HIV mixes with someone else's blood. This is how many of the people suffering from haemophilia have become infected with HIV. They picked up the virus from the blood clotting agent factor VIII which had been donated by HIV-infected people. Now blood, and blood products like factor VIII are screened for HIV before being given to patients.

Avoiding sexually transmitted diseases means avoiding sexual intercourse with a person who is infected. *How can you tell if someone has a sexually transmitted disease?* The short answer is, you cannot, but the chances of becoming infected are considerably reduced if you only have sex within the context of a stable relationship and do not have a lot of sexual partners.

People who are worried that they have been infected with a sexually transmitted disease can go to a special clinic (most large hospitals have one) where they are examined and if necessary treated. Antibiotic drugs like penicillin and streptomycin are used to treat syphilis and gonorrhea. They will cure the disease providing treatment is started early enough. Nobody need know that treatment has been given; the hospital keeps the visit to the special clinic confidential.

Viral diseases like herpes cannot be cured with antibiotics. AIDS is a special problem for which there is no known cure at present. There are drugs that slow down the progress of HIV and scientists world-wide are trying to find new drugs and vaccines to fight the disease.

1 Briefly describe the route taken by ejaculated sperm from where they are produced to the oviduct of the woman.

2 The uterus can be the most powerful muscle in the body. Why does it need to be so powerful?

3 (a) A diaphragm is fitted over the cervix: how does it work as a contraceptive?
(b) How do condoms (or sheaths) work as contraceptives?

4 Complete the following paragraph using the words below. Each word may be used once, more than once or not at all.

fertilisation vagina testes weeks semen bladder urethra
sperm duct seven sperm seminal cervix penis uterus sexual
ovaries prostate oviduct

An egg is released by one of the two _____ about every four
_____ . It passes into the _____ . It may take up to _____
days to reach the _____ . If _____ is to take place the egg must
be met by _____ before, or just after, it reaches the _____ .
Sperm are produced in the tubules of the _____ in vast quantities.
Ejaculation forces the sperm from the epididymis, into the _____ . The
_____ vesicle, and _____ gland add their secretions to the
sperm, forming _____ . This leaves the body through the urethra
running through the _____ .

5 Name three substances which show a net movement into foetal blood across the placenta, and three substances that show a net movement out of the foetal blood across the placenta.

6 Why is birth a considerable shock to the baby?

7 Complete the following paragraph using the words provided below. Each word may be used once, more than once or not at all.

cervix uterus placenta oxygen oviducts oxygenated wastes
amniotic vagina muscles implants

Once fertilisation has occurred, normally in one of the _____ the
embryo grows, moves into the uterus and _____ into its wall. The
_____ develops which provides a surface for the exchange of materials
with the mother's blood. _____ and food cross into the foetal blood,
whereas carbon dioxide and other _____ enter the mother's circulation.
The developing foetus is surrounded and protected by the _____ fluid.
At birth the _____ dilates, and powerful contractions of the
_____ of the uterus push the baby out through the _____ .

39.6 **Growth and development**

FIRST
THOUGHTS

The cotyledons of plants like the broad bean stay below ground during germination. During germination of plants like the French bean the cotyledons are carried above ground by the developing shoot.

How plants grow

Trees and other living things grow as the number of cells making up the body increases. Growth can be measured as an increase in an organism's mass, length or number of cells and the data can be represented as a growth curve. Figure 39.6A shows the growth curve of a broad bean seed as the embryo inside it develops into a new plant.

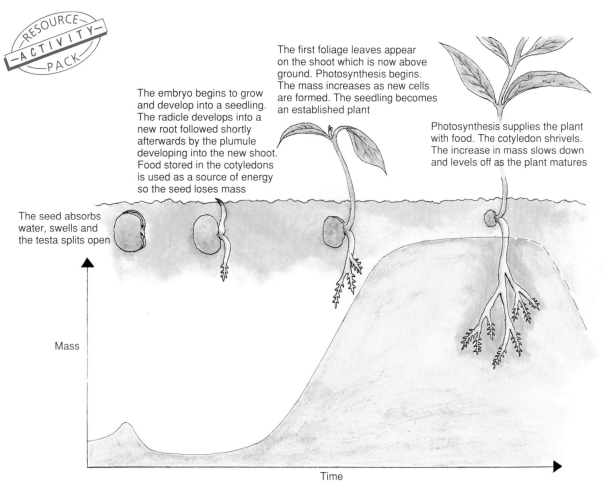

The embryo begins to grow and develop into a seedling. The radicle develops into a new root followed shortly afterwards by the plumule developing into the new shoot. Food stored in the cotyledons is used as a source of energy so the seed loses mass

The first foliage leaves appear on the shoot which is now above ground. Photosynthesis begins. The mass increases as new cells are formed. The seedling becomes an established plant

Photosynthesis supplies the plant with food. The cotyledon shrivels. The increase in mass slows down and levels off as the plant matures

The seed absorbs water, swells and the testa splits open

Mass

Time

Figure 39.6A ● Growth curve of a broad bean from seed to mature plant. The stages of growth from the embryo to the time when the seedling no longer depends on stored food is called germination

LOOK AT LINKS
for **xylem** and **phloem**
See Theme J, Topic 38.1.

The growth curves of nearly all annual plants look like Figure 39.6A. The dotted line represents flowering time followed by the formation of fruits and seeds which are then dispersed. The plant then quickly loses mass and eventually dies.

Figure 39.6B shows a root tip. Behind the tip of the developing root of a germinating seed there is a region where cells divide very quickly. Behind the region of dividing cells is another region where cells become longer, growing to ten times or more their original length.

As the cells get longer they become different from one another: we say that they become **differentiated**. Some form the sieve cells of the phloem, others form xylem cells. Differentiation in the shoot is more complicated than in the root since the developing shoot produces leaves and flowers.

Differentiation therefore, lays down the tissues of the plant body. The word **primary** is used to describe these tissues because they are the first tissues to develop. Plants which have only primary tissues are called **herbaceous** plants.

● *Where does growth occur in plants?*
In animals most cells can divide by mitosis. This means that nearly all parts of the body can grow. In plants only some cells divide by mitosis. These cells form the growing points of a plant, mostly at the tips of the shoots and roots.

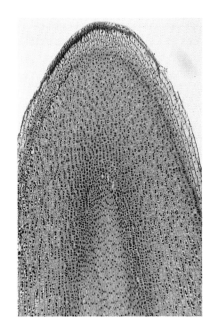

Figure 39.6B ● The growing root tip

IT *Seed Germination*
(program)

The program shows experiments to find out the best conditions for seeds to germinate. The factors that matter are light level, temperature, oxygen level and the presence of water. Find out how well the seeds develop under conditions which you select.

Figure 39.6C ● Annual rings in the cut end of the trunk of a beech tree

LOOK AT LINKS
Buttercups are herbaceous plants; beech trees are perennials. Wood makes the difference.
See Theme A, Topic 3.5.

Trees grow year after year because they contain cells which divide to produce more and more xylem. Such growth is called secondary growth because the new xylem develops after differentiation during germination has laid down the primary tissues. This is how wood forms. It is impregnated with lignin which gives it extra strength.

In countries like the UK with a temperate climate, wood grows seasonally. The cycle is repeated each year to form cylinders of wood, which in cross-section appear as annual rings (see Figure 39.6C).

What controls growth and development?

The zygote of a multicellular organism looks very simple under the microscope but it is the starting point for the development of a new individual. The instructions for development are contained in its genes. These are duplicated many times as the embryo develops. Even though all the cells of the multicellular individual have the same set of genes, different types of cell develop (differentiate) to do different biological jobs. *How does the same set of genes produce the many different kinds of cell which make up the individual organism?* It seems that part of the time only some genes are active in each cell type.

Development is an exact sequence of events which lays down the different features of the embryo in the right place at the right time. This means that the genes which produce these features must be switched on and off in the right order. **Hormones** seem to play an important part in switching genes on and off. The hormone thyroxine, for example, controls the growth and development of amphibian tadpoles into adults. The change is called **metamorphosis**. When the production of thyroxine in a tadpole is stopped, the tadpole does not metamorphose into an adult but grows into a giant tadpole.

Hormones also control insect development. The hormone ecdysone makes the young insect grow and moult its outer body covering, the exoskeleton. It does this in the correct sequence by switching on the genes which control these processes at the right time in development.

LOOK AT LINKS
for **hormones**
See Theme J, Topic 40.4

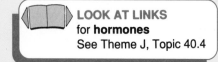

How insects grow

The growth curve for insects is not like the smooth growth curve for plants shown in Figure 39.6A or that for humans shown in Figure 39.6G. It is stepped (see Figure 39.6D).

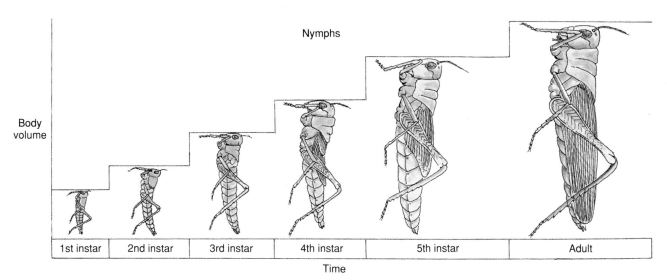

Figure 39.6D ● Growth curve of a locust – each stage in between moults is called an instar. A locust nymph passes through five instars before it becomes an adult. It increases in size at every moult.

Insects grow like this because the hard exoskeleton that surrounds the body cannot stretch. An increase in length occurs only when the old exoskeleton is removed (called moulting or ecdysis) and replaced by a new one. The body tissue expands while the exoskeleton is still soft and stretchy.

Insects change a lot as they moult and grow into adults. The changes are another example of metamorphosis. In insects like locusts, metamorphosis is gradual. Young locusts (called hoppers) look rather like miniature adults except that the wings and sex organs are not developed. With each moult (five in all) the hoppers get bigger as Figure 39.6D shows. At the last moult they become adults with fully developed wings and sex organs. This gradual change is called **incomplete metamorphosis** and the young of insects which show incomplete metamorphosis are called nymphs (see Figure 39.6E).

Figure 39.6E ● Nymphs and adults (a) Locust   (b) Earwig

Figure 39.6F ● Larvae, pupae and adults. The larvae of different insects do not look alike. Butterfly and moth larvae have a distinct head and short, stumpy legs. They are called caterpillars. Blowfly larvae are much simpler; they are called maggots.

Metamorphosis is more dramatic in insects like butterflies, moths and flies. The young are called larvae and do not look at all like the adult. They moult and grow but then turn into pupae. The final changes into the adult take place inside the pupa. When the changes are complete the adult emerges from the pupa, dries off and flies away. This dramatic change from young to adult is called **complete metamorphosis** (see Figure 39.6F).

How humans grow

A baby grows to become a child; children develop into adolescents who become adults at around the age of 20 years. These are the stages signposting the route of human growth and development. Figure 39.6G shows how different parts of the body increase in size during the first twenty years of a person's life. Notice that different parts of the body grow at different rates because cell division occurs more quickly in some parts than in others. A child's head is bigger in proportion to the rest of the body compared with an adult's. Growth of arms and legs speeds up during adolescence resulting in the proportions of head and body we see in adults.

IT'S A FACT

The heart beats roughly the same number of times during the lifetime of most mammals, but the heart rate varies. Small animals have a short life and fast heart rate; large animals live longer and have a slower heart rate. On this basis humans live three times longer than expected! We do not know why.

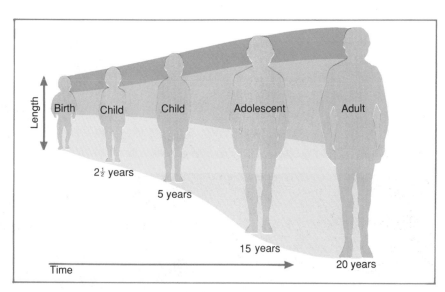

Figure 39.6G ● Human growth

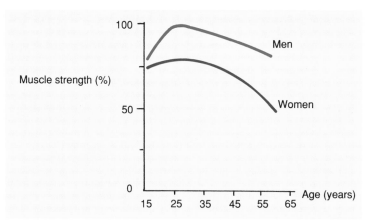

Figure 39.6H ● Muscle strength in men and women of different ages

Ageing begins in the middle twenties. By ageing we mean not only advancing years but also loss of fitness. Different aspects of fitness peak at different times, and individuals vary, especially between the sexes. For example Figure 39.6H shows the peak and decline of average muscular strength in men and women as they grow older.

Exercise helps to slow the ageing process so that early death from heart disease, for example, is less likely. Slowing down ageing does not mean living longer (although this may happen) but rather that good health is enjoyed for a much greater part of life.

CHECKPOINT

❶ Which region of the root tip contributes most to the extension of the root through the soil? Give reasons for your answer.

❷ Where in the root tip are you likely to find:
(a) the smallest cells,
(b) cells containing the highest percentage of water?

❸ Complete the following paragraph using the words provided below. Each word may be used once, more than once or not at all.

nucleus expand mitosis grow newly differentiate transport large
water dividing small osmosis elongation

Roots _____ at their tips. The cells of the region immediately behind the root tip divide by _____ . Repeated divisions mean that there are _____ numbers of _____ cells. Further back these _____ formed cells begin to _____ due to the uptake of _____ by _____ . This expansion produces rapid _____ of the root through the soil. We say that they _____ .

❹ Figure 39.6A shows the growth curve of a broad bean during germination. Study it and answer the following questions.
(a) Define the word 'germination'.
(b) Why does the mass of seed increase as germination begins?
(c) After the initial increase, why does the germinating plant then lose mass?
(d) After losing mass why does the germinating plant then increase in mass?

❺ The diagram below shows changes in the proportions of the human body from birth to adulthood. Analyse the changes in proportions of the head and the rest of the body in relation to total body length at each stage of development. Write a brief report of your analysis suggesting reasons for the changes.

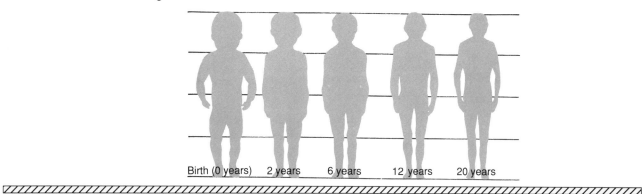

Birth (0 years)   2 years   6 years   12 years   20 years

TOPIC 40 RESPONSES AND CO-ORDINATION

40.1 Plant responses: growth movements

FIRST THOUGHTS

Plants really do move – not in the same way as animals which use muscles, but by the way they grow in response to stimuli. Read on and find out about this.

'Responses' and 'stimuli' are everyday words but what do we mean when we talk about living things responding to stimuli? Think of it like this. The environment is changing all the time. Some changes are long-term, others short-term. Because these changes cause plants and animals to take action, the changes are called **stimuli**. The actions which plants and animals take are called **responses**. Being able to respond to stimuli means that living things can alter their activities according to what is going on around them (see Figure 40.1A).

Figure 40.1A ● Responses to stimuli
(a) Some species of the mimosa plant close up when touched. *What is the stimulus: what is the response?*

(b) People respond to loud noises by trying to shut them out. *Why can loud noise be dangerous?*

(c) Stimuli come from the environment inside the body as well as outside. *What is the stimulus: what is the response?*

Plant growth movements

Do you keep plants in the house? If you do you may have noticed that they bend towards the window. Plants do this because light is a stimulus. Plants respond by growing towards the light (see Figure 40.1B). The benefit to the plant of this response is clear: the leaves receive as much light as possible for photosynthesis. Stems twist and turn and flowers and leaves move in daily rhythms to follow the light.

Plant movements are growth movements in response to stimuli. There are two kinds of growth movement:

- **Nastic movements** are responses to stimuli which come from all directions. For example, temperature change is the stimulus for tulip and crocus flowers to open and close. They open when the temperature rises and close when it falls.
- **Tropic movements (tropisms)** are responses to stimuli which come from one direction. Tropisms are positive if the plant grows towards the stimulus; negative if it grows away (see Figure 40.1C).

Figure 40.1B ● Responding to light – these plants have bent towards the window

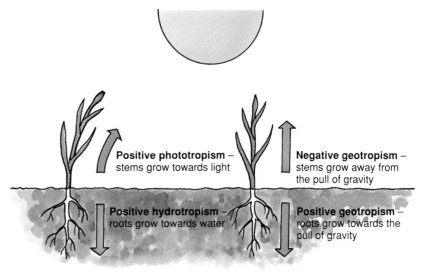

Positive phototropism – stems grow towards light

Negative geotropism – stems grow away from the pull of gravity

Positive hydrotropism – roots grow towards water

Positive geotropism – roots grow towards the pull of gravity

Figure 40.1C ● Different tropisms

● **Control of growth movements**

Many factors affect the growth of plants. Important among them are compounds called **plant growth substances**. Auxin was the first plant growth substance to be discovered. It is produced in shoot tips. Under the influence of auxin the cellulose walls of plant cells become more elastic and the cells elongate rapidly. Figure 40.1D shows how auxin enables the plant to grow towards the light.

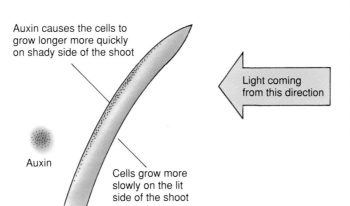

Auxin causes the cells to grow longer more quickly on shady side of the shoot

Light coming from this direction

Auxin

Cells grow more slowly on the lit side of the shoot

Figure 40.1D ● Auxin distribution. There is more auxin in the side of the shoot tip in the shade. The shoot bends towards the light because auxin makes the cells grow faster.

Experiment 1

Key

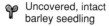 Uncovered, intact barley seedling

Uncovered barley seedling with its shoot tip (5 mm) removed

Covered, intact barley seedling

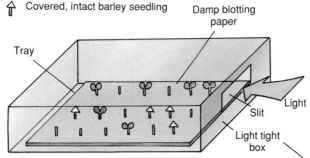

Tray

Damp blotting paper

Light

Slit

Light tight box

Barley seedlings about 25 mm high are grown in a light tight box with a slit at one end. Foil caps on some seedlings exclude light from the shoot tip

Two days later

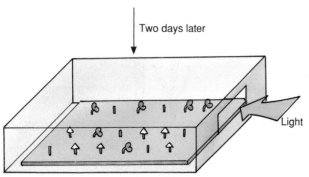

Light

The seedlings with their shoot tips removed or covered by foil caps do not grow towards the light. The uncovered, intact seedlings grow towards the light

Figure 40.1E ● (a) Does the whole shoot or just the shoot tip respond to light?

Experiment 2

Key

Intact barley seedling

Barley seedling with tip cut off. Tip placed on a slip of metal foil and replaced on the rest of the shoot. The metal foil prevents diffusion of chemicals from the shoot tip to the rest of the shoot

Barley seedling with tip removed. Tip placed on agar block and replaced on the rest of the shoot.
The agar block allows diffusion of chemicals from the shoot tip to the rest of the shoot.

Barley seedling with tip cut off. An agar block is placed on the remaining part of the shoot

Barley seedling with tip cut off. An agar block is soaked in a mash made of the shoot tip and then placed on top of the remaining part of the shoot

Barley seedling with tip cut off. An agar block is soaked in a solution of auxin and then placed on top of the remaining part of the shoot

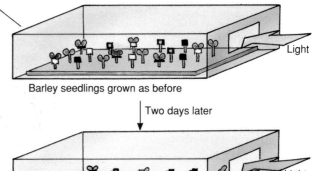

Light

Barley seedlings grown as before

Two days later

Light

The seedlings with their tips cut off and replaced with plain agar blocks and the seedlings with their tips separated from the rest of the shoot by metal foil do not grow towards the light. The other seedlings grow towards the light.

(b) Is it a chemical produced in the shoot tip or just the presence of the shoot tip itself which causes the response to light?

Two experiments designed to investigate the responses of plants to light are illustrated in Figure 40.1E. Examine the diagrams carefully. *What conclusions do you draw from the results of the experiments? Is it the shoot tip that responds to light? Is there a chemical in the shoot tip which controls growth?*

After the discovery of auxin the search was on for other plant growth substances. Today we know that a range of substances control plant growth.

The **herbicide** 2, 4-D is a synthetic auxin. It kills plants by making them grow too fast. However, narrow-leafed plants, including the food crops barley, wheat and oats are not affected by 2, 4-D at concentrations which destroy broad-leaved plants like docks, daisies and dandelions. Farmers spray wheat with 2, 4-D. The treatment kills the broad-leaved weeds which would otherwise compete with the wheat crop for growing space, nutrients and water. The yield of wheat increases and the extra money the farmer receives more than offsets the cost of buying and using the chemical.

IT'S A FACT

Growers control ripening by keeping fruit in sheds in an atmosphere that contains ethene. As little as one part of ethene per million parts of air is enough to speed up ripening.

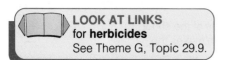
LOOK AT LINKS
for **herbicides**
See Theme G, Topic 29.9.

CHECKPOINT

❶ Comment critically on the evidence that shoot tips respond to light.

❷ Complete the paragraph below using the words provided. Each word may be used once, more than once or not at all.

tip   phototropism   auxin   geotropism   elongate   nastic   towards   faster

The _____ of the shoot produces a growth substance called _____ which causes cells behind the tip to _____ . When the shoot is lit from one side, _____ accumulates on the shaded side. The cells on the shaded side grow _____ and the shoot bends _____ the light. The response of the plant is called positive _____ .

FIRST THOUGHTS
o
o
o

40.2 ⬤ Senses and the nervous system

Stimuli are converted by receptors into signals to which the body can respond. The signals are called nerve impulses. Neurones (nerve cells) conduct nerve impulses to muscles which respond by contracting. Muscles are called effectors. Nerves are formed from bundles of neurones and are the link between stimulus and response. The sequence reads: stimulus → receptor → nerves → effector → response. Remember the sequence as you read this section.

Figure 40.2A ● Dog and man respond vigorously to stimuli

IT   **The Nervous System** (program)

The Nervous System 1 and 2 contain diagrams of the central nervous system, the structure of the brain, nerves and neurones.

RESOURCE ACTIVITY PACK

Look at Figure 40.2A – it illustrates important points about the way animals respond to stimuli.

Eyes and ears contain specialised **sensory receptor** cells which convert stimuli into signals the body can respond to. The signals are minute electrical disturbances called **nerve impulses**. They are messages for the man's leg muscles to start working hard. The muscles are called **effectors** because they respond to nerve impulses. Specialised cells called **neurones** (nerve cells) conduct nerve impulses to their destination. Each second, thousands of nerve impulses arrive at the muscle cells making them contract vigorously.

The sensory cells of the man's eyes and ears in Figure 40.2A are linked by neurones to the cells of his leg muscles. Sensory cells and muscle cells are at the beginning and end of the process that allows the man to respond to the fierce dog. The process runs

Stimulus → Receptor → Nerves → Effector → Response

LOOK AT LINKS
The structure and function of the eye is examined in Theme H, Topic 32.5.

LOOK AT LINKS
The structure and function of the ear is examined in Theme H, Topic 31.3.

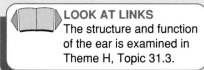

Who's behind the science

In 1829 Louis Braille, who was blind from the age of three, invented a system of writing for the blind. Letters are represented by different combinations of raised dots on paper. The dots are then read by touch.

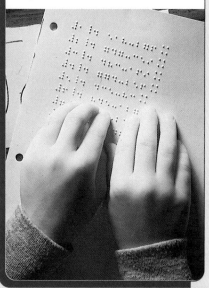

IT'S A FACT

The fastest nerve impulses in humans travel at 8 m/s.

═══ **SCIENCE AT WORK** ═══

Computer scientists developing artificial intelligence are studying the pathways of the human brain. A computer that thinks for itself is not likely to be developed for many years yet!

The senses

Our senses keep us in touch with the world around us. Each one consists of sensory cells adapted to detect a particular type of stimulus. The sensory cells of the eye detect light. The sensory cells of the ear detect sound. The sensory cells of the nose and tongue detect different chemicals. These different types of sensory cell are parts of complex organs located in the head. These organs are called organs of special sense. The rest of the body has sensory cells too. Different sensory cells detect pressure, pain, cold and heat.

Neurones

Neurones link sensory cells with effectors. In all animals they are similar in structure and in the way they work. Figure 40.2B shows a human motor neurone. A nerve impulse can travel along an axon in milliseconds. It takes more than one neurone to link the cell of a sensory receptor with an effector cell. A number of neurones link up to form a route to take nerve impulses to their destination.

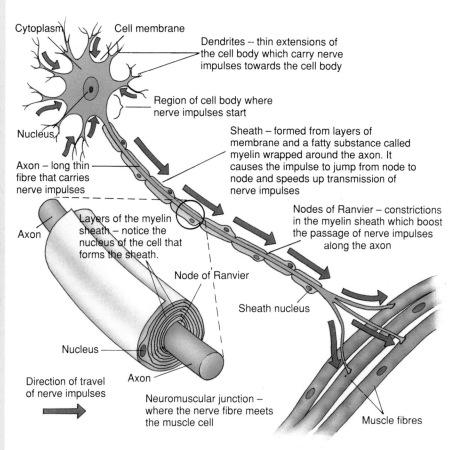

Figure 40.2B ● Human motor neurone causing a muscle to contract. The axons passing to the leg muscles can be up to a meter in length

Minute gaps called **synapses** separate neurones from one another. Each synapse separates the ends of the axon of one neurone from the dendrites of the next (see Figure 40.2C). When nerve impulses arrive at the end of the axon they stimulate the production of a special chemical called neurotransmitter which diffuses across the synapse to the dendrites of the neighbouring neurone. The neurotransmitter stimulates the dendrites to fire off a new nerve impulse.

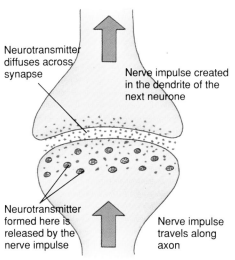

Neurotransmitter diffuses across synapse

Nerve impulse created in the dendrite of the next neurone

Neurotransmitter formed here is released by the nerve impulse

Nerve impulse travels along axon

Figure 40.2C ● A synapse

The dendrites of different neurones may form synapses with many incoming axons. This allows for an enormous number of linkages. Nerve impulses, therefore, may be switched from one pathway to another within the billions of neurones that make up the nervous system.

● *Nerves and nervous systems*

Neurones are grouped together into bundles called nerves (see Figure 40.2D) which pass to all parts of the body forming a nervous system. Most animals have a front end and a rear end. The front end forms a head which leads the rest of the body into new environments. The ability to detect changes in front of the body, therefore, is especially important. In *Planaria*, for example, sensory cells grouped together into simple organs are concentrated in the head for this purpose (see Figure 3.5J).

Figure 40.2E shows that in different animals some nerves form cords of tissue which run the length of the body. The plan of the nervous system is similar for all the animals shown although they are classified in different phyla. At the head end the nerve cord expands into a brain or a brain-like swelling which makes numerous connections with the sense organs in the head. The sense organs feed information as nerve impulses to the brain. The brain interprets the information and sends nerve impulses through the nerve cords and nerves to effectors. This is how information about its environment travels through an animal so that its effectors can respond in a useful way. The process is called **co-ordination**.

The nerve cord(s) and brain form the **central nervous system**. The nerves that join the central nervous system form the **peripheral nervous system**.

Single neurones

Covering around the group of neurones

Figure 40.2D ● A nerve

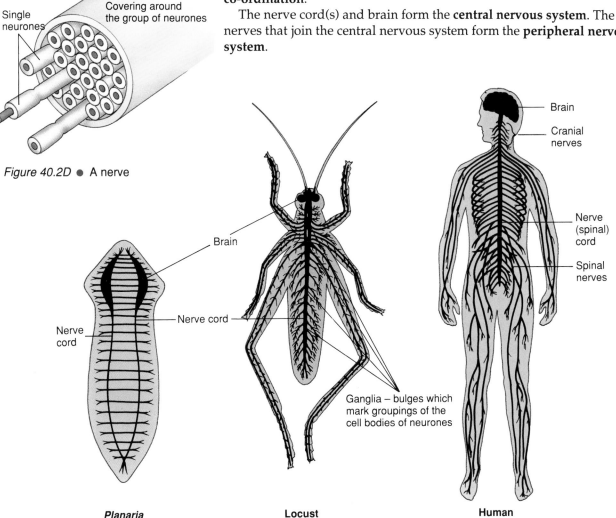

Brain

Cranial nerves

Nerve (spinal) cord

Spinal nerves

Brain

Nerve cord

Nerve cord

Ganglia – bulges which mark groupings of the cell bodies of neurones

Planaria

Locust

Human

Figure 40.2E ● Plans of the nervous systems of *Planaria*, the locust and the human

Nerve
(program)

The basic processes of the nervous system are shown in the program. The second part contains simulations of sciatic nerve experiments.

● *Reflex responses*

If you touch a hot stove you automatically move your hand away. We call the response a **reflex response** and the nerves involved form a **reflex arc** (see Figure 40.2F).

Different types of neurone form a reflex arc. A synapse separates each type of neurone from the next neurone in the arc.

● **Sensory neurones** transmit nerve impulses from sensory receptors to the central nervous system. (Figure 40.2F.) When you touch a hot object a pain-sensitive receptor cell in your finger detects the stimulus – heat – which triggers off nerve impulses. These are transmitted to the nerve cord by sensory neurones.

● **Relay neurones** receive nerve impulses from the sensory neurones and pass them to the motor neurones.

● **Motor neurones** receive nerve impulses from the central nervous system and transmit them to the effector. (Figure 40.2F.) In this case your arm muscles then contract, lifting your finger out of harm's way.

Reflex actions often occur before the brain has had time to process the information. However, when the brain catches up with the events it then takes over and brings about the next set of reactions. These reactions could be a shout of pain or a decision to switch off the stove.

The bundles of neurones running up and down the nerve cord are called ascending and descending fibres. They form a zone of tissue called **white matter**. The white colour comes from the pale myelin sheaths that cover the axons. In the core of the nerve cord lies an H-shaped mass of **grey matter** that consists mainly of the cell bodies and axons of relay neurones.

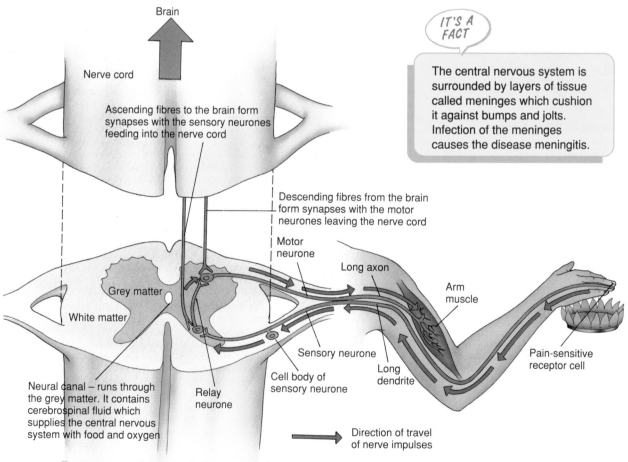

IT'S A FACT

The central nervous system is surrounded by layers of tissue called meninges which cushion it against bumps and jolts. Infection of the meninges causes the disease meningitis.

Brain

Nerve cord

Ascending fibres to the brain form synapses with the sensory neurones feeding into the nerve cord

Descending fibres from the brain form synapses with the motor neurones leaving the nerve cord

Motor neurone

Long axon

Arm muscle

Grey matter

White matter

Sensory neurone

Cell body of sensory neurone

Long dendrite

Pain-sensitive receptor cell

Neural canal – runs through the grey matter. It contains cerebrospinal fluid which supplies the central nervous system with food and oxygen

Relay neurone

Direction of travel of nerve impulses

Transverse section through the nerve cord

Figure 40.2F ● A reflex arc

● Conditioned reflexes

The influence of the brain on reflex responses was first investigated in a scientific way by the Russian physiologist Ivan Pavlov (1849–1936).

Pavlov noticed that when food was placed in a dog's mouth the flow of saliva increased. He also noticed that the flow of saliva increased as soon as the animal smelt his hand, even before the food was placed in its mouth. The salivary reflex was made stronger by following Pavlov's personal smell with the taste of food. After a period of presenting the dog with both the personal smell and the taste of food, the personal smell alone was enough to make the dog produce as much saliva as if it were given food.

Pavlov used the word 'conditioned' to describe the dog's response because it could be switched on by a non-food stimulus which the dog associated with the meal. Later work showed that in conditioned dogs new nerve pathways had been made. These connected the salivary reflex with other nerve circuits of the nerve cord.

Pavlov also conditioned dogs to salivate in response to other stimuli – the ringing of a bell for example. Conditioning fades unless it is periodically reinforced. Conditioning by personal smell, therefore, must be reinforced from time to time with a meal if the dog's salivary reflex is to remain conditioned. Try out the experiment on your dog or cat if you have one.

Figure 40.2G ● Ivan Pavlov

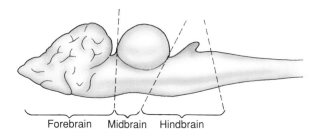

Forebrain   Midbrain   Hindbrain

Figure 40.2H ● Section lengthways through a frog's brain

● How the brain works

In vertebrates the brain consists of three regions: forebrain, midbrain and hind-brain. This three-part structure can be seen clearly in adult amphibia (see Figure 40.2H) but is less obvious in adult mammals because of the expansion of the forebrain. In humans the forebrain forms the cerebrum which is so large that it almost covers the rest of the brain (see Figure 40.2I).

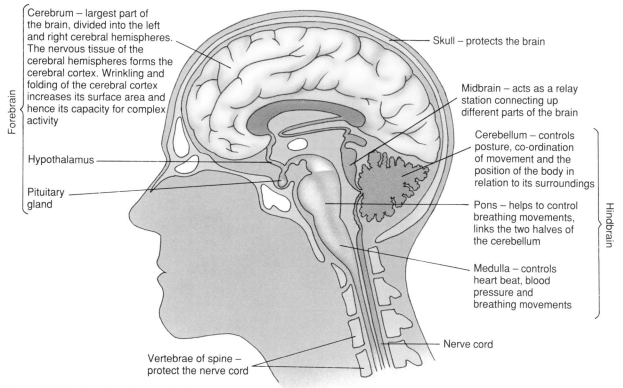

Forebrain

Cerebrum – largest part of the brain, divided into the left and right cerebral hemispheres. The nervous tissue of the cerebral hemispheres forms the cerebral cortex. Wrinkling and folding of the cerebral cortex increases its surface area and hence its capacity for complex activity

Hypothalamus

Pituitary gland

Skull – protects the brain

Midbrain – acts as a relay station connecting up different parts of the brain

Cerebellum – controls posture, co-ordination of movement and the position of the body in relation to its surroundings

Pons – helps to control breathing movements, links the two halves of the cerebellum

Hindbrain

Medulla – controls heart beat, blood pressure and breathing movements

Nerve cord

Vertebrae of spine – protect the nerve cord

Figure 40.2I ● Section through the human head showing the different parts of the brain

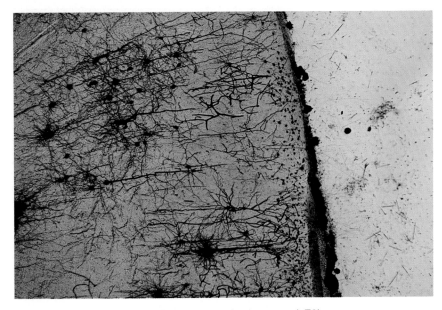

Figure 40.2J ● Multipolar neurones in the brain cortex (x70)

Figure 40.2J shows some of the neurones in the brain. They are called multipolar neurones because each one has numerous dendrites which can form synapses with incoming axons. Scientists estimate that up to six million cell bodies make up 1 cm³ of brain matter and that each neurone is connected to as many as 80 000 others.

The human brain weighs approximately 1.3 kg. It is the body's thinking and control centre. Reactions under the brain's control are called voluntary reactions. Memory and learning are also under the brain's control (see Figure 40.2I).

The different regions of the cerebral cortex each have different functions (see Figure 40.2K).

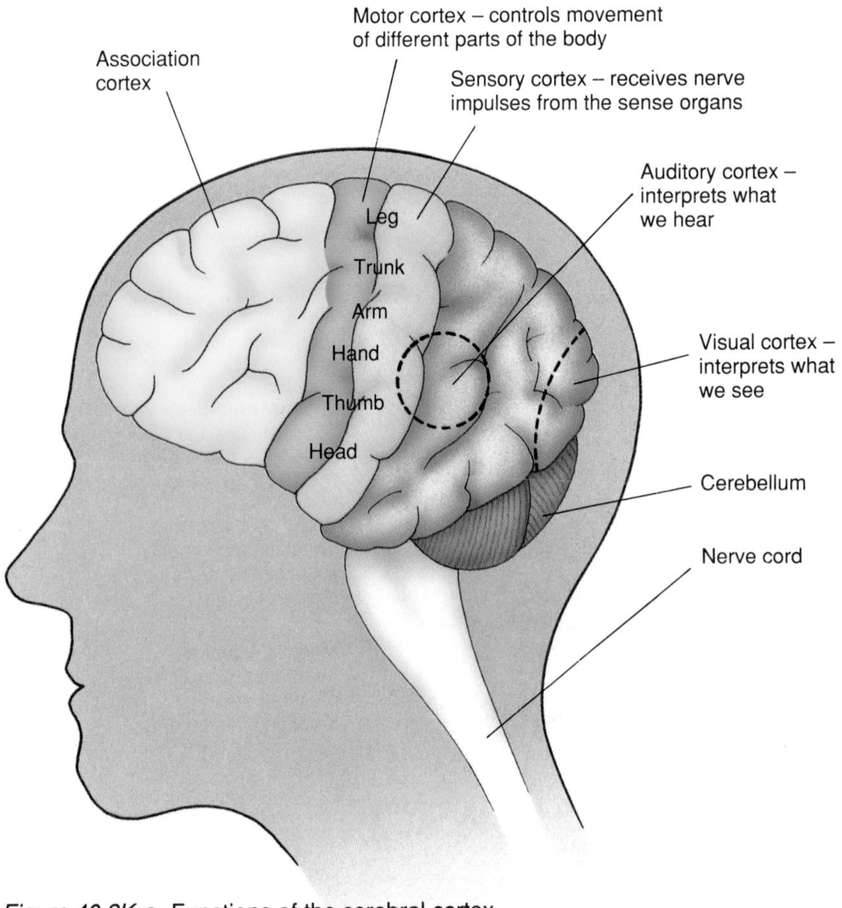

● **Intelligence**

What is intelligence? A difficult question. It includes the ability to decide how to tackle a problem and the ability to change your approach if it does not work.

Intelligence is not determined by a fixed centre in the association cortex. It depends on the way nerve fibres connect together in the different parts of the cortex and the way they connect the cortex with the rest of the brain. These nerve fibres form association pathways.

Association cortex

Motor cortex – controls movement of different parts of the body

Sensory cortex – receives nerve impulses from the sense organs

Auditory cortex – interprets what we hear

Leg
Trunk
Arm
Hand
Thumb
Head

Visual cortex – interprets what we see

Cerebellum

Nerve cord

Figure 40.2K ● Functions of the cerebral cortex

=== **SCIENCE AT WORK** ===

The brain is insensitive to pain. This means that during surgical operations which expose the brain, the patient needs only a local anaesthetic and can therefore report the effects of stimulating different areas of the cortex with, for example, very tiny electric shocks.

CHECKPOINT

❶ (a) What is a response?

(b) The diagram below shows a reflex arc.
   (i) Explain briefly what is happening at the points labelled A–G on the diagram.
   (ii) Name the parts numbered 1–3.

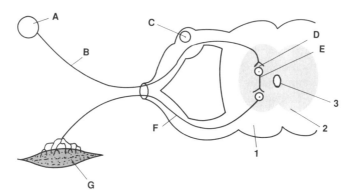

❷ Complete the following paragraph using the words provided below. Each word may be used once, more than once or not at all.

largest   nerve cord   axons   skull   vertebrae   cerebral hemispheres

The brain and _____ make up the central nervous system. They control many bodily activities and are well protected. The brain is enclosed in the _____ and the spinal cord runs through a channel in the _____ . The cerebrum is divided into two _____ . It is the _____ part of the human brain.

❸ The diagram opposite shows a motor nerve cell. Name the parts labelled A–F on the diagram and explain their function.

❹ We respond to stimuli all the time. When a door bell rings (stimulus), we answer the door (response): when we feel hot (stimulus), we take jumpers and coats off (response).
   (a) List at least seven stimuli to which you have responded today and state your responses.
   (b) Name the sensory receptors responsible for detecting the stimuli.
   (c) Briefly state the role (i) sensory receptors, (ii) nerves, (iii) muscles or glands, play in the chain of events from stimulus to response.

❺ Match each of the biological terms in Column A with their functions in Column B.

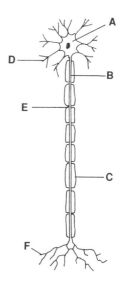

Column A	Column B
Cerebellum	Transmits nerve impulses from the central nervous system to a muscle
Medulla	Transmits nerve impulses from a sense receptor to the central nervous system
Relay neurone	Controls learning and memory
Cerebrum	Controls pulse, breathing movements and other involuntary actions
Sensory neurone	Controls balance
Motor neurone	Links a sensory neurone with a motor neurone or relay neurone

40.3 Hormones

FIRST THOUGHTS

Hormones are chemicals produced by animals to regulate their bodies' activities.

LOOK AT LINKS
Hormones control metamorphosis in amphibia and insects. For more information see Theme J, Topic 39.6.

Each meal or snack that you eat provides your body with a surge of glucose. Glucose is an important source of energy but high levels seriously disrupt the body's cells and cause them to function very inefficiently.

Your body keeps the level of glucose constant by means of **hormones**. These substances regulate the concentration of glucose in the blood and cope with the surge of glucose at meal-times. The different ways in which the body keeps its internal environment from changing is called **homeostasis**. The control of glucose levels is one example of homeostasis.

Hormones are chemicals produced by animals and plants to regulate the organisms' activities. In animals they are produced in the tissues of ductless glands called **endocrine glands** and released into the blood system. Hormones circulate in the blood and cause specific effects on the body. (See Figure 40.3A.)

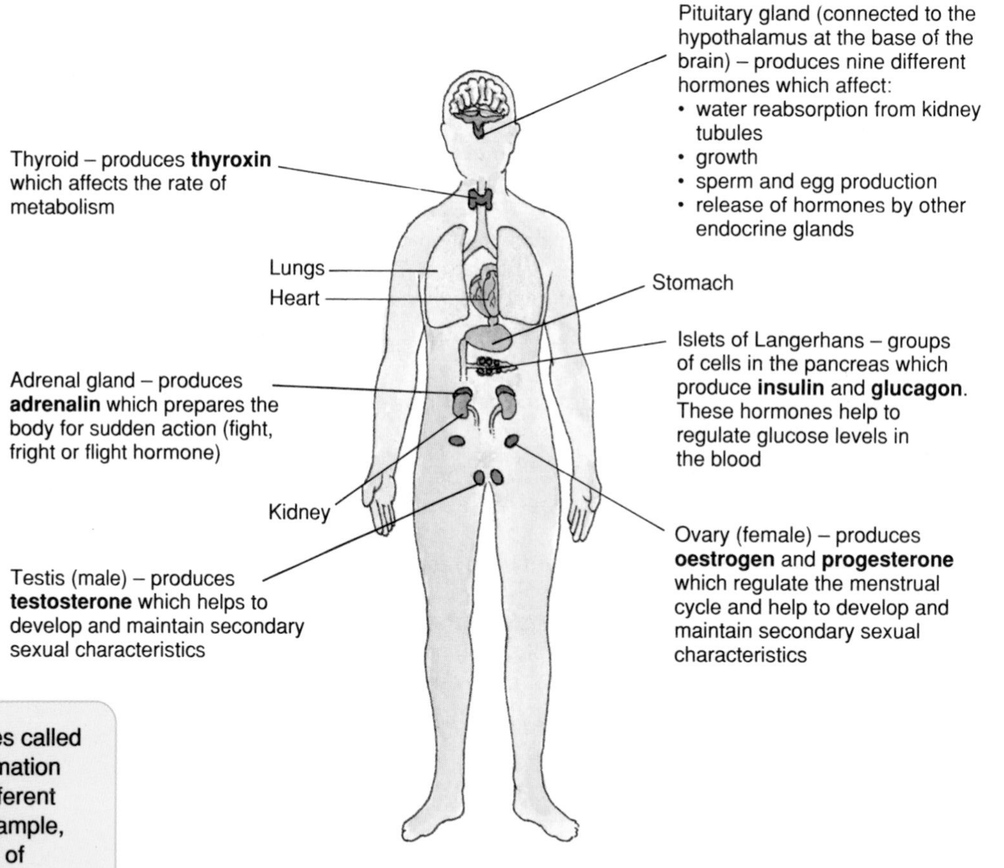

Pituitary gland (connected to the hypothalamus at the base of the brain) – produces nine different hormones which affect:
• water reabsorption from kidney tubules
• growth
• sperm and egg production
• release of hormones by other endocrine glands

Thyroid – produces **thyroxin** which affects the rate of metabolism

Lungs
Heart

Stomach

Islets of Langerhans – groups of cells in the pancreas which produce **insulin** and **glucagon**. These hormones help to regulate glucose levels in the blood

Adrenal gland – produces **adrenalin** which prepares the body for sudden action (fight, fright or flight hormone)

Kidney

Ovary (female) – produces **oestrogen** and **progesterone** which regulate the menstrual cycle and help to develop and maintain secondary sexual characteristics

Testis (male) – produces **testosterone** which helps to develop and maintain secondary sexual characteristics

IT'S A FACT

Hormone-like substances called pheromones carry information between individuals. Different species of insect, for example, produce their own types of pheromone. Individuals release pheromones into their environment where they are smelt or tasted by fellow individuals close-up. For example, worker bees release a pheromone called geraniol which attracts other workers to them; ants release an 'alarm' pheromone which warns fellow ants when their nest is invaded by ants from another colony.

Figure 40.3A ● Hormones are made in tissues called endocrine glands – they are released into the blood which transports them around the body

The tissue on which a particular hormone (or group of hormones) acts is called a **target tissue**. A hormone affects its target tissue more slowly than a nerve impulse affects a muscle. This is because nerve impulses move rapidly along neurones. Muscles therefore can respond very quickly to changing circumstances. The action of most hormones is longer-term.

Insulin
(program)

Use the program to find out how human blood-sugar level is controlled. You can take control of the system by changing sets of hormone levels.

In teenagers the body matures under the control of hormones over several years. In girls, oestrogen controls broadening of the hips and breast development. In boys, testosterone controls beard growth, broadening of the shoulders and the deepening of the voice. These developments (called secondary sexual characteristics) mark the start of puberty and continue through adolescence. Puberty begins in girls at age 11–13 and in boys at age 13–14. Because of the changing balance of hormones in the body, adolescents may experience swings of mood and also skin troubles such as spots and acne. Usually these problems have cleared up by the early twenties.

Hormone regulation of blood glucose

To keep the level of glucose in the blood constant hormones balance the glucose-producing and glucose-using processes of the body.
- The hormone thyroxine increases the rate at which glucose is oxidised in **cellular respiration**. This **decreases** the level of glucose in the blood.
- The hormone insulin also **decreases** the level of glucose in the blood. It does this by promoting the conversion of glucose into glycogen.
- The hormone glucagon **increases** the level of glucose in the blood by promoting the conversion of glycogen into glucose.

If the pancreas does not produce enough insulin a condition called **diabetes mellitus** occurs. The glucose level in the blood becomes dangerously high and can cause blindness or kidney failure. Concentrations of glucose become so high that the kidneys cannot reabsorb all the glucose and glucose is excreted in the urine. A simple test for glucose in the urine of a patient can tell a doctor if a patient is **diabetic.**

Diabetics suffer from thirst and tiredness. If the diabetes is not too severe, a carefully chosen low-sugar diet can control the condition. If the diabetes is severe, diabetics are taught to inject themselves regularly with insulin to lower their blood glucose levels (see Figure 40.3B). Getting the dose of insulin right is not always easy. If too much insulin is injected, the glucose level in the blood falls too low and diabetics can suffer from unpleasant side effects. Diabetics soon learn to recognise the symptoms and eat a little sugar to boost blood glucose to the right level.

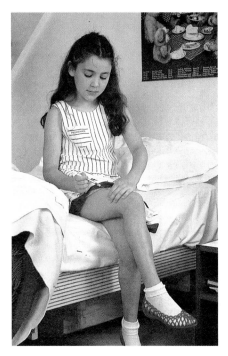

Figure 40.3B ● A diabetic child injecting herself with insulin

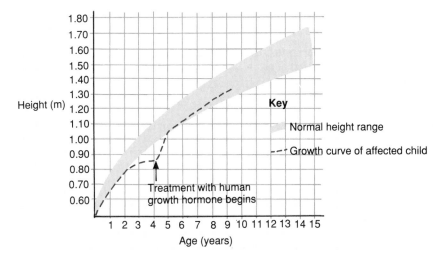

Figure 40.3C ● Human growth curve. How long after treatment begins does it take for the affected child to 'catch up' with other children?

Hormones, growth and muscle building

If a child's pituitary gland does not produce enough growth hormone then the child will not grow to a normal height. Providing the condition is diagnosed at an early age, the affected child can be given a growth hormone to make up for the deficiency. The child puts on a growth spurt and soon 'catches up' with other children of the same age (see Figure 40.3C).

IT'S A FACT

The hormone thyroxine contains the element iodine. If a person's diet does not contain enough iodine the thyroid gland does not produce enough thyroxine. As a result the person's metabolic rate is lowered and the person feels sluggish and tired. Under-production of thyroxine also causes the thyroid gland to enlarge – a condition called **goitre**.

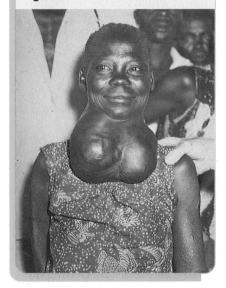

Figure 40.3D ● The muscles you need for strength events

At some time or other you have probably seen athletes straining to lift heavy weights or put the shot long distances. Athletes train very hard to build up the muscles needed to compete in these 'strength' events (see Figure 40.3D). A few, however, cheat and inject themselves with hormones called **anabolic steroids** which develop their muscles even further, giving them an unfair advantage over other competitors.

Anabolic steroids mimic the effect of the hormone testosterone which in men controls the development of secondary sexual characteristics. Testosterone also increases the rate of protein synthesis (in women as well as men). This is why athletes who take anabolic steroids develop bigger and stronger muscles. The side-effects of anabolic steroids are very unpleasant. Liver damage is possible and women can develop male secondary sexual characteristics. Men can become sexually impotent.

Anabolic steroids are on the list of drugs banned by the International Olympic Committee. Any athlete caught using them can be prohibited from taking part in future sporting events.

CHECKPOINT

❶ What are hormones and how are they transported round the body?

❷ Complete the following paragraph using the words provided below. Each word may be used once, more than once or not at all.

oestrogen   target   long-term   testosterone   nervous   short-term
transports   progesterone   adrenalin   thyroxine   blood   sexual

The endocrine tissues secrete hormones directly into the _____ which _____ them all over the body. The tissues affected by hormones are called _____ tissues. The uterus, for example, responds to the hormones _____ and _____ . The action of most hormones is _____ . Female secondary _____ characteristics, for example, develop under the influence of _____ , male secondary _____ characteristics develop under the influence of _____ . The adrenal gland secretes _____ which prepares the body for sudden action. The rapidity of its effect is more like that of the _____ system than that of other hormones.

SUPPORT AND MOVEMENT

41.1 Support in plants and animals

All living things are supported in some way. Think what would happen to your body without the support of the skeleton. It would collapse into a shapeless heap.

RESOURCE
ACTIVITY
PACK

LOOK AT LINKS
for **xylem** and **phloem**
See Theme J, Topic 38.1.

LOOK AT LINKS
for **turgor pressure**
See Theme D, Topic 19.2.

Support in plants

Figure 41.1A ● Bundles of xylem and phloem in the stem of an oak

Plants are supported by the strands of **xylem** and **phloem** that run in vascular bundles from the roots, through the stem to the leaves and flowers (see Figure 41.1A). Rings of lignin strengthen the walls of the xylem cells. Non-woody (herbaceous) plants are supported by the firmness of their cells. The pressure of the cell contents against the cell wall makes a plant cell **turgid**. Individual cells press against each other and hold the plant upright. Wood is formed from lignified xylem and gives even more support. This is why trees can grow to be tall and heavy.

Support in animals

Most animals are supported by a skeleton. There are three main types of skeleton:

- **Endoskeletons** are found in vertebrates. The skeleton, which lies inside the body surrounded by the soft tissue, is made of hard bone and cartilage. (See Figure 41.1B(a)).
- **Exoskeletons** are found in insects and their relatives. The skeleton is made of hard chitin segments which surround the body like armour plate. (See Figure 41.1B(b)).
- **Hydrostatic skeletons** are found in the larger worms. They consist of body spaces filled with fluid under pressure. Hydrostatic skeletons are firm but flexible. (See Figure 41.B(c)).

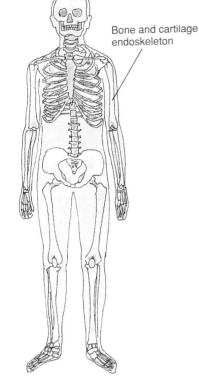

Bone and cartilage endoskeleton

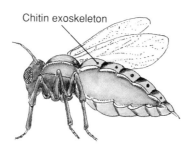

Chitin exoskeleton

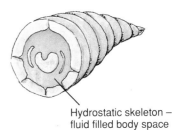

Hydrostatic skeleton – fluid filled body space

Figure 41.1B ● (a) The endoskeleton of a human

(b) The exoskeleton of an insect

(c) The hydrostatic skeleton of a worm

41.2 🌊 How muscles work

Hydrostatic skeletons are firm but flexible. The parts of exoskeletons and endoskeletons, however, are rigid. Their flexibility comes from **joints** which are made wherever two parts of a skeleton meet. The joints are pivots for limbs which form a system of levers. Muscles move limbs by pulling on them like a set of pulleys.

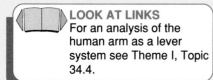

LOOK AT LINKS
For an analysis of the human arm as a lever system see Theme I, Topic 34.4.

Figure 41.2A compares the arrangement of muscles in the locust leg and the human arm. The muscles are in pairs which stretch across the joint. One muscle of a pair has the opposite effect to that of its partner. We call them **antagonistic** pairs. For example, contraction of the biceps muscle lifts the lower arm (flexing); contraction of the triceps muscle straightens (extends) the arm (see Figure 41.2B). When the biceps contracts the triceps relaxes and vice versa. The antagonistic pairs of muscles in the locust leg work in a similar way.

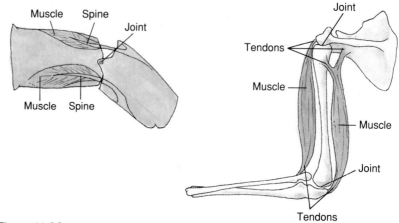

Figure 41.2A ●
(a) Locust leg – notice that the exoskeleton surrounds the muscles which are attached to its inside surface by inward projecting spines

(b) Human arm – notice that the endoskeleton is surrounded by the muscles which are attached to the outside surface by tough tendons

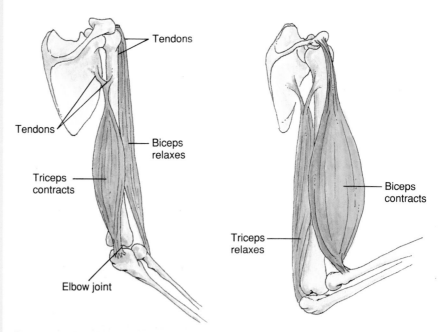

Figure 41.2B ● Moving the lower arm – the biceps and the triceps are an antagonistic pair of muscles

(a) Smooth muscle (x20)

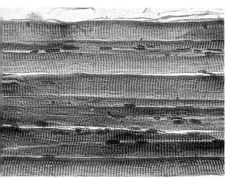

(b) Skeletal muscle (x20)

(c) Cardiac (heart) muscle (x20)

Figure 41.2C ● The three types of muscle viewed under a microscope

Types of muscle

Animals are able to move from place to place because of the action of muscles which pull on the skeleton. Moving from place to place is called locomotion. Muscular contractions are also responsible for other forms of movement. As heart muscle contracts and relaxes rhythmically it propels blood through the blood vessels. **Peristalsis** is brought about by contraction and relaxation of the muscles in the wall of the intestine. There are three types of muscle in the human body – smooth muscle, skeletal muscle and cardiac muscle (see Figure 41.2C).

● *Smooth muscle*

Smooth muscle contracts and relaxes slowly and steadily and does not become tired. These properties are ideal for the continuous movement of substances through the organs of the body. In mammals, smooth muscle is found in the walls of the intestine, blood vessels and air passages. Smooth muscle receives nerve impulses from the **autonomic nervous system** (which acts without conscious control from the brain). Contractions of smooth muscle therefore occur automatically. This is why smooth muscle is called **involuntary** muscle.

● *Skeletal muscle*

Skeletal muscle is often called striated (striped) muscle. It consists of fibres which are crossed with alternate light and dark bands. Skeletal muscle becomes tired after prolonged periods of activity but is otherwise ideal for moving parts of the skeleton. Its contractions are quick, strong and usually voluntary. Conscious messages from the brain control the strength and speed of contractions. The fibres of skeletal muscle receive branches from the axons of **motor neurones**. The muscle fibres contract when nerve impulses reach them.

● *Cardiac muscle*

Cardiac (heart) muscle is striated, like skeletal muscle. Its fibres are branched and connect with one another. This structure lets nerve impulses spread throughout the whole tissue, co-ordinating its contractions. Cardiac muscle never becomes tired. Its action is **involuntary**.

How fish swim

Fish swim by pushing their bodies and fins against the water. Their stream-lined shape helps to reduce resistance to the movement of their bodies through the water (see Figure 41.2D overleaf).

Blocks of muscle attached to each side of the fish's vertebral column move the body from side to side and drive the fish forward (see Figure 41.2E overleaf). The blocks of muscle on either side of the vertebral column form antagonistic pairs. The vertebral column itself is flexible and acts like a lever.

A gas-filled sac called the swim bladder helps to control buoyancy. When the swim bladder is full of gas the density of the fish decreases and the fish rises: when gas is removed, the density of the fish increases and the fish sinks. Cartilaginous fish such as sharks do not have swim bladders. If they stop swimming they slowly sink to the bottom.

LOOK AT LINKS
for **buoyancy**
See Theme I, Topic 35.6.

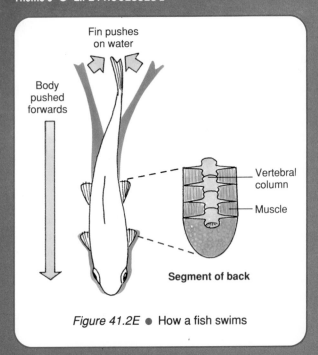

Figure 41.2E ● How a fish swims

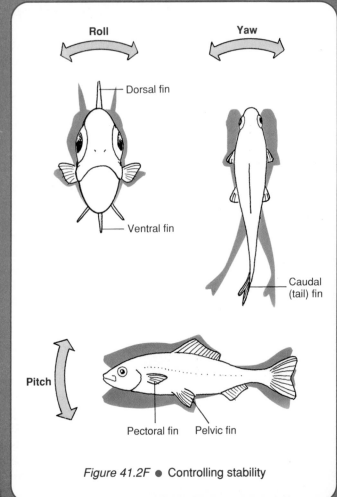

Figure 41.2F ● Controlling stability

Figure 41.2D Sharks are efficient swimmers – they have very streamlined bodies

Figure 41.2F shows how fish use their fins to control their direction of movement and their stability. The dorsal and ventral fins prevent **rolling** (rotation of the body about the long axis) and **yawing** (side to side movement of the front part of the body). The pectoral and pelvic fins prevent **pitching** (the tendency to nose dive).

41.3 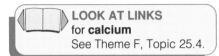 The skeleton

The vertebrate skeleton is made mostly of bone (see Figure 41.3A). It also contains cartilage which is softer than bone because it contains less **calcium** and phosphate. The amount of cartilage in the skeleton depends on the species and the age of an animal. The skeleton of sharks is made entirely of cartilage. In adult mammals, however, cartilage is found in only a few places. Cartilage covers the ends of limb bones where it helps to reduce friction in the joints as bones move upon one another.

LOOK AT LINKS
for **calcium**
See Theme F, Topic 25.4.

IT

Pixel Perfect
(DTP)

Use the *Pixel Perfect* system to create your own wall display of human anatomy. With the class working in groups you could cover topics such as the eye and ear, teeth, the skeleton, digestion, respiration, blood circulation, excretion, muscles and joints and the nervous system.

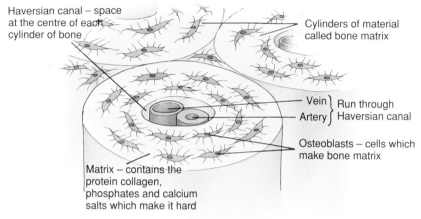

Figure 41.3A ● The structure of living bone (x200)

The human skeleton

The human skeleton is illustrated in Figure 41.3B. The bones of the skeleton are connected to one another at joints. Strap-like ligaments hold joints together. Tendons attach muscles to the skeleton. As muscles contract and relax across joints they move the different parts of the skeleton.

The human skeleton consists of two parts: the **axial skeleton** and the **appendicular skeleton**.

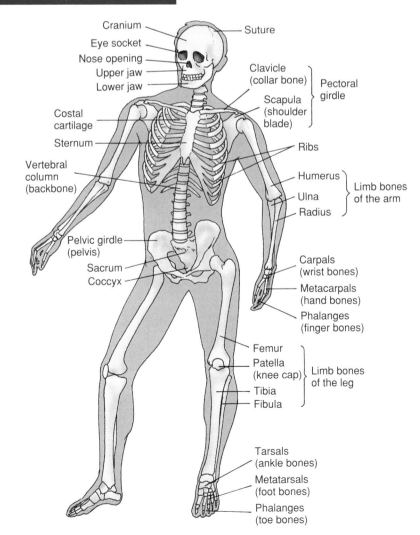

Figure 41.3B ● The human skeleton

● *The axial skeleton*

The axial skeleton consists of the skull, vertebral column and the ribs. These bones protect vital organs and tissues and form a strong support for the body. The skull and the vertebral column form a protective sheath of bone around the brain and spinal cord.

- **The skull** consists of plates of bone fused together to form the cranium which encloses and protects the brain. A hinged joint allows powerful muscles to move the lower jaw against the fixed upper jaw.
- **The vertebral column** (backbone) consists of a series of bones called **vertebrae** arranged like a curved rod (see Figure 41.3C). The vertebral column supports the skull and the limb girdles (pectoral and pelvic girdles). A cavity called the **neural canal** runs through the centre of each vertebra forming a continuous space in the vertebral column through which the spinal cord runs. At the top of the vertebral column the spinal cord passes through a hole in the skull and expands into the brain.
- **The ribs** form a curved bony cage around the heart and lungs (see Figure 41.3B). At the front they are attached by the costal cartilages to a bone called the sternum. At the back they form joints with the thoracic vertebrae. Each rib has ridges to which the intercostal muscles are attached. The costal cartilages and the joints make the ribs flexible. The intercostal muscles, the diaphragm and the muscles of the abdomen move them. Breathing depends on these movements.

IT'S A FACT

A slipped disc happens when the intervertebral disc bursts or is forced out from its position between the centrums. The person suffers considerable pain because of the pressure on the spinal cord.

LOOK AT LINKS
for more about breathing movements
See Theme F, Topic 26.2.

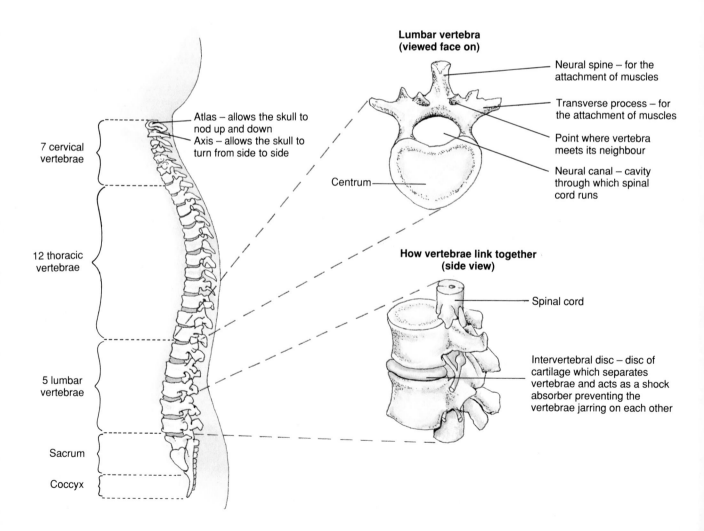

Figure 41.3C ● The vertebral column

The Human Skeleton

The Human Skeleton is a set of diagrams. You can look at the skeleton from front, side and rear and also at several individual components, including the skull.

IT'S A FACT

The fossil remains of vertebrates are usually parts of skeletons. Bone is very hard and therefore preserves well.

LOOK AT LINKS
for **artificial hip joints**
See Theme I, Topic 34.4.

● *The appendicular skeleton*

The appendicular skeleton consists of the limb girdles and limb bones. We use the hind limbs (legs and feet) for walking and running. Our upright position means that the forelimbs (arms and hands) are free for other activities.

● **The pelvic girdle** links the legs with the vertebral column (see Figure 41.3B). The pelvic girdle, which is made of two bones fused together, gives a solid framework that helps to bear the weight of the body. It is joined rigidly to the base of the vertebral column. The rigid arrangement of bones allows forces on the leg to be transmitted to the rest of the body.

● **The pectoral girdle** links the arms with the vertebral column. It is made up of the scapulas (shoulder blades) and clavicles (collar bones). This arrangement is not as effective as the pelvic girdle in transmitting force from the limbs to the body but it gives the shoulders and arms great freedom of movement.

● **The limb bones** in humans consist of long bones which form joints at the elbow in the arm and the knee in the leg. The upper long bone of each limb is attached to a limb girdle. The lower long bones are attached to the hand or the foot by a set of bones which form the wrist or the ankle. The joints with the pectoral and pelvic girdles and the joints at wrist, ankle, elbow and knee enable the limbs to move freely.

Joints

A joint is a meeting of two bones. Some joints are fixed. The bones of the skull, for example, meet at fixed joints called **sutures** (see Figure 41.3B). Other types of joint are not fixed:

● **Ball and socket joints** are formed where the upper long bones of the arms and legs meet their respective girdles. Figure 41.3D shows how the rounded end of the femur fits into a cup-shaped socket in the pelvic girdle.

● Figure 41.3E shows the **hinge joint** of the elbow. Hinge joints are also found in the fingers and knee.

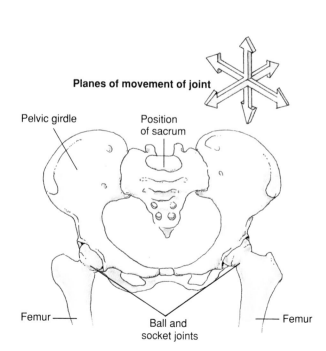

Figure 41.3D ● Ball and socket joint (hip joint)

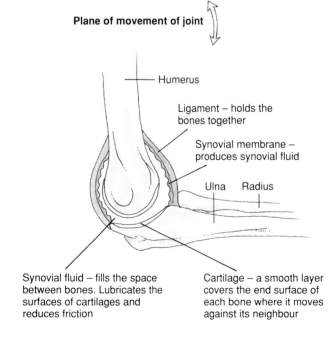

Figure 41.3E ● Hinge joint (elbow joint)

CHECKPOINT

① Study the diagram of the arm below and answer the following questions.

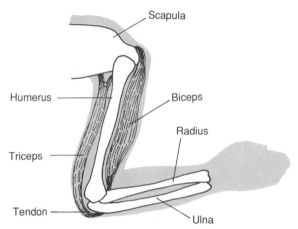

(a) Which muscle contracts when the arm is raised?
(b) Which muscle contracts when the arm is straightened?
(c) Why are the biceps and triceps called an antagonistic pair of muscles?
(d) How are the arm muscles attached to the arm bones?
(e) What type of joint is formed between the humerus and the scapula?

② Match each of the bones in Column A with its description in Column B.

Column A	Column B
Cranium	Consists of vertebrae fused together
Rib cage	Upper arm bone
Sternum	Protects the brain
Sacrum	Moves as you breathe
Clavicle	Ribs are attached to it
Femur	Called the collar bone
Humerus	Upper leg bone

③ (a) Distinguish between the hydrostatic skeleton, exoskeleton and endoskeleton.
(b) Say what features the hydrostatic skeleton, exoskeleton and endoskeleton have in common.

④ Give explanations for the following statements.
(a) Pregnant women should be encouraged to drink milk.
(b) The sutures of the skull are fixed joints.
(c) The human femur is stronger than the humerus.
(d) Breathing depends on the movement of the ribs.
(e) Women usually have broader hips than men.

⑤ Distinguish between smooth muscle, cardiac muscle and skeletal muscle. Explain how each type of muscle is suited to the job it performs.

⑥ Complete the following paragraph using the words listed below. Each word may be used once, more than once or not at all.

levers calcium support collagen joint rigidity muscles movement
contract food bones protect

The _____ of the skeleton _____ and _____ the soft
tissues of the body. The limb bones are _____ which move because
_____ attached to them _____ . Where bones meet a
_____ is formed. Bone consists of the protein _____ and
_____ salts. Blood vessels in the bone supply _____ and
oxygen.

? THEME QUESTIONS

● Topic 38

1 The diagram below, labelled A to K, shows a ventral view of a mammalian heart and blood vessels.

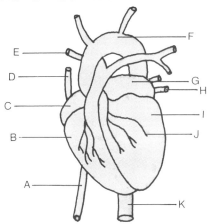

(a) State precisely where the blood in D and E would go to next.
(b) Write the letter of the part which contracts to send blood to the brain.
(c) (i) What effect may heavy smoking have on J?
  (ii) How may this affect the heart as a whole?

(LEAG)

2 The figure below is a histogram showing the rate of blood flow to various organs.

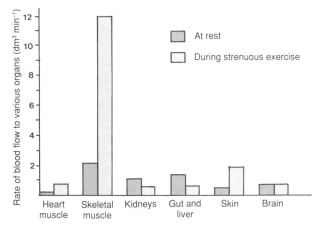

(a) Copy the table below and record the volume of blood flowing per minute to each of the organs when the body is at rest, and when the body is undergoing strenuous exercise.

	Volume of blood (dm³/min)	
	At rest	During strenuous exercise
Heart muscle		
Skeletal muscle		
Kidneys		
Gut and liver		
Skin		
Brain		

(b) What is the total volume of blood per minute being pumped by the left ventricle to all these organs when the body is (i) at rest (ii) undergoing strenuous exercise?
(c) If the pulse rate when the body is at rest is 70 beats per minute, what volume of blood is pumped out by the left ventricle at each heart beat?
(d) If the pulse rate during strenuous exercise is 160 beats per minute, what volume of blood is pumped out by the left ventricle at each heart beat?
(e) Account for the changes in the rate of blood flow to the following organs as a result of undergoing strenuous exercise.
  (i) Heart muscle
  (ii) Skeletal muscle
  (iii) Brain
  (iv) Gut and liver

(MEG)

● Topic 39

3 (a) Describe the events which occur after the release of sperms into the vagina of a human female until implantation of the embryo.
(b) The chart below shows how the thickness of the uterus lining and the levels of two hormones A and B, made in the ovaries, vary during the menstrual cycle. The first month is a normal menstrual cycle but fertilisation occurs during the second month.

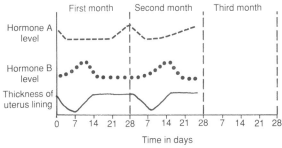

(i) Say when was the most likely time of ovulation in the first month.
(ii) During which period in the second month is fertilisation likely to have occurred?
(c) Copy and complete the chart above to show what happens, following fertilisation, to:
(i) the uterus lining in the third month,
(ii) the levels of hormones A and B in the third month.
(d) One type of contraceptive pill contains a mixture of hormones A and B.
(i) Explain briefly how this pill works as a contraceptive.
(ii) If she is using the contraceptive pill, it is usual for a woman to take a hormone pill each day for 21 days and then to take a pill without any hormones for the next 7 days. What is the advantage of taking the hormones for 21 days only?

(NEA)

4 The diagrams show sections through the flower of a tomato plant, the same flower after fertilisation and the ripe tomato fruit.

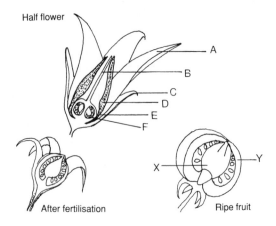

Half flower

After fertilisation   Ripe fruit

(a) Name the structures labelled A, B, C, D, E and F.
(b) State **three** changes which have occurred in the flower after fertilisation.
(c) What are the functions of the structures labelled X and Y on the fruit?

(NEA)

● *Topic 40*

5 Look at the diagram of the nervous system of a small mammal.

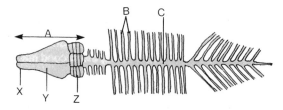

(a) Name the structures labelled A, B and C on the diagram.
(b) Which **two** main parts of the mammal's skeleton would have to be removed before you could see the above structures?
(c) In order to display the nervous system as in the diagram, would the animal be dissected from the dorsal or the ventral surface?
(d) Which is the correct statement:
    C is hollow.
    C is solid.
(e) Parts B link sense organs to the central nervous system. Name **three** sense organs found in a mammal.
(f) State the function (work) of part X.
(g) State **one** function of part Z.
(h) What is part Y called?

(WJEC)

6 A young plant is grown in a pot as shown in diagram A. It was then turned on its side as in B, and the result after several days is shown in diagram C. The pot is shown in section.
(a) Name **two** factors which could be responsible for the growth of the stem as shown in C.
(b) Name **one** factor which could be responsible for the growth of the roots in the direction shown in C.

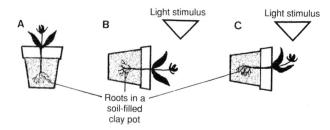

Light stimulus   Light stimulus

Roots in a
soil-filled
clay pot

(c) To make the responses shown in the diagram possible, the growing points produce a chemical substance. Name this substance.
(d) State the advantages of these responses in (i) the stem and (ii) the root, to the plant when growing in its natural habitat.

(WJEC)

● *Topic 41*

7 The diagram below shows a section through the ball and socket joint in the human hip.

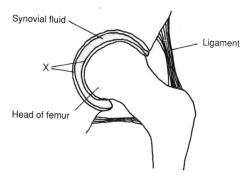

Synovial fluid

Ligament

X

Head of femur

(a) Name the structure X.
(b) The ligament is playing a part in holding the bones together. As well as being strong, suggest another important property of the ligament.
(c) What is the function of the synovial fluid in the joint?
(d) The diagram below shows the positions of the bones and main muscles of the legs of a human when running. (For clarity, each muscle is shown on one leg only.)

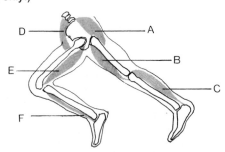

(i) Explain the term 'antagonistic muscles', illustrating your answer by reference to **two** sets of antagonistic muscles from the muscles labelled A to F on the diagram.
(ii) Suggest why muscle C is more powerfully developed than muscle F.

(NEA)

THEME K

Electricity

In winter, a power cut in the electricity supply to our homes makes life very difficult. *If you knew that a power cut was to be made in your area tonight, what plans would you make?* Get some candles for lighting, use overcoats to keep warm, check the batteries in your radio, fill a flask with a hot drink before the power cut. Electricity keeps factories, shops, hospitals and offices operating. How did people manage before the electricity supply network was established?

In this theme, you will find out what electricity is, how it is measured, what it can be used for and how it is generated and distributed. Everyone uses electricity at home, at school or at work. After studying this theme, you should appreciate the benefits and dangers of electricity as well as

TOPIC 42 ELECTRIC CHARGES

42.1 Charging things up

Tiny sparks created by static electricity can be very dangerous in the wrong place. Read on to find out why.

LOOK AT LINKS
for **the atom**
See Theme C, Topic 11.3.

SCIENCE AT WORK

Operating theatres in hospitals are fitted with antistatic floors. Theatre staff and equipment might otherwise become charged and produce sparks. This would be highly dangerous in an operating theatre because anaesthetic vapour can be explosive.

Comb your hair with a plastic comb and then see if the comb can 'pick up' small bits of paper. Running a comb through your hair charges the comb up so it attracts paper. If you rub a plastic rule on a dry cloth, the rule and the cloth become charged. If you sit in a plastic chair, especially if your clothes are made from nylon materials, your clothes and the chair become charged when you get up from the chair. Electric charge on an object is often called **static electricity**.

Objects charge up because they gain or lose electrons. The electron is the smallest particle of the **atom**. The electron carries a fixed negative charge. Every atom has a positively charged nucleus that is surrounded by electrons (Figure 42.1A). An atom is uncharged because it contains equal amounts of positive and negative charge.

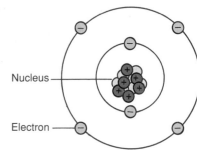

Figure 42.1A ● An uncharged atom - the positive charges balance the negative charges

An uncharged object that gains electrons becomes negatively charged. Objects that lose electrons become positively charged. Certain **insulators** like polythene become negatively charged when rubbed with a dry cloth; electrons are transferred from the cloth to the polythene by rubbing. Other insulators (e.g. perspex) become positively charged when rubbed with a dry cloth because electrons are transferred from the perspex to the cloth during rubbing (Figure 42.1B).

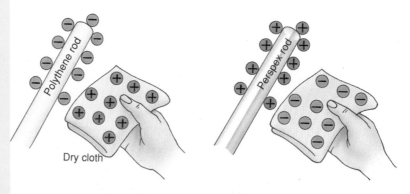

Figure 42.1B ● Charging by friction
(a) Polythene rod rubbed with a dry cloth; the rod becomes negatively charged
(b) Perspex rod rubbed with a dry cloth; the rod becomes positively charged

Conductors such as metal objects can be charged if they are insulated from the ground. A conductor in electrical contact with the ground is said to be electrically 'earthed'. Electrons can move freely through conductors and pass to or from the ground if the conductor is earthed. However, if a conductor is insulated from the ground, electrons cannot pass from it to earth. The conductor is therefore capable of holding electric charge.

Investigating static electricity

Charged objects exert forces on each other due to their charge. Objects with the same charge repel each other; objects with opposite charge attract each other. Figure 42.1C shows how to test this.

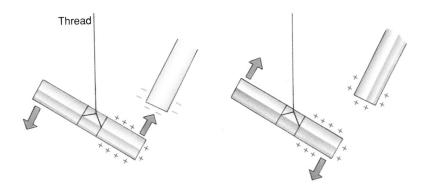

Figure 42.1C ● The law of force for charges
(a) Opposite charges attract (b) Like charges repel

An insulated conductor can be charged either by **direct contact** or by **induction** from a charged insulator. Direct contact between the charged insulator and the conductor transfers charge to the conductor from the charged insulator. It gives the conductor the same type of charge as the insulator. Figure 42.1D shows charging by induction. Charging by induction gives the conductor an opposite charge to the insulator and no charge is gained or lost by the insulator.

The gold leaf electroscope can be used to find out if an object is charged and what type of charge it carries. The electroscope itself may be charged by direct contact or by induction. Figure 42.1E shows how the electroscope works.

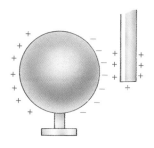

(a) The charged rod is held near the sphere

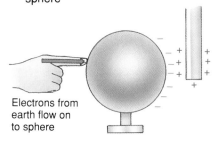

Electrons from earth flow on to sphere

(b) The sphere is earthed briefly

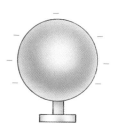

(c) The rod is removed. The sphere is left with an opposite charge to the rod
Figure 42.1D ● Charging by induction

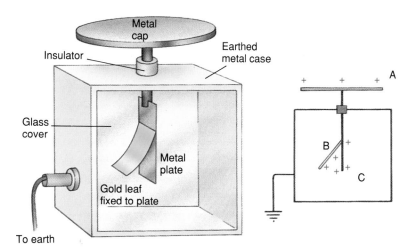

Figure 42.1E ● The gold leaf electroscope

When the electroscope is charged at A, B becomes charged the same as the metal plate C. Like charges repel, so the leaf rises at B

A silo containing chocolate powder exploded as it was being filled. The explosion destroyed the silo and severely damaged the silo building. Three people were injured in the explosion and were taken to hospital. The silo had recently been modified by replacing the metal inlet pipe with a plastic pipe. Investigators think that pinpricks found on this pipe were caused by sparks, which made the powder explode.

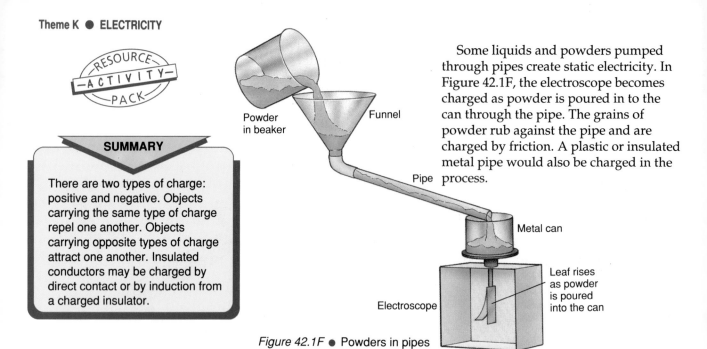

RESOURCE -ACTIVITY- PACK

Powder in beaker

Funnel

Pipe

Metal can

Leaf rises as powder is poured into the can

Electroscope

Some liquids and powders pumped through pipes create static electricity. In Figure 42.1F, the electroscope becomes charged as powder is poured in to the can through the pipe. The grains of powder rub against the pipe and are charged by friction. A plastic or insulated metal pipe would also be charged in the process.

Figure 42.1F ● Powders in pipes

SUMMARY

There are two types of charge: positive and negative. Objects carrying the same type of charge repel one another. Objects carrying opposite types of charge attract one another. Insulated conductors may be charged by direct contact or by induction from a charged insulator.

CHECKPOINT

❶ Explain each of the following:
   (a) If you walk on a nylon carpet and then touch a metal radiator you may get a shock.
   (b) Getting out of a car seat can give you a shock.
   (c) Taking off a pullover can produce lots of crackles and tiny sparks.

❷ Graham is testing the charge gained by powdered milk when it passes through a plastic pipe. He uses a gold leaf electroscope as in Figure 42.1F, and he charges it by pouring the powder into the can through the pipe.
   (a) When a negatively charged rod is brought near the electroscope, the leaf falls. What type of charge is on the electroscope?
   (b) What type of charge is gained by (i) the powder, (ii) the pipe?
   (c) A spark from the pipe during pumping could ignite the powder and make it explode. An explosion is more likely to happen with fine powders than with coarse powders. Why?

❸ In a factory, workers near a conveyor belt complain of electric shocks. Tests show that this is because the belt becomes charged as it passes round a roller.
   (a) Explain why anyone standing near the charged belt can become charged by touching an earthed bench near the belt.
   (b) What measures would you recommend to overcome this problem?

❹ (a) Oil flowing from a pipe can produce static electricity due to friction between the pipe and the oil. Why must the pipe be earthed to ensure that static electricity does not build up on it?
   (b) Things that are charged up soon become dusty. Why?

Conveyor belt

Charge on belt

+ + + + + + +

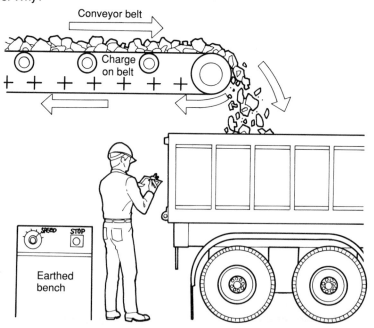

Earthed bench

42.2 ⬙ Electric fields

FIRST THOUGHTS

A stroke of lightning is a massive discharge of electricity to the ground from a thundercloud. In this section, you will find out how thunderclouds are discharged safely.

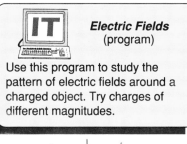

IT

Electric Fields
(program)

Use this program to study the pattern of electric fields around a charged object. Try charges of different magnitudes.

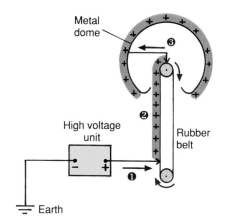

- ❶ Positive charge is 'sprayed' on to the belt
- ❷ The belt is driven by a motor and carries the charge up
- ❸ The charge is taken off the belt and the dome becomes charged up

Figure 42.2A ● The Van de Graaff generator

The **Van de Graaff generator** is a machine for charging things up. When it is switched on, charge builds up on its dome. This happens because charge is deposited on the bottom of the belt, as shown in Figure 42.2A. This charge is then carried up to the dome by the belt. Any insulated object connected to the dome is charged too. If too much charge builds up on the dome, the dome discharges itself by letting sparks fly to any nearby object.

Any charged object brought near a charged dome experiences a force due to the dome. This is because the dome creates a force field round itself which acts on any other charged object near it. This field is called an **electric field**. It can be pictured as **lines of force**. These are the paths that free positive charges would take in the field. Figure 42.2B shows the electric field pattern near a charged dome.

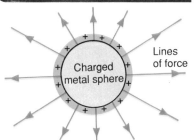

Figure 42.2B ● The electric field near a charged sphere

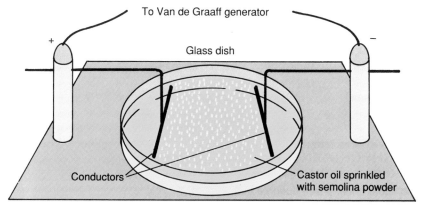

Figure 42.2C ● Field patterns (a) A uniform field (b) A concentrated field

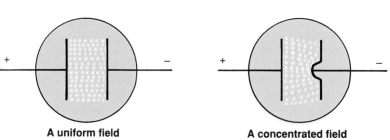

A uniform field　　　**A concentrated field**

Electric field patterns

You can see the patterns of an electric field using the apparatus in Figure 42.2C. Two conductors, connected to a Van de Graaff generator are submerged in castor oil sprinkled with semolina powder. The semolina powder forms patterns because the powder grains line up along the lines of force of the field. The field between two oppositely charged parallel plates is said to be uniform because the lines are parallel to one another. If a conductor is curved the lines of force are concentrated where the curve is greatest, because this is where the charge is most concentrated.

LOOK AT LINKS
for **ions**
See Theme C, Topic 13.2.

Lightning conductors under thunderclouds create very strong electric fields in the surrounding air. Air molecules near the tip of the conductor become **ionised** due to electrons being pulled off. The ions then discharge the thundercloud so no lightning flash is produced (Figure 42.2D).

SCIENCE AT WORK

Electrostatic paint sprays are used to coat car body panels on assembly lines. The spray gun is designed to produce tiny charged droplets of paint. The car body is oppositely charged to the paint spray. As a result, the charged droplets are attracted to the car body panel. The droplets can travel along the lines of force of the field to reach hidden parts of the panel.

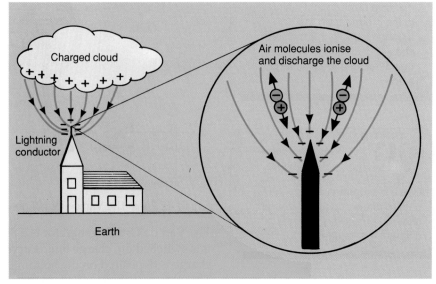

Figure 42.2D ● The lightning conductor

The action of a pointed conductor such as a lightning conductor can be shown using a Van de Graaff machine. A drawing pin is fixed to the uncharged dome, as shown in Figure 42.2E. When the machine is switched on, the dome does not charge up as it would without the drawing pin. Instead the charge on the dome concentrates at the tip of the pin, making the electric field near the tip very strong. Air molecules near the tip become ionised and discharge the dome.

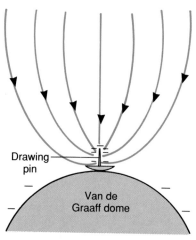

Figure 42.2E ● Discharging due to ions

SUMMARY

The charge on a conductor is most concentrated where the conductor surface is most curved. If the electric field near a charged object is strong enough, air molecules in the field become ionised and can discharge the object.

CHECKPOINT

❶ (a) Why is it dangerous to stand under a tree during a thunderstorm?
(b) Explain why a lightning conductor fitted to the top of a building reduces the risk of a lightning strike damaging the building.

❷ Susan is investigating the gold leaf electroscope. She can make the leaf rise by charging the electroscope from her plastic comb. She discovers that the leaf falls slowly if there is an upturned drawing pin on the cap of the electroscope. She also discovers that holding a burning match near the electroscope makes the leaf fall.
(a) Explain why the leaf rises or falls in each case.
(b) Susan's teacher then demonstrates to the class that radioactivity near the electroscope makes the leaf fall. What do you think radioactivity does to the air near the electroscope?

❸ Dust extractors in power station chimneys are very effective at stopping ash being carried by flue gases into the atmosphere. The flue gases are passed through a negatively charged wire grid. The grid is fixed inside an earthed metal tube. Particles of ash passing through the grid become negatively charged from the grid. The diagram shows the idea.

(a) Why are the particles attracted to the metal tube?

(b) Copy the diagram and sketch the lines of force between the wire and the plates.

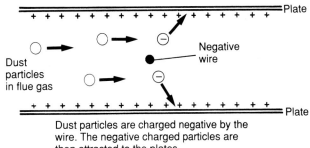

Dust particles are charged negative by the wire. The negative charged particles are then attracted to the plates

---

42.3 📖 Charge and current

An electric current in a wire is a flow of charge due to electrons moving along the wire. Read on to find out how charge is measured and how much charge is carried by a single electron.

The ping-pong ball experiment in Figure 42.3A shows that an electric current is a flow of charge. The ball has a coat of conducting paint. When the electrostatic generator is switched on, the metal plates become oppositely charged. The ball moves to touch one plate and becomes charged the same as the plate. Since like charged objects repel, the ball is then forced to the opposite plate. It therefore continues to move to and fro between the plates.

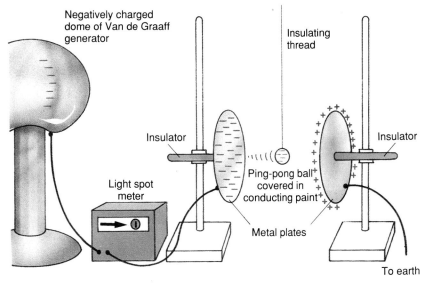

Figure 42.3A ● The ping-pong ball experiment

The ball transfers charge from one plate to the other each time it moves across the gap. Figure 42.3A shows how this happens. The meter registers a tiny current because electrons pass through it from the generator to replace the electrons carried from the negative plate by the ball.

How do you think the meter reading changes if the plates are moved closer together? The ball bounces to and fro more rapidly. This makes the reading increase because the ball is 'ferrying' charge across the gap at a greater rate than before. The current through the meter is due to the flow of charge from the generator to the plates.

Electric current is measured in **amperes**, A. The ampere is defined in terms of the magnetic effect of an electric current. All other electrical units are derived from the ampere.

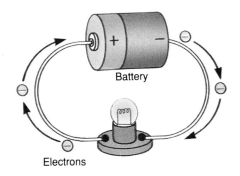

Figure 42.3B ● Charge flow

Electric charge is measured in **coulombs**, C. One coulomb is defined as the amount of charge passing a point in a circuit each second when the current is one ampere. In other words, a current of one ampere is equal to a rate of flow of charge of one coulomb per second.

For a steady current in a circuit

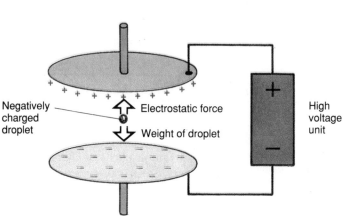

Charge passed	=	Current	x	Time
(coulombs)		(amperes)		(seconds)
Q	=	It		

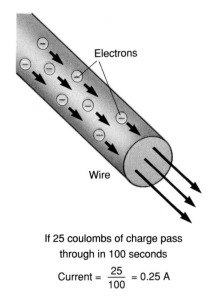

If 25 coulombs of charge pass through in 100 seconds

$$\text{Current} = \frac{25}{100} = 0.25 \text{ A}$$

Figure 42.3C ● Current equals charge flow per second

Figure 42.3D ● An oil droplet in balance

The charge carried by an electron was first measured by Robert Millikan in 1915. He studied the motion of charged oil droplets between oppositely charged parallel plates, as shown in Figure 42.3D. From his measurements, he worked out that the electron carried a charge of 1.6×10^{-19} C.

Work out for yourself how many electrons must pass each second along a wire carrying a current of one ampere. *In other words, how many electrons are needed to make a total charge of one coulomb?* You should find 6.2×10^{18} electrons are needed.

Measuring electrolysis

A metal object can be copper-plated by using the object as the cathode in an **electrolytic** cell containing copper sulphate solution. Copper ions from the solution are attracted to the cathode where they are discharged and form a layer of copper on the cathode.

What factors control the thickness of the layer of copper deposited on the cathode? In a factory where metal ornaments are copper-plated, too little copper deposited on the ornaments would make them unattractive and unsaleable; too much copper would make the ornaments expensive and uneconomic.

The thickness of the copper layer depends on the number of copper ions attracted to the cathode and on the surface area of the cathode. Each copper ion arriving at the cathode is discharged by gaining two electrons from the battery. Thus a steady flow of electrons round the circuit means that the mass of copper on the cathode increases at a steady rate.

The electric current caused by the flow of electrons round the circuit can be measured using an **ammeter** as shown in Figure 42.3E. Table 42.1 gives some measurements made by several groups in a class investigating how the mass of copper deposited depends on the current and time taken. The measurements are plotted in Figure 42.3F.

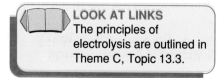

LOOK AT LINKS
The principles of electrolysis are outlined in Theme C, Topic 13.3.

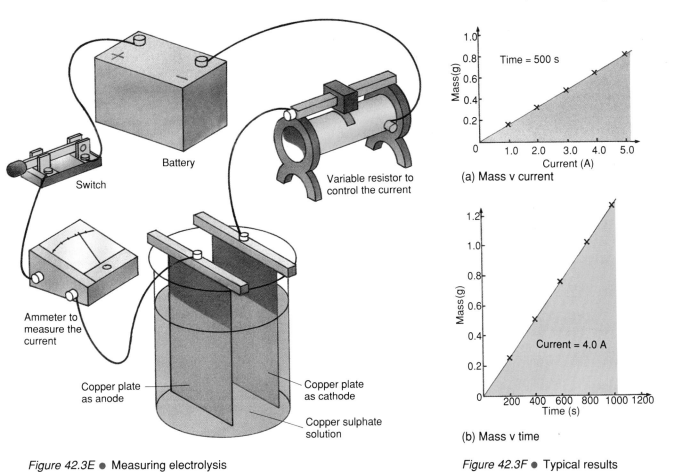

Figure 42.3E ● Measuring electrolysis

Figure 42.3F ● Typical results

Table 42.1 ● Measuring electrolysis

Mass deposited in 500 s (g)	0	0.16	0.33	0.48	0.65	0.82
Current (A)	0	1.0	2.0	3.0	4.0	5.0

Mass deposited at 4.0 A (g)	0	0.26	0.53	0.78	1.05	1.31
Time taken (s)	0	200	400	600	800	1000

What conclusions can you draw from these results? The graphs show that the mass deposited is proportional to the current and the time taken.
This can be written as an equation

Mass deposited = Constant x Current x Time

However, current x time gives the charge passed, so the mass deposited is proportional to the charge passed

Mass deposited = Constant x Charge passed

Use the graphs in Figure 42.3F to work out the mass deposited per unit of charge. This is the constant in the equation above.
To understand what the equation means, remember each copper ion discharged at the cathode increases the mass of copper on the cathode and takes two electrons from the battery. Thus the mass deposited is proportional to the number of copper ions discharged. This is proportional to the number of electrons and hence the charge from the battery. Hence the mass deposited is proportional to the charge from the battery.

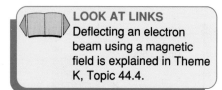

LOOK AT LINKS
Deflecting an electron beam using a magnetic field is explained in Theme K, Topic 44.4.

LOOK AT LINKS
The electron microscope uses an electron beam to form images of tiny structures.
See Theme D, Topic 19.1.

Electron beams

Television tubes and computer VDUs (visual display units) use electron beams to build up pictures on the screen. Figure 42.3G shows how an electron beam is produced by an **electron gun** in an electron deflection tube, which is a special tube designed to show some of the properties of electron beams. The filament is heated by passing an electric current through it. Electrons in the hot filament gain sufficient energy to leave the filament. This is called **thermionic emission**. These electrons are attracted towards the anode A, which is a metal plate with a hole in it. Some of the electrons pass through the hole and emerge as a narrow beam. There must be a vacuum in the tube, otherwise gas atoms would stop the electrons from the filament reaching the anode.

A high-voltage unit is connected across the deflecting plates P and Q in Figure 42.3G. The electron beam is attracted towards the positive plate. *What does this tell you about the type of charge carried by an electron?* Another way to deflect an electron beam is to use a magnetic field. Television tubes and VDUs contain magnetic deflecting coils.

The **oscilloscope** is an instrument used to display electrical signals on a screen. Figure 42.3H shows the internal construction of the oscilloscope tube. An electron beam passes between two pairs of deflecting plates and hits the screen, producing a spot of light on the screen. The electrical signal is supplied to the input terminals which are connected to the Y-deflecting plates. Different signals deflect the electron beam by different amounts.

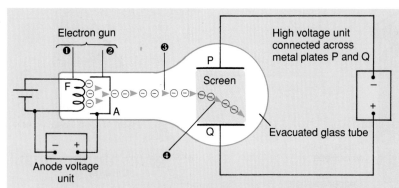

❶ The filament F is heated by passing an electric current through it. Electrons in the filament gain sufficient energy to leave the filament. This process is called thermionic emission.
❷ The anode A attracts electrons from the filament. Some of the electrons pass through the hole in the anode to form an electron beam.
❸ The beam of electrons passes into the electric field between deflecting plates P and Q.
❹ The electrons in the beam are attracted towards the positive plate Q. They pass over the screen to leave a visible trace.

Figure 42.3G ● An electron deflection tube

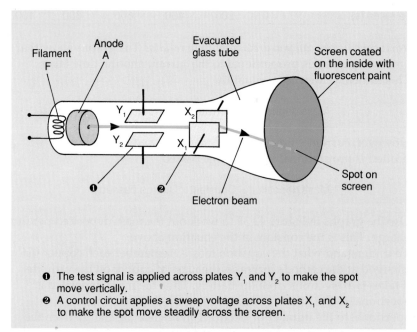

❶ The test signal is applied across plates Y₁ and Y₂ to make the spot move vertically.
❷ A control circuit applies a sweep voltage across plates X₁ and X₂ to make the spot move steadily across the screen.

Figure 42.3H ● (a) The construction of an oscilloscope tube

(b) An oscilloscope in use

One of the control circuits in the oscilloscope is used to apply a **sweep** voltage to the X-deflecting plates. This makes the spot on the screen sweep horizontally across the screen. At the same time, the 'test' signal applied to the Y-plates makes the spot move vertically. The result is that the spot produces a trace on the screen which shows how the voltage varies with time (Figure 42.3I).

SUMMARY

An electric current is a flow of charge. Current is measured in amperes. The unit of charge is a coulomb. Metals conduct electricity due to the passage of electrons. Television tubes, VDUs and oscilloscopes use electron beams to produce their displays.

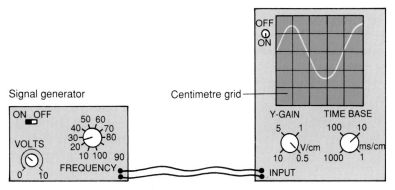

Figure 42.3I ● Using an oscilloscope

CHECKPOINT

❶ Look at the ping-pong ball experiment in Figure 42.3A.
   (a) What would be the effect on the meter reading of moving the plates further apart?
   (b) Explain in terms of electrons how the ball transfers charge from one plate to the other as it swings back and forth between the plates.

❷ (a) A wire carries a steady current of 3.5 A. How much charge passes along the wire in (i) 1 s (ii) 1 minute (iii) 10 minutes?
   (b) A charge of 200 C is to be passed along a wire in 40 seconds. What will be the average current?
   (c) What would the current be if the same charge were passed in 10 seconds?
   (d) How long would it take to pass a charge of 500 C along a wire if a steady current of (i) 0.5 A (ii) 1.0 mA were passed along the wire?

❸ Consider the electron deflection tube shown in Figure 42.3G.
   (a) Why does the beam bend towards plate Q?
   (b) Increasing the voltage at the anode makes the electrons in the beam travel faster. How would this affect the trace on the screen?
   (c) How would the trace on the screen be affected if the voltage across plates P and Q was increased?

❹ Figure 42.3I shows an oscilloscope used to display an alternating signal of constant frequency and amplitude.
   (a) What is the amplitude (i.e. height above the centre) of the trace in millimetres?
   (b) The Y-gain control knob is set at 0.5 V/cm. Work out the amplitude of the trace in volts.
   (c) How would the trace appear if the frequency was doubled with the amplitude unchanged?

❺ In a copper-plating experiment, 0.40 g of copper was deposited by a current of 2.0 A in 600 s.
   (a) How many coulombs of charge were used?
   (b) What mass of copper would have been deposited by (i) 4.0 A in 600 s (ii) 2.0 A in 300 s (iii) 4.0 A in 300 s?
   (c) What mass is deposited by 1 C of charge?
   (d) The mass of a copper ion is 1.1×10^{-22} g. Use the information above to work out its charge. How many electrons is the copper ion short of?

42.4 Batteries

In this section, you will find out how a battery works and what a rechargeable battery is. You will even find out how to save money when you buy batteries.

How many electrical items do you have that use batteries? Calculators, digital watches, cameras, radios and cassette recorders all use batteries. They are used in cars, hearing aids, torches, toys and many other items. Batteries vary in size from the tiny batteries used in digital watches to heavy duty car batteries.

A **cell** produces electricity. Lots of cells joined together form a **battery** of cells. A battery pushes electrons round a circuit from the negative terminal to the positive terminal. Early scientists did not know about electrons and they imagined the charge from a battery flowed round the circuit from the positive pole to the negative pole. That is why current directions in circuits are always marked from 'positive to negative'.

A battery is necessary in a circuit to push electrons round the circuit. In Figure 42.4B, electrons deliver energy from the battery to the lamp.

The **voltage** of the battery is a measure of the energy delivered by the electrons to the lamp. Battery voltage is sometimes called **electromotive force** or e.m.f.

The unit of voltage is the **volt**. A battery with a voltage of one volt is able to deliver one joule of energy for each coulomb of charge that passes through it. In other words, the voltage of a battery is the number of joules per coulomb that the battery can deliver when it is connected in a circuit.

Primary cells do not produce electricity when the chemicals in the cell are used up. They must be replaced by fresh cells. A simple primary cell can be made using a copper plate and a zinc plate, as shown in Figure 42.4C. Zinc is more reactive than copper in dilute sulphuric acid. Zinc atoms leave the plate and go into the solution as ions. The zinc plate becomes negatively charged and the copper plate becomes positively charged. Hydrogen ions from the sulphuric acid (which are positive) are attracted to the copper plate where they gain electrons from the copper plate and are discharged as gas. The bubbles of hydrogen gas stop further hydrogen ions reaching the copper plate. As a result, the cell voltage drops.

Figure 42.4A ● Different batteries

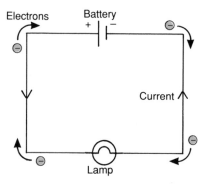

Figure 42.4B ● The current convention

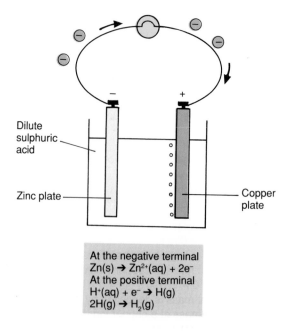

At the negative terminal
$Zn(s) \rightarrow Zn^{2+}(aq) + 2e^-$
At the positive terminal
$H^+(aq) + e^- \rightarrow H(g)$
$2H(g) \rightarrow H_2(g)$

Figure 42.4C ● A primary cell

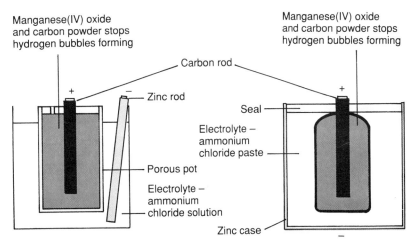

Figure 42.4D ● More primary cells (a) The Leclanché cell (b) A dry cell

SUMMARY

Batteries and cells convert chemical energy into electrical energy. Primary cells are not rechargeable, whereas secondary cells are. The voltage of a cell is the number of joules per coulomb that the cell can deliver in a circuit.

Some more primary cells are shown in Figure 42.4D. The Leclanché cell contains manganese(IV) oxide to stop hydrogen gas forming. The dry cell is based on the Leclanché cell but the electrolyte is in the form of a paste.

Secondary cells are rechargeable. This means that after use, a secondary cell can be recharged to be used again. When it is recharged, electrical energy is converted back to chemical energy inside the cell. The lead–acid accumulator is one of the most common secondary cells. Each cell has a voltage of 2 V. A 12 V car battery can be made using six of these cells. Nickel–cadmium cells are also rechargeable. These are much lighter than lead acid cells and they last longer before needing to be recharged.

CHECKPOINT

❶ Make a list of electrical devices you have that are battery-operated. Write down if the batteries are rechargeable and what type they are.

❷ Marie needs to replace the two 1.5 V batteries in her radio cassette. She is thinking of buying a battery charger at £6.50 and two 1.5 V rechargeable batteries at £1.50 each. The cheapest non-rechargeable 1.5 V batteries cost 50p each but need to be replaced every four weeks.
 (a) How much will she save over a year if she buys rechargeable cells and the battery charger?
 (b) Long-life non-rechargeable cells are on sale in the shop when she buys the rechargeable cells. Each long-life cell lasts six times longer than an ordinary cell although it costs £3.50. Do you think she should have bought these instead?

❸ Milk floats are electric vehicles that run off batteries. List some of the advantages and disadvantages of this type of electric vehicle.

❹ (a) If the headlamps of a car are switched on without the engine running, the car battery runs down. Why is it difficult to start the car then?
 (b) Cars are often difficult to start on cold, damp mornings. Why is it sensible not to use the car heater until the car engine has been started?

❺ A 12 V battery is capable of delivering 1.0 A of current for 100 hours.
 (a) How many coulombs of charge pass round a circuit in which the current is 1.0 A for 100 hours?
 (b) How much energy is available from the battery?
 (c) How long will it take to recharge the battery if the charging current is 2.0 A?

TOPIC 43 CIRCUITS

43.1 Batteries and bulbs

FIRST THOUGHTS

The simple circuits in this section must be mastered before attempting the more complicated circuits in later sections.

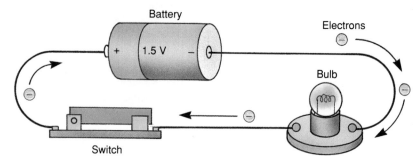

Figure 43.1A ● Lighting a torch bulb
(a) Making connections (b) Circuit diagrams

Figure 43.1A shows how to make a circuit to light a lamp bulb using a 1.5 V dry cell. When the switch is closed, electrons are forced round the circuit by the battery. The electrons deliver energy from the battery to the lamp bulb. They pass from the negative terminal round the circuit to the positive terminal, where they re-enter the battery.

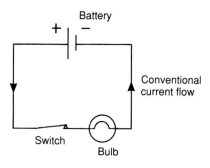

However, the convention is for electric current to be considered as flowing from positive to negative. The convention was decided before the discovery of electrons.

The **voltage** across the bulb is the amount of energy delivered to the bulb by each coulomb of charge passing through it. This is sometimes called **potential difference**. One volt of potential difference is equal to one joule of energy per coulomb of charge. The term 'potential difference' (or p.d.) is used for the voltage between two points in a circuit.

Investigating simple circuits

Set up each of the four circuits in Figure 43.1B using bulbs and dry cells identical to the ones used in Figure 43.1A. *How does the brightness of each bulb compare with the bulbs in the circuit in Figure 43.1A?*

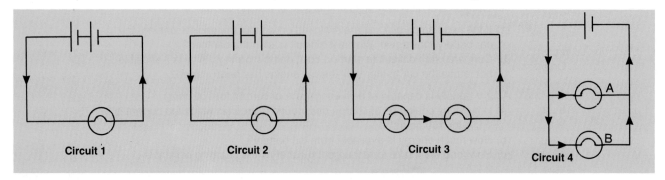

Circuit 1   Circuit 2   Circuit 3   Circuit 4

Figure 43.1B ● Comparing brightnesses

The nerves in your body send their messages to your brain electrically. When a nerve sends a signal, the voltage of each section is changed by the previous section. In this way, a 'voltage pulse' travels along the nerve fibre.

- **Circuit 1** *Why is the bulb much brighter than the bulb in the Figure 43.1A circuit? How much voltage is across the bulb?*
- **Circuit 2** This has two batteries and a lamp bulb like Circuit 1, yet the bulb does not light up. *Can you explain why?*
- **Circuit 3** The same current passes through each bulb. Unscrew one of the bulbs from its holder. The other bulb goes out too. The two bulbs are connected **in series**. Components in series always take the same current. The bulbs light normally even though two batteries are used. The battery voltage is shared or divided between the two bulbs.
- **Circuit 4** The current through bulb A is not the same as through bulb B. Unscrew one bulb and the other bulb remains lit. The two bulbs are connected **in parallel**. Each bulb is connected across the cell terminals. The p.d. across each bulb is therefore the same. Circuit components in parallel always have the same p.d.

Circuit training

More circuit components are shown in Figure 43.1C. *Can you think where they may be used?*

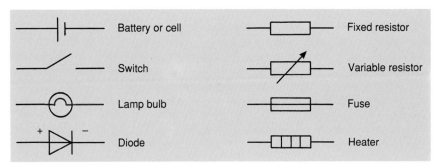

Figure 43.1C ● Circuit components

- You would damage a portable radio if you put the batteries in the wrong way round (so current flowed in the wrong direction). For a simple torch bulb circuit it does not matter which way the current flows, but radios contain more complicated components. A diode could be used as shown in Figure 43.1D, then if the battery were put into the circuit incorrectly the diode would not let any current pass.

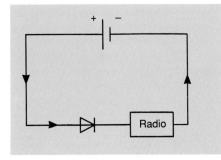
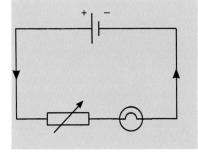

Figure 43.1D ● Using a diode   *Figure 43.1E ● Using a variable resistor*

- To vary the brightness of a torch bulb you could use a variable resistor in series with the bulb as shown in Figure 43.1E. Adjusting the knob of the variable resistor alters the amount of current flowing through the bulb and therefore affects its brightness.
- Some circuits can be damaged if the battery current is too great. A fuse connected in series with the battery will protect the circuit. If the current exceeds the fuse 'rating', the fuse wire melts and the circuit is broken so no current flows.

CHECKPOINT

❶ (a) Set up each of the circuits shown in Figure 43.1B.
  (b) How could you check that the bulbs are identical and that each cell has the same voltage?
  (c) Which circuit would use up chemical energy most quickly? Explain your answer.

❷ In each of the circuits shown below the switch is used to 'short-circuit' one of the components. This means the current passes through the short-circuit instead of through the component. What happens to the brightness of each torch bulb in each circuit when the switch is closed?

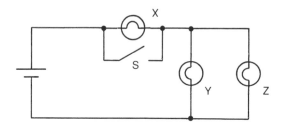
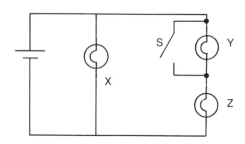

❸ Design and test a circuit that will:
  (a) light up two bulbs so that one bulb is brighter than the other,
  (b) light up two bulbs, one with constant brightness and the other with variable brightness.

❹ Simon tests a diode by connecting it in series with a bulb, a battery and a variable resistor. The bulb does not light at first so he adjusts the variable resistor. It still does not light so he reverses the connections to the diode. The bulb still does not light so he adjusts the variable resistor once more. Now it lights up.
  (a) Sketch the circuit diagram for the successful circuit.
  (b) Why did the bulb not light up when he first adjusted the variable resistor?
  (c) Why did the bulb not light up when he reversed the diode before adjusting the variable resistor again?
  (d) Sketch the circuit he started with.

43.2 💡 Electricity in the home

FIRST THOUGHTS

Mains electricity is dangerous. Study this section carefully to appreciate the safety features of the electric circuits in the home.

Make a list of all the electrical appliances in your home. *Which ones are not battery-powered?* These appliances need to be plugged in to the 'mains' to work. In the UK, the voltage of the mains is 240 V. Voltages above about 50 V can be lethal. **Never fiddle with mains appliances and fittings.**
  Heating appliances include electric kettles, immersion heaters, electric irons, hair driers and electric fires. All heating appliances contain a heating

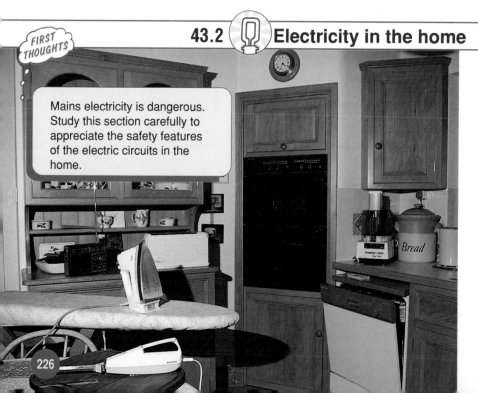

Figure 43.2A ● Household machines

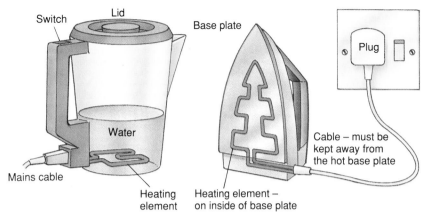

Switch

Lid

Base plate

Plug

Cable – must be kept away from the hot base plate

Water

Mains cable

Heating element

Heating element – on inside of base plate

Figure 43.2B ● Heating elements

element that converts electrical energy into heat energy. These appliances must be plugged into a mains socket. Electric cookers are always connected permanently to the mains using special wiring because they take much more current than other appliances.

Washing machines, fridges, tumble driers and electric drills each contain a **motor** that converts electrical energy into kinetic energy. Washing machines and tumble driers also contain heating elements. These appliances also have to be plugged into the mains.

Light sockets and switches are on a separate circuit to the wall plug sockets. The currents in the lighting circuit are much smaller than the currents in the wall socket circuit.

Make your own database of the electrical appliances used in your house. For each appliance, make a note of:
• the name,
• its power rating (in watts),
• the average time it is used for,
• any other information you want to include.
Use the database to compare different appliances.

Power

How much energy per second does each mains appliance use? Most appliances are labelled to tell you. For example, an electric kettle may be labelled '240 V, 3 kW'. This tells you that the kettle operates from 240 V mains and uses 3000 watts (i.e. 3 kW) of electrical power. This means it uses 3000 joules of electrical energy per second.

The current passed by a mains appliance can be worked out if the power and voltage are known, using the following equation

$$\text{Electrical power (watts)} = \text{Current (amperes)} \times \text{Voltage (volts)}$$

The voltage is the number of joules per coulomb delivered to the appliance by charge passing through it.

The current is the number of coulombs per second passing through the appliance.

So Current x Voltage $= \dfrac{\text{Coulombs}}{\text{Seconds}} \times \dfrac{\text{Joules}}{\text{Coulombs}} = $ Power in watts (J/s)

Fuses

Every mains appliance has a fuse in its plug. The fuse is designed to cut off the current if the appliance passes more current than it is supposed to. To work out the **fuse rating** of an appliance, first calculate the current it passes. For example, a 3 kW, 240 V electric kettle normally passes 3000 W / 240 V = 12.5 A of current. The mains plug of the kettle should therefore be fitted with a 13 A fuse, which will melt if a current greater than 13 A passes through it.

● *Safety matters*

Always fit a fuse with the recommended rating to a given appliance. If not, the appliance could become lethal, or it might overheat and cause a fire if a fault develops. If an appliance repeatedly 'blows' its fuse, then the appliance has a fault and should be taken to a qualified repair technician.

Household circuits

Any mains appliance is supplied with electrical energy from the electricity mains via two wires, the **live** wire and the **neutral** wire. The live wire is at 240 V and the neutral wire is earthed at the electricity supply station.

When you switch an appliance on or off at home, no other appliance is affected. For example, switching your electric kettle off does not affect your television. This is because household sockets are wired in parallel with each other. The wall sockets are part of a circuit called the **ring main**. Figure 43.2C shows part of the ring main for a typical house. Light sockets are part of the lighting circuit, which is separate from the ring main. Separate circuits supply electricity to an electric cooker or an electric shower.

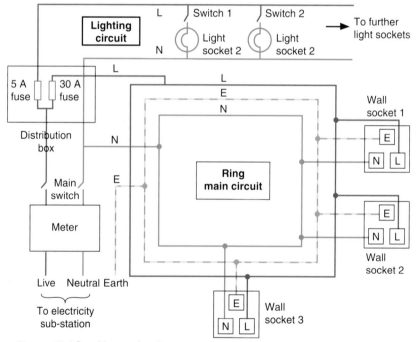

Figure 43.2C ● Home circuits

Every home is fitted with a **domestic electricity meter** that records the electrical energy supplied to all the appliances and lights in the home. The main switch disconnects all the circuits in the home from the electricity supply. This switch must be turned off whenever any of the mains circuits or sockets is being checked, repaired or extended.

The circuits are connected to the electricity supply at the **distribution box**. Each circuit is protected by a fuse in the live wire at the distribution box, which protects the circuit wires from passing too much current, which can make the wires over-heat. For example, suppose the live wire to a light socket becomes disconnected from the socket and touches the neutral wire. This is an example of a **short-circuit**. The current passing along the wires increases and the fuse blows, cutting the socket off from the live wire. If the fuse did not blow, the increase in current would make the wires very hot, which could cause a fire.

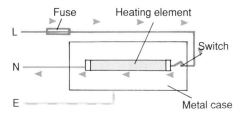

(a) Safe

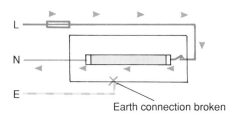

(b) Unsafe

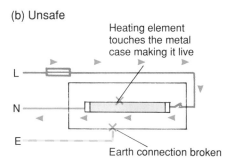

(c) Deadly

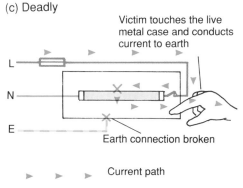

▶ ▶ ▶   Current path

(d) Electrocution

Figure 43.2D ● The importance of earthing

The ring main is made up of three separate wires. The **live** wire is always at 240 V. Electricians always switch the ring main off at the fuse box if any part needs to be rewired. Electricity passes through an appliance via the live wire and the **neutral** wire. The neutral wire is connected to the ground (i.e. earthed) at the power station.

The **earth** wire is earthed at the home. This is important for safety. For example, if the live wire in an appliance broke and touched the metal case of the appliance, anyone touching the case would be electrocuted, because the electric current would pass through the body to earth. To prevent the case becoming 'live', it is connected to the earth wire of the ring main.

Fuses are not designed to protect users from electrocution. Suppose the heating element of an electric radiator makes contact with the metal case of the radiator, which is not earthed correctly. Current passes between the live and the neutral wire through the heating element so the heater appears to work safely. However, someone touching the case would provide a pathway for current to pass between the live case and earth; since electrocution can result from currents as small as 50 mA passing through the body, the fuse would not prevent such a small extra current passing along the live wire. If the case had been earthed correctly, it would not become live as a result of the heating element touching it (Figure 43.2D).

Circuit breakers are designed to switch off if the current in the live wire differs from the current in the neutral wire. This might happen if the appliance develops a fault and a small current leaks to earth, as in the radiator example above. The fuse would not blow but the circuit breaker would 'trip' and disconnect the appliance from the mains.

Figure 43.2E shows a **3-pin plug** used to connect an appliance to the ring main. The fuse in it is to protect the appliance and is always connected in the live wire. If it melts, it cuts the appliance off from the live wire of the ring main.

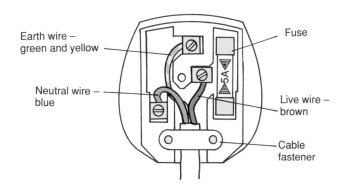

Figure 43.2E ● Inside a three-pin plug

Costing electricity

A domestic electricity meter measures electricity used in **kilowatt-hours**. This is the amount of energy used by a one kilowatt appliance in one hour and is equal to 3.6 million joules. Electricity bills always tell you the 'unit' price of electricity. This is the cost of one kilowatt-hour of electrical energy.

The energy used by an appliance can be worked out if its power rating is known. For example, a three kilowatt heater switched on for two hours would use six kilowatt-hours. This would make the meter reading increase by six 'units'. Table 43.1 (overleaf) gives some more examples.

Watts in your home
(program)

Use this simulation program to study different electrical devices in the home. *Which, on this program, are the cheapest to run? Which are the dearest?* Try to explain why.

Table 43.1 ● Using electricity

Appliance	Power (kW)	Time appliance is used for (hours)	Number of units used
Heater	3.0	2.0	6.0
Lamp	0.1	24.0	2.4
Hair drier	0.2	0.5	0.1
Cooker oven	5.0	2.5	12.5

To check the amount of electricity used by a particular appliance, switch off all the other appliances in the house and read the meter. Then use the appliance for a given time and read the meter again after that time. The increase in the meter reading should equal the number of kilowatts multiplied by the number of hours (i.e. the number of kilowatt-hours).

Worked example Figure 43.2F shows two photographs of a domestic electricity meter taken one week apart. How much electricity did this household use in one week?

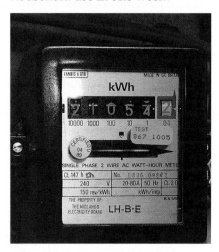

Figure 43.2F ● (a) Initial meter reading   (b) Meter reading after one week

Solution

Initial meter reading = 21 054.2 units
Reading after one week = 21 778.0 units
Number of units used in one week = 723.8 units

SUMMARY

The current passed by an appliance can be worked out from the equation

Power = Current x Voltage

The fuse rating is determined by the current. The energy used can be calculated using the equation

Energy = Power x Time

The unit of electrical energy measured by domestic electricity meters is the kilowatt-hour, which is equal to 3.6 MJ

CHECKPOINT

❶ Explain each of the following:
  (a) A mains plug should always be fitted with the 'correct' fuse.
  (b) An appliance with a frayed mains cable should not be used until the cable has been replaced.
  (c) The cable of an electric iron must never be allowed to touch the iron when the iron is hot.

❷ Prakesh's father has asked him to fit a plug and a fuse to a new electric iron. The appliance is rated at 240 V, 1000 W.
  (a) What current does the appliance take when it uses 1000 W of power?

(b) Prakesh has a 3 A fuse, a 5 A fuse and a 13 A fuse. Which one should he use in the plug?

(c) The iron has a control dial for different fabrics, as shown in the diagram. Explain how it works.

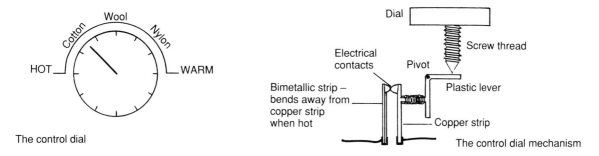

The control dial

The control dial mechanism

(d) What is likely to happen if the iron is used on full power on a nylon shirt?

❸ (a) Work out the number of 'units' of electricity used when
  (i)   a 3 kW electric heater is used for 4 hours,
  (ii) a 100 W lamp is used for 10 hours,
  (iii) a 300 W hair drier is used for 10 minutes,
  (iv) a 2.5 kW electric kettle is used for 5 minutes.

(b) If the unit price of electricity is 5.5p, work out the cost of using the heater for two hours, the lamp for five hours, and the kettle four times for five minutes each time.

❹ Electric cookers are connected permanently to the mains. The fuse is in the fuse box. Usually this is a 30 A fuse. How much power does a cooker use when it takes 30 A at 240 V? How many units of electricity would it use in three hours and what would be the cost at 5.5p per unit?

43.3 🔓 Electrical measurements

FIRST THOUGHTS

In this section, you will find out how to measure currents and voltages in low voltage circuits.

Measuring current

Debbie has brought a battery-operated vacuum cleaner to school to ask her science teacher to check it. The cleaner is rated at 12 V, 85 W and is for use in her parents' caravan. It does not work when connected to the 12 V socket in the caravan.

When it is connected to a 12 V battery, the cleaner should take 7.1 A. You should be able to work this out from the voltage and power ratings. An **ammeter** can be used to measure the current passing through the cleaner. Debbie's teacher connects the cleaner in series with an ammeter and a 12 V battery, as shown in Figure 43.3A. The ammeter reads 7.0 A when the cleaner is switched on. The teacher suggests that the wiring in the caravan might be at fault. *Can you think of any other reasons why the cleaner will not work in the caravan?*

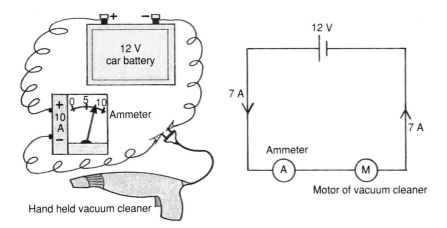

Figure 43.3A ● Using an ammeter
(a) Checking a low voltage vacuum cleaner (b) Circuit diagram

Does it matter which side of the cleaner plug the ammeter is connected to? All the components are in series so they pass the same current. The ammeter position does not matter. Figure 43.3B shows how two ammeters could be used to show this.

The circuit diagram for the caravan is shown in Figure 43.3C. In addition to the cleaner, the circuit includes two 12 V lamps. Debbie borrows the ammeter to test the lamps. She connects the ammeter in series with the battery, as shown in Figure 43.3D, and tests each lamp in turn. Her results are as follows

Lamp bulb X only ON	Ammeter reading = 2.0 A
Lamp bulb Y only ON	Ammeter reading = 1.0 A
Both lamp bulbs ON	Ammeter reading = 3.0 A

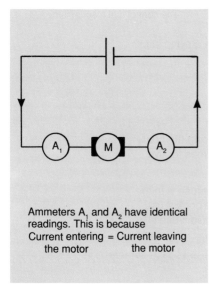

Ammeters A_1 and A_2 have identical readings. This is because
Current entering = Current leaving
the motor   the motor

Figure 43.3B ● Components in series pass the same current

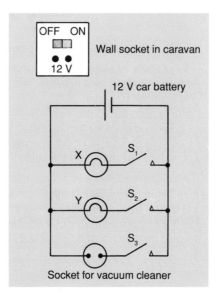

Figure 43.3C ● The caravan circuit diagram

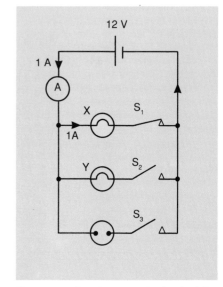

Figure 43.3D ● Lamp bulb X only ON

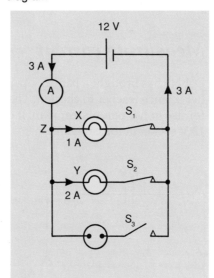

Figure 43.3E ● Lamp bulbs X and Y ON

With both lamp bulbs on, the ammeter registers the current taken by X and the current taken by Y. Figure 43.3E shows the circuit when X and Y are both on. The current entering junction Z from the ammeter is 3.0 A; at the junction, this current splits into 2.0 A that passes through X and 1.0 A that passes through Y.

> The total current entering a junction is always equal to the total current leaving the junction

Measuring potential difference

In the caravan, the lamp bulbs work so the battery must be working. The cleaner worked in school but does not work in the caravan. Perhaps the voltage of the 12 V battery is not reaching the socket of the cleaner. Debbie borrows a **voltmeter** from school to find out.

A voltmeter measures the voltage (i.e. potential difference) between two points in a circuit. This is a measure of the work done to push charge round the circuit. It is similar to the pressure in the water pipes of a central heating system. A p.d. across the socket terminals is necessary to push current through the vacuum cleaner when it is plugged in.

Debbie connects the voltmeter between the socket terminals and then switches the socket on. The voltmeter still reads zero. *Can you suggest what the fault might be?* Think about a central heating system in which no pressure is getting through to a radiator. A blockage in a water pipe could cause this. *What could prevent the voltage from a battery reaching a socket?*

Investigating potential difference

The unit of p.d. is the **volt**. Suppose the p.d. across a resistor is one volt; this means that every coulomb of charge passing through it must do one joule of work to get through. In other words, one volt is one joule per coulomb.

Let's consider a practical problem to understand more about the meaning of p.d. Figure 43.3F shows two bulbs and a dimmer (i.e. variable resistor) connected in series with each other and a 6 V battery. Claire sets the circuit up and adjusts the dimmer so that the bulbs are at normal brightness. Graham then uses the voltmeter and measures the p.d. across each bulb and the dimmer as 2.5 V across each bulb and 1.0 V across the dimmer. The battery voltage is shared between the two bulbs and the dimmer because they are in series (Figure 43.3F). Each bulb lights up normally because the p.d. across each is 2.5 V.

Circuit Boards
(program)

Use this program to revise your knowledge of electric circuits. Try connecting bulbs in different ways. Connect an ammeter into your circuit. Experiment with different cells and different arrangements.

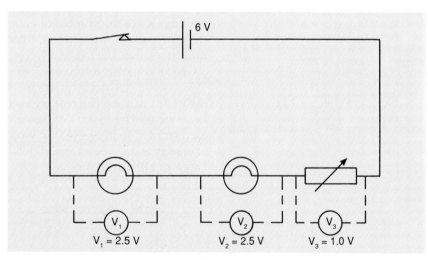

Figure 43.3F ● Sharing voltage

Why do the p.d.s across the bulbs and dimmer add up to the battery voltage? The p.d. across a component is the number of joules delivered to the component by each coulomb of charge passing through it. Since the two bulbs and the dimmer are in series, each coulomb of charge from the battery passes through each component, delivering 2.5 J to each bulb and 1.0 J to the dimmer. Hence each coulomb of charge delivers a total of 2.5 + 2.5 + 1.0 = 6 J of energy from the battery to the circuit components. The battery therefore supplies 6 J of electrical energy to each coulomb of charge passing through it, which is 6 V.

> For components in series connected to a battery, the battery voltage is equal to the sum of the potential differences across each component.

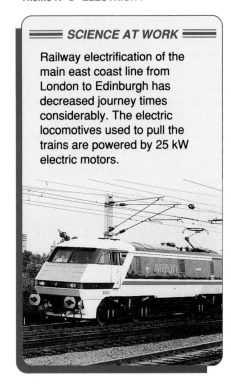

Measuring power

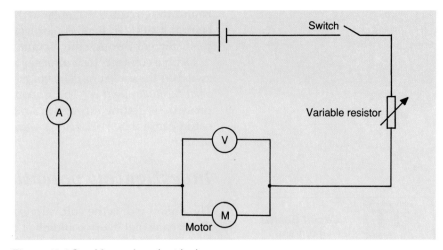

Figure 43.3G ● Measuring electrical power

How much power does an electric model train use? Figure 43.3G shows how the power used by the model train may be measured. The variable resistor is adjusted until the voltmeter reads exactly 6.0 V. The power of the train is given by

$$\text{Power} = \text{Current} \times \text{Potential difference}$$

A **joulemeter** measures the electrical energy used directly in joules. Figure 43.3H shows a joulemeter being used to measure the energy supplied to a heater. The reading must be taken before the heater is switched on and then again after it is switched off. The difference in the readings gives the number of joules supplied to the heater. To calculate the power used by the heater, divide the number of joules used by the time in seconds the heater was on. Suppose the heater used 7210 joules in 300 seconds. *What is its power?*

Domestic electricity meters measure the electrical energy used by mains appliances. The reading in joules would be enormous. *How many joules are used by a 1000 watt heater in one hour?* The heater uses 1000 joules each second, so in one hour it would use 3.6 million joules. This amount of energy is defined as one kilowatt-hour. Domestic meters are marked in 'units' of kilowatt hours.

▼ SUMMARY ▼

Current is measured using an ammeter. An ammeter must always be connected in series with the appliance taking the current to be measured.

Potential difference is measured using a voltmeter. Voltmeters are always connected in parallel with the appliance whose potential difference is being measured.

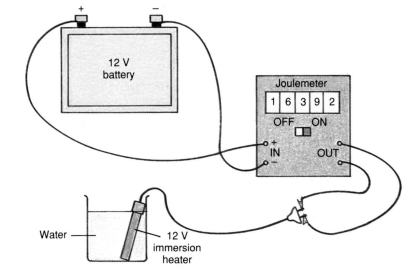

Figure 43.3H ● Using a joulemeter

CHECKPOINT

❶ (a) Work out the current through each lamp bulb in circuits A–C below.
(b) What is the p.d. across each lamp bulb in circuits D–F below?

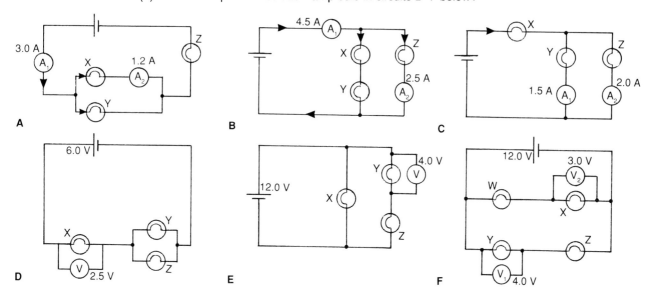

A   B   C

D   E   F

❷ Claire has repaired the faulty wire in the caravan circuit and she decides to see if the lamp bulbs both work when the vacuum cleaner is switched on. The circuit is shown in the diagram below.

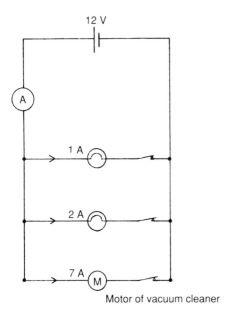

Motor of vacuum cleaner

(a) What do you think the ammeter will read when all three appliances are switched on?
(b) How much energy does each appliance use per second when switched on?
(c) How much energy does the battery supply each second when all three appliances are switched on?

❸ The circuit below is to test car headlamp bulbs.

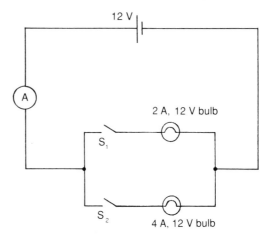

(a) What is the reading on the ammeter when (i) S_1 is closed, (ii) S_2 is closed, (iii) both switches are closed?
(b) How much charge passes through each bulb each second when both switches are closed?
(c) The battery has a voltage of 12 V. How much energy is delivered to each bulb each second when both switches are closed?

❹ Julie has a low voltage immersion heater designed to run off a car battery to warm water in a cup. The heater is rated at 12 V, 5 A.
(a) How much energy should it use in (i) 1 second, (ii) 5 minutes?
(b) How could Julie check its energy usage using a joulemeter and a 12 V battery?

43.4 Resistance

After studying this section, you should know how to work out currents, voltages and resistances in circuits.

In a central heating system, the pump forces water through the radiators and the pipes. If the pipes are narrow, the pump has to do more work than if the pipes are wide. Narrow pipes resist the flow of water much more than wide pipes do. The flow rate depends on the pressure from the pump and the 'resistance' of the pipes.

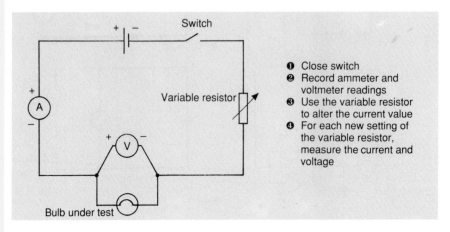

❶ Close switch
❷ Record ammeter and voltmeter readings
❸ Use the variable resistor to alter the current value
❹ For each new setting of the variable resistor, measure the current and voltage

Figure 43.4A ● Investigating components

The blood system of the body is like a 'water circuit'. The heart forces blood through the arteries, capillaries and veins. The flow rate depends on the pressure from the heart and the 'resistance' of the blood vessels.

In an electric circuit, the current depends on the battery voltage and the components in the circuit. Figure 43.4A shows how to investigate the link between current and voltage for different components. The measurements can be plotted on a graph of current (on the vertical axis) against voltage. Figure 43.4B shows some typical results for a lamp bulb, diode and wire.

Resistance is defined as voltage/current. The unit of resistance is the **ohm** (Ω, the Greek letter 'omega').

$$R = \frac{V}{I}$$

where V = potential difference in volts
I = current in amperes
R = resistance in ohms

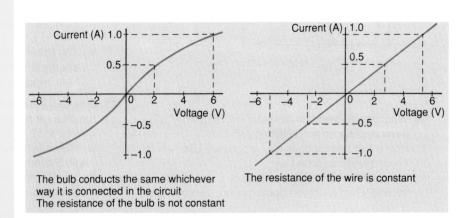

The bulb conducts the same whichever way it is connected in the circuit
The resistance of the bulb is not constant

The resistance of the wire is constant

Figure 43.4B ● (a) Testing a lamp bulb   (b) Testing a wire

Figure 43.4B ● (continued)
(c) Testing a diode

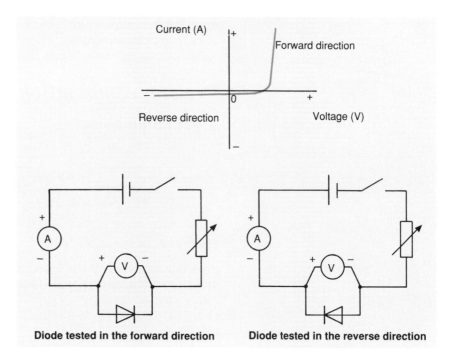

Diode tested in the forward direction   Diode tested in the reverse direction

The equation can be used to work out *R* or *V* or *I* if the other two quantities are known. For example, suppose a heater has a resistance of 8.0 Ω and it is to be connected to a 12 V battery. The current taken is given by p.d./resistance = 12 V/8 Ω = 1.5 A.

Consider the graphs in Figure 43.4B. *What can you tell from them about the resistance of each component?*

- The diode has a much greater resistance when connected in its 'reverse' direction compared with its 'forward' direction. In reverse, very little current passes through it.
- The lamp bulb has more resistance as the current increases. From Figure 43.4B, *I* = 0.5 A when *V* = 2.0 V and *I* = 1.0 A when *V* = 6.0 V. The resistance at 0.5 A is 4.0 Ω (= 2.0 V/0.5 A); at 1.0 A, the resistance is 6.0 Ω (= 6.0 V/1.0 A).
- The wire has constant resistance. This does not depend on the current passed. From Figure 43.4B, *I* = 0.5 A when *V* = 2.5 V and *I* = 1.0 A when *V* = 5.0 V. Both these readings from the graph give 5.0 Ω for the resistance of the wire.

The resistance of the human body can be as low as 1000 Ω. If the hands are wet, electrical contact is more effective than when they are dry, since water conducts electricity, and the resistance can be even lower than 1000 Ω. Shocks can be lethal if the current passed through the body is greater than about 50 mA. This means that voltages over about 50 V (= 0.050 A x 1000 Ω) can be dangerous.

Figure 43.4C ● Different resistors

A **resistor** is a component designed to have a specific resistance. Accurate resistors can be made from metal wires. Figure 43.4C shows two different types.

Ohm's Law states that the current through a metallic conductor at constant temperature is proportional to the p.d. thus p.d./current is constant.

In other words, the resistance of a metallic conductor is constant, provided the temperature is constant. The resistance of a metal increases as its temperature increases. The filament of a lamp bulb is a metal wire. As the current increases it gets hotter and so its resistance increases.

Resistor combination rules

● *Resistors in series*

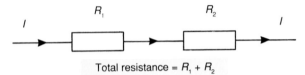

Total resistance = $R_1 + R_2$

Figure 43.4D ● Resistors in series

Consider the two resistors R_1 and R_2 in Figure 43.4D. R_1 and R_2 carry the same current because they are in series. Let the current = I
Hence p.d. across R_1, $V_1 = I R_1$
and   p.d. across R_2, $V_2 = I R_2$

Since Total p.d. across R_1 and $R_2 = V_1 + V_2$
then   Total p.d. $= I R_1 + I R_2$

$$\text{Total resistance, } R = \frac{\text{Total p.d.}}{\text{Current}} = \frac{I R_1 + I R_2}{I} = R_1 + R_2$$

For two resistors R_1 and R_2 in series, the total resistance R is equal to the sum of the individual resistances.

Worked example A 6V battery is connected in series to resistors of 1Ω, 2Ω and 3Ω as shown in Figure 43.4E. What is the current and p.d. for each resistor?

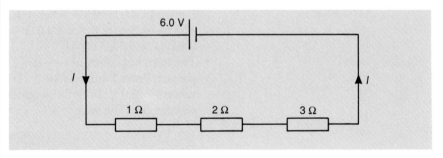

Figure 43.4E ●

Solution The total resistance = 1 + 2 + 3 = 6 Ω (using the above rule).
Hence

$$\text{Battery current, } I = \frac{\text{Battery voltage}}{\text{Total resistance}} = \frac{6V}{6\Omega} = 1A$$

Each resistor passes this current. The p.d. across each resistor can be worked out from current x resistance.
Hence

p.d. across 1 Ω = 1 x 1 = 1 V
p.d. across 2 Ω = 1 x 2 = 2 V
p.d. across 3 Ω = 1 x 3 = 3 V

Note that the battery voltage is equal to the sum of the resistor voltages because they are in series.

IT *Electric Circuits* (program)

With this simulation program, try adding different components to an electric circuit. Try:
• resistors in series and parallel,
• changing the value of resistance,
• changing the number of cells in the circuit.

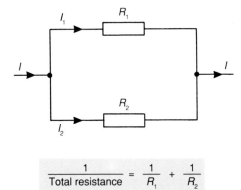

$$\frac{1}{\text{Total resistance}} = \frac{1}{R_1} + \frac{1}{R_2}$$

Figure 43.4F ● Resistors in parallel

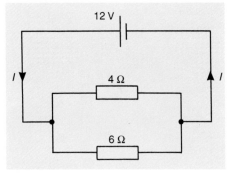

Figure 43.4G ●

● Resistors in parallel

Consider two resistors R_1 and R_2 connected in parallel as shown in Figure 43.4F. The voltage is the same across the two resistors. Let this voltage $= V$

Hence   Current through R_1, $I_1 = \dfrac{V}{R1}$

and   Current through R_2, $I_2 = \dfrac{V}{R_2}$

Therefore   Total current $I = I_1 + I_2 = \dfrac{V}{R_1} + \dfrac{V}{R_2}$

Since   Total resistance, $R = \dfrac{\text{Voltage}}{\text{Total current}}$

then $\dfrac{1}{R} = \dfrac{I}{V} = \dfrac{V/R_1 + V/R_2}{V} = \dfrac{1}{R_1} + \dfrac{1}{R_2}$

For two resistors R_1 and R_2 in parallel, the total resistance R is given by

$$\frac{1}{R} = \frac{1}{R_1} + \frac{1}{R_2}$$

Worked example 1   A 4 Ω resistor and a 6 Ω resistor are joined in parallel and then connected to a 12 V battery, as shown in Figure 43.4G. Work out the total resistance and the battery current.

Solution   The total resistance R is given by

$$\frac{1}{R} = \frac{1}{4} + \frac{1}{6} = \frac{6+4}{(4 \times 6)} = \frac{10}{24}$$

Therefore $R = \dfrac{24}{10} = 2.4\ \Omega$

Battery current, $I = \dfrac{\text{Battery voltage}}{\text{Total resistance}}$

$$= \frac{12}{2.4} = 5.0\ \text{A}$$

Worked example 2   For the circuit shown in Figure 43.4H, work out (a) the total resistance and (b) the battery current.
Solution   (a) Work out the resistance of Y and Z in parallel first, using

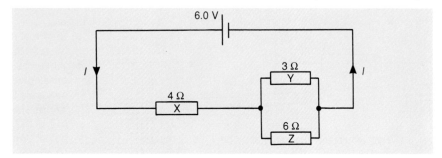

Figure 43.4H ●

the parallel combination rule.

$$\frac{1}{R} = \frac{1}{3} + \frac{1}{6} = \frac{1}{2}$$

So   Combined resistance $R = 2\ \Omega$

The total resistance is the resistance of X in series with the combined resistance of Y and Z.

Hence   Total resistance = 4 + 2 = 6 Ω

(b) Battery current, $I = \dfrac{\text{Battery voltage}}{\text{Total resistance}} = \dfrac{6}{6} = 1.0$ A

CHECKPOINT

❶ Consider each of the circuits (a)–(c) in the diagram below. What is the ammeter reading when:
   (i) switch S_1 alone is closed,
   (ii) switch S_2 alone is closed,
   (iii) both switches are closed?

   (iv) What is the total resistance of the circuit when both switches are closed?

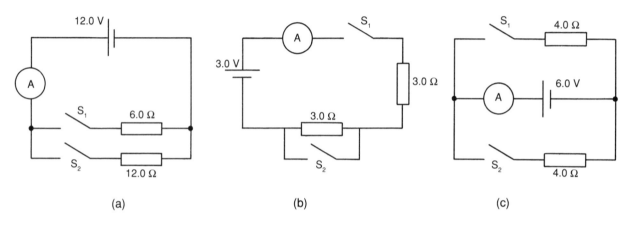

(a)   (b)   (c)

❷ (a) What is the total resistance of a 3 Ω and a 6 Ω resistor when they are joined (i) in series, (ii) in parallel?
   (b) What is the total resistance of a 3 Ω, a 5 Ω and a 6 Ω resistor when they are joined (i) in series, (ii) in parallel?
   (c) The diagram below shows another way to join the three resistors together. Show that the total resistance is 7 Ω.

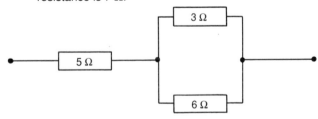

   (d) What would the total resistance be if a 6 Ω resistor was used in place of (i) the 5 Ω resistor, (ii) the 3 Ω resistor?

❸ The table shows results taken in an experiment to determine the resistance per metre of a wire.

Length of wire (m)	0	0.20	0.41	0.60	0.79	1.00
Resistance (Ω)	0	1.2	2.4	3.5	4.8	6.1

   (a) Plot a graph of resistance (on the y-axis) against length.
   (b) What is the resistance per metre of the wire?
   (c) What length of wire would pass a current of 0.5 A when joined in series with a 10 Ω resistor and a 6 V battery?

❹ Rachel wants to fix a broken set of fairy lights. There are 20 lights in all, joined in series. They are all supposed to light up when the set is plugged in to 240 V mains.
   (a) Before she plugs the set in to the mains, she checks the condition of the wires. Why is this important?
   (b) While checking the wires, she notices that bulbs are missing from two of the light sockets. Her father suggests the sockets of the missing bulbs could be 'short-circuited'. Rachel tells him that it is dangerous to use the set with fewer than the correct number of bulbs. Why?
   (c) Rachel buys some new bulbs, which she fits to the missing sockets. When she plugs the set in, they still do not work. With the set unplugged, she removes each bulb in turn from its socket to test it using a battery. What should the voltage of the battery be?
   (d) Each bulb is designed to take a current of 0.06 A. Work out its resistance and the total resistance of the whole set of 20 bulbs.

MAGNETISM

TOPIC 44

44.1  Permanent magnetism

FIRST THOUGHTS

Have you ever used a magnetic compass to find your bearings? Read on to find out the difference between Magnetic North and True North.

Cupboard doors are often fitted with magnetic catches to keep them closed. These catches are more reliable than spring-loaded catches which sometimes snap. A magnetic catch contains a small magnet. Magnets can attract or repel each other and can attract iron and steel. *How would you design a pair of magnetic catches to keep a cupboard door shut?* You would need to make sure the catches attract each other. Otherwise, the door would never stay closed.

Investigating bar magnets

When you dip a bar magnet into iron filings you find that the filings cling to the ends of the magnet. The ends are called **poles** because that is where the magnetism seems to be concentrated.

Figure 44.1A shows a bar magnet suspended from a string. The magnet lines up with one end pointing north and the other pointing south. This is because of the Earth's magnetism.

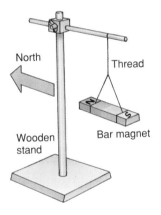

Figure 44.1A ● Direction finding

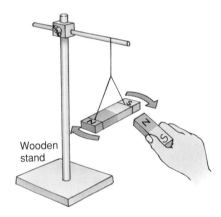

Figure 44.1B ● Like poles repel; unlike poles attract

When another magnet is held near one end of the suspended magnet, as in Figure 44.1B, the ends either attract or repel each other. The magnets attract each other when a north pole is held near a south pole, and repel each other if similar poles are held near each other.

> Like poles repel; unlike poles attract

When a nail is held near either end of the suspended bar magnet the magnet attracts the nail. Any iron or steel object is attracted by a magnet. See how many paper clips you can hang in a chain from the pole of a bar magnet. *How would you use this to compare the strength of two magnets?*

Figure 44.1C shows how to magnetise an iron nail using a bar magnet. *How can you find the polarity of each end of the nail?*

Cobalt and nickel can also be magnetised. Oxides of these metals in powder form are used to make **ceramic magnets** and to coat magnetic tapes.

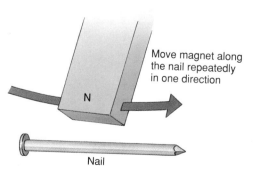

Figure 44.1C ● Making a magnet

Magnetic fields

Put a sheet of paper on a bar magnet and sprinkle some iron filings on the paper. The filings form a pattern which is shown in Figure 44.1D. The space round a magnet is called a **magnetic field**. Any other magnet in this space experiences a force due to the first magnet. In Figure 44.1D, the filings form lines that end on or near the poles of the magnet. These are called **lines of force**. By convention, the direction of these lines is always from the north pole to the south pole of the magnet.

Some further magnetic field patterns are shown in Figure 44.1E. A horseshoe magnet has a very strong field between its poles.

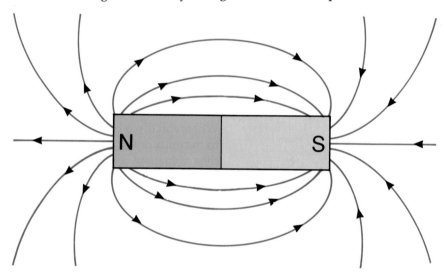

Figure 44.1D ● The magnetic field near a bar magnet

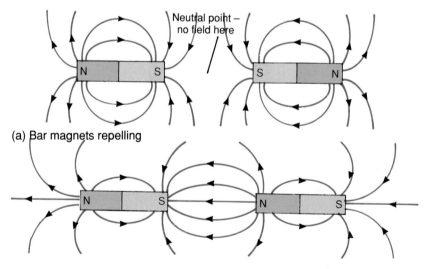

(a) Bar magnets repelling

(b) Bar magnet attracting

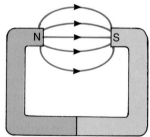

(c) U-shaped magnet
Figure 44.1E ● Magnetic field patterns

Electrostatic and Magnetic Fields
(program)

Try comparing electric fields and magnetic fields with this program. *What are the main differences?* Experiment with different types of field.

The Earth's magnetism

Have you ever used a magnetic compass on your travels? A compass always points north. It is used as a direction finder. Compasses have been used for thousands of years by travellers.

Compasses do not actually point to the Earth's North Pole (True North). They point to Magnetic North. This is where the Earth's magnetism is concentrated in the Northern hemisphere. Map readers using a compass need to know the **angle of variation** for their locality. This is the angle between True North and Magnetic North.

Scientists have plotted the Earth's magnetic field accurately. The pattern is like that of a bar magnet. However, since it is thought the Earth is partly molten inside, the idea of a giant bar magnet cannot explain the Earth's magnetism.

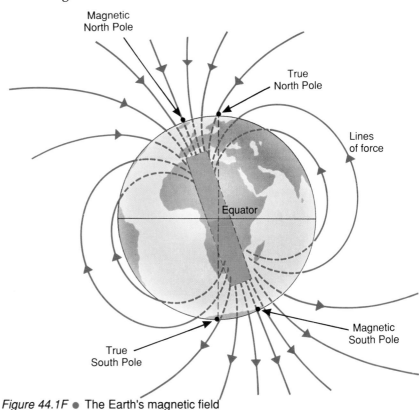

SUMMARY

Magnets are made from certain metals and alloys like iron or steel. When two magnets are held near each other, like poles repel and unlike poles attract. A compass is a magnet on a pivot. It is used to find the direction of magnetic north.

Figure 44.1F ● The Earth's magnetic field

CHECKPOINT

❶ (a) How would you find out which pole of a bar magnet is its north pole?
   (b) How would you find out if a steel ruler is magnetised?
   (c) Given two bar magnets, how would you find out which is strongest?

❷ (a) How would you magnetise a steel needle?
   (b) How would you test that it is magnetised?
   (c) Is it possible to make a magnet with a single pole? Cut a magnetised steel needle in half. You will find each half is a bar magnet. What will happen if you cut one of the halves in two? Does this produce a magnet with a single pole?

❸ How could you compare the strengths of two bar magnets using a plotting compass and a metre rule? With the aid of one or more diagrams, outline your method to find out which magnet is the strongest.

44.2 ⬚ Electromagnetism

FIRST THOUGHTS

In this section you will find out how electricity is used to create magnetism. This is called electromagnetism.

=== **SCIENCE AT WORK** ===

Brain scanning machines use solenoids to create very strong magnetic fields. Hydrogen atoms in a strong magnetic field can be made to emit radio signals. The human brain can be 'imaged' using a computerised brain scanner to map the brain's hydrogen atoms. The patient's head must be positioned in the solenoid.

When insulated wire is wrapped round an iron nail and the ends of the wire are connected to a battery the nail becomes capable of picking up iron filings and paper clips. This is a simple **electromagnet**. The nail has been magnetised by the current in the wire. Disconnect the wire from the battery and the paper clips fall off. The nail loses most of its magnetism when the current is switched off.

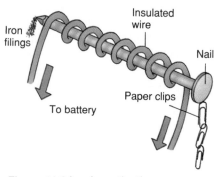

Figure 44.2A ● Investigating electromagnetism

The passage of an electric current along a wire creates a magnetic field around the wire. Figure 44.2B shows how the pattern of the magnetic field around a long, straight wire can be seen by using iron filings and a plotting compass. The lines of force due to a straight current-carrying wire are circles, centred on the wire. The field is strongest near the wire. The direction of the field is reversed if the direction of the current is reversed.

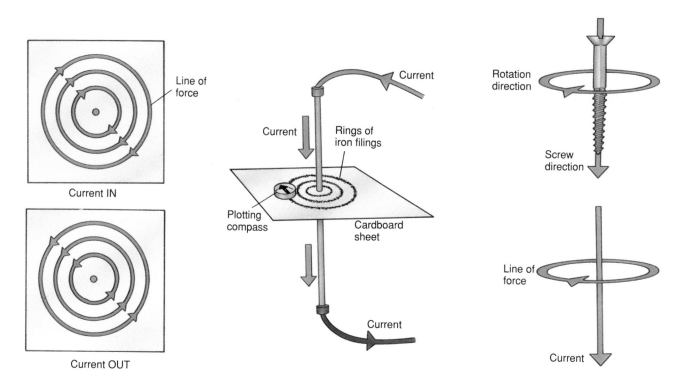

(a) Lines of force.
(Top views of cardboard sheet)

(b) Practical arrangement

(c) The corkscrew rule gives the field direction

Figure 44.2B ● The magnetic field near a long straight wire

A **solenoid** is a long coil of wire. The magnetic field pattern created by a current-carrying solenoid is like that of a bar magnet. However, unlike a bar magnet the field lines pass through the solenoid along its axis (Figure 44.2C). *How can the field created by the solenoid be made stronger?* Using more windings or a bigger current are two ways. Inserting an iron bar into the centre of the solenoid is another way.

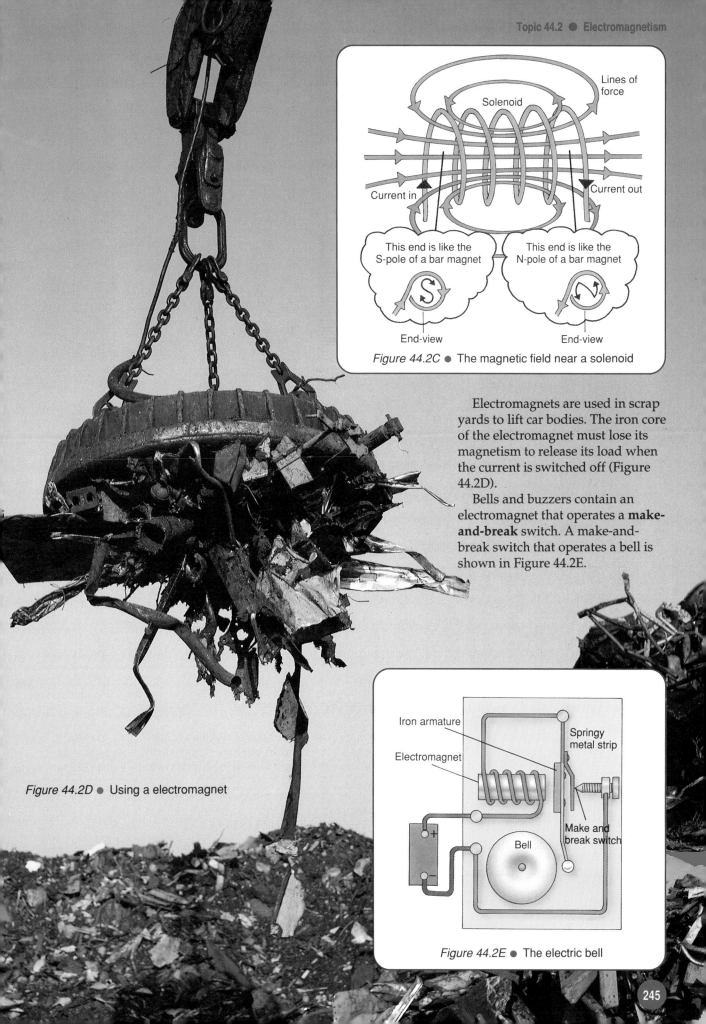

Figure 44.2C ● The magnetic field near a solenoid

Solenoid

Lines of force

Current in

Current out

This end is like the S-pole of a bar magnet

This end is like the N-pole of a bar magnet

End-view

End-view

Electromagnets are used in scrap yards to lift car bodies. The iron core of the electromagnet must lose its magnetism to release its load when the current is switched off (Figure 44.2D).

Bells and buzzers contain an electromagnet that operates a **make-and-break** switch. A make-and-break switch that operates a bell is shown in Figure 44.2E.

Figure 44.2D ● Using a electromagnet

Iron armature

Electromagnet

Springy metal strip

Make and break switch

Bell

Figure 44.2E ● The electric bell

When the bell is connected to a battery, the iron armature is pulled on to the electromagnet. This opens the make-and-break switch and the electromagnet switches off. When the electromagnet switches off, the armature springs back and the make-and-break switch closes again so the whole cycle repeats itself.

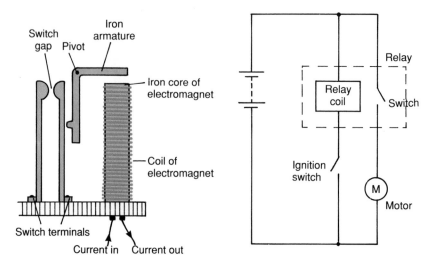

Figure 44.2F ● A relay (a) Construction (b) Circuit

Relays are used in control circuits to switch machines on or off. Figure 44.2F shows the construction of a relay. When current passes through the electromagnet the iron armature is pulled on to the electromagnet. The armature turns about the pivot and closes the switch gap. In this way, a small current can be used to switch on a much greater current. For example, when the ignition switch of a car is operated, a current of a few amperes passes through a relay coil and the relay switch closes. This lets a much greater current pass through the starter motor.

Magnetic tape is used to record computer programs and sound. When you record sound, a microphone in the recorder converts the sound into an electrical signal. This signal is supplied to an electromagnet in the recording head. The tape passes against the recording head and is magnetised by the electromagnet according to the signal. To play the signal back, the tape is passed against the replay head. This produces an electrical signal that 'drives' a loudspeaker.

Current matters

The direction of current on a circuit diagram is always shown from 'positive to negative'. This rule was put forward by André Ampère in the early nineteenth century. Ampère showed how to measure the direction and size of an electric current.

How did he decide on 'positive to negative'? Electricity is a difficult topic and you can perhaps appreciate why this is so when we look at how famous scientists like Ampère struggled to understand electricity.

The attractive power of amber when rubbed was known to the philosophers of Ancient Greece. William Gilbert was a sixteenth century physician who discovered that other materials such as glass, ebonite and resin are also capable of attracting bits of straw and paper when they are rubbed. Gilbert introduced the word 'electricity' from the Greek word for 'amber' to describe the attractive power of these materials. The idea that rubbing any of these materials 'charges' it (i.e. fills it) with electricity dates from the mid-seventeenth century. The term 'electric charge' was introduced at this time.

What happens when charged materials are brought near to each other?

Further experiments were carried out by Charles Dufay in France in the early eighteenth century. He found that:

- glass repels glass,
- ebonite repels ebonite,
- ebonite attracts glass,
- resin repels resin,
- resin repels ebonite.

What do you think happens with resin and glass?

Dufay showed that all electrified materials could be placed in one of two lists which he called 'resinous' and 'vitreous'; any material in either list repels all the materials in the same list and attracts all the materials in the other list. In other words, Dufay showed that like charges repel and unlike charges attract.

Benjamin Franklin, an eighteenth century American scientist, investigated these effects in more detail. He deduced that the two types of electric charge can be described as positive and negative because they cancelled each other out in equal amounts. The charge on glass rubbed with silk was defined as positive. He thought of electricity as a positive fluid and ordinary matter as being negative. Too much electricity in an object made it positive, too little made it negative.

Machines for creating electric charge and producing artificial lightning were invented during the eighteenth century. In 1798, a different principle for producing electricity was discovered by an Italian scientist called Alessandro Volta. He invented the first battery and used it to make electricity pass through a conductor. Figure 44.2G(b) shows the construction of Volta's battery.

Volta used the electricity from the silver end to charge an electroscope. He discovered that the electroscope became charged when it was touched with a wire joined to the silver end of the battery with the other end of the battery earthed. When a negatively charged rod was brought near the electroscope, the electroscope leaf rose showing that the charge on the electroscope was also negative. Volta deduced that the silver end of the battery was therefore negative and the other end positive. In honour of Volta's contributions to science, the unit of potential difference, the volt, is named after him.

The invention of the battery led to further investigations into the properties of current electricity. Hans Oersted, a Danish scientist, discovered the magnetic effect of an electric current in 1820. This led to the invention of the electromagnet by William Sturgeon in England in 1826 and the invention of further electromagnetic devices such as the relay and the electric bell.

André Ampère was a French scientist who discovered that an electric current has direction and size. Before Ampère, some scientists thought that positive electricity went round an electric circuit from the positive pole of the battery and negative electricity went the other way round from the negative pole at the same time. Ampère observed that a magnetic compass near a wire was deflected when the current was switched on.

More importantly, he noticed that the deflection was in the opposite direction

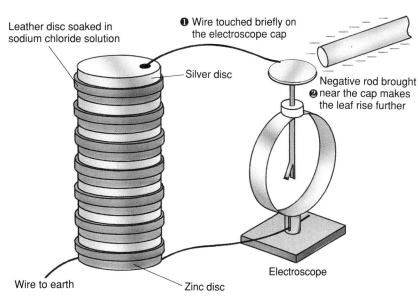

Leather disc soaked in sodium chloride solution

❶ Wire touched briefly on the electroscope cap

Silver disc

Negative rod brought ❷ near the cap makes the leaf rise further

Electroscope

Wire to earth

Zinc disc

Figure 44.2G ● (a) Alessandro Volta (b) Volta's battery

when the battery was reversed in the circuit. This cannot be explained if there is a flow of positive electricity and a flow of negative electricity at the same time. Ampère realised that one type of electricity only flows round a circuit.

Which type of electricity is responsible for current electricity through wires? Ampère had no evidence to decide this so he suggested that an electric current is a flow of positive charge. This is why the direction of electric current in a circuit is always considered to be from positive to negative. He went on to show how the magnetic effect of an electric current can be used to measure the size of the current. The importance of his work was recognised by naming the unit of electric current after him.

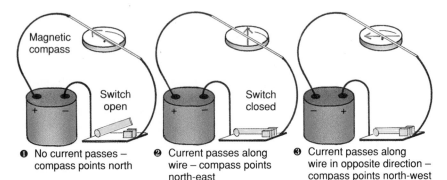

Figure 44.2H ● (a) André Ampère   (b) Current directions

CHECKPOINT

① Sketch the pattern of magnetic lines of force for each of the following:
(a) a vertical wire carrying current upwards,
(b) an air-filled solenoid,
(c) a solenoid with an iron core.

② (a) Current is passed through an air-filled solenoid. An unmagnetised iron bar is then inserted into the solenoid. How does this affect a plotting compass near the end of the solenoid?
(b) A bar magnet is held near the end of the solenoid to repel the solenoid. What happens:
(i) if the magnet is turned round,
(ii) if the current is switched off,
(iii) if the current is switched off then reversed in direction?

③ Results from an experiment to find out how the weight supported by an electromagnet varies with current are given below.

Current (A)	0	0.5	1.0	1.5	2.0	2.5	3.0
Weight (N)	0	0.5	1.5	2.4	3.3	3.8	4.0

(a) Use these results to plot a graph of weight (on the vertical axis) against current.
(b) Do you think there is a limit to weight that can be supported?

④ Karen and Paul have made a 'shaky hand' tester (shown opposite) to use at the school fair. The idea is that the bell rings if contact is made between the metal ring and the copper wire. Unfortunately the bell is not working.
(a) Karen tests the electromagnet coil of the bell with a battery and light bulb. What did she do to make this test?
(b) The electromagnet does work. Paul notices that the make and break contacts are dirty. He cleans them with a small file. Why does this make a difference?
(c) Now the bell works. Explain how it works.

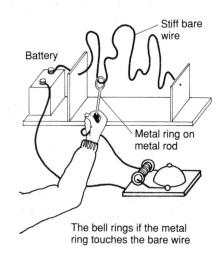

44.3 Motors and meters

A current-carrying wire creates magnetism. How is this magnetism affected by permanent magnets? Read on to find out.

How many appliances can you think of that contain an electric motor? At home, electric motors are used in appliances such as vacuum cleaners, washing machines, food mixers and electric shavers. *Can you think of any other appliances in your home which contain electric motors?*

The motor effect

A current-carrying wire creates a magnetic field. *What happens if a magnet is held near the wire?* Figure 44.3A(a) shows a horseshoe magnet held near a current carrying wire. The wire is pushed up by the magnet. This is called the **motor effect**.

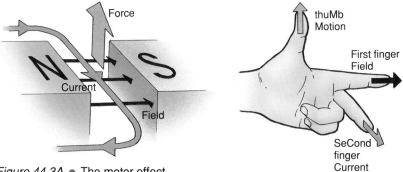

Figure 44.3A ● The motor effect
(a) The force on a current-carrying conductor (b) The left-hand rule

If the magnet is turned round so that its north and south poles swap positions, the wire is pushed down by the magnet. Reversing the direction of the magnetic field reverses the direction in which the wire moves. Reversing the current also has this effect. The **left-hand rule** tells you the direction of the force which moves the wire when you know the direction of the current and the direction of the magnetic field. Figure 44.3A(b) shows you how to remember the left-hand rule.

Loudspeakers, meters and motors are designed to make use of the motor effect. All these devices work because current-carrying wires are being moved by magnets.

● The loudspeaker

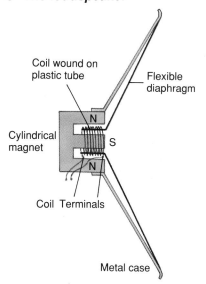

Figure 44.3B shows a loudspeaker. When varying current is passed through the coil, the magnet is forced in and out of the coil. This makes a flexible cone called the diaphragm move in and out, creating sound waves in the surrounding air.

Figure 44.3B ● A loudspeaker

● *The moving coil meter*

A model moving coil meter is shown in Figure 44.3C. When current is passed through the coil, the coil turns. Each side carries a current across the lines of the magnetic field so each side experiences a force.

Because the current is in opposite directions on each side, the force on one side is in the opposite direction to the force on the other side. If the current is increased, the coil turns more. This is how the moving coil meter works.

When the current is switched off, the coil returns to its starting position. When the current is reversed, the coil turns in the opposite direction.

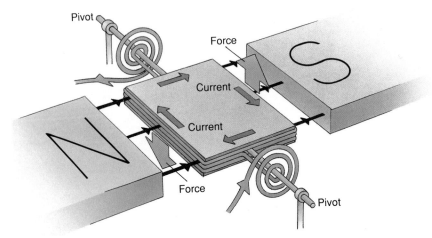

Figure 44.3C ● Making a meter

Figure 44.3D shows the construction of an accurate moving coil meter. Most ammeters and voltmeters with a pointer are constructed like this. Current enters the coil via the upper hairspring and leaves via the lower hairspring. The magnetic force on each side of the coil makes it turn, winding up the hairsprings. When the current is switched off, the hairsprings unwind and the coil returns to its 'zero' position. The iron drum produces a radial magnetic field which makes the coil deflection proportional to the current. This gives a linear scale.

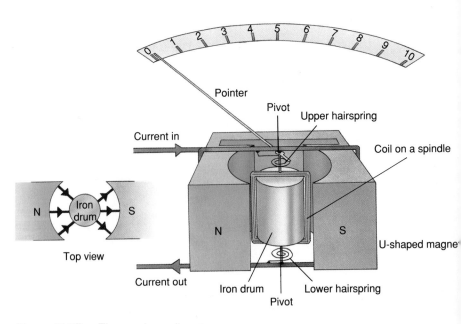

Figure 44.3D ● The moving coil meter

● *The moving coil motor*

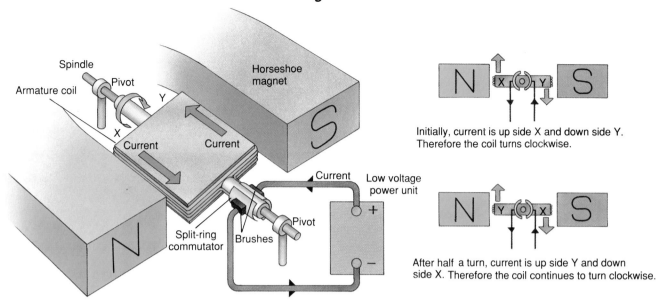

Figure 44.3E ● The simple electric motor

Initially, current is up side X and down side Y. Therefore the coil turns clockwise.

After half a turn, current is up side Y and down side X. Therefore the coil continues to turn clockwise.

A simple electric motor is shown in Figure 44.3E. When current is passed through the **armature coil**, side X of the coil is forced up and side Y down. This is because each side carries current in opposite directions in the magnetic field.

The **commutator** ensures that the coil turns continuously in the same direction. After each half-turn, the commutator reverses the direction of current round the coil. Since the sides of the coil move through 180° each half-turn, the overall effect is to give the coil a push in the same direction every half-turn.

In a practical motor, the **brushes** are made of graphite, held against the commutator by springs. Graphite is used because it conducts electricity and it lubricates the rotating commutator.

The motor can be made to turn in the opposite direction by reversing the battery connections or turning the magnet round.

The motor can be made to turn faster by increasing the current, using a stronger magnet or using a coil with more turns. Commercial motors are made with several coils on the same armature. The coils are equally spaced on the armature. Each coil is connected to its own section of the commutator. This design ensures the motor runs smoothly.

Figure 44.3F ● A practical motor

The definition of the ampere

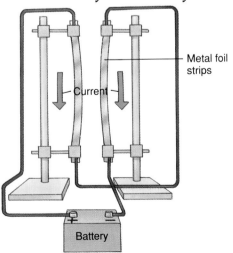

Do current-carrying wires exert forces on each other? Figure 44.3G shows how to test this using strips of metal foil as lightweight wires. The strips attract each other when the current is the same direction in both. They repel when the current is in opposite directions.

Figure 44.3G ● The force between two current-carrying wires

The ampere, the unit of current, is defined from this effect. One ampere is that current in two infinitely-long parallel wires 1.0 m apart that causes a force of 2×10^{-7} N on each metre of wire.

CHECKPOINT

❶ (a) A loudspeaker converts energy from one form to another. What form does it use and what form is this turned into?
(b) Outline the energy changes that take place when an electric motor is connected to a battery.
(c) A battery-operated toy car is driven by a simple electric motor. What would be the effect on the motion of the car if (i) a lighter battery of the same voltage was used, (ii) a heavier battery of the same voltage was used, (iii) a motor with a stronger magnet was used?

❷ (a) Make a labelled sketch of a moving coil meter and explain how it works.
(b) In a moving coil meter, describe the function of (i) the iron drum, (ii) the hairsprings, (iii) the zero adjuster.
(c) A moving coil meter is made so that its pointer deflects exactly to the end of the scale when the current is 1.0 A. However, its magnet gradually becomes weaker. How does this affect its accuracy?

❸ (a) How many electric motors are there in your home? Make a list of all the appliances in your home that contain electric motors.
(b) The power supplied to an electric motor is equal to the product of its current and its voltage. An electric drill operating at 240 V is used to drill into a wall. It takes several minutes to do this and the motor becomes quite warm. Why does it become warm when used in this way?

❹ An electric mixer has a three-speed control switch and an on/off switch. This is achieved using two identical resistors, as shown in the figure opposite.
(a) The speed control switch can be set at X or at Y or at Z. Which position gives the lowest speed 'slow', which position gives 'medium' speed and which position gives 'fast'?
(b) The figure does not show the on/off switch. Sketch the circuit and show where the switch should be.

Food mixer

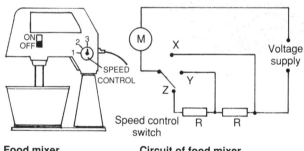

Circuit of food mixer

44.4 🔆 The television tube

Thousands of technicians and engineers work in television. Perhaps your future might lie in making television programmes.

The demonstration electron tube in Figure 44.4A shows a beam of electrons passing over a special screen inside the tube. The electrons cause a visible trace along the screen. When a magnet is brought near the tube, as shown, the electrons are pushed downwards. Placing a current-carrying coil near the tube would have the same effect. Electrons moving across the lines of force of a magnetic field are pushed by the field. The

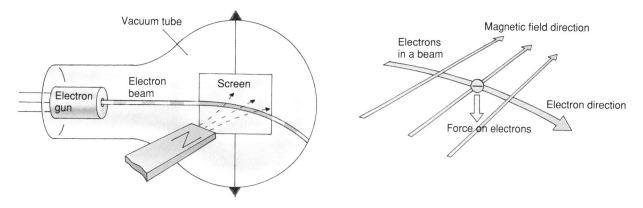

Figure 44.4A ● Electron beams in a magnetic field
(a) The electron tube

(b) Magnetic force on moving electrons

> **SCIENCE AT WORK**
>
> The electron microscope uses a beam of electrons to form an image of a specimen. The beam is focussed using magnetic fields.

same happens to electrons moving along a current-carrying wire in a magnetic field. The force on the wire is because the moving electrons are pushed by the field.

When you watch television, you are watching pictures built up on the television screen by beams of electrons. The screen is the flat end of a special electron tube called the **television tube**. The screen is formed by coating the inside of the tube at the flat end with a special chemical. A spot of light is emitted from the screen at the point where an electron beam strikes it.

Each beam is produced by an **electron gun** at the narrow end of the tube. A black and white television tube contains a single electron gun. A colour tube contains three electron guns.

The electron beam is deflected by magnetic coils at the narrow end of the tube so that the spot traces lines across the screen. In a black and white television tube, the television signal is used to vary the brightness of the spot as it moves across the screen. Figure 44.4B shows how a picture is built up on the screen in this way.

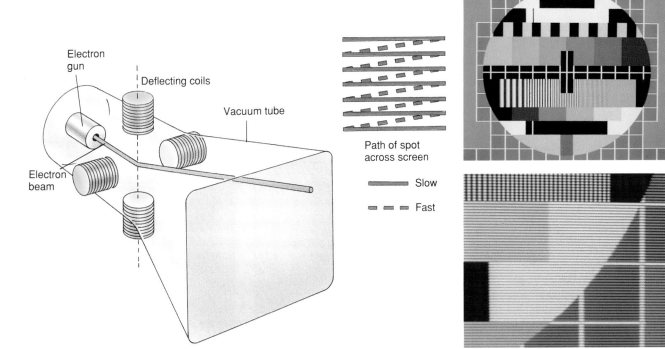

Figure 44.4B ● The television tube

Colour television tubes use three electron guns. The screen is designed so that one gun makes it emit red light, one gun makes it emit green light and the remaining gun makes it emit blue light. Red, blue and green are the primary colours of light. Different mixtures of these colours give any other colour. This is how the picture on a colour television is formed.

Figure 44.4C shows how a colour television works. The screen of a colour television is a matrix of dots of special chemicals. There are three types of dots. Each type of dot produces a primary colour of light when electrons in a beam hit it. A shadow mask is used to ensure that each type of dot can only be hit by electrons from one particular gun. In this way, one gun produces a red picture, one gun produces a green picture and one gun gives a blue picture. The pictures overlap so the viewer sees the correct colours on the screen (Figure 44.4D).

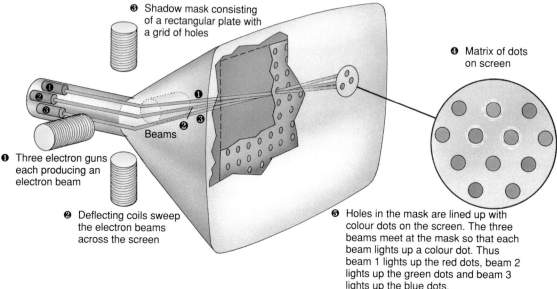

❸ Shadow mask consisting of a rectangular plate with a grid of holes

❹ Matrix of dots on screen

❶ Three electron guns each producing an electron beam

Beams

❷ Deflecting coils sweep the electron beams across the screen

❺ Holes in the mask are lined up with colour dots on the screen. The three beams meet at the mask so that each beam lights up a colour dot. Thus beam 1 lights up the red dots, beam 2 lights up the green dots and beam 3 lights up the blue dots.

Figure 44.4C ● How a colour television tube works

Figure 44.4D ● Colour pictures

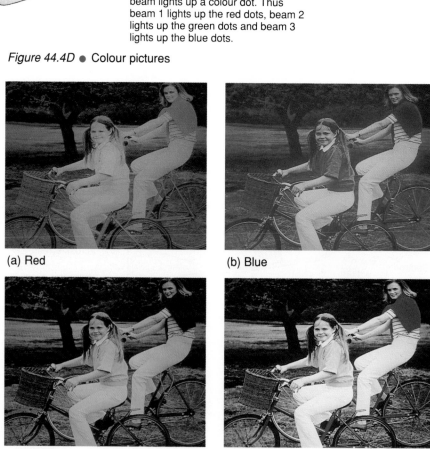

(a) Red

(b) Blue

(c) Green

(d) Full colour

SUMMARY

Television pictures are built up by beams of electrons. A colour television tube contains three electron guns, producing pictures in red, green and blue light. These pictures overlap to produce the actual colour picture on the screen.

CHECKPOINT

❶ (a) When a television is switched off, a spot that fades away is sometimes seen on the screen. What causes the spot and why does it fade away?
(b) Why does static electricity build up on television screens?

❷ (a) A colour television shows a picture of the Union Jack. How many of its three electron guns are used to produce (i) the red part, (ii) the blue part, (iii) the white part of the picture?
(b) Make a sketch of what you would see on the screen if the red gun stopped working.

❸ The picture on a colour screen is renewed 25 times each second. Each time, the electron beam traces out 625 lines on the screen.
(a) How long does the beam take to trace out a single line?
(b) How would the picture differ if the number of lines on the screen was much less than 625?
(c) How would the picture differ if it was renewed at just fives times each second?

❹ Most homes have at least one television. Where else would you expect to find televisions in use?

❺ Satellite TV offers a wide range of channels for those prepared to invest in a receiver dish and a decoder.
(a) To receive satellite television, why is it essential to have a suitable dish?
(b) The television signal from the satellite must be decoded. This is because the broadcasting station put the signal into its own code. Why is the signal coded by the television station?

44.5 Generators and transformers

In this section, you will find out how electricity is produced and distributed.

Electricity provides us with instant energy in our homes at the flick of a switch. Distant power stations generate electricity which is then transmitted to our homes through a network of cables called the **National Grid**. How did people manage before electricity reached the home? If you have ever suffered a power cut at home, you should know the problems of coping without electricity.

The principle of generating electricity was discovered by Michael Faraday in 1831. He showed that when a magnet is pushed in and out of a coil, a voltage is 'induced' in the coil. If the coil is part of a complete circuit, the induced voltage drives a current round the circuit. This effect is known as **electromagnetic induction** (Figure 44.5A).

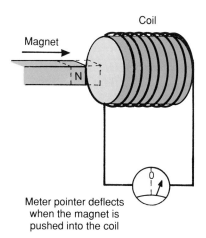

Magnet

Coil

N

Meter pointer deflects when the magnet is pushed into the coil

Figure 44.5A ● (a) Electromagnetic induction (b) Michael Faraday

255

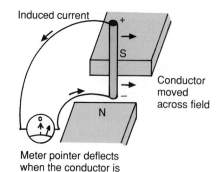

Figure 44.5B ● Induced voltage in a moving conductor

Meter pointer deflects when the conductor is moved across the field

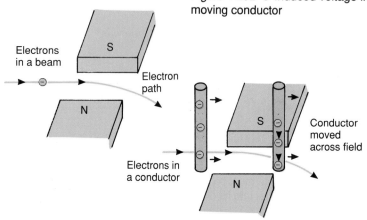

(a) Electrons in a beam crossing the magnetic field are pushed down

(b) Electrons in a conductor moved across the magnetic field are pushed down

Figure 44.5C ● Explaining induced voltage

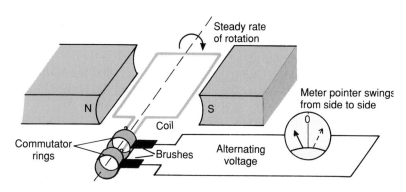

(a) Construction

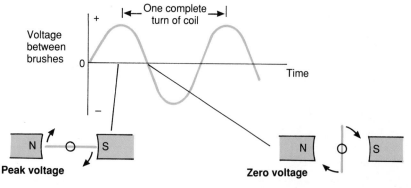

Peak voltage   Zero voltage

(b) Alternating voltage
Figure 44.5D ● The a.c. generator

Investigating electromagnetic induction

Figure 44.5B shows another way to induce a voltage in a wire. When the wire is moved between the poles of the horseshoe magnet, a voltage is induced across its ends. The induced voltage pushes current round the circuit through the meter.

Why should a voltage be induced when a wire moves across a magnetic field? A wire contains many free electrons because it is made of metal. When the wire is moved across the field as in Figure 44.5C, the electrons are moved with it. But the field pushes the electrons along the wire. So a voltage is created across the ends of the wire.

What happens if the wire stops moving? No voltage is induced in a wire that is stationary relative to the magnet. Move the magnet but keep the wire fixed and a voltage is induced. This happens whenever the wire moves relative to the magnet.

How can the induced voltage be made larger? You could use a stronger magnet or use more wire or move the wire faster.

What happens if the wire is moved along the lines of force of the field rather than across them? No voltage is produced now. The direction of motion of the wire must cut across the lines of force.

The alternating current generator

Figure 44.5D(a) shows a coil in a magnetic field. The coil is connected to a sensitive centre-reading meter. When the coil is turned at a steady rate, the meter pointer swings repeatedly from one side of the zero mark to the other side. The current through the meter repeatedly changes from one direction to the other and back. This is known as **alternating current** as opposed to direct current which passes in one direction only.

The effect happens because the voltage induced in the coil alternates, as in Figure 44.5D(b). This type of generator is sometimes called an **alternator**. If the coil is turned too fast, the meter pointer cannot keep up with the changes. But a lamp bulb would remain lit.

The voltage is biggest when the coil sides cut through the lines of force of the field. As the coil turns from this position, the voltage drops to zero and then reverses polarity as the coil sides cut across the field lines once more. Graphite brushes press against the commutator rings to make continuous contact with the coil.

Power to the people

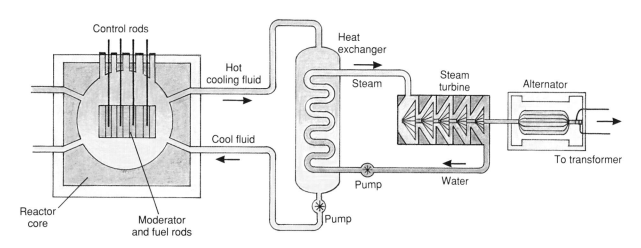

Figure 44.5E ● A nuclear power station

Power station alternators are designed to deliver alternating current to the National Grid. The frequency of the current must be exactly 50 Hz. This is achieved by making the alternator coil rotate steadily at a precise rate of 50 turns per second. In most power stations, **turbine engines** drive the alternators round at steady speed, making the alternators deliver electrical energy to the National Grid system.

Most power stations use fuel to heat water to create steam. The high-pressure steam is then used to turn the turbine wheels. The rotating turbine shaft is used to make the alternator turn steadily. Thus chemical energy from the fuel is converted to electrical energy at the power station and the electrical energy is delivered through the National Grid to consumers far away from the power station.

The advantage of the National Grid system for supplying energy is that the fuel is burned at power stations. Before the National Grid system, factories obtained power from coal-fired steam engines at each factory. They made the atmosphere in industrial areas very polluted.

However, by burning fossil fuels, power stations increase carbon dioxide levels in the atmosphere, thereby contributing to the greenhouse effect. Power stations emissions contain dust and gases that dissolve in water in the atmosphere to produce **acid rain**.

Nuclear power stations use enriched uranium to heat water to create steam. The uranium nuclei split apart, releasing fast-moving neutrons which then split more uranium nuclei, creating a chain-reaction. The fast-moving neutrons heat the reactor core and a cooling fluid is pumped through the core to transfer heat from the core to a heat exchanger where steam is produced (Figure 44.5E).

IT'S A FACT

Before the National Grid was set up, each town had its own power station. Voltage levels and frequencies differed from one town to the next. Some towns had constant voltage levels instead of alternating voltage. The overall system was very inefficient and was rationalised in 1926 when the National Grid was set up.

LOOK AT LINKS
for **steam turbines**
See Theme I, Topic 37.2.

LOOK AT LINKS
for **acid rain**
See Theme E, Topic 23.5.

Nuclear reactors do not produce carbon dioxide or acid rain. However, the spent nuclear fuel is highly radioactive and must be stored in safe conditions for hundreds of years until harmless. *Can you think of any further drawbacks to nuclear power stations?*

Hydroelectric power stations use water pressure to drive the turbines. A hydroelectric power station is usually sited near the base of a mountain with an upland lake so the water from the lake can be piped down to the station. *Can you think of any environmental problems associated with hydroelectric power stations?*

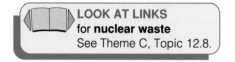

LOOK AT LINKS
for **nuclear waste**
See Theme C, Topic 12.8.

● *The National Grid*

The National Grid takes alternating current from power stations and delivers it to factories and homes. The output voltage from a power station is usually about 25 000 V. The voltage in a house is 240 V. **Transformers** are used to change the voltage levels.

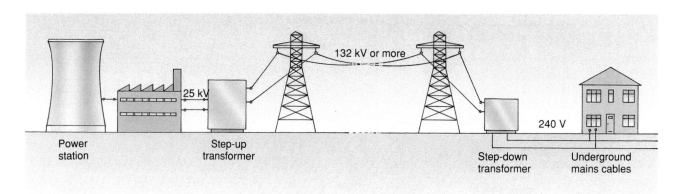

Figure 44.5F ● The National Grid

The output voltage of a power station must be 'stepped up' by transformers before being supplied to the National Grid. High voltages are better than low voltages for transmitting electrical power. At the consumer end of the National Grid, the voltage level must be stepped down before being supplied to homes and factories.

Figure 44.5G shows a model of a power line at high voltage and a model of a power line at low voltage. The high voltage line is much more efficient than the same power line at low voltage.

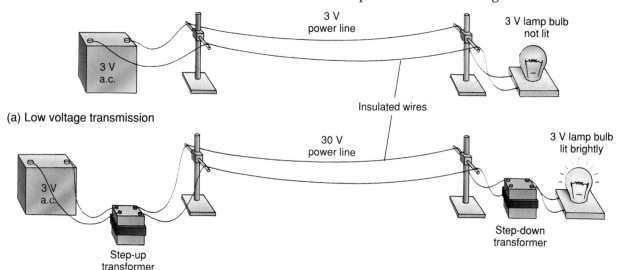

(a) Low voltage transmission

(b) High voltage transmission
Figure 44.5G ● Model power lines

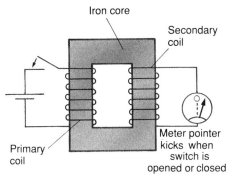

Figure 44.5H ● Investigating transformers

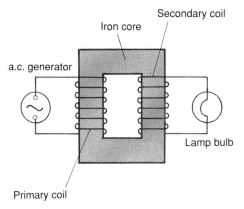

Figure 44.5I ● Using a transformer

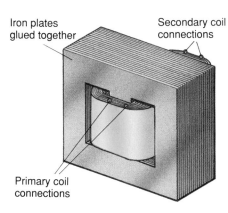

(a) A practical transformer

(b) Circuit symbol
Figure 44.5J ● Transformers in circuits

Investigating transformers

Wind two coils of wire on an iron core. Connect one coil in series with a battery and switch; connect the other coil to a centre-reading meter. Open and close the switch repeatedly. You will find the meter pointer kicks one way then the other way each time the switch is opened and closed.

Why does this happen? Each time the switch is closed, the iron core is magnetised. When the switch is opened, the core loses its magnetism. The magnetism passes through the second coil. Each time the magnetism changes, a voltage is induced in the second coil. This makes the meter pointer kick. Changing the current in the first coil induces a voltage in the second coil (Figure 44.5H).

The coils are called the **primary** and **secondary** coils. If the primary coil is connected to an alternating current generator, an alternating voltage is induced in the secondary coil. Figure 44.5I shows an experiment to demonstrate the idea. The lamp bulb connected to the secondary coil lights up when the primary coil is connected to the power unit. If the two coils are separated, the lamp bulb goes dim because the magnetism from the primary coil no longer passes through the secondary coil.

How can the lamp bulb in Figure 44.5I be made brighter?
- The primary current could be increased. This makes the magnetism of the coil stronger giving a bigger induced voltage.
- Increasing the frequency is another way. Remember Faraday's discovery that the faster the magnet is moved, the greater the induced voltage. A higher frequency makes the magnetism in the core change faster, giving a bigger induced voltage in the secondary coil.
- Using more turns on the secondary coil increases the lamp brightness. Each turn 'picks up' a certain voltage. The more turns that are used, the greater the induced voltage. You could use voltmeters to show that the ratio of the secondary voltage to the primary voltage is the same as the turns ratio. This is called the transformer rule

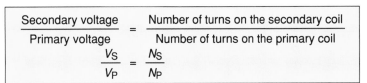

$$\frac{\text{Secondary voltage}}{\text{Primary voltage}} = \frac{\text{Number of turns on the secondary coil}}{\text{Number of turns on the primary coil}}$$
$$\frac{V_S}{V_P} = \frac{N_S}{N_P}$$

Practical transformers are designed to step alternating voltages up or down. Figure 44.5J shows the construction and circuit symbol for a practical transformer. A low voltage power unit contains such a transformer to step the mains voltage of 240 V down to the output level of the power unit. A television or radio operating from the mains also contains a step-down transformer.

The efficiency of most practical transformers is very high. For an ideal transformer delivering power, the power it can supply from its secondary coil is equal to the power supplied to its primary coil. Since electrical power is given by current multiplied by voltage, the following equation holds for an 'ideal' transformer.

> Primary current x Primary voltage = Secondary current x Secondary voltage
> $$I_P V_P = I_S V_S$$

The equation shows that if the voltage is stepped down, the current is stepped up. Also, if the voltage is stepped up, the current is stepped down. This is why voltages are stepped up on power lines. The current is stepped down so there is much less electrical heating of power lines.

Electricity in the UK
(program)

Use this database to investigate electricity use in the United Kingdom.

Worked example A transformer is to be used to 'step down' an alternating voltage from 240 V to 12 V. The primary coil has 1200 turns.
(a) Work out the number of turns on the secondary coil.
(b) The secondary coil is used to light a 12 V, 24 W bulb. What will be the current in the primary coil?

Solution
(a) Primary voltage = 240 V, Secondary voltage = 12 V, Primary turns = 1200

Using the transformer rule $\dfrac{V_S}{V_P} = \dfrac{N_S}{N_P}$

$$\frac{12}{240} = \frac{N_S}{1200}$$

Therefore Number of secondary turns, $N_S = \dfrac{12 \times 1200}{240} = 60$

(b) The power of the lamp is 24 W. Since power = current x voltage, the lamp current is therefore 2 A (= 24W/12V). This is the secondary current. To work out the primary current, use the equation

$$I_P\, V_P = I_S\, V_S$$

From the equation above $I_P \times 240 = 12 \times 2$

So Primary current, $I_P = \dfrac{12 \times 2}{240} = 0.1$ A

SUMMARY

When a wire cuts across the lines of force of a magnetic field, a voltage is induced across the ends of the wire. If the wire is part of a complete circuit, the induced voltage causes current to pass round the circuit. The effect happens if the wire is fixed and the magnetic field changes.

CHECKPOINT

① The north pole of a bar magnet is pushed into a coil, as in Figure 44.5A. The meter pointer deflects to the right as shown. Which way would it deflect if:
(a) the north pole is then withdrawn from the coil,
(b) a south pole is pushed into the coil instead,
(c) a south pole is withdrawn from the coil?

② Karen is showing Sarah how to generate a voltage by passing a wire between the poles of a horseshoe magnet. The wire is connected to a centre reading meter. The meter pointer kicks to the left of centre when the wire is moved sharply through the field.
(a) What happens when the wire is moved (i) sharply in the reverse direction, (ii) slowly in the original direction?
(b) The wire is doubled back on itself and passed through the field. Karen explains to Sarah that one part of the wire cancels out the other part. How could you demonstrate this is so?

③ (a) The figure opposite shows the voltage output of an alternator as a graph of voltage against time. Sketch similar graphs for the same alternator turned (i) more quickly, (ii) more slowly.
(b) The output voltage from a power station is stepped up to supply power to the National Grid. This means that the currents passing through the grid cables are smaller than they would be if the voltage had not been stepped up. Why is less power wasted by stepping the voltage up?
(c) A transformer with 1000 turns on its primary coil and 50 turns on its secondary coil is used to step down an alternating voltage of 240 V. The primary coil is in a circuit with a 1 A fuse. Work out:
(i) the secondary voltage,
(ii) the maximum current in the secondary coil when it is in a circuit,
(iii) the maximum power the transformer can deliver.

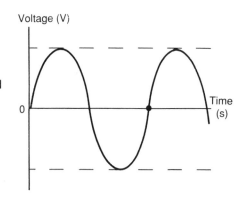

Voltage (V)

Time (s)

ELECTRONICS

45.1 Electronics

FIRST THOUGHTS

Electronics has revolutionised many activities. In this section, you will find out the difference between digital and analogue electronics.

LOOK AT LINKS
Silicon is an element with unusual electrical properties.
See Theme C, Topic 9.1.

Make a list of all the electronic gadgets that you have used. Perhaps you have a video recorder or microcomputer to put on your list. Do not forget the phone or the television remote control unit. You may have been shopping at a supermarket with laser bar-code readers at the tills or perhaps have seen a cash dispensing machine used outside a bank.

These are all examples of electronic systems that handle information. The development of **microelectronics** has made all these systems possible. Twenty or more years ago, electronic circuits used **valves** to move information round. Valves are bulky glass vacuum tubes that need high voltages to work and consequently get hot. Valves have been replaced by **silicon chips**. A single silicon chip no bigger than a thumbnail contains the equivalent of hundreds of valves. Chips do not get hot and they use very little power so they can work off small batteries.

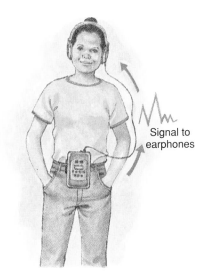

Signal to earphones

(a) An analogue system

Figure 45.1A ● A valve and a silicon chip

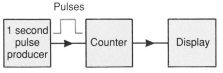

Pulses

(b) A digital watch system
Figure 45.1B ●

SUMMARY

Digital systems have just two possible voltage levels, referred to as high and low. In analogue systems, the voltages can be at any value between the limits set by the power supply.

Which two electronic gadgets do you and your friends use most often? Digital watches and personal stereos probably top the list. A personal stereo radio uses one or more chips to boost the tiny radio signal picked up by the aerial inside the stereo. The circuit in the stereo which is used to make the signal stronger is called an amplifier. The circuit is an example of an **analogue** system. Analogue means that voltages in the system can be at any value between the limits set by the power supply.

A digital watch contains a complicated electronic system designed to count and display voltage pulses produced at a rate of one per second. A small battery is all that is needed to supply power to the system.

The electronic circuit in the watch is an example of a **digital** system. Digital means that the voltage at any point in the system is either zero (i.e. low) or at a fixed positive value (i.e. high). No other values of voltage are possible in a digital system. Digital circuits are useful for making decisions, storing information, counting and many other things.

45.2 Electronic logic

What was the last decision you made? Did you make a logical decision? Read on to find out how electronic circuits make logical decisions.

Decisions are made by each one of us all the time. Each decision involves making a choice of some sort. Using **logic** allows us to make decisions. Suppose you are about to go out and you are thinking about whether or not you should wear a coat. Your decision would probably depend on your answer to two questions

Question A: Is it raining?
Question B: Is it cold outside?
Decision to be made: Shall I wear a coat?

If you answer YES to A or B, then you would take your coat. This situation where the 'output' depends on the 'inputs' can be shown by a **truth table**. Figure 45.2A shows the truth table for this situation. In the truth table, YES is shown by 1 and NO by 0. So the output is 1 if A OR B is 1.

INPUTS		OUTPUT
Is it raining?	Is it cold?	Shall I wear a coat?
0	0	0
0	1	1
1	0	1
1	1	1

1 = YES   0 = NO

Figure 45.2A ● A truth table

Warning systems are designed to give a warning under certain conditions. For example, a door alarm in a car is designed to warn if any of the car doors is open. The truth table in Figure 45.2B shows how this system operates in a two-door car. The alarm works if door A OR door B is open.

The alarm in Figure 45.2B is ON or OFF depending on the settings of the doors. A switch in each door provides an input signal to an electronic circuit that controls an alarm buzzer. The output signal from the circuit switches the buzzer on or off. This depends on the condition of the input signals. In other words, the output state is decided by the input states.

IT

Logic Gates
(program)

Use this program to study the behaviour of different types of logic gates. Then try to put them in a sequence – investigate what happens with four gates.

INPUTS		OUTPUT
Door A	Door B	Buzzer
0	0	0
1	0	1
0	1	1
1	1	1

0 = Door closed   0 = Buzzer off
1 = Door opened   1 = Buzzer on

Figure 45.2B ● A warning system

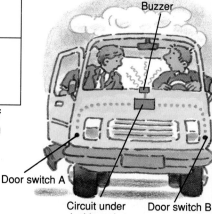

Buzzer

Door switch A

Circuit under dashboard

Door switch B

Gate	Symbol	Function (High voltage = 1, Low voltage = 0)	Truth Table INPUTS A B	OUTPUT
OR	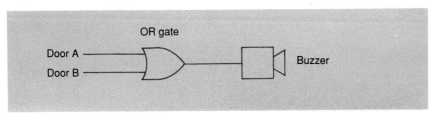 A, B, OUTPUT	OUTPUT = 1 if A OR B = 1	0 0 0 1 1 0 1 1	0 1 1 1
AND	A, B, OUTPUT	OUTPUT = 1 if A AND B = 1	0 0 0 1 1 0 1 1	0 0 0 1
NOR	A, B, OUTPUT	OUTPUT = 0 if A OR B = 1	0 0 0 1 1 0 1 1	1 0 0 0
NAND	A, B, OUTPUT	OUTPUT = 0 if A AND B = 1	0 0 0 1 1 0 1 1	1 1 1 0
NOT	OUTPUT, INPUT	OUTPUT = 1 if INPUT = 0 OUTPUT = 0 if INPUT = 1	0 1	1 0

Figure 45.2C ● Logic gates

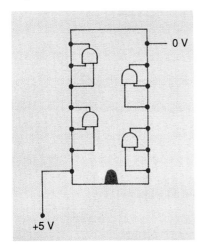

Figure 45.2D ● Door alarm

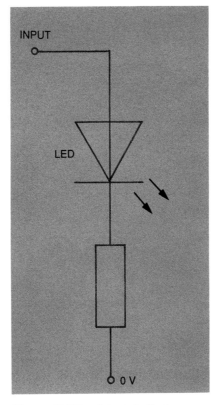

Figure 45.2E ● An AND chip

Figure 45.2F ● A logic indicator

SUMMARY

Only two voltage levels are possible in a digital circuit. The output voltage of a logic gate depends on the voltage level at each input terminal of the gate.

Logic gates

The circuit controlling the car door alarm in Figure 45.2B is called a logic gate because it is designed to make a decision. Any logic gate has one or more input terminals and an output terminal. The voltage at the output (i.e. the output state) depends on the voltages at the input terminals (i.e. the input states). This may be described by a truth table. We will only consider what a logic gate does: not how it does it. The circuit symbols and truth tables of some common logic gates are shown in Figure 45.2C.

Figure 45.2D shows how the car door alarm control circuit is made using an OR gate. Check for yourself that its truth table is the same as in Figure 45.2B. *What would happen if an AND gate was used instead?*

Logic gates are made in chip form. Figure 45.2E shows an AND chip. It contains four AND gates, each with two input terminals and an output terminal. The chip has twelve pins for these terminals and two pins for the supply voltage.

An indicator is used to display the output state of a logic gate. Figure 45.2F shows how an indicator may be made using a light-emitting diode (LED) and a resistor. The LED lights up when a '1' is applied to the input terminal of the indicator.

To supply a '1' to a logic gate input terminal, the terminal can be connected to the positive terminal of the gate's voltage supply unit. Connecting the input to the negative terminal (which is usually earthed) applies a '0' signal at the input. An indicator is connected to the output terminal to observe the output state.

❶ Copy and complete the truth table for each of the logic systems (a) to (j) shown below.

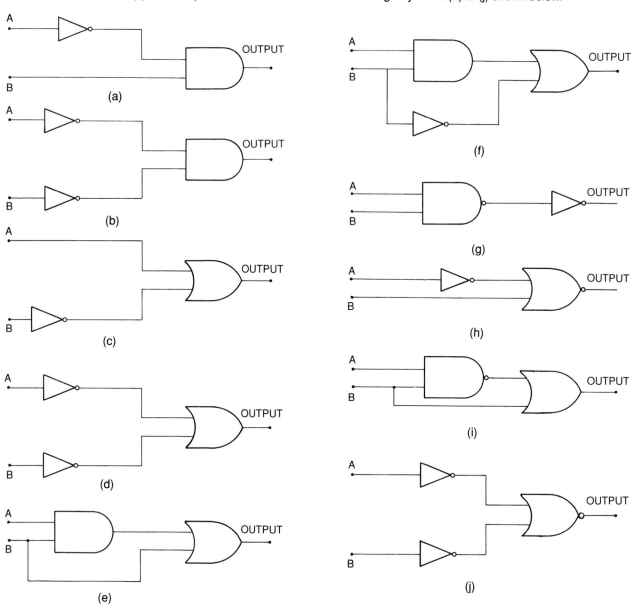

❷ A comparator is a logic circuit that gives a '1' at its output terminal only when the logic state of its input terminals are the same. The diagram shows its truth table.

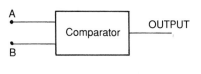

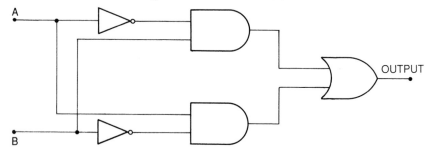

A	B	OUTPUT
0	0	1
0	1	0
1	0	0
1	1	1

(a) Simon has designed a comparator using some logic gates. His design is shown above. Unfortunately, there is a fault in his design. Make a truth table for the system he has designed.

(b) Redesign Simon's system so it works correctly.

③ Design a logic system, using two-input gates, for a four-door car to warn if any of the doors are open when the handbrake is off.

④ A burglar alarm system fitted in an apartment is designed so that the alarm is activated if a key-operated switch is 'on' and the entrance door is open or a pressure pad under the carpet behind the door is activated. The figure below shows the system and part of its truth table.

INPUTS			OUTPUT
Door switch	Key switch	Pressure pad	Alarm
OPEN = 1 CLOSED = 0	ON = 1 OFF = 0	ON = 1 OFF = 0	ON = 1 OFF = 0
0	0	0	0
1	0	0	
0	0	1	0
1	0	1	
0	1	0	0
1	1	0	
0	1	1	1
1	1	1	

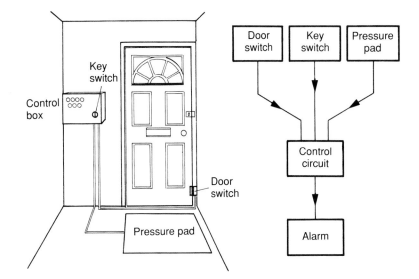

(a) Copy and complete the truth table.
(b) Anyone entering the apartment has 20 seconds to turn the key switch off after opening the door or else the alarm is activated. Why is this delay necessary?
(c) Why is the pressure pad essential?

⑤ Design a system to warn if a car seat belt is unfastened when the seat is occupied. Assume the seat belt unit supplies a '1' to a suitable logic system when the belt is locked and a switch under the seat supplies a '1' when the seat is occupied.

FIRST THOUGHTS

45.3 Electronics at work

In this section, you will find out how electronic sensors work and what they can be used for.

RESOURCE ACTIVITY PACK

The car door alarm system in Figure 45.2B uses switches as **input sensors**. These signals sense (detect) when a door is open and send a signal to the control circuit. The circuit operates the alarm buzzer. The buzzer is an **output device**, designed to convert an electrical signal into sound. The whole system is designed in three parts, the input sensors, the control circuit and the output device. Many electronic systems are designed in this way.

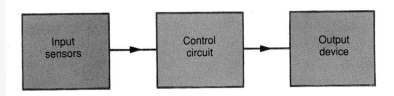

Figure 45.3A ● A control system

Input sensors

A sensor is a device that produces an electrical signal in response to a change in a physical variable such as temperature or light intensity or pressure.

A simple pressure sensor is shown in Figure 45.3B. With sufficient pressure on the switch, the switch closes and connects the output terminal of the sensor to the positive terminal of the voltage supply. The LED lights up when this happens.

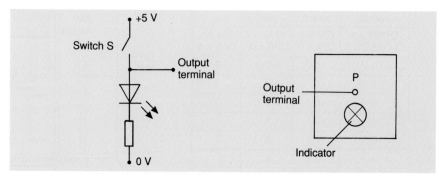

Figure 45.3B ● A pressure sensor (a) Circuit (b) Symbol

A moisture sensor has a gap in its circuit, as shown in Figure 45.3C. The gap is formed by two wires fixed on an insulator. When the gap becomes moist, it conducts electricity. The result is that the voltage at the output terminal of the sensor rises.

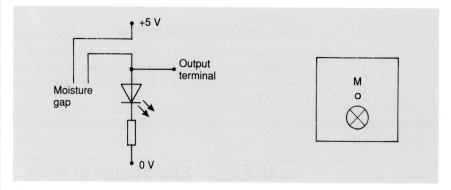

Figure 45.3C ● A moisture sensor (a) Circuit (b) Symbol

The light sensor in Figure 45.3D uses a **light dependent resistor** (LDR) and a resistor to form a potential divider. The LDR's resistance drops when the intensity of light on it increases. This makes the output voltage of the sensor rise. In darkness, the voltage drops.

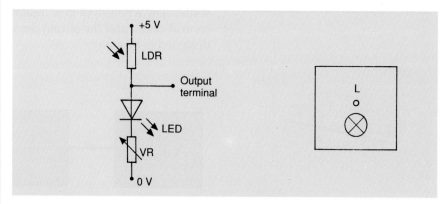

Figure 45.3D ● A light sensor (a) Circuit (b) Symbol

The LDR is made from silicon. When light falls on silicon, electrons break free from the silicon atoms. This is why the resistance drops. Extra electrons become available to carry current.

Figure 45.3E shows a temperature sensor. Temperature sensors use a thermistor in series with a resistor. The resistance of a thermistor drops as its temperature rises. This makes the output voltage of the sensor rise. Falling temperature makes the voltage fall.

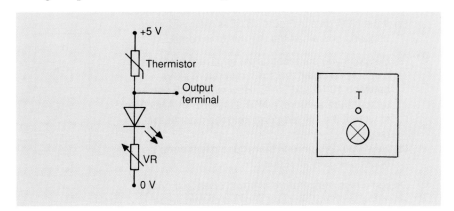

Figure 45.3E ● A temperature sensor (a) Circuit (b) Symbol

A thermistor, like an LDR, is made from silicon. Raising the temperature of silicon enables electrons to break free from silicon atoms. The thermistor must be in a light-proof cover. *Why?*

Using sensors

● *A low-temperature warning indicator*
Tomato growers need to make sure that plants are protected from frost. Figure 45.3F shows a system to do this. When the temperature of the sensor falls below a certain value, the sensor output is zero. A NOT gate is used to convert this to a '1'. This is supplied to one of the inputs of an OR gate. The other input is supplied by a 'test' switch. This is used to check the indicator works.

● *A night-time rain alarm*
Your parents might find this useful when wet clothes are left outside on the washing line at night. In darkness, the light sensor supplies a '0' to the NOT gate which therefore supplies a '1' to one of the inputs of the AND gate. The moisture sensor supplies the other AND input. The buzzer sounds the alarm if rain falls on the moisture sensor at night. Figure 45.3G shows the night-time rain alarm system.

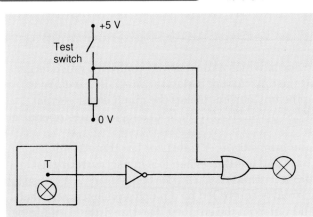

Figure 45.3F ● A low temperature indicator

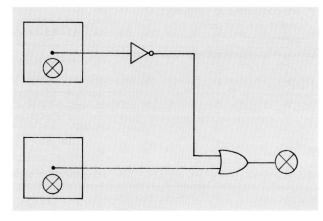

Figure 45.3G ● A night-time rain alarm

CHECKPOINT

① In Figure 45.3E, the variable resistor VR in the temperature sensor can be adjusted to alter the temperature at which the indicator switches on.
   (a) Suppose the resistance of VR is increased. Does this raise or lower the temperature at which the indicator switches on when the thermistor is cooled?
   (b) If the NOT gate in Figure 45.3F is removed what happens now when the thermistor is cooled?

② (a) Suppose you are responsible for a rare plant that can only survive if the soil temperature stays between 10 °C and 30 °C. How would you use two temperature sensors, a NOT gate and an AND gate to warn if the soil temperature goes outside this range?
   (b) How would you check that your system does operate exactly as required?

③ Design a high temperature alarm to operate a buzzer when the temperature goes above a certain value. Include a 'test' switch to check if the buzzer works when the switch is closed.

④ A certain camera is fitted with a light sensor to warn if there is not enough light in the room. This causes a LED to light up in the viewfinder when a button switch on the camera is pressed.
   (a) Unfortunately the system shown in the figure opposite is designed incorrectly. What makes the LED in the system shown light up?
   (b) Redesign the system shown so it operates as intended.

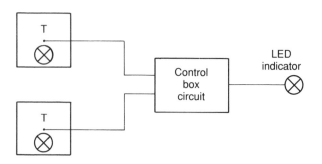

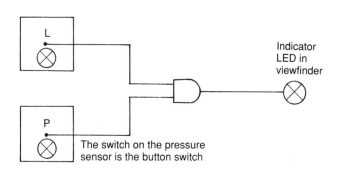

The switch on the pressure sensor is the button switch

FIRST THOUGHTS

45.4 Transistors and relays

A garage that opens its doors automatically when lit up by car headlights is fitted with light sensors. The door is opened by electric motors. The sensors are connected to transistors and relays that switch the motors on.

An LED indicator or a low-power buzzer may be used to display the output state of a logic gate. When the voltage at the output terminal of the gate goes 'high', the buzzer or the LED is activated. However, a lamp or a motor cannot be activated directly by a logic gate. The gate is unable to supply sufficient current.

Transistors

The **transistor** is a device in which a tiny current controls a much larger current. Switching off the tiny current makes the much larger current switch off; increasing the tiny current makes the much larger current increase. A transistor can boost the current from a logic gate to operate a lamp.

Transistors are made from silicon. A transistor has three terminals, called the **collector**, **base** and **emitter**. When it is in use, current goes in at its collector and out from its emitter. The important feature of a transistor is that the collector current is controlled by a much smaller current that goes in at the base (and out from the emitter). The transistor is said to be switched ON when current enters its collector (Figure 45.4A).

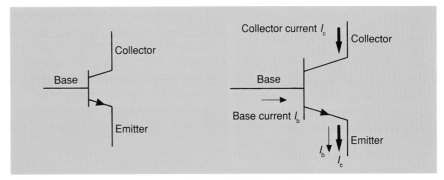

Figure 45.4A ● The transistor (a) Symbol (b) Current flow

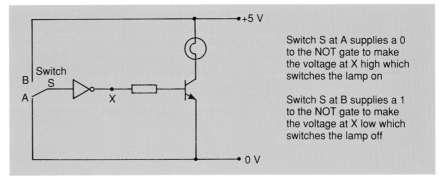

Switch S at A supplies a 0 to the NOT gate to make the voltage at X high which switches the lamp on

Switch S at B supplies a 1 to the NOT gate to make the voltage at X low which switches the lamp off

Figure 45.4B ● Using a transistor

The circuit in Figure 45.4B shows a transistor connected to a logic gate to operate a lamp. When the output voltage from the logic gate is 'high', a tiny current enters the base of the transistor to switch the transistor on. Hence current passes through the lamp into the collector of the transistor (and out from the emitter).

When making transistor circuits, two key rules must be observed:
- The polarity of the voltage supply must be correct.
- The base current should be limited to prevent the collector current becoming large enough to overheat the transistor. If this happens, the transistor may stop working altogether. A resistor in series with the base terminal is used to limit the base current.

Relays

A light-operated garage door would be very useful for lazy motorists. The car headlamps could activate a light sensor. This would then send a signal to a control circuit to operate an electric motor which would then open the door. However, the motor could not be switched on directly by a transistor; the motor needs much more current than a transistor can pass. A **relay** is used to switch the motor on. The relay coil is connected to the transistor, as shown in Figure 45.4C.

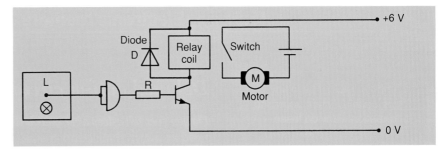

Figure 45.4C ● Using a relay

SUMMARY

A transistor is a three-terminal device in which a large current (the collector current) is controlled by a small current (the base current). The base current may be supplied by a logic gate. The transistor can be used to switch a lamp or a relay on or off.

When the transistor in Figure 45.4C is switched on (by the output of the logic gate going 'high'), current passes through the relay coil into the collector of the transistor. The relay coil is therefore energised and thus closes the relay switch. This turns the motor on.

A diode must be connected in parallel with the relay coil as shown. This is to protect the transistor when it is switched off. If the diode was not included, the relay coil would induce a large voltage across the transistor when switched off. This voltage would damage the transistor.

CHECKPOINT

1 The figure below shows a circuit with two lamps labelled X and Y.
  (a) When the switch is closed, Y lights up but X does not. Explain why this happens.
  (b) What would you expect to see if X and Y were interchanged?

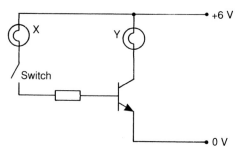

2 Marvin the Magician is showing an audience a trick using the circuit shown opposite. He has connected an LDR between X and Y and the room lights have been dimmed so the lamp is off.
  (a) He strikes a match and holds it near the LDR. The lamp lights up. Why?
  (b) The match goes out but the lamp stays on. Can you explain this?
  (c) He covers the lamp briefly with his hands and the lamp goes out. Why?

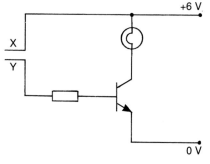

3 Transistors can fail to work correctly. Brendan has made the circuit shown in question 2 but it doesn't seem to be working correctly.
  (a) The lamp does not come on when the gap XY is short-circuited. Brendan thinks the lamp may have failed but it could be the transistor at fault. How could he test the lamp without taking it out of the circuit?
  (b) Brendan discovers that there is a piece of solder joining the base and emitter of the transistor. Why would this stop the circuit working?

4 A motorised washing line that brings the washing in if it rains or if it becomes too cold would be very useful. Design a circuit that will switch a motor on either if it rains or if the temperature falls below a certain value.

FIRST THOUGHTS

45.5 Electronic memory

Computer memories in tiny chips enable instant access to information. How do these memories work? Read on to find out.

Delayed action circuits

*Do you ever fall asleep after your bedside alarm has woken you up? If so, you need an alarm that sounds twice – the second time a few minutes after the first time. This type of alarm has a **time-delay circuit**.*

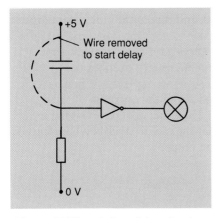

Figure 45.5A ● A time delay circuit

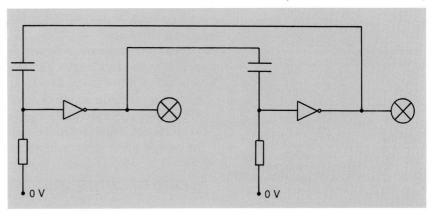

Figure 45.5B ● An astable circuit

A time-delay circuit works by charging a capacitor up. A capacitor is a device that stores charge. The capacitor is in series with a resistor. As the capacitor charges up, the voltage across the capacitor rises and the voltage across the resistor falls. The voltage changes can be used to change the output state of a logic gate after a delay. The gate switches an indicator or a buzzer on. Figure 45.5A shows a time-delay circuit.

To start the circuit working, the capacitor is discharged by connecting a wire across its terminals. The indicator goes off because the NOT gate has a '1' applied to its output. As soon as the wire across the capacitor is removed, the capacitor starts charging up and the voltage at the NOT gate input gradually falls. After a certain time, this voltage becomes low enough to switch the indicator back on.

Increasing the resistance increases the time delay before the indicator switches back on.

The circuit 'remembers' to switch on after a delay. It is sometimes called a **monostable** circuit. This is because there is only one stable state for its output.

An indicator is easier to notice if it switches on and off repeatedly. This can be achieved using two time-delay circuits linked to each other, as in Figure 45.5B. This type of circuit cannot remember which indicator to keep on. The circuit is sometimes called an **astable** circuit. Each indicator repeatedly switches from one state to the other automatically.

When one indicator comes on, it switches the other one off for a time; when this one comes back on, it turns the first one off for a time and so on. The output voltage at each gate repeatedly switches on then off. Each on–off cycle is a single pulse. The circuit is a pulse-producing circuit.

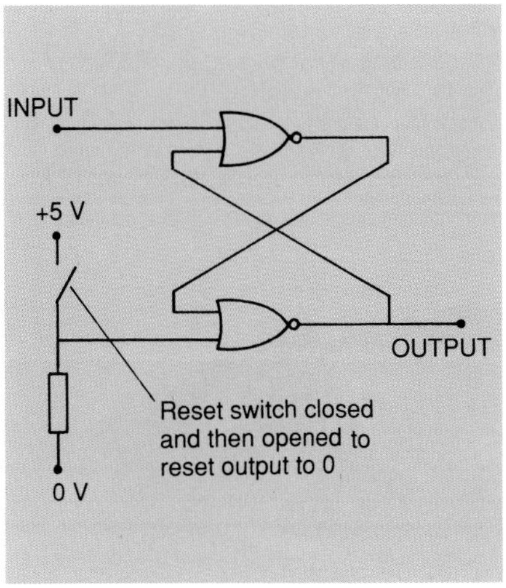

Storing and counting circuits

Karen and Rubinda are designing an alarm system activated by opening a door or stepping on a pressure pad. They have made and tested the circuit satisfactorily; however, they have just realised that an intruder just needs to step off the pressure pad and the alarm stops. They want a circuit that will 'remember' if the pressure pad is stood on, even after the pressure is removed.

Figure 45.5C shows how this can be achieved using two NOR gates. When a '1' is applied to the input, the output becomes '1' and stays at '1', even after the input drops to '0'. The circuit is sometimes called a **latch**. In the alarm circuit, the latch continues to supply a '1' to the warning buzzer, even after the pressure on the pad is removed. The '1' is stored by the latch.

Calculators and computers store bits of data in the form of '0's and '1's. The type of circuit used to store a bit of data is called a **bistable** circuit. It

Figure 45.5C ● A simple latch

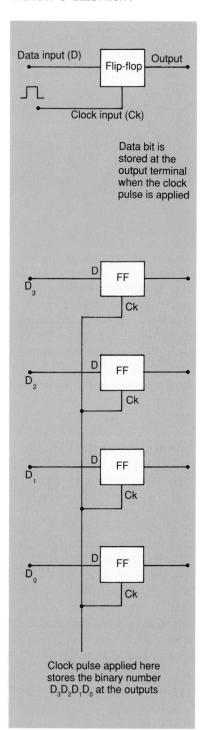

Data input (D) | Flip-flop | Output

Clock input (Ck)

Data bit is stored at the output terminal when the clock pulse is applied

D_3 | D | FF
Ck

D_2 | D | FF
Ck

D_1 | D | FF
Ck

D_0 | D | FF
Ck

Clock pulse applied here stores the binary number $D_3 D_2 D_1 D_0$ at the outputs

Figure 45.5D ● Using a flip-flop

has two stable states, one for storing a '0' and one for a '1'. It is sometimes called a **flip-flop**.

The flip-flop shown in Figure 45.5D stores a bit of data when a pulse is applied to its 'clock' input. To store a four-bit binary number (e.g. 1100), each bit is applied to the data input of a separate flip-flop. When a clock pulse is applied, the four bits are 'latched' on to the outputs.

Flip-flops are made using logic gates. The exact design of the logic circuits is not important to the user; what the circuit does is what matters. The circuits are usually manufactured on chips.

Memory chips

A microcomputer stores data in its memory chips. Each memory chip contains many flip-flops for storing bits of data. The chip is designed like a stack of boxes, with each box able to hold eight bits. An eight-bit binary number is called a **byte**. Each box has an address which must be used to store a byte of data in that box. Figure 45.5E shows the organisation of a simple memory chip.

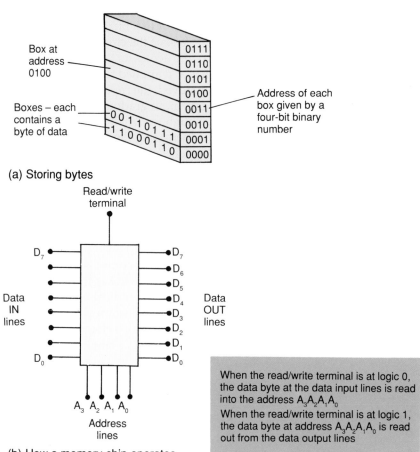

Box at address 0100

Boxes – each contains a byte of data

0111
0110
0101
0100
0011
0010
0001
0000

0 0 1 1 0 1 1 1
1 1 0 0 0 1 1 0

Address of each box given by a four-bit binary number

(a) Storing bytes

Read/write terminal

D_7 ... D_0 Data IN lines

D_7 D_6 D_5 D_4 D_3 D_2 D_1 D_0 Data OUT lines

A_3 A_2 A_1 A_0

Address lines

When the read/write terminal is at logic 0, the data byte at the data input lines is read into the address $A_3 A_2 A_1 A_0$
When the read/write terminal is at logic 1, the data byte at address $A_3 A_2 A_1 A_0$ is read out from the data output lines

(b) How a memory chip operates

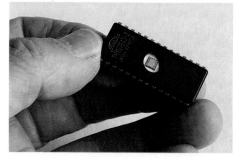

(c) A memory chip
Figure 45.5E ● Electronic memory

The capacity of a microcomputer's memory is usually expressed in **kilobytes** (= 1024 bytes) or **megabytes** (= 1024 x 1024 bytes). Before the invention of memory chips, data was stored on tapes; to retrieve data from a tape, the location of data on the tape must be found and this takes time. However, data can be retrieved from memory chips almost instantly because all the locations or boxes are equally accessible.

Your memory is like a memory chip because you can remember things fast and easily. If you couldn't, you would need to keep looking things up in reference books. That is how computers had to work before memory chips were invented. Memory chips enable instant access to data and that is why microcomputers and wordprocessors work so fast.

The graph in Figure 45.5F shows the growth of the chip memory capacity since the memory chip was invented. Scientists think it will eventually be possible to make a single flip-flop as small as a hundred atoms. This would give a single chip a memory capacity of a million million million bytes or more.

> ## SUMMARY
>
> - The output of an astable circuit repeatedly changes from 0 to 1 and back automatically.
> - When the output of a monostable circuit is changed from 0 to 1, it reverts back to 0 after a delay.
> - A bistable circuit has two stable states and may be used to store a bit of data.

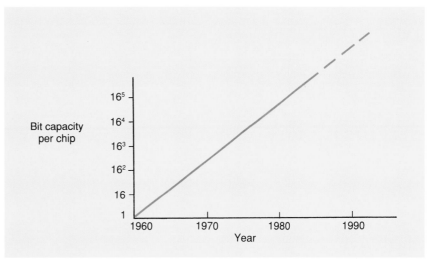

Figure 45.5F ● The growth of electronic memory

CHECKPOINT

❶ A time-delay circuit is needed in a burglar alarm system. This time delay is needed to allow the user time to switch the system on inside the house and then leave.
  (a) What would happen if the time delay was too short?
  (b) When the system is installed, the time delay is adjusted by the installation engineer to suit the user. How can the time delay for the circuit in Figure 45.5A be made longer?

❷ (a) When a bus or lorry reverses, an alarm sounds very loud to warn pedestrians. The figure opposite shows a circuit that switches a buzzer on and off repeatedly when the gear lever is put into reverse. What type of logic gate should be in the control box?
  (b) At a pedestrian crossing, a bleeper sounds when the 'cross now' sign lights up. Design a system to light an LED and sound a bleeper for a fixed time when a button is pressed.

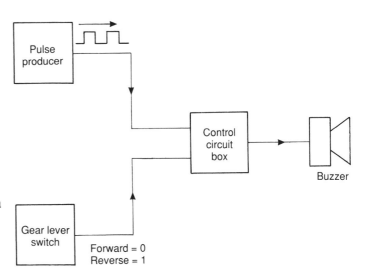

③ (a) Eight flip-flops are needed to store a single byte. How many flip-flops are contained in a 16 kilobyte chip?

(b) Write down the binary number for (i) 31, (ii) 12.

(c) Give your date of birth and then convert it into binary code as two bytes.

④ (a) Use Figure 45.5F to estimate when a chip with a memory capacity of some million million bytes is likely to be developed.

(b) Present memory chips can retrieve a data byte within microseconds. How long would it take to search through all the bytes in a one megabyte chip?

(c) Scientists are trying to find ways of making chips work faster. Why is this important?

45.6 Electronic control

FIRST THOUGHTS

Computer controlled devices are programmed to follow sets of instructions. You need to have studied the previous sections to grasp the topics in this section.

Programmable control

Lights that flash on and off help to enliven the atmosphere at a disco. The lights could be switched on and off **manually**, but the operator would soon get fed up and would probably disappear into the crowd. Using electronics, the lights can be **programmed** to switch on and off automatically in any chosen sequence.

Figure 45.6A shows how this can be done using a memory chip. The program is stored in the first eight addresses of the chip's memory. Each address contains eight bits of data. When each address is read, the four bits, D_3, D_2, D_1 and D_0, are used to switch the four indicators on or off. The addresses are read repeatedly in sequence to make the indicators switch on and off repeatedly.

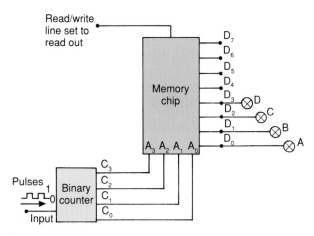

Sample program

Number of pulses counted	Address A_3 A_2 A_1 A_0	Data byte read out D_7 D_6 D_5 D_4 D_3 D_2 D_1 D_0
0	0 0 0 0	0 0 0 0 0 0 0 1
1	0 0 0 1	0 0 0 0 0 0 1 1
2	0 0 1 0	0 0 0 0 0 1 1 1
3	0 0 1 1	0 0 0 0 1 1 1 1
4	0 1 0 0	0 0 0 0 0 0 0 1
5	0 1 0 1	0 0 0 0 0 0 1 0
6	0 1 1 0	0 0 0 0 0 1 0 0
7	0 1 1 1	0 0 0 1 0 0 0 0

Pulses 0–3 switch indicators A, B, C, D on one by one
Pulses 4–7 switch the indicators on one at a time

Figure 45.6A ● Programmable memory

Number of pulses counted	Address A_3 A_2 A_1 A_0	Data byte read out D_7 D_6 D_5 D_4 D_3 D_2 D_1 D_0	State of indicators D_2(red) D_1(amber) D_0(green)		
0	0 0 0 0	0 0 0 0 0 1 0 0	ON	OFF	OFF
1	0 0 0 1	0 0 0 0 0 1 1 0	ON	ON	OFF
2	0 0 1 0	0 0 0 0 0 0 0 1	OFF	OFF	ON
3	0 0 1 1	0 0 0 0 0 0 1 0	OFF	ON	OFF
4	0 1 0 0	0 0 0 0 0 1 0 0	ON	OFF	OFF

Figure 45.6B ● Traffic lights program

Traffic lights are programmed to operate in a particular sequence. Figure 45.6B shows how this is done using a memory chip. The chip is programmed by 'writing' bits of data into each address. These bits are then 'read' out to switch the indicators on or off as programmed.

Microcomputers can be programmed to switch devices on and off. Data can be supplied to or from the computer at terminals called **ports**. A port has a number of **lines**. The logic state of each line can be set at 0 or 1 by means of a suitable program. Each device is connected to an interface circuit which is then connected to a port. The interface is to protect the computer's circuits. The microcomputer can be programmed to supply bits of data to the port in any desired sequence to switch devices on or off. Figures 45.6C and D show how a microcomputer may be used to control a buggy driven by two electric motors.

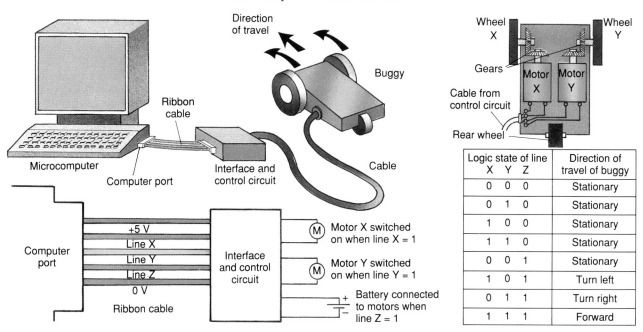

Logic state of line X Y Z			Direction of travel of buggy
0	0	0	Stationary
0	1	0	Stationary
1	0	0	Stationary
1	1	0	Stationary
0	0	1	Stationary
1	0	1	Turn left
0	1	1	Turn right
1	1	1	Forward

Figure 45.6C ● A computerised buggy

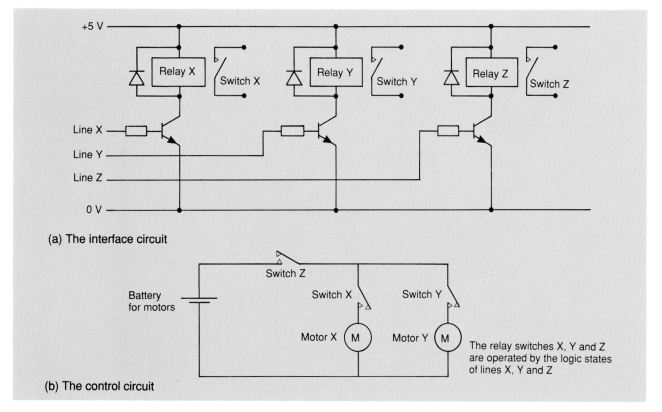

(a) The interface circuit

(b) The control circuit

The relay switches X, Y and Z are operated by the logic states of lines X, Y and Z

Figure 45.6D ● Inside the interface and control circuit

275

Feedback

In factories, lots of jobs are repetitive and are done by machines. These machines are often called **robots**. They are programmed to perform routine jobs repeatedly without stopping. For example, a lifting robot may be used to fix the windscreen on to a car. *How does the robot know when the windscreen is correctly in place?* Pressure sensors feed a signal back to the control unit of the robot when the windscreen is in place.

Radio-controlled model cars also use feedback. If the car moves in the wrong direction, the controller uses a joystick on the control unit to make the car move back on to the correct path. The controller feeds a signal back to the car. This is an example of **manual feedback** because someone must watch the car's path and correct it if necessary. The lifting robot uses **automatic feedback** using sensors; no one is needed to watch the windscreen being placed.

Automatic feedback can be used to make a buggy follow a line drawn on the floor. Two LDRs are used as 'eyes' looking at the floor. If the buggy strays from its path, one of the LDR's moves off the line and sends a signal to one of the motors. This moves the buggy back on course. (See Figure 45.6E.)

LDRs

Wheel Y

On/off switch

Wheel X

Broad black line on white floor

LDR X switches motor Y on or off
LDR Y switches motor X on or off

(a) Using LDRs

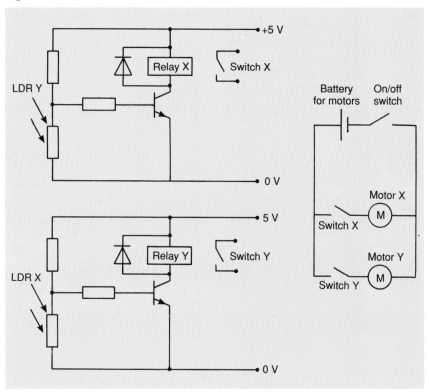

(b) The control circuit

LDR X	LDR Y	Direction of travel of buggy
Black	Black	Straight ahead (Both motors ON)
Black	White	Turn left (Motor X OFF, motor Y ON)
White	Black	Turn right (Motor X ON, motor Y OFF)

When each LDR is over the black strip, its resistance is high so the relay in its circuit is energised
If one of the LDRs moves off the black strip, its resistance falls because it receives more light from the white background. This turns the relay in its circuit off

(c) LDR control

Figure 45.6E ● An automated buggy

SUMMARY

Computers can be used to control machines automatically.
Feedback is necessary to ensure machines do not go out of control.

CHECKPOINT

① (a) In Figure 45.6A, state which indicators are switched on by each of the following four-bit addresses (i) 0 1 0 1, (ii) 0 0 0 0, (iii) 0 1 1 0.

(b) Write down the sequence of four-bit addresses that would make A flash on and off repeatedly, keep B off throughout, make C off every time A flashes on, and keep D on throughout.

② A computer is used to switch motorway warning lights on. Each set of lights consists of four indicators at the corners of a square sign, as shown in the figure opposite.

(a) What binary number must be supplied to the four lines of the output port to switch all the indicators (i) on, (ii) off?

(b) What would be seen if these two numbers were supplied alternately and repeatedly?

(c) What binary numbers should be supplied to switch A and B on and C and D off?

(d) How could A and B be flashed on and off alternately with C and D off?

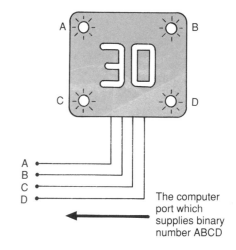

③ Kerry and Helen have designed and built a computer-controlled buggy shown opposite. The buggy has two motors which are switched on or off together. Each motor can go either forward or reverse independently of the other motor. A three-bit binary number supplied to the port by the computer is used to control the motors (see table opposite).

(a) Write down what each of the following binary numbers would do to the buggy (i) 111, (ii) 000, (iii) 110, (iv) 101.

(b) Write down the sequence of numbers that would make the buggy travel clockwise round the sides of a square.

④ A factory manager is considering ordering a computer controlled lathe to make machine parts. The machine costs £55,000. It can make 20 parts per hour compared with the five parts per hour a manual operator can make on a lathe costing £10,000. The manual operator costs £10 per hour.

(a) How many manual lathes are needed to produce 20 parts per hour?

(b) How much extra does the computer controlled lathe cost compared with the manual lathes for the same production?

(c) Why is the real cost of the manual lathes much higher?

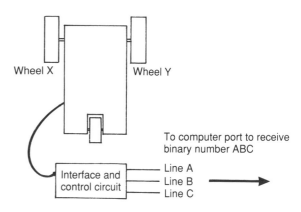

	A	B	C
Logic 0	Motors off	Wheel X forwards	Wheel Y forwards
Logic 1	Motors on	Wheel X reverse	Wheel Y reverse

FIRST THOUGHTS

45.7 Using microcomputers in science

In this section, you will find out some of the immediate benefits of microcomputers.

With so much work to do for GCSEs, you might perhaps find it helpful if a microcomputer could do some of it for you. No doubt you use a calculator when doing maths; perhaps you have used a word processor when writing up an essay or report. In the science laboratory, it is possible to use a microcomputer to make measurements automatically and to work out calculations. Meanwhile, you could be catching up on some overdue homework.

LOOK AT LINKS
for **ticker timer**
See Theme I, Topic 36.2.

Suppose you have to investigate the acceleration of a trolley down a runway to find out how the slope of the runway affects the motion. You could use a **ticker timer**. A much easier method would be to use a microcomputer to time the trolley as it passes through each of two light gates, as in Figure 45.7A. The computer can also be programmed to time how long the trolley takes to go from one gate to the other and to work out the acceleration for you. All you need to do (after setting the experiment up and programming the computer) is to release the trolley and then write down its acceleration from the microcomputer's visual display unit (VDU) afterwards.

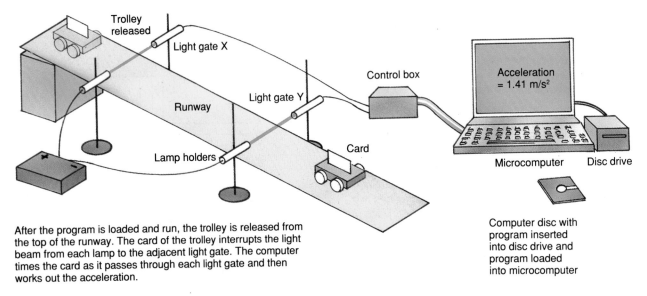

After the program is loaded and run, the trolley is released from the top of the runway. The card of the trolley interrupts the light beam from each lamp to the adjacent light gate. The computer times the card as it passes through each light gate and then works out the acceleration.

Computer disc with program inserted into disc drive and program loaded into microcomputer

Figure 45.7A ● Using a microcomputer to determine acceleration

LOOK AT LINKS
for **thermistors**
See Theme B, Topic 7.1.

Microcomputers can be programmed to receive data from suitably designed sensors. For example, Figure 45.7B shows a microcomputer being used to measure and display temperature. The sensor contains a **thermistor** connected into an electronic circuit. The circuit supplies a voltage to the microcomputer that varies with temperature. The microcomputer can be programmed by the user to measure the temperature at regular intervals and to plot a graph of temperature against time on its VDU.

Data recorders are pre-programmed to record data. This means that the user does not have to supply a program because the program is already stored in one of the recorder's memory chips. The user needs only to select the required program using the keypad.

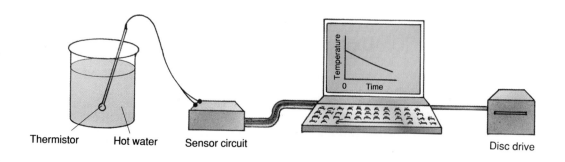

Figure 45.7B ● Measuring temperature

Many physical quantities such as light intensity, pH value, speed, pressure can be measured using a microcomputer or a data recorder. For use with a microcomputer, the sensor has to be connected to one of the microcomputer's ports via an interface circuit. This is a circuit designed to protect the microcomputer. Data recorders are usually designed so that a sensor can be connected directly to the data recorder's input terminals. Figure 45.7C shows a pH sensor that can be connected directly to a microcomputer or a data recorder.

Figure 45.7C ● pH sensor connected to a microcomputer

SUMMARY

Microcomputers and data recorders can be connected to specially designed sensors to measure and record physical quantities such as temperature, light intensity, pH values, etc. A sensor must be connected to a microcomputer via an interface circuit.

CHECKPOINT

① Does adding weight to a trolley make it accelerate faster down an incline? How could you investigate this, using the apparatus shown in Figure 45.7A and some additional weights?

② Simon and Linda want to use a microcomputer to investigate whether the temperature of the water in a beaker changes when common salt is dissolved in the water.
(a) What type of sensor is needed?
(b) With the help of their teacher, they have set the apparatus up and written a suitable program. How can they check the accuracy of the temperature probe? (Hint: they must measure something of known temperature.)

③ A certain data recorder is capable of taking and storing 1024 readings at any one of several different rates. These rates, selected by a dial on the recorder, are listed below.

A 1000 readings per second   E 10 readings per minute
B 100 readings per second   F 1 reading per minute
C 10 readings per second   G 10 readings per hour
D 1 reading per second   H 1 reading per hour

Select the most appropriate range for each of the following tasks:
(a) Recording the changing light intensity in a greenhouse over 12 hours from sunrise to sunset.
(b) Investigating the current growth in a light bulb when the bulb is switched on.
(c) Recording the growth of a plant using a movement sensor.
(d) Recording the temperature of a certain liquid near its freezing point when it suddenly solidifies due to a 'seed' crystal being dropped into it.

④ The figure opposite shows the results from an experiment in which an alkaline solution was added drop-by-drop to some dilute sulphuric acid in a beaker. A microcomputer was used to measure and display the pH value of the contents of the beaker against the volume of alkali added.
(a) Explain the shape of the curve.
(b) What volume of alkali neutralised the acid exactly?
(c) Sketch the curve you would expect for pH-value against volume added if the acid had been added to the alkali.

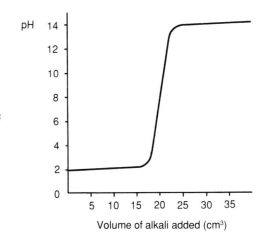

45.8 🔦 Electronics and communications

Whatever career you choose, you will undoubtedly use electronics to communicate with other people.

IT'S A FACT

The Domesday Project is a computer database, compiled in 1985, giving information about every village and town in the United Kingdom. Much of the material for the project was written in schools. Nine centuries earlier, William the Conqueror ordered the Domesday Book, a survey of the every village in the country. The entire project, consisting of the equivalent of thousands of books, is stored on two special discs. To find out about a particular topic the user is prompted through a sequence of options displayed on the VDU.

Figure 45.8A ● Using a fax machine

Stephanie is an architect working in her office at home on the design of a sports centre to be built in a nearby town. The builder has just telephoned her to find out how her work is progressing. Stephanie uses her fax machine to send a drawing of the roof design to the builder.

Using the telephone, you can speak to relatives and friends locally and internationally. A fax machine uses a telephone line to send a written message or a drawing to any other fax machine in just a few minutes.

We send and receive information to and from each other all the time. We get most of our information from what we see and hear. The 'mass media' (radio, television, newspapers, etc.) supply information to millions of people. Books and computer data bases store information which can be referred to when required.

Information is stored by computers as bytes of data, each byte consisting of a sequence of 0's and 1's. Figure 45.8B shows a simple computer program to store and retrieve the phone numbers of your friends.

```
10   INPUT  "NAME TO BE FOUND"; N$
20   READ  L$, L%
30   IF  N$ = L$  THEN  50
40   GOTO  20
50   PRINT  "NUMBER IS"; L%
60   DATA  CLAIRE, 52713, JOHN, 25413, RUBINDA, 36214, SARAH, 42138
70   DATA  DATA  MICHELLE, 76344, SEPHIDA, 44213
```

LOOK AT LINKS
The genetic code is a biological method of transmitting information. See Theme D, Topic 19.3.

Notes: 1 Write your own information for lines 60, 70, etc.
        2 The program is suitable for an Electron or BBC microcomputer

Figure 45.8B ● A personal telephone directory

Figure 45.8C ●

(a) The Highway Code: what does this mean?

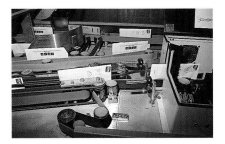

(b) A sorting machine reading postcode dots

(c) Reading bar codes

To retrieve a number, type in the appropriate name on the keyboard and the number is displayed on the VDU. As each letter of the name is typed in, an eight-bit byte is sent from the keyboard to the microcomputer's memory. All the letters and symbols on the keyboard are coded so that each gives a different eight-bit byte. The code is known as ASCII (American Standard Code for Information Interchange).

Many different codes exist for sending information. The reason for using a code may be to give rapid transfer of information (as with ASCII) or perhaps to protect information (as with secret codes). Some more codes are described below.

• **The Highway Code** is a list of regulations that must be obeyed by road users. Traffic signs supply information at a glance to motorists. The motorist must remember what each sign means. (Figure 45.8C(a).)

• **Postal codes** allow letters and parcels to be sorted and delivered rapidly. When you send a letter, be sure to write on the post code of the destination. After your letter has been collected from the post box, it is taken to the nearest sorting office where the post code is read and then coded as a sequence of dots printed on the envelope. These dots glow in ultraviolet light and can be read 'automatically' by sorting machines which channel your letter to its destination. Your letter may pass through several sorting machines in different offices before it is delivered to its destination. (Figure 45.8C(b).)

• **Bar codes** are used in many supermarkets at the check-outs. Each item on the shelves has a bar code printed on it. The assistant at the cash-till passes each item's bar code across the bar-code reader; the description and price of the item is displayed and printed out on the till receipt. The supermarket manager can keep track of stocks of items and the consumer gets a print-out of the description and price of each item bought. The information about each item is held in the memory of a computer which is linked to every till in the supermarket. (Figure 45.8C(c).)

Communication links

Computers in different towns can be linked using the telephone system. To send information from one computer to another, each byte is converted into a stream of pulses of light or electricity. The pulses are transmitted down telephone lines.

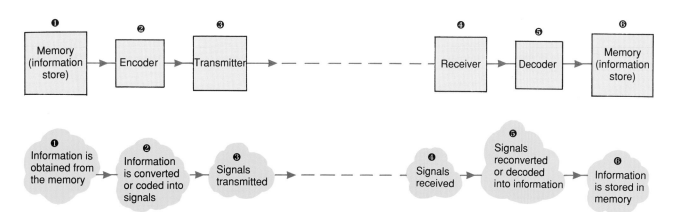

Figure 45.8D ● Sending information

Computer records are data bases holding vast amounts of information. The Inland Revenue computers store information about every working adult in the country. Hospital computers hold personal medical records. Banks and building societies use computers to store financial information about customers. Ministry of Defence computers hold vital information about national defence.

How secure is the information held in computer data bases? If computers send information using the phone network, what safeguards prevent unauthorised access to such information? Security codes are used to stop illegal entry to data bases. To gain access, the correct security code must be keyed in.

How secure is information when it is being transmitted? Optical fibres and microwave links are gradually replacing copper wires in the phone network. Figure 45.8E shows how a phone conversation is carried by a pair of copper wires. If several pairs of wires are twisted together, 'crossed lines' may occur and phone callers may hear other calls in the background. In fact, such phone lines can easily be 'tapped' to find out what is being said. *Are optical fibres and microwave links more secure from tapping than copper wires?*

LOOK AT LINKS
for **telecommunications**
See Theme H, Topic 33.3.

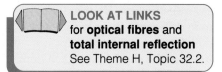

LOOK AT LINKS
for **optical fibres** and **total internal reflection**
See Theme H, Topic 32.2.

Figure 45.8E ● How a phone call is carried

A single pair of wires can be made to carry several phone calls at the same time. This uses a technique known as pulse code modulation (PCM). Each audio signal is sampled (i.e. measured) 8000 times per second. Each sample is converted into a binary number and transmitted as a sequence of very brief pulses. In the time between one pulse and the next, pulses from other calls are transmitted (Figure 45.8F). A single pair of wires is capable of transmitting about two million pulses each second.

A microwave beam is capable of carrying hundreds of phone calls at the same time. Microwaves are electromagnetic waves with frequencies of approximately 10^{10} Hz. By switching the beam on and off extremely fast, it can be used to send about 1000 million pulses per second. Using PCM, many phone calls can be carried at the same time. A single microwave beam can even carry all the signals for a television channel.

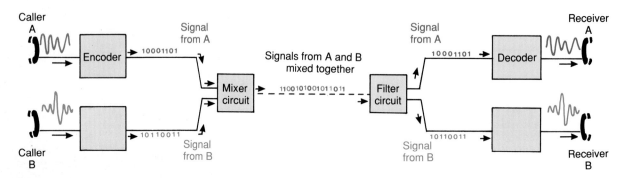

Figure 45.8F ● Pulse code modulation

Microwave towers in cities and towns are used to transmit and receive microwave beams. The microwaves travel in a straight line between the towers and are unaffected by weather conditions. Satellites in geostationary orbits receive and transmit microwave beams from ground stations to carry international phone calls.

Optical fibres are used to guide light over long distances. The frequency of light used is approximately 10^{14} Hz which is 10 000 times higher than typical microwave frequencies. Thus, a light beam can be used to carry many more pulses each second than a microwave beam. A single optical fibre, using PCM, can carry more than 30 000 phone calls or 30 television channels at the same time.

The glass in an optical fibre is extremely clear. A semiconductor laser is used to send light pulses along an optical fibre. Where the fibre bends, the light rays are **totally internal reflected** where they touch the fibre boundary.

Optical fibres can carry much more information than copper wires and glass is much cheaper than copper. New developments such as home shopping, local television stations and video phones will become possible as optical fibres replace copper wires.

Figure 45.8G ● Microwave traffic
(a) The BT tower, 189 m high, is used to send and receive microwaves to and from other towers throughout the UK

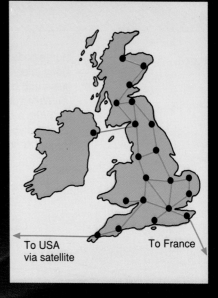

(b) The UK microwave network

To USA via satellite

To France

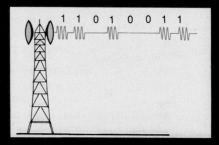

1 1 0 1 0 0 1 1

(c) A microwave beam carrying data

SUMMARY

Computers store and transfer information as bytes of data, each byte consists of a sequence of 1's and 0's. The phone network is used to link computers in different locations. Copper wires in the network are being replaced by optical fibres and microwave beams which can carry much more information.

CHECKPOINT

❶ Morse code was invented to send information in the form of electrical pulses along telegraph wires. The code is shown below. Each dot represents a short pulse and each dash a long pulse.
   (a) Write your name in Morse code.
   (b) Write a short sentence and convert it to Morse code.
   (c) Send your sentence in Morse code to a friend who then has to decode it and send a reply back in Morse code.

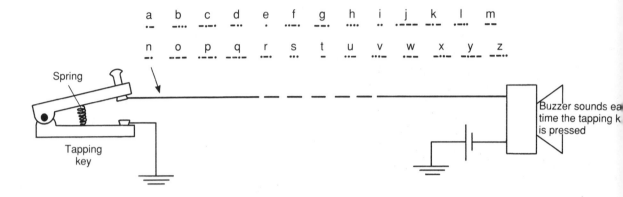

❷ Make a list of ten points of information you have gained over the past 24 hours. If possible, include in your list at least one point from the radio, one from the TV, one from a friend and one using neither sight nor sound. Write down how you gained each point on your list.

❸ To obtain money using a bank card, the holder puts the card into the dispensing machine and then keys in his or her personal identification number (PIN) before keying in the amount of money required.
   (a) Under no circumstances should the PIN be written on the bank card. Why?
   (b) The card holder is usually allowed three attempts to key in his or her PIN number. After that, the machine keeps the card. Why does the bank not allow unlimited attempts?
   (c) If the holder loses his or her card, why is it important to inform the bank as soon as possible?

❹ Braille enables blind people to read. It consists of raised dots on paper, as shown below.
   (a) Use a pin to write a short message on a sheet of paper in Braille.
   (b) Ask a friend to decode the message and write a reply.

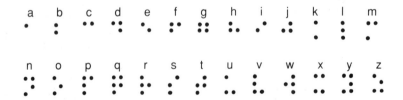

❺ (a) How is it possible for light to be guided along an optical fibre that is bent?
   (b) Why do optical fibres need to be made from extremely clear glass?
   (c) Why is an optical fibre link more secure from being 'tapped' than (i) a link using copper wires, (ii) a microwave link?

? THEME QUESTIONS

1 (a) When a plastic ruler is rubbed on a piece of wool it becomes charged. Give one simple test you could use to show the ruler was charged.

(b) The hoses used at petrol filling stations to transfer petrol from the pumps to cars are made of a special type of rubber which conducts electricity. Explain why.

(c) The figure shows a direct electric current passing down a length of wire. When an electric current passes through a wire it produces a magnetic field around the wire. Copy and complete the figure by drawing the magnetic field around the wire.

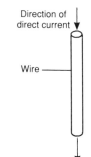

(d) Copy and complete the two graphs below by showing how the voltage of an a.c. current and a d.c. current vary with time.

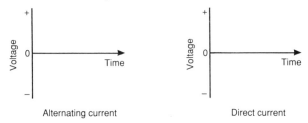

Alternating current   Direct current

(e) Billy uses a 'power pack' to provide electrical energy for his train set. It contains a transformer like the one shown.

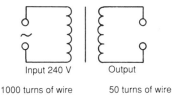

Input 240 V   Output
1000 turns of wire   50 turns of wire

Use the formula

$$\frac{\text{Output voltage}}{\text{Input voltage}} = \frac{\text{Number of turns of wire on output coil}}{\text{Number of turns of wire on input coil}}$$

to calculate the output voltage of this transformer.

(f) A circuit diagram of Billy's power pack is shown below.

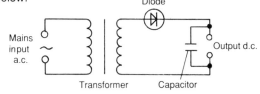

Transformer   Capacitor

Explain how this circuit is able to convert an a.c. into a smoothed d.c. current.

(LEAG)

2 The information below is taken from the instruction book for an electric cooking pot. Use it to help you answer the questions which follow it.

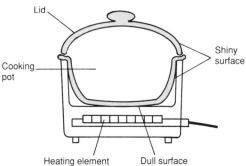

The Devon cooker is designed to cook food slowly throughout the day or night to produce tender food. It may be used to cook soups and stews directly in the pot, or as a water bath for steam puddings.

The Devon has two settings: HIGH: 115 watts (W)
                                              LOW: 95 watts (W)

The Devon must be fitted with a three-pin plug that has the normal 13 amp fuse replaced by a 3 amp fuse.

The Devon works on the normal 240 volts mains supply.

(a) One recipe needs the Devon cooker set on HIGH (115 W) for two hours.

(i) How much electrical energy will the Devon use in one second?

(ii) Calculate the amount of electrical energy the Devon will use while cooking the food.

(iii) Explain how the amount of energy gained by the food in the cooked recipe compares with your answer to (ii).

(b) Suggest an explanation for the instruction:
The Devon must be fitted with a three-pin plug that has the normal 13 amp fuse replaced by a 3 amp fuse.
(Any calculation should be shown clearly.)

(SEG)

3 An electric kettle is marked

3 pints/1.7 litres
2400 watts
230/240 volts

(a) If the mains voltage is 240 V what current will flow through the kettle after it is switched on?

(b) What difference would you notice if the kettle was used in a country where the mains voltage is 120 V?

(MEG)

4 The purpose of an electricity sub-station is to reduce the voltage at which electrical energy is transmitted down to the 240 volts which we use in our homes.

(a) What name do we give to the device which achieves this in a sub-station? Draw a simple labelled diagram to show how such a device works.

(b) If one hundred homes, all connected to one such device, arrange to draw a current of 20 amperes

each, what is the minimum current which must flow into the sub-station from the grid?
(Assume that the transmission voltage is 10 000 volts.)

(c) When a table lamp is switched on, it gives what seems to be a steady light. But the voltage applied to the bulb is changing many times each second from 240 V to 0 V. Explain in as much detail as you can how you would find out whether the brightness of the bulb changes over a short period of time. What results would you expect?

(MEG)

5 Mr Dewar controls the temperature of the room where his wines ferment using an electric convector heater. The heater is controlled by the following circuit.

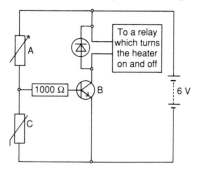

(a) Explain how heat is transferred around the fermenting room.
(b) Some electric heaters have a fan built into them. What advantage is this?
(c) Name the electronic components labelled A, B and C in the figure above.
(d) How does the resistance of component C vary with temperature?
(e) Explain how the circuit in the figure operates. You may assume that the room is colder than Mr Dewar wants it when he installs the system.

(LEAG)

6 A student designed a circuit for an alarm. It is shown in the diagram below.

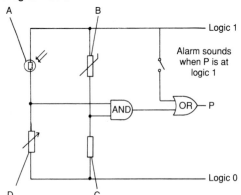

(a) Name the components labelled A–D in the circuit. Select names from the following list:
switch   resistor   variable resistor   cell   thermistor   lamp   diode   light dependent resistor   light-emitting diode
(b) Which logic gate in the circuit is responsible for the fact that:
(i) the alarm sounds when a settee is burning

vigorously, but not when a light is turned on in the room,
(ii) the switch can be used to test the alarm in a cold, dark room.
(c) Explain why this alarm might fail to sound when there is a fire. Assume that there is no electrical fault.

(MEG)

7 The table shows corresponding values of potential difference across a torch bulb and the current passing through it.

Potential difference (V)	0	0.02	0.1	0.5	1.0	1.65	2.3	3.1	4.0
Current (A)	0	0.04	0.08	0.12	0.16	0.20	0.24	0.28	0.32

(a) Draw a circuit diagram of a circuit which could have been used to obtain these data.
(b) On graph paper, plot a graph of current on the y-axis against potential difference on the x-axis.
(c) (i) Use the graph to find the potential difference across the bulb when the current through it was 0.25 A.
(ii) Calculate the resistance of the bulb filament when the current through it was 0.25 A.
(d) (i) State how the resistance of the bulb filament changes when the current through it is increased.
(ii) Why does the resistance change in this way?
(e) In the circuit shown below, assume that the battery and ammeters have negligible resistance and that the voltmeter draws a negligible current. Calculate:
(i) the resistance of the two resistors in parallel,
(ii) the total resistance of the circuit,
(iii) the reading on A_1,
(iv) the reading on V,
(v) the reading on A_2,
(vi) the power dissipated in the 2 ohm resistor.

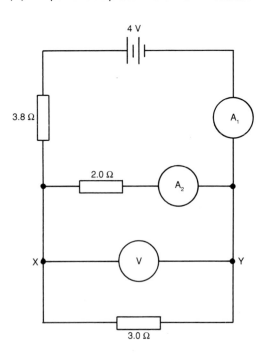

(NEA)

THEME L

Our Natural Resources

The chemical industry plays a central part in our lives. It provides the fertilisers which enable us to grow enough food, the pesticides which prevent crops from being eaten by insects or smothered by weeds and the treatments which make our water safe to drink. The chemical industry provides the building materials for our homes and the fabrics for the clothes we wear. When we are ill, we have a whole range of painkillers, antiseptics, antibiotics and anaesthetics to comfort us. When we want to enjoy a sport, the chemical industry offers us a choice of footballs, tennis racquets, golf balls, climbing ropes, canoes, sailing dinghies, all of them made from synthetic materials.

The chemical industry provides all these materials by using the Earth's resources and human ingenuity. Chemists study the rates of chemical reactions and the heat changes which take place; they calculate how much product a reaction should give and find out the best conditions in which to carry out a reaction. All these steps are involved in the design of the industrial plants which transform natural resources into the materials we need.

TOPIC 46 CHEMICAL REACTION SPEEDS

46.1 Why reaction speeds are important

Who is interested in the speeds of chemical reactions? If you were a cheese manufacturer, you would be interested in speeding up the chemical reactions which produce cheese. The more tonnes of cheese you could produce in a month, the more profit you would make. If you were a butter manufacturer, you would want to slow down the chemical reactions which make your product turn rancid.

In a chemical reaction, the starting materials are called the **reactants**, and the finishing materials are called the **products**. It takes time for a chemical reaction to happen. If the reactants take only a short time to change into the products, that reaction is a **fast reaction**. The **speed** or **rate** of that reaction is high. If a reaction takes a long time to change the reactants into the products, it is a **slow reaction**. The speed or rate of that reaction is low.

Many people are interested in knowing how to alter the speeds of chemical reactions. The factors which can be changed are:
- the size of the particles of a solid reactant,
- the concentrations of reactants in solution,
- the temperature,
- the presence of light,
- the addition of a catalyst.

A **catalyst** is a substance which can alter the rate of a chemical reaction without being used up in the reaction.

46.2 Particle size and reaction speed

Carbon dioxide can be prepared in the laboratory by the reaction

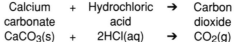

Calcium carbonate	+	Hydrochloric acid	→	Carbon dioxide	+	Calcium chloride	+	Water
$CaCO_3(s)$	+	$2HCl(aq)$	→	$CO_2(g)$	+	$CaCl_2(aq)$	+	$H_2O(l)$

One of the reactants, calcium carbonate (marble) is a solid. You can use this reaction to find out whether large lumps of a solid react at the same speed as small lumps of the same solid. Figure 46.2A shows a method for finding the rate of the reaction. It can be used when one of the products is a gas. As carbon dioxide escapes from the flask, the mass of the flask and contents decreases.

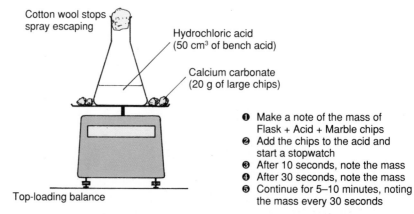

Cotton wool stops spray escaping

Hydrochloric acid (50 cm³ of bench acid)

Calcium carbonate (20 g of large chips)

Top-loading balance

❶ Make a note of the mass of Flask + Acid + Marble chips
❷ Add the chips to the acid and start a stopwatch
❸ After 10 seconds, note the mass
❹ After 30 seconds, note the mass
❺ Continue for 5–10 minutes, noting the mass every 30 seconds

Figure 46.2A ● Apparatus for following the loss in mass when a gas is evolved

The reaction starts when the marble chips are dropped into the acid. The mass of the flask and contents is noted at various times after the start of the reaction. The mass can be plotted against time. Figure 46.2B shows typical results.

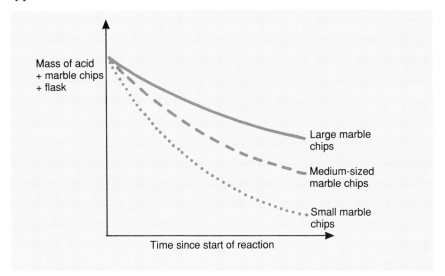

Figure 46.2B ● Results obtained with different sizes of marble chips

The results show that the smaller the size of the particles of calcium carbonate, the faster the reaction takes place. The difference is due to a difference in surface area. There is a larger surface area in 20 g of small chips than in 20 g of large chips. The acid attacks the surface of the marble. It can therefore react faster with small chips than with large chips.

SUMMARY

Reactions in which one reactant is a solid take place faster when the solid is divided into small pieces. The reason is that a certain mass of small particles has a larger surface area than the same mass of large particles.

CHECKPOINT

❶ When potatoes are cooked, a chemical reaction occurs. What can you do to increase the speed at which potatoes cook?

❷ There is a danger in coal mines that coal dust may catch fire and start an explosion. Explain why coal dust is more dangerous than coal.

❸ 'Alko' indigestion tablets and 'Neutro' indigestion powder are both alkalis. Which do you think will act faster to cure acid indigestion? Describe how you could test the two remedies in the laboratory with a bench acid to see whether you are right.

46.3 Concentration and reaction speed

Many chemical reactions take place in solution. One such reaction is

Sodium thiosulphate	+	Hydrochloric acid	→	Sulphur	+	Sodium chloride	+	Sulphur dioxide	+	Water
$Na_2S_2O_3(aq)$	+	$2HCl(aq)$	→	$S(s)$	+	$2NaCl(aq)$	+	$SO_2(g)$	+	H_2O

Sulphur appears in the form of very small particles of solid. The particles do not settle: they remain in suspension. Figure 46.3A overleaf shows how you can follow the speed at which sulphur is formed.

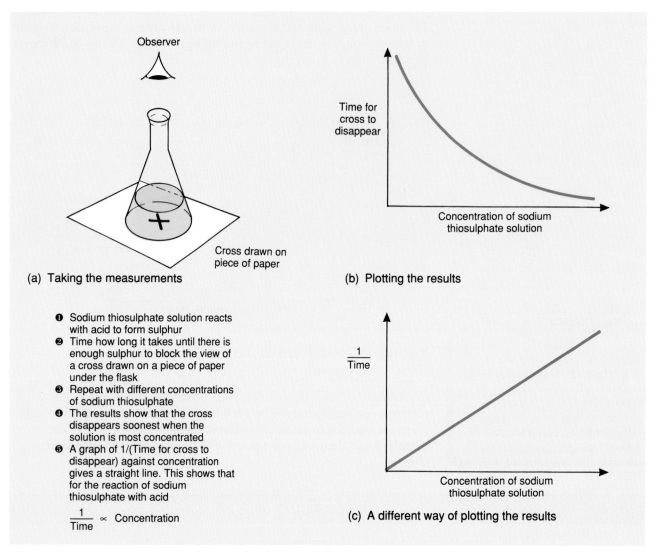

- ❶ Sodium thiosulphate solution reacts with acid to form sulphur
- ❷ Time how long it takes until there is enough sulphur to block the view of a cross drawn on a piece of paper under the flask
- ❸ Repeat with different concentrations of sodium thiosulphate
- ❹ The results show that the cross disappears soonest when the solution is most concentrated
- ❺ A graph of 1/(Time for cross to disappear) against concentration gives a straight line. This shows that for the reaction of sodium thiosulphate with acid

$$\frac{1}{Time} \propto Concentration$$

Figure 46.3A ● Experiment on reaction speed and concentration

Rates of Reaction
(program)

Use this simulation program to study how a chemical reaction is affected by temperature, concentration and particle size.

SUMMARY

For the reactions in solution mentioned here, the speed of the reaction is proportional to the concentration of the reactant (or reactants). That is, the speed doubles when the concentration is doubled.

The faster a reaction takes place, the shorter is the time needed for the reaction to finish. To be more precise, the speed of the reaction is **inversely proportional** to the time taken for the reaction to finish

Speed of reaction ∝ 1/Time

You can see from Figure 46.3A(c) above that

1/Time ∝ Concentration

Therefore

Speed of reaction ∝ Concentration

In this experiment, only one concentration was altered. A variation is to keep the concentration of sodium thiosulphate constant and alter the concentration of acid. Then the speed of the reaction is found to be proportional to the concentration of the acid. If the acid concentration is doubled, the speed doubles. The reason for this is that the ions are closer together in a concentrated solution. The closer together they are, the more often the ions collide. The more often they collide, the more chance they have of reacting.

CHECKPOINT

① Molly is asked to investigate the marble chips–acid reaction. She must find out what effect changing the concentration of the acid has on the speed of the reaction. Explain how Molly could adapt the experiment shown in Figure 46.2A to carry out her investigation.

46.4 Pressure and reaction speed

 **LOOK AT LINKS**
The effect of pressure on gas density is discussed in Theme B, Topic 7.2.

Pressure has an effect on reactions between gases. The speed of the reaction increases when the pressure is increased. The reason is that increasing the pressure pushes the gas molecules closer together. The molecules therefore collide more often, and the gases react more rapidly.

46.5 Temperature and reaction speed

LOOK AT LINKS
The effect of temperature on the motion of molecules is discussed in Theme B, Topic 5.4.

IT **Chemical Collisions**
(program)

What factors affect the rate of reaction between two gases? Use this program to investigate.

SUMMARY

The speed of a reaction between gases increases when the pressure is increased. The speed of a reaction increases when the temperature is raised. Some chemical reactions are speeded up by light.

You met the reaction between sodium thiosulphate and acid in Topic 46.3. This reaction can also be used to study the effect of temperature on the speed of a chemical reaction. Warming the solutions makes sulphur form faster. There is a steep increase in the speed of the reaction as the temperature is increased.

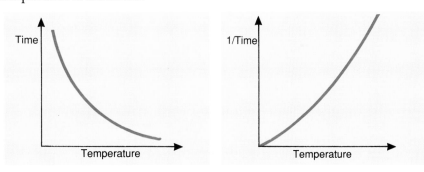

Figure 46.5A ● The effect of temperature on the speed of reaction

This reaction goes approximately twice as fast at 30 °C as it does at 20 °C. It doubles in speed again between 30 °C and 40 °C and so on.

At the higher temperature, the ions have more kinetic energy. Moving through the solution more rapidly, they collide more often and more vigorously and so there is a greater chance that they will react.

46.6 Light and chemical reactions

LOOK AT LINKS
for **photographic film**
See Theme D, Topic 17.4.
for **photosynthesis**
See Theme F, Topic 25.1.

Heat is not the only form of energy that can speed up reactions. Some chemical reactions take place faster when they absorb light. The formation of silver from silver salts takes place when a **photographic film** is exposed to light. In sunlight, green plants are able to carry on the process of **photosynthesis**.

==

CHECKPOINT

❶ Polly's project is to find out what effect temperature has on the speed at which milk goes sour. Suggest what measurements she should make.

❷ Ismail's project is to find out whether iron rusts more quickly at higher temperatures. Suggest a set of experiments which he could do to find out.

❸ You are asked to study the reaction

   Magnesium + Sulphuric acid → Hydrogen + Magnesium sulphate

You are provided with magnesium ribbon, dilute sulphuric acid, a thermometer and any laboratory glassware you need. Describe how you would find out what effect a change in temperature has on the speed of the reaction. Say what apparatus you would use, what measurements you would make and what you would do with your results.

❹ Magnesium reacts with cold water slowly

   Magnesium + Water → Magnesium hydroxide + Hydrogen

If there is phenolphthalein in the water, it turns pink, showing that an alkali has been formed.
Describe experiments which you could do to find the effect of increasing the temperature on the speed of this reaction. Say what you would measure and what you would do with your results. With your teacher's approval, try out your ideas.

==

46.7 Catalysis

A reaction used to prepare oxygen is

$$\text{Hydrogen peroxide} \rightarrow \text{Oxygen} + \text{Water}$$
$$2H_2O_2(aq) \rightarrow O_2(g) + 2H_2O(l)$$

Figure 46.7A shows how the oxygen can be collected and measured in a gas syringe.

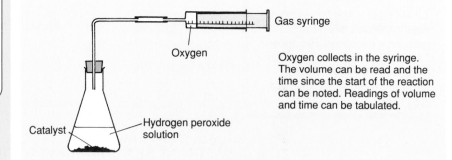

Figure 46.7A ● Collecting and measuring a gas

The formation of oxygen is very slow at room temperature. The reaction can be speeded up by the addition of certain substances, for example manganese(IV) oxide. When manganese(IV) oxide is added to hydrogen peroxide, the evolution of oxygen takes place much more rapidly (see Figure 46.7B). Manganese(IV) oxide is not used up in the reaction. At the end of the reaction, the manganese(IV) oxide can be

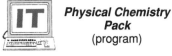

IT *Physical Chemistry Pack* (program)

Use the *Rates of Reaction* part of this program to study the effect of different reaction conditions on the decomposition of hydrogen peroxide.

RESOURCE
–ACTIVITY–
PACK

LOOK AT LINKS
You have learned how the chemical reactions that take place in animals and plants are catalysed by **enzymes**.
See Theme D, Topic 18.4.

LOOK AT LINKS
You will see how valuable catalysts are in industry in Theme L, Topic 51.

SUMMARY

Some chemical reactions can be speeded up by adding a substance which is not one of the reactants, which is not used up in the reaction. Such a substance is called a catalyst.

filtered out of the solution and used again. A substance which increases the speed of a chemical reaction without being used up in the reaction is called a **catalyst**. Different reactions need different catalysts.

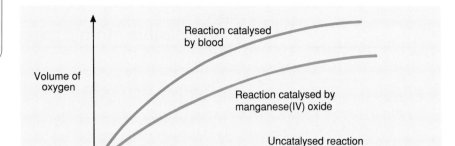

Figure 46.7B ● Catalysis of the decomposition of hydrogen peroxide

Any individual catalyst will only catalyse a certain reaction or group of reactions. Platinum catalyses a number of oxidation reactions. Nickel catalyses hydrogenation reactions. Industries make good use of catalysts. If manufacturers can produce their product more rapidly, they make bigger profits. If they can produce their product at a lower temperature with the aid of a catalyst, they save on fuel. The reactions which make plastics take place under high pressure. The construction of industrial plastics plants which are strong enough to withstand high pressure is expensive. A plastics manufacturer therefore tries to find a catalyst which will enable the reaction to give a good yield of plastics at a lower pressure. Then the plant will not have to withstand high pressures. Less costly materials can be used in its construction. Industrial chemists are constantly looking for new catalysts.

Some reactions only give good yields of product at high temperatures. Such a reaction costs a manufacturer high fuel bills. Industrial chemists look for a catalyst which will make the reaction take place more readily at a lower temperature. This will cut running costs and increase profits.

CHECKPOINT

❶ Catalysts A and B both catalyse the decomposition of hydrogen peroxide. The following figures were obtained at 20 °C for the volume of oxygen formed against the time since the start of the reaction.

Time (minutes)	0	5	10	15	20	25	30	35
Volume of oxygen with catalyst A (cm³)	0	4	8	12	16	17	18	18
Volume of oxygen with catalyst B (cm³)	0	5	10	15	16.5	18	18	18

(a) Plot a graph to show both sets of results.
(b) Say which is the better catalyst, A or B.
(c) Explain why both experiments were done at the same temperature.
(d) Explain why both sets of figures stop at 18 cm³ of oxygen.
(e) Add a line to your graph to show the shape of the graph you would obtain for the uncatalysed reaction.

❷ Someone tells you that nickel oxide will catalyse the decomposition of hydrogen peroxide to give oxygen. How could you find out whether this is true? Draw the apparatus you would use and state the measurements you would make.

TOPIC 47   CHEMICAL CALCULATIONS

FIRST THOUGHTS

47.1 Relative atomic mass

Every dot of ink on this page is big enough to have a million hydrogen atoms fitted across it from side to side.

The masses of atoms are very small. Some examples are:
- Mass of hydrogen atom, H = 1.4×10^{-24} g.
- Mass of mercury atom, Hg = 2.8×10^{-22} g.
- Mass of carbon atom, C = 1.7×10^{-23} g.

Chemists find it convenient to use **relative atomic masses**. The hydrogen atom is the lightest of atoms, and the masses of other atoms can be stated *relative to* that of the hydrogen atom. On the original version of the relative atomic mass scale:
- Relative atomic mass of hydrogen = 1.
- Relative atomic mass of mercury = 200 (a mercury atom is 200 times heavier than a hydrogen atom).
- Relative atomic mass of carbon = 12 (a carbon atom is 12 times heavier than a hydrogen atom).

Chemists now take the mass of one atom of carbon-12 as the reference point for the relative atomic mass scale. On the present scale

$$\text{Relative atomic mass of element} = \frac{\text{Mass of one atom of the element}}{(1/12) \text{ Mass of one atom of carbon-12}}$$

Since relative atomic mass (symbol A_r) is a ratio of two masses, the mass units cancel, and relative atomic mass is a number without a unit.

The relative atomic masses of some common elements are listed in Table 47.1. You will find a complete list in the Appendix.

Table 47.1 ● Some relative atomic masses

Element	A_r	Element	A_r
Aluminium	27	Magnesium	24
Barium	137	Mercury	200
Bromine	80	Nitrogen	14
Calcium	40	Oxygen	16
Chlorine	35.5	Phosphorus	31
Copper	63.5	Potassium	39
Hydrogen	1	Sodium	23
Iron	56	Sulphur	32
Lead	207	Zinc	65

SUMMARY

The relative atomic mass, A_r, of an element is the mass of one atom of the element compared with $1/12$ the mass of one atom of carbon-12.

CHECKPOINT

❶ Refer to Table 47.1.
  (a) How many times heavier is one atom of nitrogen than one atom of hydrogen?
  (b) What is the ratio

  Mass of one atom of mercury / Mass of one atom of bromine?

  (c) How many atoms of oxygen are needed to equal the mass of one atom of bromine?
  (d) How many atoms of sodium are needed to equal the mass of one atom of lead?

47.2 Relative molecular mass

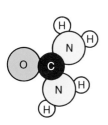

Figure 47.2A ● Atoms in a molecule of urea

The mass of a molecule is the sum of the masses of all the atoms in it. The relative molecular mass (symbol M_r) of a compound is the sum of the relative atomic masses of all the atoms in a molecule of the compound (see Figure 47.2A).

Worked example   Find the relative molecular mass of urea.

Solution   Formula of compound is CON_2H_4
1 atom of C (A_r 12) = 12
1 atom of O (A_r 16) = 16
2 atoms of N (A_r 14) = 28
4 atoms of H (A_r 1) = 4
Total   = 60
Relative molecular mass, M_r, of urea = 60

Many compounds consist of ions, not molecules. The formula of an ionic compound represents a **formula unit** of the compound; for example, $CaSO_4$ represents a formula unit of calcium sulphate, not a molecule of calcium sulphate. The term relative molecular mass can be used for ionic compounds as well as molecular compounds.

SUMMARY

The relative molecular mass of a compound is equal to the sum of the relative atomic masses of all the atoms in one molecule of the compound or in one formula unit of the compound.
M_r = Sum of A_r values

CHECKPOINT

① Work out the relative molecular masses of these compounds:

CO CO_2 SO_2 SO_3 $NaOH$ $NaCl$ CaO $Mg(OH)_2$ Na_2CO_3

$CuSO_4$ $CuSO_4.5H_2O$ $Ca(HCO_3)_2$

47.3 Percentage composition

From the formula of a compound you can find the percentage by mass of the elements in the compound.

Worked example 1   Find the percentage by mass of (a) calcium (b) chlorine in calcium chloride.

Solution   First find the relative molecular mass of calcium chloride, formula $CaCl_2$.

$M_r = A_r(Ca) + 2A_r(Cl)$
$= 40 + (2 \times 35.5) = 111$

Percentage of calcium = $\dfrac{40}{111} \times 100 = 36\%$

Percentage of chlorine = $\dfrac{71}{111} \times 100 = 64\%$

You can see that the two percentages add up to 100%.

Worked example 2 Find the percentage of water in crystals of magnesium sulphate-7-water.

Solution Find the relative molecular mass of $MgSO_4.7H_2O$.

1 atom of magnesium (A_r 24)	= 24
1 atom of sulphur (A_r 32)	= 32
4 atoms of oxygen (A_r 16)	= 64
7 molecules of water = $7 \times [(2 \times 1) + 16]$ = 126	
Total = M_r	= 246

> **SUMMARY**
>
> You can calculate the percentage by mass composition of a compound from its formula.

$$\text{Percentage of water} = \frac{\text{Mass of water in formula}}{\text{Relative molecular mass}} \times 100$$

$$= \frac{126}{246} \times 100 = 51.2\%$$

The percentage of water in magnesium sulphate crystals is 51%.

CHECKPOINT

You do not need calculators for these problems.

❶ Find the percentage by mass of;
(a) calcium in calcium bromide, $CaBr_2$,
(b) iron in iron(III) oxide, Fe_2O_3,
(c) carbon and hydrogen in ethane, C_2H_6,
(d) sulphur and oxygen in sulphur trioxide, SO_3,
(e) hydrogen and fluorine in hydrogen fluoride, HF,
(f) magnesium, sulphur and oxygen in magnesium sulphate, $MgSO_4$.

❷ Calculate the percentage by mass of water in:
(a) copper(II) sulphate-5-water, $CuSO_4.5H_2O$ (take A_r (Cu) = 64),
(b) sodium sulphide-9-water, $Na_2S.9H_2O$.

47.4 The mole

> **FIRST THOUGHTS**
>
> Chemical equations tell us which products are formed when substances react. Equations can also be used to tell us what mass of each product is formed. The key to success is the mole concept.

A reaction of industrial importance is

Calcium carbonate → Calcium oxide + Carbon dioxide
$CaCO_3(s)$ → $CaO(s)$ + $CO_2(g)$

Cement manufacturers use this reaction to make calcium oxide (quicklime) from calcium carbonate (limestone). The mole concept makes it possible to calculate what mass of calcium oxide will be formed when a certain mass of calcium carbonate dissociates.

The mole concept dates back to the nineteenth century Italian chemist called Avogadro. This is how he argued:

The relative atomic masses of magnesium and carbon are: A_r (Mg) = 24, A_r (C) = 12.
Therefore we can say:
Since one atom of magnesium is twice as heavy as one atom of carbon,
then one hundred Mg atoms are twice as heavy as one hundred C atoms,
and five million Mg atoms are twice as heavy as five million C atoms.

Imagine a piece of magnesium that has twice the mass of a piece of carbon. It follows that the two masses must contain equal numbers of atoms: two grams of magnesium and one gram of carbon contain the same number of atoms; ten tonnes of magnesium and five tonnes of carbon contain the same number of atoms.

The same argument applies to the other elements. Take the relative atomic mass in grams of any element:

| 12 g carbon | 24 g magnesium | 32 g sulphur | 40 g calcium | 56 g iron | 80 g bromine | 207 g lead |

All these masses contain the same number of atoms. The number is 6.022×10^{23}.

> The amount of an element that contains 6.022×10^{23} atoms (the same number of atoms as 12 g of carbon-12) is called one **mole** of that element.

The symbol for mole is **mol**. The ratio $6.022 \times 10^{23}/\text{mol}$ is called the Avogadro constant. When you weigh out 12 g of carbon, you are counting out 6×10^{23} atoms of carbon. This amount of carbon is one mole (1 mol) of carbon atoms. Similarly, 46 g of sodium is two moles (2 mol) of sodium atoms. You can say that the **amount** of sodium is two moles (2 mol). One mole of the compound ethanol, C_2H_6O, contains 6×10^{23} molecules of C_2H_6O, that is, 46 g of C_2H_6O (the molar mass in grams). To write 'one mole of oxygen' will not do. You must state whether you mean one mole of oxygen atoms, O (with a mass of 16 grams) or one mole of oxygen molecules, O_2 (with a mass of 32 grams).

Molar mass

The mass of one mole of a substance is called the **molar mass**, symbol M. The molar mass of carbon is 12 g/mol. The molar mass of sodium is 23 g/mol. The molar mass of a compound is the relative molecular mass expressed in grams per mole. Urea, CON_2H_4, has a relative molecular mass of 60; its molar mass is 60 g/mol. Notice the units: relative molecular mass has no unit; molar mass has the unit g/mol.

> Amount (in moles) of substance $= \dfrac{\text{Mass of substance}}{\text{Molar mass of substance}}$
>
> Molar mass of element = Relative atomic mass in grams per mole
>
> Molar mass of compound = Relative molecular mass in grams per mole

Worked example 1 What is the amount (in moles) of sodium present in 4.6 g of sodium?

Solution A_r of sodium = 23. Molar mass of sodium = 23 g/mol

$$\text{Amount of sodium} = \frac{\text{Mass of sodium}}{\text{Molar mass of sodium}} = \frac{4.6\text{ g}}{23\text{ g/mol}} = 0.2\text{ mol}$$

The amount (moles) of sodium is 0.2 mol.

IT *The Mole Concept* (program)

Use this program to investigate the idea of a 'mole'. Listen to the tape and work through the program at the same time.

SUMMARY

The number of atoms in 12.000 g of carbon-12 is 6.022×10^{23}. The same number of atoms is present in a mass of any element equal to its relative atomic mass expressed in grams. This amount of any element is called **one mole** (1 mol) of the element. The ratio $6.022 \times 10^{23}/\text{mol}$ is called the Avogadro constant. The number of moles of a substance is called the **amount** of that substance. The mass of one mole of an element or compound is the **molar mass**, M, of that substance.

M of an element $= A_r$ expressed in g/mol

M of a compound $= M_r$ expressed in g/mol

Worked example 2 If you need 2.5 mol of sodium hydroxide, what mass of sodium hydroxide do you have to weigh out?

Solution Relative molecular mass of NaOH = 23 + 16 + 1 = 40

Molar mass of NaOH = 40 g/mol

$$\text{Amount of substance} = \frac{\text{Mass of substance}}{\text{Molar mass of substance}}$$

$$2.5 = \frac{\text{Mass}}{40}$$

Mass = 40 x 2.5 = 100 g

You need to weigh out 100 g of sodium hydroxide.

CHECKPOINT

❶ State the mass of:

(a) 1.0 mol of aluminium atoms,
(b) 3.0 mol of oxygen molecules, O_2,
(c) 0.25 mol of mercury atoms,
(d) 0.50 mol of nitrogen molecules, N_2,
(e) 0.25 mol of sulphur atoms, S,
(f) 0.25 mol of sulphur molecules, S_8.

❷ Find the amount (moles) of each element present in:
(a) 100 g of calcium,
(b) 9.0 g of aluminium,
(c) 32 g of oxygen, O_2,
(d) 14 g of iron.

❸ State the mass of:
(a) 1.0 mol of sulphuric acid, H_2SO_4,
(b) 0.5 mol of nitrogen dioxide molecules, NO_2,
(c) 2.5 mol of magnesium oxide, MgO,
(d) 0.10 mol of calcium carbonate, $CaCO_3$.

 The masses of reactant and product

Have you grasped the mole concept? In this section you will find out how it is used to obtain information about chemical reactions.

As well as knowing what products are formed in a chemical reaction, chemists want to know **what mass** of product is formed from a given mass of starting material. For example, calcium oxide (quicklime) is made by heating calcium carbonate (limestone). Manufacturers need to know what mass of limestone to heat to yield the mass of quicklime they want.

Worked example 1 What mass of limestone (calcium carbonate) must be decomposed to yield 10 tonnes of calcium oxide (quicklime)?

Solution First write the equation for the reaction

Calcium carbonate → Calcium oxide + Carbon dioxide
$CaCO_3(s)$ → $CaO(s)$ + $CO_2(g)$

The equation tells us that

1 mol of calcium carbonate forms 1 mol of calcium oxide.

Using the molar masses $M(CaCO_3) = 100$ g/mol, $M(CaO) = 56$ g/mol,

100 g of calcium carbonate forms 56 g of calcium oxide.

The mass of calcium carbonate needed to make 10 tonnes of calcium oxide is therefore given by

$$\text{Mass of } CaCO_3 = \frac{100}{56} \times (\text{Mass of CaO}) = \frac{100}{56} \times 10 = 17.8 \text{ tonnes}$$

Worked example 2 What mass of aluminium can be obtained by the electrolysis of 60 tonnes of pure aluminium oxide, Al_2O_3?

Solution The equation comes first.

$$\text{Aluminium oxide} \rightarrow \text{Aluminium} + \text{Oxygen}$$
$$2Al_2O_3(s) \rightarrow 4Al(s) + 3O_2(g)$$

From the equation you can see that

1 mole of aluminium oxide forms 2 mol of aluminium.

Using the molar masses $M(Al) = 27$ g/mol, $M(Al_2O_3) = 102$ g/mol,

102 g of aluminium oxide form 54 g of aluminium.

The mass of aluminium obtained from 60 tonnes of aluminium oxide is therefore given by

$$\text{Mass of aluminium} = \frac{54}{102} \times \text{Mass of aluminium oxide}$$

$$= \frac{54}{102} \times 60 = 31.8 \text{ tonnes}$$

SUMMARY

The equation for a chemical reaction shows how many moles of product are formed from one mole of reactant. Using the equation and the molar masses of the chemicals, you can find out what mass of product is formed from a certain mass of reactant. In chemical calculations, the balanced equation for the reaction is the key to success.

CHECKPOINT

You do not need calculators for these problems.

1 What mass of magnesium oxide, MgO, is formed when 4.8 g of magnesium are completely oxidised?

2 Hydrogen will reduce hot copper(II) oxide, CuO, to copper:

Hydrogen + Copper(II) oxide → Copper + Water

(a) Write the balanced chemical equation for the reaction.
(b) Calculate the mass of copper that can be obtained from 4.0 g of copper(II) oxide. Use A_r (Cu) = 64

3 What mass of sodium bromide, NaBr, must be electrolysed to give 8 g of bromine, Br_2?

4 Ammonium chloride can be made by neutralising hydrochloric acid with ammonia:

$$HCl(aq) + NH_3(aq) \rightarrow NH_4Cl(aq)$$

What mass of ammonium chloride is formed when 73 g of hydrochloric acid are completely neutralised by ammonia?

47.6 Percentage yield

Calculations based on chemical equations give the **theoretical yield** of product to be expected from a reaction. Often the actual yield is less than the calculated yield of product. The reason may be that some product has remained in solution or on a filter paper and has not been weighed with the final yield. The percentage yield of a product is given by:

$$\text{Percentage yield} = \frac{\text{Actual mass of product}}{\text{Calculated mass of product}} \times 100$$

Worked example A student calculates that a certain reaction will yield 7.0 g of a salt. Her product weighs 6.3 g. What percentage yield has she obtained?

Solution

$$\text{Percentage yield} = \frac{\text{Actual mass of product}}{\text{Calculated mass of product}} \times 100$$

$$= \frac{6.3}{7.0} \times 100 = 90\%$$

CHECKPOINT

You will need a calculator to solve some of these problems.

❶ When 6.4 g of copper were heated in air, 7.6 g of copper(II) oxide, CuO, were obtained.

$$2Cu(s) + O_2(g) \rightarrow 2CuO(s)$$

(a) Calculate the mass of copper(II) oxide that would be formed if the copper reacted completely. (Use A_r (Cu) = 64)
(b) Calculate the percentage yield that was actually obtained.

❷ When 28 g of nitrogen and 6 g of hydrogen were mixed and allowed to react, 3.4 g of ammonia formed.

$$N_2(g) + 3H_2(g) \rightarrow 2NH_3(g)$$

(a) What is the maximum mass of ammonia that could be formed?
(b) What percentage of this yield was obtained?

❸ A student passed chlorine over heated iron until all the iron had reacted. He collected 16.0 g of iron(III) chloride, $FeCl_3$. What percentage yield had he obtained?

❹ A student neutralised 98 g of sulphuric acid, H_2SO_4, with ammonia, NH_3. On evaporating the solution until the salt crystallised, she obtained 120 g of ammonium sulphate, $(NH_4)_2SO_4$.
(a) Write a balanced chemical equation for the reaction.
(b) Calculate the theoretical yield of ammonium sulphate.
(c) Calculate the actual percentage yield.
(d) What do you think happened to the rest of the ammonium sulphate?

❺ Copper(II) sulphate can be made by neutralising sulphuric acid with copper(II) oxide:

$$CuO(aq) + H_2SO_4(aq) \rightarrow CuSO_4(aq) + H_2O(l)$$

The salt crystallises as copper(II) sulphate-5-water, $CuSO_4.5H_2O$.
(a) Calculate the mass of crystals that can be made from 8.0 g of copper(II) oxide and an excess (more than enough) of sulphuric acid. Use A_r (Cu) = 64.
(b) A student obtained 22 g of crystals from this preparation. What percentage yield was this?

47.7 Finding formulas

FIRST THOUGHTS

All those fascinating formulas in chemistry books – where do they come from? In this section you can find out.

The formula of a compound is worked out from the percentage composition by mass of the compound.

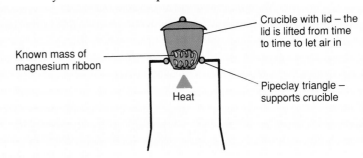

Crucible with lid – the lid is lifted from time to time to let air in

Known mass of magnesium ribbon

Pipeclay triangle – supports crucible

Heat

Figure 47.7A ● Heating magnesium

Worked example Finding the formula of magnesium oxide.
First, an experiment must be done to find the mass of oxygen that combines with a weighed amount of magnesium. Figure 47.7A shows a weighed quantity of magnesium being heated until it has been converted completely into magnesium oxide. Then the magnesium oxide must be weighed. The mass of oxygen that has combined with the magnesium is found by subtraction. A typical set of results is given below.

[1] Mass of crucible = 19.24 g
[2] Mass of crucible + magnesium = 20.68 g
[3] **Mass of magnesium** = [2] – [1] = 1.44 g
[4] Mass of crucible + magnesium oxide = 21.64 g
[5] **Mass of oxygen combined** = [4] – [2] = 0.96 g

Solution The results are used in this way:

Element	Magnesium	Oxygen
Mass	1.44 g	0.96 g
A_r	24	16
Amount in moles	1.44/24 = 0.060	0.96/16 = 0.060
Divide through by 0.060	1 mole Mg	1 mole O
Formula is	MgO	

The formula MgO is the simplest formula which fits the results. Other formulas, such as Mg_2O_2, Mg_3O_3, etc. also fit the results. MgO is the **empirical formula** for magnesium oxide.

The empirical formula of a compound is the simplest formula which represents the composition by mass of the compound.

SUMMARY

The empirical formula of a compound shows the symbols of the elements present and the ratio of the number of atoms of each element present in the compound.

CHECKPOINT

You do not need calculators for these problems.

1 Find the empirical formulas of the following compounds:
(a) a compound of 3.5 g of nitrogen and 4.0 g of oxygen,
(b) a compound of 14.4 g of magnesium and 5.6 g of nitrogen,
(c) a compound of 5.4 g of aluminium and 9.6 g of sulphur.

❷ Calculate the empirical formulas of the compounds which have the following percentage compositions by mass:
(a) 40% sulphur, 60% oxygen,
(b) 50% sulphur, 50% oxygen,
(c) 20% calcium, 80% bromine,
(d) 39% potassium, 1% hydrogen, 12% carbon, 48% oxygen.

❸ Find the empirical formulas of the compounds formed when
(a) 18 g of beryllium form 50 g of beryllium oxide,
(b) 11.2 g of iron form 16.0 g of an oxide of iron,
(c) 2.800 g of iron form 5.325 g of an iron chloride.

47.8 Concentration

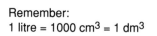

Remember:
1 litre = 1000 cm³ = 1 dm³

One way of stating the concentration of a solution is to state the mass of solute in one litre of solution, for example in grams per litre, g/l. Chemists find it more useful to state the amount in moles of a solute present in one litre of solution (see Figure 47.8A).

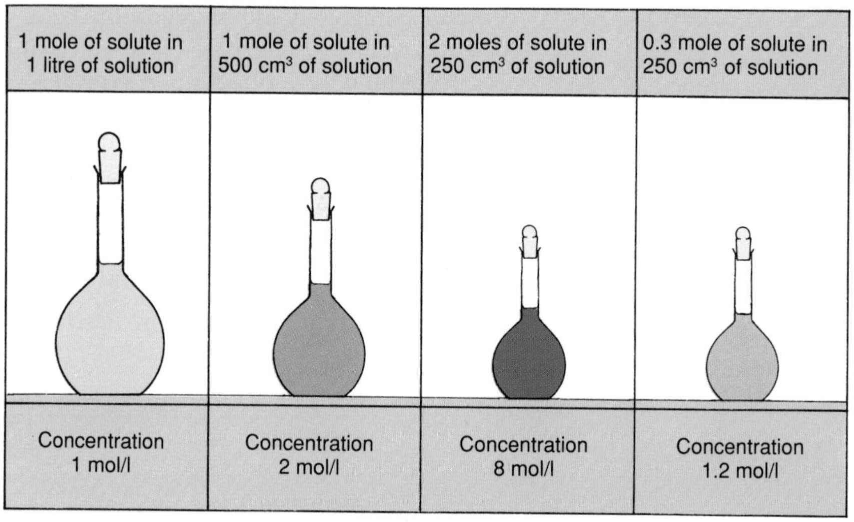

1 mole of solute in 1 litre of solution	1 mole of solute in 500 cm³ of solution	2 moles of solute in 250 cm³ of solution	0.3 mole of solute in 250 cm³ of solution
Concentration 1 mol/l	Concentration 2 mol/l	Concentration 8 mol/l	Concentration 1.2 mol/l

Figure 47.8A ● Concentrations of solutions in moles per litre (mol/l)

$$\text{Concentration in moles per litre} = \frac{\text{Amount of solute in moles}}{\text{Volume of solution in litres}}$$

Rearranging,

Amount of solute (mol) = Volume of solution (l) × Concentration (mol/l)

Worked example 1 Calculate the concentration of a solution that was made by dissolving 100 g of sodium hydroxide and making the solution up to 2.0 litres.

Solution Molar mass of sodium hydroxide, $NaOH = 23 + 16 + 1 = 40$ g/mol

$$\text{Amount in moles} = \frac{\text{Mass}}{\text{Molar mass}} = \frac{100 \text{ g}}{40 \text{ g/mol}} = 2.5 \text{ mol}$$

Volume of solution = 2.0 litre

$$\text{Concentration} = \frac{\text{Amount in moles}}{\text{Volume in litres}} = \frac{2.5 \text{ mol}}{2.0 \text{ l}} = 1.25 \text{ mol/l}$$

SUMMARY

The concentration of a solute in a solution can be stated as:
(a) grams of solute per litre of solution, g/l,
(b) moles of solute per litre of solution, mol/l.

$$\text{Concentration (mol/l)} = \frac{\text{Amount of solute (mol)}}{\text{Volume of solution (l)}}$$

Worked example 2   Calculate the amount in moles of solute present in 75 cm^3 of a solution of hydrochloric acid which has a concentration of 2.0 mol/l.

Solution   Amount (mol) = Volume (l) x Concentration (mol/l)

Amount of solute, HCl = $(75 \times 10^{-3}) \times 2.0$
        = 0.15 mol

Note that the volume in cm^3 has been changed into litres to make the units correct:

Amount (**moles**) = Volume (**litres**) x Concentration (**moles per litre**)

CHECKPOINT

❶ Calculate the concentrations of the following solutions.
 (a) 30 g of ethanoic acid, $C_2H_4O_2$, in 500 cm^3 of solution.
 (b) 8.0 g of sodium hydroxide in 2.0 l of solution.
 (c) 8.5 g of ammonia in 250 cm^3 of solution.
 (d) 12.0 g of magnesium sulphate in 250 cm^3 of solution.

❷ Find the amount of solute in moles present in the following solutions.
 (a) 1.00 l of a hydrochloric acid solution of concentration 0.020 mol/l.
 (b) 500 cm^3 of a solution of potassium hydroxide of concentration 2.0 mol/l.
 (c) 500 cm^3 of sulphuric acid of concentration 0.12 mol/l.
 (d) 100 cm^3 of a 0.25 mol/l solution of sodium hydroxide.

❸ Solutions which are injected into a vein must be isotonic with the blood. They contain 8.43 g/l of sodium chloride.
 (a) What is the concentration of sodium chloride in mol/l?
 (b) What does 'isotonic' mean? Why must the solutions be isotonic with blood?

❹ A woman mixes a drink containing 9.2 g of ethanol, C_2H_6O, in 100 cm^3 of solution. What is the concentration of ethanol in the solution (in mol/l)?

❺ A number of brands of indigestion tablets were tested. The volume of acid which one tablet could neutralise was found. The results are shown in the table below.

Brand	Price of 100 tablets (£)	Volume of 0.01 mol/l acid neutralised by one tablet (cm³)
Fizzo	0.80	3.0
Calmo	0.90	3.5
Paingo	1.20	4.0
Settlo	1.50	4.5

 (a) Calculate the amount (mol) of acid needed to neutralise 100 tablets of each brand.
 (b) Work out which brand gives the best value for money.

TOPIC 48 FUELS

48.1 Methane

FIRST THOUGHTS

○
○
○

Developing countries need more fuel. Industrial countries have difficulty in disposing of all their waste. One solution to both problems is biogas. You can find out about biogas in this section.

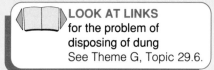

LOOK AT LINKS
for the problem of disposing of dung
See Theme G, Topic 29.6.

LOOK AT LINKS
for the **energy crisis**
See Theme B, Topic 8.4.

=== *SCIENCE AT WORK* ===

Every year, 25 million tonnes of organic waste goes into landfill sites in the UK. Biogas forms as the rubbish decays. Most landfill operators burn biogas to get rid of it. Others sink pipes into the landfill and pump out biogas for sale. In Bedfordshire, biogas from a landfill is used to heat the kilns in a brickworks. On Merseyside, biogas is used to heat the ovens in a Cadburys' biscuit factory.

SUMMARY

Biogas is formed when biomass (plant and animal matter) decays in the absence of air. The chief component of biogas is methane. Biogas can be collected from landfill rubbish sites, from sewage works and on farms. It can be burned as a fuel. Biogas generators are common in India and China. Methane accumulates in coal mines, where it can cause explosions.

Father Conlon and Father Williams are monks at Bethlehem Abbey in Northern Ireland. In 1987 they won a 'pollution abatement technology award'. They feed manure from their farm into a **biomass digester**. Biomass is material of plant or animal origin. Bacteria feed on biomass and make it decay. Under anaerobic conditions (in the absence of air), a gas called **biogas** forms. Biogas is a fuel, and the monks burn it to provide the monastery with heating. The solid remains of the biomass form an odourless compost which they bag and sell as a fertiliser for use on gardens, potato farms and golf courses.

Many farms in the UK now have biomass digesters. There are millions of such digesters in India and China. India's huge cattle population supplies plenty of dung for digestion. The biogas produced is used as a fuel for cooking and heating. It burns with a hotter, cleaner flame than cattle dung. The residual sludge which gathers in the digester is a better fertiliser than raw dung. Both the gas and the sludge are clean and odourless.

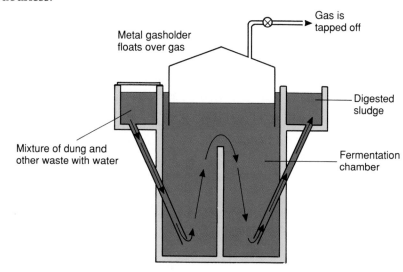

Figure 48.1A ● A biomass digester

Figure 48.1B ● A gas rig in the North Sea

The chief component of biogas is **methane**. Methane is the gas we burn in Bunsen burners and gas cookers. It is the valuable fuel we call **natural gas** or **North Sea gas**. Reserves of North Sea gas are usually found together with North Sea oil. Methane is also the gas called **marsh gas** which bubbles up through stagnant water. It collects in coalmines, and methane explosions have been the cause of many pit disasters.

❶ (a) What are the advantages of biogas generators for developing countries?
 (b) Why does India have plenty of cattle dung?
 (c) In what ways is biogas a more convenient fuel than dung?
 (d) What advantages do biogas generators have for industrial countries?

❷ (a) What is biomass? Briefly describe how biomass can be fermented to produce biogas. What other product is formed?
 (b) What are the problems in adapting the process to produce fuel gas for domestic use?
 (c) Can you point out any situations in which a biogas generator might both save money and also benefit the environment?

48.2 Alkanes

FIRST THOUGHTS

Methane is one member of a family of compounds, the alkanes. Composed of hydrogen and carbon only, the alkanes are hydrocarbons. You will meet another family of hydrocarbons, the alkenes, in Topic 51.3.

Methane is a **hydrocarbon**, a compound of hydrogen and carbon. With formula CH_4, it is the simplest of the hydrocarbons. Figure 48.2A shows how, in a molecule of methane, four covalent bonds join hydrogen atoms to a carbon atom.

Hydrocarbons are **organic compounds**. Originally, the term 'organic compound' was applied to compounds which were found in plant and animal material, for

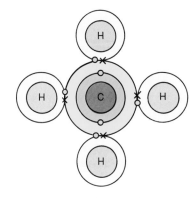

Figure 48.2A ● Bonding in methane

example sugars, fats and proteins. All these compounds contain carbon, and the term 'organic compound' is now used for all carbon compounds, whether they have been obtained from plants and animals or made in a laboratory. However, simple compounds like carbon dioxide and carbonates are not usually described as organic compounds. Most organic compounds are covalent. The salts of organic acids contain ionic bonds.

Methane is one of a **series** of hydrocarbons called the **alkanes**. The next members of the series are ethane, C_2H_6, propane, C_3H_8 and butane, C_4H_{10} (see Figure 48.2B). Many hydrocarbons have much larger molecules.

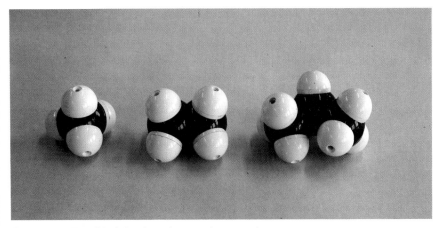

Figure 48.2B ● Models of methane, ethane and propane

As well as molecular formulas, CH_4, C_2H_6 and C_3H_8, the compounds have **structural formulas**. A structural formula shows the bonds between atoms.

$$H-\overset{\displaystyle H}{\underset{\displaystyle H}{C}}-H \qquad H-\overset{\displaystyle H}{\underset{\displaystyle H}{C}}-\overset{\displaystyle H}{\underset{\displaystyle H}{C}}-H \qquad H-\overset{\displaystyle H}{\underset{\displaystyle H}{C}}-\overset{\displaystyle H}{\underset{\displaystyle H}{C}}-\overset{\displaystyle H}{\underset{\displaystyle H}{C}}-H$$

Methane   Ethane   Propane

Each compound differs from the next in the series by the group

$$-\overset{\displaystyle H}{\underset{\displaystyle H}{C}}-$$

Table 48.1 ● The alkanes

Alkane	Formula C_nH_{2n+2}
Methane	CH_4
Ethane	C_2H_6
Propane	C_3H_8
Butane	C_4H_{10}
Pentane	C_5H_{12}
Hexane	C_6H_{14}
Heptane	C_7H_{16}
Octane	C_8H_{18}

A set of chemically similar compounds in which each member differs from the next in the series by a CH_2 group is called a **homologous series**. Table 48.1 lists the first members of the **alkane series**. Their formulas all fit the general formula C_nH_{2n+2}, for example for pentane $n = 5$, giving the formula C_5H_{12}. The alkanes are described as **saturated** hydrocarbons. This means that they contain only single bonds between carbon atoms. This is in contrast to the **alkenes**. The alkanes are unreactive towards acids, bases, metals and many other chemicals. Their important reaction is combustion.

Isomerism

Sometimes it is possible to write more than one structural formula for a molecular formula. For the molecular formula C_4H_{10}, there are two possible structures

$$H-\overset{\displaystyle H}{\underset{\displaystyle H}{C}}-\overset{\displaystyle H}{\underset{\displaystyle H}{C}}-\overset{\displaystyle H}{\underset{\displaystyle H}{C}}-\overset{\displaystyle H}{\underset{\displaystyle H}{C}}-H$$

Butane

(a)

$$H-\overset{\displaystyle H}{\underset{\displaystyle H}{C}}-\overset{\displaystyle H}{\underset{\displaystyle C}{C}}-\overset{\displaystyle H}{\underset{\displaystyle H}{C}}-H$$
$$\overset{\displaystyle |}{H-\overset{\displaystyle H}{\underset{\displaystyle H}{C}}-H}$$

(b)   Methylpropane

The difference is that (a) has an unbranched chain of carbon atoms and (b) has a branched chain. The formulas belong to different compounds, which differ in boiling point and other physical properties. The compound with formula (a) is called butane; the compound with formula (b) is called methylpropane. These compounds are **isomers**. Isomers are compounds with the same molecular formula and different structural formulas.

LOOK AT LINKS
for **alkenes**
See Theme L, Topic 51.3.

❶ Explain what is meant by a 'homologous series'.

❷ (a) Explain what is meant by the term 'alkane'.
(b) Why are alkanes very important in our way of life?
(c) Where do we obtain alkanes?
(d) The molecular formula for propane is C_3H_8. Write the structural formula for propane.
(e) What information does the structural formula of a compound give that the molecular formula does not give?
(f) Explain what is meant by the term 'isomerism'. Illustrate your answer by referring to pentane, C_5H_{12}.

48.3 Combustion

SUMMARY

The combustion of hydrocarbons is exothermic. The products of complete combustion are carbon dioxide and water. Incomplete combustion produces carbon and poisonous carbon monoxide.

Hydrocarbons burn in a plentiful supply of air to form carbon dioxide and water. The reaction is **exothermic**: energy is released.

Methane + Oxygen → Carbon dioxide + Water; Energy is released
$CH_4(g) + 2O_2(g)$ → $CO_2(g) + 2H_2O(l)$

Butane + Oxygen (in Camping Gaz) → Carbon dioxide + Water; Energy is released

Octane + Oxygen (in petrol) → Carbon dioxide + Water; Energy is released

Revise what you learned about combustion in Theme E, Topic 21.7.

❶ (a) What harmless combustion products are formed when hydrocarbons burn in plenty of air?
(b) When does incomplete combustion take place?
(c) What are the products of incomplete combustion? What is dangerous about incomplete combustion? How can it be avoided?

48.4 Petroleum oil and natural gas

FIRST THOUGHTS

Prospecting for oil is an even more important business than prospecting for gold. *How do prospectors find oil? And how was oil formed in the first place?* You can find out in this section.

In some parts of the world, a black, treacle-like liquid seeps out of the ground. At one time, farmers in Texas, USA, used to burn this substance to get rid of it when it formed troublesome pools on their land. The black liquid was called **crude oil**. It is now regarded as one of the most valuable resources a country can have. The petrochemicals industry obtains valuable fuels such as petrol, and thousands of useful materials such as plastics, from crude oil. Natural gas is found in the same deposits as crude oil.

Oil and gas are **fossil fuels**. They were formed millions of years ago when a large area of the Earth was covered by sea. Tiny sea creatures called plankton died and sank to the sea bed, where they became mixed

LOOK AT LINKS
for **oil** and **natural gas**
See Theme B, Topic 8.2.

LOOK AT LINKS
for **sedimentary rocks**
See Theme A, Topic 2.5.

IT'S A FACT

Have you heard of the petrol tree? The gopher tree grows well in desert areas. Its sap contains about 30% hydrocarbons. Petrol could be made from the sap of this tree.

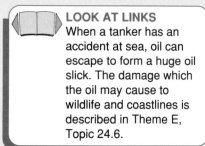

LOOK AT LINKS
When a tanker has an accident at sea, oil can escape to form a huge oil slick. The damage which the oil may cause to wildlife and coastlines is described in Theme E, Topic 24.6.

SUMMARY

Crude oil and natural gas were formed by the slow bacterial decay of animal and plant remains in the absence of oxygen. These fuels are found in many parts of the world.

LOOK AT LINKS
for **fractional distillation**
See Theme D, Topic 15.8.

308

with mud. Bacteria in the mud began to bring about the decay of the creatures' bodies. Decay took place slowly because there is little oxygen dissolved in the depths of the sea. As the covering layer of mud and silt grew thicker over the years, the pressure on the decaying matter increased. Bacterial decay at high pressure with little oxygen turned the organic matter into crude oil and natural gas.

The sediment on top of the decaying matter became compressed to form rock. Rocks formed in this way are called **sedimentary rocks**. Some of these rocks are porous: they contain tiny passages through which liquid and gas can pass. Others are impermeable: they do not let any substances through. Ground water carries crude oil and natural gas upward through porous rocks. They may reach the surface, but more often they become trapped by a **cap rock** of impermeable rock (see Figure 48.4A). There the crude oil and natural gas remain unless an oil prospector drills down to them.

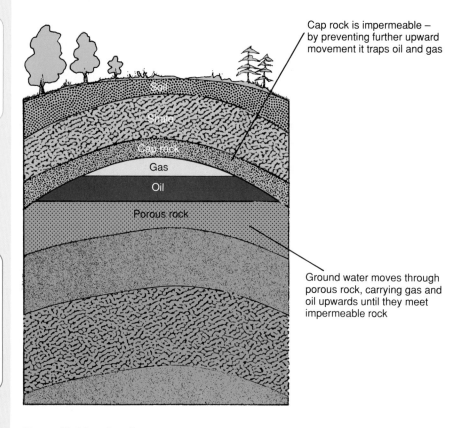

Cap rock is impermeable – by preventing further upward movement it traps oil and gas

Ground water moves through porous rock, carrying gas and oil upwards until they meet impermeable rock

Figure 48.4A ● An oil trap

Many countries have deposits of oil and gas, for example the USA, the USSR, Iran, Nigeria and the countries in the Arabian Gulf. The UK and Norway have oil and gas beneath the North Sea. The UK has piped ashore oil and gas since 1972. There are two ways of getting oil ashore from an oil well in the sea. One way is to lay a pipeline along the sea bed and pump the oil through it. The other method is to use 'shuttle tankers' which pick up the oil from the oilfield and transport it to a terminal on land. Natural gas is almost always brought ashore by pipeline.

Crude oil is transported from oil wells to refineries. Pipelines carry oil overland. Tankers carry oil overseas.

Crude oil does not burn very easily. **Fractional distillation** is used to separate crude oil into a number of important fuels. The fractions are separated on the basis of their boiling point range. They are not pure compounds: they are mixtures of alkanes with similar boiling points.

Figure 48.4B   An oil rig being towed out to sea

Table 48.2 ● Petroleum fractions and their uses

Fraction	Approximate boiling point range (°C)	Approximate number of carbon atoms per molecule	Use
Petroleum gases	below 25	1–4	Petroleum gases are liquefied and sold in cylinders as 'bottled gas' for use in gas cookers and camping stoves. They burn easily at low temperatures. Smelly sulphur compounds must be removed to make bottled gas pleasant to use and non-polluting.
Gasoline (petrol)	40–75	4–12	Petrol is liquid at room temperature, but vaporises easily at the temperature of vehicle engines.
Naphtha	75–150	7–14	Naphtha is used by the petrochemicals industry as the source of a huge number of useful chemicals, e.g. plastics, drugs, medicines, fabrics (see Figure 48.4C overleaf).
Kerosene	150–240	9–16	Kerosene is a liquid fuel which needs a higher temperature for combustion than petrol. The major use of kerosene is as aviation fuel. It is also used in 'paraffin' stoves.
Diesel oil	220–250	15–25	Diesel oil is more difficult to vaporise than petrol and kerosene. The diesel engine has a special fuel injection system which makes the fuel burn. It is used in buses, lorries and trains.
Lubricating oil	250–350	20–70	Lubricating oil is a viscous liquid. With its high boiling point range, it does not vaporise enough to be used as a fuel. Instead, it is used as a lubricant to reduce engine wear.
Fuel oil	250–350	Above 10	Fuel oil has a high ignition temperature. To help it to ignite, fuel oil is sprayed into the combustion chambers as a fine mist of small droplets. It is used in ships, heating plants, industrial machinery and power stations.
Bitumen	Above 350	Above 70	Bitumen has too high an ignition temperature to be used as a fuel. It is used to tar roads and to waterproof roofs and pipes.

IT'S A
FACT

A petroleum fraction called **white spirit** is widely used as a solvent. In November, 1988, a fire at King's Cross underground station in London killed 30 people. Under the escalators, investigators found empty drums that had held 150 litres of white spirit. The staff use white spirit for cleaning the treads of the escalators. The presence of flammable white spirit could help to explain the speed with which the fire spread.

Alkanes with small molecules boil at lower temperatures than those with large molecules. Alkanes with large molecules are more viscous than alkanes with small molecules. The fractions also differ in the ease with which they burn: in their **flash points** and **ignition temperatures**.

- When a fuel is heated, some of it vaporises. When the fuel reaches a temperature called the **flash point**, there is enough vapour to be set alight by a flame. Once the vapour has burned, the flame goes out.
- The **ignition temperature** of a fuel is higher than its flash point. It is the temperature at which a mixture of the fuel with air will ignite and continue to burn steadily.

The use that is made of each fraction depends on its boiling point range, flash point, ignition temperature and viscosity; see Table 48.2.

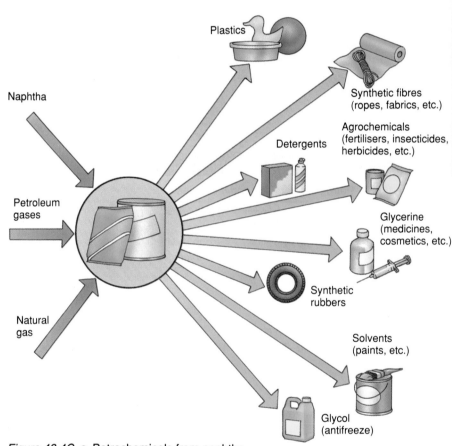

Figure 48.4C ● Petrochemicals from naphtha

Cracking

We use more petrol, naphtha and kerosene than heavy fuel oils. Fortunately, chemists have found a way of making petrol and kerosene from the higher-boiling fractions, of which we have more than enough. The technique used is called **cracking**. Large hydrocarbon molecules are cracked (split) into smaller hydrocarbon molecules. A heated catalyst (aluminium oxide or silicon(IV) oxide) is used.

| Vapour of hydrocarbon with large molecules and high b.p. | CRACKING → passed over a heated catalyst | Mixture of hydrogen and hydrocarbons with smaller molecules and low b.p. |

SUMMARY

Crude oil is separated into useful components by fractional distillation. The use that is made of each fraction depends on its boiling point range, ignition temperature and other properties. The fuels obtained from crude oil are listed in Table 48.2. Cracking is used to make petrol and kerosene from heavy fuel oils. The petrochemicals industry makes many useful chemicals from petroleum.

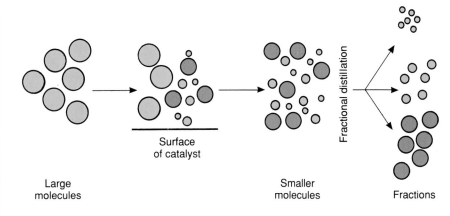

Large molecules   Surface of catalyst   Smaller molecules   Fractional distillation   Fractions

Figure 48.4D ● Cracking

CHECKPOINT

① The use of crude oil fractions in the UK is as follows:
Road transport 37%
Heating and power for industry 21%
Heating and power for other consumers 19%
Making chemicals 11%
Power stations 8%
Heating houses 4%
Show this information in the form of a pie-chart or a bar graph.

② The figure below shows the percentage of crude oil that distils at various temperatures.
(a) From the graph, read the percentage of crude oil that distils:
   (i)   below 70 °C,   (ii) between 120 and 170 °C,
   (iii) between 170 and 220 °C,   (iv) between 220 and 270 °C,
   (v)   between 270 and 320 °C,   (vi) above 320 °C.
(b) Draw a pie-chart to show these figures.
(c) The percentages vary from one sample of oil to another. North Sea oil contains a larger percentage of lower boiling point compounds than Middle East oil does. Which oil should sell for a higher price? Explain your answer.

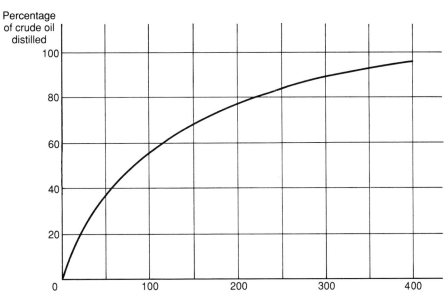

3 A barrel of Middle East oil contains 160 litres. From it are obtained:

natural gas (7 litres) kerosene (7 litres)
petrol (9 litres) gas oil (41 litres)
naphtha (23 litres) fuel oil (73 litres)

Show these figures as a pie-chart.

4 (a) How are petrol and kerosene obtained from crude oil?
(b) What is the name of the process for converting heavy fuel oil into petrol?
What are the economic reasons for carrying out this reaction?

5 (a) What is crude oil?
(b) Why is it described as a fossil fuel?
(c) What useful substances are obtained from crude oil?
(d) Why is an increase in the price of crude oil such a serious matter?

FIRST THOUGHTS

48.5  Coal

Coal is an important source of energy. It fuelled the Industrial Revolution and is still a major source of energy in the UK today.

Between 200 and 300 million years ago, the Earth was covered with dense forests. When plants and trees died, they started to decay. In the swampy conditions of that era, they formed peat. Gradually, the peat became covered by layers of mud and sand. The pressure of these layers and high temperatures turned the peat into coal. The mud became shale and the sand became sandstone. Coal is a fossil fuel: it was formed from the remains of living things.

Many countries have coal deposits. The largest coal-mining countries are the USSR, the USA, China, Poland and the UK. Coal is a mixture of carbon, hydrocarbons and other compounds. When it burns, the main products are carbon dioxide and water.

SUMMARY

Coal is a fossil fuel derived from plant remains. Most of the coal mined is burned in power stations. The destructive distillation of coal gives useful products.

Carbon (in coal) + Oxygen → Carbon dioxide
Hydrocarbons (in coal) + Oxygen → Carbon dioxide + Water

In the UK, three-quarters of the coal used is burned in power stations. The heat given out is used to raise steam, which drives the turbines that generate electricity.

If air is absent when coal is heated, coal does not burn. It decomposes to form coke and other useful products. The process is called **destructive distillation**.

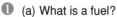

CHECKPOINT

1 (a) What is a fuel?
(b) Why are coal and oil called fossil fuels?
(c) State two properties that make a fuel a 'good' fuel.
(d) Where is most of the coal that we use burned?
(e) What use is made of coal apart from burning it?

CHEMICAL ENERGY CHANGES

49.1 Exothermic reactions

FIRST THOUGHTS

In many places in this book, we refer to the importance of energy. One means by which energy is converted from one form into another is by chemical reactions.

LOOK AT LINKS
for **carbohydrates**
See Theme D, Topic 18.2.

LOOK AT LINKS
for **hydrates**
See Theme D, Topic 17.3.

LOOK AT LINKS
for **acids** and **alkalis**
See Theme D, Topic 16.

LOOK AT LINKS
for **aerobic respiration**
See Theme F, Topic 26.1.

Our bodies obtain energy from the combustion of foods, and our vehicles obtain energy from the combustion of hydrocarbons. Reactions of this kind, which give out energy, are **exothermic reactions** (ex = out; therm = heat). You will meet many such reactions. Some are described below.

Combustion

Topic 48.3 described the combustion of the fuels:
- coal (carbon + hydrocarbons),
- natural gas (largely methane, CH_4),
- petrol (a mixture of hydrocarbons, e.g. octane, C_8H_{18})

We use the heat from these exothermic reactions to warm our homes and buildings and to drive our vehicles.

Figure 49.1A ● They all use exothermic reactions

- An oxidation reaction in which heat is given out is **combustion**. The oxidation of sugars in our bodies is combustion.
- Combustion accompanied by a flame is **burning**. When coal is burned in a fireplace, you see the flames.
- A substance which is oxidised with the release of energy is a fuel. Both sugars and coal are fuels.

Respiration

We use the combustion of foods to supply our bodies with energy. Important among 'energy foods' are **carbohydrates**. Glucose, a sugar, is oxidised to carbon dioxide and water with the release of energy. This exothermic reaction, which takes place inside plant cells and animal cells, is called **aerobic respiration**.

Neutralisation

When an acid neutralises an alkali, heat is given out.

Figure 49.1B ● Energy from respiration

Hydrogen ion	+	Hydroxide ion	→	Water	Heat is given out
$H^+(aq)$	+	$OH^-(aq)$	→	$H_2O(l)$	

SUMMARY

In exothermic reactions, energy is released. Examples are:
• the combustion of hydrocarbons,
• respiration,
• neutralisation,
• hydration of anhydrous salts.

Hydration

Many anhydrous salts react with water to form hydrates. During hydration, heat is given out.

Anhydrous copper(II) sulphate	+	Water	→	Copper(II) sulphate-5-water	Heat is given out
$CuSO_4(s)$	+	$5H_2O(l)$	→	$CuSO_4.5H_2O(s)$	

49.2 Endothermic reactions

LOOK AT LINKS
for **photosynthesis**
See Theme F, Topic 25.1.

LOOK AT LINKS
Calcium oxide is used in the manufacture of cement and concrete.
See Theme L, Topic 51.1.
Calcium oxide is also used to make calcium hydroxide (slaked lime), which is used as a fertiliser.
See Theme G, Topic 29.7.

SUMMARY

In endothermic reactions, energy is taken in from the surroundings. Examples are:
• photosynthesis,
• thermal decomposition,
• the reaction between steam and coke.

Photosynthesis

Plants manufacture sugars in the process of **photosynthesis**. They convert the energy of sunlight into the energy of the chemical bonds in sugar molecules. Photosynthesis is an **endothermic reaction**: it takes in energy.

Carbon dioxide + Water $\xrightarrow[\text{in the leaves of green plants}]{\text{catalysed by chlorophyll}}$ Glucose + Oxygen Energy is taken in

$$6CO_2(g) + 6H_2O(l) \rightarrow C_6H_{12}O_6(aq) + 6O_2(g)$$

Thermal decomposition

Many substances decompose when they are heated. An example is calcium carbonate (limestone).

Calcium carbonate	→	Calcium oxide	+	Carbon dioxide	Heat is taken in
$CaCO_3(s)$	→	$CaO(s)$	+	$CO_2(g)$	

This is an important reaction because it yields **calcium oxide** (quick lime).

The reaction between steam and coke

The endothermic reaction between steam and hot coke produces carbon monoxide and hydrogen. This mixture of flammable gases is used as fuel.

Carbon (coke)	+	Steam	→	Carbon monoxide	+	Hydrogen	Heat is taken in
$C(s)$	+	$H_2O(g)$	→	$CO(g)$	+	$H_2(g)$	Heat is taken in

CHECKPOINT

1 Give an example of a reaction which is of vital importance in everyday life and which is (a) exothermic and (b) endothermic. Explain why the reactions you mention are so important.

2 The reaction shown below is exothermic.

Anhydrous copper(II) sulphate + Water → Copper(II) sulphate-5-water

Describe or illustrate an experiment by which you could find out whether this statement is true.

49.3 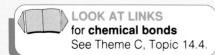 **Heat of reaction**

Why is energy (heat and other forms of energy) given out or taken in during a chemical reaction? That is the question for this section.

LOOK AT LINKS
for **chemical bonds**
See Theme C, Topic 14.4.

Chemical bonds are forces of attraction between the atoms or ions or molecules in a substance. To break these bonds, energy must be supplied. When bonds are created, energy is given out. In a chemical reaction, bonds are broken, and new bonds are made.

Figure 49.3A shows the breaking and making of bonds when methane burns.

$$\text{Methane} + \text{Oxygen} \rightarrow \text{Carbon dioxide} + \text{Water}$$
$$CH_4(g) + 2O_2(g) \rightarrow CO_2(g) + 2H_2O(l)$$

The energy given out when the new bonds are made is greater than the energy taken in to break the old bonds. This reaction is therefore **exothermic**.

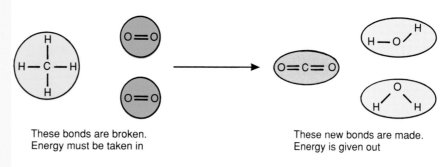

These bonds are broken.
Energy must be taken in

These new bonds are made.
Energy is given out

In this reaction, the energy given out is greater than the energy taken in – this reaction is exothermic

Figure 49.3A ● Bonds broken and made when methane burns

Figure 49.3B shows the breaking and making of bonds in the reaction

$$\text{Carbon (coke)} + \text{Water (steam)} \rightarrow \text{Carbon monoxide} + \text{Hydrogen}$$
$$C(s) + H_2O(g) \rightarrow CO(g) + H_2(g)$$

In this reaction, the energy taken in to break the old bonds is greater than the energy given out when the new bonds form. The reaction is therefore **endothermic**.

The bonds in H_2O must be broken.
Energy must be taken in

As the bonds in CO and H_2 are made, energy is given out

In this reaction, the energy taken in is greater than the energy given out. This reaction is endothermic

Figure 49.3B ● Bonds broken and made when steam reacts with hot coke

Energy diagrams

In a chemical reaction, the reactants and the products possess different chemical bonds. They therefore possess different amounts of energy. A diagram which shows the energy content of the reactants and the products is called an **energy diagram**.

Figure 49.3C is an energy diagram for an exothermic reaction. It shows the energy content of the reactants and the products.

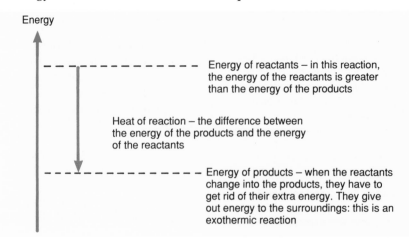

Energy

Energy of reactants – in this reaction, the energy of the reactants is greater than the energy of the products

Heat of reaction – the difference between the energy of the products and the energy of the reactants

Energy of products – when the reactants change into the products, they have to get rid of their extra energy. They give out energy to the surroundings: this is an exothermic reaction

Figure 49.3C ● An energy diagram for an exothermic reaction (e.g. the combustion of methane)

Figure 49.3D shows an energy diagram for an endothermic reaction. Marked on both energy diagrams is the heat of reaction

Heat of reaction = Energy of products – Energy of reactants

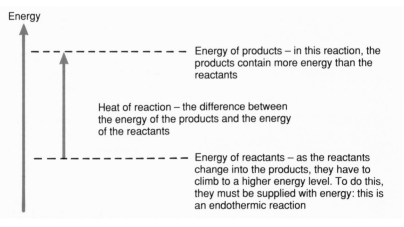

Energy

Energy of products – in this reaction, the products contain more energy than the reactants

Heat of reaction – the difference between the energy of the products and the energy of the reactants

Energy of reactants – as the reactants change into the products, they have to climb to a higher energy level. To do this, they must be supplied with energy: this is an endothermic reaction

Figure 49.3D ● An energy diagram for an endothermic reaction (e.g. the reaction between coke and steam)

SUMMARY

In a chemical reaction, energy must be supplied to break chemical bonds in the reactants. Energy is given out when new chemical bonds are made during the formation of the products. The difference between the energy content of the products and the energy content of the reactants is the heat of reaction.

CHECKPOINT

❶ Draw an energy diagram for the neutralisation of hydrochloric acid by sodium hydroxide solution. If you have forgotten whether it is exothermic or endothermic, see Topic 49.1. Mark the heat of reaction on your diagram.

❷ Draw an energy diagram for the combustion of petrol to form carbon dioxide and water. Mark the heat of reaction on your diagram.

❸ Is photosynthesis exothermic or endothermic? What are the reactants and what are the products? Illustrate your answer by an energy diagram.

❹ Describe the reaction that takes place when magnesium ribbon is heated in air. What do you see that shows the reaction is exothermic? What forms of energy are released? Draw an energy diagram for the reaction.

TOPIC 50  *METALS*

FIRST THOUGHTS

50.1 Metals and alloys

> Metals and alloys have played an important part in history. The discovery of bronze made it possible for the human race to advance out of the Stone Age into the Bronze Age. Centuries later, smiths found out how to extract iron from rocks, and the Iron Age was born. In the nineteenth century, the invention of steel made the Industrial Revolution possible.

Metals are strong materials. They are used for purposes where strength is required. Metals can be worked into complicated shapes. They can be ground to take a cutting edge. They conduct heat and electricity. As science and technology advance, metals are put to work for more and more purposes.

Alloys

An alloy is a mixture of metallic elements and in some cases non-metallic elements also. Many metallic elements are not strong enough to be used for the manufacture of machines and vehicles which will have to withstand stress. Alloying a metallic element with another element is a way of increasing its strength. Steel is an alloy of iron with carbon and often other metallic elements. Duralumin is an alloy of aluminium with copper and magnesium. This alloy is much stronger than pure aluminium and is used for aircraft manufacture (Figure 50.1A).

Alloys have different properties from the elements of which they are composed. Brass is made from copper and zinc. It has a lower melting point than either of these metals. This makes it easier to cast, that is, to melt and pour into moulds. Brass musical instruments have a more pleasant and sonorous sound than instruments made from either of the two elements copper or zinc.

Figure 50.1A ● Concorde

> **LOOK AT LINKS**
> Some uses of metals have been described in Theme C, Topic 9.

> **SUMMARY**
> An alloy is a mixture of metals, with, in some cases, non-metallic elements also. Alloys have different properties from the elements of which they are composed.

50.2 The metallic bond

Metals possess their remarkable and useful properties because of the type of chemical bond between the atoms: the metallic bond.

A piece of metal consists of positive metal ions and free electrons (see Figure 50.2A). The free electrons are the outermost electrons which break free when the metal atoms form ions. Free electrons move about between the metal ions. This is what prevents the metal ions from being driven apart by repulsion between their positive charges.

LOOK AT LINKS
for **the conduction of electricity**
See Theme K, Topic 43.1.

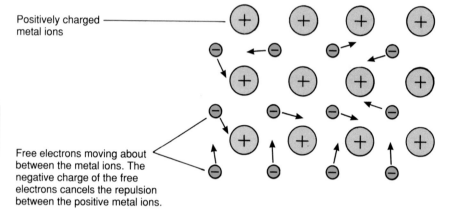

Positively charged metal ions

Free electrons moving about between the metal ions. The negative charge of the free electrons cancels the repulsion between the positive metal ions.

Figure 50.2A ● The metallic bond

SUMMARY

The metallic bond is a strong bond. It gives metals their strength and allows them to conduct electricity.

The metallic bond explains how metals **conduct electricity**. It also explains how metals can change their shape without breaking. When a metal is bent, the shape changes but the free electrons continue to hold the metal ions together.

50.3 The chemical reactions of metals

You have already met the reaction between metals and acids in Theme D, Topic 16.1 and the reaction between metals and air in Theme E, Topic 21.5. In this section, you will find out how to classify metals on the basis of the vigour of their chemical reactions.

Reactions of metals with air

Many metals react with the oxygen in the air (see Table 50.1).

Table 50.1 ● The reactions between metals and oxygen

Metal	Symbol	Reaction when heated in air	Reaction with cold air
Potassium	K		
Sodium	Na		
Calcium	Ca		
Magnesium	Mg	Burn in air to form oxides	React slowly with air to form a surface film of the metal oxide. This reaction is called **tarnishing**
Aluminium	Al		
Zinc	Zn		
Iron	Fe		
Tin	Sn	When heated in air, these metals form oxides without burning	
Lead	Pb		
Copper	Cu		
Silver	Ag		Silver tarnishes in air
Gold	Au	Do not react	Do not react
Platinum	Pt		

Reactions of metals with water

Table 50.2 ● Reactions of metals with cold water and steam

Metal	*Reaction with water*
Potassium 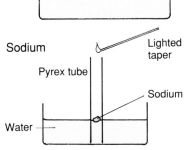 The hydrogen that is formed burns Potassium reacts violently with water	A violent reaction occurs. Hydrogen and potassium hydroxide solution, a strong alkali, are formed. The reaction is so exothermic that the hydrogen burns. The flame is coloured lilac by potassium vapour. Potassium + Water → Hydrogen + Potassium hydroxide $2K(s)$ + $2H_2O(l)$ → $H_2(g)$ + $2KOH(aq)$ Potassium is kept under oil to prevent water vapour and oxygen in the air from attacking it.
Sodium 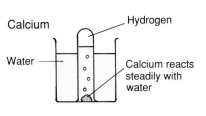	Reacts slightly less violently than potassium does. Hydrogen and sodium hydroxide solution, a strong alkali, are formed. The hydrogen formed burns with a yellow flame. The flame colour is due to the presence of sodium vapour. Sodium + Water → Hydrogen + Sodium hydroxide $2Na(s)$ + $2H_2O(l)$ → $H_2(g)$ + $2NaOH(aq)$ Sodium is kept under oil to prevent water vapour and oxygen in the air attacking it.
Calcium 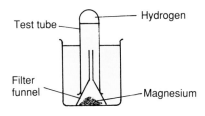	Reacts readily but not violently with cold water to form hydrogen and calcium hydroxide solution, the alkali limewater. Calcium + Water → Hydrogen + Calcium hydroxide $Ca(s)$ + $2H_2O(l)$ → $H_2(g)$ + $Ca(OH)_2(aq)$
Magnesium 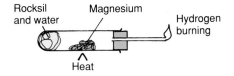	Reacts slowly with cold water to form hydrogen and magnesium hydroxide. Magnesium + Water → Hydrogen + Magnesium hydroxide $Mg(s)$ + $2H_2O(l)$ → $H_2(g)$ + $Mg(OH)_2(aq)$
	Burns in steam to form hydrogen and magnesium oxide. Magnesium + Steam → Hydrogen + Magnesium oxide $Mg(s)$ + $H_2O(g)$ → $H_2(g)$ + $MgO(s)$
Aluminium	Aluminium has a surface layer of aluminium oxide which is unreactive. When the oxide layer is removed, aluminium reacts readily with water to form hydrogen and aluminium oxide.
Zinc 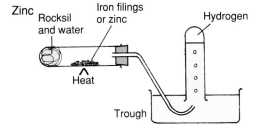	Reacts with steam to form hydrogen and zinc oxide. Zinc + Steam → Hydrogen + Zinc oxide $Zn(s)$ + $H_2O(g)$ → $H_2(g)$ + $ZnO(s)$

(continued overleaf)

Table 50.2 ● Reactions of metals with cold water and steam (continued)

Metal	Reaction with water
Iron	Reacts with steam to form hydrogen and the oxide, Fe_3O_4, tri-iron tetraoxide, which is blue-black in colour. $\quad$ Iron $\quad+\quad$ Steam $\quad\rightarrow\quad$ Hydrogen $+$ Tri-iron tetraoxide $\quad$ $3Fe(s)\ +\ 4H_2O(g)\ \rightarrow\quad 4H_2(g)\quad+\quad\quad Fe_3O_4(s)$
Tin Lead Copper Silver Gold Platinum	Do not react

Reactions of metals with dilute acids

Table 50.3 ● The reactions of metals with dilute acids

Metal	Reaction with dilute acid
Potassium Sodium Lithium	The reaction is dangerously violent **Do not try it**
Calcium Magnesium Aluminium Zinc Iron Tin Lead	These metals react with dilute hydrochloric acid to give hydrogen and a solution of the metal chloride, e.g. $\quad$ Zinc $+$ Hydrochloric acid $\rightarrow$ Hydrogen $+$ Zinc chloride $\quad$ $Zn(s) +\quad\quad 2HCl(aq)\quad\quad\rightarrow\quad\ H_2(g)\quad+\quad ZnCl_2(aq)$ The vigour of the reaction decreases from calcium to lead. Lead reacts very slowly. With dilute sulphuric acid, the metals give hydrogen and sulphates.
Copper Silver Gold Platinum	These metals do not react with dilute hydrochloric acid and dilute sulphuric acid. (Copper reacts with dilute nitric acid to form copper nitrate. Nitric acid is an oxidising agent as well as an acid.)

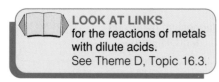

LOOK AT LINKS
for the reactions of metals with dilute acids.
See Theme D, Topic 16.3.

CHECKPOINT

See Theme E, Topic 21.6 if you need to revise.

❶ State whether the oxides of the following elements are acidic or basic or neutral.
   (a) iron   (d) sulphur
   (b) carbon   (e) zinc
   (c) copper

❷ Write (a) word equations (b) balanced chemical equations for the combustion of the following elements in oxygen to form oxides.
   (i) zinc   (iii) sodium
   (ii) magnesium (iv) carbon

❸ (a) Which are attacked more by acid rain: lead gutters or iron fall pipes?
   (b) Food cans made of iron are coated with tin. How does this help them to resist attack by the acids in foods?

❹ Write word equations and symbol equations for the reactions between:
   (a) magnesium and hydrochloric acid,
   (b) iron and hydrochloric acid to form iron(II) chloride,
   (c) zinc and sulphuric acid,
   (d) iron and sulphuric acid to form iron(II) sulphate.

50.4 The reactivity series

There are over seventy metallic elements. One way of classifying them is to arrange them in a sort of league table, with the most reactive metals at the top of the league and the least reactive metals at the bottom. This section shows how it is done.

Structure and Bonding
(program)

Find the section of the program on the reactivity series. Use it to investigate the properties of different metals in the series.

Chemistry Super Stars
(program)

Test your chemistry skill using the game in this program on the reactivity of metals. Try to identify the metals involved.

SUMMARY

• Many metals react with oxygen; some metals burn in oxygen. The oxides of metals are bases.
• A few metals (for example sodium) react with cold water to give a metal hydroxide and hydrogen. Some metals react with steam to give a metal oxide and hydrogen.
• Many metals react with dilute acids to give hydrogen and the salt of the metal.
Metals fall into the same order of reactivity in all these reactions. This order is called the reactivity series of the metals.

There are over 70 metals in the Earth's crust. Table 50.4 summarises the reactions of metals with oxygen, water and acids. You will see that the same metals are the most reactive in the different reactions.

Table 50.4 ● Reactions of metals

Metal	Reaction when heated in oxygen	Reaction with cold water	Reaction with dilute hydrochloric acid
Potassium Sodium Lithium	Burn to form oxides	Displace hydrogen; form alkaline hydroxides	React dangerously fast
Calcium Magnesium Aluminium Zinc Iron		Slow reaction	Displace hydrogen; form metal chlorides
		No reaction, except for slow rusting of iron; all react with steam	
Tin Lead Copper	Oxides form slowly without burning	Do not react, even with steam	React very slowly
Silver Gold Platinum	Do not react		Do not react

The metals can be listed in order of **reactivity**, in order of their readiness to take part in chemical reactions. This list is called the **reactivity series** of the metals. Table 50.5 shows part of the reactivity series.

Table 50.5 ● Part of the reactivity series

Metal	Symbol	
Potassium	K	
Sodium	Na	
Calcium	Ca	
Magnesium	Mg	
Aluminium	Al	
Zinc	Zn	Reactivity
Iron	Fe	decreases
Tin	Sn	from top
Lead	Pb	to bottom
Copper	Cu	
Silver	Ag	
Gold	Au	
Platinum	Pt	

If you have used aluminium saucepans, you may be surprised to see aluminium placed with the reactive metals high in the reactivity series. In fact, aluminium is so reactive that, as soon as aluminium is exposed to the air, the surface immediately reacts with oxygen to form aluminium oxide. The surface layer of aluminium oxide is unreactive and prevents the metal from showing its true reactivity.

① In some parts of the world, copper is found 'native'. Why is zinc never found native?

② The ancient Egyptians put gold and silver objects into tombs. Explain why people opening the tombs thousands of years later find the objects still in good condition. Why are no iron objects found in the tombs?

③ The following metals are listed in order of reactivity:

sodium > magnesium > zinc > copper

Describe the reactions of these metals with (a) water, (b) dilute hydrochloric acid. Point out how the reactions illustrate the change in reactivity.

FIRST THOUGHTS

50.5 Metals in the Periodic Table

The reactivity series is one way of classifying metals. The Periodic Table of the elements, which you met in Theme C, Topic 11.5, is another.

LOOK AT LINKS
Silicon and germanium are on the borderline between metals and non-metals. They are semiconductors. For the importance of semiconductors in computers, see Theme C, Topic 9.1 and Theme K, Topic 45.

SUMMARY

The Periodic Table is a well-known method of classifying the elements. Group 1 contains the most reactive metals, the alkali metals. Group 2 contains other reactive metals, the alkaline earths. Aluminium is in Group 3. Less reactive metals are in Group 4 and in the block of transition metals. Groups 5, 6, 7 and 0 contain the non-metallic elements.

													Metals			Non-metals			0
1	2			H										3	4	5	6	7	He
Li	Be													B	C	N	O	F	Ne
Na	Mg				Transition metals									Al	Si	P	S	Cl	Ar
K	Ca	Sc	Ti	V	Cr	Mn	Fe	Co	Ni	Cu	Zn	Ga	Ge	As	Se	Br	Kr
Rb	Sr	Y	Zr	Nb	Mo	Tc	Ru	Rh	Pd	Ag	Cd	In	Sn	Sb	Te	I	Xe
Cs	Ba	La	Hf	Ta	W	Re	Os	Ir	Pt	Au	Hg	Tl	Pb	Bi	Po	At	Rn

Table 50.6 ● The Periodic Table

In Table 50.6 you see how a line has been drawn across the Periodic Table to separate the metallic elements (on the left) from the non-metallic elements (on the right). On the far left are the very reactive metals lithium, sodium and potassium. These metals are called the **alkali metals** because their hydroxides are strong alkalis. They form ions of formula M^+ and occupy Group 1 of the Periodic Table. The metals of Group 1 are at the top of the reactivity series. The metals in Group 2 form ions of formula M^{2+}. They are called the **alkaline earths**. They are lower in the reactivity series than Group 1 metals. Aluminium is in Group 3. The less reactive metals, tin and lead, are in Group 4.

The metals in between Group 2 and Group 3 are called the **transition metals**. They include iron, copper, silver, gold and zinc. Transition metals form more than one kind of ion, for example iron forms the ions Fe^{2+} and Fe^{3+}. The ions of transition metals are often coloured. Transition metals and their ions often act as catalysts. Vanadium(V) oxide is used as a catalyst in the manufacture of sulphuric acid. Iron and molybdenum catalyse the manufacture of ammonia.

LOOK AT LINKS
The differences between the physical properties of metallic and non-metallic elements are summarised in Theme C, Table 9.1.

Table 50.7 summarises the differences between the chemical properties of metallic and non-metallic elements.

Table 50.7 ● Chemical properties of metallic and non-metallic elements

Metallic elements	Non-metallic elements
Metals which are high in the reactivity series react with dilute acids to give hydrogen and a salt of the metal	Non-metallic elements do not react with dilute acids
Metallic elements form positive ions, e.g. Na^+, Zn^{2+}, Fe^{3+}	Non-metallic elements form negative ions, e.g. Cl^-, O^{2-}
Metal oxides and hydroxides are bases, e.g. Na_2O, CaO, $NaOH$. If they dissolve in water they give alkaline solutions, e.g. $NaOH$	Many oxides are acids and dissolve in water to give acidic solutions, e.g. CO_2, SO_2. Some oxides are neutral and insoluble, e.g. CO
The chlorides of metals are ionic crystalline solids, e.g. $NaCl$	The chlorides of the non-metals are covalent liquids or gases, e.g. $HCl(g)$, $CCl_4(l)$

SUMMARY

Metallic and non-metallic elements differ in:
- their reactions with acids,
- the acid–base nature of their oxides,
- the nature of their chlorides,
- the type of ions they form.

50.6 Predictions from the reactivity series

FIRST THOUGHTS

The classifications you have been learning about are useful: they enable you to make predictions about chemical reactions.

Competition between metals for oxygen

Aluminium is higher in the reactivity series than iron. When aluminium is heated with iron(III) oxide, a very vigorous, exothermic reaction occurs

$$\text{Aluminium} + \text{Iron(III) oxide} \rightarrow \text{Iron} + \text{Aluminium oxide}$$
$$2Al(s) + Fe_2O_3(s) \rightarrow 2Fe(s) + Al_2O_3(s)$$

This reaction is called the **thermit reaction** (therm = heat). It is used to mend railway lines because the iron formed is molten and can weld the broken lines together (see Figure 50.6A).

Figure 50.6A ● Using the thermit reaction

SUMMARY

Reactive metals displace metals lower down the reactivity series from their compounds.

Displacement reactions

Metals can displace other metals from their salts. A metal which is higher in the reactivity series will displace a metal which is lower in the reactivity series from a salt. Iron will displace lead from a solution of lead nitrate.

CHECKPOINT

❶ Which metal is best for making saucepans: zinc, iron or copper? Explain your choice.

❷ Gold is used for making electrical contacts in space capsules. Explain (a) why gold is a good choice and (b) why it is not more widely used.

❸ A metal, romin, is displaced from a solution of one of its salts by a metal, sarin, A metal, tonin, displaces sarin from a solution of one of its salts. Place the metals in order of reactivity.

❹ The following metals are listed in order of reactivity, with the most reactive first:

Mg, Zn, Fe, Pb, Cu, Hg, Au

List the metals which will:
(a) occur 'native',   (b) react with cold water,
(c) react with steam,   (d) react with dilute acids,
(e) displace copper from copper(II) nitrate solution.

50.7 Uses of metals and alloys

As you read through this section, think about the reasons which lead to the choice of a metal or alloy for a particular purpose.

Metals and alloys have thousands of uses. The purposes for which a metal is used are determined by its physical and chemical properties. Sometimes a manufacturer wants a material for a particular purpose and there is no metal or alloy which fits the bill. Then metallurgists have to invent a new alloy with the right characteristics. Table 50.8 gives some examples.

Table 50.8 ● What are metals and alloys used for?

Metal/Alloy	Characteristics	Uses
Aluminium (Duralumin is an important alloy)	Low density Never corroded Good electrical conductor Good thermal conductor Reflector of light	Aircraft manufacture (Duralumin) Food wrapping Electrical cable Saucepans Car headlamps
Brass (alloy of copper and zinc)	Not corroded Easy to work with Sonorous Yellow colour	Ships' propellers Taps, screws Trumpets Ornaments
Bronze (alloy of copper and tin)	Harder than copper Not corroded Sonorous	Coins, medals Statues, springs Church bells

TRY THIS

To see some beautiful crystals, stand a piece of iron wire in a solution of lead nitrate. **Take care** – remember lead salts are poisonous.

IT'S A FACT

One cm³ of gold can be hammered into enough thin gold leaf to cover a football pitch. Gold foil is used for decorating books, china, etc.

IT'S A FACT

At the launch of the 'Platinum 1990' exhibition, the Johnson Matthey precious metals group presented a £300,000 wedding dress made of platinum. They had made it by lining super-thin platinum foil with paper, shredding the platinum–paper combination into strands and weaving the strands into a fabric. The Japanese designer who made the dress sent instructions to the exhibition, *Ironing the dress is strictly forbidden*.

Table 50.8 ● What are metals and alloys used for? (continued)

Metal/Alloy	Characteristics	Uses
Copper	Good electrical conductor Not corroded	Electrical circuits Water pipes and tanks
Gold	Beautiful colour Never tarnishes Easily worked	Jewellery Electrical contacts Filling teeth
Iron	Hard, strong, inexpensive, rusts	Motor vehicles, trains, ships, buildings
Lead	Dense Unreactive	Protection from radioactivity Was used for all plumbing (Lead is no longer used for water pipes as it reacts very slowly with water)
Magnesium	Bright flame	Distress flares, flash bulbs
Mercury	Liquid at room temperature	Thermometers Electrical contacts Dental amalgam for filling teeth
Silver	Good electrical conductor Good reflector of light Beautiful colour and shine (tarnishes in city air)	Electrical contacts Mirrors Jewellery
Sodium	High thermal capacity	Coolant in nuclear reactors
Solder (alloy of tin and lead)	Low melting point	Joining metals, e.g. in an electrical circuit
Steel (alloy of iron)	Strong	Construction, tools, ball bearings, magnets, cutlery, etc.
Tin	Low in reactivity series	Coating 'tin cans'
Titanium	Low in density Stays strong at high and low temperatures	Supersonic aircraft
Zinc	High in reactivity series	Protection of iron and steel; see Table 50.11.

SUMMARY

Metals and alloys are essential for many different purposes. Metals and alloys are chosen for particular uses because of their physical properties and their chemical reactions.

///////// CHECKPOINT //////////

❶ Name the metal which is used for each of these purposes. Explain why that metal is chosen.
(a) Thermometers
(b) Window frames
(c) Sinks and draining boards
(d) Radiators
(e) Water pipes
(f) Household electrical wiring
(g) Scissor blades

❷ Explain the following:
(a) Some mirrors have aluminium sprayed on to the back of the glass instead of silver, which was used previously.
(b) Although brass is a colourful, shiny material, it is not used for jewellery.
(c) Titanium oxide has replaced lead carbonate as the pigment in white paint.

50.8 **Compounds and the reactivity series**

The stability of metal oxides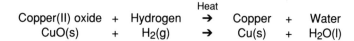

- Reactive metals form compounds readily.
- The compounds of reactive metals are difficult to split up.

Magnesium is a reactive metal, and magnesium oxide is difficult to reduce to magnesium.

Copper is an unreactive metal, and copper(II) oxide is easily reduced to copper. Hydrogen will reduce hot copper(II) oxide to copper.

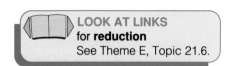

LOOK AT LINKS
for **reduction**
See Theme E, Topic 21.6.

$$\begin{array}{ccccccc} & & & & \text{Heat} & & \\ \text{Copper(II) oxide} & + & \text{Hydrogen} & \rightarrow & \text{Copper} & + & \text{Water} \\ \text{CuO(s)} & + & H_2(g) & \rightarrow & \text{Cu(s)} & + & H_2O(l) \end{array}$$

Carbon is another reducing agent. When heated, it will reduce the oxides of metals which are fairly low in the reactivity series. Reduction by carbon is often the method employed to obtain metals from their ores.

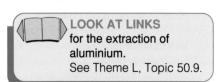

LOOK AT LINKS
for the extraction of aluminium.
See Theme L, Topic 50.9.

$$\begin{array}{ccccccc} & & & & \text{Heat} & & \\ \text{Zinc oxide} & + & \text{Carbon} & \rightarrow & \text{Zinc} & + & \text{Carbon monoxide} \\ \text{ZnO(s)} & + & C(s) & \rightarrow & \text{Zn(s)} & + & \text{CO(g)} \end{array}$$

Neither hydrogen nor carbon will reduce the oxides of metals which are high in the reactivity series. Aluminium is high in the reactivity series; its oxide is difficult to reduce. The method used to obtain aluminium from aluminium oxide is electrolysis.

If a metal is very low in the reactivity series, its oxide will decompose when heated. The oxides of silver and mercury decompose when heated.

The stability of other compounds

When compounds are described as stable it means that they are difficult to decompose (split up) by heat. Table 50.9 shows how the stability of the compounds of a metal is related to the position of the metal in the reactivity series.

The sulphates, carbonates and hydroxides of the most reactive metals are not decomposed by heat. Those of other metals decompose to give oxides.

▼ **SUMMARY**

The oxides of metals low in the reactivity series (e.g. Cu) are easily reduced by carbon and hydrogen. The oxides of metals high in the reactivity series are difficult to reduce.
Compounds of metals low in the reactivity series are decomposed by heat. Compounds of metals high in the reactivity series are stable to heat.

Table 50.9 ● Action of heat on compounds

Cation	Anion				
	Oxide	*Chloride*	*Sulphate*	*Carbonate*	*Hydroxide*
Potassium Sodium Calcium	No decomposition				
Magnesium Aluminium Zinc Iron Lead Copper	No decomposition	No decomposition	Oxide and sulphur trioxide $MO + SO_3$ Some also give SO_2	Oxide and carbon dioxide $MO + CO_2$	Oxide and water $MO + H_2O$
Silver Gold	Metal + oxygen Not formed		Metal + $O_2 + SO_3$	Metal + $O_2 + CO_2$	Do not form hydroxides

Extraction of metals from their ores

One of the important jobs which chemists do is to find ways of extracting metals from the rocks of the Earth's crust.

Metals are found in rocks in the Earth's crust. A few metals, such as gold and copper, occur as the free metal, uncombined. They are said to occur 'native'. Only metals which are very unreactive can withstand the action of air and water for thousands of years without being converted into compounds. Most metals occur as compounds.

Rock containing the metal compound is mined. Then machines are used to crush and grind the rock. Next a chemical method must be found for extracting the metal. All these stages cost money. If the rock contains enough of the metal compound to make it profitable to extract the metal, the rock is called an ore.

Figure 50.9A ● 'Native' copper

The method used to extract a metal from its ore depends on the position of the metal in the reactivity series (see Table 50.10).

Table 50.10 ● Methods used for the extraction of metals

Metal	Method
Potassium Sodium Calcium Magnesium	The anhydrous chloride is melted and electrolysed
Aluminium	The anhydrous oxide is melted and electrolysed
Zinc Iron Copper Lead	Found as sulphides and oxides. The sulphides are roasted to give oxides; the oxides are reduced with carbon
Silver Gold	Found 'native' (as the free metal)

Sodium

Sodium is obtained by the electrolysis of molten dry sodium chloride. The same method is used for potassium, calcium and magnesium. This is an expensive method of obtaining metals because of the cost of the electricity consumed.

Aluminium – the 'newcomer' among metals ▨

Aluminium is mined as **bauxite**, an ore which contains aluminium oxide, $Al_2O_3.2H_2O$. This ore is very plentiful, yet aluminium was not extracted from it until 1825. Another 60 years passed before a commercial method of extracting the metal was invented. *What was the problem?*

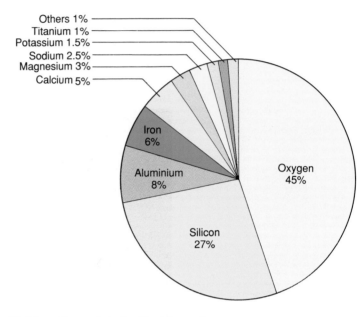

Others 1%
Titanium 1%
Potassium 1.5%
Sodium 2.5%
Magnesium 3%
Calcium 5%
Iron 6%
Aluminium 8%
Oxygen 45%
Silicon 27%

Figure 50.9B ● Elements in the Earth's crust

A Danish scientist called Hans Christian Oersted succeeded in obtaining aluminium from aluminium oxide in 1825. First he made aluminium chloride from aluminium oxide. Then he used potassium amalgam (an alloy of potassium and mercury) to displace aluminium from aluminium chloride.

The German chemist Friedrich Wöhler altered the method somewhat. He used potassium (instead of potassium amalgam).

A French chemist, Henri Sainte-Claire Déville, tackled the problem of scaling up the reaction. He used sodium in the displacement reaction. In 1860 he succeeded in making the reaction yield aluminium on a large scale. The price of aluminium tumbled. Instead of being an expensive curiosity, it became a useful commodity. With its exceptional properties, aluminium soon found new uses, and the demand for the new metal increased.

Aluminium was expensive because of the cost of the sodium used in its extraction. Chemists were keen to find a less costly method of extracting the new metal. Many thought it should be possible to obtain aluminium by electrolysing molten aluminium oxide. The difficulty was the high melting point, 2050 °C, which made it impossible to keep the compound molten while a current was passed through it.

The big breakthrough came in 1886. Two young chemists working thousands of miles apart made the discovery at the same time. An American called Charles Martin Hall, aged 21, and a Frenchman called Paul Héroult, aged 23, discovered that they could obtain a solution of aluminium oxide by dissolving it in molten cryolite, Na_3AlF_6, at 700 °C. On passing electricity through the melt, the two men succeeded in obtaining aluminium. Their method is still used. The Hall-Héroult cell is shown in Figure 50.9C. Anhydrous pure aluminium oxide must be obtained from the ore and then electrolysed in the cell.

SCIENCE AT WORK

In 1985, a firm in Northampton had the idea of buying empty aluminium drink cans for recycling. They installed machines which pay 1p for every two aluminium cans fed in but not for steel cans. *How can the machines tell the difference between aluminium cans and steel cans?*

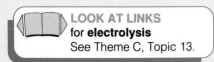

LOOK AT LINKS
for **electrolysis**
See Theme C, Topic 13.

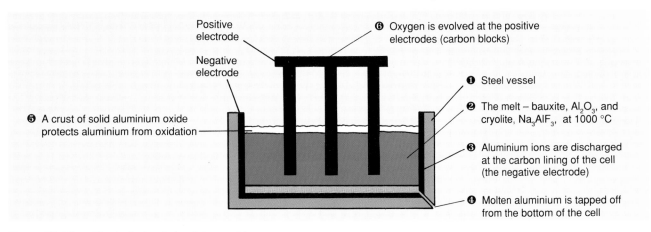

Positive electrode

Negative electrode

❻ Oxygen is evolved at the positive electrodes (carbon blocks)

❶ Steel vessel

❷ The melt – bauxite, Al_2O_3, and cryolite, Na_3AlF_3, at 1000 °C

❸ Aluminium ions are discharged at the carbon lining of the cell (the negative electrode)

❺ A crust of solid aluminium oxide protects aluminium from oxidation

❹ Molten aluminium is tapped off from the bottom of the cell

Figure 50.9C ● Electrolysis of aluminium oxide

Iron

Siting a Blast Furnace
(program)

Your task is to site a blast furnace on an imaginary island. *What factors do you take into account in siting the furnace?*

Many countries have plentiful resources of iron ores, **haematite**, Fe_2O_3, **magnetite**, Fe_3O_4 and **iron pyrites**, FeS_2. The sulphide ore is roasted in air to convert it to an oxide. The oxide ores are reduced to iron in a **blast furnace** (Figure 50.9D). Iron ore and coke and limestone are fed into the furnace. Iron ores and limestone are plentiful resources. Coke is made by heating coal.

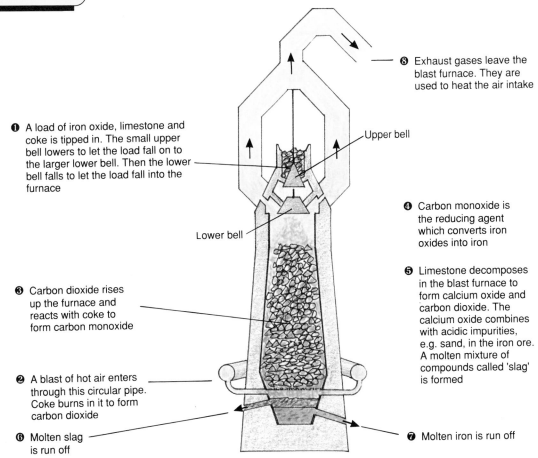

❽ Exhaust gases leave the blast furnace. They are used to heat the air intake

❶ A load of iron oxide, limestone and coke is tipped in. The small upper bell lowers to let the load fall on to the larger lower bell. Then the lower bell falls to let the load fall into the furnace

Upper bell

Lower bell

❹ Carbon monoxide is the reducing agent which converts iron oxides into iron

❺ Limestone decomposes in the blast furnace to form calcium oxide and carbon dioxide. The calcium oxide combines with acidic impurities, e.g. sand, in the iron ore. A molten mixture of compounds called 'slag' is formed

❸ Carbon dioxide rises up the furnace and reacts with coke to form carbon monoxide

❷ A blast of hot air enters through this circular pipe. Coke burns in it to form carbon dioxide

❻ Molten slag is run off

❼ Molten iron is run off

Figure 50.9D ● A blast furnace is a tower of steel plates lined with heat-resistant bricks. It is about 50 m high.

The chemical reactions which take place in the blast furnace are:

Step 2

$$\text{Carbon (coke)} + \text{Oxygen} \xrightarrow{\text{Heat}} \text{Carbon dioxide}$$
$$C(s) + O_2(g) \rightarrow CO_2(g)$$

Step 3

$$\text{Carbon dioxide} + \text{Carbon (coke)} \xrightarrow{\text{Heat}} \text{Carbon monoxide}$$
$$CO_2(g) + C(s) \rightarrow 2CO(g)$$

Step 4

$$\text{Iron(III) oxide} + \text{Carbon monoxide} \xrightarrow{\text{Heat}} \text{Iron} + \text{Carbon dioxide}$$
$$Fe_2O_3(s) + 3CO(g) \rightarrow 2Fe(s) + 3CO_2(g)$$

Step 5

(a)
$$\text{Calcium carbonate (limestone)} \xrightarrow{\text{Heat}} \text{Calcium oxide} + \text{Carbon dioxide}$$
$$CaCO_3(s) \rightarrow CaO(s) + CO_2(g)$$

(b)
$$\text{Calcium oxide} + \text{Silicon(IV) oxide (sand)} \xrightarrow{\text{Heat}} \text{Calcium silicate(slag)}$$
$$CaO(s) + SiO_2(s) \rightarrow CaSiO_3(l)$$

The blast furnace runs continuously. The raw materials are fed in at the top, and molten iron and molten slag are run off separately at the bottom. The slag is used in foundations by builders and road-makers. The process is much cheaper to run than an electrolytic method. With the raw materials readily available and the cost of extraction low, iron is cheaper than other metals.

Electrons flow through the external circuit from the positive electrode to the negative electrode

❶ The electrolyte is copper(II) sulphate solution

❷ The negative electrode is a strip of pure copper. Copper ions are discharged and copper atoms are deposited on the electrode. The strip of pure copper becomes thicker $Cu^{2+}(aq) + 2e^- \rightarrow Cu(s)$

❸ The positive electrode is a lump of impure copper. Copper atoms supply electrons to this electrode and become copper ions which enter the solution. The lump of impure copper becomes smaller $Cu(s) \rightarrow Cu^{2+}(aq) + 2e^-$

❹ Anode sludge, this is the undissolved remains of the lump of impure copper

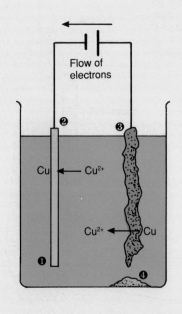

Figure 50.9E ● Purification of copper

Copper

Copper is low in the reactivity series. It is found 'native' (uncombined) in some parts of the world. More often, it is mined as the sulphide. This is roasted in air to give impure copper. Pure copper is obtained from this by the **electrolytic** method shown in Figure 50.9E.

After the cell has been running for a week, the negative electrode becomes very thick. It is lifted out of the cell, and replaced by a new thin sheet of copper. When all the copper has dissolved out of the positive electrode, a new piece of impure copper is substituted.

Other metals are present as impurities in copper ores. Iron and zinc are more reactive than copper, and their ions therefore stay in solution while copper ions are

SUMMARY

The method used for extracting a metal from its ores depends on the position of the metal in the reactivity series. Very reactive metals, such as sodium, are obtained by electrolysis of a molten compound. Less reactive metals, such as iron, are obtained by reducing the oxide with elements such as carbon or hydrogen. The metals at the bottom of the reactivity series occur 'native'.

discharged. Silver and gold are less reactive than copper. They do not dissolve and are therefore present in the anode sludge. They can be extracted from this residue.

Silver and Gold

Silver and gold, are found 'native'. A new deposit of gold was discovered in the Sperrin mountains Northern Ireland in 1982.

CHECKPOINT

❶ The Emperor Napoleon invested in the French research on new methods of obtaining aluminium. He was interested in the possibility of aluminium suits of armour for his soldiers. What advantage would aluminium armour have had over iron or steel?

❷ (a) Arrange in order of the reactivity series the metals copper, iron, zinc, gold and silver.
   (b) Arrange the same metals in order of their readiness to form ions, that is, the ease with which the reaction $M(s) \rightarrow M^{n+}(aq) + ne^-$ takes place.
   (c) Arrange the same metals in order of the ease of discharging their ions, that is, the ease with which the reaction $M^{n+}(aq) + ne^- \rightarrow M(s)$ takes place.
   (d) Refer to Figure 50.9E showing the electrolytic purification of copper. Use your answers to (b) and (c) to explain why copper is deposited on the negative electrode but iron, zinc, gold and silver are not.

❸ Explain why (a) the human race started using copper, silver and gold long before iron was known and (b) iron tools were a big improvement on tools made from other metals.

❹ Give the names of metals which fit the descriptions A, B, C, D and E.
   A Reacts immediately with air to form a layer of oxide and then reacts no further.
   B Reacts violently with water to form an alkaline solution.
   C Reacts slowly with cold water and rapidly with steam.
   D Is a reddish-gold coloured metal which does not react with dilute hydrochloric acid.
   E Can be obtained by heating its oxide with carbon.

FIRST THOUGHTS

50.10 Iron and steel

The machines that manufacture our possessions, our means of transport and the frameworks of our buildings: all these depend on the strength of steel.

The iron that comes out of the blast furnace is called **cast iron** (or pig iron). It contains three to four per cent carbon. The carbon content makes it brittle, and cast iron cannot be bent without snapping. The impurity makes the melting point lower than that of pure iron so that cast iron is easier to cast – to melt and mould – than pure iron. Cast iron expands slightly as it solidifies. This helps it to flow into all the corners of a mould and reproduce the shape exactly. By casting, objects with complicated shapes can be made, for example the cylinder block of a car engine (which contains the cylinders in which the combustion of petrol vapour in air takes place).

Figure 50.10A ● Wrought iron

Iron which contains less than 0.25% carbon is called wrought iron. Wrought iron is strong and easily worked (Figure 50.10A). Nowadays, mild steel has replaced wrought iron.

Steel

Steel is made by reducing the carbon content of cast iron, which makes it brittle, to less than one per cent. Carbon is burnt off as its oxides, the gases carbon monoxide, CO, and carbon dioxide, CO_2. Iron is less easily oxidised. The sulphur, phosphorus and silicon in the iron are also converted into acidic oxides. These are not gases, and a base, such as calcium oxide, must be added to remove them. The base and the acidic oxides combine to form a slag (a mixture of compounds of low melting point).

Figure 50.10B shows a basic oxygen furnace. In it, cast iron is converted into steel. One converter can produce 150–300 tonnes of steel in an hour.

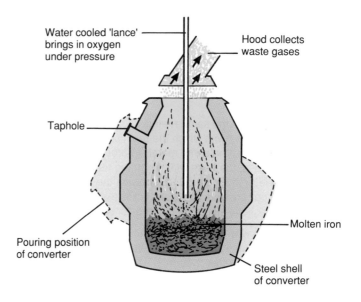

Water cooled 'lance' brings in oxygen under pressure

Hood collects waste gases

Taphole

Molten iron

Pouring position of converter

Steel shell of converter

Figure 50.10B ● A basic oxygen furnace holding 150–300 tonnes of steel

There are various types of steel. They differ in their carbon content and are used for different purposes. Low-carbon steel (mild steel) is pliable; high-carbon steel is hard.

Alloy steels

Many elements are alloyed with iron and carbon to give alloy steels with different properties. They all have different uses, for example nickel and chromium give stainless steel, manganese and molybdenum increase strength, and vanadium increases springiness.

SUMMARY

Cast iron (up to 4% carbon) is easy to mould, but is brittle. Wrought iron (the purest form of iron) is easily worked without breaking. Low-carbon steel (mild steel) is pliable; high-carbon steel is hard. Alloy steels contain other elements in addition to iron and carbon. Different steels are suited to different uses.

CHECKPOINT

❶ What is the difference between cast iron and wrought iron in (a) composition (b) strength and (c) ease of moulding? Name two objects made from cast iron and two objects made from wrought iron.

50.11 Rusting of iron and steel

> The rusting of iron is an expensive nuisance. Replacing rusted iron and steel structures costs the UK £500 million a year. In this section we look at some remedies.

Iron and most kinds of steel rust. Rust is hydrated iron(III) oxide, $Fe_2O_3 \cdot nH_2O$ (n, the number of water molecules in the formula, varies).

Some of the methods which are used to protect iron and steel against rusting are listed in Table 50.11. Some methods use a coating of some substance which excludes water and air. Other methods work by sacrificing a metal which is more reactive than iron.

Figure 50.11A ● Rust protection

(a) Paint protects the car

(b) Chromium plating protects the bicycle handlebars

(c) Galvanised steel girders

(d) Zinc bars protect the ship's hull

Table 50.11 ● Rust prevention

Method	Where it is used	Comment
A coat of paint	Ships, bridges, cars, other large objects (see Figure 50.11A(a))	If the paint is scratched, the exposed iron starts to rust. Corrosion can spread to the iron underneath the paintwork which is still sound.
A film of oil or grease	Moving parts of machinery, e.g. car engines	The film of oil or grease must be renewed frequently.
A coat of plastic	Kitchenware, e.g. draining rack	If the plastic is torn, the iron starts to rust.
Chromium plating	Kettles, cycle handlebars (see Figure 50.11A(b))	The layer of chromium protects the iron beneath it and also gives a decorative finish. It is applied by electroplating.
Galvanising (zinc plating)	Galvanised steel girders are used in the construction of buildings and bridges (see Figure 50.11A(c))	Zinc is above iron in the reactivity series: zinc will corrode in preference to iron. Even if the layer of zinc is scratched, as long as some zinc remains, the iron underneath does not rust. Zinc cannot be used for food cans because zinc and its compounds are poisonous.
Tin plating	Food cans	Tin is below iron in the reactivity series. If the layer of tin is scratched, the iron beneath it starts to rust.
Stainless steel	Cutlery, car accessories, e.g. radiator grille	Steel containing chromium (10–25%) or nickel (10–20%) does not rust.
Sacrificial protection	Ships (see Figure 50.11A(d))	Blocks of zinc are attached to the hulls of ships below the waterline. Being above iron in the reactivity series, zinc corrodes in preference to iron. The zinc blocks are sacrificed to protect the iron. As long as there is some zinc left, it protects the hull from rusting. The zinc blocks must be replaced.

LOOK AT LINKS
The conditions which make iron rust are water and air and acidity. If salts are present, rusting is accelerated.
See Theme E, Topic 21.9.

The Earth contains huge deposits of iron ores. We need iron for our machinery and for our means of transport. During the twentieth century, we have used more metal than in all the previous centuries put together. If we keep on mining iron ores at the present rate, the Earth's resources may one day be exhausted. We allow tonnes of iron and steel to rust every year. We throw tonnes of used iron and steel objects on the scrap heap. The Earth's iron deposits will last longer if we take the trouble to collect scrap iron and steel and recycle it, that is, melt it down and reuse it.

SUMMARY

Exposure to air and water in slightly acidic conditions makes iron and steel rust. Some of the treatments for protecting iron and steel from rusting are:
• oil or grease,
• a protective coat of another metal, e.g. chromium, zinc, tin,
• alloying with nickel and chromium,
• attaching a more reactive metal, e.g. magnesium or zinc, to be sacrificed.

Figure 50.11B ● Scrap iron dump

CHECKPOINT

❶ Say how the rusting of iron is prevented:
(a) in a bicycle chain,
(b) in a food can,
(c) in parts of a ship above the water line,
(d) in parts of a ship below the water line,
(e) in a galvanised iron roof.

❷ 'The Industrial Revolution would not have been possible without steel.' Say whether or not you agree with this statement. Give your reasons.

❸ The map opposite shows possible sites, A, B, C and D, for a steelworks. Say which site you think is the best, and explain your choice. You will have to consider the need for:
• iron ore, coke (from coal), limestone,
• a work-force,
• transporting iron and steel to customers,
• removing slag.

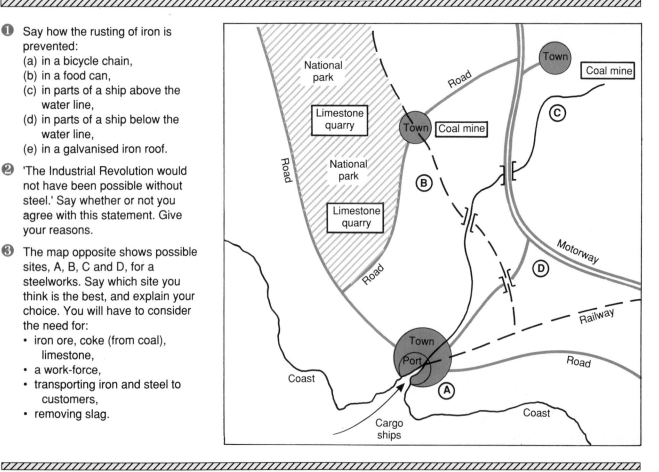

50.12 Aluminium

Aluminium is the most plentiful metal in the Earth's crust, yet aluminium was not manufactured until the nineteenth century. The twentieth century has seen aluminium finding more and more vitally important uses.

LOOK AT LINKS
for methods of reducing heat loss.
See Theme B, Topic 7.8.

Uses of aluminium

Aluminium is a metal with thousands of applications. Some of these are listed in Table 50.12. Pure aluminium is not a very strong metal. Its alloys, such as duralumin (which contains copper and magnesium), are used when strength is needed.

Table 50.12 ● Some uses of aluminium and its alloys

Property	Use for aluminium which depends on this property
Never corroded (except by bases)	Door frames and window frames are often made of aluminium. 'Anodised aluminium' is used. The thickness of the protective layer of aluminium oxide has been increased by anodising (making it the positive electrode in an electrolytic cell).
Low density	Packaging food: milk bottle tops, food containers, baking foil. The low density and resistance to corrosion make aluminium ideal for aircraft manufacture. Alloys such as duralumin are used because they are stronger than aluminium.
Good electrical conductor	Used for overhead cables. The advantage over copper is that aluminium cables are lighter and need less massive pylons to carry them.
Reflects light when polished	Car headlamp reflectors
Good thermal conductor	Saucepans, etc.
Reflects heat when highly polished	Highly polished aluminium reflects heat and can be used as a thermal blanket. Aluminium blankets are used to wrap premature babies. They keep the baby warm by reflecting heat back to the body. Firefighters wear aluminium fabric suits to reflect heat away from their bodies.

The cost to the environment

Bauxite is found near the surface in Australia, Jamaica, Brazil and other countries. The ore is obtained by open cast mining (Figure 50.12A). A layer of earth 1 m to 60 m thick is excavated, and the landscape is devastated. In some places, mining companies have spent money on restoring the landscape after they have finished working a deposit.

Figure 50.12A ● An open cast bauxite mine

Pure aluminium oxide must be extracted from bauxite before it can be electrolysed. Iron(III) oxide, which is red, is one of the impurities in bauxite. The waste produced in the extraction process is an alkaline liquid containing a suspension of iron(III) oxide. It is pumped into vast red mud ponds.

Jamaica has a land area of 11 000 km². Every year, 12 km² of red mud are created. The Jamaicans are worried about the loss of land. Even when it dries out, red mud is not firm enough to build on. They also worry about the danger of alkali seeping into the water supply. The waste cannot be pumped into the sea because it would harm the fish.

Purified aluminium oxide is shipped to an aluminium plant. The electrolytic method of extracting aluminium is expensive to run because of the electricity it consumes. Aluminium plants are often built in areas which have hydroelectric power (electricity from water-driven generators). This is relatively cheap electricity. The waterfalls and fast-flowing rivers which provide hydroelectric power are found in areas of natural beauty. Local residents often object to the siting of aluminium plants in such beauty spots.

There may be other difficulties over hydroelectric power. Purified aluminium oxide has to be transported to a remote area and aluminium has to be transported away. If there are not enough local workers, a workforce may have to be brought into the area and provided with housing. Often it pays to build an aluminium plant in an area which has a big population and good transport, even if the cost of electricity is higher.

The exhaust gases from aluminium plants contain fluorides from the electrolyte. Before leaving the chimney, the exhaust gases are 'scrubbed' with water. The waste water, which contains fluoride, is discharged into rivers. The remaining exhaust gases are discharged into the atmosphere through tall chimneys. In the past, fluoride emissions have been known to pollute agricultural land, killing grass and causing lameness in cattle. Farmers sued for the damage to their cattle. Aluminium plants now take more care to control fluoride emission.

IT
Industrial Chemistry
(program)

Use the program to investigate:
• The making of sulphuric acid.
• The factors involved in siting an aluminium plant.
Make a list of the factors involved in both production processes.

SUMMARY

Aluminium has brought us many benefits. There is, however, a cost to the environment. The open cast mining of bauxite spoils the landscape. The purification creates unsightly red mud ponds. The extraction can cause pollution through fluoride emission.

Factors which decide the siting of aluminium plants include
• the cost of electricity,
• the cost of transporting the raw material and the product,
• the availability of a workforce.

Figure 50.12B ● Recycling aluminium

① The map below shows possible sites for aluminium plants. Give the advantages and disadvantages of each of the sites A, B, and C. Say which you think is the best site.

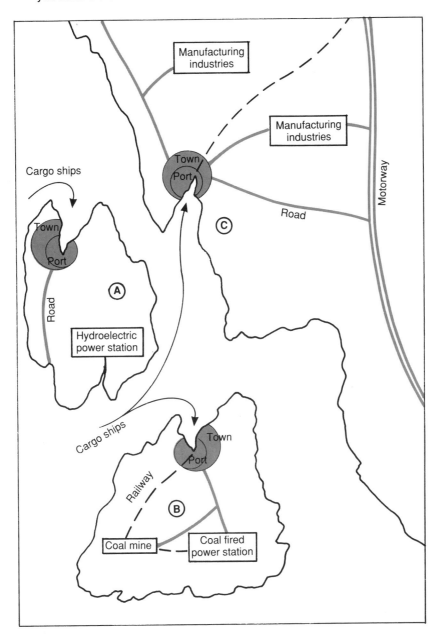

② The percentages of some metals recycled in the UK are shown below.
(a) Explain what 'recycled' means.
(b) Plot the figures as a bar chart or as a pie chart.
(c) Why is lead easy to recycle?
(d) How can iron be separated from other metals for recycling?
(e) What resources are saved by recycling aluminium?

Metal	Aluminium	Zinc	Iron	Tin	Lead	Copper
Percentage recycled	28	30	50	30	56	19

TOPIC 51

THE CHEMICAL INDUSTRY

The UK quarries 90 million tonnes of limestone and chalk each year. Most of it is used in the building industry.

RESOURCE
-ACTIVITY-
PACK

Limestone

Figure 51.1A ● Concrete and glass

All around you, you can see buildings made of concrete, steel and glass. Concrete is used in the construction of all kinds of homes, schools, factories, skyscrapers, power stations and reservoirs. All our forms of transport depend on the concrete which is used in roads and bridges, docks and airport runways. For extra strength, for example in bridges, reinforced concrete is strengthened by steel supports.

The starting point in the manufacture of concrete is limestone or chalk. Both these minerals are forms of calcium carbonate. First, limestone or chalk is used with shale or clay to make cement. A small percentage of calcium sulphate (gypsum) is also needed (see Figure 51.1B). Figure 51.1C shows how concrete is made from cement.

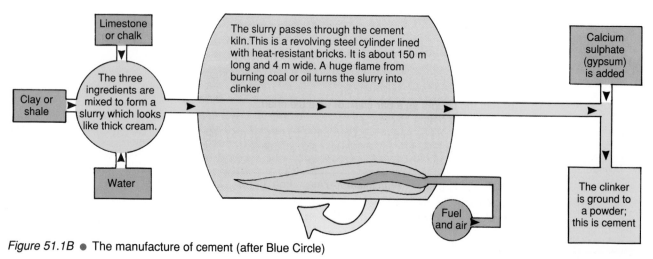

Figure 51.1B ● The manufacture of cement (after Blue Circle)

Limestone or chalk

Clay or shale

The three ingredients are mixed to form a slurry which looks like thick cream.

Water

The slurry passes through the cement kiln. This is a revolving steel cylinder lined with heat-resistant bricks. It is about 150 m long and 4 m wide. A huge flame from burning coal or oil turns the slurry into clinker

Fuel and air

Calcium sulphate (gypsum) is added

The clinker is ground to a powder; this is cement

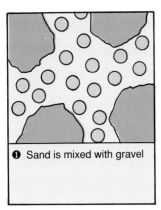
❶ Sand is mixed with gravel

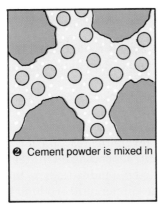
❷ Cement powder is mixed in

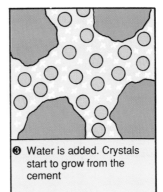
❸ Water is added. Crystals start to grow from the cement

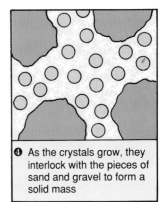
❹ As the crystals grow, they interlock with the pieces of sand and gravel to form a solid mass

Figure 51.1C ● Making concrete (after Blue Circle)

Chalk and limestone are calcium carbonate, $CaCO_3$. Clay and shale consist largely of silicon(IV) oxide, SiO_2, and aluminium oxide, Al_2O_3, with some other compounds. The chemical reactions which occur between them produce cement, which consists chiefly of calcium silicate, $CaSiO_3$, and calcium aluminate, $CaAl_2O_4$. A little calcium sulphate (gypsum) is added to slow down the rate at which concrete sets.

The UK has large deposits of both limestone and chalk. Limestone is quarried by blasting a hillside with an explosive. Chalk is dug out by mechanical excavators. Both methods devastate the landscape. It happens that these minerals often occur in regions of great natural beauty (Figure 51.1D). We have to balance the damage to our countryside against the useful materials which industry can obtain from limestone and chalk. Mining companies are required to restore the countryside after they exhaust a deposit of limestone or chalk (Figure 51.1E). Limestone is used in the manufacture of iron in blast furnaces, in the manufacture of glass and in the manufacture of lime.

SUMMARY

Concrete is a strong and versatile construction material. It is made from cement, sand, gravel and water. Cement is made from chalk or limestone and clay or shale. The quarrying of vast quantities of these raw materials creates environmental problems.

Figure 51.1D ● A limestone quarry

Figure 51.1E ● Restoring the scenery

Lime

When calcium carbonate is heated strongly, it dissociates (splits up) to give calcium oxide and carbon dioxide.

LOOK AT LINKS
for the use of lime in agriculture.
See Theme D, Topic 16.2.

LOOK AT LINKS
You can find out about the use of carbon dioxide in fire-extinguishers in Theme E, Topic 21.8.

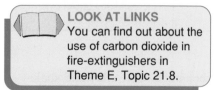

Calcium carbonate $\rightleftharpoons$ Calcium oxide + Carbon dioxide
$$CaCO_3(s) \rightleftharpoons CaO(s) + CO_2(g)$$

The reaction is a **reversible** reaction: it can go from left to right and also from right to left, depending on the temperature and the pressure. The reaction is carried out industrially in towers called **lime kilns** (see Figure 51.1F). At the temperature of a lime kiln, 1000 °C, calcium carbonate dissociates. The through draft of air carries away carbon dioxide as it is formed and prevents it from recombining with calcium oxide. Otherwise there would be an acid–base reaction between the acid gas, carbon dioxide, and the base, calcium oxide.

Figure 51.1G ● Enjoying a 'carbonated' drink

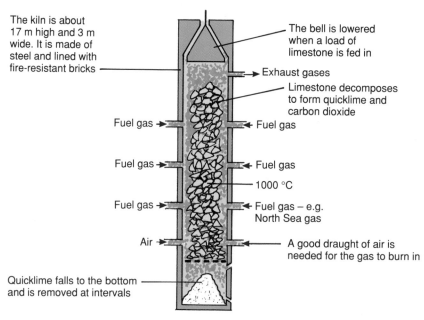

The kiln is about 17 m high and 3 m wide. It is made of steel and lined with fire-resistant bricks

The bell is lowered when a load of limestone is fed in

Exhaust gases

Limestone decomposes to form quicklime and carbon dioxide

Fuel gas → ← Fuel gas

Fuel gas → ← Fuel gas

1000 °C

Fuel gas → ← Fuel gas – e.g. North Sea gas

Air → A good draught of air is needed for the gas to burn in

Quicklime falls to the bottom and is removed at intervals

Figure 51.1F ● A lime kiln

Calcium oxide is called **lime** or **quicklime**. It reacts with water to form calcium hydroxide, which is called **slaked lime**.

Calcium oxide + Water → Calcium hydroxide
$$CaO(s) + H_2O(l) \rightarrow Ca(OH)_2(s)$$

On building sites, calcium hydroxide, slaked lime, is mixed with sand to give **mortar**. Mortar is used to hold bricks together. As mortar is exposed to the air, it becomes gradually harder as it reacts with carbon dioxide in the air to form calcium carbonate.

Calcium oxide, lime, is used in agriculture. Farmers spread it on fields to neutralise excess acid in soils.

The carbon dioxide produced in lime kilns is also useful. Carbon dioxide dissolves to a slight extent in water to give a solution of the weak acid, carbonic acid, H_2CO_3. Under pressure, the solubility of carbon dioxide increases. The basis of the soft drinks industry is dissolving carbon dioxide in water under pressure, and adding flavourings. When the cap is taken off a bottle, the pressure is decreased, and carbon dioxide comes out of solution.

SUMMARY

When calcium carbonate (limestone) is heated in lime kilns, calcium oxide (quicklime) and carbon dioxide are produced. On building sites, calcium oxide is used to make mortar. On farms, it is used to neutralise excessive acidity of soils. Carbon dioxide is used in the soft drinks industry and as a fire extinguisher.

Glass

Glass is a mixture of calcium silicate, $CaSiO_3$, and sodium silicate, Na_2SiO_3. In structure, it resembles silicon(IV) oxide, SiO_2, (sand), which is a crystalline substance with a macromolecular structure (see Figure 51.1H). In glass, many of the Si—O bonds have been broken, and the structure is less regular. X-rays show that glass does not have the orderly packing of atoms found in other solids. Glass is neither a liquid nor a crystalline solid. It is a **supercooled liquid**: it appears to be solid, but has no sharp melting point.

● *Some new uses for glass*

Craftsmen worked with glass for thousands of years without knowing anything about its structure. When chemists began to study glass, they made many advances in glass technology. New types of glass were invented. Some of these are described in this section.

Pyrex® glass will stand sudden changes in temperature without cracking. It is made by adding boron oxide during the manufacture of glass.

Window glass consists of plates of glass which are the same thickness all over. Formerly, plates were made by grinding a sheet of glass to the required thickness and smoothness. In the process, 30% of the sheet was wasted. The Pilkington Glass Company invented the **float glass** process. Molten glass flows on to a bath of molten tin (Figure 51.1I). As the glass cools and solidifies, the top and bottom surfaces are both perfectly smooth and planar. While it is still soft, the glass is rolled to the required thickness and then cut into sections.

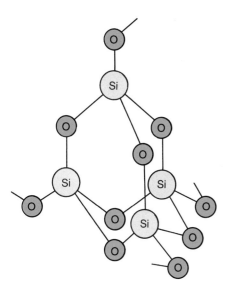

Figure 51.1H ● The structure of silicon(IV) oxide (silica)

Figure 51.1I ● Float glass

Photosensitive glass is used in sunglasses which darken in bright light and lighten again when the light fades. The glass includes silver chloride.

Glass ceramic is almost unbreakable. It is made by heating photosensitive glass in a furnace. Glass ceramic is used in ovenware, electrical insulation, the nose cones of space rockets and the tiles of space shuttles.

Soluble glass has important uses. In many tropical countries, the disease, **bilharzia** (or schistosomiasis) is a blight. The snails which carry the disease can be killed by copper salts in quite low concentrations. The copper compounds can be incorporated into a soluble glass. Pellets of the copper-containing soluble glass can be put into the water. As they dissolve, they release copper compounds gradually into the snail-infested water. To make a soluble glass, phosphorus(V) oxide, P_2O_5, is used instead of silicon(IV) oxide.

FIRST THOUGHTS

The recipe for glass is 4500 years old. Egyptians discovered it when they melted sand with limestone and sodium carbonate. To their surprise, they obtained a transparent material, glass. Egypt is one of the few countries where sodium carbonate occurs naturally.

LOOK AT LINKS
for **bilharzia**
See Theme G, Topic 29.3.

SUMMARY

The glass industry makes:
- Pyrex® glass,
- plate glass,
- light-sensitive glass,
- glass ceramic,
- soluble glass.

CHECKPOINT

① (a) Why must a bottle of a carbonated soft drink have a well-fitting cap?
(b) Why can you not see bubbles inside the closed bottle?
(c) Why can you see bubbles when the bottle is opened?

② 'Spreading calcium hydroxide on soil reduces the acidity of the soil.' Describe an experiment which you could do to check whether this statement is true.

③ 'Mortar reacts with the air to form calcium carbonate.' Describe experiments which you could do on new mortar and old mortar to find out whether this statement is true.

FIRST THOUGHTS

o
o
o

51.2 Agricultural chemicals

In Theme G, Topic 29.7, we saw the importance to farmers of synthetic fertilisers. In this topic, we look at the role of the chemical industry in supplying these fertilisers.

Making ammonia

The first nitrogen-containing fertiliser which the farmers of Europe used was sodium nitrate. They had to import it across the Atlantic from Chile. There were disadvantages to this practice. European chemists tackled the problem of making nitrogenous fertilisers. Nitrogen was the obvious starting material because every country has plenty of it in the air. Making nitrogen combine with other elements proved to be a problem. The problem was solved by a German chemist called Fritz Haber. In 1908, he succeeded in combining nitrogen with hydrogen to form ammonia

$$\text{Nitrogen} + \text{Hydrogen} \rightleftharpoons \text{Ammonia}$$
$$N_2(g) + 3H_2(g) \rightleftharpoons 2NH_3(g)$$

This reaction is reversible: it takes place from right to left as well as from left to right. Some of the ammonia formed dissociates (splits up) into nitrogen and hydrogen. A mixture of nitrogen, hydrogen and ammonia is formed. To increase the percentage of ammonia formed in the reaction, a high pressure and a low temperature are used. A low temperature reduces the dissociation of ammonia, but it also makes the reaction very slow. Modern industrial plants use a compromise temperature and speed up the reaction by means of a catalyst. (The buildings and equipment in which a manufacturing process is carried out are called a **plant**.) The yield of ammonia is about 10%. Ammonia is condensed out of the mixture. With a boiling point of –33 °C, which is higher than that of most gases, ammonia is easily liquefied. The nitrogen and hydrogen which have not reacted are recycled through the plant (see Figure 51.2A).

The hydrogen for the Haber process is obtained from natural gas. The process takes place in a number of stages. The overall reaction is:

$$\text{Natural gas (methane)} + \text{Steam} \rightarrow \text{Hydrogen} + \text{Carbon monoxide}$$
$$CH_4(g) + H_2O(g) \rightarrow 3H_2(g) + CO(g)$$

Carbon monoxide is oxidised to carbon dioxide and removed to leave hydrogen.

▼ SUMMARY

The starting point in the manufacture of fertilisers is the manufacture of ammonia from nitrogen and hydrogen by the Haber process. Hydrogen is obtained from natural gas, and nitrogen is obtained from air.

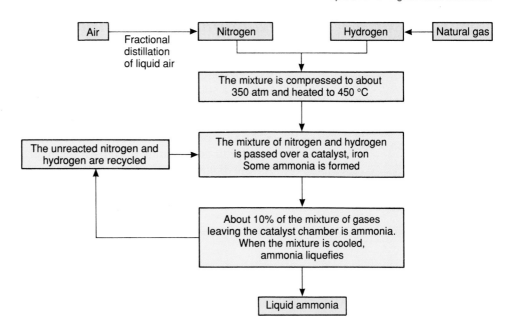

Figure 51.2A ● A flow diagram for the Haber process

● *Making fertilisers from ammonia*

A concentrated solution of ammonia can be used as a fertiliser. It is easier to store solid fertilisers, such as ammonium salts (see Figure 51.2D). Being a base, ammonia is neutralised by acids to yield ammonium salts

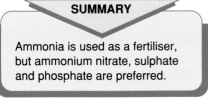

Ammonia + Nitric acid → Ammonium nitrate
$NH_3(aq)$ + $HNO_3(aq)$ → $NH_4NO_3(aq)$

Ammonia + Sulphuric acid → Ammonium sulphate
$2NH_3(aq)$ + $H_2SO_4(aq)$ → $(NH_4)_2SO_4(aq)$

Ammonia + Phosphoric acid → Ammonium phosphate
$3NH_3(aq)$ + $H_3PO_4(aq)$ → $(NH_4)_3PO_4(aq)$

SUMMARY

Ammonia is used as a fertiliser, but ammonium nitrate, sulphate and phosphate are preferred.

Manufacture of nitric acid

Nitric acid is made by the oxidation of ammonia (see Figure 51.2B).

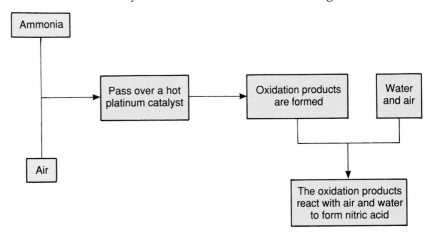

Figure 51.2B ● A flow diagram for the manufacture of nitric acid

SUMMARY

Nitric acid is made by the oxidation of ammonia.

In addition to its importance in the fertiliser industry, nitric acid is used in the manufacture of explosives, such as TNT (trinitrotoluene), and dyes.

Manufacture of sulphuric acid

Sulphuric acid is made by the **contact process**. Sulphur dioxide and oxygen combine in contact with a catalyst, vanadium(V) oxide. Air is used as a source of oxygen. Sulphur dioxide is obtained by:
- Burning sulphur (deposits of sulphur occur in many countries).
- As a by-product of the extraction of metals from sulphide ores.
- As a by-product of the removal of unwanted, unpleasant-smelling sulphur compounds from petroleum oil and natural gas.

A flow diagram for the industrial process is shown in Figure 51.2C.

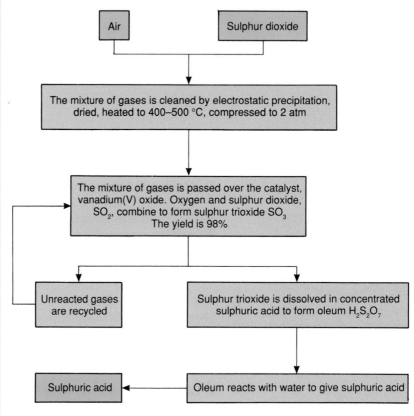

Figure 51.2C ● The contact process

Sulphur trioxide reacts with water to give sulphuric acid

Sulphur trioxide + Water → Sulphuric acid
$$SO_3(s) \quad + H_2O(l) \rightarrow \quad H_2SO_4(l)$$

It is dangerous for industry to carry out the reaction in this way. As soon as sulphur trioxide meets water vapour, it reacts to form a mist of sulphuric acid. It is safer to absorb the sulphur trioxide in sulphuric acid to form oleum, $H_2S_2O_7$, and then convert the oleum into sulphuric acid.

Sulphuric acid is important in the fertiliser industry because it is needed for the manufacture of phosphoric acid. It has many other uses, such as the manufacture of paints, pesticides and plastics.

Manufacture of phosphoric acid

Phosphoric acid is made from the widespread ore calcium phosphate by a reaction with sulphuric acid.

Calcium phosphate + Sulphuric acid → Phosphoric acid + Calcium sulphate

LOOK AT LINKS
The importance of fertilisers is discussed in Theme D, Topic 17.4 and Theme G, Topic 29.7. The most popular fertilisers are those that contain compounds of nitrogen, phosphorus and potassium: the NPK fertilisers.

Making NPK fertilisers

Figure 51.2D shows a flow diagram for the manufacture of NPK fertilisers. It shows how ammonium nitrate and ammonium phosphate are manufactured. There is no need to make potassium chloride because there are plentiful deposits of it in the UK.

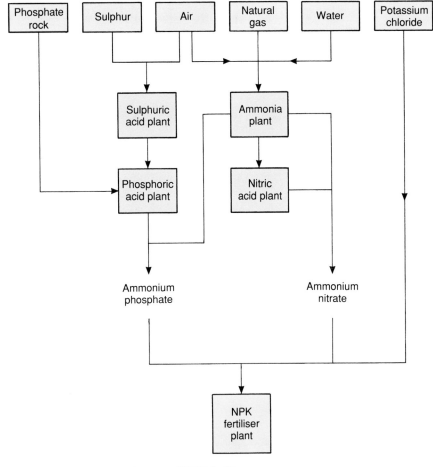

Figure 51.2D ● Manufacture of NPK fertilisers

SUMMARY

Ammonium nitrate and ammonium phosphate are manufactured. Potassium chloride is mined. The three salts are mixed to make NPK fertilisers.

CHECKPOINT

❶ State two advantages of the fertiliser ammonium phosphate over the insoluble salt calcium phosphate.

❷ What methods do farmers use for applying (a) ammonia and (b) ammonium sulphate?

❸ Why are farmers prepared to pay a lot for fertilisers? Why do all fertilisers contain nitrogen?

❹ What is the advantage of using nitrogen as a starting material in the manufacture of fertilisers? What difficulty had to be overcome before manufacture started? Who solved the difficulty and how?

❺ NPK fertilisers are popular. What do the letters NPK stand for? Explain why it is important that fertilisers contain (a) N, (b) P and (c) K. (See Theme G, Topic 29.7 if you need to revise.)

❻ State three routes by which nitrogen from the air finds its way into the soil. Why is the nitrogen content of the air not used up?

51.3 🖐 Plastics and fibres

The toys you see in Figure 51.3A are made of plastics. The clothes you see in Figure 51.3B are made of synthetic fibres. Both types of material are polymers. In this topic, you will find out what a polymer is.

Figure 51.3A ● Plastics

Figure 51.3B ● Fibres

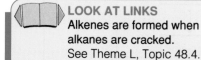

LOOK AT LINKS
Alkenes are formed when alkanes are cracked.
See Theme L, Topic 48.4.

Alkenes

Ethene is a hydrocarbon of formula C_2H_4 (see Figure 51.3C). There is a double bond between the carbon atoms.

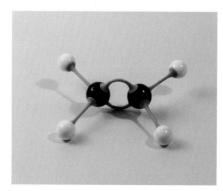

Figure 51.3C ● (a) A model of ethene   (b) The formula of ethene

Ethene and other hydrocarbons which contain double bonds between carbon atoms are described as **unsaturated** hydrocarbons. The double bond will open to allow another molecule to add on. Unsaturated hydrocarbons will add hydrogen to form **saturated** hydrocarbons. For example, ethene adds hydrogen to form ethane, which is an **alkane**. Reactions of this kind are called **addition reactions**; see Figure 51.3D. Saturated hydrocarbons, such as alkanes, contain only single bonds between carbon atoms.

Ethene + Hydrogen → Ethane

Figure 51.3D ● The addition reaction between ethene and hydrogen

Propene is an unsaturated hydrocarbon which resembles ethene (see Figure 51.3E). Ethene and propene are members of a **homologous series**, that is, a set of similar compounds whose formulas differ by CH_2. They are called **alkenes** (see Table 51.1). The general formula is C_nH_{2n}.

SUMMARY

Alkenes are unsaturated hydrocarbons. They possess a double bond between carbon atoms. They are a homologous series of general formula C_nH_{2n}.

```
H   H   H
|   |   |
C = C — C — H
|       |
H       H
```

Figure 51.3E ● The formula of propene

Table 51.1 ● The first members of the alkene series

Alkene	Formula, C_nH_{2n}
Ethene	C_2H_4
Propene	C_3H_6
Butene	C_4H_8
Pentene	C_5H_{10}
Hexene	C_6H_{12}
Heptene	C_7H_{14}
Octene	C_8H_{16}

Reactions of alkenes

● *Hydrogenation*

Animal fats, such as butter, are solid. Vegetable oils, such as sunflower seed oil, are liquid. More vegetable oil is produced than we need for cooking, and insufficient butter is produced to satisfy the demand for solid fat. It is therefore profitable to convert vegetable oils into solid fats. Manufacturers make use of the fact that fats are saturated, while oils are unsaturated. Hydrogenation (the addition of hydrogen) is used to convert an unsaturated oil into a saturated fat. The vapour of an oil is passed with hydrogen over a nickel catalyst.

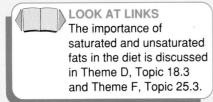

LOOK AT LINKS
for **fats** and **oils**
See Theme D, Topic 18.3.

$$\text{Vegetable oil (unsaturated) + Hydrogen} \xrightarrow[\text{nickel catalyst}]{\text{pass over heated}} \text{Solid fat (saturated)}$$

The product is margarine. The process can be modified to leave some of the double bonds intact and yield soft margarine.

LOOK AT LINKS
The importance of saturated and unsaturated fats in the diet is discussed in Theme D, Topic 18.3 and Theme F, Topic 25.3.

● *Hydration*

Water will add to alkenes. A molecule of water can add across the double bond. Combination with water is called **hydration**. The product formed by the hydration of ethene is ethanol, C_2H_5OH.

Ethene + Water → Ethanol

```
      H                        H
      |                        |
  H — C   H               H — C — H
      ‖ + |                    |
  H — C   O — H           H — C — O — H
      |                        |
      H                        H
```

Ethanol is the compound we commonly call **alcohol**. It is an important industrial solvent. The industrial manufacture is

LOOK AT LINKS
for **ethanol**
See Theme L, Topic 51.4.

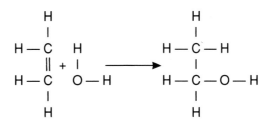

$$\text{Ethene + Steam} \xrightarrow[\text{(phosphoric acid), under pressure}]{\text{pass over a heated catalyst}} \text{Ethanol}$$

Only about 10% of ethene is converted to ethanol. The unreacted gases are recycled over the catalyst

● **Addition polymerisation**

The double bond in ethene enables many molecules of ethene to join together to form a large molecule.

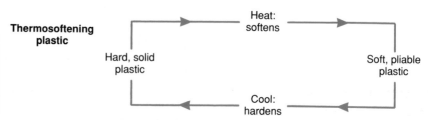

This reaction is called **addition polymerisation**. Many molecules (30 000–40 000) of the **monomer**, ethene, **polymerise** (i.e. join together) to form one molecule of the **polymer**, poly(ethene). The conditions needed for polymerisation are high pressure, a temperature of room temperature or higher and a catalyst.

$$\text{Ethene} \xrightarrow[\text{over a heated catalyst}]{\text{pass at high pressure}} \text{Poly(ethene)}$$

$$n\text{CH}_2\text{—CH}_2 \xrightarrow[\text{catalyst}]{\text{heat, pressure,}} \text{—}(\text{CH}_2\text{—CH}_2)_n$$

Poly(ethene) is better known by its trade name of **polythene**. It is used for making plastic bags, kitchenware (buckets, bowls, etc.), laboratory tubing and toys. It is flexible and difficult to break.

Plastics

Polymers such as poly(ethene) and other polyalkenes are **plastics**. Plastics are materials which soften on heating and harden on cooling. They are therefore useful materials from which to mould objects. There are two kinds of plastics: **thermosoftening plastics** and **thermosetting plastics**.

Thermosoftening plastics can be softened by heating, cooled and resoftened many times. Thermosetting plastics can be softened by heat only once.

LOOK AT LINKS
The ways in which the uses of materials depend on their properties are mentioned in Theme B, Topic 4.6.

Thermosoftening plastic

Hard, solid plastic → Heat: softens → Soft, pliable plastic

Soft, pliable plastic → Cool: hardens → Hard, solid plastic

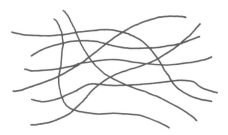

Thermosetting plastic

Heat: softens → Cool: hardens

Hard, solid plastic → Soft, pliable plastic → Permanently hard plastic

The reason for the difference in behaviour is a difference in structure (see Figure 51.3F).

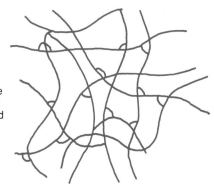

Thermosoftening plastics consist of long polymer chains. The forces of attraction between chains are weak

(a) Part of the structure of a thermosoftening plastic

When a thermosetting plastic is softened and moulded, the chains react with one another. Cross-links are formed and a huge three-dimensional structure is built up. This is why thermosetting plastics can be formed only once

(b) Part of the structure of a thermosetting plastic
Figure 51.3F ●

Manufacturers find thermosoftening plastics very convenient to use. They can buy thermosoftening plastic in bulk in the form of granules, then melt the material and press it into the shape of the object they want to make. Thermosoftening plastics are easy to colour. When a pigment is added to the molten plastic and thoroughly mixed, the moulded objects are coloured all through. This is much better than a coat of paint which can become chipped. Thermosetting plastics have important uses too. Materials used for bench tops must be able to withstand high temperatures without softening. 'Thermosets' are ideal for this use.

● *Condensation polymerisation*

The chief thermosetting polymers are not poly(alkenes). Many of them are made by another type of polymerisation called **condensation polymerisation**. For this to occur, the monomer must possess two groups of atoms which can take part in chemical reactions. When the reactive groups in one molecule of monomer react with the groups in other molecules of monomer, large polymer molecules are formed (see Figure 51.3G). In the reaction, small molecules are eliminated, e.g. H_2O, HCl, NH_3. The elimination of water gave the name **condensation** to this type of polymerisation.

SUMMARY

Addition polymerisation is the addition of many molecules of monomer to form one molecule of polymer. Thermosoftening and thermosetting plastics have advantages for different uses.

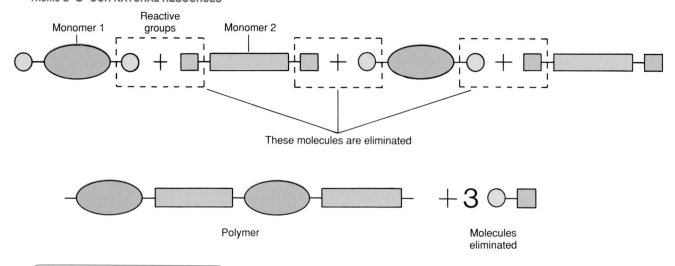

These molecules are eliminated

Polymer

Molecules
eliminated

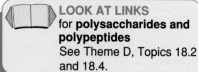

LOOK AT LINKS
for **polysaccharides and polypeptides**
See Theme D, Topics 18.2 and 18.4.

Figure 51.3G ● Condensation polymerisation

Examples of condensation polymers are:
• epoxy resins, which are used in glues,
• polyester resins, which are used in glass-reinforced plastics,
• polyurethanes, which are used in varnishes.
• See Table 51.2 for nylon, terylene and rayon.

SUMMARY

Condensation polymerisation is the reaction between many molecules of monomer to form one molecule of polymer with the elimination of a small molecule such as a molecule of water.

● **Methods of moulding plastics**
Different methods are used for moulding thermosoftening and thermosetting plastics (see Figures 51.3H, I, J, K).

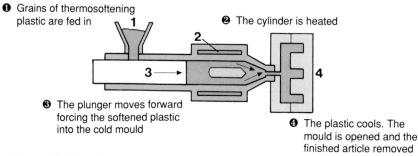

❶ Grains of thermosoftening plastic are fed in

❷ The cylinder is heated

❸ The plunger moves forward forcing the softened plastic into the cold mould

❹ The plastic cools. The mould is opened and the finished article removed

Figure 51.3H ● For thermosoftening plastics, injection moulding is used for many objects, e.g. milk bottle crates and construction kits

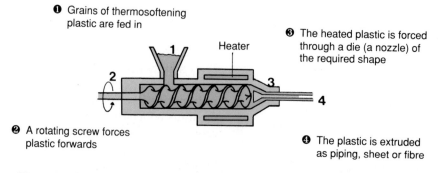

❶ Grains of thermosoftening plastic are fed in

❸ The heated plastic is forced through a die (a nozzle) of the required shape

❷ A rotating screw forces plastic forwards

❹ The plastic is extruded as piping, sheet or fibre

Figure 51.3I ● For thermosoftening plastics, the extrusion method is used to make threads of fabric, pipes and tubes, e.g. insulation for electrical cable

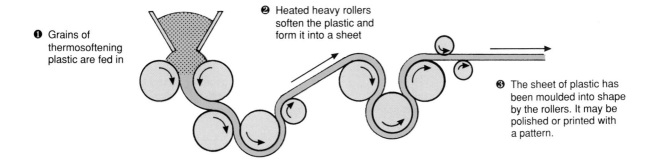

❶ Grains of thermosoftening plastic are fed in

❷ Heated heavy rollers soften the plastic and form it into a sheet

❸ The sheet of plastic has been moulded into shape by the rollers. It may be polished or printed with a pattern.

Figure 51.3J ● For thermosoftening plastics, calendering is used to make large sheets of plastic, e.g. floor coverings and car seat covers

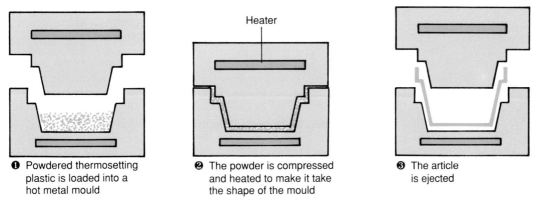

Heater

❶ Powdered thermosetting plastic is loaded into a hot metal mould

❷ The powder is compressed and heated to make it take the shape of the mould

❸ The article is ejected

Figure 51.3K ● The usual method of shaping thermosetting plastics is compression moulding

Some manufacturers mix gases with plastics to make low density plastic foams. These foams are used in packaging, for thermal insulation of buildings, for insulation against sound and in the interior of car seats. Sometimes it is necessary to strengthen plastics by the addition of other materials. Boat hulls, plastic panels in cars, instrument panels and wall-mounted hand-driers are just a few of the articles which are made of GRP (glass-fibre-reinforced plastic) (see Figure 51.3L).

SUMMARY

Different methods are used for moulding thermosoftening plastics (which can be softened by heat many times) and thermosetting plastics (which can be softened by heat only once before setting permanently).

Figure 51.3L ● GRP boat

Polyalkenes

Table 51.2 ● Some poly(alkenes) and their uses

Poly(ethene); trade name Polythene

Monomer Polymer

$$\underset{\underset{H}{|}}{\overset{\overset{H}{|}}{C}} = \underset{\underset{H}{|}}{\overset{\overset{H}{|}}{C}} \qquad \left(\underset{\underset{H}{|}}{\overset{\overset{H}{|}}{C}} - \underset{\underset{H}{|}}{\overset{\overset{H}{|}}{C}} \right)_n$$

Polythene is used to make plastic bags. High density polythene is used to make kitchenware, laboratory tubing and toys.

Poly(chloroethene); trade name PVC

Monomer Polymer

$$\underset{\underset{H}{|}}{\overset{\overset{Cl}{|}}{C}} = \underset{\underset{H}{|}}{\overset{\overset{H}{|}}{C}} \qquad \left(\underset{\underset{H}{|}}{\overset{\overset{Cl}{|}}{C}} - \underset{\underset{H}{|}}{\overset{\overset{H}{|}}{C}} \right)_n$$

PVC is used to make wellingtons, raincoats, floor tiles, insulation for electrical wiring, gutters and drainpipes.

Poly(propene); trade name Polypropylene

Monomer Polymer

$$\underset{\underset{H}{|}}{\overset{\overset{H}{|}}{C}} = \underset{\underset{H}{|}}{\overset{\overset{CH_3}{|}}{C}} \qquad \left(\underset{\underset{H}{|}}{\overset{\overset{H}{|}}{C}} - \underset{\underset{H}{|}}{\overset{\overset{CH_3}{|}}{C}} \right)_n$$

Polypropylene is resistant to attack by chemicals. Since it does not soften in boiling water, it can be used to make hospital equipment which must be sterilised. Polypropylene is drawn into fibres which are used to make ropes and fishing nets.

Poly(tetrafluoroethene); trade names PTFE and Teflon

Monomer Polymer

$$\underset{\underset{F}{|}}{\overset{\overset{F}{|}}{C}} = \underset{\underset{F}{|}}{\overset{\overset{F}{|}}{C}} \qquad \left(\underset{\underset{F}{|}}{\overset{\overset{F}{|}}{C}} - \underset{\underset{F}{|}}{\overset{\overset{F}{|}}{C}} \right)_n$$

PTFE is a hard plastic which is not attacked by most chemicals. Few substances can stick to its surface. It is used to coat non-stick pans and skis.

Perspex

Monomer

$$\underset{\underset{H}{|}}{\overset{\overset{H}{|}}{C}} = \underset{\underset{CH}{|}}{\overset{\overset{CO_2CH_3}{|}}{C}}$$

Perspex finds many applications because it is transparent and can be used instead of glass. It is more easily moulded than glass and less easily shattered.

Polystyrene

Monomer

$$\underset{\underset{H}{|}}{\overset{\overset{H}{|}}{C}} = \underset{\underset{C_6H_5}{|}}{\overset{\overset{H}{|}}{C}}$$

Polystyrene is a hard, brittle plastic used for making construction kits. Polystyrene foam is made by blowing air into the softened plastic. It is used for making ceiling tiles, insulating containers and packaging materials.

RESOURCE ACTIVITY PACK

SUMMARY

Some important poly(alkenes) are:
- poly(ethene),
- poly(chloroethene),
- poly(propene),
- poly(tetrafluoroethene),
- perspex,
- polystyrene.

LOOK AT LINKS
Cellulose is a polysaccharide. It forms the walls of plant cells. Over 3000 sugar molecules join to form one cellulose molecule.
See Theme D, Topic 18.2.

SUMMARY

Some important condensation polymers are nylon, terylene, bakelite, melamine and rayon.

SUMMARY

Some disadvantages in the use of plastics are:
- Clothes made of synthetic fibres do not absorb perspiration.
- Most plastics are non-biodegradable.
- They ignite easily, and some burn to form toxic products.

Table 51.3 ● Some condensation polymers and their uses

Polymer	Properties	Uses
Nylon	A polyamide Thermosoftening m.p. 200 °C High tensile strength	Textile fibre used in clothes; also in ropes, fishing lines and nets
Terylene	A polyester Thermosoftening	Important in clothing manufacture
Bakelite	Thermosetting An electrical insulator Insoluble in water and organic solvents Not attacked by chemicals	Electrical appliances, e.g. switches, sockets, plugs. Casings for radios and telephones
Melamine	Similar to bakelite	Kitchen surfaces, bench tops
Rayon	Made from cellulose by reshaping, that is breaking the long chains of sugar molecules in cellulose into shorter chains and then rejoining them	Important in clothing manufacture

● Some drawbacks

Nylon and terylene do not absorb water well. Clothes made of these fibres do not absorb perspiration and allow it to evaporate. Nylon, terylene and other polyesters are usually mixed with natural fibres such as wool and cotton. The mixtures absorb water and are therefore more comfortable to wear.

Many refreshment stands serve coffee and soft drinks in disposable cups. These are often made of polystyrene. All the plastic cups, plates and food containers which people use and throw away have to be disposed of. This is difficult to do because plastics are **non-biodegradable**. They are not decomposed by natural biological processes. Some plastic waste is burned in incinerators and the heat generated is used. Other plastics cannot be disposed of in this way because they burn to form poisonous gases, for example, hydrogen chloride, carbon monoxide and hydrogen cyanide. Much plastic waste is buried in landfill sites. One third of the plastics manufactured is used for packaging: it is made to be used once and thrown away. As the mass of non-biodegradable plastic waste increases, more land is used up to bury the waste.

Chemists are working on the problem. They have invented some **biodegradable** plastics, that is plastics which can be broken down by micro-organisms. One type has starch incorporated into the plastic. When bacteria feed on the starch, the plastic partially breaks down. Other new types of plastic are completely biodegradable.

There are some dangers in the use of plastics. Plastic foams are used as insulation in many buildings. Furniture is often stuffed with plastic foam. If there is a fire, burning plastics spread the fire rapidly. This is because plastics have lower ignition temperatures than materials like wood, metal, brick and glass. There is another danger too: some burning plastics give off poisonous gases.

SUMMARY

Plastics are petrochemicals obtained from oil. Earth's resources of oil are limited. Should we use oil as fuel or save it for the petrochemicals industry?

Oil: a fuel and a source of petrochemicals

Industry is constantly finding new uses for plastics. The raw materials used in their manufacture come from oil. At first the price of oil was low and plastics were cheap materials. As the price of oil has risen, this is no longer true. The Earth's resources of oil will not last for ever. We should be thinking about whether we ought to be burning oil as fuel when we need it to make plastics and other petrochemicals.

CHECKPOINT

① Say what materials the following articles were made out of before plastics came into use. Say what advantage plastic has over the previous material, and state any disadvantage.
   (a) gutters and drainpipes
   (b) toy soldiers
   (c) dolls
   (d) motorbike windscreens
   (e) lemonade bottles
   (f) buckets
   (g) electrical plugs and sockets
   (h) wellingtons
   (i) furniture stuffing
   (j) electrical cable insulation
   (k) dustbins

② (a) What does the word 'plastic' mean?
   (b) Plastics can be divided into two types, which behave differently when heated. Name the two types. Describe how each behaves when heated. Say how the difference in behaviour is related to (i) the use made of the plastics and (ii) the molecular nature of the plastics.

③ Study the following list of substances.

   nylon sucrose ethane styrene olive oil starch
   margarine glass silk rubber melamine

   (a) List the naturally occurring polymers.
   (b) List the synthetic polymers.
   (c) Name the substance which is not a polymer but can easily be converted into one.
   (d) List the substances which are not polymers and which cannot easily polymerise.

④ PVC is used in the manufacture of drainpipes and plastic bags.
   (a) Calculate the relative molecular mass of the monomer, $CH_2 = CHCl$.
   (b) The M_r of the polymer is 40 000. Calculate the number of molecules of monomer which combine to form one molecule of polymer.
   (c) What method could be used to mould PVC pipes?
   (d) If you needed to mould a straight length of PVC pipe to make it fit round a curve in a drainage system, how would you do this?
   (e) Used PVC bags have to be disposed of. Burning PVC bags in an incinerator would cause pollution. Name two pollutants that would be released into the atmosphere.

51.4 Alcohols, acids and esters

Ethanol

Ethanol is the best-known member of a series of compounds called alcohols. Ethanol is a drug. It is classified as a depressant. This means that it depresses (suppresses) feelings of fear and tension and therefore

Timothy's idea of a good time is to go down to the pub and have a few beers with his friends. Sometimes, however, he wakes up the next day with a throbbing headache and a feeling of nausea. He has a 'hangover'. The substance which has produced these effects is **ethanol**, a liquid which we usually call **alcohol**.

LOOK AT LINKS

The effects of alcohol on behaviour and health are described in Theme F, Topic 25.3. People who abuse alcohol, that is, drink it in more than moderate quantities, become addicted to alcohol, and their health suffers.

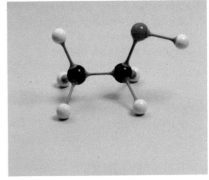

Figure 51.4A ● Ethanol and relaxation   *Figure 51.4B* ● Ethanol

makes people feel relaxed. The body can absorb ethanol quickly because it is completely soluble in water.

The alcohols

Ethanol is a member of a homologous series of compounds called **alcohols**. Alcohols possess the group

$$-\overset{|}{\underset{|}{C}}-O-H$$

and have the general formula $C_nH_{2n+1}OH$ (see Table 51.4). The formulas are written as CH_3OH, etc. rather than CH_4O to show the —OH group and show that they are alcohols. The members of the series have similar physical properties and chemical reactions. Ethanol is the only alcohol that is not poisonous. Methanol is very toxic: drinking only small amounts of methanol can lead to blindness and death.

Table 51.4 ● The alcohols

Alcohol	Formula, $C_nH_{2n+1}OH$
Methanol	CH_3OH
Ethanol	C_2H_5OH
Propanol	C_3H_7OH
Butanol	C_4H_9OH

Alcohols are a homologous series of formula $C_nH_{2n+1}OH$. Ethanol is the only alcohol which is safe to drink in moderate quantities. Regular abuse of alcohol ruins your health. The alcohols have important industrial uses.

The use of ethanol is not restricted to drinking. Ethanol is an important solvent. It is used in cosmetics and toiletries, in thinners for lacquers and printing inks. Being volatile (with b.p. 78 °C), the solvent evaporates and leaves the solute behind. Other alcohols also are used as solvents for paints, lacquers, shellacs and industrial detergents. The big advantage of alcohols as solvents is that they are miscible with water and many organic liquids.

Manufacture of ethanol

The traditional method of making ethanol is the fermentation of carbohydrates. The sugar glucose can be converted into ethanol by the enzyme zymase, which is present in yeast. Carbon dioxide is produced in the reaction, which is called **fermentation**.

SUMMARY

Alcoholic drinks are made from sugars by fermentation. The reaction is catalysed by an enzyme in yeast. Starches can be hydrolysed to sugars and then fermented to give ethanol. Industrial ethanol is made by the hydration of ethene.

LOOK AT LINKS
for **the hydration of ethene**
See Theme L, Topic 51.3.

IT'S A FACT

In the original breathalyser test, a motorist suspected of having too much ethanol in his or her blood had to breathe out through a tube containing some orange potassium dichromate(VI) crystals. Ethanol changes the colour of this powerful oxidising agent from orange through green to blue. If the crystals turned green, it showed that the motorist was 'over the limit'.

SUMMARY

Ethanol is oxidised to ethanoic acid.

$$\text{Glucose} \xrightarrow{\text{enzyme in yeast}} \text{Ethanol} + \text{Carbon dioxide}$$
$$C_6H_{12}O_6(aq) \quad\quad 2C_2H_5OH(aq) + 2CO_2(g)$$

Fruit juices contain sugars. When yeast is added, the sugar ferments to form ethanol. When the ethanol content of the solution reaches 14%, it kills the yeast. This is the maximum ethanol concentration in wine. More concentrated solutions of ethanol (spirits, e.g. gin) are obtained by distillation.

Ethanol can also be made from starchy crops, such as potatoes, malt, barley and hops. Malt (germinated barley) is added to allow an enzyme in malt to hydrolyse starch to a mixture of sugars. Then yeast is added to ferment the sugars.

$$\text{Starch} + \text{Water} \xrightarrow{\text{enzyme in malt}} \text{Sugar}$$
$$(C_6H_{10}O_5)_n(aq) + nH_2O(l) \quad\quad nC_6H_{12}O_6(aq)$$

Ethanol is sold in four main forms.
- Absolute alcohol: 96% ethanol, 4% water.
- Industrial alcohol or methylated spirit: 85% ethanol, 10% water, 5% methanol. The methanol is added to make the liquid unfit to drink.
- Spirits: gin, rum, whisky, brandy, etc. which contain about 35% ethanol.
- Fermented liquors: wines (12–14% ethanol), beers and ciders (3–7% ethanol). These contain flavourings and colouring matter.

Ethanol for industrial use is not made by fermentation. It is made by the **hydration of ethene**.

Oxidation of ethanol

Wine turns sour if it is open to the air. The reason is that ethanol is oxidised by air if certain micro-organisms are present. The product is ethanoic acid. Vinegar is 3% ethanoic acid.

$$\text{Ethanol} + \text{Oxygen} \xrightarrow{\text{certain microorganisms}} \text{Ethanoic acid} + \text{Water}$$
$$C_2H_5OH(aq) + O_2(g) \quad\quad CH_3CO_2H(aq) + H_2O(l)$$

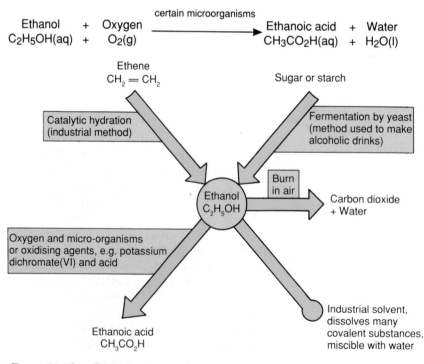

Figure 51.4C ● Ethanol

Gasohol

The cost of petroleum oil has risen since the oil crisis of 1973. Countries which have to import oil want to find alternatives. The major use of petroleum oil fractions is in vehicle engines. Petrol engines are designed to operate over a temperature range at which petrol will vaporise. Any fuel added to petrol must vaporise at the engine temperature and it must dissolve in petrol. Ethanol has the same boiling point as heptane, and it dissolves in petrol. Ethanol burns well in vehicle engines, producing 70% as much heat per litre as petrol does. A petrol engine will take 10% ethanol in the petrol without any adjustments to the carburettor (which controls the ratio of air to fuel in the cylinders). A mixture of petrol and ethanol is described as **gasohol**. The combustion of ethanol produces carbon dioxide and water: there is little atmospheric pollution.

To invest in the production of ethanol by fermentation, a country needs land available for growing suitable crops. It needs plenty of sunshine to ripen the crops quickly and supply sugar or starch for fermentation. Brazil has already started using ethanol as a vehicle fuel. Brazil has very little oil, but plenty of land and sunshine. Most of the petrol sold there contains 10% ethanol. This reduces Brazil's expenditure on oil imports. By the year 2000, Brazil hopes to provide for 75% of its motor fuel needs by using 2% of its land for growing crops for fermentation (Figure 51.4D).

Figure 51.4D ● Petrol pumps in Brazil selling 'Alcool' gasohol

Ethanoic acid

Ethanoic acid has the structural formula

$$\begin{array}{c} \text{H} \\ | \\ \text{H}-\text{C}-\text{C} \\ | \qquad \diagdown \text{O}-\text{H} \\ \text{H} \end{array} \diagup\!\!\!\!^{\displaystyle O}$$

Ethanoic acid is a member of a homologous series called **carboxylic acids**. It is a weak acid. It reacts in the same way as mineral acids but more slowly. The salts are **ethanoates**. A 3% solution of ethanoic acid is **vinegar**. It is used as a preservative because micro-organisms cannot grow in vinegar. Ethanoic acid and other organic acids react with alcohols to form sweet-smelling liquids called **esters**.

LOOK AT LINKS
To obtain more agricultural land, Brazil is clearing rain forest. The cost to the environment is discussed in Theme M, Topic 53.8.

The Ethanol Question
(program)

Use this simulation to study the factors affecting the chemical reactions involved in producing ethanol. Try your hand at producing ethanol yourself, at a competitive selling price.

SUMMARY

Ethanol can be added to the petrol in vehicle engines. Brazil is a country with no oil but with plenty of arable land and a sunny climate. Brazil is growing crops which can be fermented to give ethanol. Ethanol is a clean fuel: it burns to form carbon dioxide and water.

LOOK AT LINKS
for **weak and strong acids**
See Theme D, Topic 16.1.

LOOK AT LINKS
Animal fats and vegetable oils are esters.
See Theme D, Topic 18.3.

SUMMARY

Ethanoic acid is a carboxylic acid. It is a weak acid. It reacts in the same way as mineral acids but more slowly. Carboxylic acids react with alcohols to form esters. Esters are used as food additives and as solvents. Solvent abuse is a dangerous habit.

● *Esters*

Many esters are liquids with fruity smells. They occur naturally in fruits. They are used as food additives to improve the flavour and smell of processed foods. Other esters are used as solvents, for example in glues. People can get 'high' by inhaling esters. Some people enjoy the sensation so much that they become 'glue sniffers'. It is really the solvent, which may be a hydrocarbon or an ester, that they want to inhale. This dangerous habit is called **solvent abuse**. It produces the same symptoms as ethanol abuse. In addition, sniffers who are 'high' on solvents become disoriented. They may believe that they can jump out of windows or off bridges or walk through traffic. Many deaths occur from solvent abuse both through disoriented behaviour and from sniffers passing out and suffocating on their own vomit.

CHECKPOINT

❶ (a) Explain what is meant by fermentation.
   (b) Name a commercially important substance which is made by this method. Say what it is used for.

❷ (a) Why does wine turn sour when it is left to stand?
   (b) Suggest two methods of slowing down the rate at which wine turns sour.

❸ What are the dangers of drinking (a) ethanol and (b) methanol?

❹ Petrol is produced by distillation and by 'cracking'.
   (a) Explain what cracking is.
   (b) Say where the energy used in (i) distillation and (ii) cracking comes from.
   (c) Say where the energy used in fermentation comes from.

❺ Europe has a surplus of grain. Someone proposes building plants to obtain ethanol from the surplus cereals. Say what advantages this would bring to
   (a) the environment (b) the farmer (c) the motorist (d) industry
   (e) the tax payer.
   Can you see anything wrong with the idea? Explain your answers.

❻ 'Ethanoic acid is a weaker acid than hydrochloric acid.'
   Describe an experiment which you could do to show that this is a true statement.

51.5 Chemistry helps medicine

Chemotherapy is the treatment of illness by chemical means. Chemicals can cure diseases and relieve pain. Advances in chemotherapy have made life safer, longer and more free from pain than it was a century ago. Some of the chemicals which are used in medicine are mentioned in this section.

Painkillers

Aspirin is the most popular pain-killer. It was first sold in 1899. Each person in the UK swallows an average of 200 aspirins a year. Many other medicines, e.g. APC, contain aspirin. When you swallow aspirin, there is slight bleeding of the stomach wall. To reduce irritation of the stomach wall, you should always swallow plenty of water with aspirin. **Codeine** is a stronger pain-killer, used in headache tablets and in cough medicines.

   Morphine is a substance with an amazing ability to relieve intense pain. The problem with morphine is that it is **addictive**. It is only used in cases of dire necessity, for example when soldiers are wounded in battle.

Morphine can only be obtained by doctors. **Heroin** is a pain-reliever which is even more potent and more addictive than morphine. Heroin is not used in medicine because it is so addictive. Drug-dealers like to get their customers to try heroin because they will soon become 'hooked' and come back to buy again and again.

Tranquillisers and sedatives

One person in twenty takes **tranquillisers** every day. Tranquillisers are substances which relieve tension and anxiety. With so many people taking tranquillisers over long periods of time, some doctors are worried about long-term effects. Research workers are now investigating whether there is any danger in taking tranquillisers for a long time.

Many people take **sedatives** (sleeping tablets). Drugs called **barbiturates** are used for this purpose. They are habit-forming. People who rely on barbiturates sometimes kill themselves accidentally by taking an overdose. These drugs are also used in the treatment of high blood pressure and mental illness.

LOOK AT LINKS
for **adrenalin**
See Theme J, Topic 40.3.

Stimulants

Adrenalin is a substance which the body produces when it needs to prepare for action: for 'fight or flight'. It is a **stimulant**: it makes the heart beat faster and makes a person ready for strenuous action.

Amphetamines (pep pills) have similar effects on the body. Some people take amphetamines to keep themselves awake; other people want to pep themselves up and make themselves more entertaining. People can become addicted to amphetamines. A person taking amphetamines becomes excitable and talkative, with trembling hands and enlarged pupils.

Who's behind the science

Laughing gas was discovered by Sir Humphrey Davy (see Theme C, Topic 13.3). At first it was used only as a curiosity at parties. One of these parties was attended by a dentist, Horace Morton. He decided to try laughing gas as an anaesthetic on his patients. Morton obtained better results by using ether. The use of chloroform spread rapidly after Queen Victoria took it during the birth of one of her children in 1853.

Anaesthetics

Anaesthetics made modern surgery possible. Before the days of anaesthetics, a surgeon asked his patient to drink some brandy or smoke some opium to deaden the pain. Then the surgeon did the operation as quickly as he could. Sometimes patients died from pain and shock. After anaesthetics came into use, surgeons were able to take time to do the best operation they could, rather than the fastest. They were able to explore new techniques.

The first anaesthetics to be used were chloroform (1846), ether (1847) and dinitrogen oxide (laughing gas). There were some drawbacks to using these gases. In large doses, chloroform is harmful. Ether is very flammable, and it has been the cause of fires in hospitals in the past. Dinitrogen oxide (laughing gas) does not produce a very deep anaesthesia; however it is suitable for use in dentistry. Research workers have found a better anaesthetic, **fluothane**, which was first used in 1956. It has been so successful and free from side-effects that most operations are now done under fluothane.

Antiseptics

Another advance in surgery came with antiseptics. A century ago, many patients survived operations but died later in the wards. A surgeon called James Lister realised that the patients' wounds were becoming infected. He sprayed the operating theatre and the wards with a mist of

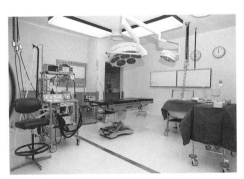

Figure 51.5A ● A modern operating theatre

The power of sulphonamide drugs was discovered by Gerhardt Domagh. The first human being on whom he tested the drug was his own daughter. She was dying of 'child-bed fever', a bacterial infection which can attack women who have just had a baby. Happily, the drug worked. Domagh received the Nobel prize in 1939.

The old treatment for syphilis was to apply a paste of heavy metal salts (salts of arsenic, lead, mercury and antimony) to the skin. The metal salts killed the micro-organism that caused the disease, but many patients experienced metal poisoning. Paul Ehrlich reasoned that, if he could attach one of these metals to a dye which was able to stain the micro-organism, the metal–dye compound might target the micro-organism 'like a magic bullet' without attacking body tissues. Ehrlich and his team of research workers set to work. At the 606th attempt they were successful. They called their new compound salvarsan. Ehrlich received the Nobel prize in 1908.

phenol and water. His experiment produced immediate results: the death rate fell. Phenol had killed micro-organisms that would otherwise have infected surgical wounds. Phenol is an **antiseptic**. It is unpleasant to use. Solid phenol will burn the skin, and its vapour is toxic. Research chemists made other compounds which work as well as phenol and are safer to use. TCP® and Dettol® are antiseptics which contain trichlorophenol.

Antibiotics

Infectious diseases, such as tuberculosis and pneumonia, used to kill thousands of people every year. The grim picture changed in 1935 with the discovery of the **sulphonamides**. They are antibiotics: substances which fight disease carried by bacteria. Infectious diseases are no longer a serious threat. In surgery too, powerful antibiotics have made having an operation safer than it was at the beginning of this century.

Alexander Fleming was a research bacteriologist in a London hospital. When the First World War began, he joined the Medical Corps. He was distressed by what he saw in his field hospital. Soldiers who did not seem to be mortally wounded when they arrived in the hospital died later from infections. Bacteria in mud and dirty clothing had infected their wounds, and gangrene set in. Watching men die a slow, painful death, Fleming wished that his work as a bacteriologist would enable him to discover a substance that would kill bacteria: a **bactericide**. After the war, Fleming went back to his research. One day, he found a mould called *Penicillium* on a dish of bacteria which he was culturing. To his amazement, he saw that the mould had killed bacteria. From the mould, he prepared an extract which he called **penicillin**. Would this be the powerful bactericide he had been hoping for? Sadly, although penicillin worked in the laboratory, it did not work in patients. Substances in the blood made the bactericide inactive.

In 1940, work on penicillin recommenced. The Second World War had started, and a powerful bactericide was needed urgently. Two chemists, Howard Florey and Ernst Chain, succeeded in making a stable extract of penicillin. They tested it, first on mice and then on human patients. The tests were successful, and the USA built a plant for the mass-production of penicillin. In 1942, penicillin was used in hospitals on the battle field. The results were spectacular. No longer did soldiers die from minor wounds. In 1944, Fleming was knighted. Later, Fleming, Florey and Chain shared the Nobel Prize for medicine.

Penicillin has been widely used to treat a variety of infections. One disadvantage is that penicillin cannot be taken by mouth. It is broken down by acids, in this case the hydrochloric acid in the stomach. A more recent antibiotic, **tetracycline**, does not share this drawback. Tetracycline is a 'broad spectrum' antibiotic which can be used against many kinds of bacteria.

CHECKPOINT

❶ Your Uncle Bert is always swallowing aspirins. Explain to him (a) why he should not take too many aspirins and (b) why he should take water with aspirins.

❷ (a) A singer you know feels so tired that she is thinking of taking pep pills before giving a performance. Explain to her why this is not a good idea in the long run.
(b) What is the body's natural stimulant? How does it work?

❸ Briefly explain how surgery has changed as a result of (a) the discovery of anaesthetics and (b) the discovery of antiseptics.

❹ Morphine is a very powerful pain reliever. Why do doctors prescribe it for so few patients? For what types of patient is morphine prescribed?

❺ Why do doctors never prescribe heroin as a pain-killer?

❻ Someone you know takes barbiturates to help her to get to sleep. Suggest to her what else she could do, instead of taking pills, to get to sleep.

❼ (a) Before the time of James Lister, surgeons did not change their operating gowns between patients. What was wrong with this practice?
   (b) What did James Lister do to improve surgery?

❽ (a) What did Sir Alexander Fleming do to merit a Nobel prize for medicine?
   (b) He had a piece of luck in his research, but his success was not due to luck. What else went into his discovery?

51.6 The chemical industry

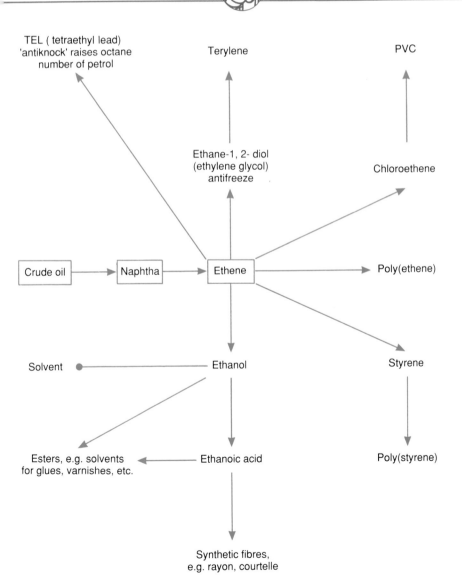

The chemical industry can be divided roughly into ten sections.
1 **Heavy chemical industry**: oils, fuels, etc. (see Topic 48).
2 **Agriculture**: fertilisers, pesticides, etc. (see Topic 51.2).
3 **Plastics**: poly(ethene), poly(styrene), PVC, etc. (see Topic 51.3).
4 **Dyes**
5 **Fibres**: nylon, rayon, courtelle, etc. (see Topic 51.3).
6 **Paints, varnishes**, etc.
7 **Pharmaceuticals**: medicines, drugs, cosmetics, etc. (see Topic 51.5).
8 **Metals**: iron, aluminium, alloys, etc. (see Topic 50).
9 **Explosives**: dynamite, TNT, etc. (see Topic 51.2).
10 **Chemicals from salt**: sodium hydroxide, chlorine, hydrogen, hydrochloric acid, etc. (see Theme C, Topic 13.6 and Theme D, Topic 17.1).

Figure 51.6A shows some of the petrochemicals which are obtained by the route

Petroleum oil → Naphtha → Ethene → Petrochemical

Figure 51.6A ● Some petrochemicals

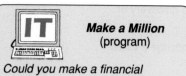

Make a Million
(program)

Could you make a financial success in industry? Use the program to find out. The industrial processes you can choose from include:
- manufacturing acid,
- electrolysis,
- fractionating,
- generating electricity.

Is the chemical industry the place for you? Have you a legal brain or a financial brain? Are you good at relating to other people? Have you a flare for advertising and marketing? Are you an engineer? Are you a scientist who wants to spend his or her time in the laboratory inventing new products? Do you want to be part of the workforce that runs the plant and is responsible for maintaining a high-quality product? These questions span a huge variety of people. It takes a different type of ability to work at finance from the ability to do scientific research. If you add up the numbers of people who can answer 'Yes' to just one of these questions, the sum total is the number of people employed by the chemical industry. Figure 51.6B shows how they work together.

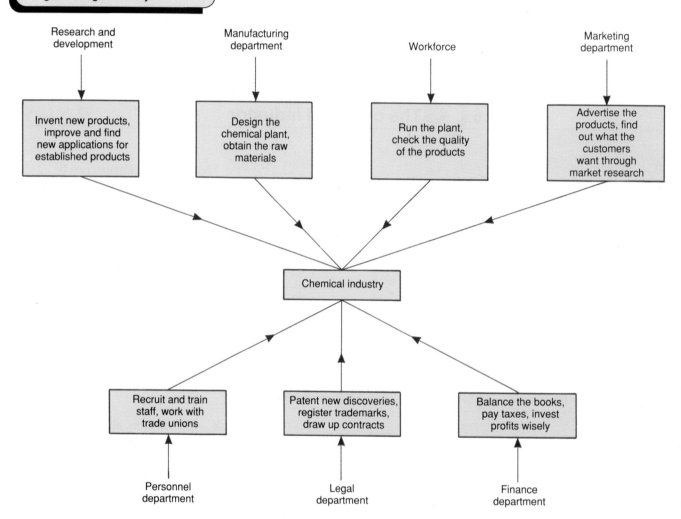

Figure 51.6B ● How different parts of the chemical industry work together

? THEME QUESTIONS

● **Topic 46**

1 Zinc reacts with sulphuric acid to give hydrogen. Mention three ways in which you could speed up the reaction.

2 In a set of experiments, zinc was allowed to react with sulphuric acid. Each time, 0.65 g of zinc was used. The volume of acid was different each time. The volume of hydrogen formed each time is shown in the table.

Volume of sulphuric acid (cm^3)	Volume of hydrogen (cm^3)
5	45
15	135
20	180
25	215
30	235
35	240
40	240

Plot, on graph paper, the volume of hydrogen produced against the volume of acid used. From the graph, find out:
(a) where the reaction is most rapid (and explain why),
(b) what volume of sulphuric acid will produce 100 cm^3 of gas,
(c) what volume of gas is produced if 10 cm^3 of sulphuric acid is used,
(d) what volume of sulphuric acid is just sufficient to react with 0.65 g of zinc.

● **Topic 48**

3 The flow chart below shows the main stages in the production of sugar from sugar cane plants.

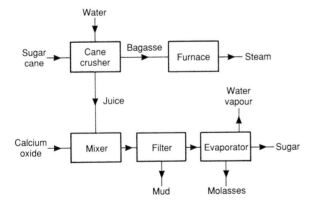

(a) (i) Suggest why water is added to the cane-crusher.
(ii) What do you think 'bagasse' is?
(iii) Suggest **two** reasons why the bagasse is used as a fuel for the furnace.
(iv) Explain the reason for the filter.
(v) Explain what happens inside the evaporator.
(b) Sugar cane plants are grown in Brazil to make sugar and to make fuel for cars. To make fuel the sugar is

fermented to make ethanol. Fermentation involves a micro-organism like yeast respiring in an oxygen-free atmosphere.
(i) Apart from ethanol name **one** other substance produced in this reaction.
(ii) Suggest **one** effect this reaction would have on its environment.
(iii) Give **one** way in which this reaction is different from aerobic respiration.
(c) The ethanol produced is used in cars and other road vehicles instead of petrol. It contains fewer impurities than petrol and burns more easily. This means that it has several advantages over petrol. Suggest **two** of these advantages and explain each one.
(d) (i) In Britain research is being carried out on cars powered by electricity. Suggest **one** reason why, apart from the cost, Brazil has **not** spent money on this research. Explain your answer.
(ii) Draw up a table to show **three** advantages and **three** disadvantages of electric-powered vehicles compared with petrol-powered vehicles.

(SEG)

● **Topic 50**

4 The following metals are listed in order of decreasing reactivity. X and Y are two unknown metals.

K X Ca Mg Al Zn Y Fe Cu

(a) Will X react with cold water?
(b) Will Y react with cold water?
(c) Will Y react with dilute hydrochloric acid?
Explain how you arrive at your answers.
(d) What reaction would you expect between zinc sulphate solution and (i) X (ii) Y?
(e) Which is more easily decomposed, XCO_3 or YCO_3?

5 Look at the following pairs of chemicals. If a reaction happens, copy the word equation, and complete the right hand side.
(a) Copper + Oxygen →
(b) Calcium + Hydrochloric acid →
(c) Copper + Sulphuric acid →
(d) Carbon + Lead(II) oxide →
(e) Hydrogen + Calcium oxide →
(f) Aluminium + Tin(II) oxide →
(g) Gold + Oxygen →
(h) Zinc + Copper(II) sulphate solution →
(i) Magnesium + Sulphuric acid →
(j) Hydrogen + Silver oxide →
(k) Carbon + Magnesium oxide →
(l) Lead + Copper(II) sulphate solution →
(m) Hydrogen + Potassium oxide →

6 Explain these statements about aluminium.
(a) Although aluminium is a reactive metal, it is used to make doorframes and windowframes.
(b) Although aluminium conducts heat, it is used to make blankets which are good thermal insulators.

(c) Although aluminium oxide is a common mineral, people did not succeed in extracting aluminium from it until seven thousand years after the discovery of copper.

(d) Recycling aluminium is easier than recycling scrap iron.

7 (a) Explain how steel is made from cast iron.

(b) Explain what advantages steel has over cast iron.

(c) Explain how the following methods protect iron against rusting: painting, galvanising, tin-plating, sacrificial protection.

8 Imagine that you live in a beautiful part of Northern Ireland. A firm called Alumco wants to build a new aluminium plant in your area so that they can use a river as a source of hydroelectric power.

(a) Write a letter from a local farmer to the Secretary of State for Northern Ireland. Say what you fear may happen as a result of pollution from the plant.

(b) Write a letter from a group of environmentalists to the Secretary of State, opposing the plan and giving your reasons.

(c) Write a letter from an unemployed couple to the Secretary of State saying that you welcome the coming of new industry to the area.

(d) Write a letter from the local Council to the Secretary of State. Tell him or her that there is very little unemployment in the area. Say that the new plant would have to bring in workers from outside the region. Explain that there is not enough housing in the area for newcomers.

(e) Write a letter from Alumco to the Secretary of State for Northern Ireland. Tell the Secretary of State of the importance of aluminium. Point out the many uses of aluminium. Explain that to keep up with increasing demand you have to build another plant to supply aluminium.

(If five letters are too many for you, divide the work among the class. Then get together to read out the letters. Have a discussion to decide what the Secretary of State ought to do.)

● *Topic 51*

9 This flow diagram shows the Haber process for making ammonia gas.

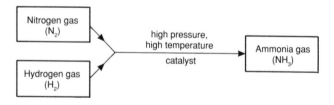

(a) A catalyst is used because it makes the process cheaper.

(i) What effect does a catalyst have on a chemical reaction?

(ii) Explain how using a catalyst can make the process cheaper.

(b) Write a balanced chemical equation for the reaction which takes place during the Haber process.

(c) Most of the ammonia gas from the Haber process is made into fertilisers such as ammonium sulphate.

Ammonia gas can be compressed to form liquid ammonia. In some countries this liquid is injected into the soil as a fertiliser.

(i) Give **one** reason why fertilisers are added to soil.

(ii) Suggest which acid is used to make ammonium sulphate.

(iii) Suggest and explain **two** reasons for injecting liquid ammonia *into* the soil rather than spraying it *onto* the surface.

(iv) The world use for fertilisers has been increasing for several years. Suggest an explanation for this increase.

(SEG)

10 The USA produces 8 million tonnes of sulphuric acid a year as a by-product in the smelting of sulphide ores.

(a) Calcium oxide is used to neutralise the acid by the reaction:

Calcium oxide + Sulphuric acid → Calcium sulphate + Water

Write the chemical equation for the reaction. Calculate the mass of calcium oxide needed to neutralise 8 million tonnes of sulphuric acid.

(b) Calculate the mass of calcium carbonate (limestone) that must be heated in a lime kiln to make the calcium oxide used in (a).

11 Borosilicate glass has very good resistance to heat and to sudden temperature changes. It does not react with many chemicals and is strong. Identical pieces of glass were placed in different boiling liquids for eight hours. The graphs in the figure show how the mass of each piece of glass changed.

(a) (i) Draw a labelled diagram to show the laboratory apparatus you could use to boil the acid.

(ii) State **two** safety precautions you would need to take when using this apparatus.

(b) The change in mass is given in milligrams. What is the symbol for milligrams?

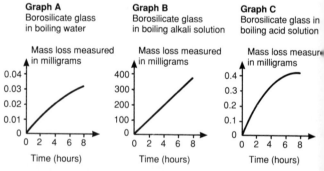

(c) (i) What pattern connects the mass change of the glass pieces in each liquid?

(ii) Describe **two** ways in which the mass loss shown in graph B is different from that shown in graph A and graph C.

(d) (i) The test using acid was carried out at 105 degrees Celsius (°C). Using your understanding of particle behaviour, explain why the rate of mass loss is greater at this temperature than at room temperature.

(ii) Suggest **one** other method of increasing the rate of mass loss.

(SEG)

THEME M
Ecology

You have probably heard the phrase the 'balance of nature'. It refers to the delicate balance that exists between living things and their environment. The human race has done much to upset this balance through selfishness, ignorance and greed. Everyday we read in the newspapers and see on television examples of 'environmental disasters'. Most of these are the result of our thoughtless exploitation of the environment. Now people are becoming aware that the human race is responsible for preserving the environment of planet Earth and each one of us can play a part in protecting our environment.

ECOSYSTEMS

52.1 Ecosystems, habitats and communities

FIRST THOUGHTS

Ecology is the study of how living things interact with each other and with their environment – the study of the balance of nature. The people involved in this study are called ecologists.

LOOK AT LINKS
for **species**
See Theme A, Topic 3.4.

If, as ecologists, we are to carry out a scientific study we need to look at a localised part of the environment called an **ecosystem**. Ecosystems exist in great variety both on land and in water (see Figure 52.1A).

All ecosystems are made up of two parts: the **living** and the **non-living**. The non-living part of an ecosystem is called the **habitat**. It is the place where organisms live and therefore has the conditions which they need for their existence such as light, oxygen and a suitable temperature. The living part of an ecosystem is the plants and animals that inhabit the habitat and is known as the **community**. Each community is made up of many populations of plants and animals. A **population** is a group of individuals of the same **species**. Each population in the community is adapted to living in a particular habitat.

Figure 52.1A ● Ecosystems

Figure 52.1B ● Adapting to environmental conditions

(a) Periiwinkles resist drying up by shutting their opercula (trap doors) when the tide goes out

(b) Limpets stick firmly to the rocks when the tide goes out and their tough shells protect them from extremes of temperature

(c) Gulls are major predators on rocky shores

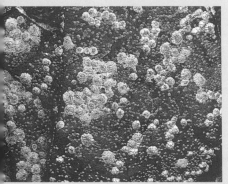

(e) Barnacles attach themselves to rocks and compete for space with each other and with seaweeds

In a sea-shore ecosystem there are many different animal and plant populations in the community. Each of these has been successful in adapting to a number of environmental conditions which occur on the seashore:

- **Tides**. Many animals and plants remain on the shore after the tide has gone out. They must be able to withstand the harsh conditions.
- **Evaporation**. Organisms have to conserve their body water otherwise they would dry up (see Figure 52.1B (a)).
- **Temperature**. Air temperature tends to fluctuate more quickly and to a greater extent than the temperature of the sea (see Figure 52.1B (b)).
- **Predators**. Shore animals have to contend with sea birds when the tide is out and with predatory fish when the tide is in (see Figure 52.1B (c) and (d)).
- **Food and space**. Seaweeds compete for space on the rocks and for light to carry out photosynthesis. Animals compete for food and for shelter (see Figure 52.1B (e)).
- **Wave action**. When the tide comes back in seaweeds and seashore animals have to withstand the battering of waves (see Figure 52.1B (f)).

(d) Predatory fish return to the shore with the tide

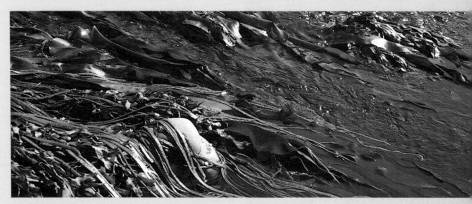

(f) Seaweeds are able to bend with the waves and are covered with slimy mucilage which protects them from being torn to pieces

Figure 52.1C ●

(a) Competition

(b) Predation

(c) Parasites

(d) Grazer

(e) Decomposers

Each ecosystem has a particular set of **environmental factors** to which animals and plants have to be adapted if they are to survive. These include:

- Light – which is needed by plants in order to carry out photosynthesis.
- Oxygen – for respiration.
- Carbon dioxide – for photosynthesis in plants.
- Water – as an essential constituent of cells.
- Temperature – which affects the rate at which reactions take place in cells.
- Nutrients – which are essential for growth, energy and reproduction.

The presence of other organisms within the community gives rise to the following factors:

- **Competition**. Individuals in a population of plants or animals have to compete not only with each other but with other species as well (see Figure 52.1C (a)).
- **Predation**. A predator is an animal that has to kill to feed. The prey must evade the predator if it is to survive (see Figure 52.1C (b)).
- **Parasites and disease**. A parasite usually lives on or within the host organism, using the host or the host's food supply as its own source of food (see Figure 52.1C (c)). Some diseases are caused by parasites.
- **Grazers** are animals that feed entirely upon plants (see Figure 52.1C (d)).
- **Decomposers** are organisms such as **bacteria** and **fungi** which break down dead and decaying material (see Figure 52.1C (e)).
- **The effect of humans**. People affect ecosystems in a number of ways. Industry, farming, forestry and housing have all contributed to the loss or deterioration of many natural ecosystems.

Look at the two very different ecosystems in Figure 52.1D. One represents a pond the other a town or city ecosystem. In each case make a list of the environmental factors that will affect the organisms that live there.

We will see that although ecosystems may appear to be very different, their structures are based upon feeding and energy transfer and therefore follow a common pattern. All the ecosystems together make up the **biosphere**.

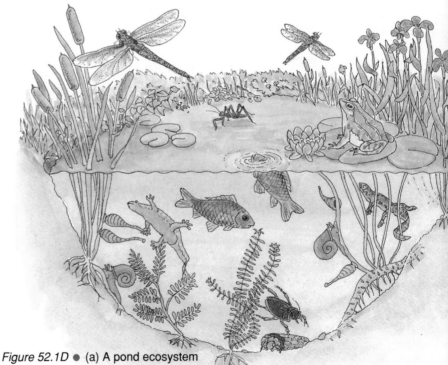

Figure 52.1D ● (a) A pond ecosystem

IT'S A FACT

The leaves of a tree differ depending on their position. Those at the top are in direct sunlight a lot of the time. These 'sun leaves' are smaller in area and are packed with chloroplasts. The 'shade leaves' found lower in the tree canopy, have a much larger area and far fewer chloroplasts. They contribute very little to photosynthesis.

LOOK AT LINKS
for **bacteria** and **fungi**
See Theme A, Topic 3.5.

SUMMARY

Ecosystems are the basic unit of study in ecology. They are made up of the habitat (non-living surrounding) and the community (living plants and animals). A community consists of populations of plants and animals. Each population must be adapted to the conditions that exist in the ecosystem if it is to survive.

CHECKPOINT

❶ Match the list of terms below with the descriptions that follow.

habitat   biosphere   population   competition   community   ecosystem

(a) All the ecosystems on the Earth.
(b) A group of individuals of the same species.
(c) Organisms that interact within the same ecosystem.
(d) Made up of the habitat and the community.

❷ Match the animals and plants in Column A below with their correct habitats in Column B:

Column A	Column B
Lichen	Wood
Trout	Path
Hawthorn	Rocky shore
Groundsel	Pond
Squirrel	Moorland
Heather	River
Frog	Hedge
Crab	Wall

❸ Environmental conditions differ in different habitats. In each case, choose two physical conditions, e.g. climate, soil, wave action and suggest the problems that they would pose for animals and plants living in the following habitats:
(a) Fast-flowing mountain stream.
(b) Coniferous plantation.
(c) Saltmarsh.
(d) Acid heathland.

❹ Distinguish, as clearly as possible, between the following:
(a) Ecosystem and habitat.
(b) Population and community.
(c) Competitors and predators.
(d) Grazers and decomposers.

(b) A town ecosystem

52.2 ● Community structure

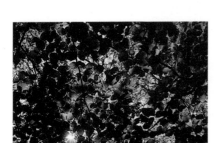

Figure 52.2A ● Green plants trap the radiant energy of sunlight

LOOK AT LINKS
for **teeth**
See Theme F, Topic 25.4.

Producers and consumers

In any community, the organisms can be classified by their method of feeding. Basically, either they can make their own food or they can't.

Autotrophs are able to make their own food from simple substances such as carbon dioxide and water. Green plants are autotrophs. They use light as a source of energy to make sugars. Many bacteria are also autotrophs. Some obtain their energy from light and others from simple chemical reactions. Since autotrophs ultimately provide food for all the other members of the community, we call them **producers**. (See Figure 52.2A).

Heterotrophs cannot make their own food so they have to eat it. For this reason they are called **consumers**:
● **Primary consumers** are herbivores. They eat producers (see Figure 52.1C(d)).
● **Secondary consumers** are carnivores. They eat herbivores (see Figure 52.1C(b)).
● **Tertiary consumers** are carnivores that eat secondary consumers.
Each category of feeding is known as a **trophic level** (from the Greek *trophos* which means 'a feeder'). *But how do we know what an animal feeds upon?* We can get a good idea by looking at **teeth** and other feeding structures. We can also investigate contents of the animal's gut or study its feeding behaviour.

Decomposers

Some consumers obtain their energy from dead and decaying material and are called decomposers. These are mainly bacteria and fungi and they perform an important role in the cycling of nutrients. As they break down dead material, they make it available as nutrients for the growth of new plants. (See Figure 52.2B.)

IT'S A FACT

Animal plankton contains the immature larvae of many sea-shore animals. The larvae of crabs look very different from the adults. They also feed upon different food and are carried by currents to eventually settle on new parts of the shore.

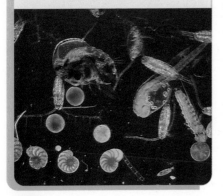

Figure 52.2B ● Decomposition

Food chains and food webs

Feeding methods are a useful way of showing the relationships that exist in a community. We can highlight these by means of **food chains**. These show the passage of food (and therefore energy) from one organism to another. Food chains always start with a producer. The food then passes to a primary consumer, next to a secondary consumer and so on. The number of links (producer and consumers) in a food chain may vary, but is seldom more than five. (See Figure 52.2C.)

Food chains can show the feeding in any community. The arrows represent the transfer of food between different trophic levels. So it is easy to see the particular role that each organism plays in the community. The role of an organism is known as its **niche**. The niche can be identified in other ways apart from feeding, for example it may depend upon where the organism makes its home or how it reproduces.

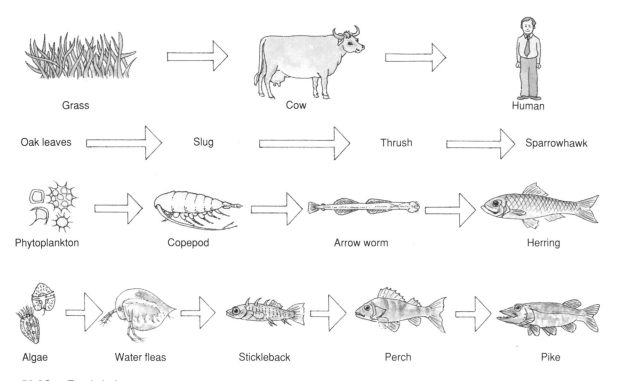

Figure 52.2C ● Food chains

Several food chains exist in a community and these will link up to form a **food web** (see Figure 52.2D). This is because the diet of an animal consists of a number of different species. A food web represents a more complete picture of the feeding relationships in a community.

SUMMARY

Producers are able to make their own food. They include green plants and some bacteria. Producers provide food for primary consumers (herbivores). These in turn provide food for secondary consumers (carnivores). Decomposers feed upon dead and decaying material. These feeding relationships can be shown by the use of food chains and food webs. The role that an animal of plant plays in a community is known as its niche.

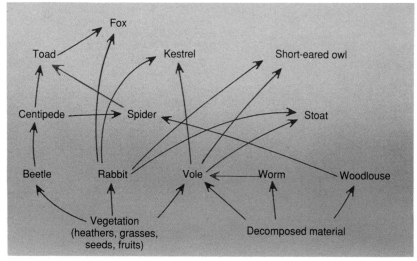

Figure 52.2D ● Food web for a moorland community

❶ Study the food web and answer the questions which follow.

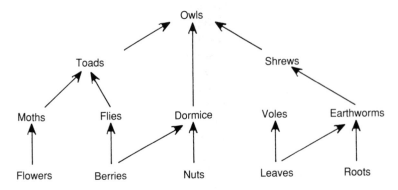

(a) From the diagram name (i) two primary consumers, (ii) one secondary consumer.
(b) Construct, using the food web above, two different food chains, each with four links. The arrows should point from eaten to eater.
(c) Explain why every food chain must begin with a green plant.
(d) If all the owls were killed, what would happen to the size of the populations of (i) dormice, (ii) earthworms?
(e) In the food web shown, the moths depend upon the flowers and the dormice depend upon the hazel tree for food. Give one example to show how (i) the flowers may depend on the moths, (ii) the hazel tree may depend upon the dormice.

(WJEC)

52.3 Ecological pyramids

Food chains and food webs can describe the feeding relationships that occur in a community. However they give us no information about the numbers of individuals involved. It takes many plants to support a few herbivores. Similarly there must be far more prey than there are predators. (See Figure 52.3A.)

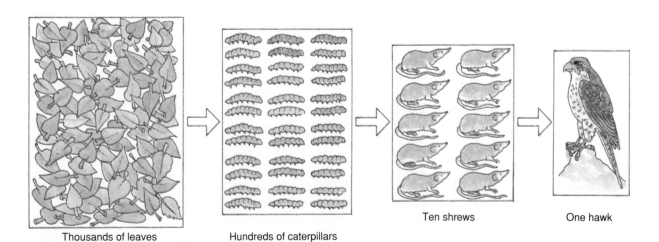

Thousands of leaves   Hundreds of caterpillars   Ten shrews   One hawk

Figure 52.3A ● More plants than herbivores - more prey than predators

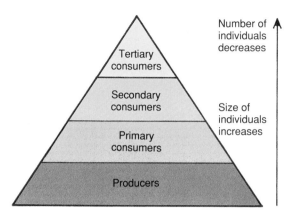

Figure 52.3B ● Pyramid of numbers

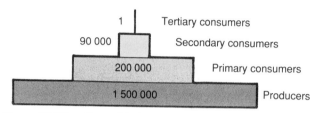

Figure 52.3C ● Pyramid of numbers for a grassland community in 0.1 hectare

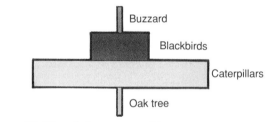

Figure 52.3D ● Oak tree pyramid

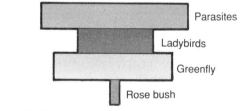

Figure 52.3E ● Inverted pyramid

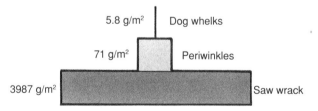

Figure 52.3F ● Biomass pyramid for a rocky shore community

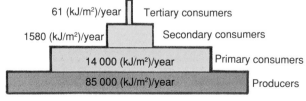

Figure 52.3G ● Pyramid of energy for a river

Pyramids of number

Pyramids of number give information about the numbers of individuals in each trophic level. They are drawn up by counting the number of individuals in a certain area, say one square metre. These numbers are then plotted like bar charts but horizontally (see Figure 52.3B). The producers are placed at the base of the pyramid. Above them are placed the primary consumers. The secondary consumers are placed on top of these and so on. Note that as we go up the pyramid:

- The numbers of individuals decrease.
- The size of each individual increases.

Figure 52.3C shows a pyramid of numbers drawn from some results taken from a grassland community.

A problem with this method is that it fails to take into account the size of the organisms at each trophic level. For instance one oak tree will support many more herbivores than one grass plant. Figure 52.3D shows a pyramid of this kind. Pyramids appear top heavy if we include parasites since many parasites will feed on the secondary consumers. Such a pyramid is said to be inverted as shown in Figure 52.3E.

Pyramids of biomass

One way of overcoming this problem of the size of organisms, is to chart the **biomass** at each trophic level. A representative sample of the organisms at each trophic level is weighed. The mass is then multiplied by the estimated number in the community. In practice the dry mass is used since fresh mass varies so much with water content. The sample is heated in an oven at 110 °C until there is no further change in mass (this is often neither practicable nor desirable if it involves destroying animals and plants in the process). Figure 52.3F shows a biomass pyramid for a rocky shore community.

Biomass pyramids also have their drawbacks:

- Some organisms grow at a much faster rate than others, for example grass does not have a large biomass, but it carries on growing at a very fast rate.
- The biomass of an individual can vary during the year – a beech tree will have a much greater biomass in June than it has in November. *Why do you think this is?*

Pyramids of energy

Pyramids of energy provide the most accurate representation of the feeding relationships in a community. They give information about the amount of new tissue at each trophic level over a certain period of time. They make it possible to compare different communities accurately. They can also be used to

Lake Web and Bio-wood (program)

In an environment such as a lake or a wood, survival depends on making decisions about what to eat, what to ignore and what to escape from. Try surviving in *Lake Web* or *Bio-wood*.

compare the production of food by different methods of farming. Figure 52.3G shows an energy pyramid for a river.

Shortening the food chain

Look at the pyramid of numbers in Figure 52.3H. It shows the estimated numbers of individuals that could be supported on 1000 tonnes of grass in ten months.

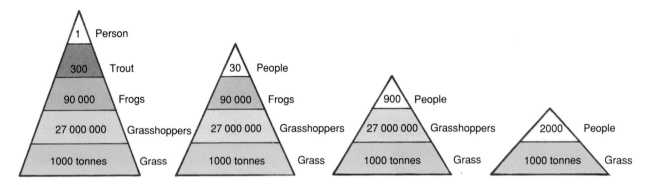

Figure 52.3H ● Shortening the food chain

If the food chain was shortened and people decided to eat frogs instead of trout, 30 people could be supported in this way (assuming that a person could get by on 10 frogs a day). *What would happen if the food chain were shortened still further and people ate grasshoppers?* Assuming that 100 grasshoppers a day would keep one person satisfied, then 900 people could be supported. If we now eliminate the grasshoppers from the food chain, then by feeding on grass alone, 2000 people could live on land that could only support one person when his or her diet was trout.

What message is there for us from this exercise? It tells us that a vegetarian diet can sustain far more people. By eliminating links in the food chain, more individuals at the end of the food chain can be fed. *Why do you think that the diets of people in underdeveloped countries tend to be made up mostly of plants?* In the Western developed countries people have a varied diet including large amounts of poultry, fish, lamb, beef and pork. *What does this tell you about the economies of these countries?*

With the huge increase in the world's population, what is likely to happen to the price of meat and what may be the inevitable change in human diets in the future?

SUMMARY

Pyramids of number tell us about the numbers of individuals at each trophic level. Biomass pyramids give information about the mass of material present. More accurate are energy pyramids that show the transfer of energy through a community. A short food chain can support far more people than one with many links in the chain.

CHECKPOINT

① The diagram below shows a food web.

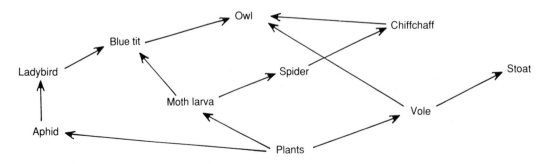

(a) Name the ultimate source of energy for all the organisms in this food web.
(b) From this food web name one example of a secondary consumer.
(c) Construct a food chain which includes examples of animals from four different feeding levels in this food web.
(d) If all the spiders were killed by disease, suggest the effects this could have on the food web shown.

52.4 Energy flow through ecosystems

We have talked about the passage of food between trophic levels, but it is far more accurate to describe the passage or flow of energy through an ecosystem. Energy can be converted. For example, the radiant energy of sunlight is converted into the chemical bond energy in carbohydrates during photosynthesis.

Energy flow through producers

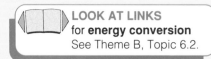

LOOK AT LINKS
for **energy conversion**
See Theme B, Topic 6.2.

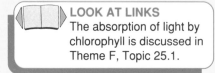

LOOK AT LINKS
The absorption of light by chlorophyll is discussed in Theme F, Topic 25.1.

The energy in all ecosystems has its origin in sunlight. Green plants (and some bacteria) are the only organisms that can use this energy to convert carbon dioxide and water into carbohydrates. Photosynthesis is far less efficient than we may imagine, because much of the sunlight that falls on to plants, is not absorbed. The light may not be absorbed because:
- much of it is reflected from the surface of the leaf,
- a large amount passes straight through the leaf,
- only light falling in the range of wavelengths from 380 nm (red) to 720 nm (blue) can be absorbed by chlorophyll.

The overall efficiency of energy conversion in photosynthesis is less than 8%.

What does the plant do with this energy? The plant needs energy to drive its own chemical reactions during respiration. The remainder of the energy is used in growth and repair, which increase the biomass of the plant. This represents the food and energy that is available to primary consumers and so can be transferred up to a higher trophic level. Some energy will be transferred from the plant when leaves are shed, when fruits and seeds are dispersed and eventually when the plant dies. Decomposers will benefit from this since they will gain energy from the dead plant tissues. Figure 52.4A summarises the energy flow through a green plant.

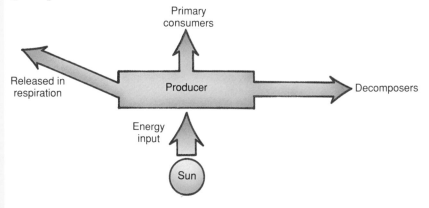

Figure 52.4A ● Energy flow through a green plant

Energy flow through consumers

Transfer of energy from producers to primary consumers, that is from plants to herbivores also involves a loss of energy. It is estimated that for every 100 g of plant material eaten, only 10 g ends up as herbivore biomass. This represents an effective loss of energy between trophic levels of approximately 90%. The reasons for the inefficiency of this transfer of energy are:

- Some of the plant material passes out of the body of the herbivore as faeces without being digested.
- A lot of energy is used in respiration by the herbivore.
- Some energy passes to decomposers in dead remains.

Similar losses of energy from the ecosystem occur between each subsequent trophic level. Carnivores are able to achieve a 20% efficiency. That is to say, 20% of the herbivore biomass ends up as carnivore biomass. This is possible because proteins are more efficiently digested than are carbohydrates.

● The energy budget of a primary consumer

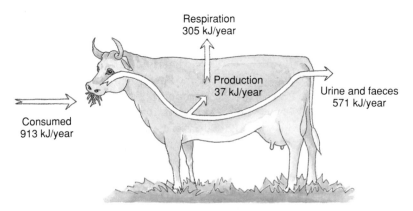

Figure 52.4B ● The energy intake and output of a cow

SUMMARY

Energy enters ecosystems as sunlight and leaves it as heat. Only a fraction of the light falling on a leaf will end up as new plant biomass. There is great loss of energy from the ecosystem as it flows between trophic levels.

Figure 52.4B shows the energy intake and output of a cow. Of the energy in the grass which a cow eats, over half is passed out of the body in faeces. Some goes to increase cow biomass (production). A lot of energy is lost from the body as heat produced in respiration and in the urine. The energy budget of the cow can be summarised in the following equation:

$$\text{Energy intake} = \text{Energy transfer in respiration} + \text{Energy transfer in production} + \text{Energy in urine} + \text{Energy in faeces}$$

CHECKPOINT

❶ Look at Figure 52.4B.
(a) Would you say that the cow is efficient in converting grass into biomass (production)? Explain your answer.
(b) What percentage of the energy intake is present in faeces and urine? Faeces provide a rich food source for a number of organisms. Name some of them.
(c) What percentage of the energy intake is used up in respiration?
(d) Cows spend a great deal of their time grazing. In view of your other answers, why do you think this is?
(e) How do you think the energy budget of a secondary consumer would compare with the example here?

❷ Look at the figure below and answer the following questions (the size of the arrows represents the relative amounts of energy passed on at each stage).

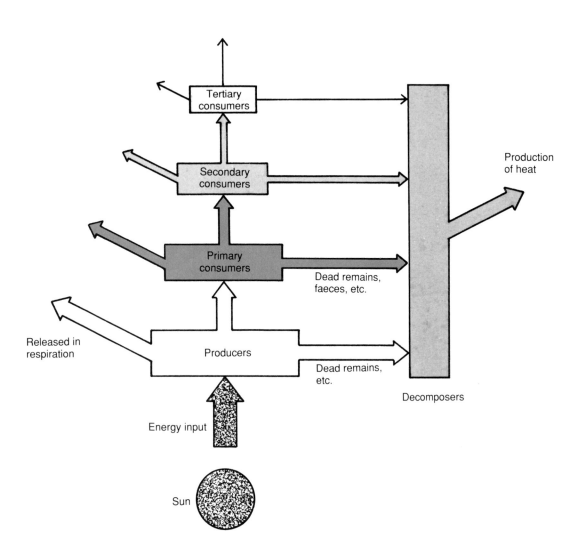

(a) What is the original source of energy for the ecosystem?
(b) How is energy eventually lost from the ecosystem?
(c) Would you say that the transfer of energy through the ecosystem was a cyclical process where the energy is reused or a flow in one direction? Give reasons for your choice.
(d) In what ways is energy lost from (i) the producers and (ii) the consumers?
(e) Predict what might happen to the biomass of the primary consumers when the rate of photosynthesis increases.
(f) How might an increase in the number of primary consumers affect
  (i) the number of producers,
  (ii) the number of secondary consumers?

❸ From every one square metre of grass it eats, a cow obtains 3000 kJ of energy. It uses 100 kJ for growth, 1000 kJ are lost as heat and 1900 kJ are lost in faeces.
(a) What percentage of the energy in one square metre of grass
  (i) is used in growth,
  (ii) passes through the gut and is not absorbed?
(b) If beef has an energy value of 12 kJ per gram, how many square metres of grass are needed to produce 100 g of beef?

52.5 Decomposition and cycles

Decomposition

Figure 52.5A ● Animal decomposition

Eventually all plants and animals die. You may have seen the remains of a blackbird caught by the family cat, a hedgehog run over and left at the side of the road or a dead gull washed up on the shore (see Figure 52.5A). In autumn dead leaves form a carpet on the ground (see Figure 52.5B). All this dead material eventually disappears. *Where does it go?*

Figure 52.5B ● Plant decomposition

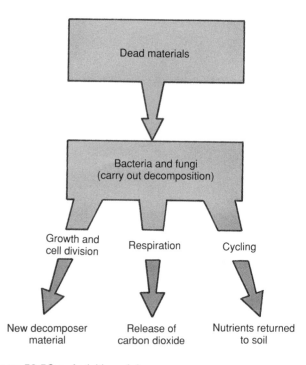

Figure 52.5C ● Activities of decomposers

In the UK decomposition is quicker in the summer than in the winter. Maggots are able to decompose up to 80% of small mammal and bird carcasses in the summer. In the winter, there are few maggots around so decomposition is mainly carried out by microbes.

There are many animals that feed upon dead remains, we call them **scavengers**. Crows, maggots, woodlice and vultures all make a living by feeding upon dead material. However scavengers cannot account for the removal of all dead material and even without them it would slowly disappear anyway due to the action of decomposers. These are microbes, mainly fungi and bacteria, that break down dead material and also make food go rotten. They release enzymes which digest the dead remains in just the same way as food in your gut is digested. The simple products of digestion are absorbed by the decomposers and used for their own growth. (See Figure 52.5C.)

Cycles

LOOK AT LINKS
for **the carbon cycle**
See Theme E, Topic 20.6.

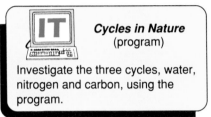

LOOK AT LINKS
for **the nitrogen cycle**
See Theme E, Topic 20.5.

IT   *Cycles in Nature*
(program)

Investigate the three cycles, water, nitrogen and carbon, using the program.

SUMMARY

Decomposers break down dead remains and release nutrients into the ecosystem. These nutrients are absorbed by plants and passed along food chains. Nutrients such as carbon, nitrogen and sulphur are continuously being cycled through ecosystems.

Not all of the products of decomposition are used to make new fungi and bacteria: most are returned to the soil as nutrients. These nutrients are then made available to plants and in turn to animals for growth. This cycling of nutrients is vital if life is to continue. Most living matter (95%) is made up of just six elements: carbon, hydrogen, nitrogen, oxygen, phosphorus and sulphur.

A constant supply of nutrients containing these elements is essential if living organisms are to continue to make important compounds like proteins, fats and carbohydrates. Figure 52.5D shows the pattern of cycling nutrients which takes place in all ecosystems, on land, in freshwater and in the sea.

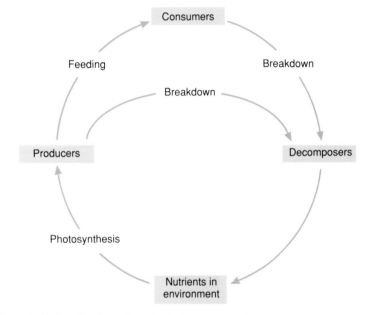

Figure 52.5D ● Cycling of nutrients in an ecosystem

52.6 The effect of humans on ecosystems

Our effect upon ecosystems is highlighted daily in the newspapers and on television (see Figure 52.6A). Not a day goes by without our hearing of a new environmental crisis: the pollution of our air and water, soil erosion and the creation of deserts, the population explosion and the shortages of food and shelter, destruction of natural habitats such as tropical rain forests and vanishing wildlife.

Figure 52.6A ● Environmental disaster - deforestation in the Amazon

The depletion of the ozone layer, acid rain, the increase in the greenhouse effect have all brought home to us the fact that our planet is fragile. Disasters such as oil spills and chemical leaks bring environmental problems to our attention, but less serious incidents happen everyday. *What is our response?* It is easy to think that these disasters are far too vast and are impossible to cope with. *But why?* Over the past fifty years we have made great strides in reducing poverty. Improvements have come in health: infant mortality has been reduced and many diseases can now be controlled. Advances have also been made in combatting food shortages, improving welfare and education. In 1990 some nations began to reduce their stocks of arms. If all nations did this, there would be more money to spend on undoing the damage which we have done to the Earth. One thing is sure, we cannot continue to use the Earth as a rubbish tip. This would only be storing up unsolvable problems for future generations. We have only one Earth.

Agricultural chemicals

Between 1945 and 1975, the world's food output doubled. This 'Green Revolution' was brought about by improved agricultural technology, advances in crop breeding and the use of agricultural chemicals. The rapid rise in production now seems to be slowing and a number of unexpected side-effects are surfacing. The structure and properties of the soil seem to have been changed. Over-use of fertilisers, the addition of lime to counter acidity and constant ploughing have taken their toll. The Soviet Union in the 1950s and 60s made huge efforts to produce more grain. It is now suffering the after-effects. There are areas where the soil is exhausted and the land has to remain fallow.

● *Fertilisers*

Fertilisers improve crop growth by giving the plants nutrients that they need, such as nitrates and phosphates (see Figure 52.6B). Some of these chemicals are not taken up by crops and find their way into our waterways when they are washed through the soil by rain. Once this agricultural 'run-off' gets into the surface waters it can have adverse effects on the environment.

Figure 52.6B ● Applying artificial fertiliser

IT'S A FACT

The cottony-cushion scale insect became a pest in the orange groves of California when accidentally introduced from Australia. It had no natural predators in California so scientists went to Australia and found a species of ladybird. They introduced this species to California where it quickly reduced the scale insect numbers so that it was no longer a pest. This is an example of biological control.

Figure 52.6C Crops are often sprayed with herbicides and insecticides

LOOK AT LINKS
for **dioxin**
See Theme G, Topic 29.9.

● *Herbicides*

Herbicides are chemicals used to eliminate weeds. Weeds compete with the crop plant for light, space, water and soil nutrients. They can seriously reduce crop yield. Many herbicides are made from the chemical dinitrophenol. During the manufacture of dinitrophenol, a harmful impurity is formed called **dioxin**.

● *Insecticides*

LOOK AT LINKS
for **insecticides**
See Theme G, Topic 29.10.

Insecticides are chemicals that kill pest insects. The use of insecticides has saved millions of lives. Malaria, typhus and yellow fever are all carried by insects. It is estimated that without pesticides, crop losses of 45% would occur in the tropics. However insecticides have proved to have dangerous side effects.

Alternative methods of controlling pests are being explored. **Biological control** involves the introduction of the pest's natural predator in order to reduce its numbers. A classic example of biological control comes from Australia, where farmers planted the prickly-pear cactus in an attempt to keep wallabies from eating their crops. The prickly-pear grew so well that it covered millions of acres of grassland and became a greater nuisance than the wallabies had been. The answer to the problem was found by introducing a moth from Argentina. The moth's caterpillars fed on the cactus. The spread of the cactus was halted and much of the land reclaimed for agricultural use. Parasitic wasps have also been used successfully to control many crop pests throughout the world.

LOOK AT LINKS
for **radioactive decay**
See Theme C, Topic 12.2.

Radiation

Radiation probably represents the most feared type of pollutant. Sources of non-natural radiation come from the testing and use of nuclear weapons and from leakages from nuclear reactors (see Figure 52.6D). Radioactive waste from the latter is a mixture of different isotopes. These all **decay** (give off radiation) at different rates. The half-life of a radioactive isotope is the time taken for its activity to decay to half of its original level.

Figure 52.6D ● A nuclear reactor

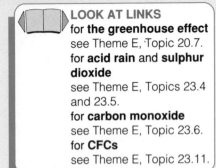

LOOK AT LINKS
for **the greenhouse effect**
see Theme E, Topic 20.7.
for **acid rain** and **sulphur dioxide**
see Theme E, Topics 23.4 and 23.5.
for **carbon monoxide**
see Theme E, Topic 23.6.
for **CFCs**
see Theme E, Topic 23.11.

Polluting gases

- **Carbon dioxide** is not only produced when we breathe, it is released into the atmosphere whenever fossil fuels, such as coal, oil and natural gas are burnt. Carbon dioxide enhances the **greenhouse effect**.
- **Sulphur dioxide** is released into the atmosphere when fossil fuels are burnt. Together with oxides of nitrogen in car exhaust fumes, sulphur dioxide eventually falls as **acid rain**.
- **Carbon monoxide** is produced by car exhausts. Haemoglobin in red blood cells takes up carbon monoxide in preference to oxygen.
- **CFCs** (chlorofluorohydrocarbons) are used in refrigerators and as propellants in aerosol sprays. It has been found that the release of CFCs into the atmosphere is destroying the ozone layer.

Pollution of lakes and rivers

Our waterways are often the sink of domestic, industrial and agricultural wastes.

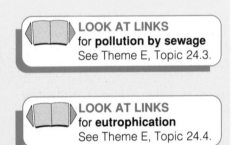

LOOK AT LINKS
for **pollution by sewage**
See Theme E, Topic 24.3.

LOOK AT LINKS
for **eutrophication**
See Theme E, Topic 24.4.

● *Sewage*
Sewage is often discharged into our rivers and is the biggest single pollutant (see Figure 52.6E). Its effects resemble those of **eutrophication**. It encourages rapid growth of bacteria which use up oxygen from the water during respiration. The result is that the river will be depleted of fish and many invertebrates because of the lack of oxygen. It takes time for the sewage to be broken down by the bacteria, so the amount of dissolved oxygen in the river only reaches its original, unpolluted level some way downstream.

LOOK AT LINKS
for **thermal pollution**
See Theme E, Topic 24.2.

● *Heat*
Water is used to cool many industrial processes. The largest user is the electricity industry in its power stations (see Figure 52.6F). Water is returned to the river at a higher temperature than the river temperature. Oxygen becomes less soluble in water as the temperature increases.

Pollution of the seas

We are at long last beginning to realise that the dumping of waste into our seas is storing up long-term problems for the future. Our rivers empty toxic chemicals into the sea as they drain from the land and are discharged as waste from industries. They include:

- **Fertilisers and sewage** increase the growth of algae and threaten the balance of natural ecosystems such as the Great Barrier Reef in Northern Australia. The rapid growth of the algae is killing the coral, which grows best in low nutrient concentrations.
- **Insecticides** such as DDT, aldrin and dieldrin, used in the protection of crops, also drain off the land into rivers. Shellfish are able to concentrate pesticides in their tissues.
- **Radionuclides** can also reach high levels in tissues. They can be found in high concentrations near coastal nuclear power stations.
- **Toxic metals** such as mercury, cadmium, copper and lead can also be concentrated up food chains. **Minamata disease** is one of the most striking examples of the adverse effects of heavy metal pollution. Cadmium has been found in high concentrations in the bodies of fish in the Bristol Channel. Lead concentrations in the North Sea have increased three-fold and copper dumped off the Dutch coast resulted in the deaths of thousands of fish.

LOOK AT LINKS
for **Minamata disease**
See Theme E, Topic 24.1.

● *Oil pollution*

Modern oil tankers carry millions of tonnes of unrefined, crude oil. The pollution from spillages that we see in the media is made worse by the practice of washing out oil tanks at sea. The advent of large scale offshore drilling brings further risk. Names like the *Exxon Valdez*, *Torrey Canyon* and *Amoco Cadiz* conjure up familiar pictures of oil covered beaches. The sufferers include fish-eating birds, whose feathers become clogged, so they are unable to fly and soon die of exposure, drowning or starvation (see Figure 52.6G). Marine mammals such as seals and sea otters can be affected by the oil penetrating their fur. The detergents sprayed on the shorelines of Britain to disperse the oil were toxic to much intertidal life.

Figure 52.6E ● Sewage - the biggest water pollutant

Figure 52.6F ● Power station cooling towers

Figure 52.6G ● Oiled sea bird

LOOK AT LINKS
for **oil pollution**
See Theme E, Topic 24.6.

SUMMARY

Much threatens the delicate balance of life in our ecosystems due to the intervention of man. We have a duty of care to redress this balance and protect it for future generations.

TOPIC 53 POPULATIONS

53.1 Population growth

Figure 53.1A ● Populations come in all shapes and sizes

A **population** is a group of individuals of the same species living in a particular habitat (see Figure 53.1A). The following are all populations:

- aphids on a sycamore tree,
- barnacles on a rocky shore,
- bacteria growing on a food medium in a petri dish,
- duckweed on the surface of a pond,
- a shoal of herring in the sea.

One of the reasons ecologists study populations is to gain information about the rate at which their numbers change. Such studies are of practical use if the species is a pest or if it causes disease. For instance, population studies of the locust are important since a swarm of locusts can devour a harvest. Studies of mosquito populations can help scientists to control the spread of malaria. Investigations into the human population explosion are very important for the future of mankind.

Why do individuals live in populations? There may be a number of reasons:

- The habitat provides food, shelter and other vital factors.
- Individuals come together to breed.
- Individuals may gain more protection as a population, for example a shoal of fish or a colony of gulls.

However, overcrowding may result in competition within the population. Individuals may compete for food, space, light and other resources. Inevitably some will not survive this competition and numbers may decline.

Think about a plant or animal species colonising a new area. A few individuals enter the new habitat. Provided there are no predators and that there is no shortage of food, the individuals will thrive and reproduce. At first their numbers will increase slowly. Later, as the population grows, so does the rate of increase (2 becomes 4 then 8, 16, 32, 64, 128, 256, 512 and so on). This sort of growth where each generation is double the size of the previous one is the maximum rate of growth and is called exponential growth. Exponential growth can only take place under ideal environmental conditions. It cannot go on for long. Eventually limiting factors such as lack of food and overcrowding cause the rate of increase to slow and eventually to level off. After this the population remains constant as long as the rate at which individuals are born is equal to the rate at which individuals die. (See Figure 53.1B.)

TRY THIS

A population growth curve like the one in Figure 53.1B can quite easily be produced by growing some yeast cells in sugar solution. Every half hour take up a small sample with a pipette and look at a drop of it under the microscope. By counting the number of yeast cells in the microscope's field of view, you can follow the development of the yeast population. The exercise is more accurate if a counting slide is used. The slide is divided into squares and the number of yeast cells in each square is counted at the same magnification each time.

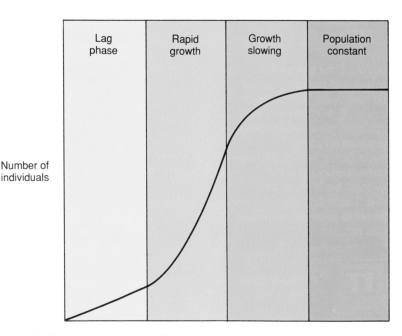

| Lag phase | Rapid growth | Growth slowing | Population constant |

Number of individuals

Figure 53.1B ● Population growth curve

53.2   Checks on population increase

So what prevents populations increasing? It could be lack of food, overcrowding, or perhaps the build up of poisonous waste products produced by the individuals of the population itself. A number of environmental factors limit the growth of populations. These environmental factors act as natural checks which prevent the population from growing too large. Among them are:

• **Food, water and oxygen**. These affect the growth of most populations. Individuals in the population compete for them and if they are in short supply then some individuals will not survive and the population will level off or decline.

• **Light**. Light is especially necessary for green plants which carry out photosynthesis. Plants compete for light in areas of dense vegetation. (See Figure 53.2A.)

Figure 53.2A ● Competing for light

IT'S A FACT

Lemmings are mouse-like animals that feed on grasses and roots in the mountains of Norway. Every few years the population grows rapidly due to increased breeding. Overcrowding occurs and large numbers emigrate to the lowlands. Many die or are killed. Those that reach the sea attempt to swim out and drown in the process.

Old Park Farm
(program)

What is happening to the bat population? Use the program to investigate bats' roosting and feeding areas and to find out about the ecological problems which threaten the bat population.

- **Lack of shelter.** Animals compete for shelter in order to avoid predators or harsh climate (see **Climate** below).
- **Overcrowding.** Overcrowding often leads to unhygienic conditions which favour the spread of disease. It also results in stress.
- **Predators.** These are natural checks on population increase. The size of a predator population depends on the numbers of prey. An increase in the number of predators means that more prey will be caught and the number of prey will fall. The predators' food supply is reduced and this leads in turn to a drop in the number of predators.
- **Accumulation of toxic wastes.** Natural waste products such as carbon dioxide and nitrogenous waste such as ammonia and urea become toxic if they are allowed to build up. Obviously, as the population increases, more waste is produced and this can restrict further growth.
- **Disease.** Disease can spread very quickly through large populations. Monocultures of arable crops are susceptible to disease-causing organisms.
- **Climate.** Harsh weather conditions can reduce populations. Animals and plants can die if the temperature is very high or very low. Drought and flood, storms and gales all take their toll on populations.

Sometimes populations decrease dramatically in a short space of time. They do not level off but crash dramatically. This may occur because the population runs out of food or if it has been overcome by disease. The danger is often a temporary or a seasonal affair. For example, the numbers of aphids on a rose bush decline very quickly if ladybirds start to prey on them.

53.3 Population size

Golden Eagle
(program)

As chief warden of a Scottish Wildlife reserve, you have been asked to double the Golden Eagle population. Use the program to try this. You will find it helpful to make notes of things you try.

Birth rates as well as death rates will determine the size of a population. Some species are capable of phenomenal increases in population. Many insects lay hundreds of eggs, frogs lay thousands and fish produce millions.

Few animals stay in one place, they tend to move into and out of the habitat in which the population lives. We call the movement of individuals into a population **immigration** and the movement of individuals out of a population **emigration** (see Figure 53.3A). In a stable population

$$\text{Birth rate} + \text{Immigration rate} = \text{Death rate} + \text{Emigration rate}$$
$$(B) \qquad\qquad (I) \qquad\qquad (D) \qquad\qquad (E)$$

If the population is increasing then

$$B + I \text{ will be more than } D + E$$

If a population is declining then

$$D + E \text{ will be more than } B + I$$

Estimating the size of a population

Ecologists often need to estimate the size of a particular population when they are carrying out a scientific study. In the case of plants there is usually little difficulty. A quadrat is laid down on the vegetation (a quadrat is a sampling device which consists of a metal or wooden

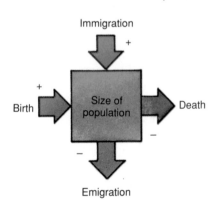

Figure 53.3A ● Factors affecting the size of a population

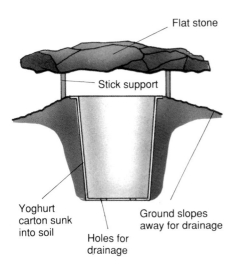

Flat stone

Stick support

Yoghurt carton sunk into soil

Holes for drainage

Ground slopes away for drainage

Figure 53.3B ● A pitfall trap is one way of trapping small animals prior to counting

rectangle, usually one metre square). The number of individuals of a particular plant occurring within the quadrat is then counted. The number of quadrats needed to cover the habitat is estimated and multiplied by the number of plants per quadrat to give the total population.

Sampling animals is more difficult. Animals tend to move about – they certainly do not stay in a quadrat. Also many animals only come out at night so they have to be trapped before they can be counted (see Figure 53.3B). Ecologists use a method called mark, release, recapture to estimate many animal populations. It works like this:

- Collect a number of animals from the habitat.
- Mark the captured animals. Ecologists try to make the mark in some way that is harmless and does not make the animals conspicuous to predators, for example, a small dot in a dull colour on a beetle's carapace.
- Release the marked animals into the same habitat they came from and leave them for a day or two to mix freely back into the rest of the population.
- Make a second collection of a similar number of animals from the same habitat. Note the number of marked individuals in this second sample.
- The total population of each species can be estimated by using the following

$$\text{Total population} = \frac{\text{Number in first catch} \times \text{Number in second catch}}{\text{Number of marked individuals in second catch}}$$

Worked example 20 ground beetles were caught in a pitfall. They were each marked with a small dot of paint and when it was dry, they were released. After two days a second sample of 18 beetles was caught. Of these, six were marked individuals from the first occasion. Estimate the total population of beetles.

Solution
Number in first catch = 20
Number in second catch = 18
Number of marked individuals in second catch = 6
Total population $= \dfrac{20 \times 18}{6} = 60$

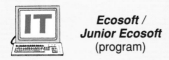

IT

Ecosoft / Junior Ecosoft
(program)

If you have collected data from fieldwork or laboratory activities, you can put them into the programs *Ecosoft* or *Junior Ecosoft*. These programs help you to sort out and present the data attractively and clearly.

CHECKPOINT

❶ By using a net to sweep long grass, 90 froghoppers (small insects) were collected. Each was marked and released back into the grass. The next day a second sweep produced 80 froghoppers and of these six had a mark on them. Estimate the total population of froghoppers in the field.

❷ It is important that the handling and marking of animals causes them no harm. Explain why it is also important that:
(a) the mark does not rub off too soon,
(b) the mark does not make the animal conspicuous.

❸ On the seashore, periwinkles are excellent animals for this sort of exercise. They are easy to find under rocks and seaweed and are most active when the tide is in. A sample of 18 periwinkles was marked and released and after a period of four days, 26 were collected. Of these, 12 were marked individuals. Estimate the periwinkle population for the stretch of shoreline.

53.4 Human populations

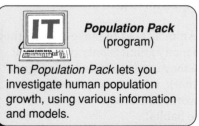
The human population is presently growing at an alarming rate, but it
has not always been so. For thousands of years the rate of population
increase was fairly slow. The huge increase that we see today has really
only occurred over the last 300 years (see Figure 53.4A). We can see from
Figure 53.4B that this rate of increase is far greater in so-called under-
developed countries than in Europe and North America. *Why is this?*

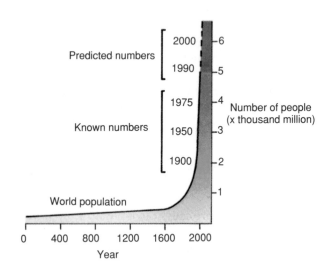

Figure 53.4A ● World population growth based on present
trends

Figure 53.4B ● Where the population is growing

There are many factors which contribute to this population increase:
- Improved agriculture has meant greater food production.
- Public health has improved, for instance there are cleaner water
  supplies and improved sanitation.
- Medical provision such as vaccination has improved and new drugs
  have been introduced to combat disease.
- Advances have been made in the control of disease-causing organisms.

All these factors contribute to lower infant mortality and increased life
expectancy. The average life expectancy has increased, in Europe and
North America, to 68 for men and 73 for women. In India, the figures
have for a long time been less than half these ages because of the high
death rate among infants. However, with improved health and living
conditions, the average life expectancy in India has risen to 56.

There are unforeseeable population checks, such as famine, floods,
war, earthquakes and other natural and man-made disasters. In
Bangladesh between 1970 and 1975, famine, floods and fighting resulted
in a yearly death rate of 30 per 1000. The rapid spread of Acquired
Immune Deficiency Syndrome (AIDS) particularly in developing
countries, could not have been predicted a few years ago. However
the overall trend is one of rapid increase in the world's population.
Estimates suggest that at the current rate, it could double in the next
30 years. *But the Earth has limited resources and limited space, so what are
we to do?* Clearly the biggest objective must be to reduce the birth
rate. This will involve education in under-developed countries and may
also challenge the religious and moral principles of many.

The rate of population growth is influenced by the proportion of young people in the population, in particular by women of child-bearing age. The figure below shows population pyramids for India and the USA. The base of the pyramid shows the percentage of children below the age of five years in each population. The oldest people appear at the top of the pyramids.

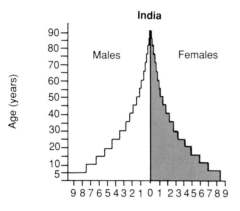

Percentage of the population in each age group
(For India 1% = approximately 4 million people)

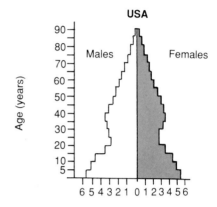

Percentage of the population in each age group
(For USA 1% = approximately 2 million people)

❶ (a) (i) Which country has the higher number of children below the age of 5 years?
    (ii) Which country has the higher number of old people over 80 years?
(b) Which country has (i) the higher birth rate (ii) the lower death rate?
(c) Explain your answers to (a) and (b) above.

❷ (a) What forecast can you make about the numbers of child-bearing women in each country in 15 years time?
(b) What will happen to the birth rate in each country as a result?

❸ (a) Which of the population pyramids of these two countries most resembles the pattern found in Britain?
(b) What is likely to happen to the number of adult workers in relation to elderly dependents as the average age of the population increases?
(c) What implications does this have for (i) health and social services and (ii) employment in this country?

53.5   Competition

We all have an idea of what is meant by competition. In a race, all the competitors strive as hard as they can to win, but at the end there is only one winner. In nature, the same thing happens. Individuals compete for resources that are in short supply. These may include food, space, light and other things that are vital for life. Clearly only those individuals able to compete successfully will survive so competition restricts the size to which a population will grow. Competition between individuals is of two types:
• Competition between individuals of the same species.
• Competition between individuals of different species.

● Competition between individuals of the same species

This sort of competition arises from the fact that plants and animals tend to produce far more offspring than the habitat can support. They do this to ensure the survival of the species and to enable the population to colonise new areas. As a result, there will be competition between individuals and only those that are the best adapted will survive to breed. They will be the ones who pass on their genes to the next generation. This competition is called 'survival of the fittest'. By this we mean that only as the result of a 'struggle for existence' do the best adapted individuals survive to breed and pass on their characteristics to the next generation. Competition will therefore contribute to natural selection. (See Figure 53.5A.)

LOOK AT LINKS
for **natural selection**
See Theme N, Topic 55.

Figure 53.5A ● Competition between individuals of the same species

● Competition between individuals of different species

There will be competition for scarce resources between the different species in a community. Weeds compete successfully with crops. They germinate rapidly and grow quickly to establish themselves before the crop matures. They occupy space and take light, water and minerals from the soil, which could have been used by the crop. By the time the crop plants have grown to their full height, the weeds will already have flowered and set seed, so ensuring their survival.

Animals of different species quite often compete for food. For instance predators like owls and weasels compete for the same prey, for example shrews. Different species of fly larvae will compete for the limited food available within a cow pat. Animals also compete for territory, for shelter and for nesting sites. Many different species are able to co-exist in a particular habitat because they occupy different **niches**.

Competition is most intense when different species attempt to fill the same niche. For example, *Elminius*, the Australian barnacle arrived on the UK shores during the Second World War when it hitched a ride on the

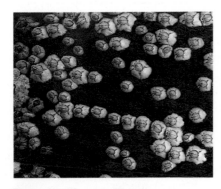

Figure 53.5B ● (a) *Elminius*

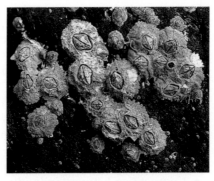

(b) *Semibalanus*

(c) *Chthamalus*

LOOK AT LINKS
for **niches**
See Theme M, Topic 52.2.

hulls of ships. There are two common native species of barnacle, *Semibalanus* and *Chthamalus* (see Figure 53.5B). In many situations, *Elminius* is able to 'out compete' both *Semibalanus* and *Chthamalus*, the reasons for this include:

- *Elminius* is more tolerant to low salinity.
- *Elminius* can withstand lower temperatures than *Chthamalus*.
- *Elminius* can withstand higher temperatures than *Semibalanus*.
- The feeding rate and rate of growth of *Elminius* are faster than those of *Semibalanus* and *Chthamalus*.

The ability of *Elminius* to fill its niche at the expense of the two native species of barnacle, demonstrates **competitive exclusion**. Competitive exclusion means that two species cannot co-exist if they both have the same niche.

Succession

What was it like when plants first colonised a habitat? We can get a good idea if we look at an area of ground that has been disturbed, perhaps by developers, by farming or by fire. Within a few weeks some weed and grass species will have grown. These species are known as **pioneers**, since they are the first to colonise. With the passage of time the pioneer plants may be replaced by a wider range of taller herb species. These may in turn be replaced by other more competitive scrub vegetation. This gradual change in the composition of the species is known as **succession**.

We can see succession taking place if arable land is neglected or on a smaller scale, if we do not mow the lawn. Other plant species soon appear: in the lawn, daisies and dandelions, on arable land, poppies and thistles. In most lowland areas of Britain the process of succession would eventually end as deciduous woodland if we were to let it, but it would take over 150 years. By then, the numbers of different species would have increased and the community as a whole would have become more complex and more stable. This sort of community changes very little and is known as a **climax community** (see Figure 53.5C). Other examples of climax communities include tropical rain forests and coral reefs. They contain a huge variety of different species so it is vital that we conserve them by protecting them from destruction.

TRY THIS

Why not persuade your teacher or your parents to allow a small area of lawn at school or at home to remain uncut? You will be surprised how many different plants appear. These will flower and attract insects and soon you will have provided a refuge for wildlife right on your doorstep!

SUMMARY

Competition exists both within a single species and between different species. Only those animals and plants that are the best adapted will survive this competition to fill a niche, others will be excluded. The sequence of changes in plants, which ends at a climax community is called succession.

Figure 53.5C ● A climax community - deciduous woodland

53.6 🐸 Predators and prey

Predator–Prey Relationships (program)

How do the populations of predators and prey change over yearly periods? The program lets you investigate.

Predators are animals that catch and kill other animals called prey. Thus predation has a major effect upon the number of the prey population. It is also true to say that the prey will have an effect upon the predator population. If the prey is scarce then some of the predators will starve.

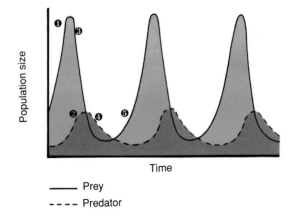

Figure 53.6A ● Predator–prey relationship

Figure 53.6A shows the relationship between the numbers of predators and prey. The relationship is self-regulating as we shall see. Notice that the since predators tend to reproduce more slowly, the predator cycle is smaller than the prey cycle and also lags behind it.

The events taking place in the predator–prey cycle are as follows:
❶ If conditions such as food supply are good, then the prey will breed and increase in number.
❷ Since there is now more food available, the predator will thrive and its numbers will increase.
❸ The rate of predation will now increase and as a result the number of prey will decline.
❹ Since there is now less food available to the predator, many will starve.
❺ With fewer predators, the prey numbers will increase again and so it goes on.

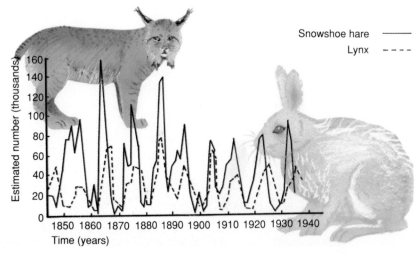

Figure 53.6B ● The lynx and the snowshoe hare predator–prey cycle

Other factors will affect the size of both populations. The incidence of disease, harsh climate and lack of shelter will all play their part. The most widely documented example of this predator–prey cycle is that of the snowshoe hare and its predator, the lynx. Records of their numbers were kept by the Hudson Bay Fur Company in Canada between 1845 and 1935. The numbers of hare and lynx pelts brought in by trappers were recorded. The fluctuations in the numbers of predator and prey are shown in Figure 53.6B.

What makes a successful predator?

A predator must be able to hunt and kill efficiently. *But how can a predator make life easier for itself?*

- By not being dependent on one particular species for prey there is less risk of starvation. If the numbers of one species of prey decline the predator can switch to another.
- Catching young, old and sick prey. The predator needs to expend less energy if its prey can be caught easily. A result is the weeding out of weaker individuals in the prey population. Those that remain are the best adapted individuals, who pass on their genes to the next generation.
- Catching large prey will provide more food for the predator per kill.
- Migrating to areas where prey is more plentiful.

However well adapted the predator becomes, it should not be too successful or else it risks the possibility of wiping out its food source. The predators most at risk of doing this are humans.

The prey's guide to survival

In order to avoid being captured, many prey species have a great variety of adaptations. These deter the predator, though they are never completely successful.

- Many try to out-run, out-swim or out-fly the predator.
- Staying in large groups, for example herds of antelope and shoals of fish, is an attempt to distract the predator from concentrating on one particular individual (see Figure 53.6C).
- Some animals, such as bees and wasps, will sting to avoid capture. Others just taste horrible, for instance ladybirds, so the predator thinks twice before eating one again.
- Some prey species possess warning colours that tell the predator to 'keep clear'. The hoverfly has striking yellow and black stripes that remind the predator of a wasp or bee (see Figure 53.6D). A hungry frog that has been stung previously by a wasp will think again before it attempts to eat a hoverfly. In fact, the hoverfly has no sting, so it is quite harmless.
- Camouflage is often used by prey to escape capture. The problem is that it is also used by the predator to avoid being seen when stalking the prey. Many animals try to blend in with their surroundings. Others try to look like something else, twigs or leaves for instance (see Figure 53.6E).
- Some prey species try shock tactics. They try to startle their predators into abandoning their attack. The eyed hawkmoth can quickly open its wings to reveal a pair of huge, coloured eye-spots. This often has the effect of scaring off a hungry bird (see Figure 53.6F).

Figure 53.6C ● Hiding in the crowd

Figure 53.6D ● A hoverfly displaying the 'danger' colours of a wasp

Figure 53.6E ● Two camouflaged moths

Figure 53.6F ● The eyed hawkmoth

Man the predator

Can you think of a modern day example of how man hunts and kills his food?
Most of our food, animal and vegetable, is produced by farming, but one
activity in which man remains the primitive hunter is fishing (see Figure
53.6G).

Over the past 50 years, the intensity of fishing in many areas has
increased to such an extent that fish stocks are threatened. In many cases
the size of a particular stock has been so reduced that it is no longer
profitable to fish. In more severe cases the entire stock has been brought
to the verge of extinction.

Figure 53.6G ● A trawler in action

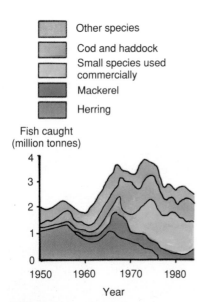

Other species

Cod and haddock

Small species used
commercially

Mackerel

Herring

Fish caught
(million tonnes)

Figure 53.6H ● Total catches of fish in
the North Sea

This situation of overfishing has been brought about by improved technology, which has made it possible to increase the amount of fish caught dramatically. The power of fishing vessels has increased, making it possible to use bigger nets. The nets are now plastic. They are stronger, lighter and almost transparent in the water. Sonar has made it possible to detect fish shoals exactly, so the net can be positioned in such a way that an entire shoal is trapped. Refrigeration enables a catch to be preserved so factory ships can stay at sea for longer periods of time and roam further afield.

The rise in world fish landings after the Second World War was truly remarkable (see Figure 53.6H). Between 1940 and 1970, landings increased from 20 million tonnes per year to 70 million tonnes per year. Since then landings have not increased significantly. *Why is this?* If we look at the catch effort curve (see Figure 53.6I), we can see that an increase in fishing effort will, for a time, bring about an increase in the catch. The maximum which is reached is termed the **maximum sustainable yield**. If this level of fishing effort is exceeded, then landings will be reduced. This overfished situation can be solved only if the intensity of fishing is reduced. By reducing catches, the fisherman would, in the long term, have bigger landings of better quality fish. But this is not what happens – faced with declining catches the fisherman tries to catch more fish. So a situation of extreme overfishing is reached where both the existence of the stock and the fisherman's livelihood are threatened.

Another example of man's greed and short-sightedness is the over-exploitation of the whale for its meat and oil. Predation by man has been the main cause of the decline in a number of whale species (see Figure 53.6J). In the 1940s the blue whale had been hunted almost to the point of extinction. Having exhausted the stock of blue whales, whaling fleets turned instead to another species, the fin whale. Over the 1960s hunting reduced their numbers to danger level. The sei whale was the next to be over-exploited and its numbers fell dramatically …

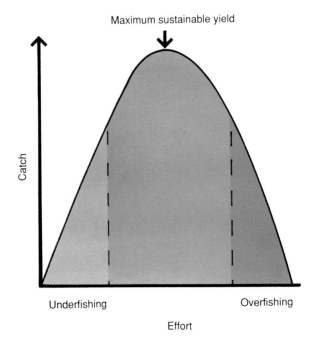

Figure 53.6I ● The catch–effort curve for fishing

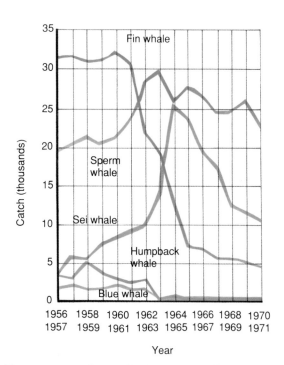

Figure 53.6J ● The decline in numbers of whale species due to overfishing

53.7 Parasitism and other associations

Parasites often cause a sense of revulsion in people, because of the harm that they can cause. In fact, probably every living animal has some of these uninvited guests, the only exceptions to this are the parasites themselves. Some parasites cause disease and death and therefore reduce the size of a population (see Figure 53.7A).

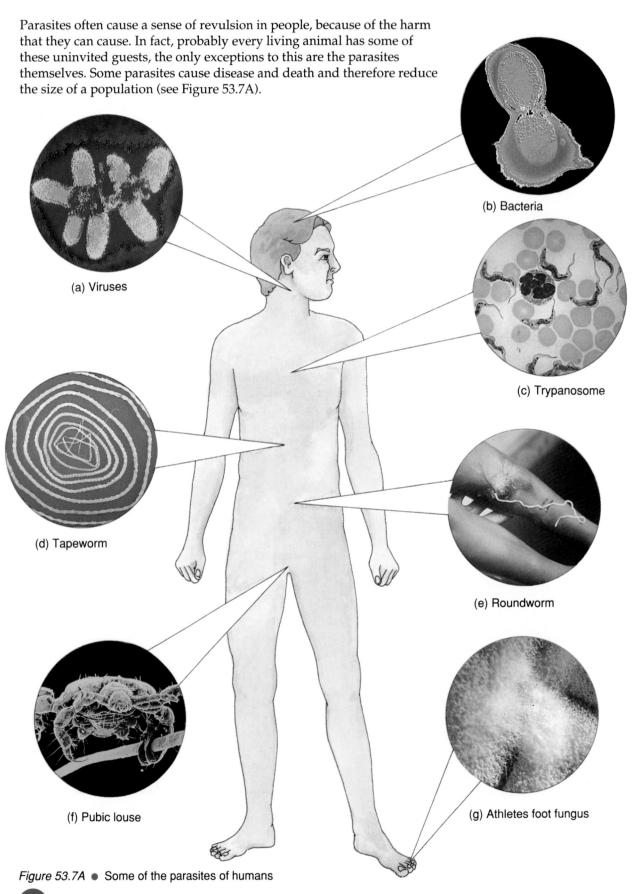

(a) Viruses

(b) Bacteria

(c) Trypanosome

(d) Tapeworm

(e) Roundworm

(f) Pubic louse

(g) Athletes foot fungus

Figure 53.7A ● Some of the parasites of humans

Parasitism is one of a number of different associations that can exist between two organisms. **Symbiosis** is a general term for close associations in which either one of the partners benefits to the detriment of the other or both benefit or neither appears to benefit. Benefits can be food, shelter or protection.

Table 53.1 ● Some associations

Association	How each participant is affected
Competition	Neither population benefits, they inhibit each other
Predation	The predator benefits at the expense of the prey
Parasitism	The parasite benefits to the detriment of the host
Commensalism	One participant, the commensal, benefits whilst the other, the host, is unaffected
Mutualism	The association benefits both partners

Parasitism

Parasitism is a one-sided relationship between two organisms. The parasite obtains food at the host's expense, either by consuming the host itself or by consuming the host's food supply. Parasites of humans include fungi, bacteria, viruses, protozoa, worms and arthropods. Microbes that cause disease are termed **pathogens**. When an animal is healthy, it has little difficulty supporting all its parasites with food. However, if the animal is weakened by starvation or drought for instance, then parasites can have a fatal effect upon it.

There is a great variety of parasites. The degree to which they are tied to the host varies. **Ectoparasites** attach themselves to the outside of the host and many only form temporary associations, for example, a tick will attach itself to a cow long enough to take a blood meal and then drop off. An **endoparasite** lives inside the host's body which becomes the parasite's habitat, giving it food, shelter and protection. The malarial parasite only leaves the human body when it is carried to a new host by a mosquito.

The lousiest animal in the world is a small mammal about the size of a rabbit called the hyrax. It harbours 25 different species of lice.

Some wasps have parasitic larvae. The adult wasp lays its eggs inside the body of another insect such as a caterpillar. The larvae hatch out and entirely consume the caterpillar from the inside. After forming pupae, the adult wasps eventually emerge.

● *Parasitic adaptions*

Parasites have very specialised life styles. This is particularly true of endoparasites which have to adapt to living inside a host that may well react adversely to them. To cope with their mode of existence, parasites have evolved a number of adaptations.

- Endoparasites often have poorly developed organs of locomotion and digestion. They move very little and many absorb the pre-digested food of the host.
- They have poorly developed senses of sight, hearing and smell as there are few stimuli they are likely to encounter. Parasitic flowering plants have no roots and may lack chloroplasts. *Why is this?*
- Many endoparasites have well developed organs for attachment to the host, for example the hooks and suckers of the tapeworm.
- Parasites such as the flea have specialised mouthparts for penetrating the host's tissue.
- If the endoparasite is to live inside the host, then it must be able to resist the host's **immune reactions**. For this reason parasitic roundworms have a thick resistant cuticle.
- The host tissue may lack oxygen. This is true of the human intestine where the hookworm lives.

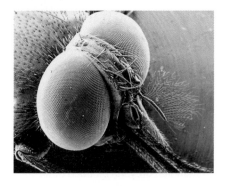

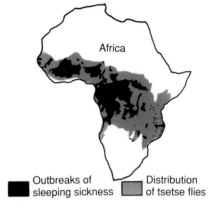

Figure 53.7B ● Tsetse fly and sleeping sickness

● How do parasites find new hosts?

If a parasite cannot ensure that some of its offspring are able to infect a new host, then the species will die out. Parasites have numerous adaptations that have enabled them to meet this aim.

- Many are capable of producing hundreds of thousands of eggs every day in the hope that some will find their way to a new host.
- Some are hermaphrodite, that is they have male and female reproductive organs. Consequently when one mates with a partner, both donate sperm and twice as many fertilised eggs are produced.
- In some parasites the male and female get very attached to each other, literally. In the case of the fluke that causes bilharzia, the male carries the female in a groove in his body to ensure that they will mate.
- Many parasites use another organism to transmit their offspring to the host. Many insects acts as **vectors** in this way. The tsetse fly transmits the protozoan that causes sleeping sickness from one person to another. The flies have piercing mouthparts that penetrate the human skin like a hypodermic needle and then inject the protozoan into a new host (see Figure 53.7B).
- In some cases, the parasite may use a secondary host to enable it to complete its life cycle. The pork tapeworm has two hosts in its life cycle. A human is the primary host and a pig the secondary host. The tapeworm lives in the human intestine. Its millions of eggs are passed out in the faeces and some may be eaten by a pig. These hatch out and the larvae find their way into the muscle of the pig. If this is eaten as under-cooked pork, then the adult tapeworm will develop in the new primary host (see Figure 53.7C).

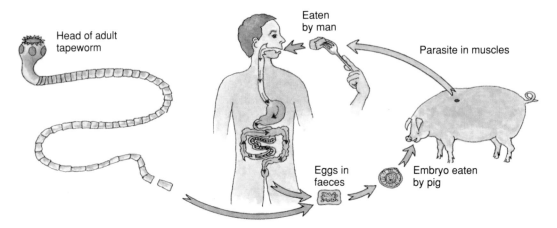

Figure 53.7C ● Life cycle of the pork tapeworm

IT'S A FACT

Pilot fish are commensals that accompany large sharks wherever they swim. Since sharks are messy feeders the pilot fish are able to pick up scraps of food. No one knows why the shark tolerates the pilot fish. If a shark is caught its companions will reluctantly swim off to find another protector.

Mutualism

Mutualism is an association between organisms of different species in which each partner benefits. Sometimes the partners become so dependent upon each other that they are unable to exist separately.

The roots of legumes such as peas, beans and clover, have lumps on them called **root nodules**. These contain **nitrogen-fixing bacteria**. The bacteria can convert nitrogen from the air into compounds which the plant can use to make protein. In return, the bacteria obtain carbohydrates from the plant's roots. Many bacteria and protozoa live in the large intestines of mammals. They break down the cellulose in plant material to sugars. They are especially important to herbivores in helping them to digest the cellulose which forms a large part of their diet. In return, the microbes get some of the food and a warm environment.

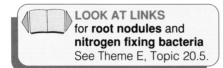
LOOK AT LINKS
for **root nodules** and
nitrogen fixing bacteria
See Theme E, Topic 20.5.

A looser example of mutualism is that between oxpecker birds and animals such as buffaloes and antelopes. The oxpecker removes ticks and other ectoparasites from the skin of the game animal and often alerts it if predators approach. Cleaner fish do a similar job for larger fish, removing lice and other ectoparasites.

Commensalism

This is an association between two organisms of different species, in which one benefits without harming the other. The sea anemone is able to hitch a ride on the crab. The crab is a messy feeder and scraps of food float towards the sea anemone which picks them up in its tentacles (see Figure 53.7D). In this example, the sea anemone is the commensal, its presence is of no advantage or disadvantage to the crab.

SUMMARY

Parasites live in or on their hosts to which they cause harm. In order to be successful, parasites have evolved many adaptations. Some parasites use vectors and secondary hosts to ensure the spread of their offspring.

Figure 53.7D ● Crab and sea anenome

CHECKPOINT

❶ Why are under-nourished people more likely to be affected by parasites than people who are well-fed?

❷ Look at the figure below. It shows the life cycle of the malarial mosquito. The female mosquito is the vector of the protozoan, *Plasmodium*, that causes malaria.
   (a) Suggest ways in which the eggs, larvae and pupae of the mosquito are well adapted for living in water.
   (b) Attempts to control the parasite aim to break the life cycle of the vector. Suggest ways in which each of the stages in the life cycle could be eradicated.
   (c) How can the adult mosquito be prevented from biting people and so spreading the disease?

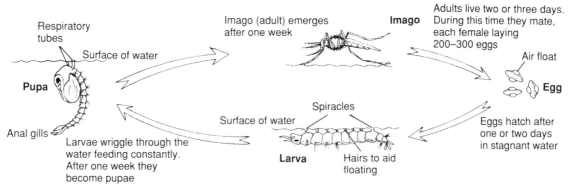

53.8 Conservation

The Amazon rain forest is thought to supply us with one third of the world's oxygen. Its destruction means a build up of carbon dioxide, enhancing the greenhouse effect.

Habitat destruction and exploitation have meant that thousands of species of plants and animals have been brought to the verge of extinction. In the face of economic development, the growth of human populations and the increase in agriculture to feed them, habitats are vanishing quickly and their species with them. The destruction of tropical rain forests means that 500 to 1000 species of plants are becoming extinct every year. They are disappearing even before they can be discovered by man and their potential value, for instance in providing new medicines, is wasted. Animal species are now disappearing at the rate of one species per day. Humans, through greed and ignorance, are felling forests that not only harbour a huge diversity of species, but provide the oxygen we breathe and use up carbon dioxide.

Figure 53.8A ● Species are disappearing from the rain forest at a rate of 500 to 1000 a year

Figure 53.8B ● The Kenyan authorities burned hundreds of tonnes of poached ivory to prevent it reaching the market-places of the world

Ecology and Conservation
(program)

Slapton Ley is a nature reserve in Devon. It needs good management. *Can you do the job?* The videodisc gives you the background information. You can control the reserve by computer. Beware – other people might have different ideas about how to manage the reserve.

Ecodisc
(videodisc)

Use the program to look at a woodland and a pond foodweb. You can then change the balance of the ecosystem. Finish off with the quiz.

We can benefit future generations by preserving our environment. We have a duty of care to manage wild species which can be of direct use to us in terms of food and other materials. We must realise that over-exploitation of non-renewable resources will leave us poorer in the future. It is also in our interests to safeguard the existence of species that are a part of the delicate balance of nature in our world. There are many animals that we shall never see. The giant otter, wood bison, Parma wallaby, spectacled bear and Atlantic walrus are thought to be extinct or close to extinction. The destruction of habitats to enable agriculture to feed ever more human mouths is one cause. The over-exploitation of species for commercial use is another. In a world where species are disappearing so fast, perhaps we should look again at the sort of legacy we wish our children to inherit.

Many of the species that are approaching a premature end, could in fact become food for us if they were managed. The Saiga antelope in the USSR has been saved from the brink of extinction and has now increased to numbers that allow some animals to be killed for food. The same is true of the American bison and the eland.

Plant and animal breeders combine desirable characteristics to produce improved strains, e.g. crops with high yields and farm animals with more meat. To produce the new varieties, breeders often use the original wild ancestors of modern stock. If we fail to preserve rare breeds their gene banks will not be available for use at some future date.

We have to take action if fish and whale stocks are to be conserved. There has been a serious decline in the numbers of many marine molluscs from tropical waters, such as cowries, scallops, cone shells and clams. This is because too many are harvested and exported to the USA and Europe, leaving too few to breed.

In the 1970s there was a large increase in the amount of illegal ivory poaching. During the decade half of the elephants in Kenya were lost to poaching and Uganda lost 90% (see Figure 53.8B). Approximately 50 tonnes of ivory is used in Europe each year, equivalent to 10 000 elephants. Illegal poaching also concentrates the profits in the hands of a few. Proper management with the sale of ivory from animals that have died naturally and from those killed to control numbers, would help to improve the economies of some African countries.

Figure 53.8C ● The fur trade

Figure 53.8D ● Birdcages and birds for sale. Many of the birds sold in such markets are endangered species.

SUMMARY

Conservation of species and protection of their habitats has had a low priority in the eyes of the nations of the world in the past. It must constantly be brought to their attention that the world's resources are limited. If we do not act we will pay a high price in terms of the loss of beautiful, fascinating and essential wildlife.

Sometimes the conservation of wildlife can be a personal responsibility of each of us. The trade in furs and other animal skins is an obvious example (see Figure 53.8C). If we stopped buying furs, then the slaughter would stop, and after all there are plenty of imitation furs available. Prosperity increased in the 1960s and more women were able to afford furs. In 1968 the USA imported 10 000 leopard skins, 1000 cheetah skins, 13 000 jaguar skins and 130 000 ocelot skins. Similar numbers were imported into Europe. The shooting and trapping took their toll on the wild species. At last the Convention on International Trade in Endangered Species (CITES) asked governments to pass laws to protect threatened species. But some governments have yet to recognise CITES and widespread poaching and illegal trading still occur.

The trade in exotic birds takes 10 million birds from the wild every year; about half of these die even before they reach their destination. High prices are paid for parrots, waxbills, lovebirds and other exotic species. Also birds of prey, such as the peregrine falcon are exported to be used in falconry. Despite the protection of CITES illegal trafficking continues, with the loss of many birds in transit (see Figure 53.8D).

People have introduced new species of animals into many countries. Some of these have been beneficial; others have upset the native animal species. Cattle have been introduced into the Americas, Australia and Africa, where there has been a large increase in meat production. On the other hand, rabbits were introduced into Australia only to become a pest and to threaten native species. Rats have spread all round the world on ships and have carried their diseases with them.

The news has not all been bleak. In the early 1970s, the tiger was on the verge of extinction, with just 1800 left. Hunting, trapping and the destruction of its natural habitat were the main causes. In 1973, the World Wildlife Fund, with the co-operation of the Indian government, launched 'Operation Tiger'. They attempted not only to save the tiger but also to conserve a whole ecosystem. Laws were passed to protect the species and tiger reserves were set up. Poachers were given very stiff sentences. The operation has resulted in a dramatic increase in the tiger population.

Captive breeding programmes have also seen some species saved from extinction. The Arabian oryx has been bred in captivity in Phoenix Zoo, Arizona. Herds have since been set up in other parts of the world and some even released into the wild in Oman. Other species saved by captive breeding include Przewalski's horse, the European bison and Pere David's deer.

Some years ago, a number of international organisations combined forces to put forward the World Conservation Strategy (WCS). This plan was to persuade nations to pass laws which would protect plant and animal species from destruction and preserve their habitats. The WCS aim is to conserve the natural processes and cycles of the biosphere. If this aim is achieved, then habitats will be preserved and ecosystems will be saved. The WCS plans to preserve the Earth's variety of species by controlling the killing of animals and the destruction of plants. Some governments agree with the WCS aims, but have so far failed to put the programme into action. Other governments are indifferent. At present, all hope of progress in conservation lies with the independent organisations.

? THEME QUESTIONS

● **Topic 52**

1 The diagram shows a food web.

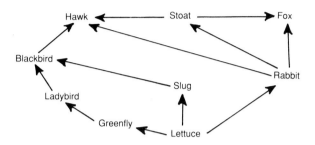

(a) Which of the following statements is true?
  (i) Hawks eat slugs
  (ii) Stoats eat hawks
  (iii) Blackbirds eat ladybirds
  (iv) Foxes eat blackbirds

(b) Which of the animals in the list below could die off if all the rabbits were removed?
  (i) Slug (ii) Greenfly (iii) Ladybird (iv) Stoat

(c) The number of plants and animals were counted at three different places in a pond. The results are shown in the table below.

Place	Numbers counted			
	Small fish	Water flea	Duck	Small plants (Algae)
1	4	500	1	10 000
2	1	700	0	8000
3	3	680	1	7000
Totals				

  (i) Copy and complete the table.
  (ii) Use the names in the table to draw a pyramid of numbers.

(d) Explain why all the plants in the pond were found near the surface.

(e) Plants are food for the pond animals. Give **two** other ways in which these animals depend on the plants.
(WJEC)

2 The diagram shows some of the feeding relationships in a British oak wood.

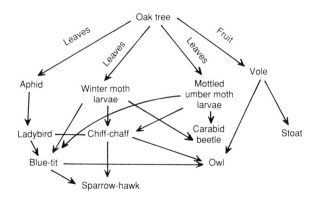

(a) (i) Name the source of energy for **all** the organisms in this food web.
  (ii) Name **three** substances which the oak tree could obtain from the environment and which would contribute to its structure.

(b) From the diagram, select
  (i) one carnivore,
  (ii) one producer,
  (iii) one food chain which includes **four** different organisms.

(c) Draw a simple diagram to compare the likely numbers of each of the species in the food chain which you have selected in (b) (iii).

(d) Explain how energy is lost to the environment from the food web.

(e) In some years there are exceptionally large numbers of winter moth and mottled umber moth larvae. Describe **two** probable effects of this on other organisms in the food web.

(f) Each autumn the oak trees shed their leaves. Explain how the elements contained in the cellulose in the leaves are made available for the growth of trees in subsequent years. (JMB)

3 When sewage effluent was discharged into a river, the oxygen concentration at the point of discharge rapidly dropped.
(a) Suggest why this happened.
(b) The numbers and types of organisms in a part of a non-polluted river are shown below.

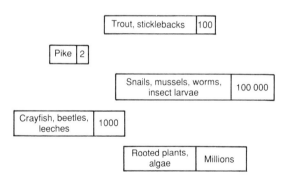

Construct a pyramid of numbers, (not to scale) using all this data.

(c) (i) Name the organism you would remove if you wanted to increase the number of trout in the river.
  (ii) State one further effect of removing this organism from the river. (WJEC)

4 In 1963, it was decided to kill mosquitoes by spraying a lake where they lived with a pesticide. The pesticide used is not poisonous to vertebrates unless it is in a concentration of 950 parts per million (p.p.m.). In 1964, large numbers of fish-eating birds were found dead in the lake. Study the table and the pyramid of numbers for the lake (overleaf), then answer the questions.

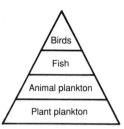

Organism	Concentration of pesticide (p.p.m.)
Plant plankton	1
Animal plankton	10
Fish	100
Fish-eating birds	1000

(a) Name the producers.

(b) Name the primary consumers.

(c) Explain why fish survived in the lake in 1964 but not fish-eating birds.

(d) Explain what you would expect to happen to the population of fish in the lake during 1965 if spraying continued.

(e) Explain what you would expect to happen to the population of animal plankton as a result of (d).

(f) Name a heavy metal which can act as a poison.

(WJEC)

● **Topic 53**

5 The graph shows the average weight/day of haddock caught by trawlers in the North Sea from 1905–1960.

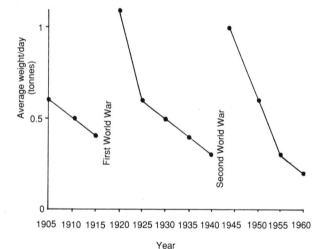

During the World Wars, fishing trawlers were very much reduced. During peace time, the number of trawlers remained the same.

(a) Explain the decrease in the weight of haddock caught between 1920 and 1940.

(b) Explain how the lack of fishing during the war years helped to conserve the haddock.

(c) In 1960 the captains of two trawlers were prosecuted for using nets with a mesh smaller than is permitted.
  (i) Explain why a large mesh helps to conserve fish stocks.
  (ii) Suggest **three** other ways of conserving haddock in the North Sea.

(d) Suggest **two** factors which could directly affect the rate of growth of a haddock from the newly hatched fish to the adult. (WJEC)

6 Read the following extract from a newspaper article and answer the questions which follow:

LADYBIRDS TO SAVE EUCALYPTS

An Australian ladybird has been successfully introduced into New Zealand to *biologically control* the eucalyptus tortoise beetle, which has a hard exoskeleton, by eating its eggs.

The adult and larval stages of the beetle eat eucalypt leaves. This results in heavy and repeated leaf loss which may cause the death of the trees.

In Australia the tortoise beetle is controlled by *parasites* and predators and other beetles compete with it for food. In New Zealand there are no such predators and the use of *insecticides* has proved an unsatisfactory method of control.

In August, overwintering adult beetles emerge from under loose bark of eucalypts, feed and then mate. Eggs are laid on the underside of young leaves. The larvae which hatch feed on the new shoots. About November, mature larvae drop to the ground and pupate in the soil. Adults emerge and the cycle is repeated.

(a) Using organisms from the article above complete a food chain containing a producer, a herbivore and a carnivore.

(b) Suggest a suitable definition for **each** of the terms which are in italic in the passage.

(c) Suggest a possible reason why the use of insecticides has been ineffective in controlling the eucalyptus beetle.

(d) The tortoise beetle is a pest in New Zealand but not in Australia. Suggest a reason for this.

(e) What would be the best month to release the ladybirds in New Zealand for the most effective control of the beetle?

(f) State a precaution which would have to be taken prior to the release of the Australian ladybirds into the eucalypt trees of New Zealand. (WJEC)

7 Study the following data concerning whale hunting.

A	B	C
Species of whale	Number caught in 1971–2	Estimated maximmum that can be caught without reduction of population size
Antarctic Sei whale	5449	5500
Pacific Sei whale	4710	5000
Fin whale	3992	3000
Sperm whale	13 551	20 000

(a) Which of the four whales listed is likely to become extinct?

(b) From the figures in the table, give **one** reason for **not** banning whale hunting totally.

(c) Besides knowing the total number of whales in a population, state two other facts which must be known to produce the estimates in column C.

(d) Name **two** animals other than whales, in danger of extinction, which are receiving protection. (WJEC)

THEME N
Genetics and Evolution

TOPIC 54 INHERITANCE AND GENETICS

54.1 From generation to generation

Glance around your classmates. Almost certainly you look different from one another. However, you each look something like your parents or even grandparents because you inherited their DNA and, therefore, the characteristics that DNA controls. The study of the patterns of heredity (the ways in which offspring resemble or differ from their parents) is called genetics.

Blending inheritance

Figure 54.1A ● Three generations of a family. *What characteristics do you think they have in common?*

IT'S A FACT

People used to think that blood was responsible for offspring inheriting a mix of their parents' characteristics. Even today we speak of 'blood relation', 'royal blood' and 'blood line'.

Early on in our history parents must have noticed that their children did not look exactly like them. Each child shows a mixture of the mother's and father's characteristics. The idea grew up that the parents' characteristics are somehow blended in their children. Differences between a child and his or her parents were supposed to be due to the mixing effect. 'Stronger' characteristics in one of the parents were thought to account for differences between brothers and sisters.

If parents' characteristics really do blend in their offspring what colour flowers would you expect in the offspring of red and white flowers? What colour flowers would you expect in the offspring of the offspring? Would the red and the whites of the original parents ever be seen again? Figure 54.1B shows you what does happen when the original parents are pure-breeding red and white roses. Does Figure 54.1B support or contradict the ideas of blending inheritance?

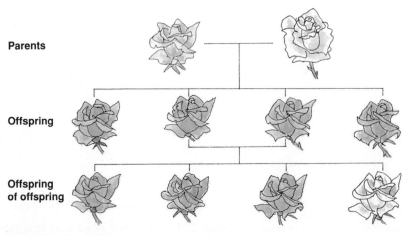

Parents

Offspring

Offspring of offspring

Figure 54.1B ● Inheritance of flower colour in pure-breeding roses

54.2 Enter Gregor Mendel

Like any other branch of science, genetics has its own vocabulary. Before you start reading about Gregor Mendel's experiments you need to know the meaning of a few words. Checking the genetics glossary will help you.

Genetics glossary

- **pure-breeding** characteristics that 'breed true' appearing unchanged generation after generation
- **parental generation** (symbol **P**) individuals that are pure-breeding for a characteristic
- **first filial generation** (symbol F_1) the offspring produced by the parental generation
- **second filial generation** (symbol F_2) the offspring of the first filial generation
- **dominant characteristic** any characteristic that appears in the F_1 offspring of a cross between parents with contrasting characteristics such as tallness and shortness in pea plants
- **recessive characteristic** any characteristic present in the parental generation that misses the F_1 generation but reappears in the F_2 generation

Mendel's experiments

The work of Gregor Mendel marks the beginning of modern genetics. At the monastery where Mendel was a monk, he kept a small garden plot where he experimented with breeding the garden pea (*Pisum sativum*). He observed the way in which its characteristics were inherited from one generation to the next.

Mendel's choice of the garden pea for his experiments was fortunate:
- Pea plants are easy to grow.
- Pea plants have different characteristics which breed true, appearing unchanged generation after generation (for example height of plant, colour of seed).
- The petals of the pea flower enclose the stamens and the carpels. Cross pollination, therefore, does not usually occur. If pea plants could naturally cross pollinate, Mendel's experiments would have been unsuccessful. *Can you think why?*

Who's behind the science

Gregor Mendel was born in 1822. He was the son of an Austrian farmer. As a young man he entered the Augustinian monastery in the town of Brünn (now Brno in Czechoslovakia) and was ordained as a priest at the age of 25. Mendel trained in mathematics and natural history at the university of Vienna and then taught in the high school at Brünn.

Figure 54.2A ● The pea plant and its flower showing how the petals enclose the stamens and carpels

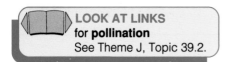
LOOK AT LINKS
for **pollination**
See Theme J, Topic 39.2.

Mendel's success also lay in the methodical way he planned his work. He only studied one characteristic at a time in thousands of pea plants and his mathematical training allowed him to analyse his results.

To prevent self-pollination in the plants in his experiments, Mendel prised open the flower buds before the pollen matured and removed the anthers. He then pollinated the flowers with pollen from other mature plants and tied small, muslin bags over the pollinated flowers to prevent any stray pollen settling on the flowers.

Mendel took pollen from **pure-breeding** short plants and dusted it onto the stigmas of **pure-breeding** tall plants and vice versa. These plants were the **parental generation**. He collected and grew the seeds they produced. (See Figure 54.2B.)

It did not matter if Mendel took pollen from tall or short parent plants, the F_1 **generation** were always tall. He called 'tallness' a **dominant** characteristic.

Mendel then let the F_1 generation self-pollinate. He collected and grew their seeds. The 'shortness' characteristic that skipped the F_1 generation re-appeared in the F_2 **generation**. Mendel called 'shortness' a **recessive** characteristic. (See Figure 54.2C.)

How characteristics are inherited

Introductory Genetics (program)

This set of three programs is designed to clarify your ideas about genetics and inheritance. Test your understanding with the questions following each program.

From his results Mendel realised that parents passed 'something' on to their offspring which made them look like their parents. When these offspring became parents they passed on the 'something' to their offspring, and so on from generation to generation. Today, we call the 'something' which parents pass to offspring **genes**.

Mendel reasoned that sexually reproduced offspring receive the same number of genes from each parent and that any particular characteristic, therefore, must be controlled by a pair of genes. Paired genes controlling a particular characteristic are called **alleles**. They may be identical to one another or different. An individual with identical alleles controlling a particular characteristic is called a **homozygote** (*homo-* means the same); an individual with different alleles controlling a characteristic is called a **heterozygote** (*hetero-* means different).

Mendel concluded that alleles must separate when **gametes** form. We know that the separation of alleles occurs at **meiosis** and that only one allele goes to each gamete. Mendel, however did not know this. Nearly 30 years went by after his experiments with peas before meiosis was discovered.

LOOK AT LINKS
for **gametes** and **meiosis**
See Theme J, Topic 39.1.

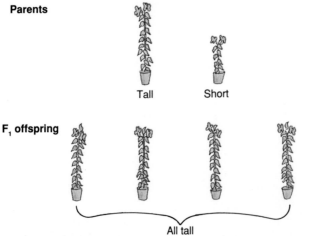

Parents

Tall   Short

F_1 **offspring**

All tall

Figure 54.2B ● The F_1 offspring of tall and short parents are all tall

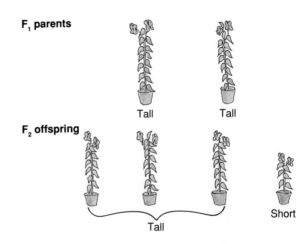

F_1 **parents**

Tall   Tall

F_2 **offspring**

Tall   Short

Figure 54.2C ● F_1 parents produce a mixture of tall and short F_2 offspring

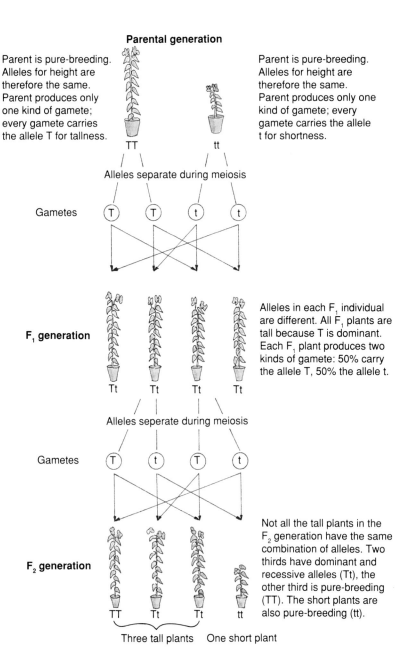

Parental generation

Parent is pure-breeding. Alleles for height are therefore the same. Parent produces only one kind of gamete; every gamete carries the allele T for tallness.

TT

Parent is pure-breeding. Alleles for height are therefore the same. Parent produces only one kind of gamete; every gamete carries the allele t for shortness.

tt

Alleles separate during meiosis

Gametes   (T) (T) (t) (t)

F₁ generation

Tt   Tt   Tt   Tt

Alleles in each F₁ individual are different. All F₁ plants are tall because T is dominant. Each F₁ plant produces two kinds of gamete: 50% carry the allele T, 50% the allele t.

Alleles seperate during meiosis

Gametes   (T) (t) (T) (t)

F₂ generation

TT   Tt   Tt   tt

Not all the tall plants in the F₂ generation have the same combination of alleles. Two thirds have dominant and recessive alleles (Tt), the other third is pure-breeding (TT). The short plants are also pure-breeding (tt).

Three tall plants   One short plant

Figure 54.2D ● How alleles controlling a characteristic pass from one generation to the next. *Which plants are homozygotes and which are heterozygotes? Why are only homozygotes pure-breeding?*

Mendel used letter symbols to simplify his observations. Capital letters symbolised alleles for dominant characteristics and small letters symbolised alleles for recessive characteristics. For example, he used **T** for the allele which produced tallness in pea plants and **t** for the allele which produced shortness, and set out the crosses between plants diagrammatically (see Figure 54.2D).

Mendel repeated his experiments using other pairs of characteristics. For example, he crossed purple flowered plants with white flowered plants. He always found that the flowers in the F₁ generation were purple. In other words, purple was a dominant characteristic; white was a recessive characteristic. Table 54.1 summarises the different pairs of dominant and recessive characteristics studied by Mendel in his experiments.

Table 54.1 ● Dominant and recessive characteristics in pea plants. (Note: axial flowers sprout along the stem; terminal flowers at the end.)

Characteristic	Dominant	Recessive
Seed shape	Round seed	Wrinkled seed
Seed colour	Yellow seed	Green seed
Seed coat colour	Coloured seed coat	White seed coat
Pod shape	Smooth pod	Wrinkled pod
Pod colour	Green pod	Yellow pod
Flower position	Axial flowers	Terminal flowers
Plant height	Tall stem	Short stem

1 The table shows the results of breeding experiments with pea plants beginning with parents pure-breeding for tallness and shortness.

Cross	Original parental cross	F₁ plants from parental cross	F₂ plant from F₁ cross
Height	Tall x short	All tall	779 tall: 268 short

(a) Explain how you can tell from the results that tallness is dominant and shortness is recessive.
(b) To the nearest whole number, what is the ratio of tall to short plants in the F₂ generation?
(c) All the F₁ plants are tall. Explain how the combination of their alleles is different from that of the parent tall plant.
(d) Copy and complete the diagram opposite to explain the F₂ results obtained from crossing within the F₁ generation.

2 What is the distinction between genes and alleles?

3 Match the terms in Column A with their definitions in Column B.

Column A	Column B
Gene	A gene which can express itself despite the presence of another version of the gene
Recessive gene	Portion of DNA molecule which controls a specific characteristic such as eye colour in humans and height in pea plants
Dominant gene	A plant which will always breed true for a particular characteristic
Pure-breeding plant	A gene not expressed in the presence of another version of the gene

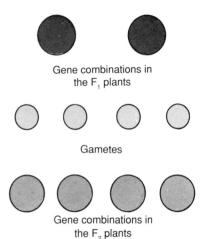

Gene combinations in the F₁ plants

Gametes

Gene combinations in the F₂ plants

54.3 Genes at work

In this section you will find out about some interesting examples of human genetics.

LOOK AT LINKS
for **blood groups**
See Theme J, Topic 38.2.

Genetics of human blood groups

Sometimes a characteristic is controlled by more than two alleles. Human blood groups, for example, are controlled by three, A, B and O. An individual has two out of the three alleles.

The A and B alleles control production of the antigens which determine a person's blood group. The A and B alleles are dominant to the O allele but not to each other. So, if the A and B alleles are both present, then the person's blood group is AB. If neither the A nor B alleles are present, then the person's blood group is O. (See Table 54.2.)

Table 54.2 ● The genetics of blood groups (Notice that blood groups A and B each have two possible combinations of alleles)

Alleles	Antigen on red blood cells	Blood group
AA or AO	A	A
BB or BO	B	B
AB	A and B	AB
OO	None	O

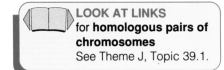
LOOK AT LINKS
for **homologous pairs of chromosomes**
See Theme J, Topic 39.1.

Inheritance of sex

Figure 54.3A shows the chromosomes of a man and a woman. In each case a photograph of all the chromosomes from the nucleus of a body cell has been cut up and the chromosomes arranged into **homologous pairs** and in order of size.

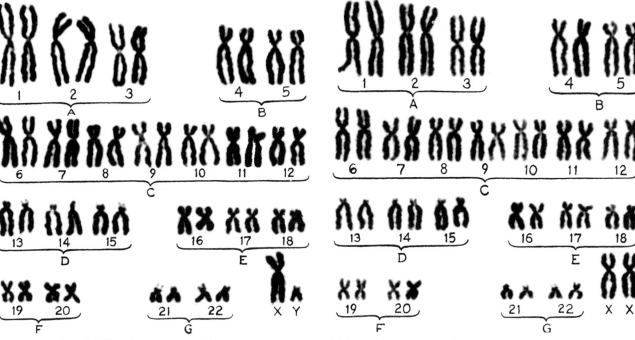

Figure 54.3A ● (a) The chromosomes of a man

(b) The chromosomes of a woman

Of the 23 pairs of chromosomes in each photograph, the chromosomes in each of 22 pairs are similar in size and shape in both the man and the woman. Notice, however, that the chromosomes of the 23rd pair in the man are different from the 23rd pair in the woman. These are the sex chromosomes. The larger chromosomes are called the X chromosomes; the smaller chromosome is called the Y chromosome.

Since the body cells of a woman each carry two X chromosomes, meiosis can only produce eggs containing an X chromosome. Each body cell of a man, however, carries an X chromosome and a Y chromosome, so meiosis produces two types of sperm. Of the sperms produced, 50% carry an X chromosome and 50% carry a Y chromosome. A baby's sex depends on whether the egg is fertilised by a sperm carrying an X chromosome or one carrying a Y chromosome (see Figure 54.3B). The birth of almost equal numbers of girls and boys is governed by the production of equal numbers of X and Y sperms at meiosis.

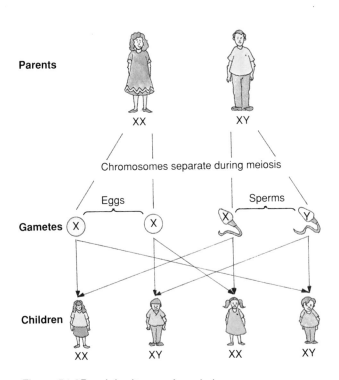

Figure 54.3B ● Inheritance of sex in humans

411

Human genetic diseases

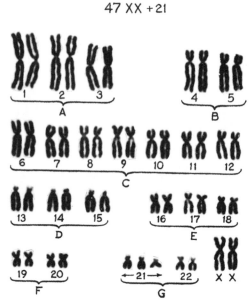

47 XX + 21

Figure 54.3C ● (a) A child with a variety of Down's syndrome working alongside pupils in a normal school class

(b) The chromosomes of a person with Down's syndrome

IT'S A FACT

There are slightly more boys born than there are girls. Scientists are not sure why, but in the past it was just as well because girls had slightly more chance of surviving childhood than boys. Perhaps girls are tougher. Nowadays, developments in medical care mean that the death of young children of either sex is comparatively rare in developed countries.

IT **Sex Determination** (program)

What are the chances of an offspring being male or female? How does this affect the population overall? Find out, using the program.

Down's syndrome is one of the most familiar conditions resulting from a genetic abnormality. It is called a syndrome because it involves a number of disorders. People with Down's syndrome are usually short and stocky. They are more likely to suffer from infectious diseases, find speech difficult and have abnormalities of the heart and other organs. Most are also slightly mentally handicapped, which often improves with treatment. Some are above average in intelligence.

Figure 54.3C shows the chromosomes of a person with Down's syndrome. Carefully examine the 21st set of chromosomes and compare them with the 21st set in Figure 54.3A. *Can you see the extra one making 47 chromosomes in all?* A defect occurring during cell division produces the extra copy of chromosome 21. It is the presence of the extra chromosome that causes Down's syndrome.

Defects occurring during cell division can also affect the numbers of sex chromosomes (set 23). In humans a combination of an X and a Y chromosome (XY) produces male children. However, XXY, XXXY and XXXXY combinations also produce males. The combinations XXX and X0 (only one X chromosome present) as well as the normal combination XX produce female children. Men and woman with these unusual combinations of sex chromosomes are usually sterile and suffer from other abnormalities.

● *Sex linkage*

Haemophilia is a genetic condition in which the blood does not clot properly after an injury. In its most common form the person fails to produce the clotting agent factor VIII. The allele responsible for haemophilia is recessive and is located on the X chromosome. Therefore, haemophilia is a **sex-linked** disease.

Although women may carry the defective allele on one of the X chromosomes, they do not usually suffer from haemophilia. This is

📖 LOOK AT LINKS
for **factor VIII** and **haemophilia**
See Theme J, Topic 38.2.

because the normal allele on the other X chromosome is dominant. The dominant allele masks the effect of its recessive partner and ensures enough factor VIII is made for normal blood clotting to take place. A woman who carries the recessive allele on one of the X chromosomes is called a **carrier**. Although she does not suffer from the disease she is able to pass it on to her children. For a woman to have haemophilia she would have had to receive the recessive allele for the characteristic from both her mother and her father. Since the recessive allele is rare, this only happens very occasionally.

Men have one X chromosome and one Y chromosome. The Y chromosome does not carry as many genes as the X chromosome. If a man inherits the recessive allele for haemophilia on the X chromosome, there is no dominant allele on the Y chromosome to mask the effect of the recessive allele. No factor VIII is produced and the man suffers from haemophilia.

Haemophilia is a genetic disease with a royal connection. Queen Victoria was a carrier of the haemophilia allele. One of her sons and two of her daughters inherited the defective allele. Although haemophilia is usually rare, various intermarriages caused the defective allele to spread among the royal families of Europe.

Figure 54.3D is a **pedigree chart** of Queen Victoria's family. A pedigree chart shows genetic data about related individuals through a number of generations.

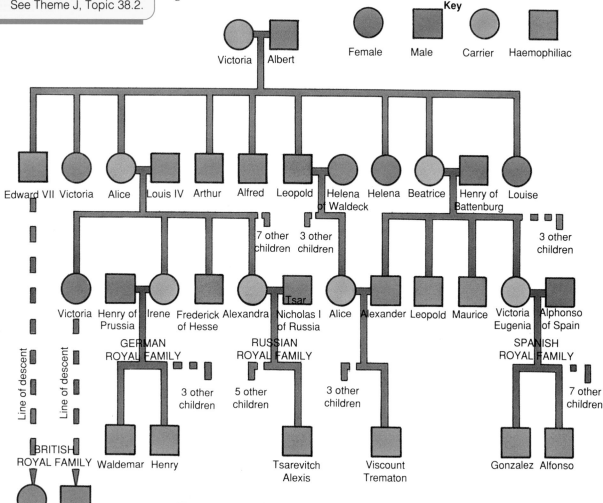

Figure 54.3D ● Distribution of the haemophilia allele in Queen Victoria's descendants. (Notice that there are no female haemophiliacs and that the British Royal Family escaped the disease because Edward VII did not inherit the defective allele.)

Red–green colour-blindness is another sex-linked disorder caused by a recessive allele on the X chromosome. As with haemophilia, women can be carriers but rarely suffer from the disorder. Red–green colour-blindness occurs in 8% of men but only 0.04% of women.

Shall we start a family?

A couple thinking of starting a family can be especially anxious that any children they have are fit and healthy. If either partner has a family history of genetic disease, the couple may want to know what the chances are of handing on the problem to any children they have. A pregnant woman may want to know if the baby she is carrying has inherited a particular disease. An older woman may wish to evaluate the risk of having a baby with Down's syndrome (the likelihood of having a child with Down's syndrome increases with the mother's age). These are just some of the worries that people can have about starting a family.

Scientists and doctors have developed techniques which allow them to diagnose genetic disorders in prospective parents and in babies developing in the uterus.

LOOK AT LINKS
for **base pairs** and **DNA**
See Theme D, Topic 18.5.

LOOK AT LINKS
for **amniotic fluid**
See Theme J, Topic 39.5.

LOOK AT LINKS
for **ultrasound scanners**
See Theme H, Topic 31.2.

- **Genetic probes**. For some types of genetic disorder, differences between the defective allele responsible for the disorder and its normal partner can be detected with genetic probes. The probes detect differences in the sequences of **base pairs** on the **DNA**. Genetic probes give very accurate results. (Figure 54.3E(a).)
- **Amniocentesis**. **Amniotic fluid** contains living cells from the foetus. These cells, once removed, can be grown in the laboratory and examined for genetic disorders. A thin needle is used to withdraw fluid from the amniotic cavity. Doctors work out where the foetus is in the uterus by using an **ultrasound scanner**. (Figure 54.3E(b).)
- **Statistical evidence**. The risk of having a child with a genetic disorder is well documented for some disorders such as Down's syndrome. (Figure 54.3E(c).)

Figure 54.3E ● (a) A genetics laboratory where the results from genetic probes are analysed

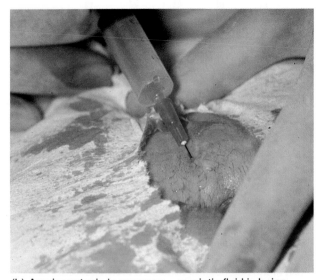

(b) Amniocentesis in progress – amniotic fluid is being withdrawn through a thin needle piercing the abdomen of a pregnant woman

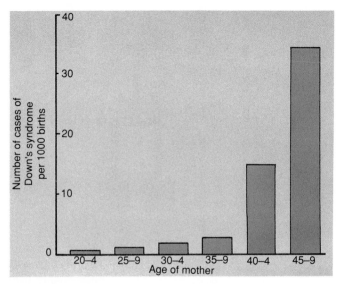

(c) Statistical evidence – the risk of having a baby with Down's syndrome

Any prospective or expectant parents who have reason to be worried about genetic disorders can attend **genetic counselling**. During genetic counselling, statistical evidence and results from amniocentesis and genetic probes are discussed by the couple and a specially trained genetic counsellor. The counselling helps couples to make informed choices about whether to start a family if there is a chance of having children with genetic disorders. It also helps expectant mothers and their partners to decide whether to continue with a pregnancy when they know their baby has a genetic disorder.

CHECKPOINT

❶ Defective alleles on the X chromosome are the cause of red–green colour-blindness. How do you account for the difference in the occurrence of red–green colour-blindness between men and woman?

❷ Explain why the sex of a baby is determined by the father and not the mother. How does this account for the birth of almost equal numbers of boys and girls?

❸ Women carry the defective allele for haemophilia but do not usually suffer from the disease. Explain why this is so.

54.4 ● Variation: genes and the environment

Look at your classmates, the members of your family and your friends. They have different coloured hair, different coloured eyes, different shaped faces. They all show variations in the different characteristics that make up physical appearance.

Figure 54.4A shows another human characteristic that varies: height. The average height of the adult population lies at the centre of the curve. Most people have heights close to the average. Only a few individuals are really short or really tall compared with the majority.

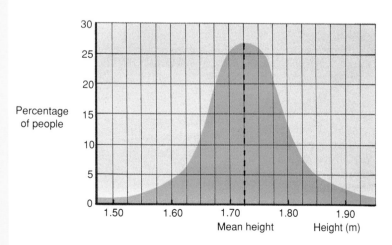

Figure 54.4A ● Variation in height of the adult human population

Figure 54.4B ● (a) Special training and a high protein diet have produced this weight-lifter's bulging muscles. Compare him with the other person who has a less strenuous life style.

(b) High winds and salt spray have made this tree lop-sided. The other tree, planted in a sheltered site, is unaffected by prevailing winds and grows vertically.

The outward appearance of an organism is called its **phenotype**; the genes contained in its cells form its **genotype**. Our appearances (our phenotype) vary because each of us inherits a different combination of alleles (our genotype). The same is true of all the members of all the different species of organism living now and in the past. Appearances, however, are not solely determined by the alleles that living things inherit. Figure 54.4B shows how the environment plays a part as well. The characteristics produced by the environment are said to be **acquired**. Acquired characteristics are not inherited.

CHECKPOINT

❶ Inherited characteristics and acquired characteristics are sources of variation in species.
(a) Distinguish between inherited and acquired characteristics.
(b) Which type of characteristic is important for the evolution of new species? Try to give reasons for your answer.

FIRST THOUGHTS

54.5 The growth of modern genetics

Developments in cell biology and molecular biology have helped to explain the results of Mendel's breeding experiments. Discovering the structure of DNA and the nature of genes has opened up the possibility of manufacturing processes based on biotechnology. This section tells you about these exciting prospects.

Mendel reported the results of his experiments in 1865 at a meeting of the Brünn Natural History Society. Nobody really understood what he was talking about. His paper was published the following year but was ignored (Figure 54.5A). Mendel continued his breeding experiments with pea plants until 1871 when he was made Abbot of the monastery. His new duties gave him little time for further research. He died in 1884.

There matters rested until 1900 when Mendel's work was re-discovered by three biologists working independently of one another. The growth of modern genetics dates from their recognition of the importance of Mendel's work.

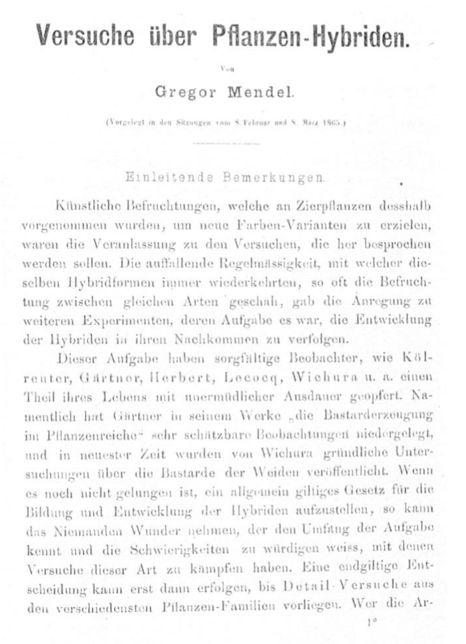

In the interval between the publication of Mendel's paper and its re-discovery, important advances had been made in cell biology. New ways of staining cells showed that the nucleus contained strands of material that took up dyes very strongly. They were called chromosomes, which literally means 'coloured bodies'. Mitosis and meiosis were seen for the first time.

Early work on genetics depended on breeding experiments to establish the effect of genes on the appearances of organisms. Questions about what genes are and how they produce their effects were not tackled until new techniques in molecular biology were developed. Figure 54.5B shows how developments in genetics, cell biology and molecular biology were brought together to give a full explanation of Mendel's observations. Today the techniques of cell biology and molecular biology have revolutionised genetics. New discoveries are stimulating the growth of biotechnology bringing benefits to agriculture, industry and medicine.

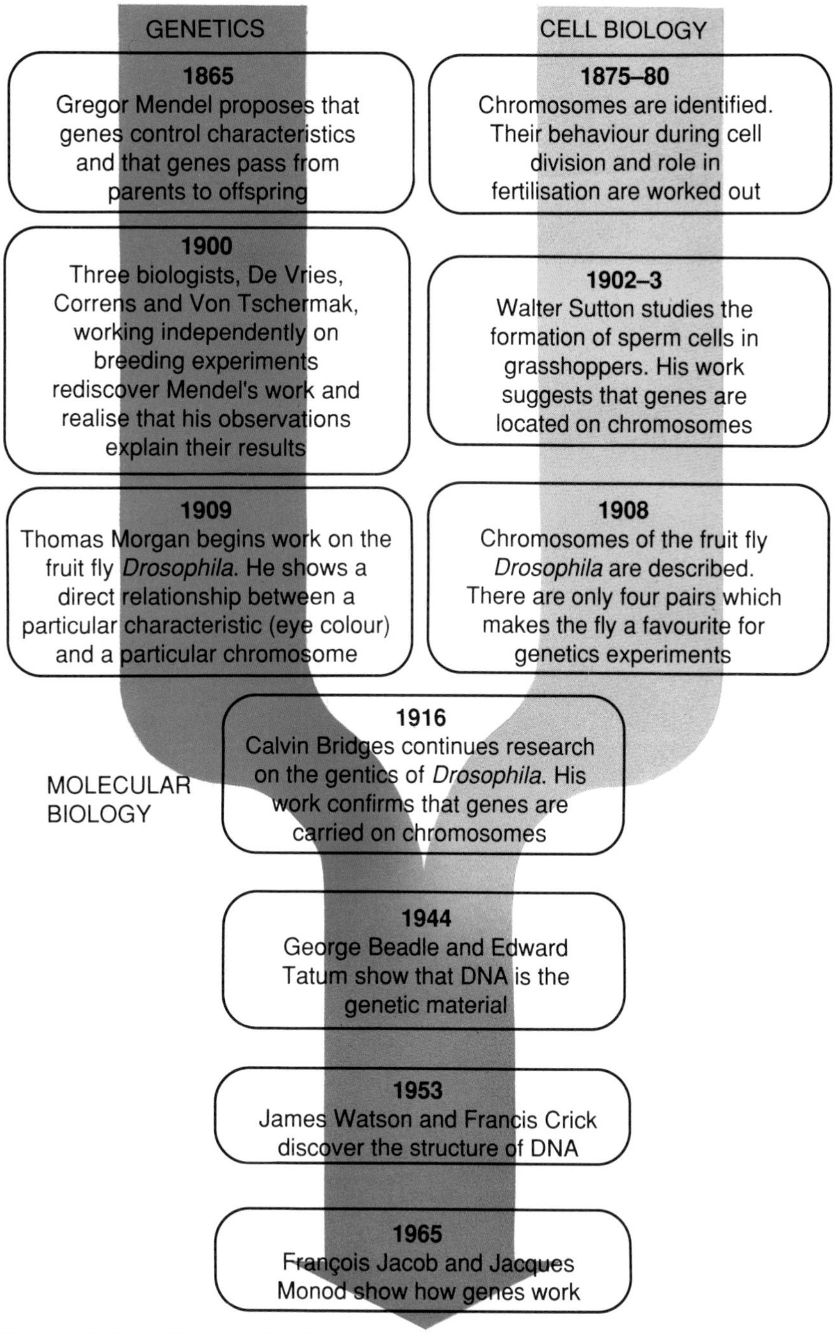

Versuche über Pflanzen-Hybriden.

Von

Gregor Mendel.

(Vorgelegt in den Sitzungen vom 8. Februar und 8. März 1865.)

Einleitende Bemerkungen.

Künstliche Befruchtungen, welche an Zierpflanzen desshalb vorgenommen wurden, um neue Farben-Varianten zu erzielen, waren die Veranlassung zu den Versuchen, die hier besprochen werden sollen. Die auffallende Regelmässigkeit, mit welcher die-selben Hybridformen immer wiederkehrten, so oft die Befruch-tung zwischen gleichen Arten geschah, gab die Anregung zu weiteren Experimenten, deren Aufgabe es war, die Entwicklung der Hybriden in ihren Nachkommen zu verfolgen.

Dieser Aufgabe haben sorgfältige Beobachter, wie Köl-reuter, Gärtner, Herbert, Lecocq, Wichura u. a. einen Theil ihres Lebens mit unermüdlicher Ausdauer geopfert. Na-mentlich hat Gärtner in seinem Werke „die Bastarderzeugung im Pflanzenreiche" sehr schätzbare Beobachtungen niedergelegt, und in neuester Zeit wurden von Wichura gründliche Unter-suchungen über die Bastarde der Weiden veröffentlicht. Wenn es noch nicht gelungen ist, ein allgemein giltiges Gesetz für die Bildung und Entwicklung der Hybriden aufzustellen, so kann das Niemanden Wunder nehmen, der den Umfang der Aufgabe kennt und die Schwierigkeiten zu würdigen weiss, mit denen Versuche dieser Art zu kämpfen haben. Eine endgiltige Ent-scheidung kann erst dann erfolgen, bis Detail-Versuche aus den verschiedensten Pflanzen-Familien vorliegen. Wer die Ar-

Figure 54.5A ● The title page of Mendel's paper. Almost all of the notebooks containing the results of his experiments were destroyed soon after his death.

IT'S A FACT

The fruit fly *Drosophila* is a small fly which feeds on the sugar it finds in rotting fruit. The fly has been studied intensively and today more is known about its genetics than any other animal. It is ideal for genetic experiments because:
• It reproduces quickly (a generation every two weeks),
• It is easy to keep,
• Its cells each have only four pairs of chromosomes in the nucleus (the fewer chromosomes the better for genetic experiments),
• It has giant chromosomes in the salivary glands (giant chromosomes are easy to see under the microscope).

GENETICS

1865
Gregor Mendel proposes that genes control characteristics and that genes pass from parents to offspring

1900
Three biologists, De Vries, Correns and Von Tschermak, working independently on breeding experiments rediscover Mendel's work and realise that his observations explain their results

1909
Thomas Morgan begins work on the fruit fly *Drosophila*. He shows a direct relationship between a particular characteristic (eye colour) and a particular chromosome

CELL BIOLOGY

1875–80
Chromosomes are identified. Their behaviour during cell division and role in fertilisation are worked out

1902–3
Walter Sutton studies the formation of sperm cells in grasshoppers. His work suggests that genes are located on chromosomes

1908
Chromosomes of the fruit fly *Drosophila* are described. There are only four pairs which makes the fly a favourite for genetics experiments

MOLECULAR BIOLOGY

1916
Calvin Bridges continues research on the genetics of *Drosophila*. His work confirms that genes are carried on chromosomes

1944
George Beadle and Edward Tatum show that DNA is the genetic material

1953
James Watson and Francis Crick discover the structure of DNA

1965
François Jacob and Jacques Monod show how genes work

Figure 54.5B ● The growth of modern genetics

Improving the oil palm

We use vegetable oil in the home for cooking and industry uses huge quantities for making margarine, detergents and soaps. *Where does the oil come from?* Rapeseed is a major source but the fruits of the oil palm tree and sunflower seeds are even more important (see Figure 54.5C). Oil palm oil and sunflower oil provide 30% of the world's supply of vegetable oil.

(a) Oil palm   (b) Sunflower   (c) Rape

Figure 54.5C ● Major sources of vegetable oil

PARENTS

Trees producing fruit with a thick shell around the seed are crossed with trees producing fruit without a shell around the seed

HYBRID OFFSPRING

The thin-shelled fruit of some of the hybrid offspring produce a lot of oil

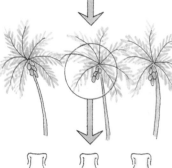

It is only possible to find out which offspring will have fruit that produces a lot of oil by growing plants from the hybrid seeds. This takes about three years

TISSUE CULTURE

A tree is selected that has fruit which produce a lot of oil. Root tissue from the selected tree is placed in a medium which contains all the nutrients needed for growth. Auxin is used to stimulate growth

CLONE FORMATION

Plants develop from the root tissue. They are genetically the same (clones) since they come from the same parent. All the clones have fruit which produce a lot of oil

Oil palm trees grow in the tropics. Each year trees produce about one tonne of oil per hectare. Some trees, however, produce much more. Breeding new stocks of trees from these high yielding varieties seems an obvious way of improving oil production. Unfortunately breeding oil palms is a slow, unreliable process. Trees vary greatly in oil content even when bred from good oil producing parents. Scientists have turned to **cloning** techniques to produce a consistent supply of high yielding trees (see Figure 54.5D).

Genetics Maize (program)

Use the program to investigate monohybrid inheritance. The program looks at the grain colour of corn cobs.

Figure 54.5D ● Breeding programme for the oil palm. Oil palms are produced which yield up to six times more oil than oil palms bred by traditional methods (Note: a hybrid is the offspring of a cross between two genetically unlike individuals)

54.6 ● Biotechnology

Figure 54.6A ● Traditional products of biotechnology

LOOK AT LINKS
for **fermentation**
See Theme L, Topic 51.4.

LOOK AT LINKS
for **yeast**
See Theme A, Topic 3.5.

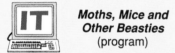

IT ***Moths, Mice and Other Beasties*** (program)

Moths, Mice and Other Beasties is a set of five programs on genetics. You can use this, and the worksheets that go with it, to go over the work you have done on genetics.

Using biotechnology

The word **biotechnology** describes the way we use plant cells, animal cells and micro-organisms to produce substances that are useful to us. Although the word biotechnology is new, the processes of biotechnology have a long history. The use of moulds to make cheese, and bacteria to make vinegar are early examples. For thousands of years we have exploited **yeast** to make wine, beer and bread. The ancient civilisations of Egypt and China knew that lactic acid bacteria preserved milk by turning it into yoghurt (Figure 54.6A).

Before the First World War glycerol and propanone (which are used in the manufacture of explosives) were made by bacteria. After the war the petrochemical industry expanded and the manufacture of glycerol and propanone from oil replaced these early examples of industrial biotechnology. However, rising oil costs have revived interest in the production of these chemicals by biotechnology.

In 1928 Alexander Fleming reported that the mould *Penicillium notatum* made a substance that killed bacteria. The substance was called penicillin: the first of a family of antibiotic drugs made by biotechnology.

Modern biotechnology is branching out in new and exciting ways. Central to success is our understanding that the products of biotechnology are the result of the action of genes. We now know what genes are, how they work and how to manipulate them to our advantage.

● DNA technology

A person's DNA is as unique as their fingerprints. DNA fingerprinting can help to identify criminals in cases where the criminal's body cells are found at the scene of the crime. Except in the case of identical twins, the chances of two people having the same DNA fingerprint are millions to one.

Figure 54.6B shows how DNA fingerprints help to identify criminals. The X-ray film shows the DNA maps made from a semen stain found at the scene of a rape, the body cells of a suspect and the body cells of the victim. *Do you think the police have caught the right man?*

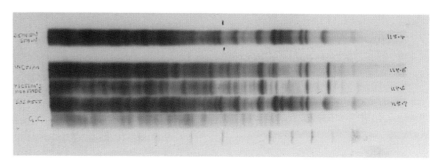

Figure 54.6B ● DNA fingerprinting

● Biosensors

An **antibody** will only attach itself to a particular **antigen**; an enzyme will only catalyse a particular reaction. Biosensors use the sensitivity of these reactions and microelectronic circuits to detect minute amounts of chemicals. In the future, biosensors will help scientists to diagnose disease and to monitor pollution in the environment.

● *Monocional antibodies*

White blood cells produce millions of antibodies to defend the body from attack by bacteria, viruses, fungi and other potentially dangerous antigens. It is difficult to separate different antibodies into pure samples of the antibodies required to fight specific antigens. The problems can be overcome by fusing white cells that produce a particular antibody with a type of rapidly dividing cancer cell. The fused cells only produce the antibody required. Pure samples of antibodies made in this way are called monoclonal antibodies.

Monoclonal antibodies have a wide range of uses. Scientists hope to be able to use monoclonal antibodies to treat cancer. Some types of cancer cell make proteins (antigens) that are different from proteins made by healthy cells. If monoclonal antibodies can be made that attach to only abnormal proteins, then it should be possible to target the cancer cells with drugs without affecting the healthy cells (Figure 54.6C).

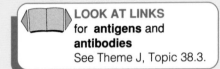

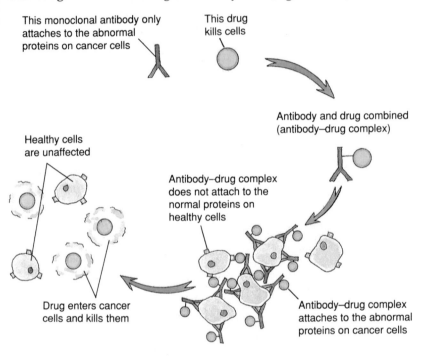

This monoclonal antibody only attaches to the abnormal proteins on cancer cells

This drug kills cells

Antibody and drug combined (antibody–drug complex)

Healthy cells are unaffected

Antibody–drug complex does not attach to the normal proteins on healthy cells

Drug enters cancer cells and kills them

Antibody–drug complex attaches to the abnormal proteins on cancer cells

Figure 54.6C ● How monoclonal antibodies could be used to treat cancer

Genetic engineering

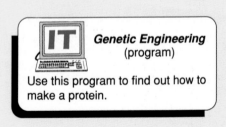

In the early 1970s a type of enzyme (called a restriction enzyme) which cuts DNA into pieces was discovered in several species of bacteria. The discovery marked the beginning of genetic engineering. It made possible the transfer of genes from one type of cell (usually human) to another type of cell (usually a bacterium). The technique enables bacteria to make products which normally they would not make. These products include new medicines, fuels and foods. Figure 54.6D explains how scientists use genetic engineering to make the human hormone **insulin**.

Insulin was the first substance made by genetic engineering to be given to humans. In 1980 volunteer diabetics successfully tried out genetically engineered insulin and by 1982 it was in general use. Before then, insulin was obtained from slaughtered cattle and pigs. It was expensive to produce and in limited supply. The chemical structure of the animal insulin is also different from human insulin; some diabetics reacted allergically to it. Genetically engineered insulin is cheaper, available in large quantities and chemically the same as human insulin.

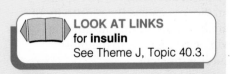

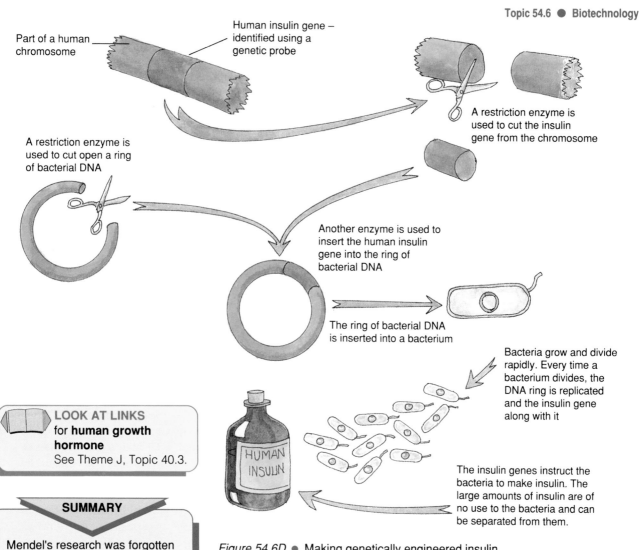

Part of a human chromosome

Human insulin gene – identified using a genetic probe

A restriction enzyme is used to cut the insulin gene from the chromosome

A restriction enzyme is used to cut open a ring of bacterial DNA

Another enzyme is used to insert the human insulin gene into the ring of bacterial DNA

The ring of bacterial DNA is inserted into a bacterium

Bacteria grow and divide rapidly. Every time a bacterium divides, the DNA ring is replicated and the insulin gene along with it

HUMAN INSULIN

The insulin genes instruct the bacteria to make insulin. The large amounts of insulin are of no use to the bacteria and can be separated from them.

LOOK AT LINKS
for **human growth hormone**
See Theme J, Topic 40.3.

SUMMARY

Mendel's research was forgotten until it was re-discovered at the beginning of the twentieth century. Developments in cell biology helped to explain the significance of his results. Our ability to manipulate genes has led to the development of biotechnology.

Figure 54.6D ● Making genetically engineered insulin

Other genetically engineered hormones, including **human growth hormone** and the hormone that controls the absorption of calcium into bones, are being produced by methods similar to those for producing insulin. Using human genes to produce substances like hormones helps to prevent the harmful side-effects that can come from products obtained from animal tissues. It also reduces the use of animals for medical research.

CHECKPOINT

❶ Why did a full understanding of the results of Mendel's breeding experiments with pea plants depend on the discovery of chromosomes and their behaviour during meiosis?

❷ Why is the fruit fly *Drosophila* ideal for experiments in genetics?

❸ What is a clone? Illustrate your answer with named examples.

❹ Why are some diabetics allergic to injections of insulin obtained from the tissues of slaughtered cattle and pigs?

❺ Imagine that you are a scientist who thinks it would be better to produce a hormone-type drug by genetic engineering. Make a flow plan that sets out the different stages of your research. Use scientific language to explain the biological reasoning behind each stage of the plan.

55.1 Evolution: the growth of an idea

Species of living organisms change over the course of time. This change is called evolution. How evolution takes place was a puzzle until Charles Darwin discovered the principles of natural selection. In this section you can find out how the idea developed in Darwin's mind.

The variety of life today almost certainly owes its origins to a scenario billions of years ago similar to the one in Figure 55.1B. *How do the events in Earth's history take us from such beginnings to the present day?* Present-day living things are descended from ancestors that have gradually changed through thousands of generations. We call the process **evolution**.

Look at the picture strip of Earth's **geological eras** at the bottom of the page. It is a timetable showing major events during the evolution of life from its beginnings to the appearance of the first human beings approximately 2.5 million years ago.

Charles Darwin

The British naturalist Charles Darwin was the first person to work out a theory explaining **how** species can evolve. In 1831 Darwin was invited to join the company of HMS *Beagle* on a world voyage which included a survey of the South American coast. The journey took five years. During the *Beagle's* time around South America, Darwin took over as the ship's naturalist. He collected fossils and specimens of plants and animals on expeditions inland. He made many observations about the wildlife he encountered.

On one April day in 1832 Darwin collected 68 different species of small beetle from the rain forest around Rio de Janeiro in Brazil. What puzzled him was that there should be so many different species of one kind of insect. *How did such variety come about?*

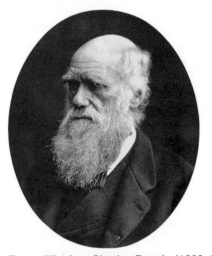

Figure 55.1A ● Charles Darwin (1809–82)

Geological era — Earth's origins

Mars

Mercury   Venus

Sun

Earth

Seas full of organic molecules

Bacteria-like cells form stony pillars called stromatolites. These form some of Earth's oldest rocks

Time scale (millions of years ago)   4800   4400   4000   3600   3200   2800

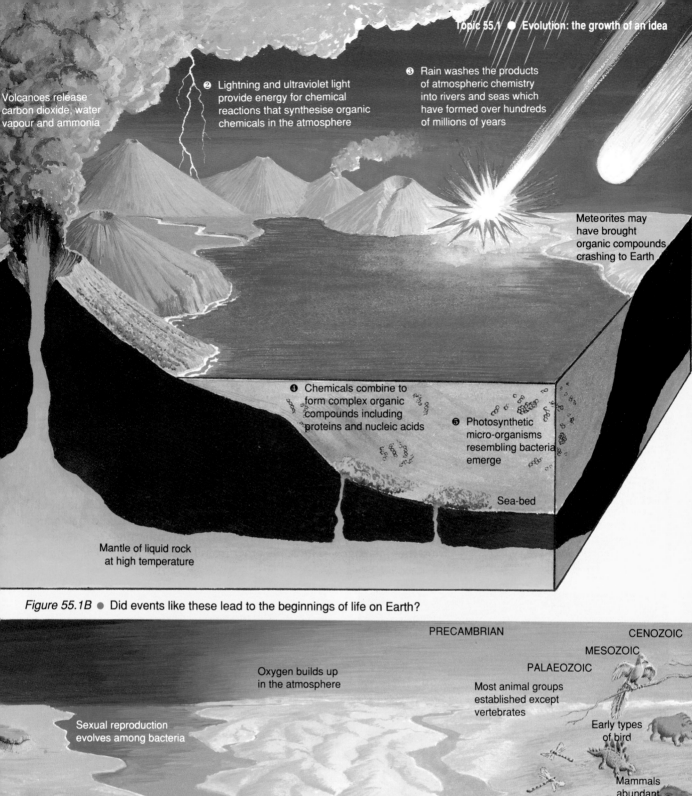

Volcanoes release carbon dioxide, water vapour and ammonia

❷ Lightning and ultraviolet light provide energy for chemical reactions that synthesise organic chemicals in the atmosphere

❸ Rain washes the products of atmospheric chemistry into rivers and seas which have formed over hundreds of millions of years

Meteorites may have brought organic compounds crashing to Earth

❹ Chemicals combine to form complex organic compounds including proteins and nucleic acids

❺ Photosynthetic micro-organisms resembling bacteria emerge

Sea-bed

Mantle of liquid rock at high temperature

Figure 55.1B ● Did events like these lead to the beginnings of life on Earth?

PRECAMBRIAN

CENOZOIC

MESOZOIC

PALAEOZOIC

Oxygen builds up in the atmosphere

Most animal groups established except vertebrates

Early types of bird

Sexual reproduction evolves among bacteria

Mammals abundant

First insects appear on land

Reptiles abundant

Early land plants

First flowering plants

Simple multicellular animals appear such as worms and jellyfish

Fish abundant

Humans appear

423

2400   2000   1600   1200   800   400

Figure 55.1C ● HMS *Beagle* during her voyage around South America

As the *Beagle* sailed up the Pacific coast of South America, Darwin noticed that one type of organism gave way to another. He also noticed that many of the animals were different from those he had seen on the Atlantic coast.

Its South American survey complete, the *Beagle* set sail for the Pacific islands of the Galapagos on 7 September 1835. Once ashore, Darwin observed that the wildlife of the islands was similar to the wildlife he had seen on the South American mainland. However, he noticed differences in detail. The birds shown in Figure 55.1D are cormorants. One comes from the Galapagos islands, the other from Brazil. *What differences can you see between them?*

(a) Galapagos Islands cormorant

(b) Brazilian cormorant

Figure 55.1D ● Flying demands a lot of energy. The absence of predators on the Galapagos Islands means that cormorants do not have to fly away to escape danger. Birds with small wings, therefore, are at an advantage. However, predators threaten Brazilian cormorants. Birds with large wings can fly away and are at an advantage even though they use a lot of energy.

Each of the Galapagos Islands Darwin visited was inhabited by tortoises which were similar to the mainland forms but much larger. He noticed something else: the tortoises on each island were slightly different, so he could tell which island particular tortoises came from (Figure 55.1E). Darwin wondered why the tortoises were different from island to island.

(a) Isla Isabela tortoise

(b) Isla Espanola tortoise

Figure 55.1E ● Tortoises from Isla Isabela (formerly Albemarle) and Isla Espanola (formerly Hood), two of the Galapagos islands. Isla Isabela is well watered and the tortoises wallow in the pools. Isla Espanola is arid and here the tortoises browse on the water-filled stems of cacti and juicy leaves and berries. Notice the shape of the shell of the tortoises from each island. *Can you account for the differences?*

In Darwin's day, most people believed that each species was fixed and unchangeable; but Darwin could not agree. The variety of species discovered on his expeditions in South America and the Galapagos islands convinced him that species are not fixed but change through time; that is, they evolve. *The puzzle was, what mechanism brought about their evolution?*

● *The influence of Lyell and Malthus*

Just before Darwin set sail in the *Beagle*, he was given the first volume of a newly published book *Principles of Geology* by Charles Lyell (Figure 55.1F). The second and third volumes were sent to him during the voyage.

Lyell believed that the Earth's rocks were very old and that natural forces had produced continuous geological change during the course of the Earth's history. Lyell explained that the age of rocks could be estimated from the types of fossil they contained. He also stated that the fossil record was laid down over hundreds of millions of years.

Darwin reasoned from Lyell's work that if rocks and rock formations have changed slowly, over long periods of time, living things might have a similar history.

Another piece of the jigsaw fell into place soon after Darwin's return to England. One day he was reading *An Essay on the Principle of Population* written in 1798 by the Reverend Thomas Malthus (Figure 55.1G). In the essay Malthus stated that a population would increase indefinitely unless it was kept in check by shortages of resources such as food, water and living space.

Darwin understood that living organisms produce more offspring than can normally be expected to survive. A beech tree, for example, produces thousands of seeds each year. Hundreds of seedlings sprout from the seeds but only one or two grow into mature trees (Figure 55.1H). He also understood that the supply of food, amount of space and other resources in the environment are limited. Only those organisms with the structures and the way of life that suited (adapted) them to make best use of these

Figure 55.1F ● Sir Charles Lyell (1797–1875) greatly influenced Darwin's view of Earth and its history. Darwin met Lyell on his return to England and they became great friends.

Figure 55.1G ● Reverend Thomas Malthus

LOOK AT LINKS
Characteristics of the sexually reproduced members of a generation vary because each member inherits different combinations of alleles from its parents.
See Theme N, Topic 54.2.

limited resources survived long enough to reproduce (see Figures 55.1D and 55.1E). Less well-suited organisms left fewer offspring or did not survive to reproduce at all. Therefore, variations which were favourable for survival accumulated from one generation to the next, while less favourable variations died out (became extinct). Darwin called this process natural selection. He realised that this is the mechanism of evolution. At last he understood how species change through time.

Figure 55.1H ● Hundreds of seedlings are growing in an area about 10 m². Very few will grow to maturity. Most perish, crowded out by the two or three that grow the fastest.

FIRST THOUGHTS

55.2 Artificial selection

By choosing particular characteristics, breeders have developed new varieties of plants and animals. The examples described in this section illustrate the process of breeding and its importance in support of Darwin's idea.

Darwin was a cautious man. He knew that other people who had proposed theories of evolution before him had been ignored and disliked. After the *Beagle's* voyage, he spent the next twenty years gathering more evidence to support his ideas. His search for evidence led him to investigate the work of breeders of animals and plants.

Figure 55.2A shows two very different breeds of dog. Centuries of selecting dogs with particular characteristics such as size, colour, length of coat and shape of ear have resulted in a wide variety of breeds. The corgi, spaniel, labrador and bulldog are just a few examples. *How many other breeds can you think of?*

Dog breeders have taken advantage of the large amount of variation in the characteristics of the members of generations of dogs and chosen the characteristics which they want to be passed on to the next generation. The dogs with these characteristics have been allowed to reproduce and so the genes controlling the selected characteristics have been passed to their offspring. This process of choosing which characteristics should pass to the next generation and which should not is called **artificial selection**. (See Figure 55.2B.)

Figure 55.2A ● The same species?

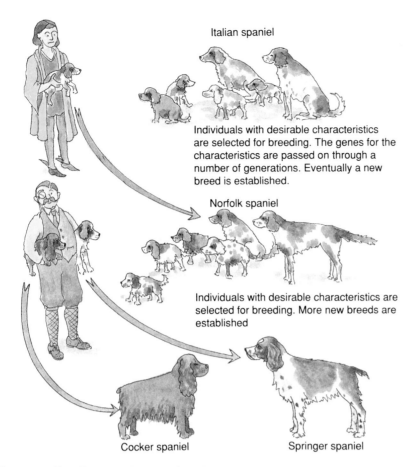

Italian spaniel

Individuals with desirable characteristics are selected for breeding. The genes for the characteristics are passed on through a number of generations. Eventually a new breed is established.

Norfolk spaniel

Individuals with desirable characteristics are selected for breeding. More new breeds are established

Cocker spaniel

Springer spaniel

Figure 55.2B ● The artificial selection of desired characteristics produces breeds of dog that look very different from their ancestors

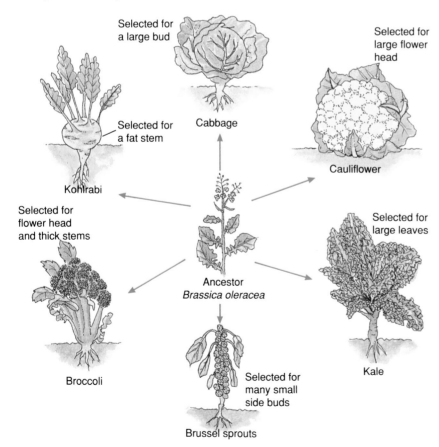

Selected for a large bud

Selected for large flower head

Cabbage

Cauliflower

Selected for a fat stem

Kohlrabi

Selected for flower head and thick stems

Selected for large leaves

Ancestor *Brassica oleracea*

Kale

Broccoli

Selected for many small side buds

Brussel sprouts

Figure 55.2C ● A variety of vegetables bred from a single ancestral species

Generations of artificial selection have resulted in the great variety of dog breeds we know today. All dogs belong to the same species, *Canis familiaris*, and are descended from the same ancestral species even though they look very different from one another.

Figure 55.2C shows another example of artificial selection. Varieties of vegetable have been produced by choosing different characteristics which make good eating and breeding for each one. All the plants belong to the same species, *Brassica oleracea* (a relative of the mustard plant), and are descended from the same ancestral species.

Darwin added the experience of breeding pigeons to his observations of other people's work. He saw that by mating pigeons with different characteristics, new varieties of pigeons could be produced. All the pigeons in Figure 55.2D belong to the species *Columba livia*.

Darwin reasoned that if artificial selection produced change in domestic animals and plants, natural selection should have the same effect on wildlife. The only difference was that artificial selection by human beings produced new varieties in a relatively short time, selection by nature took much longer.

Figure 55.2D ● The many varieties of domestic pigeon

55.3 The Origin of Species

Darwin hesitated from publishing his ideas on natural selection, but in 1858 he had an unpleasant surprise. He received a letter and an essay from Alfred Russel Wallace who was a naturalist living and working in Malaya (Figure 55.3A). In the letter, Wallace asked for Darwin's opinion as a respected naturalist on the essay which set out the principles of natural selection as the mechanism for evolutionary change. This was a terrible blow to Darwin who had worked patiently on the same ideas for 20 years.

Like Darwin, Wallace was led to the idea of natural selection through reading Malthus' essay on population. Over the years, Darwin had discussed natural selection with only a few close friends and fellow scientists. They had urged him to publish his ideas. When Wallace's letter arrived, Darwin was stung into action.

Both scientists recognised the other's contribution and acted most generously over the matter. They agreed to the joint publication of their ideas which appeared in the *Journal of the Linnean Society* for 1858.

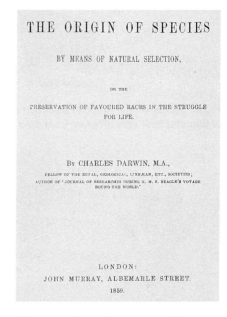

Figure 55.3A ● Alfred Russel Wallace

Figure 55.3B ● Title page of *The Origin of Species*

Although Wallace was a distinguished naturalist in his own right, he realised that Darwin's ideas were more thoroughly worked out than his own. For the rest of his life Wallace insisted that Darwin take most of the credit. After the publication of the joint paper, Darwin hastily prepared a fuller account of his work. *The Origin of Species* was published in 1859 (Figure 55.3B).

In the book Darwin brought together so much evidence that evolution was established as a viable theory. However, the position of natural selection was less secure. Many scientists thought it likely that natural selection was the mechanism of evolution but wanted more evidence. Not until the development of modern genetics, beginning with the discovery of Mendel's work, was natural selection generally accepted as the mechanism for evolutionary change. Understanding genetics allows us to understand why organisms vary. Natural selection works on these variations to produce evolutionary change.

IT'S A FACT

Although Mendel published his theories of heredity in 1866, Darwin never knew about them. It was only after their deaths that Darwin's work on natural selection and Mendel's work on genetics were brought together to give an explanation of evolutionary change.

❶ Briefly explain your understanding of evolution.

❷ Why do you think studying life in the past helps us to understand biology today?

❸ What is an ancestor?

❹ What is a descendant?

❺ What is meant by the term 'natural selection'?

FIRST THOUGHTS

55.4 Evolution in action

In this section you can read about examples of evolutionary change.

LOOK AT LINKS
for **populations**
See Theme M, Topic 52.

Members of a species do not live in isolation. They are part of a **population**. No two individuals of a population are the same genetically (except identical twins). Some individuals have genes controlling characteristics which are better suited for survival than the genes of other members of the population. The individuals with the favourable characteristics are more likely to reproduce successfully and have offspring more likely to survive than the individuals with less favourable characteristics. The result is evolution (see Figure 55.4A).

Evolution is still happening

When a new *insecticide* is used against an insect pest, a small amount is enough to kill most of the population. However, a few individuals are not affected because they have genes which code for enzymes that help to break down the insecticide into harmless substances. These individuals are resistant to the insecticide. These are the insects that survive and reproduce. The majority of their offspring inherit the genes for the enzymes that break down insecticide. In this way the number of resistant insects in the population increases.

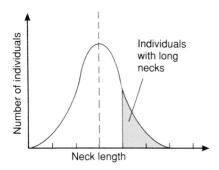

A long neck enables giraffes to browse on the leaves of trees. This is an advantage during the dry season when grass and other food plants are in short supply. This passes more genes for long necks on to the next generation

Short-necked ancestor of the giraffe

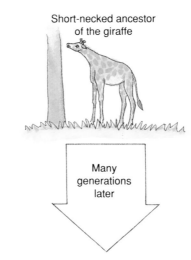

Many generations later

Long-necked descendants

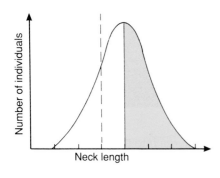

Figure 55.4A ● Passing on favourable characteristics

Insects reproduce quickly so resistance spreads quickly through the population. More and more insecticide has to be used until it becomes so inefficient and so expensive that an alternative insecticide has to be found. Even then, the effect is only temporary because the insect pest soon develops resistance to the new insecticide (Figure 55.4B). The insecticide acts as the agent of selection.

Resistance to antibiotics has evolved in bacteria in much the same way as resistance to insecticides has evolved in insects. Populations of bacteria always contain a few individuals with genes that make them resistant to an antibiotic. These individuals survive and reproduce. The new generation inherits the genes for resistance. Resistance develops rapidly in bacteria because they reproduce rapidly (in some species a new generation is produced every 20 minutes). The antibiotic acts as the agent of selection.

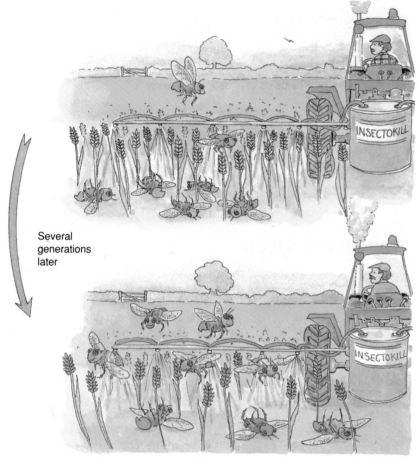

Several generations later

Figure 55.4B ● Resistance of insect pests to insecticide

The Blind Watchmaker/Insect (program)

Using *The Blind Watchmaker* or *Insect* you can select which offspring survive and produce the next generation. Mutation occurs, allowing you to design your own evolving creature.

IT'S A FACT

The insecticide DDT was used to control insect pests during the Second World War. In 1947 the first cases of resistance to the new compound were reported in houseflies. Since then resistance in houseflies has developed so that some varieties are resistant to one hundred times the dose of DDT needed to kill unresistant flies. Today, hundreds of insect species are resistant to a range of insecticides.

Figure 55.4C shows two forms of the peppered moth *Biston betularia*. The speckled, pale moth (called the peppered variety) is found most often in the countryside where it merges into the light-coloured background of lichen covered trees and rocks. In towns and cities air pollution kills the lichens leaving trees and other surfaces bare and sooty. The black moth (called the melanic variety) is the most common form in this environment where it merges into the dark background.

Figure 55.4C ● Can you see the moths?

Birds eat moths whose colour does not merge into the background because they are more easily seen. Natural selection (in the form of moth-eating birds) favours the melanic variety in urban areas and the peppered variety in the countryside (Figure 55.4D).

IT'S A FACT

Resistance in bacteria means that antibiotics become less effective for the treatment of disease. Doctors try to get round the problem by using different types of antibiotic and by making sure that patients are given an antibiotic only if it is absolutely necessary. In hospitals, the pressure of selection by antibiotics is so intense that strains of bacteria resistant to a range of antibiotics rapidly evolve.

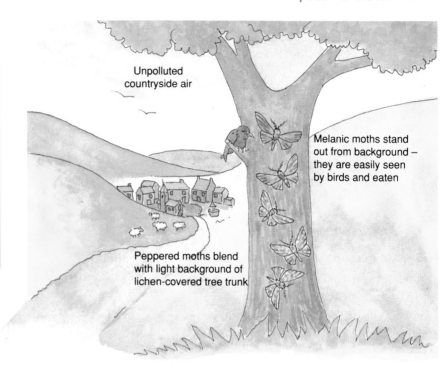

Unpolluted countryside air

Melanic moths stand out from background – they are easily seen by birds and eaten

Peppered moths blend with light background of lichen-covered tree trunk

Polluted air of industrial area

Melanic moths blend with black background of soot-covered tree trunk

Peppered moths stand out from black background – they are easily seen by birds and eaten

Figure 55.4D ● Maintaining the balance between the peppered and melanic varieties of the moth *Biston betularia*

CHECKPOINT

① Look at Figures 55.1D and 55.1E on pages 424 and 425. Explain in your own words the evolution of flightless cormorants and different varieties of tortoise on the Galapagos Islands. In your explanation mention variation, favourable characteristics, ancestors and descendants.

② Look at Figure 55.4A. The graphs show the variation in length of neck in giraffes and their ancestors. What do the graphs tell you about the process of evolutionary change? Why do long necks in giraffes favour survival?

③ Briefly summarise the reasons for the differences in abundance of peppered moths and melanic moths in the countryside and industrial areas.

④ Why is the bird in Figure 55.4D an agent of natural selection?

55.5 The vertebrate story

LOOK AT LINKS
for **vertebrates**
See Theme A, Topic 3.5.

FIRST THOUGHTS

Fish, amphibians, reptiles, birds and mammals are vertebrates. Their ancestors lived in the sea about 500 million years ago. This section traces the evolution of the vertebrates.

The Earth's surface consists of layers of rock. The more recently formed a layer is, the nearer it is to the Earth's surface. Undisturbed rock layers follow on like the chapters of a book. The fossils in each rock layer are a record of life on Earth at the time when the layer was formed. The sequence of fossils traces the history of life on Earth.

The rock layers of the Grand Canyon have lain undisturbed for hundreds of millions of years (Figure 55.5A). They have been exposed by the Colorado River eroding the soft rock. Today the river flows through a gorge 1.6 kilometres deep. The layers of rock at the bottom of the canyon are 2000 million years old. To travel down one of the trails from the rim to the bottom is to travel back in time. The fossils in each layer represent a particular stage in the evolution of life (Figure 55.5B).

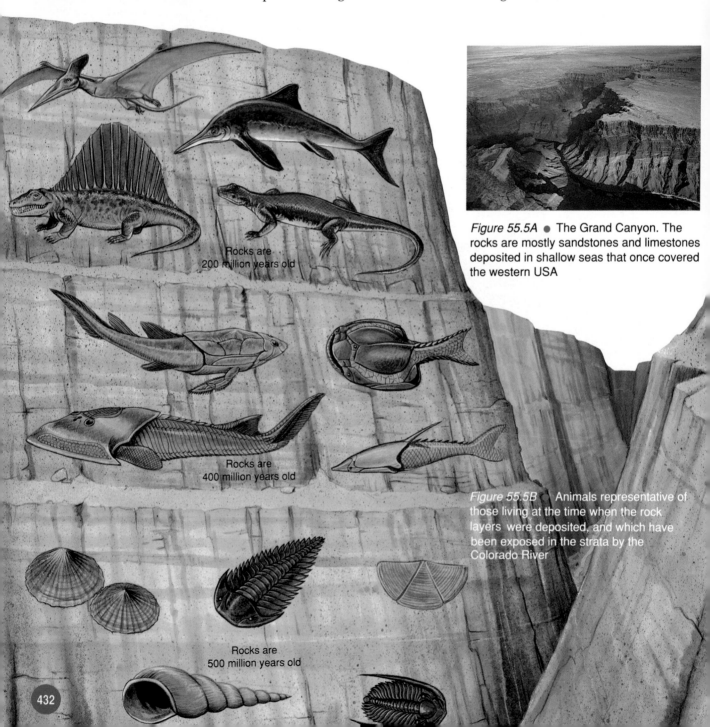

Rocks are 200 million years old

Rocks are 400 million years old

Rocks are 500 million years old

Figure 55.5A ● The Grand Canyon. The rocks are mostly sandstones and limestones deposited in shallow seas that once covered the western USA

Figure 55.5B   Animals representative of those living at the time when the rock layers were deposited, and which have been exposed in the strata by the Colorado River

LOOK AT LINKS
Rock layers can be deformed. Sometimes they can be vertical or even upside down.
See Theme A, Topic 2.6.

IT'S A FACT

Everyone believed that the coelocanth (a type of fish) had been extinct for 200 million years. Then in 1938 a fisherman caught one in the Indian Ocean. Since then a number of specimens have been caught. The fin bones and muscles of the coelocanth differ from those of other fish living today. Coelocanths resemble the fossil remains of *Eusthenopteron*.

The vertebrate story begins in the rock layers dated at about 400 million years old. The fossil bones of ancient types of fish are found here. In the younger rocks near the surface, fossils of reptiles appear for the first time. In the deeper, older layers there are no fossil bones at all although there are shells and impressions of invertebrate animals that lived in the sea 500 million years ago or more.

What do the rocks of the Grand Canyon tell us about the evolution of life? Careful study of the fossils in successive layers of rock reveals that:
- Representatives of the major invertebrate groups were in existence by 500 million years ago.
- Fish were the first vertebrates to appear about 400 million years ago.
- Reptiles appeared about 200 million years after the fish.
- Birds and mammals appeared more recently, too late to be represented as fossils in the rocks of the Grand Canyon.

The sequence of fossils also tells us that the older the fossils, the more they differ from present-day living things. From the fossil record we can conclude that organisms change through time. In other words, present-day living things are a product of evolution.

The invasion of land

Eusthenopteron was a type of fish that lived about 375 million years ago. These fish had lungs and were able to gulp air. Breathing air enabled them to survive periods of drought when the lakes and marshes in which they lived dried out. They also had strong fins which allowed them to move on land. There was abundant invertebrate food on the banks of the pools in which they lived; insects and plants had moved onto land about 25 million years before the appearance of *Eusthenopteron*.

As *Eusthenopteron*, and other fish like it, could live for part of the time out of water they were more likely to survive and leave behind new generations of air-breathing descendants. The vertebrate invasion of land had begun.

Figure 55.5C ● Eusthenopteron

Amphibians

Frogs, newts and salamanders and all other amphibians are descendants of the earliest land dwellers (Figure 55.5D). The adults usually live on land, but need water for breeding. The female lays her eggs in water. They are fertilised in water and hatch into tadpoles which swim and have gills. The tadpole grows: legs develop, it loses its tail and its gills are replaced by lungs. The change from tadpole to adult is called a metamorphosis.

Figure 55.5D ● Ichthyostega – an early type of amphibian that lived about 350 million years ago

The amphibian body is covered with soft skin through which the body quickly loses water in a dry atmosphere. This is why you find frogs and toads on land only where it is damp.

Reptiles

Reptiles, descended from an ancient type of amphibian, completed the move from water to land around 200 million years ago. Over the next 130 million years an enormous variety of reptiles appeared: land giants, agile runners, fliers, swimmers. They dominated the environment (Figure 55.5E).

Reptiles are true land animals. The most important features which allow them to be so are:
- Horny scales which waterproof the skin.
- Well developed legs.
- An egg which is surrounded by a hard impermeable shell. The liquid inside the egg provides the developing embryo with its own 'private pool'. This allows reptiles to breed away from water.

About 70 million years ago many species of reptile became extinct. Today tortoises, turtles, snakes, lizards and crocodiles are virtually all that remain. Why so many species of reptile became extinct is not clear. However, before they became extinct two quite different groups of reptile had given rise to the ancestors of birds and mammals.

IT'S A FACT

The extinction of most reptiles occurred in a relatively short period of time. The extinction of dinosaurs in North America, for example, happened over 12 million years. This seems like a very long time to us but it is an instant compared with the 4000 million years of life on Earth. Think of it like this: if the 4000 million years of life on Earth occupied one day, the reptiles would have died out in the space of five minutes.

Dimorphodon – although the dinosaur probably lacked the muscles for flapping flight, it had a wingspan of two metres and probably glided

Megalosaurus – a large carnivorous dinosaur

Scelidosaurus – herbivorous dinosaur

Compsognathus – chicken-sized dinosaur with powerful legs for running

Plesiosaurus – long necked reptile well adapted for swimming in the sea

Ichthyosaurus – reptile adapted for swimming. Specimens have been found with the skeletons of embryos inside them. It seems possible that the female Icthyosaurus gave birth to live young

Figure 55.5E   155 million years ago reptiles dominated the land

LOOK AT LINKS
for **metabolism**
See Theme F, Topic 25.2.

LOOK AT LINKS
for **homoeostasis**
See Theme F, Topic 27.1
and Theme J, Topic 40.3.

RESOURCE
-ACTIVITY-
PACK

Warm-bloodedness and cold-bloodedness

The **metabolism** of cells releases heat which warms the animal body. Most enzymes which control metabolism work best at a temperature of about 37 °C. If an animal can maintain its body temperature at around 37 °C, even when the temperature outside changes, then metabolism will be at its most efficient. Birds and mammals have evolved ways of keeping the temperature at the centre of the body (the core temperature) at around 37 °C. This is why they are described as **warm-blooded** even though the temperature at the body's surface may fluctuate a little with changes in the temperature outside.

Being warm-blooded means that birds and mammals can live in places where other animals would soon perish because they cannot maintain a steady core temperature. Animals that cannot maintain a steady core temperature are called **cold-blooded**, not because they are 'cold' but because their body temperature fluctuates with the temperature of the environment. Their body temperature drops when the temperature of the environment drops and rises when the temperature of the environment rises (Figure 55.5F). Fish, amphibians and all invertebrates are cold-blooded. Many reptiles are cold-blooded but some species are able to achieve limited control of body temperature (Figure 55.5G).

IT'S A
FACT

The Earth's climate cooled around 70 million years ago. Perhaps this is one reason why many species of reptile became extinct. However, like lizards today, it seems likely that some ancient species of reptile could regulate body temperature and so offset the effects of cold weather.

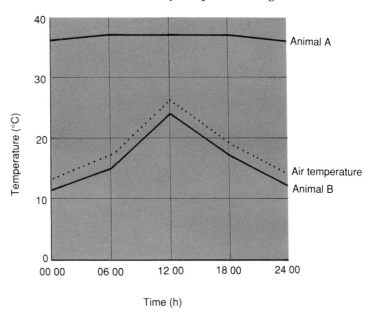

Figure 55.5F ● The body temperatures of two animals and the air temperature recorded over 24 hours. *Which animal is warm-blooded and which cold-blooded?*

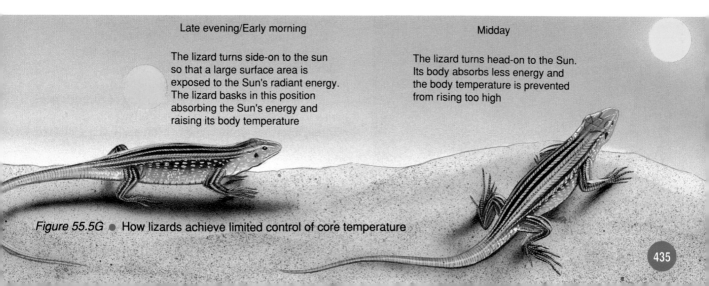

Late evening/Early morning

The lizard turns side-on to the sun so that a large surface area is exposed to the Sun's radiant energy. The lizard basks in this position absorbing the Sun's energy and raising its body temperature

Midday

The lizard turns head-on to the Sun. Its body absorbs less energy and the body temperature is prevented from rising too high

Figure 55.5G ● How lizards achieve limited control of core temperature

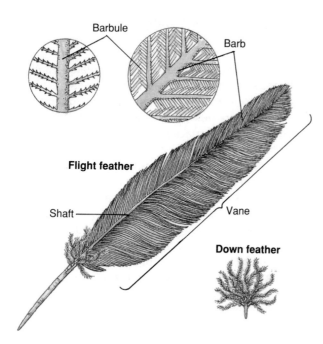

Figure 55.5H ● Feathers

Figure 55.5I ● *Archaeopteryx* was about the size of a crow.
Notice the impressions of feathers (characteristic of birds).
Archaeopteryx also had teeth in its beak (characteristic of
reptiles)

Figure 55.5J ● Hoatzin chick

Birds

A bird's body is covered with feathers. Its forelimbs
are modified for flying. Feathers make flight possible
and help to retain body heat (Figure 55.5H).

Flight feathers give the body shape and lift. Each
one has a central shaft. Either side of the shaft are
hundreds of parallel filaments called barbs which
together make the vane. Each barb has several
hundred tiny barbules along it, each carrying very
small hooks which fasten on to the hooks of the
barbules above. This arrangement gives flight
feathers their shape. Down feathers are fluffy
because they do not have hooks on their barbules.
They provide insulation.

The colour of a bird's feathers also helps to attract
mates and provide camouflage.

Birds spend a great deal of time preening
themselves to keep their feathers in good condition.
Feathers are fluffed out and the bird nibbles them,
drawing each one through its beak to remove fleas,
lice and mites. The preen gland (called the parson's
nose) lies just above the tail. It produces oil which
the bird works into the feathers to waterproof them.
Preening also repairs feathers and puts them back
into place. When the fossil remains of an early type
of bird called *Archaeopteryx* were found in 1861, it
might have been mistaken for a reptile if it had not
been for the beautifully preserved impressions of
feathers which surrounded the specimen (Figure
55.5I).

● Flying

How did flight evolve? One idea is that the reptile
ancestors of birds lived in trees and that the
evolution of feathers enabled them to glide from
branch to branch. In Figure 55.5I you can see a claw
on the leading edge of the wing. Scientists think that
this helped *Archaeopteryx* to clamber along the
branches. The chicks of the hoatzin have claws like
this and lead a similar sort of life in the tangled
branches of the South American rain forest (Figure
55.5J).

Another idea suggests that the evolution of flight
began with a feathered carnivorous reptile running
after its prey in hops and bounds, helped by its
feathered arms. According to this theory, flight
developed from long leaps after food.

No one knows the origins of flight. All we do
know is that some long extinct group of reptiles gave
rise to the feathered warm-blooded creatures we call
birds, and that *Archaeopteryx* is an early stage in their
evolution.

LOOK AT LINKS
for **flight**
See Theme I, Topic 37.3.

Mammals

(a) Duck-billed platypus

(b) Spiny anteater
Figure 55.5K ●

One of the early groups of reptile which lived 200 million years ago was the ancestor of mammals. The fossil evidence shows that at first the mammal line flourished but later it nearly died out in the 'age of reptiles' that followed. However, mammals became abundant after most of the reptile species had become extinct 70 million years ago.

Of present-day mammals, the duck-billed platypus and spiny anteater most resemble the animals that were the ancestors of the mammal line (Figure 55.5K). Both animals have a mixture of reptile and mammal features. For example, they lay eggs as reptiles do. However, they are covered with hair and suckle their young with milk as mammals do.

● Skin, hair and control of body temperature

Hair is made of the protein keratin. It grows from pockets of cells in the skin called **hair follicles**. Figure 55.5L shows hair follicles and other structures in a section of human skin. Although parts of the human body appear hairless, we can see where the hair follicles are when we are cold because the follicle muscles contract, covering the skin with small bumps which we call 'goose pimples'.

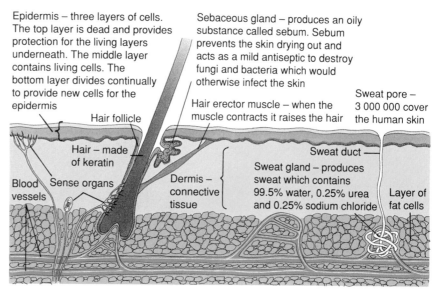

Epidermis – three layers of cells. The top layer is dead and provides protection for the living layers underneath. The middle layer contains living cells. The bottom layer divides continually to provide new cells for the epidermis

Hair follicle

Hair – made of keratin

Blood vessels

Sense organs

Sebaceous gland – produces an oily substance called sebum. Sebum prevents the skin drying out and acts as a mild antiseptic to destroy fungi and bacteria which would otherwise infect the skin

Hair erector muscle – when the muscle contracts it raises the hair

Dermis – connective tissue

Sweat pore – 3 000 000 cover the human skin

Sweat duct

Sweat gland – produces sweat which contains 99.5% water, 0.25% urea and 0.25% sodium chloride

Layer of fat cells

Figure 55.5L ● Section through the human skin

Hair and other mechanisms help to control the body's temperature:
- Hairs raised by the erector muscles trap a layer of air which insulates the body in cold weather (air is a poor conductor of heat). In warm weather the hair is lowered and no air is trapped.
- Fat insulates the body and reduces heat loss.
- Sweat cools the body because it carries heat energy away from the body as it evaporates.
- Millions of temperature-sensitive sense receptors cover the skin. Nerves connect them to the brain which controls the body's response to changes in temperature in the environment.
- When it is warm, blood vessels in the skin dilate. More blood flows through the vessels in the skin and loses heat to the environment. In cold weather, the blood vessels in the skin constrict and less heat is lost to the environment.

Figure 55.5M ● A grey kangaroo carrying her offspring in her marsupium

● *Present-day mammals*

Apart from the duck-billed platypus and the spiny anteater, the class mammals includes two groups: the marsupials and the placentals. Marsupial mammals include the kangaroo, wallaby and koala bear. They give birth to offspring which are at an early stage of development. The offspring crawl into their mother's pouch (called the marsupium) and attach themselves to the nipples of her milk glands. Inside the pouch they grow and develop until they can look after themselves (Figure 55.5M).

Placental mammals include moles, bats, rodents, whales, monkeys and humans (Figure 55.5N). They give birth to offspring which are at a later stage of development than marsupials. The embryo is attached to the wall of the uterus by the placenta through which it obtains nourishment.

Mammals are successful animals. They colonise every environment: from polar ice caps to tropical forests to hot deserts. They fill the air, land and sea.

Humans are relative newcomers to the scene. Our ancestors first appeared approximately 2.5 million years ago. They were as we are – curious. We use words to communicate our curiosity, construct codes of moral behaviour and ask questions about our relationship with the world of nature. We have even invented a way of investigating such questions. It is called Science!

Figure 55.5N ● Some of the many placental mammals

SUMMARY

It is possible that there is life somewhere else in the Universe, but we do not know of it yet. For the time being, therefore, Earth is unique. It is filled with life – a product of 4000 million years of evolution.

? THEME QUESTIONS

● **Topic 54**

1 The diagram shows some of the features of the inheritance of sex.

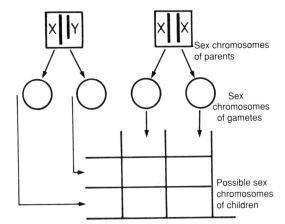

(a) Copy the diagram and indicate the sex of each parent.

(b) Complete your copy of the diagram by drawing in the spaces provided, the chromosomes present in the gametes and in the children.

(c) The diagram shows the chromosomes taken from a cell of an adult human.

(i) State whether the chromosomes are from a male or female.

(ii) Give one reason for your answer. (WJEC)

2 Diagram A shows the chromosomes of a body cell from a female insect. Diagram B shows the chromosomes of a body cell from a male insect of the same species.

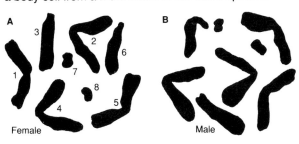

(a) Using the numbers, arrange the chromosomes of the female into groups of matching pairs. The first matching pair is shown.

4 matches with 2

(b) Carefully draw the pair of chromosomes in the male which do not match.

(c) Name the structures concerned with heredity which are found arranged along chromosomes.

(d) How many chromosomes would be found in a sperm produced by this insect?

(WJEC)

3 A farmer used sperms from a pure bred prize bull to artificially inseminate (fertilise) 15 cows whose coat colour was red. All the calves produced were black coated.

(a) State what can be deduced about the gene for red coat colour in these cows.

(b) State the phenotype of the prize bull.

(c) Using suitable symbols state the genotypes of the following:

(i) the calves,

(ii) the cows,

(iii) the prize bull.

(d) Copy the boxes below and show the result of the cross between the prize bull and a cow.

Gametes ↓ →		

(e) From the animals he now has, show how the farmer could obtain another animal with the same genotype as the prize bull by copying and completing the diagram below.

Gametes → ↓		

(WJEC)

4 A fruit grower discovered among his red currant bushes one plant bearing only white berries. He saved the seed and from these he grew plants which only produced white berries.
(a) What is the name given to a new characteristic which suddenly appears in an organism and is inherited?
(b) The character for white berries was found to be recessive to the character for red berries. In a copy of the box and key below show how it is possible for two plants, heterozygous for the red berry gene, to produce a plant with white berries.

Key
Red berries

White berries

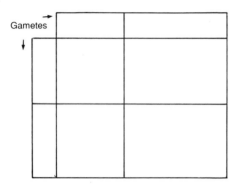

(WJEC)

5 The diagram below shows the offspring of crosses between pure bred Aberdeen Angus bulls, which are black, and pure Redpoll cows, which are red. The ratio of the colours of the offspring of the first generation is also shown. Coat colour is controlled by a single gene which has two forms (alleles): one for black and one for red coat colour.

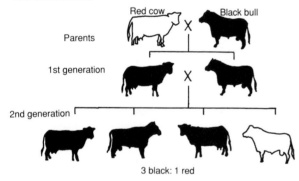

3 black: 1 red

(a) What letters are suitable to represent the two forms (alleles) of the gene?
(b) Make a rough copy of the diagram.
(i) Draw a circle around each animal in the diagram which is definitely homozygous for the gene for coat colour.
(ii) Draw a square around each animal in the diagram which is definitely heterozygous for the gene for coat colour.
(c) Explain why some of the animals in the diagram could be either homozygous or heterozygous for the gene for coat colour.

(LEAG)

● *Topic 55*
6 Snails are eaten by thrushes. Some snails have shells that are very striped, others unstriped. Every September for several years a scientist counted all the snails he could find in an area of grassland. Here are the results:

Year	% covered by grass	Number of snails with ... very striped shells	unstriped shells
1971	98	58	13
1972	25	24	22
1973	5	2	33
1974	97	34	10
1975	96		
1976		9	43
1977	98	68	13

(a) State:
(i) a probable number of snails you would have expected to find in 1975,
(ii) a probable percentage cover of grass in 1976.
(b) (i) All the snails were of the same type (species). During the seven years of study a single specimen was found with a completely black shell. What word could be used to describe this unusual form of the species?
(ii) Choose the best answer. The term which best **explains** the results in the table is
1 heredity   3 conservation
2 natural selection 4 artificial selection.

(WJEC)

7 Charles Darwin suggested that natural selection is a way in which species either adapt to changing conditions or become extinct.
(a) Suggest the meaning of the terms (i) adapt, (ii) extinct.
(b) The peppered moth can be light coloured or dark. It is eaten by birds. Here is an account of an investigation which took place before the Clean Air Act of 1956.
Both light and dark coloured moths were released in two different areas and as many as possible were re-captured. One group was released near an industrial area; the other was released in a non-industrial area. The results were:

	% Re-captured Light coloured	Dark coloured
Non-industrial area	12.5	6.3
Industrial area	13.1	27.5

(i) Use this data to explain Darwin's original suggestion concerning natural selection.
(ii) Since the Clean Air Act, industrial areas have become much less polluted. Explain how this influenced the number of light coloured moths surviving in these areas.
(c) Explain why it might be an advantage for the species to produce dark mutations occasionally, even in a clean environment.

(WJEC)

Teachers' Notes

Activities

● Theme H

Waves 1 and 2   This is a very useful set of simulations, especially for reinforcing basic points which teachers hope to show in practical work. With little initial guidance, pupils can explore the behaviour of single pulses in a range of situations. Waves can then be investigated by changing from single pulses to sets of pulses. Both longitudinal and transverse pulses and waves are possible. Topics which can be investigated include reflection, interference, refraction, ripple tanks, Young's Fringes and Lissajous figures.
Hardware: BBC
Supplier: Resource, Exeter Road, Wheatley, Doncaster

Young's Fringes   This MUSE programme shows how two-slit interference arises and shows how the pattern is related to wavelength, slit separation and screen position. The emphasis is on a simple diagrammatic presentation, without algebraic derivations.
Hardware: BBC
Supplier: MUSE, Houghton-on-the-hill, Leicester

Sound/Ripples   The *Ripples* section contains animations of ripple tank phenomena. The *Sound* section includes basic information on production and nature of longitudinal waves. The user can specify tones by amplitude and frequency; the resulting waves can then be heard and modelled on the screen.
Hardware: BBC, Econet, Archimedes
Supplier: AVP, Chepstow, Gwent

Blindspot   One of the programs from the *Reactions, Blindspot and Body Types* disk. The *Blindspot* program models the structure of the eye at a simple, introductory level. It includes an experiment enabling the user to investigate and measure their own blindspot. Other programmes on this disk could be used with Theme J.
Hardware: BBC, Nimbus
Supplier: AVP, Chepstow, Gwent

Colour/Optics   The *Optics* section ties in with Topic 32, with sections on concave and convex lenses and concave and convex mirrors. The *Colour* section is a simple, interactive program which links effectively with the spectrum in Topic 33. The program allows the users to move patches of colour around the screen and to simulate coloured light falling on coloured objects.
Hardware: BBC, Archimedes, Econet
Supplier: AVP, Chepstow, Gwent
Alternatives: Computer models of ray diagrams are plentiful. Others include *Lenses* (AVP), *Light and Colours* (AVP), *Lens Ray Tracing* (Salford Science Software), *Camera* (Science in Process Software Pack One), *Understanding Waves* (Harmony Software).

Other software which uses a colour monitor to good effect includes *Light and Colours* (AVP), *Colours* (Science in Process Software Pack Three), *Colour Topics* (Philip Harris).

There is a choice of software on the topic of the eye. Some examples are *Biology Disc 1* (Vision Software), *Eye* (Longman Micro Software), *The Eye and the Ear* (AVP) and *The Human Eye* (Garland).

Pulsmod and *Sigtran*   Each program contains a disk, a students' booklet with questions and a teachers' guide with answers. They allow the user to investigate sampling and digital and analogue communication, at the user's own pace. Both programs are interactive.
Hardware: BBC, Econet, Nimbus
Supplier: British Telecom Education Service

● Theme I

Moments   This program illustrates the principle of moments with a simple lever system consisting of a plank of fixed length, a fulcrum and a number of weights. Students may add, move or remove masses in order to balance the lever. There are four demonstration options and a problem setting option. Five levels of difficulty are permitted. A set of worksheets is supplied with the program to support practical work.
Hardware: BBC, Nimbus
Supplier: Science Education Software, Dolgellau, Gynedd

Bridge Building   The program allows students to evaluate three different types of bridge (beam, Warren, arch). Pupils can choose different features of the bridge, e.g. material, arch depth, and evaluate the different factors important in bridge building.
Hardware: BBC
Supplier: Longman Micro Software, Harlow, Essex

Working Under Pressure   This is a simulation program in which students are placed in the role of pipeline planning engineers. Students have to make

decisions about pipe diameters and the location of gas compressors. They test their pipe against a range of demands for gas from one or two towns served by the pipeline. The pipeline design can then be tested against variables such as weekday and weekend demands, or levels of demand ten years ahead. Computations of pressure drop and quantity of gas delivered for different lengths and diameters of pipes are made using a 'pipeline' calculator which is part of the program.
Hardware: BBC, Nimbus
Supplier: British Gas Education Service, PO Box 46, Honslow

Floating and Sinking This program can extend some of the practical work done in the laboratory. The program allows students to study the behaviour of different objects, of various sizes, made of different materials, in a range of liquids.
Hardware: BBC
Supplier: Longman/Logotron Ltd., Cambridge

Upthrust and Flotation A simulation dealing with Archimedes' Principle and the forces acting upon balloons and other objects floating in, or immersed in, fluids.
Hardware: BBC, Nimbus
Supplier: AVP, Chepstow, Gwent

Motion This is a videodisc-based program presenting nearly 200 short film sequences of a wide range of examples of motion. It is an excellent resource for a range of abilities, allowing detailed exploration of motion for more able pupils.
Hardware: IVIS or Domesday interactive video systems
Supplier: Anglia College of HE, East Road, Cambridge
Note: This disc is not cheap (approx. £100 + VAT), but it may be purchased by a group of schools or a Local Education Authority. It could be used in the early stages of secondary schools for discussion of motion sequences and it is also suitable for use in a more quantitative manner higher up the school, including at sixth form level. In our view, it is good value for money.

Uniformly Accelerated Motion This program employs the tutorial technique of computer synchronised audio (voice-track used in combination with the computer). It can be used for direct learning or for revision. The essential theory of the subject is explained and illustrated not only by graphs but also by graphics animations. The program assumes the most elementary knowledge on the part of the user, but gives a thorough treatment of uniform velocity, uniform acceleration, the idea of terminal velocity and

the acceleration due to gravity. The fundamental equations of uniform velocity and uniformly accelerated motion are explained and formulated. A number of problems based on uniformly accelerated motion are included.
Hardware: BBC and audio cassette
Supplier: BBC Software Publications, 80 Wood Lane, London

Floater and *Lift* *Floater* simulates the motion of a frictionless particle in a two-dimensional frame. The particle can be allowed to move freely in a straight line and rebound elastically from the sides of the box. Alternatively, you can control the motion of the particle with a joystick (essential when using the program) which can change the direction and velocity of the particle. The program allows the user to study the displacement, velocity and acceleration of the particle as it moves within the box.

Lift involves sending a tiny figure called Mabel up and down in a lift shaft. Mabel is amazingly resilient and flexible. Her mass and her gravitational acceleration can be varied. A spring balance can also be moved with Mabel, both controlled by a joystick. As Mabel's velocity and acceleration are changed, different readings are shown on the spring balance.

A huge variety of options are available for displaying and studying the motion in both *Floater* and *Lift*.
Hardware: BBC B
Supplier: Cambridge Micro Software, CUP, Shaftesbury Road, Cambridge

Gravity Pack This package contains three programs that simulate the motion of objects under the influence of gravity. The programs allow more control than is possible in laboratory experiments, so users can explore the characteristics of gravity and gravitational fields more effectively. *The Monkey and the Hunter* is an interactive animation of a hunter trying to shoot a monkey and shows how bodies of different masses are accelerated at the same rate by gravity. *Newton's Cannon* demonstrates that if a cannonball is fired horizontally from a height it will either crash to Earth, shoot off into space or go into a stable orbit, depending on the velocity at which it if fired. *Satellites* explores the behaviour of a satellite in a gravitational field between the Earth and the Moon (this program is more suitable for sixth form students).
Hardware: BBC
Supplier: Cambridge Micro Software, CUP, Shaftesbury Road, Cambridge

Motion in Space This provides a simulation of motion in 'ideal conditions'. The program goes slightly further in creating space walking and space missions in which a female astronaut can be moved

by firing four gas jets. As the astronaut moves, the horizontal and vertical speeds are given allowing the components of motion to be studied in some detail. The fuel used and oxygen supply remaining are given on the screen. Three of the missions involve space rescues, two involve rebuilding a damaged satellite.
Hardware: BBC B
Supplier: Cambridge Micro Software, CUP, Shaftesbury Road, Cambridge

The World of Newton   This computer simulation allows the user to investigate a microworld unfettered by the complications of the real world. The program uses a small oblong object which can be moved around the screen with 'kicks'. The booklet tells you that this object 'moves on the screen according to Newton's Laws of Motion'. Different parts of the program provide entertaining challenges, e.g. *Crazy Maze*, *Beat the Clock*. This is an excellent simulation which could be used in any part of Topic 36. Ideally, a networked system of computers would make it possible for several groups of pupils to be using the program simultaneously.
Hardware: BBC
Supplier: Longman Micro Software, Harlow, Essex

Newton and the Shuttle   This program puts the student in the role of the commander of a reusable space shuttle with a mission to launch the shuttle, manoeuvre it into the correct orbit, recover a dead satellite orbiting in space and make a successful descent back to Earth. The simulation helps to show physics in action and the application of Newton's laws of motion. Helpful explanations are given in the accompanying documentation.
Hardware: BBC
Supplier: BBC Software Publications, 80 Wood Lane, London

Motion Sensor   The motion sensor is a 'range finder' which uses an ultrasonic beam to measure distance. The motion sensor connects to the back of a microcomputer, and comes with a range of friendly software and documentation. Pupils' activity sheets providing ideas for using the sensor can be obtained. It is an excellent resource for studying motion at GCSE level.
Hardware: BBC Micro, Archimedes, Nimbus
Supplier: Educational Electronics, Leighton Buzzard, Bedfordshire

● *Theme J*

There is a range of pulse sensors available from, for example, Philip Harris and Educational Electronics. Eurisen (Earl Shilton, Leics.) make a hand held 'Pulse Stick' which can beep synchronously with the user's pulse. A description of a cheap, simple pulse recorder for the BBC micro can be found in *Journal of Biological Education*, Spring 1989

Blood Circulation   A computer simulation including models of heart structure and the way that blood flows through the heart
Hardware: BBC, Econet
Supplier: AVP, Chepstow, Gwent
Alternatives: *Blood Circulation Maze Game* (Philip Harris)

ABO Blood Grouping   This provides an alternative to practical work which involves the students in taking or using blood samples. The program covers the taking of blood samples, use of antisera in blood tests, principles of blood transfusions, agglutination and the genetics of the ABO system.
Hardware: BBC, Archimedes, Nimbus
Supplier: AVP, Chepstow, Gwent
Alternatives: *Blood Groups* (Philip Harris) is an interactive program showing how blood is grouped and describing reactions between donor and recipient blood.

Graphic Hearts   A set of programs which show the structure and working of a mammalian heart.
Hardware: BBC
Supplier: Biology Health and Fitness Curriculum Project, Department of Education, Cambridge University

Seed Germination   This shows a simulated series of experiments. It could be used in advance of laboratory experiments, or after the experiments to reinforce the key learning points.
Hardware: BBC, Archimedes, Nimbus
Supplier: Philip Harris, Shenstone, Staffordshire

Female Reproductive Cycle/Fertilisation   The program includes the role of hormones in the menstrual cycle. There are animated models of fertilisation and implantation.
Hardware: BBC
Supplier: Philip Harris, Shenstone, Staffordshire

The Nervous System/Nerve   *Nerve* is aimed at the 15–19 age range but its three sections can be used separately. It is largely interactive so students may need some initial help.
Hardware: BBC, Nimbus, Archimedes
Supplier: AVP, Chepstow, Gwent

Insulin   An interactive simulation of a human physiological control system. There are three levels of complexity in the program, allowing control of up to nine hormone parameters.
Hardware: BBC
Supplier: AVP, Chepstow, Gwent

Water Balance in Plants   This program relates wilting to water balance and movement between cells.
Hardware: BBC
Supplier: AVP, Chepstow, Gwent

The Human Skeleton   This is a set of views of the skeleton, with diagrams of the skull, vertebrae, ribs, girdles and limbs.
Hardware: BBC, Archimedes
Supplier: AVP, Chepstow, Gwent

Pixel Perfect   This is a desk top publishing application. Graphic information of all kinds can be manipulated to create documents such as posters, worksheets, magazines and displays. *Digital Anatomy* is a set of anatomy diagrams which can be altered and used in *Pixel Perfect*.
Hardware: BBC, Archimedes, Econet
Supplier: AVP, Chepstow, Gwent
Note: *Pixel Perfect* is also available on CD-ROM. Packs can be obtained for science, humanities, maths, art and technology.

● **Theme K**
Electric Fields   This simulation allows students to investigate electric fields and potential around different charges in a visual way. *Electric Fields* can be used in several ways: as a teacher-run demonstration; as student-run programs to reinforce ideas learnt in class; as a way for students to learn by discovery (the pack includes six worksheets for students). The program allows up to four simulated charges of variable intensity to be placed on the screen.
Hardware: BBC
Supplier: BBC Software Publications, 80 Wood Lane, London

Electrostatic and Magnetic Fields   The package consists of two parts, *Electric Fields and Potentials*, and *Magnetic Effects of Electric Currents*. The first displays electrostatic field lines and equipotentials for a number of different situations; the second illustrates various magnetic effects such as Oersted's experiment. The package comes with a full teacher's guide which includes information about the theory behind the experiments.
Hardware: BBC
Supplier: SPA, PO Box 59, Leamington Spa, Warwickshire

Circuit Boards   This program is useful for revising work done in the laboratory on circuit boards. The screen display shows a plan view of a sixteen pillar circuit board and a side pad containing connectors, switches, bulbs, ammeters and diodes. The components can be transferred from the side pad to any position on the board following the circuit outlines provided. Bulbs light up with three levels of brightness, ammeters give readings and short circuits are possible without damaging the components or flattening the cells. The number of cells on the board can be changed at any time, switches can be opened and closed and the direction of diodes can be reversed. The display is in colour.
Hardware: BBC, Archimedes, Nimbus, PC
Supplier: AVP, Chepstow, Gwent

Electric Circuits   This is a package of four programs: *Components* gives information concerning electrical components, shows the symbols used in circuit diagrams and provides visual effects. In *Alternating and Direct Current* the difference between a.c. and d.c. is explained and the connection between a.c. and the sine curve is illustrated. Half wave and full wave rectification are introduced, first in terms of the sine curve and then by means of circuit diagrams with diodes. *Ohms Law* provides circuits with arrangements of resistors in series and in parallel. Students are able to choose the number of cells and also the value of each resistance. They are then required to calculate the total resistance and the current. Finally *Circuit Board* provides a simulation of a school circuit board. It allows one, two or three cells, an ammeter, a variable resistance, a switch and any combination of bulbs in up to three parallel circuits. The bulbs vary in brightness according to the current and if the current is too high, they blow. The ammeter records the overall current and a warning is sounded if it is over-loaded. The circuits can be modified at any time.
Hardware: BBC, Archimedes, Nimbus
Supplier: AVP, Chepstow, Gwent

Interactive Data Base on Use of Energy and Electricity in the United Kingdom   The data base contains detailed information about the past and present use of energy and electricity in Britain. It also acts as a 'simulated' laboratory that allows users to estimate the likely future demand for these commodities and see how these demands might be met. The basic data are capable of being interpreted, analysed and extrapolated at a range of levels. It is accompanied by a teachers' guide.
Hardware: BBC, Nimbus
Supplier: UKAEA Education Service, Harwell Laboratory, Oxfordshire

Watts in your home   This is a simulation showing energy/electricity use in a typical home. It provides an interesting way of comparing the costs of energy-consuming appliances in use. A very useful program.
Hardware: BBC
Supplier: Cambridge Micro Software, CUP, Shaftesbury Road, Cambridge

Logic Gates   The behaviour of five types of logic gate (AND, NAND, OR, NOR, XOR) are simulated in this program and the connecting leads displayed. This program simulates the behaviour of a sequence of logic gates designed by the user. Four gates can be connected to form a circuit. This circuit can be integrated into a single chip and this chip used as part of a new design. It is therefore possible to combine a maximum of 16 gates into a single circuit and stimulate its behaviour. Designs can be saved to and loaded from disk. Detailed notes are provided to familiarise the user with the program, and to introduce the beginner to the subject. The disk includes the simple designs used in the notes and also a full adder and binary decoder as examples of more complex circuits.
Hardware: BBC, Archimedes, Nimbus, PC
Supplier: AVP, Chepstow, Gwent

● **Theme L**
Chemical Collisions   This program allows the user to explore the factors affecting the reaction of two gases. Two sets of up to 80 coloured particles combine on the screen to form white particles only if they collide with sufficient energy. The progress of the reaction can be analysed using bar charts, graphs and by a number count. The temperature and the numbers of particles involved in the reaction can be controlled by the user.
Hardware: BBC, Apple
Supplier: Cambridge Micro Software, CUP, Shaftesbury Road, Cambridge

Rate of Reaction Simulation   This program simulates a typical experiment and is designed to allow students to observe the effects of temperature, concentration, particle size and agitation on an acid–carbonate reaction. Diagrams, tables and graphs of results are displayed on screen and may be printed out as required.
Hardware: BBC, Archimedes, Nimbus.
Supplier: Garland, 35 Dean Hill, Plymouth

Physical Chemistry Pack   This is a suite of programs. The effect of reaction conditions, including particle size of catalyst, on the rate of decomposition of hydrogen peroxide is investigated in *Rates of Reaction*. *Gas Laws* aids understanding of these difficult concepts by providing graphical displays demonstrating the relationship between volume, temperature, pressure and mass of an ideal gas. *Homogeneous Equilibrium* is an investigation of acid–alcohol equilibrium and some gas phase equilibria leading to an equilibrium law in terms of concentration. The first part seems the most useful for this age group.
Hardware: BBC, Archimedes, Nimbus.
Supplier: Longman Micro Software, Harlow, Essex

The Ethanol Question   This is a simulation designed to introduce the difficult concepts of rate of reaction and equilibrium in an industrial context where chemical reactions seldom proceed to completion. The simulation is in two parts. The first guides students through the different factors which influence the position of equilibrium in the reaction so that they can make the most of the raw materials. Part two introduces the costs associated with changing conditions and the task of producing ethanol at a competitive selling price, with guidelines given for a target price. The package includes a students' booklet, worksheets and a guide for teachers.
Hardware: BBC, Nimbus
Supplier: BP Educational Service, London

The Mole Concept   Using the technique of computer synchronised audio (a voice-track combined with computer software), the concept of a mole is demonstrated and explained. Graphics and animation help to introduce the terms, nucleus, proton, electron and relative atomic mass. The combining of two hydrogen atoms and one oxygen atom to form one molecule of water is illustrated. This leads to the mole as a representation of the number of atoms in one gram of carbon-12. The mole is shown to be the vital unit 'ingredient' in the 'recipes' for precisely calculating chemical reactions. This leads to a simulated titration experiment.
Hardware: BBC and audio cassette
Supplier: BBC Software Publications, 80 Wood Lane, London

Structure and Bonding   A set of four programs. *Atomic Structure and Bonding* explains and tests atomic structure, electronic configuration and bonding using a random selection of elements and compounds from the first 20 elements of the Periodic Table. In *Ionic and Covalent Bonding*, the cursor keys are used to select two of the first 20 elements. Providing a simple compound is possible, diagrams are drawn showing its formation. *Reactivity Series* tests the chemical properties of the most important metals. *Electrolysis* illustrates the electrolysis of a range of ionic substances, showing how their behaviour is predictable on the basis of the reactivity series.
Hardware: BBC, Nimbus, PC
Supplier: AVP, Chepstow, Gwent

Chemistry Super Stars   The four areas of *Chemistry Super Stars* provide a problem-solving/game approach in the areas of preparation and properties of salts, reactions of common compounds and the reactivity of metals. Students must solve problems set in game formats which are useful for revision. In *Reactivity*, students identify five metals from their

reactions with solutions.
Hardware: BBC, Archimedes
Supplier: Chalksoft, Spalding, Lincs

Siting a Blast Furnace   This program aims to develop an awareness of the many factors associated with industrial location. Students are able to site a blast furnace on an imaginary island. When the furnace has been located the program can be requested to produce a detailed breakdown of the component costs of one tonne of iron.
Hardware: BBC, Nimbus
Supplier: Longman Micro Software, Harlow, Essex

Industrial Chemistry Pack   *The Manufacture of Sulphuric Acid* is an investigation into aspects of a chemical industrial process. The conflicting demands of best equilibrium yield, high daily production and profitable manufacture are taken into account. *Siting an Aluminium Plant* enables students to consider some of the factors which must be considered when planning the siting and production targets of an aluminium smelting plant.
Hardware: BBC
Supplier: Longman Micro Software, Harlow, Essex

Applied Chemistry   This is a series of programs covering some of the important industrial processes. Pupils are taken through flow charts for the Haber and contact processes, with questions to test their understanding and recall. For iron, aluminium, chlorine and sodium hydroxide production, diagrams of the plant are shown and details of the process examined. In *Polymerisation*, the processes leading to the formation of several common addition and condensation polymers are shown graphically.
Hardware: BBC, Nimbus, PC
Supplier: AVP, Chepstow, Gwent

Make a Million   This is an educational game designed to be used in conjunction with classroom work. The program involves the industrial production of a variety of substances and electricity from basic raw materials. The processes involved are blasting, electrolysis, fractionating, generating electricity, and making and adding acid. Detailed study of the manufacturing processes is not necessary but the package allows and stimulates the student to make further investigations which can lead to project work. The program is a game, almost along the lines of an adventure, where the user chooses a pathway to financial success. A set of worksheets containing information about the processes covered in the program is provided with the package.
Hardware: BBC, Archimedes, Nimbus.
Supplier: AVP, Chepstow, Gwent

● *Theme M*
Old Park Farm   This is an accessible learning resource on the subject of conservation, using as an example a bat population.
Hardware: BBC with Concept Keyboard
Supplier: AB Micro Express, Wharfdale Road, Pentwyn, Cardiff

Ecology and Conservation   This is an ecological management game. Groups with competing interests plan the development of a nature reserve. It is suitable for pupils of a wide ability range, working in groups.
Hardware: BBC
Supplier: BBC Software Publications, 80 Wood Lane, London

Ecosoft/Junior Ecosoft   Data from fieldwork or from the laboratory can be manipulated and displayed. This is a very flexible package which teachers might wish to use in many areas of data management. Junior Ecosoft is nominally intended for use up to Key Stage 3 but some teachers use it for GCSE.
Hardware: BBC, Nimbus (*Ecosoft*)
Supplier: AUCBE, Edymion Road, Hatfield, Herts.

Ecodisc   This is an interactive videodisc. The disc provides a large volume of information about a nature reserve. Users manage the reserve. Target group is normally Key Stage 4 though it could be used at Key Stage 3 and at A level.
Hardware: BBC AIV System
Supplier: BBC Enterprises, 80 Wood Lane, London
Note: Schools may be able to obtain an AIV system on loan from the LEA.

Cycles in Nature   This program investigates the water, nitrogen and carbon cycles. The three cycles can be used separately.
Hardware: BBC, Nimbus, Archimedes
Supplier: AVP, Chepstow, Gwent

Ecology Foodwebs   This is a three stage package for Key Stage 4: animated guide to food webs, interactive section and quiz. It uses games style presentation.
Hardware: BBC, Archimedes
Supplier: AVP, Chepstow, Gwent

Lake Web and *Bio-Wood*   These are similar programs which challenge the user to survive in an environment. Survival depends on deciding what to eat, what to ignore and what to escape from.
Hardware: BBC
Supplier: AVP, Chepstow, Gwent

Golden Eagle   Suitable for Key Stage 3 or introduction at Key Stage 4. The user runs a wildlife reserve with the aim of doubling the Golden Eagle population. It encourages systematic record keeping

and learning from repeated attempts.
Hardware: BBC
Supplier: AVP, Chepstow, Gwent

Ecology Pack   This pack has uses at and beyond Key Stage 4. It contains these programs: *Biomass, Pond Ecology, Predator-Prey Relationships* and *Statistics for Biologists*.
Hardware: BBC, Nimbus
Supplier: AVP, Chepstow, Gwent

Population Pack   Applicable at Key Stage 4 and beyond. The pack contains programs on human population growth and on a Malthusian model of population, food and energy supplies.
Hardware: BBC, Archimedes, Nimbus
Supplier: Longman Micro Software, Harlow, Essex

Predator–Prey Relationships   The user supplies numbers, size, population, etc. The program predicts predator–prey relations over annual cycles.
Hardware: BBC
Supplier: AVP, Chepstow, Gwent

● **Theme N**
Introductory Genetics   Suitable for Key Stage 4, with accompanying material for further study. There are three programs: *Sex Determination, Dominance and Co-dominance* and *Inheritance of Blood Groupings*. Tests accompany each program.
Hardware: BBC, Archimedes, Nimbus
Supplier: Garland, 35 Dean Hill, Plymouth

Genetic Engineering   For Key Stage 4 and beyond. Production of recombinant DNA is examined, leading to the manufacture of a protein.
Hardware: BBC, Archimedes, Nimbus
Supplier: Philip Harris, Shenstone, Staffordshire

Sex Determination   This program could be used as an introduction to genetics. It illustrates randomness in producing gametes and offspring, including the effect of population size.

Hardware: BBC, Archimedes, Nimbus
Supplier: AVP, Chepstow, Gwent

Genetics Maize Program   The grain colour of corn cobs is used to demonstrate aspects of monohybrid inheritance. Results are shown both pictorially and in a genetics diagram.
Hardware: BBC, Archimedes, Nimbus
Supplier: AVP, Chepstow, Gwent

Moths, Mice and Other Beasties   There are five programs, suitable for reinforcing laboratory work on genetics. *Moths*, on selection and melanism; *Mice 1, 2, 3* on inheritance; *Snails* on predation.
Hardware: BBC, Archimedes, Nimbus
Supplier: AVP, Chepstow, Gwent

Biology Simulations   A set of programs which contains the program *Population Genetics* which illustrates changes in gene frequency in a changing population.
Hardware: BBC, Archimedes, Nimbus
Supplier: AVP, Chepstow, Gwent

The Blind Watchmaker/Insect   These programs demonstrate that variations in organisms are due to reproduction in which gene mutation occurs. Can be fascinating for almost any age. The user plays the part of the environment, determining which organisms are adaptively favoured.
Hardware: *The Blind Watchmaker*: Apple Mac Plus. *Insect*: BBC, Archimedes
Supplier: *The Blind Watchmaker*: SPA, PO Box 59, Leamington Spa, Warwickshire. *Insect*: Beebug, 117 Hatfield Road, St Albans, Herts

Survival of the Fittest   Suitable for Key Stage 4 and beyond. The program investigates genetic principles underlying evolution. It includes a population division facility.
Hardware: Nimbus
Supplier: SPA, PO Box 59, Leamington Spa, Warwickshire

Numerical Answers

CHECKPOINT 30.3
❶ (b) 2040 m
❷ (a) 200 kHz (b) 1.16 MHz (c) 1.21 MHz
(d) 648 kHz
❸ (a) 0.50 Hz (b) 20 m, 10 m/s
❹ (a) 0.664 m (b) 0.113 m (c) 13.6 mm

CHECKPOINT 31.2
❶ (a) 333 m/s
❺ 270 m

CHECKPOINT 32.3
❶ (b) 1.5

CHECKPOINT 33.2
❶ (c) 0.12 m
❷ (a) 50 kW h (b) 12.5 kW h (c) 37.5 kW h

CHECKPOINT 33.3
❶ (a) 16.7 ms (b) 2.53 s (c) 4.2 years

THEME H QUESTIONS
1 (a) (i) x (ii) w (b) 4 (d) 2 Hz (e) 120
2 (b) 9000 m (c) 1500 m/s (d) 3000 m
3 (a) (i) 126 dB
7 (b) (i) 10 μm (d) (i) 6 minutes (ii) 0.1 h
(iii) 7.2 kW h (iv) 36p

CHECKPOINT 34.1
❷ 2.5 kg, 0.02 kg, 1.0 N, 600 N
❹ 1.8 N
❺ (b) (i) 2.5 N (ii) 0.025 N (c) 5.75 N
(d) 0.575 kg

CHECKPOINT 34.3
❷ (a) 10 N to the left (b) 50 N up
(c) 500 N up the ramp
❹ (a) 2.40 N (b) 4.80 N (c) 7.20 N
❺ 3900 N

CHECKPOINT 34.4
❷ (a) 1.5 N (b) 5.67 N (c) 1.5 N (d) 5.25 N
❸ (b) 340 N (c) 1.9 m from the fulcrum

CHECKPOINT 35.1
❸ (a) 1750 Pa (b) 35 kPa

CHECKPOINT 35.2
❹ 18 kN

CHECKPOINT 35.3
❸ 7×10^6 Pa
❹ (a) 900 Pa (b) 0.54 N

CHECKPOINT 35.4
❶ (a) Greater (b) Same (c) 2500 Pa
❷ 20 m
❸ 16.3 kPa

CHECKPOINT 35.5
❷ 10 m
❹ 10.8 kN

CHECKPOINT 35.6
❸ (a) 5.0 N (b) 5.0 N (c) 0.5 kg

CHECKPOINT 36.1
❶ (a) 4.67 km/h (b) 1.30 m/s
❷ (a) 1.67 m/s
❹ (b) 2.67 m/s
❺ (a) 12 km East, 16 km South
(b) 6 hours 40 minutes

CHECKPOINT 36.2
❶ (b) 1 s (a) (i) 27 cm/s (ii) 0.27 m/s
❷ (a) 0.30 m/s^2 (b) 540 m
❹ (b) 2 m/s^2 (c) (i) 400 m (ii) 400 m
❺ 3150 m, 7 m/s^2

CHECKPOINT 36.3
❶ 6.67 m/s^2, 7.54 m
❷ (a) 10 cm (b) 10 cm/s (c) 20 cm/s^2
❸ (b) (i) 0.125 m/s^2, 400 m (ii) –0.25 m/s^2, 200 m
(c) 5 m/s
❹ (a) (i) 30 m/s (ii) 0 m/s (b) 15 m/s
(c) 5 s, –6 m/s^2
❺ (a) 109 m/s (b) 219 m/s (c) 6.83 m/s^2

CHECKPOINT 36.4
❷ (b) (ii) 0.21 s
❸ (a) 15 m/s (b) 11.25 m
❹ (a) 2.1 s (b) 0 m/s (c) 21 m/s
❺ (b) Simon's (c) 45 m (d) 20 m/s

CHECKPOINT 36.5
❷ (a) 1.5 N (b) 25 m/s^2 (c) 4.0 kg (d) 0.45 kg
❸ (a) 444 N (b) 8 kN (c) 0.056
❹ (a) 22 500 N (b) 23.7 minutes
❺ (a) 4.45 m/s (b) 1.79 ms
(c) –2500 m/s^2, 7500 N

CHECKPOINT 36.6
❸ (a) 62.5 J (b) 200 kJ (c) 1000 MJ
❹ (a) 375 KJ (c) 55 m/s
❺ (a) 1890 J (c) 9.2 m/s

CHECKPOINT 36.7
❷ (a) 6000 kg m/s (b) (i) 500 N (ii) 5000 N
❹ (a) 1.11 m/s, 1390 J (b) (i) 2.22 m/s, 56 J
(ii) 0 m/s, 4500 J
❺ 32 m/s

CHECKPOINT 36.8
❹ (b) 19.1

CHECKPOINT 37.1
❸ (a) 120 kJ (b) 750 J (c) 9.4%
❹ (a) 1.82, 0.8, 2.5 (b) A, 91%
❺ (a) 1100 J, 1000 J (b) 91% (c) 1220 N

CHECKPOINT 37.2
❹ (a) 1000 l (b) 143 l

THEME I QUESTIONS
1 (a) (ii) 1.20 m (ii) 24 J
3 (a) (i) 3 (ii) 8, 9 and 10 (b) (i) 0.2 s
(ii) 1.3 m/s
4 (a) 800 N (c) 500 N (d) 6.25 m/s^2
(e) (i) 120 kJ (ii) 320 kJ (iii) 200 kJ
5 (a) 0.0024 m^2 (b) 125 kPa (c) (i) 4 m/s
(ii) 300 s (b) (i) 150 s (e) 0.13 m/s^2 (f) 1050 m
6 (d) (i) 4200 m (ii) 10 m/s (e) 39%

THEME J QUESTIONS
2 (b) (i) 6.1 dm^3 (ii) 16.5 dm^3 (c) 0.087 dm^3
(d) 0.103 dm^3

CHECKPOINT 42.1
❷ (a) + (b) (i) + (ii) −

CHECKPOINT 42.3
❷ (a) (i) 3.5 C (ii) 210 C (iii) 2100 C (b) 5.0 A
(c) 20.0 A (d) (i) 1000 s (ii) 500 000 s
❸ (b) Smaller deflection (c) Larger deflection
❹ (a) 15 cm (b) 0.75 V
❺ (a) 1200 C (b) (i) 0.80 g (ii) 0.20 g (iii) 0.40 g
(c) 3.33 x 10^{-4} g (d) 3.3 x 10^{-19} C, 2

CHECKPOINT 42.4
❷ (a) £3.50
❺ (a) 360 000 (b) 4.32 MJ (c) 50 h

CHECKPOINT 43.2
❷ (a) 4.2 A (b) 5.0 A
❸ (a) (i) 12 (ii) 1 (iii) 0.18 (iv) 0.21 (b) 40.3p
❹ 7.2 kW, 21.6, £1.19

CHECKPOINT 43.3
❶ (a) (i) X = 1.2 A, Y = 1.8 A, Z = 3.0 A
(ii) X = Y = 2.0 A, Z = 2.5 A
(iii) X = 3.5 A, Y = 1.5 A, Z = 2.0 A
(b) (i) X = 2.5 V, Y = Z = 3.5 V
(ii) X = 12.0 V, Y = 4.0 V, Z = 8.0 V

(iii) W = 9.0 V, X = 3.0 V, Y = 4.0 V, Z = 8.0 V
❷ (a) 10.0 A (b) 12 J, 24 J, 84 J (c) 120 J
❸ (a) (i) 2.0 A (ii) 4.0 A (iii) 6.0 A (b) 2 C, 4 C
(c) 24 J, 48 J
❹ (a) (i) 60 J (ii) 18 kJ

CHECKPOINT 43.4
❶ (a) (i) 2.0 A (ii) 0.5 A (iii) 1.5 A
(b) (i) 1.0 A (ii) 0 A (iii) 1.5 A
(c) (i) 3.0 A (ii) 1.0 A (iii) 3.0 A
(d) (i) 4.0 Ω (ii) 6.0 Ω (iii) 2.0 Ω
❷ (a) (i) 9 Ω (ii) 2 Ω (b) (i) 14 Ω (ii) 1.43 Ω
(d) (i) 8.0 Ω (ii) 8.0 Ω
❸ (b) 6.0 Ω/m (c) 0.33 m
❹ (c) 12 V (d) 200 Ω, 4000 Ω
❺ (a) (i) 6.0 Ω, 2.0 A (ii) 2.4 Ω, 2.5 A
(iii) 3.0 Ω, 1.0 A (b) (i) 2 Ω, 4.0 V, 2.0 A;
6 Ω, 8.0 V, 1.33 A; 12 Ω, 8.0 V, 0.67 A
(ii) 6 Ω, 6.0 V, 1.0 A; 1 Ω, 1.5 V, 1.5 A;
3 Ω, 4.5 V, 1.5 A; (iii) 1 Ω, 1.0 V, 1.0 A;
3 Ω, 2.0 V, 0.67 A; 6 Ω, 2.0 V, 0.33 A

CHECKPOINT 44.4
❷ (a) (i) 1 (ii) 1 (iii) 3
❸ (a) 64 μs

CHECKPOINT 44.5
❸ (c) (i) 12.0 V (ii) 20 A (iii) 240 W

CHECKPOINT 45.5
❸ (a) 128 k (b) (i) 1 1 1 1 1 (ii) 1 1 0 0
❹ (a) 2005–2010 (b) approximately 1 s

CHECKPOINT 45.6
❺ (a) 4 (b) £15,000

CHECKPOINT 45.7
❹ (b) 20 cm^3

THEME K QUESTIONS
1 (e) 12 V
2 (a) (i) 115 J (ii) 828 kJ
3 (a) 10 A
4 (b) 0.48 A
7 (c) (i) 2.5 V (ii) 10 Ω (e) (i) 1.2 Ω (ii) 5.0 Ω
(iii) 0.8 A (iv) 0.96 V (v) 0.48 A (vi) 0.46 W

CHECKPOINT 47.1
❶ (a) 14 (b) 2.5 (c) 5 (d) 9

CHECKPOINT 47.2
❶ 28, 44, 64, 80, 40, 58.5, 56, 58, 106, 159.5, 249.5, 162

CHECKPOINT 47.3
❶ (a) 20% (b) 70% (c) 80% C, 20% H
(d) 40% S, 60% O (e) 2.5% H, 97.5% F
(f) 20% Mg, 27% S, 53% O
❷ (a) 36% (b) 67.5%

CHECKPOINT 47.4
❶ (a) 27 g (b) 96 g (c) 50 g (d) 14 g (e) 8 g
(f) 64 g
❷ (a) 2.5 mol (b) 0.33 mol (c) 1.0 mol
(d) 0.25 mol
❸ (a) 98 g (b) 23 g (c) 100 g (d) 10 g

CHECKPOINT 47.5
❶ 8.0 g
❷ (b) 3.2 g
❸ 10.3 g
❹ 107 g

CHECKPOINT 47.6
❶ (a) 8.0 g (b) 95%
❷ (a) 34 g (b) 10%
❸ 98%
❹ (b) 132 g (c) 91%
❺ (a) 25 g (b) 88%

CHECKPOINT 47.8
❶ (a) 1.00 mol/l (b) 0.10 mol/l (c) 2.0 mol/l
(d) 0.40 mol/l
❷ (a) 0.02 mol (b) 1.00 mol (c) 0.06 mol
(d) 0.025 mol
❸ (a) 0.144 mol/l
❹ 2 mol/l
❺ (a) 3.0×10^{-3} mol, 3.5×10^{-3} mol, 4.0×10^{-3} mol, 4.5×10^{-3} mol

CHECKPOINT 51.4
❹ (a) 61.5 (b) 650

THEME L QUESTIONS
2 (b) 11 cm³ (c) 90 cm³ (d) 35 cm³
9 (a) 4.57 million tonnes (b) 8.16 million tonnes

CHECKPOINT 52.4
❸ (a) (i) 3.33% (ii) 30% (b) 12 m²

CHECKPOINT 53.3
❶ 1200
❸ 39

Table of symbols, atomic numbers and relative atomic masses

Element	Symbol	Atomic number	Relative atomic mass	Element	Symbol	Atomic number	Relative atomic mass
Actinium	Ac	89	227	Mercury	Hg	80	201
Aluminium	Al	13	27	Molybdenum	Mo	42	96
Americium	Am	95	243	Neodymium	Nd	60	144
Antimony	Sb	51	122	Neon	Ne	10	20
Argon	Ar	18	40	Neptunium	Np	93	237
Arsenic	As	38	75	Nickel	Ni	28	59
Astatine	At	85	210	Niobium	Nb	41	93
Barium	Ba	56	137	Nitrogen	N	7	14
Berkelium	Bk	97	247	Nobelium	No	102	254
Beryllium	Be	4	9	Osmium	Os	76	190
Bismuth	Bi	83	209	Oxygen	O	8	16
Boron	B	5	11	Palladium	Pd	46	106
Bromine	Br	35	80	Phosphorus	P	15	31
Cadmium	Cd	48	112	Platinum	Pt	78	195
Caesium	Cs	55	133	Plutonium	Pu	94	242
Calcium	Ca	20	40	Polonium	Po	84	210
Californium	Cf	98	251	Potassium	K	19	39
Carbon	C	6	12	Praesodymium	Pr	59	141
Cerium	Ce	58	140	Promethium	Pm	61	147
Chlorine	Cl	17	35.5	Protactinium	Pa	91	231
Chromium	Cr	24	52	Radium	Ra	88	226
Cobalt	Co	27	59	Radon	Rn	86	222
Copper	Cu	29	63.5	Rhenium	Re	75	186
Curium	Cm	96	247	Rhodium	Rh	45	103
Dysprosium	Dy	66	162.5	Rubidium	Rb	37	85
Einsteinium	Es	99	254	Ruthenium	Ru	44	101
Erbium	Er	68	167	Samarium	Sm	62	150
Europium	Eu	63	152	Scandium	Sc	21	45
Fermium	Fm	100	253	Selenium	Se	34	79
Fluorine	F	9	19	Silicon	Si	14	28
Francium	Fr	87	223	Silver	Ag	47	108
Gadolinium	Gd	64	157	Sodium	Na	11	23
Gallium	Ga	31	70	Strontium	Sr	38	87
Germanium	Ge	32	72.5	Sulphur	S	16	32
Gold	Au	79	197	Tantalum	Ta	73	181
Hafnium	Hf	72	178	Technetium	Tc	43	99
Helium	He	2	4	Tellurium	Te	52	127
Holmium	Ho	67	164	Terbium	Tb	65	159
Hydrogen	H	1	1	Thallium	Tl	81	204
Indium	In	49	115	Thorium	Th	90	232
Iodine	I	53	127	Thulium	Tm	69	169
Iridium	Ir	77	192	Tin	Sn	50	119
Iron	Fe	26	56	Titanium	Ti	22	48
Krypton	Kr	36	84	Tungsten	W	74	184
Lanthanum	La	57	139	Uranium	U	92	238
Lawrencium	Lw	103	257	Vanadium	V	23	51
Lead	Pb	82	207	Xenon	Xe	54	131
Lithium	Li	3	7	Ytterbium	Yb	70	173
Lutecium	Lu	71	175	Yttrium	Y	39	89
Magnesium	Mg	12	24	Zinc	Zn	30	65
Manganese	Mn	25	55	Zirconium	Zr	40	91
Mendelevium	Md	101	256				

The Periodic Table of the elements

Group

1	2											3	4	5	6	7	0
																	4 He Helium 2
7 Li Lithium 3	9 Be Beryllium 4											11 B Boron 5	12 C Carbon 6	14 N Nitrogen 7	16 O Oxygen 8	19 F Fluorine 9	20 Ne Neon 10
23 Na Sodium 11	24 Mg Magnesium 12											27 Al Aluminium 13	28 Si Silicon 14	31 P Phosphorus 15	32 S Sulphur 16	35.5 Cl Chlorine 17	40 Ar Argon 18
39 K Potassium 19	40 Ca Calcium 20	45 Sc Scandium 21	48 Ti Titanium 22	51 V Vanadium 23	52 Cr Chromium 24	55 Mn Manganese 25	56 Fe Iron 26	59 Co Cobalt 27	59 Ni Nickel 28	63.5 Cu Copper 29	65 Zn Zinc 30	70 Ga Gallium 31	73 Ge Germanium 32	75 As Arsenic 33	79 Se Selenium 34	80 Br Bromine 35	84 Kr Krypton 36
85 Rb Rubidium 37	88 Sr Strontium 38	89 Y Yttrium 39	91 Zr Zirconium 40	93 Nb Niobium 41	96 Mo Molybdenum 42	99 Tc Technetium 43	101 Ru Ruthenium 44	103 Rh Rhodium 45	106 Pd Palladium 46	108 Ag Silver 47	112 Cd Cadmium 48	115 In Indium 49	119 Sn Tin 50	122 Sb Antimony 51	128 Te Tellurium 52	127 I Iodine 53	131 Xe Xenon 54
133 Cs Caesium 55	137 Ba Barium 56	139 La Lanthanum 57 *	178 Hf Hafnium 72	181 Ta Tantalum 73	184 W Tungsten 74	186 Re Rhenium 75	190 Os Osmium 76	192 Ir Iridium 77	195 Pt Platinum 78	197 Au Gold 79	201 Hg Mercury 80	204 Tl Thallium 81	207 Pb Lead 82	209 Bi Bismuth 83	210 Po Polonium 84	210 At Astatine 85	222 Rn Radon 86
Fr Francium 87	226 Ra Radium 88	227 Ac Actinium 89 †															

140 Ce Cerium 58	141 Pr Praseodymium 59	144 Nd Neodymium 60	147 Pm Promethium 61	150 Sm Samarium 62	152 Eu Europium 63	157 Gd Gadolinium 64	159 Tb Terbium 65	162 Dy Dysprosium 66	165 Ho Holmium 67	167 Er Erbium 68	169 Tm Thulium 69	173 Yb Ytterbium 70	175 Lu Lutetium 71
232 Th Thorium 90	231 Pa Protactinium 91	238 U Uranium 92	237 Np Neptunium 93	242 Pu Plutonium 94	243 Am Americium 95	247 Cm Curium 96	247 Bk Berkelium 97	251 Cf Californium 98	254 Es Einsteinium 99	253 Fm Fermium 100	256 Md Mendelevium 101	254 No Nobelium 102	257 Lr Lawrencium 103

1 H Hydrogen 1

* 58–71 Lanthanum series
† 90–103 Actinium series

Key

a	a = relative atomic mass
X	**X** = atomic symbol
b	b = atomic number

Cumulative Index

Book 1